Ius Gentium: Comparative Perspectives on Law and Justice

Volume 142

Ius Gentium is a book series which discusses the central questions of law and justice from a comparative perspective. The books in this series collect the contrasting and overlapping perspectives of lawyers, judges, philosophers, and scholars of law from the world's many different jurisdictions for the purposes of comparison, harmonisation, and the progressive development of law and legal institutions. Each volume makes a new comparative study of an important area of law. This book series continues the work of the well-known journal of the same name and provides the basis for a better understanding of all areas of legal science.

The *Ius Gentium* series provides a valuable resource for lawyers, judges, legislators, scholars, and both graduate students and researchers in globalisation, comparative law, legal theory, and legal practice. The series has a special focus on the development of international legal standards and transnational legal cooperation.

Mauro Balestrieri · Alice Cauduro
Editors

The Legal Anatomy of the Body

Health, Rights, and Politics in Times of Emergency

Springer

Editors
Mauro Balestrieri
Department of Law
University of Turin
Torino, Torino, Italy

Alice Cauduro
Department of Law
University of Turin
Torino, Torino, Italy

ISSN 1534-6781 ISSN 2214-9902 (electronic)
Ius Gentium: Comparative Perspectives on Law and Justice
ISBN 978-3-032-26433-6 ISBN 978-3-032-26434-3 (eBook)
https://doi.org/10.1007/978-3-032-26434-3

This work was supported by National Interest Project (PRIN 2022 PNRR) funded with the support of the European Union and the Italian Government.

This Springer imprint is published by the registered company Springer Nature Switzerland AG
The registered company address is: Gewerbestrasse 11, 6330 Cham, Switzerland

Preface

Over the past few decades, the relationship between law and medicine has become increasingly close, interconnected, and, at the same time, ever more complex. On one hand, medical science has deepened its understanding of health and the human body through undeniable techno-scientific advances; on the other, legal science has elaborated the basic principles for managing health, constructing concepts designed to guide society toward the pursuit of collective well-being. Underlying both of these dimensions lies one element that is fundamental and inescapable: the *body*. Health, well-being, illness, and care: each of these concepts, in the broad range of meanings that distinguish them, shares indeed a common thread, namely, the differentiation between the 'healthy' and the 'ill', between 'normality' and 'emergency'. There is nothing more pressing than a sick body in need of care: the urgency of illness has no true equivalent in other domains, and it is precisely this urgency that grounds the epistemological and scientific regime of medicine.

In recent years, legal scholarship has carefully documented the profound transformations that have reshaped both the right to health and public health. The rapid diffusion of technological development, which has enabled and continues to enable increasingly personalized, precise, and intelligent medicine; the massive use of big data, algorithms, and quantification practices, whose primary effect is a new reconfiguration of the relationship between health and illness; as well as the changes in health policies on both national and global scales, raise pressing questions about the boundaries between individual and collective interests. All of this is profoundly reshaping the balance of power between medicine and law. What seems increasingly evident at the global level is indeed a radical reconfiguration of the health paradigm within a securitarian and emergency-based logic which, for multiple reasons, now stands out as a rule rather than an exception in the international scenario. Yet at the core of this evolution remains the materiality of the body, its corporeality, its inherent vulnerability, and its precarious condition. The legal challenge posed by a sick body is precisely that of reconciling its fragility with the normative frameworks that seek to protect it, while at the same time ensuring that care, dignity, and rights remain inseparable from the condition of illness itself. From this perspective, the study of the body is intrinsically connected to the examination of social systems that safeguard individual well-being, conceived in a far broader sense than the mere restoration of normality, and attentive to real needs at both local and global level.

Building on these elements, and in particular by underscoring the preeminent role that emergencies have come to play in the regulation of both national and international health policies, the contributions gathered in this volume aim to develop a legal, historical, and critical reflection on the body in different theoretical and practical articulations. Specifically, this book brings together the work developed through lectures, workshops, seminars, and an international conference held between 2023 and 2025 at the University of Turin within the European project *Human Well-Being in Times of Tech Management of Emergency* (GA n. P20225FPNT – CUP: D53D23022210001). The contributions collected represent the culmination of a multidisciplinary and multifaceted research effort, as well as the outcome of national and international collaborations, aimed at exploring the evolving boundaries of the right to health at a time when emergencies have increasingly become the norm.

The sections of this book are designed to constitute a genealogical pathway, tracing the most significant epistemological, philosophical, political, and legal transformations in the configuration of the body and of the right to health. In this sense, the volume constitutes an 'intellectual journey' through the evolution of the relationship between law and medicine, highlighting the profound nexus between health and the state of emergency that has unfolded throughout the modern and contemporary ages.

Many friends and colleagues contributed to the realization of this project. First and foremost, we are grateful to the distinguished national and international colleagues who participated in this collaborative initiative and supported us, at every stage, in defining the themes and issues explored in the book. We also wish to thank the Department of Law at the University of Turin and those who endorsed and supported our idea, in particular our Director, Valeria Marcenò, and the Deputy Directors, Enrico Sciandrello and Fabio Longo, who strongly promoted this volume with enthusiasm and commitment. A special acknowledgment goes to Raffaella Galasso and Simona Guida, whose patience and assistance were indispensable in bringing this project to completion. Finally, our thanks extend to all the guests who took part in our events and in the discussions that surrounded them, sharing our project with genuine engagement and support.

Torino, Italy
January 2026

Mauro Balestrieri
Alice Cauduro

Contents

Editors and Contributors

About the Editors

Mauro Balestrieri is Associate Professor of Comparative Law at the University of Turin. His research explores comparative jurisprudence, legal theory, and the cultural and historical formation of legal institutions. He is co-author of *Quantitative Methods in Comparative Law* (Edward Elgar, 2023) and co-editor of *The Grand Strategy of Comparative Law* (Routledge, 2024).

Alice Cauduro is Assistant Professor of Administrative Law at the University of Turin, where she also teaches Pharmaceutical Law. Her research focuses on medical law, public health, and access to medicines. She has published extensively on these areas, starting with the open-access book *L'accesso al farmaco* (Ledizioni, 2017). During a research period at the Centre for Law, Medicine and Life Sciences, University of Cambridge, she worked on pharmaceutical expenditure governance in the UK and Italy, leading to the publication of an article in the European Journal of Health Law (2026).

Contributors

Mauro Balestrieri Department of Law, University of Turin, Torino, Italy

Alice Cauduro Department of Law, University of Turin, Torino, Italy

Mirko Djukovic Centre for Fundamental Rights, Hertie School, Berlin, Germany

Luigi Ferrajoli Department of Law, University Roma Tre, Rome, Italy

Antonio Gerace Instituto de Estudos Filosóficos, Coimbra, Portugal

Alberto Giustiniano Department of Philosophy, University of Turin, Torino, Italy

Simone Guidi Institute for the European Intellectual Lexicon and History of Ideas (CNR-ILIESI), Italian National Research Council, Rome, Italy

Tamara Hervey City St George's, University of London, London, UK

Dario Ippolito Department of Law, University Roma Tre, Rome, Italy

Giovanni Leghissa Department of Philosophy, University of Turin, Torino, Italy

Laurie Marguet University of Rouen, Rouen, France

Stephanie Palmer Faculty of Law, University of Cambridge, Cambridge, UK

Mélanie Samson Sciences Po, Paris, France

Marco Storni Centre de recherche en philosophie (PHI), Université libre de Bruxelles, Bruxelles, Belgium

Keith Syrett University of Bristol Law School, Bristol, UK

Luca Tonetti Department of Historical and Geographic Sciences and the Ancient World (DiSSGeA), University of Padua, Padua, Italy

Hannah van Kolfschooten Centre for Life Sciences Law, University of Basel, Basel, Switzerland

Isaac Weldon Centre for Advanced Studies in Bioscience Innovation Law, Faculty of Law, University of Copenhagen, Copenhagen, Denmark; Global Strategy Lab, York University, Toronto, Canada

Matija Žgur Department of Law, University Roma Tre, Rome, Italy

Introduction: Law, Body, and Health in a Post-Pandemic World

Mauro Balestrieri and Alice Cauduro

Abstract This opening chapter outline the central topics of the volume focusing especially on health law, state of exception, and the legal anatomy of the body. It first highlights the ambivalent relationship between the right to health and the state of emergency, showing how health law increasingly operates at the threshold between ordinary governance and exceptional measures. It then turns to the global dimension, emphasizing the extent to which the normalization of health emergencies has become a contingent feature of the new world order. A particular focus is placed on the evolving nexus between the body, health, and universal health care, tracing how the legal frameworks surrounding public health have undergone profound economic transformations in recent decades. The chapter concludes by reflecting on future prospects, asking what new forms of governance, rights, and vulnerabilities may emerge in the coming years, as they appear increasingly marked by the rise of medicalisation, healthism, and digital surveillance.

1 Emergency as the 'New Normal'? Legal and Technological Narratives for Public Health Management

In recent years, academic studies have seen a notable proliferation of readings engaging with the concept of 'emergency'. From law and political science, to history, economics, and health studies, the ideas of emergency and exception have been

This chapter is the result of a collaborative effort: Sections 1 and 3 were authored by Mauro Balestrieri; Sections 2 and 4 by Alice Cauduro; Section 5 was jointly written by both authors.

M. Balestrieri (✉) · A. Cauduro
Department of Law, University of Turin, Torino, Italy
e-mail: mauro.balestrieri@unito.it

A. Cauduro
e-mail: alice.cauduro@unito.it

M. Balestrieri and A. Cauduro (eds.), *The Legal Anatomy of the Body*, Ius Gentium: Comparative Perspectives on Law and Justice 142,
https://doi.org/10.1007/978-3-032-26434-3_1

explored, contested, and reframed through multiple disciplinary lenses.[1] To assert that we live in a 'state of emergency' (however methodologically, historically, or legally defined) has become almost a label, a paradoxical disclaimer accompanying our daily practices. Although this phenomenon is manifest and broadly recognised, its full complexity remains far from exhausted. The proliferation of articles, essays, and inquiries has not, in fact, yet produced a clear qualification of the problem, which often persists in ambiguous and opaque ways. What, in essence, separates normality from emergency? What limits must be preserved to prevent it from becoming a permanent state of exception? And if an emergency becomes the 'new normal', can it still be called an emergency?

The purpose of this volume and of the contributions it brings together is twofold. First, it seeks to elucidate how the body and, along with it, the notions of health and well-being accepted in recent regulations and international guidelines, emerge as the product of a specific construction (or *assemblage*) continually reshaped by legal, political, and health-related emergencies. Second, it aims to integrate law, medicine, and social sciences examining how legal and medical categories are moulded by (and in turn mould) the narratives through which they are articulated. Briefly stated, if the idea of a (permanent) 'state of emergency' reshapes our political landscape, its most immediate and tangible effects are inscribed upon the political frameworks we inhabit and upon the body itself. The body is the locus where emergency is experienced, regulated, and administered, and at the same time the primary arena in which its effects are both enacted and contested. The chapters collected in this volume, drawing on legal, philosophical, historical, and sociological perspectives, highlight the inextricable interrelation between the *semantics* of the body and those of emergency. As it is evident, the body itself is the site most persistently traversed by emergency practices: from restrictions on movement and proximity, with which we became familiar during the COVID-19 epidemic, to the forms of discrimination and exclusion experienced by the most vulnerable and marginalised, to the complex debates surrounding compulsory vaccination, the development of therapies, health screening, and the emergence of new forms of antibiotic resistance. In short, everything we experience, politically, legally, existentially, revolves around the body; and, circularly, everything that concerns the body appears to be affected and captured by the very concept of emergency. In this sense, it is important to take into account the reasons underlying this contemporary situation. The way in which we name reality, construct legal categories, and devise practices determines how we engage with and respond to the notion of emergency. Words matter; and when they are stripped of meaning, it is an entire framework of rights that collapses.[2] Within the very notion of emergency, words and things, definitions and practices, law and science, coalesce into operative regimes, moulding in turn rights and bodies.

---

[1] For a comprehensive account of the rise of 'emergency studies' in academia, see Anderson (2017) and Fusco et al. (2020).

[2] On the idea that words and language constitute the primary vehicle for understanding the meaning of law and political community, see White (1984).

In a seminal reflection on the biopolitics of health, Donna Haraway aptly captured such dynamic: '[B]odies – she claimed – are not born; they are *made*'.[3] Our body is the integrated product of practices, narratives, disciplines, and policies that surround it and incessantly *shape* it. There can be no definitive crystallisation of the body, nor any denial of the endless processes in which it is entangled: if from one side the body is situated politically, legally, and medically, at the same time it resists being contained within a single, coherent conceptual unit.[4] Our physical body is singular, and yet inevitably plural; it is something we *have*, something we *are*, and something we ceaselessly *become*. Thinking today about the concepts of health and well-being inevitably means engaging with the multifaceted and complex morphology that the body reveals. What this book seeks to do is precisely to provide a legal and interdisciplinary framework for this constantly evolving condition, in which biological, cultural, political, and technological dimensions are so inextricably intertwined.

1.1 Health Law in the State of Exception

Legal scholars widely agree that emergency cannot be defined in a precise or exhaustive manner.[5] Case by case, it is vaguely defined as a juridical *vacuum*, a form of governance by mere facts, an enactment of raw necessity, or a domain where the normal legal order is emphatically 'suspended'.[6] The underlying idea is that the concept of emergency resists clear theoretical limitations, since the events that constitute it are unpredictable and constantly open to change. In other words, we know that an emergency exists, but we cannot know in advance what will cause it. To hide behind conceptual difficulty, however, does not seem the right path for genuinely addressing the empirical and legal problem of emergency. Scholars emphasized indeed the need to combine more rigorous definitional methods with a special focus on vulnerability, hazards, and social risks, with the aim of containing any chaotic situation and avoiding dangerous expansions. Strictly speaking, the term 'emergency' evokes a situation of urgency requiring extraordinary measures and, among these measures, constitutional theory has identified the concepts of the 'state of emergency' and the 'state of exception' as their pragmatic and juridical expressions.[7] Yet in this 'dark age of definitions', jurists paradoxically appear the most willing to embrace flexibility rather than restraint. As Karin Loevy rightly argues,

---

[3] Haraway (1989), p. 10. On the post-human idea of bodies as cyborgs, see also Haraway (1991), p. 149.

[4] For an incisive overview on the philosophical, historical, and legal problem of the body, see Fraser and Greco (2005), p. 4.

[5] See Gross and Ní Aoláin (2006), p. 6.

[6] As famously argued by Agamben (2005). For an historical-political background on the idea of 'state of exception', see also Saint-Bonnet (2001).

[7] For a theoretical account, see Ferejohn and Pasquino (2004).

> [s]trikingly, while disaster scientists are deeply concerned about the question of what is a disaster, and as we've seen, what makes the question itself important (and often misleading), legal theorists seem almost completely uninterested with this question. They seem content in assuming that emergencies – in public law – are defined by their exceptionality, by the fact that they raise occasion for the use of special, exceptional powers. They are, clearly, much more interested in maintaining flexibility of legal institutions – laws, political branches, administrative agencies, and officials – to deal with the unexpected. It is remarkable that in legal theory, the emergency comes already defined as the chaotic agent, which these agencies must be able to (or fail to) handle.[8]

In some sense, we may add, the high degree of tolerance shown by legal thought towards emergency powers stems precisely from the progressive *normalisation* of exception within our constitutional fabric: a normalisation so extensive and pervasive that the very idea of 'exception' has become almost uninteresting and unremarkable.[9] In this vein, it may be said without exaggeration, that the history of health law is nothing less than a history of perpetual emergencies.[10] The H1N1 influenza pandemic, the 2014–2016 Ebola crisis in West Africa, and the 2016 Zika emergency are merely the most recent instances of a constant and systemic state of medical alert that has, in fact, always characterised the global landscape. COVID-19 represented the latest example of a disease stemming from anthropogenic and demographic changes, which acted as potential incubators of further pandemics that epidemiologists and virologists now expect with near certainty.[11] The delicacy and fragility of global health, both nationally and internationally considered, serve as a stark reminder of our existence as *mere bodies*. Human beings congregate, travel, live in proximity to exotic animals, transmit and contract their diseases, alter the environment, and are in turn affected by the habitats they inhabit. All this reflects the inevitable flow of life and events or, we might say, of history itself.

There is something paradoxical, even ironic, in all this. Despite the remarkable advances of medicine, the true history, the one that concretely shapes the lives of all living beings, remains ultimately *natural* history: the chronicle of diseases, of climate change, of the health alterations produced by the environment, and of the circulation of pathogens across the globe through the unstoppable movement of living beings.[12] If 'emergency' as such eludes precise legal definition and remains bound within its lexical ambiguity and vagueness, public health emergencies, by contrast, are perfectly evident and readily defined in all their material and future manifestations.

It is perhaps for this reason that the paradigm of emergency has become so dominant and pervasive, particularly in the field of health law. The premise for its now undisputed success and rapid diffusion lies precisely in its establishment as

---

[8] Loevy (2016), p. 66.

[9] On this point, see Fusco et al. (2020), p. 2.

[10] For a detailed analysis of the constitutional implications of public health emergencies before COVID-19, see Villarreal (2020), p. 225.

[11] Gostin (2014), p. 32.

[12] About the idea that 'in the end, all history is natural history', see Schama (2023), p. 3.

a wholly self-sufficient, coherent, and comprehensive device for governing extraordinary medical events among the political communities. The contemporary world seems to unfold along a continuum of emergencies that function as evidence of a 'second-order' regularity: what we call 'the rule' is now artificially constituted and sustained through the proliferation of states of exception.[13] The subordination of the rule to emergency rests on the presumption that all phenomena are, in principle, governable and that global affairs can be subjected to regulation: anything outside this framework is pulled back under control with stricter measures.[14] Health law does not differ from this pattern: indeed, it appears to be perennially captured within the state of exception, its legal, administrative, and military categories, since viruses spreading beyond a particular season or geographical region reveal, in biological terms, their ductility in being adaptive, constantly evolving to form new strains, and capable of rapid mutation. In short, in its theoretical openness and empirical flexibility, the concept of exception seems to become the natural (and alarming) extension of life's own mutability.

1.2 Globalisation and the Normalisation of Healthcare Emergency

As is now widely recognised, the contemporary era has been marked by transformations that have reshaped lifestyles, reconfigured political categories, and altered the very conditions of human existence.[15] The rapid acceleration of communication, the relentless expansion of commercial exchanges, and the emergence of new risks to public health arising thousands of kilometres away yet profoundly shaping individual lives, has made it increasingly evident that what is 'distant' is, in fact, ever closer. In this view, speed, globalisation, and digital interconnectedness are not necessarily synonymous with greater security or stability; rather, the acceleration of global interdependencies has become the defining feature of a 'new normal', an age marked by pervasive anxiety, heightened insecurity, and recurrent crisis.[16] Suddenly, we find ourselves inhabiting a fragile society, and it is the very notion of health that now reveals its own instability. Distinctions between 'domestic' and 'international' health problems are losing their usefulness and appear misleading.[17] What is 'local' inevitably becomes 'global', and vice versa.[18] The very demarcation between 'health'

[13] About the European situation, see Greene (2018).

[14] For these insights, see Calhoun (2004), p. 375 ff.

[15] For an effective summary about the epistemic revolution of contemporary age, see de Sousa (2020), p. 198. On the endemic fragility of the contemporary world, important reflections have been offered by Lyotard (1984).

[16] Robertson (1990), p. 27.

[17] As explicitly recognized by Frenk and Gómez-Dantés (2002), p. 95.

[18] On the idea of 'glocality' as synthesis between 'global' and 'local', see famously Robertson (1995), p. 25.

and 'illness' has become increasingly blurred due to the unwarranted expansion of disease categories, overdiagnosis, overtreatment, and medicalisation.[19] In this virtual annihilation of time and space, we become part of a single fabric which, if frayed on one side, can compromise the integrity of the whole weave.

This phenomenon is, of course, not new. Microbes and pathogens have always crossed borders, often as an inevitable consequence of commercial exchanges and migrations.[20] What appears significantly more complex today, however, is the coordination between national and supranational levels. Metaphorically speaking, it is as if the idea of pandemic and health emergency that marked our recent past had never truly disappeared.[21] The next, inevitable global contagion will once again serve as a 'critical test' for our democratic societies, and here again, the use of language will play a decisive role. Changes in the conceptualization of normality and emergency do not remain confined to a purely 'physical' or 'material' dimension of the world; rather, they rapidly transform into *cognitive* changes affecting the political ways we perceive ourselves and our relations with others. Our ways of thinking, being, and living have evolved in step with the very modes through which we conceptualise, justify, and categorise the emergencies that have shaped both our recent past and our present. In a sense, the unfolding of epidemics, recurrent crises, and states of emergencies has brought to the surface a different vision of history, making our inner fragility newly (and unexpectedly) visible.[22]

One of the most compelling ways to conceive of this condition is through the entanglement between risk, normality, and emergency in modern times. As Ulrich Beck famously observed, we have reached a paradoxical juncture in which the very routines through which we systemically act generate, in turn, consequences that are both immeasurable and exceptional.[23] Security fosters global insecurity; international rules breed global anarchy; the pursuit of control and surveillance generates new forms of global unpredictability. Within this circular (and contradictory) dynamic, emergency becomes the unstable ground upon which postmodern societies continually rely, and, precisely for this reason, a condition of necessary permanence in the future. But the real conundrum lies in the *structural* divergence between the proliferation of such risks (environmental, health-related, political, and social) and the normative frameworks that ought, in principle, to prevent their very occurrence. As Beck argued,

> the ecological and high-tech risks that have upset the public for some years now, have a new quality. In the afflictions they produce they are no longer tied to their place of origin – the industrial plant. By their nature they endanger *all* forms of life on this planet. The normative

[19] About the inner difficulty of drawing the line between health and disease in modern medicine, see Hofmann (2021).

[20] For a fascinating historical survey, see Cooper and Szreter (2021), pp. 21–43.

[21] On the relevance of metaphors and language in the conceptualization of health emergencies, see Nerlich (2022), p. 20.

[22] On the philosophical significance of this renewed 'emergence' of reality and history, see Ferraris (2022).

[23] Beck (2002), p. 40.

> bases of their calculation – the concept of accident and insurance, medical precautions, and so on – do not fit the basic dimensions of these modern threats.[24]

It is precisely in this sense that globalisation and emergency are legally 'reshaping' our lives. The risks we are facing and will inevitably continue to face are too vast and complex to be addressed within traditional legal frameworks. Emergency measures, almost as a form of paradoxical last resort, are required precisely because societies themselves *generate* on their own the very conditions that make them necessary. The 'political' and the 'unpolitical' hybridise: to manage a crisis is no longer merely a matter of organising the means for its safe and immediate resolution, but of embedding and re-articulating the entire phenomenon within an emergency framework by which it is, in turn, shaped. Most significantly, it is no coincidence that the pandemic context has popularised terms such as 'resilience', 'preparedness', and 'anticipatory governance': the idea that stirs between the lines of these apparently innocent terms is a constant anxiety for action, resolution, and containment of a threat perceived as ever imminent. There will always be an impending emergency to confront, an epidemic to contain, a disease to prevent through mechanisms of control, screening, and management. As Pitirim Sorokin famously observed, since the end of the Second World War the global order has experienced a steady proliferation of so-called emergencies which have shaped national political agendas.[25] It is therefore necessary to turn our attention to a range of disciplines that can help us understand what Beck identified as the 'normative inadequacy' of our postmodern legal societies. That is, to adopt an external vantage point from which to better grasp the inconsistencies within the contemporary frameworks of health law. Drawing on the contributions of sociology, anthropology, and the history of medicine, this volume seeks to understand the *preconditions* under which emergencies are declared, tracing a genealogy of the concept of health and its relationship with regulation, while showing how law itself has become embedded in the actual cultural transformations.

1.3 Towards a New Framework: Syndemic Legalities

As we have seen, the activation of states of emergency by governments across the world has represented the most immediate and direct political response adopted to manage population health and social well-being during recent health crises.[26] Quite naturally, such measures have raised pressing questions of constitutional legitimacy, once again demonstrating the profound connection between health law and democratic rights.[27] In a sense, it may be argued that the protection of health constitutes the central pillar of modern legal theory: the public sphere exists primarily insofar as

[24] Beck (1992), p. 22.

[25] Sorokin (1942).

[26] For an overview of states of exception declarations during the recent COVID-19 pandemic, see Grogan and Yamin (2023), pp. 354–366.

[27] West (2003), pp. 130–135.

political authority assumes responsibility for safeguarding the health and security of the population. If this is true, however, it becomes crucial to understand the rationale behind policies that have extended emergency measures and states of exception in some cases almost *sine die*.[28] And specifically, from a juridical point of view, what legal future awaits our democracies in light of global environmental conditions and the risks posed by the potential outbreak of future epidemics.

In recent specialist literature, the term that has increasingly attracted international attention is *syndemic*. Coined from the convergence of the words *synergy* and *epidemics*, it refers to the aggregation of multiple factors (such as pandemics, structural inequalities, poverty, and degraded environmental contexts) capable of generating as outcome serious public health crises. As Merrill Singer concisely formulates in her seminal study:

> [a] syndemic, in short, involves a set of enmeshed and mutually enhancing health problems that, *working together* in a context of noxious social and physical conditions, can significantly affect the overall disease burden and health status of a population.[29]

What is particularly compelling about this definition is the emphasis on the aggregated, or multi-layered, dimension of the phenomenon. According to Singer, it is not a single element that creates a syndemic, but rather a *constellation* of factors which, in their aggregation, generate something complex and potentially disruptive. In other words, the key element is not the specific source of a potential disease (viral or bacterial), but rather the conditions of structural weakness that ultimately enable its rapid spread.[30] The principal causes of a syndemic are by now well-known and extensively documented: (*i*) changing political and economic conditions that significantly deteriorate the quality of living standards; (*ii*) shifting ecological and environmental contexts such as deforestation, flooding, or climate change; (*iii*) altering demographics and social behaviours such as migration or excessive urbanisation; and, finally, (*iv*) the weakening of public health measures such as the decline in compulsory vaccination or the emergence of microbial adaptation to certain categories of drugs. What has become clearer than anything else, however, is that current global conditions almost never concern one of these factors in isolation, but invariably and persistently the interaction of at least two or more of them simultaneously. In other words, every health crisis is, by definition, multifactorial and composite.

It is precisely in the field of the right to health that the distinction between normality and exception takes on a particularly distinctive form. To speak of health, especially in relation to the body in its potential pathology, is to frame the discourse in terms that are inherently both *political* and *legal*. Public and private—the privacy of one's own body and the necessary projection of health into the public and international sphere—are two sides of the same coin. Because of the close connection

---

[28] For a critical survey, see now Ginsburg and Versteeg (2021).

[29] Singer (2009), p. xiv.

[30] For a specific focus on issues of justice, poverty, and structural vulnerabilities in the development of the recent COVID-19 pandemic, see Cowan and Mumford 2022

between the global and the local, a matter of health law can no longer be defined as purely private; on the contrary, it is intrinsically public, global, and transnational.[31]

All of this holds true not only from a strictly political or institutional standpoint, but above all from a *biological* and *ecological* perspective.[32] As numerous experts have clearly argued, the emergence of new pathogenic viruses, epidemics, and rapidly spreading diseases originates in the environmental upheavals caused primarily by the intensified exploitation of natural resources and the disruption of ecosystems through aggressive human activity.[33] Just as occurred with the recent COVID-19 outbreak, the destruction of natural habitats can easily lead to the transmission of unknown diseases with potentially uncontrollable consequences.[34] Likewise, the rapid increase in global temperatures will inevitably contribute to the creation of warmer or different environments that are more conducive to the incubation and spread of new diseases.[35] Strictly speaking, we cannot truly claim to be living in a 'post-pandemic' world; rather, we inhabit an ecosystem that is structurally predisposed to express itself precisely through pandemics: an environment, that is, naturally inclined toward the occurrence and spread of those emergency events which, once merely imagined, have now become a near-certainty.[36]

Many scholars have observed that, given the progressive deterioration of the living conditions of numerous animal and plant species, legal theory must now move towards a explicitly ecological dimension, that is, a radical change of paradigm respectful of the environment and the bio-sphere.[37] According to this view, law, in its own way, has been responsible for creating a toxic environment in which practices harmful to health were long regarded as fully legal and even appropriate. This is not a matter of reviving a naïve model of natural law, but of recognising a systemic transformation that directly concerns the life of each individual. In other words, we have entered a phase of *syndemic legalities*, where the cyclical recurrence of emergencies has ceased to be episodic and has instead crystallised into a foundational and stabilising element of the emerging global order. What is ultimately at stake is the inevitability of their recurrence, and whether our legal and political systems are prepared, or fatally unprepared, to confront this almost certain future.

As Andrew Lakoff has convincingly argued, the declaration of a public health emergency is less a suspension of law than a fictive device to activate an 'external' sphere of action. As with the Zika virus, emergency measures operated as a massive

[31] On the impossibility a drawing a clear line between the national and international levels in health emergencies, see Fidler (1996).

[32] Jenkins et al. (2020).

[33] Weiss and McMichael (2004).

[34] See Murdoch and French (2020), Barouki et al. (2021).

[35] Carlson et al. (2022).

[36] Osterholm (2005).

[37] See, most notably, Capra and Mattei (2015).

and penetrating regulatory mechanism that, in his words, 'did not point to an extra-legal state of exception but was rather a technocratic classification designed to integrate the outbreak of a novel disease into a preexisting regulatory framework'.[38] To classify a phenomenon juridically, whether as rule or emergency, norm or exception, entails its integration into an assemblage of elements that collaborate in the management of crisis, drawing together forms of knowledge and disciplines ranging from medicine to civil protection, from biology to international public health. The true paradox, however, lies precisely here. From a legal-administrative standpoint, the concept of emergency must be temporally limited; yet the management of a pandemic requires, by contrast, an extended and prolonged horizon. At the same time, while an outbreak may be local, its consequences are everywhere and nowhere. What remains, almost as an inevitable sentence, is a single imperative: the demand for continuous preparedness, a fully proactive and performative mode of governance to confront threats of whatever kind.[39]

1.4 Emergency and the Governmentality of Bodies

The recent COVID-19 pandemic has provided crucial proofs in this regard. In 2021, in response to the partially unsatisfactory management of the epidemic crisis, the European Union established the *Health Emergency Preparedness and Response Authority* (HERA), a special agency explicitly tasked with preparing, as the name itself suggests, for future pandemics.[40] The measures falling within the competence of this body include both bureaucratic coordination among Member States and the promotion of scientific research, notably through funding for the acquisition of equipment and pharmaceuticals. As demonstrated by a recent analysis, the activation of emergency measures and the formal declaration of a national 'state of emergency' during the COVID-19 pandemic have, at the domestic level, expanded executive power beyond constitutional limits.[41] The pandemic exposed serious risks to the rule of law and fundamental rights, producing institutional shifts that, despite occasional safeguards by courts and judges, often left the rapid expansion of executive power insufficiently checked. In the eyes of the public, the emergency was perceived as a 'state of siege', as a prolonged assault to our peaceful lives with no clear end in sight, which in turn gave rise to an unusual increase of military metaphors applied to medicine and health.

Once again, the analysis of the language, and more specifically of the serious speech acts made by authorities permeating the legal and political sphere, proves decisive. The measures accompanying the prevention and treatment of COVID-19, indeed, adopted a *warlike* register: an invisible enemy was moving among our bodies,

[38] Lakoff (2017), p. 3.

[39] On this aspect, see the seminal work of Quarantelli (1988).

[40] HERA (2022).

[41] Bjørnskov and Voigt (2024), p. 333.

residing within them, and gaining strength and propagation. Doctors and nurses were portrayed as soldiers on the front line, and the first victims of the virus as casualties of a global war. If terrorism has revealed the emergence of an asymmetric conflict where the enemy is no longer a clearly defined army but an anonymous individual living next door, COVID-19 strongly radicalized this logic, revealing that our real foe may simply take the form of a virus, transmitted with ease from one person to another, often without either party being aware.[42] Torn from its original location on the battlefield, the military concept of the enemy has then progressively hybridised, transfigured, and turned into an invisible and almost uncontrollable pathogen.[43] But precisely in doing so, the very idea of the enemy has been also *internalised* within our bodies, which have become the privileged vector of the virus, the object of medical scrutiny, the threat whose movement must be contained or restricted, and, ultimately, the micro-trace of a political community in crisis.

In this very sense, what the recent pandemic has revealed most starkly is the profound fragility of our societies. The spread of COVID-19 has made it clear that the true crisis was not merely a health emergency, but first and foremost a *social* one.[44] Many critics have highlighted the particularly aggressive role played by neoliberal and free-market capitalist systems, pharmaceutical companies, and international actors, as well as their tendency to protect the interests of the privileged over those of the world's poorer populations.[45] This is certainly true, but it must be placed within a broader perspective in which, once again, the discourse on bodies asserts its centrality. To speak of the management of health is to recognise that public health governance necessarily operates through a form of *governmentality*, that is, the administration of bodies, practices, and lifestyles across the population.[46] In this view, the body assumes a *liminal* status: a resource to be indexed, quantified, and studied as the primary incubator of new potential diseases, and, at the same time, something experienced as 'our own' body and, inadvertently, as a 'foreign' one. The vast apparatus of population studies encompassing statistics, quantitative methods, and medical measures of incidence, risk, and prediction, shows a medico-legal technology that is profoundly political at its core, and on whose administration the democratic future of our societies may ultimately depend.

But perhaps, the most ambitious aim of this volume is to confront what may be defined as the *enigma of health*: namely, the fact that, historically speaking, no person's health or illness has ever been purely a biological matter, but an essentially juridical conundrum.[47] From this perspective, medicine cannot be reduced to biology alone. The concept of health has its own genealogy, its own history, and its own modes of manifestation, which make it the pivotal site where diverse scientific and political

---

[42] About the metaphor of the 'enemy' for the COVID-19 virus, see Kumar et al. (2020) and Chauhan et al. (2021).

[43] Saunders (2021).

[44] Lupton and Willis (2021), p. 4.

[45] For a detailed review, see Lupton (2022), p. 41.

[46] Flear (2015), p. 21.

[47] Amato (2023), p. 16.

practices converge. This is the hard lesson of our time: that health can no longer be conceived in isolation, but must be understood as a nexus of biological, legal, political, and cultural dimensions. As we have argued, we are now beyond the neat dichotomies of normality and emergency, nature and culture, inhabiting instead a third dimension: that of the body, poised in its peculiar liminality, and traced by the subtle fil rouge that crucially binds life to law.

2 Health Between Fundamental Rights and Public Finance

The COVID-19 pandemic has not only undeniably revealed that the core of the crisis lay not merely in the governance of public health, but primarily in the social fabric; and while the body and health have long been inscribed within the juridical order as matters of public concern, the normative regulation of these domains has become increasingly entangled with economic logics, thereby heightening their complexity. The issue of public health as a crossroads between the guarantee of fundamental rights and public finance goes beyond the question of the impact of neoliberal policies on public health administrations, and primarily concerns the policies and duties of the State. This is a domain in which the social dimension of contemporary democracies is brought into direct relation with existing public institutions as expressions of liberal democracy.

Indeed, the right to health, as recognized and guaranteed by contemporary democracies, was until quite recently conceived essentially as a matter of control over the body, insofar as it was regarded as a potential issue of public hygiene. In the nineteenth century, health was primarily understood as a matter of hygiene and public sanitation, aimed at containing the emerging diseases in urban areas resulting from the Industrial Revolution and the related challenges of urbanization. Over time, this concern grew in several countries, particularly in Europe, alongside the increasing demand for broader well-being among the working population.[48] It was during this historical period that modern public health systems began to take shape, emerging as a response to the needs of the population.[49]

[48] As noted by Frazer (1950), p. 471 is 'only in the United Kingdom, in some of the Scandinavian countries and, to a lesser extent, in Germany before 1914, that the Public Health and Social Services have reached a high standard of usefulness to their communities'.

[49] As argued by Shepard (1952), p. 3: 'public health, as a community function, has grown out of necessity. It was not imposed from above but developed because the needs of the population demanded it'.

2.1 The Origins of Universal Healthcare

The establishment and evolution of public health organizations continued throughout the early twentieth century, and in the second half (between 1948 and the 1970s-80s), the experience of social reforms in the United Kingdom played a decisive role in shaping the international context, not only in Europe but also in the United States, where, however, the National Health Service (NHS) model would never take hold.[50] After the Second World War, with the establishment of the World Health Organization (WHO), health was defined as 'a state of complete physical, mental and social well-being and not merely the absence of disease or infirmity' and was recognized as a fundamental human right.[51] Over time, public authorities gradually shifted their focus from the body as an object of public control to the individual as a bearer of rights, acknowledging the importance of addressing the social determinants of health, those conditions in which people are born, grow, live, work, and age.[52] During those years, awareness grew regarding the importance of ensuring health through the provision of care services, for which the entire community must take responsibility. Within this perspective, individual health as a condition of collective well-being was effectively embodied in the Welfare State model, which seeks to comprehensively address the various dimensions of well-being, including education, workplace security and dignity, public services more broadly, and so forth.[53] Since its establishment in 1948, the NHS in the United Kingdom has been regarded as the primary representation of this model, to the extent that the two concepts have often been understood as synonymous.[54] The NHS thus became the paradigm of the 'Beveridge model', in which equality in access to healthcare, regardless of economic or social status, gives full meaning to the concept of 'universalism'. This model is characterized by the provision of essential medical care free of charge at the point of delivery and by access for all, based on individual and specific needs. In this sense, the affirmation of social rights and the Welfare State aimed to contribute to overcoming inequalities between social classes. Thus, between 1948 and the early 1980s, many European countries experienced a phase of expansion of the Welfare State centred on universalism. In healthcare, this model translated into universal access to medical care through the NHS, funded by general taxation, with a tax system designed to reflect each individual's actual ability to contribute.

Several countries in Europe, and beyond, have oriented themselves towards the 'Beveridge model' by adopting universalistic (or mixed) healthcare systems aimed

[50] Trattner (1999).

[51] See the Preamble to the Constitution of the World Health Organization signed in New York on July 22, 1946, approved by the Federal Assembly on December 19, 1946, entered into force on April 7, 1948.

[52] Parmet et al. (2020), p. 76; Chapman (2016), p. 248.

[53] See Bruce (1965), p. 259; Pierson (2006), p. 232.

[54] In this regard Jones and Lowe (2002), p. 82, have maintained that 'since its establishment in 1948, the National Health Service has been so closely identified with the welfare state that the two terms have often been considered synonymous'.

at establishing an advanced form of 'health inclusion', theoretically ensuring that everyone can access care without discrimination. Other countries, however, have adopted a different approach based on social insurance, following the 'Bismarck model', albeit strengthening state intervention to provide insurance coverage for the most vulnerable groups. Nevertheless, this distinction oversimplifies healthcare systems, given the heterogeneity of Social Health Insurance (SHI) systems and models similar to the NHS.[55]

It is important to emphasize that systems inspired by the 'Beveridge model' operate within a market framework with the objective of limiting individual dependency. In this sense, it is understood that the Welfare State, and consequently the NHS, was adopted to curb market power over individual conditions and should not be seen as an 'expression of communist ideology'; indeed, its ideological foundation combines a set of liberal values with those inspired by state intervention aimed at mitigating the consequences of excessive liberalism and capitalism.[56] From this perspective, health understood as a fundamental right is recognized and guaranteed primarily at the national level by modern constitutionalism; over time, however, the right to health has begun to be framed as a global issue, and discourse has increasingly shifted towards health at the international level.

2.2 *From Health as a Fundamental Right to Health as a Public Expenditure*

Over the course of the second half of the twentieth century, the right to health began to be recognized at the supranational level within the framework of global health,[57] primarily through the World Health Organization (WHO), whose role has gradually been established over time, albeit not without encountering various obstacles.[58] With the World Health Organization's 'Global Strategy for Health for All' (1981), the idea emerged that an individual's right to health, understood as fundamental, can only be considered guaranteed in a universalistic sense, through a public healthcare system providing care services regardless of personal, social, economic, or geographic conditions. This strategy also assigns states the responsibility for the health of their citizens.[59] Although there is now an awareness that a State that fails to attend to the health of its population undermines its economic potential, creates a risk of social instability, and threatens its global strategic capacity, international health institutions have rarely succeeded in supporting the more ambitious mission of realizing health as a human right, regardless of cost.[60]

[55] den Exter and Syrett (2020), p. 244.

[56] Tobin (2012), pp. 42–43.

[57] Coggon (2024).

[58] Gostin (2014), p. 87; Gostin et al. (2018).

[59] World Health Organization (1981), p. 34.

[60] Tobin (2012), pp. 42–43.

At the State level, the majority of countries have not adopted universalistic models, and some have effectively undermined the effectiveness of their existing national systems by moving towards a voluntary insurance-based model. Although this model includes certain provisions for the care of the underprivileged, it does not guarantee equal access to the right to health. A notable example is the United States, where even essential healthcare services for serious or chronic conditions are not universally insured.[61]

However, the universalism model began to face a crisis in Europe as early as the 1970s, when health policies started to diverge from the original Welfare State framework. This shift was driven by neoliberal demands that characterized the late twentieth century, beginning with the United Kingdom, which had established the universal healthcare system.[62] Health ceased to be solely the concern of the WHO and began to be considered by international economic institutions such as the World Trade Organization (WTO) and the World Bank. In this regard, the 1996 Global Burden of Disease (GBD) report, jointly produced by the World Bank and the WTO, is emblematic, as it proposed 'a new approach to measuring health status',[63] which aimed to measure the overall burden of disease in a population, primarily based on the Disability-Adjusted Life Year (DALY) indicator, through cost-effectiveness evaluation of healthcare interventions.

The 'new measurement of health status' proposed by the GBD introduced an integrated quantitative model that assesses both the quantity and quality of life lost due to disease, disability, and premature death. However, caution has been advised in the use of these specific types of quantitative metrics.[64] From the perspective of 'health equity', many aspects should be considered.[65] The GBD approach claims universality but fails to account for local, cultural, and regulatory contexts, as well as the dimensions of health justice, the right to health, and structural inequalities. Over time, attention has shifted from the mere absence of disease to the promotion of individuals capacities to live healthy lives.[66] The global health model, primarily driven by cost-effectiveness evaluations and cost containment, risks obscuring the political decisions and conflicts of interest that influence healthcare spending choices. In this regard, analyses of the 'philanthrocapitalism' characterizing international health actions highlight that efforts should focus on 'accountability and democratic

---

[61] For this view see Stiglitz (2012), p. 228: 'America has an inefficient health care system that delivers first-rate care to those who are lucky enough to have good insurance or wealthy enough to afford it without insurance'.

[62] On this point see Jones and Lowe (2002), p. 83: 'since the mid-1970s, the NHS has been at the heart of attempts to reform of dismantle the welfare state'; see also Streeck (2024).

[63] Murray and Lopez (1996), p. 2.

[64] According to Adams (2016), p. 1: 'specific kinds of quantitative metrics that make use of evidence-based statistical measures [...] for doing health work in global ways'.

[65] For Sen (2002), pp. 659–666: 'and is best seen as a multidimensional concept. It includes concerns about achievement of health and the capability to achieve good health, not just the distribution of health care'.

[66] Venkatapuram (2011).

decision-making in global health'.[67] In summary, if the data used to construct these mathematical analyses are often incomplete, heterogeneous, or estimated through complex, non-transparent, and difficult-to-verify statistical models, this can lead to a false objectivity that serves to reinforce pre-existing political decisions, thereby undermining any universalistic intent.

It has been highlighted that over time, advancements in healthcare technologies and their rising costs have made it increasingly difficult for healthcare systems in Europe to guarantee universal access. Moreover, the global financial crisis of 2007 and 2008 generated economic pressures significant enough to call into question the sustainability of healthcare services.[68] Restrictive public spending policies, including in healthcare, have characterized the beginning of the current century, based on the idea that excessive expenditure was the cause of the economic crisis and recession. However, it has been clarified that the crises in Europe were not caused by excessive public debt or welfare state systems, but rather by the very austerity measures themselves.[69] Indeed, 'the Welfare State was born into a world of austerity – of rationing, price control, coupons, rent restriction, and houses requisitioned for the use of the homeless'.[70]

Consequently, even the theoretical possibility of using the traditional classification of welfare systems in the healthcare sector appears to be outdated; there would be 'some evidence, in Europe, of a weak form of convergence of health systems driven more by economic constraints than by political and social attitudes'.[71] Even when comparing the United States and the European Union, the differences between the two approaches should not be overstated, because 'European nations are more frequently supplementing national commitments to provide healthcare with private mechanisms'.[72] Indeed, although with regard to access to healthcare 'the comparison between Europe and the United States reveals two very different approaches to dealing with the fundamental question of access to healthcare',[73] not even in those countries where NHS legislation is still in force is equality in access to medical care concretely guaranteed today. This evolution has not been countered by the creation of a European public space for health protection. Indeed, health remains an exclusive national competence within the European Union, much like budgets, although there is room for coordination, complementarity, and support from the EU (Art. 6 TFEU)

---

[67] Birn (2014), p. 19; Birn et al. (2017).

[68] Santuari and Sage (2020), p. 22.

[69] See Stiglitz (2012), p. 220, where he lays the theoretical foundations of its critique of austerity and its consequences on public services: 'Europe crisis is not an accident, but it's not caused by excessive long-term debts and deficit or by the welfare state. It's caused by excessive austerity […]'.

[70] Marshall (1964), p. 294.

[71] Liberati (2024), p. 2.

[72] Santuari and Sage (2020), p. 20.

[73] den Exter et al. (2020), p. 212.

which affirms the right to health as fundamental (Art. 32 CFREU) and provides for a high standard of medical care (Art. 168 TFEU).[74]

The European Union's health policy contains a fundamental contradiction within itself and each member state therefore adopts a different healthcare model. What can be said to unite the various European countries is that 'because Europe has (more or less) universal coverage, its access issues focus first and foremost on central determinations of the treatments and services that are in and out of coverage and what a *right to health* demands'.[75] We are thus witnessing the dismantling of the universalistic model, driven by the realization of the idea of the individual primarily as a market subject—either as a consumer or as a body generating collective costs to be contained. Indeed, this trend is consistent with the orientation that has characterized EU legislation since the establishment of the European Union, with the aim, among others, of creating the conditions for the free movement of goods within the single European market, even though, over time, the fundamental rights of the European Union have also been affirmed through the Charter of Fundamental Rights of the European Union (CFREU), which was granted the same legal value as the founding Treaties (2009). The tension between health and the market is well illustrated, in this respect, by EU pharmaceutical legislation, which seeks to harmonize national rules on the free circulation of medicines as goods, while at the same time pursuing the objective of protecting public health.[76] This context reflects the general EU-inspired political trend toward reducing public intervention in the economy, which is regarded as a factor limiting business competition (consider, for instance, the prohibition of State aid).

Moreover, the neoliberal orientation of European Union policies, which has indirectly affected the way in which social rights, including the right to health, are safeguarded in the various Member States, has, over the decades, been accompanied by a certain retreat in the achievements concerning the freedom of bodies from public authorities' control. Indeed, there is a tendency toward the (resurgence of) bodily control by public authorities, reflecting policies that limit individual choices, even at the risk of personal health. A notable example is the recent shift in the approach to (safe) access to voluntary termination of pregnancy in the United States.[77] Not by chance. Historically, it is on women's bodies that both the drive toward public control, through the medicalization of the choice to terminate a pregnancy, and the denial of health as a right requiring a public healthcare system have been concentrated, as

[74] As noted by Mossialos et al. (2010), p. 4: 'Health Policy in the European Union (EU) has a fundamental contradiction at ist core'; see also Hervey and McHale (2015b), pp. 535–550.

[75] den Exter et al. (2020), p. 211. On the dismantling of the NHS in England, see Roderick and Pollock (2022).

[76] Directive 2001/83/EC of the European Parliament and of the Council of 6 November 2001 on the Community code relating to medicinal products for human use.

[77] Murray and Shaw (2024), pp. 793–864.

inequalities in access have persisted both within individual States and across the European Union.[78]

More generally, the relentless pursuit of control over bodies is reflected in public security policies which, as already noted before, in turn generate insecurity. Emergencies, in fact, generate a demand for security and legitimize security policies by States, justifying a transformation of democratic decision-making processes toward a speed allegedly incompatible with parliamentary democracies. Fundamental rights and freedoms, such as freedom of movement, assembly, and expression, which, during the COVID-19 pandemic, faced unprecedented restrictions in contemporary democracies, are today subjected to normative stress by post-pandemic security policies, which have by now been normalized through the pandemic experience. This highlights how health universalism implies the ability to reconcile both a public commitment to guaranteeing health with minimal intervention in the control of bodies.

2.3 *The COVID-19 Pandemic Crisis as Opportunity for Rethinking Public Health*

However, the imperative nature of universal health guarantee can still be discerned today in theoretical studies highlighting the close connection between health and equality. In this regard, the COVID-19 pandemic has globally and indiscriminately revealed the inseparable link between the right to health and equality, as well as the public role in addressing health inequalities, which has long been central to the international debate.[79] The issue of access to COVID-19 vaccines highlighted the shortcomings and contradictions of the global health system. However, it was only in May 2025 that the 78th World Health Assembly adopted, with 124 votes in favour and 11 abstentions, the new Global Pandemic Agreement—the result of years of international negotiations initiated in response to the challenges revealed during the COVID-19 pandemic. The Agreement aims to make the world safer and more equitable in the prevention, preparedness, and response to future pandemics. Certainly, the recent pandemic has both revealed and exacerbated the well-known dynamics of market failures and the inequalities they can produce[80] and the European Union could have played an important role in guaranteeing rights, coordinating scientific research, and in the production and procurement of vaccines.

The direction in which the EU has moved has not reflected these expectations. Yet, the COVID-19 pandemic has clearly demonstrated and taught us the impossibility of

[78] As argued by Isailović (2025), p. 1: '[...] current EU legal frameworks contribute to producing a system of stratified reproductive freedom which entrenches intersectional gender-based inequalities'.

[79] Anand et al. (2005), p. 15.

[80] See Stiglitz (2012), p. xiii: 'markets, by themselves, even when they are stable, often lead to high levels of inequality, outcomes that are widely viewed as unfair'.

guaranteeing health without a collective public effort that ensures everyone's access to essential and life-saving care.

The experience of this pandemic does not seem to have called the current system into question; rather, it appears to have exacerbated existing problems.[81] The global health emergency and the inability of states and international organizations to govern it have exposed a crisis of democracy –understood not only in its formal sense but also in its substantive capacity to guarantee social rights, as established in Europe during the last century with the shift from liberal democracy, understood solely in formal terms, to social democracy, i.e., substantive democracy. Moreover, already in the second half of the last century, there was awareness that the development of the Welfare State had challenged the classical liberal model of democracy, highlighting the transformation of the role of the state. The state could no longer be limited to protecting individual freedoms but had to concretely guarantee fundamental rights (e.g., education and health). This awareness was not limited to countries where constitutional charters had explicitly assigned duties to the state; in such places, the role of the state was theoretically expanded to the point of imagining that the state bears the duty to guarantee the necessary services and fulfil social rights.[82] The 1970s and 1980s, as previously highlighted, were the decades during which the universal healthcare model was established in several European states, while simultaneously beginning to experience a crisis, starting with the NHS in the UK. Notable contributions from that era, defending the Welfare State, clearly emphasized how the greatest political support for that model was vested in the NHS. This led to the construction of its defence by reaffirming the principle that having to pay for medical care is wrong, that having to pay creates a barrier to some necessary medical treatments, that citizens are healthier than they were prior to the existence of the NHS, and that, comparatively, countries with an NHS exhibit better health outcomes.[83] Over time, in Europe, however, a certain disenchantment with the NHS appears to have grown even within its country of origin (UK).[84] In fact, the problem with guaranteeing health through universalistic systems is that legal mechanisms to compel the state to ensure such guarantees have not been theorized. What was lacking at the time was the development of a coherent theory of social State law capable of establishing itself[85] which today is instead being proposed, and which entails refunding existing institutions on new grounds and introducing appropriate safeguards for social rights through so-called 'guarantee institutions'; it is thus considered possible to reconstruct the foundations of universalism within a framework of global constitutionalism that takes social rights guarantees seriously, foremost among them the right to health,[86] in order to address the real needs of individuals and peoples. The COVID-19 pandemic has taught that only truly universal healthcare systems are capable of guaranteeing,

---

[81] Streeck (2024).

[82] Plant (1985), p. 28–29.

[83] Willcocks (1985), pp. 257–258.

[84] Syrett (2003), p. 716.

[85] Ferrajoli (1982).

[86] Ferrajoli (2022), p. 20.

especially in times of emergency, health for all and healthcare efficiency. Precisely due to the lack of effectiveness of universal health, instead of restoring to health its full meaning as a universal right, the COVID-19 emergency resulted in an exponential differentiation of health guarantees, not only between different countries worldwide, but also among individuals within the same state, based on socio-economic conditions.

3 Between Surveillance and Solidarity: Health and the Privacy Dilemma

Contemporary societies are increasingly experiencing the intensification of two, conflicting tendencies. On the one hand, as we have seen, the obligation to guarantee health as a public duty coupled with a political responsibility by States and international bodies; on the other, the opposing desire of individuals not to suffer excessive intrusions into their personal privacy. Such dichotomy appears, in every respect, to be an irreconcilable and arguably tragic conflict: depending on the perspective adopted, scholars argue, one of the two imperatives inevitably gives way, allowing the other to dominate.[87]

The recent COVID-19 pandemic has starkly demonstrated the enduring relevance of this dilemma, bringing it once more to the centre of scholarly and political debates. A clear example is the use of telemedicine and the suite of home monitoring technologies that, not only in Europe or in the United States but also across the globe, organized and managed the sensitive data of millions of patients.[88] From the simple measurement of body temperature to the constant monitoring of vital signs, these data often passed through private company servers, clouds and digital infrastructures, making them susceptible to illegitimate appropriation, theft, or cyberattacks. This represents, once again, a conundrum that is difficult and perhaps even impossible to resolve. While the effectiveness of such tools in treating patients and promptly isolating sources of infection has been widely acknowledged, they have also sparked concerns over the emergence of a digital surveillance apparatus whose effects may now be universal.[89]

The idea frequently proposed to resolve this dilemma is some form of ongoing *balancing* between these two imperatives.[90] A solution, however, that is itself not without difficulty. On the one hand, we easily and daily testify the intrinsic tendency of such technologies to constantly expand their scope and precision; on the other, the inadequacy of existing legal frameworks to effectively regulate and respond to health emergencies opens troubling questions about a potential dystopian future.[91] From

[87] For a brief overview about these two, conflicting tendencies, see Vayena (2018), p. 157.

[88] Jalali et al. (2021).

[89] Gerke et al. (2020).

[90] Lenert and McSwain (2020).

[91] Fahey and Hino (2020).

this cost-benefit perspective, some scholars have emphasized the highly positive value of infectious disease control, particularly at the international level, presenting it as the most effective means of safeguarding health as a public good.[92] Critics, by contrast, have denounced its use as yet another form of the 'mechanisation' of life. Within this clash of opposing visions, however, the true stakes of the debate become clear.

3.1 *The Geopolitical Dimensions of Public Health*

According to proponents of 'epidemic intelligence', the non-stop tracking of pathogenic agents and the quantitative and statistical measurement of diseases are vital to maintaining global public health.[93] This surveillance model represents a close observation of the living, comparing the quality of care across public and private sectors while simultaneously monitoring high-risk groups (such as the homeless, migrants, and health workers). In the case of potential pandemics, such monitoring becomes even more crucial, as it enables the immediate comparison of data and facilitates the first level of response and intervention. More importantly, if even a single country evades such monitoring tasks or refuses to share data transparently, it thereby constitutes an international threat and a political menace for the entire world population. It seems, once again, that political language heavily permeates the field of health law, acquiring not only the 'military' features already described in previous section, but also a distinctly *geopolitical* inflection.[94]

The phenomenon is not entirely new, though it is not recent either. Beginning in the mid-1950s, public health acquired a distinct surveillance dimension, initially directed at individuals and later extended to diseases more broadly. The primary aim was to enable the timely activation of appropriate measures, first at the local level and subsequently at the international level. This system may be described as a *Westphalian model*, insofar as it remained tied to territorial borders and was principally coordinated by sovereign nations, which retained the authority to control information and to decide whether, and to what extent, it could circulate. Soon, however, this model evolved and expanded, assuming an increasingly extensive scope. The emergence, after 9/11, of global terrorism, bioweapons, and the deliberate use of diseases as instruments of attack against states and civilian populations marked a decisive paradigm shift. A notable example in this regard is the Global Public Health Intelligence Network (GPHIN), an online Canadian monitoring system for potential health-related terrorist threats which, by effectively bypassing national borders, positioned itself as a new regulator in the circulation of sensitive information concerning diseases and epidemics. But, as anticipated, the first real testing ground for the emergence of a new framework was the spread of the H1N1 virus and the ensuing pandemic in

[92] For this position, see Youde (2010), p. 6.

[93] See the seminal contribution by Bloch et al. (1996).

[94] On this point, see the detailed analysis provided by Weir and Mykhalovskiy (2007).

2009, soon followed by the Ebola outbreak in West Africa in 2014. From both a political and a risk-management perspective, these events led to a marked expansion of surveillance and screening policies, though often judged inadequate.[95] This led also to an intensification of tracking activities on a global scale and to growing demands for more proactive intervention, with the aim of pushing detection *prior* to diagnosis. We thus witness the emergence of a new framework, a *post-Westphalian model*, in which health data becomes a valuable source of information and intelligence, turning health policies into more radical forms of *bio-security*.[96] What should be emphasized here is the essentially military origin of this trajectory. Initially conceived within the framework of counterterrorism, then slowly adapted to flu transmission and local contagions, the state of emergency model generated by the potential bacteriological threat progressively expanded to encompass public health more broadly, thereby imposing a regulatory regime in which the exception is absorbed into (and normalised within) the rule.[97] As David P. Fidler aptly notes,

> [t]he deepest synergy levels for biosecurity policy in intervention appear in capabilities for responses to infectious disease outbreaks. Both security and public health experts acknowledge that addressing intentionally-caused or naturally-occurring outbreaks requires similar types of interventions to control the epidemic, break any chain of transmission, treat the infected, and move society toward recovery. Such interventions include mass distribution and administration of antibiotics or vaccines, surge capacity in health care facilities to provide clinical treatment to the ill, and the capability to engage in quarantine and isolation of infected persons or those suspected of being infected.[98]

This does not, of course, imply that States have lost their relevance; on the contrary, sensitive information still circulates through national administrative structures. Yet the singular, corporeal life of the human being increasingly appears enmeshed in a spiral where the paradigm of 'universal contagion' asserts itself as the prevailing, timeless political model.[99]

There are, however, plausible grounds for maintaining that the two spheres remain separate: that the monitoring of sensitive population data does not result in a gross violation of privacy, provided it is directed towards the overarching aim of safeguarding global public health.[100] Anyway, what must be recognised beyond specific positions on the matter, is that any support for loosening the right to privacy in favour of intensified control over population' sensitive data inevitably rests on an implicit argument: that anatomy is not simply a medical science but rather an *anatomo-politics*, a domain in which the governance of bodies becomes inseparable from their biological management.[101] Echoing the writings of the French philosopher Michel

[95] For a critical view about the World Health Organization's management of such health crises, see Kamradt-Scott (2017).

[96] About the first use of this dual model in health law, see Fidler (2003).

[97] As noted by Reingold (2003), p. 77.

[98] Fidler (2007), p. 212.

[99] For this view, see famously Hardt and Negri (2000), p. 136.

[100] About the strong moral justification of pandemic surveillance, see e.g. Sorell (2023), p. 15.

[101] For this aspect, see Tesh (1988).

Foucault, an author who will recur frequently throughout this volume, the body emerges then as the fundamental precondition for public decision-making, and, at the same time, as the essential outcome for geopolitical governance.[102] We have never ceased to be a Foucauldian society and, if anything, we seem to be moving ever further in that direction. According to Foucault, indeed, anatomy and the study of body's morphologies are directly implicated as a central focus of power's interests, giving rise to what he famously called *biopower*.[103] If anatomo-politics focuses on the individual body, biopolitics extends this logic to the collective level, where governments regulate the vital processes of populations like birth and reproduction, mortality, epidemies, and the management of demographic trends.

But here lies the decisive point. Biopolitics is a politics of life, understood both as the management of living beings and as their continuous surveillance: it is about power as well as about personhood.[104] It is no coincidence that, in developing this model, Foucault drew particular inspiration from Jeremy Bentham's famous penal institution: the *Panopticon*, in which a single observer could oversee, at a glance, the entire prison population arranged around them.[105] This *panoptic sort*, as Oscar Gandy has compellingly argued, is not merely a model of reference: it represents a systemic and structural political transformation that directly affects our economies, our legal systems, our morality, and our international order.[106] Once again, within this transformation, the body persists as a continuum, as an enduring locus where political paradigms invariably converge in ways that we might not previously have imagined.

3.2 *Privacy and the Marketisation of Health*

At the heart of current debates on health surveillance and the economic logic of data extraction, the capitalist dimension of contemporary biopolitics occupies a central place. In a widely discussed volume, Shoshana Zuboff described 'surveillance capitalism' as the dominant logic within our neoliberal economies.[107] According to Zuboff, surveillance capitalism cannot be reduced to an economic logic alone; rather, it also carries profound moral and political implications, extending to a micro-analytical control of movements and behaviours that risks assuming an almost totalising character. Our cities are now increasingly approaching a paradigm of *smart health*, in which the same data-tracking and management technologies already heavily employed for geolocation services, advertising, and marketing promotions,

[102] Foucault (1977), p. 25.
[103] Foucault (1978), p. 139.
[104] As emphasized by Lyon (2007), p. 23.
[105] Elmer (2012), p. 21.
[106] Gandy Jr (2021), p. 50.
[107] Zuboff (2019).

are internalized in order to deliver care and, parallelly, to generate profit.[108] The very concept of privacy, long regarded as central to our collective and legal imagination, thus appears, almost abruptly, to have become *obsolete*.

To trace this history is, once again, to grasp the role played by the juridical concept of the body. Over the course of the twentieth century, privacy gradually attained the status of constitutional right, as testified for example in the United States, where privacy was famously defined by Warren and Brandeis as the 'right to be let alone'.[109] This is, evidently, a particularly strong and almost absolute characterization, one in which the private sphere is understood as inviolable by the State, to the extent that the individual body is emphatically framed as a kind of sacred space, a sort of *sanctuary*, into which no external interference is permissible.[110] Most notably, the recognition of a constitutional right to abortion in *Roe v. Wade* (1973) rested on a distinctive interpretation of the woman's right to privacy, understood as the legitimate exclusion of the State from any interference conflicting with her decision concerning the continuation of pregnancy.[111] But can medical surveillance, when it extends beyond the physician-patient relationship, disrupt this absolute domain of privacy? For many, rethinking privacy today means precisely recognizing how the right to health has become, in every respect, a social right, and thus an expression of a *communal spirit* to be mitigated in the light of a broader political dimension.[112] Privacy is a minor value, something that can be sacrificed in the aim of saving lives: before the individual body, which is our own, there stand many other bodies that, through ours, might live or survive. The crucial issue, then, is to determine the extent to which the solidarity that should lead individuals to accept health screenings and monitoring for the sake of collective well-being risks, at the other extreme, sliding into a form of permanent surveillance.[113]

It is precisely to address these theoretical and practical challenges that Carissa Véliz, in a recent volume, proposed a new theory of privacy adapted to the changing landscape of contemporary society.[114] According to Véliz, rather than accepting growing demands for greater intrusions into privacy in the name of the public interest, we should instead assert that a valid theory of privacy can only be sustained *within* an institutional framework that is democratic, grounded in the rule of law, and committed to protecting individual rights and guarantees. A robust theory of privacy, she argues, can succeed if situated within an institutional context that is intrinsically egalitarian, rooted in the democratic framework, and structured to uphold individual rights and legal protections. In other words, no meaningful theory of privacy can ever exist

[108] For a detailed analysis of the concept of 'smart health', see Pramanik et al. (2017).

[109] Warren and Brandeis (1890), p. 214.

[110] For a specific U.S. centred analysis of the right to privacy, see Fairchild et al. (2007).

[111] For a recent investigation on abortion, privacy, and U.S. case law, see Aseltine and Ekland-Olson (2025).

[112] As argued, for example, by Stroup et al. (2004) and Lombardo and Ross (2007).

[113] On the potential problems of balancing privacy and security considerations during pandemics, see Miller and Smith (2023), p. 51.

[114] Véliz (2024).

without a legal infrastructure capable of protecting individuals from potential abuses. Any form of digitalization is, by its very nature, also a potential form of surveillance: what is required is a solid ethical framework to ensure that every act of tracking (digital or not) is accompanied by a set of controls. From the other side, it is possible also to speak of an excess of privacy, which manifests in antisocial behaviours that fundamentally undermine the very premise of living in a shared society.

3.3 Ageing, Immortal Bodies, and the Dystopia of Perfect Health

Medicalised bodies, surveilled bodies: bodies drawn ever nearer to the nascent utopia of immortality and to the gradual erasure of death. Bodies propelled to their utmost potential, reshaped and re-inscribed, projected towards an imagined perfection of form and health. The paradigm of surveillance, united with the constant scrutiny of diseases and with the relentless monitoring of health data has, in recent years, driven medical discourse towards a new and futuristic objective: the pursuit of *ultra-age*.[115] If it is true, as the WHO asserts, that 'the pace of population ageing is much faster than in the past' and that 'between 2015 and 2050, the proportion of the world's population over 60 years will nearly double from 12% to 22%', then the pursuit of a longer and healthier life in which health and well-being are combined emerges as the cornerstone of a political agenda that is not merely local but planetary in scope.[116] How, then, can this latest emergency in the field of health law be addressed and effectively prevented? How can a living being, that is by nature mortal, nevertheless aspire to 'forget' death or at least to suspend its horizon? In a celebrated contribution, sociologist Zygmunt Bauman underscored precisely this dimension of a constant transgression of life's limits and of liberation from death as a defining feature of medical research. According to Baumann,

> [t]he truth that death cannot be escaped is not denied – it cannot be denied; but it could be held out of the agenda, elbowed out by another truth: that each *particular* case of death (most importantly, death which threatens the particular person, me, at the particular moment, now) can be resisted, postponed or avoided altogether. Death as such is inevitable; but each concrete instance of death is contingent. Death is omnipotent and invincible; but none of the specific cases of death is.[117]

In contemporary society, a strange and paradoxical mechanism emerges: on the one hand, mortality appears as something inevitable and ever-present; on the other, precisely because of this omnipresence, it is effectively displaced and concealed beneath the persistence of particular 'causes' of death. In this view, death as such ceases to exist in its entirety and is instead fragmented into micro-causes, each to be analytically addressed in advance through medical or pharmacological intervention.

---

115 On the theme of ageing, see Doron and Georgantzi (2018).

116 WHO (2022).

117 Bauman (1992), p. 5.

As Bauman observes, while death itself cannot be avoided, it is indeed possible to act in order to *prevent* heart attacks, obesity, blood clots, or certain types of cancer. The consequence of this logic is a pervasive process of medicalisation, through which the body becomes inseparable from medical technologies and biomedical progress:

> A death that has not been prevented does not undermine the authority of the medical profession. At worst it may stain the reputation of an individual doctor. But the condemnation of the individual practitioner only reinforces the authority of the art: the doctor's fault was not to use the tools and the procedures he *could use*. He is guilty precisely because the profession as a whole is capable of doing what he did not do, though should have done. [...] The means have not been invented *yet*; the equipment has not been developed, the vaccine has not been discovered, the technique has not been tested. But they will, given time and money. Conquest of no disease is *in principle* impossible.[118]

There are, strictly speaking, no defeats for medicine, but only cases that reveal its future potential, its ongoing engineering, and its massive expansion. In other words, medicine operates through powerful accelerations: through technologies and procedures awaiting deployment which, however, require constant surveillance of the body and close monitoring of the most specific dimensions of disease in order to be realised and advanced. This is what leads Bauman to argue that the horror of death has been diluted and dissected into minute *fragments*, each susceptible to be targeted, until the experience of dying itself becomes the premise for a constant observation of life in its most minute details.

We might be tempted to dismiss Bauman's interpretation as no more than a highly dystopian scenario, far removed from social reality. Yet the rise and growing success of Digital Healthcare and AI in recent years point to a picture strikingly close to the hypothesis of constant and pervasive control over all actors within the medical ecosystem.[119] Particularly significant is the use of massive repositories of medical and genetic data to anticipate the onset of disease, deliver accurate diagnoses, and trace predictive patterns. Alongside this, the proliferation of portable devices, technologies capable of producing personalised pharmaceuticals, and systems for the continuous monitoring of the body are ushering in what has been described as a 'fourth revolution' in medicine.[120] In this sense, AI emerges as the perfect corollary to Bauman's vision: a technology that promises to push death ever further away, but only by making it obsessively present in every action, every gesture, every heartbeat of the body. Even the WHO now appears aligned with this trajectory. In a recently published memorandum, it explicitly acknowledges that AI, despite the inevitable risks it entails, has become indispensable for promoting human well-being, safety, and the public interest, and that any concrete development of medicine can no longer proceed without the constant extraction of data from the human body.[121]

Surveillance stands then at the threshold of a dual project: on the one hand, a political enterprise of control and governance; on the other, a medico-scientific

---

[118] Bauman (1992), p. 6.

[119] See recently Corrales Compagnucci et al. (2022).

[120] Jayanthi et al. (2019), p. 58.

[121] WHO (2021), p. 26.

endeavour indispensable for the production of knowledge and the advancement of care. It is precisely at this intersection that the tension between privacy, public health, and democratic legitimacy becomes most acute in a logic of progressive accumulation. And, we may add, it is precisely at this juncture that rule and exception begin to coalesce, to the point of becoming hybridised. While public health was initially concerned with the emergence of specific diseases, epidemiology soon evolved into a classificatory science, expanding its observational scope to a vast array of potential diseases, like chronic conditions, psychiatric and mental illnesses, workplace injuries, traffic accidents, dietary and sedentary lifestyle-related risk factors, and so on.[122] The discourse on longevity pushes this logic even further, articulating a modernist utopia in which the prospect of mortality is increasingly censored, displaced by an ethic of extreme morality that elevates health to the status of a moral duty. Life itself has become the object of constant, meticulous, and far-reaching observation that draws the clinical gaze closer to a re-moralisation of health issues.[123] In this tyranny of health 'at all costs', life ceases to possess an autonomous meaning and is reduced to a mere instrument, subordinated to the imperative of preservation and optimisation. Every state requires healthy bodies that could work, produce, and generate wealth: efficient bodies capable of creating value, or, equally, bodies from which value can be extracted. This is not to invoke dystopian scenarios, but rather to acknowledge how the governance of living beings already operates, and how each of our lives is embedded within specific, and increasingly constitutive, political-managerial evaluations.[124] Illness undoubtedly rests on a biological foundation, yet the boundary between the 'normal' and the 'pathological' is often the result of social construction, an act of political engineering which, if left unchecked, risks producing stigma and discrimination.[125]

The central challenge contemporary societies face is that data can never be deployed in a neutral manner; its use is always embedded within circuits of production and erasure, inscription and suppression, definition and dissolution. In this sense, the collection of empirical data does not merely result in an accumulation of information; it operates as an instrument that actively produces and configures political and social realities. We are moulded by the very machinery that observes us: an apparatus which, in the act of observation, produces new meanings of what we are and to which we are, in turn, increasingly compelled to conform. But what kind of society is one in which health becomes a compulsory condition for productivity? And what model of life is it that, while seemingly centred on well-being, conceals instead a profound moral and spiritual alienation? In the collapse of the categories of normality and emergency, and in the rise of a third dimension defined by their ambiguity, future pandemics and emerging diseases will place health law at the centre of

[122] For an historical overview of this process, see Armstrong (1995) and Choi (2012).

[123] On the increasing shift of surveillance toward a microscopic, invasive, and managerial form, see also Lyon (2003), p. 15.

[124] As acknowledged by Weir and Mykhalovskiy (2010), p. 6.

[125] On this aspect, see Macnicol (2006).

yet another decisive arena of confrontation and governance.[126] Developing a solid legal theory capable of clearly determining who is entitled to access certain information, who is authorized to manage it, and who ultimately holds the right to translate it into public decision-making directly concerns the strength and quality of our future democracies.

4 Digital Health Between the Dimension of 'Post-Human Care' and the Paradigm of 'Person-Centred Care'

The transparency of information is central to the debate on contemporary democracy, particularly considering that democracy has long been understood as the government of 'visible power'.[127] From this perspective, the discussion on widespread access to information has shaped the evolution of administrative law in Europe, where the U.S. FOIA has been widely adopted, with all its limitations and implementation challenges.[128] Contemporary law provides instruments to guarantee access to information and recognizes that knowledge is indispensable for effective public participation in decision-making. Yet, even today, we experience a deficit of transparency in our democracies. The public health sector is not exempt from the tendency toward opacity on the part of public decision-makers. In an era in which healthcare systems are confronted with countless new possibilities for knowledge offered by emerging technologies, we still face informational asymmetries, often dictated by market logics; in this respect, the issue of confidentiality surrounding the prices of innovative high-cost medicines is emblematic.[129]

In this context, digital healthcare today stands at a crossroads between a 'post-human dimension of care'—characterized by the extensive use of advanced technologies, artificial intelligence, and automation, which redefine the relationship between body, identity, and medical treatment—and the simultaneously urgent and complex goal of humanizing care, understood as a 'person-centred approach' that safeguards the dignity, complexity, and real needs of the individual, beyond their mere role as a patient and cost generator for the community.

[126] For the surveillance model applied to future pandemics, see Thomas (2014).

[127] Bobbio (2014), p. 81.

[128] Pozen and Schudson (2018).

[129] According to Gautier and David (2022), p. 9: 'a more democratic way of governing pharmaceutical policies'.

4.1 *Digital Health as a Tool to Promote Knowledge in the Service of the Humanization of Care*

In addition to representing a powerful tool for scientific research, digitalization in the healthcare sector could open unprecedented scenarios of significant relevance for healthcare systems, enhancing the participation of individuals, patients, healthcare professionals, and ordinary citizens. Yet, the path towards what could be defined as the 'humanization of care', understood as 'person-centred care' in their full complexity, with real needs and not merely as a patient generating costs for the community, appears today complicated precisely by the digital revolution in healthcare. Indeed, the progressive loss of effectiveness of universal access to care within universalistic healthcare models, alongside the crisis of the networks of international health institutions, has in recent years been exacerbated by digital inequalities and by the tendency to exert control over bodies through new technologies.

If, in the twenty-first century, public healthcare has been profoundly influenced, like every other sphere of social life, by the digital technological revolution,[130] nowadays the term 'Digital Health' evokes not only various digital tools now integrated into healthcare services, but also numerous questions and challenges that the digital revolution brings with it to the healthcare sector.[131]

The COVID-19 pandemic has highlighted many of the most debated issues concerning the relationship between new technologies, health, and rights, intensifying the discourse on the use of new technologies in healthcare, primarily due to the pervasive social control they have enabled.[132] Among the digital tools encompassed by the Digital Health, it is possible to distinguish between digital devices directly involved in research and care delivery, and technologies supporting the organizational and managerial aspects of healthcare systems.

Telemedicine emerged in healthcare systems across various countries prior to the COVID-19 pandemic and has contributed to transforming the perspective on the doctor-patient relationship. Even before the range of devices connecting healthcare professionals to patients expanded and were recognized as useful for delivering care without direct physical contact, these tools began to establish themselves as a solution to bridge geographical distances that concretely limit the provision of care. Yet, the pandemic simultaneously underscored the importance of the proximity of local healthcare facilities to individuals and communities. Indeed, preventive activities—central to the medical philosophy that inspired the birth and development of public healthcare, particularly within universalistic models—primarily entail the concrete possibility of physically reaching people.[133] Public health has traditionally been understood in connection with the well-being of populations and is not considered

[130] Rizoulieres and Béranger (2021), pp. 1–6.

[131] Lupton (2014), Fontaine and Clinck (2022).

[132] Hutler et al. (2022), Rothstein (2021), pp. 666–676.

[133] For Eckstein (1959), p. 268, the first objective of the NHS was 'to remove all barriers between patient and treatment by the removal of economics barriers, the geographical redistribution of doctors and facilities [...]'.

merely a matter of healthcare services.[134] Recently, artificial intelligence and machine learning have been transforming the landscape of diagnostic and predictive services aimed at healthcare prevention, offering previously unimaginable possibilities such as personalized medicine. Robotics and virtual realities are revolutionizing surgical and rehabilitation activities, as well as medical training in general.

Numerous health and wellness applications, for which every individual is a potential consumer, are widely available on the market. Through digital devices, it is possible not only to monitor physical activity and nutrition but also to track patients' therapeutic adherence by continuously monitoring the wearer's vital parameters, thereby enabling new modes of self-monitoring and tracking.[135] In this context, the issue of control over the body by public authorities through surveillance in public health also becomes central in the digital era.[136] This can be understood as an expression of the current surveillance capitalism.[137]

The use of this variety of tools is envisaged by healthcare systems in various countries to increase access to medical care, especially in peripheral areas, to overall improve the efficiency of healthcare services, to make patients more engaged and informed, to facilitate prevention even at home, to promote personalized medicine, and to support the care of elderly individuals.[138] In these terms, Digital Health would not, in itself and as such, be a source of inequalities or a multiplier of them.

However, many healthcare systems in Europe still lack adequate technological capabilities to effectively manage these processes. Although several leading centres make extensive use of advanced technologies, healthcare administrations generally lag behind in digital organization, even in adopting basic tools such as electronic health records, which could have significantly improved healthcare delivery long ago. However, the use of big data and predictive analytics requires the capacity to collect and process large amounts of health data both to support clinical decisions and to inform health policy choices. An effort to standardize the capabilities of various healthcare facilities across regions thus appears to be a priority and a prerequisite for any discussion about using new technologies to envision the reorganization of services. The issue shifts the focus onto the proprietary, ethical, economic, and social implications of these transformations in the healthcare sector. Indeed, healthcare digitalization today theoretically enables full interoperability of health data across different healthcare facilities, primarily those within the same healthcare system. This requires the management of personal data and consequently raises concerns regarding privacy. From this perspective, the main challenges and current issues essentially relate to two areas: the first, traditionally linked to privacy and data protection, now also includes electronic informed consent; the second concerns the potential amplification of healthcare inequalities and the ineffectiveness of 'patient-centred care'.

---

[134] Gostin and Wiley (2016), Hervey and McHale (2015a).

[135] For the self-tracking see Lupton (2016).

[136] Black et al. (2019).

[137] Zuboff (2019).

[138] Andreoni and Mambretti (2021).

The universalism of access to healthcare can find valid support in certain digital tools only on the condition that it does not become a multiplier of inequality in health.[139] The digital divide and digital inequalities, which concern the inability to access or effectively use technologies, reflect new technological trends in inequality. Within the same reasoning lies the issue of the (further) risk of losing the doctor-patient relationship. Indeed, the universalism of access to care represents a model that centres on the humanization of healthcare, viewing the medical aspect of treatment as an element to be integrated with a broader attention to the person as someone in need of listening and dialogue.

In this regard, the personalization of medicine through digital healthcare must be accompanied by the universalistic humanization of care, with its attention to individual differences. The rejection of the idea of standardizing care translates into the caregiving relationship and the impossibility of completely replacing human interaction.

From this perspective, the shift from focusing on bodies to emphasizing the rights of the person should guide the development of digital health, ensuring it does not result in the depersonalization of care. In this sense, the challenge of healthcare digitalization for national health systems lies in their ability to integrate big data management, pharmacological epidemiology and medical care, into traditional epidemiology, taking into account socio-economic variables, so as to highlight the issues faced by the most marginalized populations that impact even their survival.[140] If universalism is not reconstructed in this sense, it is difficult to envision fully harnessing the potential of technology in healthcare without merely enduring its greatest challenges. The guiding principle for any use of health technology in public decision-making, from this perspective, is equality, understood primarily as the recognition and care of the specific needs of each individual and population. From this perspective, Digital Health represents a challenge in the arduous path toward what could be defined as the 'humanization of care', understood as 'care centred on the person' in their full complexity, with real needs, and not merely as a patient generating costs for the community. A healthcare digitalization that enables the personalization of care would allow gaps in healthcare systems, whether informational or organizational, to be addressed, contributing to the reduction of inequalities. The task, then, is to respond to the critical issues of healthcare digitalization from the perspective of overcoming the primacy of the market over the individual. In these terms, Digital Health does not indicate a trajectory toward post-human care but should be understood as serving the 'humanization of care', restoring to health its universalistic dimension.

---

[139] According to Blake et al. (2021), p. 413: 'as immediate COVID-19 concerns encourage greater telehealth access, safe and uniform implementation is necessary to combat the COVID-19 outbreak and general health disparities going forward. Studies on understanding how to fully engage underserved populations in telehealth are critical to expanding equity in telehealth usage'.

[140] Tognoni and Cauduro (2018), p. 165.

In conclusion, one of the central challenges posed by digital health lies in its potential to foster knowledge as a means of ensuring transparency in public decision-making processes. Within this framework, digital health should be conceived not merely as a set of technological tools, but as an instrument capable of promoting informed participation and enhancing democratic accountability in the governance of healthcare. In this sense, digital health ought to serve the broader objective of the humanization of care, understood as the affirmation of a 'person-centred model' that recognizes the complexity, dignity, and concrete needs of individuals.

5 This Book

The structure of this book deliberately follows an interdisciplinary and composite trajectory, situated along the margins of contact between law and other fields—specifically history, sociology, and the philosophy of science—on the conviction that a topic as complex as the body and its medico-legal status must be approached also, and indeed especially, through the analytical tools offered by dialogue with other domains of knowledge.

The first part, entitled *Law, Medicine, and the Early Modern Epistemology of the Body*, aims to trace a genealogy of the relationships linking the body, quantification, medical science, and health emergency. The overarching idea guiding this section is to show how medical and legal techniques have evolved in a mutually reinforcing manner in their attempt to administer and govern the body both under conditions of apparent 'normality' (health) and under those of 'emergency' (illness). The essays collected demonstrate that both law and medicine operate as techniques of observation and regulation of bodies, with the dual purpose of deciphering corporeal symptoms and assimilating them within a particular epistemic framework. What thus emerges is the significance of law as a regulatory mechanism during the first pandemics in Europe in the early modern period; of medical science in its endeavour to codify alternative states of illness and health; and of quantification as an art employed to classify, measure, and compare the health conditions of individuals. All of this, though separated by centuries, reveals the intricate ensemble of knowledges that have historically converged around the idea of the body, and how that idea has—at every stage—shifted in accordance with specific scientific and political paradigms.

The second part, *Philosophies of the Body and Legal Responses to Health Emergencies*, turns more specifically to the biopolitics of the body by examining the concept of health at the intersection between power and the governance of life. The legal-philosophical thought of Michel Foucault provides a privileged framework for rethinking the relationship between individual freedom and states of health emergency, particularly by tracing the complex nexus that links biopolitics and governmentality as techniques directed towards the control and measurement of life in contemporary society. This section therefore seeks to clarify the political—often securitarian—context that shapes certain health-related measures, especially those adopted during recurrent states of health emergency, showing how the very notion of exception has expanded to the point of being deployed continually, across a wide spectrum of circumstances. Once again, it is the body that constitutes the concrete locus where both health-related and non-health-related policies take effect within the contemporary legal landscape. *Healthism* and *medicalization* emerge, in this regard, as two paradigms of legal-medical action that—also through the intervention of states and international organisations—now set the agenda for a redefined approach to life, health, and disease. The stakes are exceptionally high, and the attendant risks, often linked to a loss of individual autonomy over one's body and the data that pertain to it, signal a profound transformation already under way, often marked by significant legal challenges.

The third part, entitled *Global Health Governance between Access, Innovation, and Regulatory Challenges*, shifts the focus from the body to the collective sphere that governs people's health. The discussion centres on questions concerning the construction of public institutional systems capable of promoting innovation in the health sector and ensuring universal access to care while respecting fundamental rights. The debate developed in the chapter aims to provide a conceptual framework for understanding the role and the tools available to public institutions in the governance of public health. The contributions therefore intertwine, from different theoretical perspectives and from the local to the global level, the issues raised by the challenges of access to healthcare within global regulation. The multiple critical dimensions of global health governance are thus examined, beginning with an analysis of legal preparedness for crises within the post-pandemic European regulatory framework, also considering the notion of 'pharmaceutical citizenship', and extending to the need to rethink existing democratic institutions. Through a continuous change of lens, the analysis further focuses on pharmaceutical policies adopted in response to emerging health emergencies.

The fourth part, *Gender, Intersectionality, and Reproductive Rights in Health Crises*, addresses the theme of policies and regulations concerning vulnerabilities, especially in times of crisis. From this perspective, the impact of emergencies on gender issues is analysed, with particular attention to women's reproductive rights, such as the right to abortion. Within the intersectional approach that every public framework must adopt in guaranteeing the rights of the invisible and thus overcoming social inequalities, it also becomes possible to delineate the scope and direction of the use of new technologies. At the heart of this reflection lies respect for the plurality of experiences and identities, to prevent AI and similar technologies from becoming tools that exacerbate existing inequalities. In this sense, intersectionality becomes crucial for understanding how public health emergencies amplify structural and social fragilities, while simultaneously offering an opportunity to rethink public health governance. It is clear how the body which lies at the centre of the analyses in this volume—exists in a constant tension between being the private space for an individual's social emancipation and a tool for mass control.

References

Adams V (ed) (2016) Metrics: what counts in global health. Duke University Press, Durham–London
Agamben G (2005) State of exception. Attell K (trans). University of Chicago Press, Chicago
Amato P (2023) Toward a fuller understanding of the enigma of health. In: Egbokhare F, Afolayan A (eds) Global health, humanity and the COVID-19 pandemic: philosophical and sociological challenges and imperatives. Palgrave Macmillan, London, pp 15–31
Anand S, Peter F, Sen A (eds) (2005) Public health, ethics, and equity. Oxford University Press, New York
Anderson B (2017) Emergency futures: exception, urgency, interval, hope. Sociol Rev 65(3):463–477
Andreoni G, Mambretti C (eds) (2021) Digital health technology for better aging: a multidisciplinary approach. Springer, Cham
Armstrong D (1995) The rise of surveillance medicine. Sociol Health Illn 17(3):393–404
Aseltine E, Ekland-Olson S (2025) Abortion in the United States: the moral and legal landscape. Routledge, London
Barouki R, Kogevinas M, Audouze K et al (2021) The COVID-19 pandemic and global environmental change: emerging research needs. Environ Int 146:106272
Bauman Z (1992) Survival as a social construct. Theory Cult Soc 9(1):1–36
Beck U (1992) Risk society: towards a new modernity. Sage, London
Beck U (2002) The terrorist threat: world risk society revisited. Theory Cult Soc 19(4):39–55
Birn AE (2014) Philanthrocapitalism, past and present: the Rockefeller Foundation, the gates foundation, and the setting(s) of the international/global health agenda. Hypothesis 12(1):e8
Birn AE, Pillay Y, Holtz TH (2017) Textbook of global health, 4th edn. Oxford University Press, New York
Bjørnskov C, Voigt S (2024) State of emergency: an economic analysis. Cambridge University Press, Cambridge
Blake H, Bihm J, Nkwanyuo R et al (2021) Beyond COVID-19: the state of telehealth equity and best practices in underserved populations. J Law Med Ethics 49(3):410–414
Bloch AB, Onorato IM, Ihle WW et al (1996) The need for epidemic intelligence. Public Health Rep 111(1):26–33
Bobbio N (2014) Il futuro della democrazia, 4th edn. Einaudi, Torino
Bruce M (1965) The coming of the welfare state, 2nd edn. B.T. Batsford Ltd, London
Calhoun C (2004) A world of emergencies: fear, intervention, and the limits of cosmopolitan order. Can Rev Sociol Anthropol 41(4):373–395
Capra F, Mattei U (2015) The ecology of law: toward a legal system in tune with nature and community. Berrett-Koehler Publishers, Oakland
Carlson CJ, Albery GF, Merow C et al (2022) Climate change increases cross-species viral transmission risk. Nature 607(7919):555–562
Chapman AR (2016) Global health, human rights, and the challenge of neoliberal policies. Cambridge University Press, Cambridge
Chauhan N, Jaggi M, Chauhan SC, Yallapu MM (2021) COVID-19: fighting the invisible enemy with microRNAs. Expert Rev Anti-Infect Ther 19(2):137–145
Choi BCK (2012) The past, present, and future of public health surveillance. Scientifica 2012:875253
Coggon J (2024) Defining global health law. J Glob Health Law 1(2):150–176
Cooper H, Szreter S (2021) After the virus: lessons from the past for a better future. Cambridge University Press, Cambridge
Corrales Compagnucci M, Wilson ML, Fenwick M, Forgó N, Bärnighausen T (eds) (2022) AI in eHealth: human autonomy, data governance and privacy in healthcare. Cambridge University Press, Cambridge
Cowan D, Mumford A (eds) (2022) Pandemic legalities: legal responses to COVID-19—justice and social responsibility. Bristol University Press, Bristol

de Sousa SB (2020) Toward a new legal common sense: law, globalization, and emancipation, 3rd edn. Cambridge University Press, Cambridge
den Exter AP, Syrett K (2020) Access to healthcare in Europe. In: Orentlicher D, Hervey TK (eds) The Oxford handbook of comparative health law. Oxford University Press, Oxford, pp 242–272
den Exter A, Hall MA, Hoffman AK et al (2020) Introduction to access to healthcare. In: Orentlicher D, Hervey TK (eds) The Oxford handbook of comparative health law. Oxford University Press, Oxford, pp 808–812
Doron I, Georgantzi N (eds) (2018) Ageing, ageism and the law: European perspectives on the rights of older persons. Edward Elgar Publishing, Cheltenham
Eckstein H (1959) The english health service. Its origins, structure, and achievements. Harvard University Press, Cambridge
Elmer G (2012) Panopticon—discipline—control. In: Ball K, Haggerty KD, Lyon D (eds) Routledge handbook of surveillance studies. Routledge, London, pp 21–29
Fahey RA, Hino A (2020) COVID-19, digital privacy, and the social limits on data-focused public health responses. Int J Inf Manag 55:102181
Fairchild AL, Bayer R, Colgrove J (2007) Searching eyes: privacy, the state, and disease surveillance in America. University of California Press, Berkeley
Ferejohn J, Pasquino P (2004) The law of the exception: a typology of emergency powers. Int J Const Law 2(2):210–239
Ferrajoli L (1982) Stato sociale e stato di diritto. Pol Dir 13(1):41–52
Ferrajoli L (2022) Per una costituzione della terra. L'umanità al bivio. Feltrinelli, Milano
Ferraris M (2022) Emergenza. Einaudi, Turin
Fidler D (1996) Globalization, international law, and emerging infectious diseases. Emerg Infect Dis 2:77–84
Fidler DP (2003) SARS: political pathology of the first post-Westphalian pathogen. J Law Med Ethics 31(4):485–505
Fidler DP (2007) Biosecurity: friend or foe for public health governance? In: Bashford A (ed) Medicine at the border: disease, globalization, and security, 1850–present. Palgrave Macmillan, London, pp 196–218
Flear ML (2015) Governing public health: EU law, regulation and biopolitics. Hart Publishing, Oxford
Fontaine Q, Clinck J (2022) The European health data space proposal: a first look at the newest piece of the EU data sharing puzzle. Eur Health Pharm Law Rev 6(2):87–94
Foucault M (1977) Discipline and punish: the birth of the prison. Sheridan A (trans). Vintage Books, New York
Foucault M (1978) The history of sexuality, vol 1. an introduction. Hurley R (trans). Pantheon Books, New York
Fraser M, Greco M (2005) Introduction. In: Fraser M, Greco M (eds) The body: a reader. Routledge, London, pp 1–42
Frazer WM (1950) A history of English public health, 1834–1939. Baillière, Tindall & Cox, London
Frenk J, Gómez-Dantés O (2002) Globalisation and the challenges to health systems. Br Med J 325:95–97
Fusco GG, Cercel C, Lavis S (2020) Introduction: untimely considerations on the state of exception. In: Cercel C, Fusco GG, Lavis S (eds) (2020) states of exception: law, history, theory. Routledge, London, pp 1–12
Gandy OH Jr (2021) The panoptic sort: a political economy of personal information, 2nd edn. Oxford University Press, New York
Gautier L, David PM (2022) 'Health for all' and the challenges for pharmaceutical policies: a critical interpretive synthesis over 40 years. Soc Sci Humanit Open 5(1):100255
Gerke S, Shachar C, Chai PR, Cohen IG (2020) Regulatory, safety, and privacy concerns of home monitoring technologies during COVID-19. Nat Med 26(8):1176–1182
Ginsburg T, Versteeg M (2021) The bound executive: emergency powers during the pandemic. Int J Const Law 19(5):1498–1535

Gostin LO (2014) Global health law. Harvard University Press, Cambridge, MA
Gostin LO, Wiley LF (2016) Public health law: power, duty, restraint, 3rd edn. University of California Press, Oakland
Gostin LO, Meier BM, Thomas R et al (2018) 70 years of human rights in global health: drawing on a contentious past to secure a hopeful future. Lancet 392(10165):2731–2735
Greene A (2018) Permanent states of emergency and the rule of law: constitutions in an age of crisis. Hart Publishing, Oxford
Grogan J, Yamin AE (2023) Mapping COVID-19 legal responses: a functionalist analysis. In: Baer S, Daly T, Landau D, Lerner H, Saunders C (eds) Democracy and pandemic emergency measures. Cambridge University Press, Cambridge, pp 354–366
Gross O, Ní Aoláin F (2006) Law in times of crisis: emergency powers in theory and practice. Cambridge University Press, Cambridge
Haraway D (1989) The biopolitics of postmodern bodies: determinations of self in immune system discourse. Differences 1(1):3–44
Haraway D (1991) A cyborg manifesto: science, technology, and socialist-feminism in the late twentieth century. In: Haraway D (ed) Simians, cyborgs and women: the reinvention of nature. Routledge, New York, pp 149–181
Hardt M, Negri A (2000) Empire. Harvard University Press, Cambridge, MA
HERA (2022) HERA work plan for 2022. European Commission 10(2):12–18. https://health.ec.europa.eu/publications/hera-work-plan-2022_en
Hervey TK, McHale JV (eds) (2015a) European Union health law: themes and implications. Cambridge University Press, Cambridge
Hervey TK, McHale JV (2015b) Conclusions. In: European Union health law: themes and implications. Cambridge University Press, Cambridge, pp 535–550
Hofmann B (2021) How to draw the line between health and disease? Start with suffering. Health Care Anal 29:127–143
Hutler B, Blasimme A, Gur-Arie R et al (2022) Assessing the governance of digital contact tracing in response to COVID-19: results of a multi-national study. J Law Med Ethics 50(4):791–804
Isailović I (2025) EU abortion law after Dobbs: states, the market, and stratified reproductive freedom. Colum J Eur L 30(1):1–48
Jalali MS, Landman A, Gordon WJ (2021) Telemedicine, privacy, and information security in the age of COVID-19. J Am Med Inform Assoc 28(3):671–672
Jayanthi P, Vinodh S, Sakthivel M (2019) Fourth industrial revolution: an impact on healthcare industry. In: Ahram T (ed) Advances in artificial intelligence, software and systems engineering. Springer, Cham, pp 57–65
Jenkins A, Watts MJ, Cameron L et al (2020) Nested ecology and emergence in pandemics. Lancet Planet Health 4(8):e302–e303
Jones M, Lowe R (2002) From Beveridge to Blair: the first fifty years of Britain's welfare state 1948–98. Manchester University Press, Manchester
Kamradt-Scott A (2017) What went wrong? The World Health Organization from swine flu to Ebola. In: Kruck A, Oppermann K, Spencer A (eds) Political mistakes and policy failures in international relations. Palgrave Macmillan, Cham, pp 193–215
Kumar R, Gupta N, Kodan P et al (2020) Battling COVID-19: using old weapons for a new enemy. Trop Dis Travel Med Vaccines 6:6
Lakoff A (2017) Unprepared: global health in a time of emergency. University of California Press, Berkeley
Lenert L, McSwain BY (2020) Balancing health privacy, health information exchange, and research in the context of the COVID-19 pandemic. J Am Med Inform Assoc 27(6):963–966
Liberati P (2024) Are European health models still different? In: Cambridge working papers in economics, vol 2441. Faculty of Economics, University of Cambridge, Cambridge, pp 1–68
Loevy K (2016) Emergencies in public law: the legal politics of containment. Cambridge University Press, Cambridge

Lombardo JS, Ross DL (2007) Disease surveillance: a public health priority. In: Lombardo JS, Buckeridge DL (eds) Disease surveillance: a public health informatics approach. Wiley, Hoboken, pp 3–14
Lupton D (2014) Critical perspectives on digital health technologies. Sociol Compass 8(12):1344–1359
Lupton D (2016) The quantified self: a sociology of self-tracking. Polity, Cambridge
Lupton D (2022) COVID societies: theorising the coronavirus crisis. Routledge, London
Lupton D, Willis K (2021) COVID society: introduction to the book. In: Lupton D, Willis K (eds) The COVID-19 crisis: social perspectives. Routledge, Abingdon, pp 1–12
Lyon D (2003) Surveillance after September 11. Polity Press, Cambridge, MA
Lyon D (2007) Surveillance studies: an overview. Polity Press, Cambridge, MA
Lyotard JF (1984) The postmodern condition: a report on knowledge. Bennington G, Massumi B (trans). University of Minnesota Press, Minneapolis
Macnicol J (2006) Age discrimination: an historical and contemporary analysis. Cambridge University Press, Cambridge
Marshall TH (1964) Class, citizenship and social development. Doubleday & Company, Garden City, NY
Miller S, Smith M (2023) Combating Covid-19: surveillance, autonomy, and collective responsibility. In: Macnish K, Henschke A (eds) The ethics of surveillance in times of emergency. Oxford University Press, Oxford, pp 47–59
Mossialos E, Permanand G, Baeten R et al (eds) (2010) Health systems governance in Europe: the role of European Union law and policy. Cambridge University Press, Cambridge
Murdoch DR, French NP (2020) COVID-19: another infectious disease emerging at the animal-human interface. N Z Med J 133(1510):12–15
Murray CJL, Lopez AD (eds) (1996) The global burden of disease: a comprehensive assessment of mortality and disability from diseases, injuries, and risk factors in 1990 and projected to 2020. Harvard School of Public Health, Cambridge, MA (for WHO and the World Bank)
Murray M, Shaw K (2024) Dobbs and democracy. Harv Law Rev 137(3):728–864
Nerlich B (2022) Pandemics, metaphors and what it means to be human. In: Martin P, de Saille S, Liddiard K, Pearce W (eds) Being human during COVID-19. Bristol University Press, Bristol, pp 20–27
Osterholm MT (2005) Preparing for the next pandemic. Foreign Aff 84(4):24–37
Pierson C (2006) Beyond the welfare state? The new political economy of welfare, 3rd edn. Polity Press, Cambridge
Plant R (1985) The very idea of a welfare state. In: Bean P, Ferris J, Whynes D (eds) Defence of welfare. Tavistock Publications, London, pp 3–30
Pozen DE, Schudson M (eds) (2018) Troubling transparency: the history and future of freedom of information. Columbia University Press, New York
Pramanik MI, Lau RY, Demirkan H, Azad MA (2017) Smart health: big data enabled health paradigm within smart cities. Expert Syst Appl 87:370–383
Quarantelli EL (1988) Disaster crisis management: a summary of research findings. J Manag Stud 25(4):373–385
Reingold AL (2003) If syndromic surveillance is the answer, what is the question? Biosecur Bioterror 1(2):77–81
Rizoulieres R, Béranger J (2021) Introduction. In: Rizoulieres R, Béranger J (eds) The digital revolution in health. Wiley-ISTE, Hoboken, NJ
Robertson R (1990) Mapping the global condition: globalization as the central concept. Theory Cult Soc 7(2–3):15–30
Robertson R (1995) Glocalization: time–space and homogeneity–heterogeneity. In: Featherstone M, Lash S, Robertson R (eds) Global Modernities. SAGE Publications, London, pp 25–44
Roderick P, Pollock AM (2022) Dismantling the National Health Service in England. Int J Health Serv 52(4):470–479

Rothstein MA (2021) Big data, surveillance capitalism, and precision medicine: challenges for privacy. J Law Med Ethics 49(4):666–676
Saint-Bonnet F (2001) L'état d'exception. Presses Universitaires de France, Paris
Santuari A, Sage W (2020) Paradigms of healthcare systems, law, and regulation: a transatlantic conversation. In: Orentlicher D, Hervey TK (eds) The Oxford handbook of comparative health law. Oxford University Press, Oxford
Saunders RA (2021) Geopolitics on the 'other side': counterpart's imaginary of a world system after the virus. Geopolitics 27(5):1574–1598
Schama S (2023) Foreign bodies: pandemics, vaccines and the health of nations. Simon & Schuster UK, London
Sen A (2002) Why health equity? Health Econ 11(8):659–666
Shepard WP (1952) Essentials of public health. Lippincott, Philadelphia
Singer M (2009) Introduction to syndemics: a critical systems approach to public and community health. Jossey-Bass, San Francisco
Sorell T (2023) Pandemic population surveillance: privacy and life-saving. In: Macnish K, Henschke A (eds) The ethics of surveillance in times of emergency. Oxford University Press, Oxford
Sorokin PA (1942) Man and society in calamity: the effects of war, revolution, famine, pestilence upon the human mind, behavior, social organization and cultural life. E. P. Dutton & Co., New York
Stiglitz JE (2012) The price of inequality. W.W. Norton & Company, New York
Streeck W (2024) Globalismo e democrazia. L'economia politica del tardo neoliberismo. Feltrinelli, Milano
Stroup DF, Brookmeyer R, Kalsbeek WD (2004) Public health surveillance in action: a framework. In: Brookmeyer R, Stroup DF (eds) Monitoring the health of populations: statistical principles and methods for public health surveillance. Oxford University Press, New York, pp 1–36
Syrett K (2003) A technocratic fix to the 'legitimacy problem'? The Blair government and health care rationing in the United Kingdom. J Health Polit Policy Law 28(4):715–746
Tesh SN (1988) Hidden arguments: political ideology and disease prevention policy. Rutgers University Press, New Brunswick, NJ
Thomas L (2014) Pandemics of the future: disease surveillance in real time. Surveillance Soc 12(2):287–300
Tobin J (2012) The right to health in international law. Oxford University Press, New York
Tognoni G, Cauduro A (2018) Farmaci (e tecnologie) come indicatore, didattico e complessivo, della storia del Sistema sanitario nazionale. Ital J Soc Policy 2:157–172
Trattner WI (1999) From poor law to welfare state: a history of social welfare in America, 6th edn. Free Press, New York
Vayena E (2018) Protecting health privacy in the world of big data: introduction. In: Cohen IG, Lynch HF, Vayena E, Gasser U (eds) Big data, health law, and bioethics. Cambridge University Press, Cambridge, pp 157–160
Véliz C (2024) The ethics of privacy and surveillance. Oxford University Press, Oxford
Venkatapuram S (2011) Health justice: an argument from the capabilities approach. Polity, Cambridge
Villarreal PA (2020) Public health emergencies and constitutionalism before COVID-19: between the national and the international. In: Albert R, Roznai Y (eds) Constitutionalism under extreme conditions. Springer, Cham, pp 217–238
Warren SD, Brandeis LD (1890) The right to privacy. Harv Law Rev 4(5):193–220
Weir L, Mykhalovskiy E (2007) The geopolitics of global public health surveillance in the 21st century. In: Bashford A (ed) Medicine at the border: disease, globalization, and security, 1850–present. Palgrave Macmillan, London, pp 240–264
Weir L, Mykhalovskiy E (2010) Global public health vigilance: creating a world on alert. Routledge, London
Weiss RA, McMichael AJ (2004) Social and environmental risk factors in the emergence of infectious diseases. Nat Med 10(Suppl 12):S70–S76

West R (2003) Reconsidering legalism. Minn Law Rev 88:119–135

White JB (1984) When words lose their meaning: constitutions and reconstitutions of language, character, and community. University of Chicago Press, Chicago

Willcocks AJ (1985) The moral basis of the welfare state. In: Bean P, Ferris J, Whynes D (eds) In defence of welfare. Tavistock Publications, London

World Health Organization (1981) Global strategy for health for all by the year 2000. World Health Organization, Geneva. https://apps.who.int/iris/bitstream/10665/38893/1/9241800038.pdf

World Health Organization (2021) Ethics and governance of artificial intelligence for health: WHO guidance. World Health Organization, Geneva. https://www.who.int/publications/i/item/9789240029200

World Health Organization (2022) Ageing and health. World Health Organization, Geneva. https://www.who.int/news-room/fact-sheets/detail/ageing-and-health

Youde J (2010) Biopolitical surveillance and public health in international politics. Palgrave Macmillan, London

Zuboff S (2019) The age of surveillance capitalism: the fight for a human future at the new frontier of power. PublicAffairs, New York

Law, Medicine, and the Early Modern Epistemology of the Body

Pestis Ius in Early Modern Pandemics: A Genealogy of Health Law in the Holy Roman Empire

Antonio Gerace

Abstract This chapter provides the first in-depth analysis of Christian Ulrich Blume's *Discursum juridicum de peste et juribus circa tempus Pestis* (1683), an underexplored juridical treatise. Moving beyond the initial legal lacunae of Roman and Canon law concerning pandemics, Blume's *Discursum* exemplifies the emergence of a coherent 'plague law' (*pestis ius*) in the Early Modern period. The study examines Blume's multi-layered methodology, which integrates juridical-philosophical sources (e.g., Aristotle, Grotius, Pufendorf), Civil law and Canon law, practical-juridical directives such as Pest-Ordnungen and specific legal precedents from the Holy Roman Empire. The analysis highlights Blume's pragmatic approach to public health, encompassing regulations on urban control, resource management, and social conduct. Crucially, the *Discursum* navigates the complexities of a multi-confessional Empire, detailing adapted roles for various clergymen (Catholic parish priests and Lutheran pastors) and even the inclusion of Jewish doctors. By asserting that 'the argument from war to plague is valid' (*a bello ad pestem argumentum valet*), Blume sanctioned extraordinary measures, reshaping legal acts, property rights, and judicial procedures. This chapter argues that Blume's work offers a vital, original perspective on how Early Modern jurists grappled with pandemic crises, seeking to impose legal and moral order amidst the chaos of the plague.

1 The Genesis of Plague Law: A Chronological Overview

After the disruptive event of the Black Death in 1347, the 'plague law' (*pestis* or *pestilentiae ius*) began to evolve into a coherent system. Neither the *Corpus Iuris Civilis* nor the *Corpus Iuris Canonici* provided specific legal frameworks to address the unique medical challenges posed by such a pandemic. By 534, Justinian's Body of Civil Law was finalized, hence years before the eruption of the 'Justinian Plague' (541–549). Notably, the *Novellae constitutiones*, compiled between 535 and the

A. Gerace (✉)
Instituto de Estudos Filosóficos, Coimbra, Portugal
e-mail: antoniogerace1987@gmail.com

M. Balestrieri and A. Cauduro (eds.), *The Legal Anatomy of the Body*, Ius Gentium: Comparative Perspectives on Law and Justice 142,
https://doi.org/10.1007/978-3-032-26434-3_2

emperor's death in 565, contains no specific constitution on plague, while mentioning only once a *tristissima pestis* in Thrace (coll. IV, tit. XIII, nov. XXXIV).[1] Moreover, by appealing to the Scriptures—but without citing a specific passage, even though the reference to Luke 21:11 is clear –,[2] Justinian recalled to Constantinople's citizens that 'pestilence' (*pestilentia*) is one of the major instruments of the 'righteous God's wrath' (*iusta Dei ira*), together with earthquakes (*terrae motus*) and famine (*fames*) (con. LXXVII). God may use them to punish two impious crimes (*impia facinora*): (1) 'illicit luxury against nature' (*illicita luxuria naturae contraria*); (2) blasphemy (*execrabilia*; βλασφημία).[3] Recent scholarship convincingly downsizes the actual impact of the Justinian Plague on the transition from Antiquity to the Middle Ages, a factor that might explain why the *Novellae* did not explicitly address such a monumental challenge. Furthermore, papyrological evidence from the period reveals 'strong continued administration and economic vitality,' while 'inscriptions reveal continuity over the plague period.'[4] In any case, the so-called 'Justinian Plague' did not lead to the development of a specific legal system designed to confront pandemic challenges.

During the Middle Ages, the Papal States, as one of the heirs of the Roman Empire, developed another significant legal system: canon law, which wielded normative power throughout Latin Europe. Canon law began its systematization with the *Decretum Gratiani* (1140) and was further developed until Pope John XXII's *Extravagantes* (1317). Again, this systematization occurred years before the outbreak of the Black Death in 1347, leaving jurists without specific canonical references for plague. It therefore comes as no surprise that the word 'plague' (*pestis*) has no medical connotation, but it is used metaphorically as a synonym for 'heresy' (*pestis haeretica*), clerics' misbehaviour, and simony (*simoniaca pestis*) within these legal texts. Moreover, such an approach remained consistent in subsequent constitutions, which were later incorporated into the *Extravagantes communes*, compiled in Paris by Jean Chapuis by the end of the fifteenth century and comprising papal decretals from Urban IV (1261–64) to Sixtus IV (1471–84). Few specific indications are reserved for other 'diseases' (*morbus*), with a particular focus on epilepsy (*caducus morbus*) to prohibit priests suffering from this condition from celebrating mass and distributing the Eucharist.[5] Other illnesses were mentioned primarily if they rendered a clergyman unable to fulfil his duties,[6] or related to leprosy, specifically concerning

---

[1] Justinian (1575), p. 86.

[2] Luke 21:11: 'there will be great earthquakes and in various places famines and plagues, and there will be dreadful portents and great signs from heaven'; 'Et terraemotus magni erunt per loca, et pestilentiae, et fames, terroresque de caelo, et signa magna erunt' (Vulgate). All Bible quotations are taken from the New Revised Standard Version Updated Edition (NRSVue) unless otherwise stated.

[3] Justinian (1575), p. 74.

[4] Mordechai et al. (2019), p. 25548.

[5] Richter (1959), p. 1.588.

[6] Richter (1959), pp. 2.481–483.

the possibility of marriage between individuals sharing this disease to avoid 'incontinence' within leprosaria.[7] This last disease clearly had a strong biblical reference, particularly Leviticus 13, where priests are meticulously instructed on how to declare someone 'impure'. However, from a juridical perspective, thirteenth-century scholars were less concerned with legal implications and more intrigued by the theological proximity of leprosy, which could be transmitted from parents to newborns, to the concept of original sin, effectively inherited.[8] The harrowing experience of the Black Death, in contrast, significantly ignited the production of more medically-oriented scholarship, notably the so-called *consilium* ('advice'), such as that authored by Gentile da Foligno,[9] while Italian cities tried to face the pandemic. Boccaccio testifies at least three measures that Florence took: 1. Clean the city from the rubbish (*Da molte immondizie purgata la città*); 2. Prohibit sick people from entering the city (*vietato l'entravi dentro a ciascuno infermo*); and 3. Collective prayers recited in procession (*umili supplicazioni non una ma molte e in processioni ordinate*),[10] measures which were consistently taken in the Italian Peninsula.[11]

Soon after the plague, jurists continued to address the epidemic as an indication of God's 'hostility' (*hostilitas*). This is exemplified by Bartolo di Sassoferrato (1313–1357), who, while commenting on the *Corpus Iuris Civilis* regarding usucaption and usurpation (*de usucapionibus et usurpationibus*), specifically mentioned the difficulties of administering justice (*iura reddere*) in 1348 due to the high mortality.[12] The first documented attempts to contain the pandemic were developed in highly vulnerable locations: cities with a strong vocation for international trade with the Balkans and the Levant, such as Ragusa (modern-day Dubrovnik). This Dalmatian city, which had already gained independence from Venice in 1358, notably implemented quarantine measures in 1377. It required incoming individuals arriving by sea and land to be isolated outside the city walls, specifically in Mercana (Mrkan) and Ragusa Vecchia (Cavtat), respectively.[13] Similar measures were subsequently adopted by Italian cities from the fifteenth century onwards, with Venice establishing the very first lazzaretto in 1423 to confine individuals arriving from infected areas.[14] Jurists hence started gathering from both civil and canon law those elements which were normed in 'normal' times, but which could be used to address the numerous challenges provoked by pandemics, such as matrimonial, burial, inheritance and criminal laws. This developing legal framework provided both prevention measures—such as territorial sanitation, public water management, and regulations for conduits and sewage –and measures to be taken during the pandemic itself. The latter included

---

[7] Richter (1959), pp. 2.690–691.

[8] Cerrito (2020).

[9] French (2001).

[10] Boccaccio (1956), p. 5.

[11] Lee (2022).

[12] Bartolus de Saxoferrato (1505), p. 100r; see Žepič (2022), p. 50.

[13] Römer (2004).

[14] Crawshaw (2013), Gensini et al. (2004).

rules for trade, assistance for the sick, the distinct roles of doctors and priests (respectively for the healing of the body and of the soul), hospital and burial management, and indeed specific rules for matters like marital relations, procedures for notarial acts, and the conduct of jurisdictional activities.

In Italy, this process was undertaken by three key-authors: the Franciscan, jurist, and theologian Giovanni Francesco da Ripa (ca. 1480–1535), and his *Tractatus juridicus de peste* (1522); 2. The lawyer Silvestro Aldobrandini (1500–1588), and his *Tractatus juridicus de peste* (1523); and finally, the jurist Girolamo Previdelli (d. ca. 1534), who is best known for having represented Henry VIII in his (unsuccessful) divorce case, but also authored a *Tractatus legalis de peste* (1524).[15] These three authors are to be considered as a kind of milestone in the elaboration of a coherent plague law, being theirs the very first attempt to do it. With the aim to provide a clear indication of how civil authorities must deal with the plague, and having in mind the shared view that the plague was the expression of God's hostility against a sinful society, Giovanni Francesco da Ripa used the strong claim *valere argumentum de bello ad pestem* ('the argument from war to the plague is valid'), applying the war state of exception to the plague, a principle that then resulted a kind of juridical literary motif.[16]

2 The Holy Roman Empire as Study Case

In his seminal work, *Crimine e giustizia in tempo di peste nell'Europa moderna* (1991), Alessandro Pastore offered a comparative overview of the intricate relationship between plague, religion, witchcraft, and law in Early Modern Europe.[17] His analysis particularly focused on the inextricably linked fields of criminal law and succession law. Pastore's research spanned various regions, including Switzerland (Geneva, Lausanne, and Freiburg), England, Scotland, and Italy (Bologna, Rome, and Genoa). Among other topics, he skilfully elucidated the two distinct levels—plebeian and erudite—of discussions surrounding the plague's origins. He also demonstrated how confessional and superstitious beliefs influenced the administration of justice, leading to the identification of 'otherness'—whether living or dead witches, or heretics—as potential agents in the plague's spread. Furthermore, Pastore highlighted how inheritance litigations consistently surged during outbreaks, contributing to increased inefficiency in tribunals and, consequently, to individuals taking justice into their own hands. At the conclusion of his book, Pastore expressed a desire for a 'thorough exploration' (*esplorazione a tappeto*) of the juridical, medical, and theological dissertations produced within the Holy Roman Empire. He specifically stressed the close connection between witchcraft and the spread of plague, suggesting

[15] Ascheri (2020). See Stanco (2020), and Vinci (2020) for further bibliography.

[16] Žepič (2022), p. 51, Riva (1598), p. 3; p. 229.

[17] Pastore (1991). Drage (1665) clearly show the strong link between witchcraft and plague. See Levack (2016) and Cole (2016).

Table 1 Publications concerning the plague. These data are retrieved through the Universal Short Title Catalogue (accessed 02 Sept 2025) (For each query, the table presents only the top six results in each of the three metrics: Region, Language, and Genre. For comparative purposes, the 'Low Countries' category in both queries consolidates the data for Northern and Southern Netherlands. This reflects a total of 490 editions for the '*pest**' query (divided respectively into 279 and 211 editions) and 218 editions for the '*peste*' query (comprising 123 editions for the Northern Netherlands and 95 for the Southern Netherlands). The British Isles have also been included in the second query to allow for a direct comparison with the first, despite the limited number of sources in the latter case)

Query: '*pest**' 5281 results. Period 1450–1700					
Region	n. ed.	Language	n. ed.	Genre	n. ed.
Holy Roman empire	2417	German	1776	Medical texts	3100
Italian states	1029	Latin	1485	Religious texts	1034
France	482	Italian	750	Ordinances	691
Low Countries	490	French	418	Univ. public.	416
Iberia	275	Dutch	299	Jurisprudence	135
British Isles	268	English	261	New books	133
Query: '*peste*' 1792 results. Period 1450–1700					
Region	n. ed.	Language	n. ed.	Genre	n. ed.
Italian states	748	Italian	640	Medical texts	1143
France	337	Latin	499	Ordinances	380
Holy Roman empire	228	French	348	Religious texts	197
Low Countries	218	Spanish	148	Univ. public.	154
Iberia	179	Dutch	107	New books	49
British Isles	3	German	28	Jurisprudence	34

that such research could yield new theoretical insights.[18] Far from attempting a 'thorough exploration'—which would necessitate the development of a comprehensive research project—the present chapter will specifically concentrate on Central Europe, and more precisely on the Holy Roman Empire, given its significant experience with a new epidemic wave between 1640 and 1720, ignited by the incessant state of war which devastated the region, such as the Thirty Years' War (1618–1648); the Swedish-Polish War (1655–1657), the Great Northern War (1700–1721); the series of wars between the Turkish Empire, the Habsburg dynasty, and the Polish-Lithuanian Commonwealth.[19] In light of this major threat to the population, it is unsurprising that a substantial body of work concerning the plague was published across Europe following the advent of the printing press. A notable portion of these publications comprised medical texts issued in German, as the accompanying Table 1 indicates.

[18] Pastore (1991), pp. 216–217; Žepič (2022), p. 50.

[19] Eckert (2020), pp. 15–17; Eckert (1996).

Notably, works dealing with jurisprudence are quite scarce, and most of them academic disputes,[20] but among these works, Christian Ulrich Blume's *Discursum iuridicum de peste, et iuribus circa tempus pestis* represents an unstudied milestone towards a coherent plague law. The next section of this book-chapter provides the very first analysis of this source, exploring how the challenge of plague was faced in the late 17th century Holy Roman Empire.

3 Blume's *Discursum*: How to Face Pandemics

The *Discursum iuridicum de peste, et iuribus circa tempus pestis* is a dissertation discussed at the Helmstedt University (*Academia Julia*) on 28th March 1683, before the dean—and influent jurist—George von Engelbrecht the Elder (1638–1705). Blume structured his *Discursum* using three distinct sets of sources. First, he established a more juridical-philosophical framework by drawing upon both classic authors, such as Aristotle (*Ethica Nicomachea*; *Politica*), and contemporary scholarship. Among these, he cited Heinrich Bocer (*De bello et duello*), Jean Bodin (*De republica*), Hugo Grotius (*De jure belli et pacis*), Thomas Hobbes (*De cive*), Samuel von Pufendorf (*Elementa Iurisprudentiae universalis*), and Caspar Ziegler (*De juribus maiestaticis*). Second, he drew more specific elements from both civil and canon laws by appealing to commentators on Justinian's *Corpus Iuris Civilis*, such as Bartolo da Sassoferrato (*Super Digestum*) and Johann Brunnemann (*Commentarius in pandectarum libros*), or to commentators on both civil and canon law, like Rolando della Valle (*Consiliorum, seu mavis responsorum iuris cum civilis, tum pontificii*). Concerning religious matters, Blume referred to both Lutheran and Roman Catholic sources. In the former case, he appealed to the decisions issued by the Faculty of Law of the (Lutheran) Helmstedt University, while in the latter case, the sources included canon law (*decretales*), Henry of Susa's *Summa*, and the decrees of the Council of Trent. Blume's inclusive approach to Catholic sources clearly demonstrates his intention to provide a juridical treatise applicable across any state of the Holy Roman Empire. Third, Blume based his *Discursum* on more practical-juridical treatises, notably the works of Ripa and Previdelli. He enhanced their writings by leveraging the rich, practical legal experience embodied in the so-called *Pest-Ordnung*. These ordinances had been issued since the beginning of the 16th century.[21] However, Blume specifically drew upon four key *Pest-Ordnung* published close to the redaction of his own work, which are frequently mentioned throughout his text and also highlight the localized presence of the plague: the Leipzig (1680)[22] and Silesian (1680) *Pest-Ordnung*,[23] the 'Sambt-Rahts-Ordnung' (1657), – likely the Helmstedt

[20] As a way of examples, Suevus (1653), Episcopius (1652), Limborch (1652) and de Vries (1682), Forster (1598).

[21] Flamm (2008), Žepič (2022), pp. 58–59.

[22] Leipzig (1680).

[23] Schlesische (1710).

Pest-Ordnung[24]—and the 'Kaiser Leopold's Ordnung', authored by the emperor's physician Johann Wilhelm von Mannagetta (1680).[25]

The author initiates his treatise by asserting that, 'by nature,' human beings cannot exist *extra societatem* (outside society), and are thus compelled to live in groups. In this initial stance, he directly contrasts with Thomas Hobbes, explicitly cited, whose views on human nature likely diverged significantly. Instead, the author appeals to the esteemed authority of Aristotle and his seminal definition of the human being as πολιτικὸν ζῷον (a political animal), a concept expounded in the Nicomachean Ethics (IX, 9) and Politics (I, 2). This Aristotelian perspective finds resonance with other prominent thinkers of the era, namely Hugo Grotius and Samuel von Pufendorf, who evidently concurred with this fundamental premise.[26] Nonetheless, within any societal structure, it becomes apparent that not all members consistently collaborate or dutifully observe their obligations. This inherent challenge necessitates the establishment of *ius*, defined as the 'rule of human actions' (*norma actionum humanarum*). Indeed, the author posits that a society, bereft of such governing rules, would inevitably collapse, much as an individual cannot subsist without the animating force of a rational soul.[27] The polity (*Respublica*) is presented as the *optima et perfectissima* (the best and most perfect) form of society. A polity comprises numerous diverse 'societies', or groups of people, all of whom must engage in cooperative endeavours. Such cooperation, however, must be rigorously subjected to 'right and laws', given the limited number of individuals who perform their duties solely out of inherent will and virtue. Consequently, laws serve a dual purpose: they can compel adherence through the imposition of harsh punishments and, conversely, they can incentivize compliance by offering rewards.[28] The temporal power holds the inherent right to promulgate laws for the common good of the polity. Concurrently, this authority extends to

---

[24] Only one reference to a 1657 Helmsted *Pest–Ordnung* was found, located in the private library of Johann Heinrich Meibom (1638–1700), a physician and resident of Helmstedt (Mscr. Meib. 380). This collection was later incorporated into the Göttingen University Library (SUB). See Meyer (1894), p. 166. However, the 1657 Helmsted *Pest–Ordnung* does not appear in the SUB's current catalogue records. In any case, Blume very likely had this document at his disposal.

[25] Mannagetta (1680).

[26] 'Hominem, nobilissimam creaturam, licet omnium rerum affluentia esset instructus, extra societatem tamen non vivere posse, sed naturaliter ad illam propendere (quicquid etiam in contrarium velint Hobbes...) omnes saniores ac prudentes asserunt. Quod prudentum suffragia attinet, Aristoteles, omnis eruditionis Princeps expresse hoc asserit ... ut et H. Grotius [... et] Pufendorf', Blume (1683), p. A1v–A1r. On *ius naturale*, see Padoa Schioppa (2017), pp. 342–358.

[27] 'Cum autem homo non semper socio tribuat, quod tribuendam ipsi erat, officiumque suum observe, sed saepius socium, ob naturalem ad dissentiendum facilitatem ... injuria afficiat, inaequalitatem introducat, siquidem, homo secretus a lege et iustitia pessimum animalium est [Arist. I Politica] necesse est, ut adsit quoddam, quod monstret agenda & non agenda vetet, quod ipsum est jus, norma actionum humanarum, quo jure absente, quemadmodum homo absque anima rationali non potest consistere, ita etiam societas absque jure est peritura', Blume (1683), p. A1v.

[28] 'Cum vero Respublica, tanquam societatum optima & perfectissima Arist. 1. Pol. 2. Ex variis societatibus constet, sequitur quod & in illa jus aliquod & LL [= leges] vigere debeant ... cum pauci sint qui amore virtutis injunctum officium faciant, sed ob ingenii humani pravitatem in vetita semper tendant, ideoque plurimi ad observandum officium metu poenarum adigentur, & praemiis allicientur, quod fieri potest jure & legibus', Blume (1683), p. A1v.

the modification, amendment, dispensation, and even abrogation of existing legislation.[29] Nevertheless, this power is not absolute; a clear limit exists. Only those laws falling under *ius civile* (civil law) are subject to and dependent on the prince's will. Within the domain of civil law, two distinct categories emerge: *iura universalia* (universal laws), which apply to all individuals under the Prince's dominion, and *iura singularia* (particular laws), which constitute specific rights or privileges bestowed upon particular individuals or institutions as exceptions to the universal law.[30] Having laid this comprehensive foundational overview of legal systems, Blume then transitions to his specific focus: the plague (*pestis*). He observes that the plague *vix* (barely) appears within civil law, where it is often categorized alongside other febrile illnesses such as typhus (*febris petechalis*) and bloody flux (*dysenteria*). Yet, regardless of the precise medical definition, Blume's paramount objective is to illustrate the principles by which justice must be administered when a plague afflicts a state.[31]

The legislative process for establishing law is perpetually contingent upon the holder of power, a dynamic shaped by the specific type of republic. In agreement with Polybius' anacyclosis model, power can manifest as a monarchy, an aristocracy, a democracy, a tyranny, an oligarchy, or an ochlocracy. The Holy Roman Empire, however, stands as a notable exception to these conventional models, characterized by its unique mixed system. In this intricate structure, the emperor is not the sole authority capable of enacting 'universal laws'. Rather, the system also incorporates the Reichsstände (*status imperii*)—the Imperial Estates—with the Emperor and Reichsstände convening collectively in the Reichstag (*comitium*), or Imperial Diet. Blume underscores this critical point, emphasizing that the emperor cannot establish any law that binds all citizens of the Empire without the explicit consent of the electors and the Reichsstände. As illustrative examples of such universal laws, Blume cites the historically significant Treaty of Passau in 1552 and the Peace of Augsburg in 1555.[32] Furthermore, the Holy Roman Empire is intricately subdivided into numerous lesser entities, within which each respective ruler possesses the right to promulgate 'particular laws' (*iura singularia*) and confer privileges. Notwithstanding this, such rulers do not possess, strictly speaking, absolute power. Their authority is derived from the emperor and is geographically circumscribed to their specific territories, enabling them to establish 'territorial law' (*ius territoriale*).[33] Consequently, each territorial administration—including, for instance, imperial cities—is vested with the authority

[29] 'Haec igitur jura & LL Majestas in Republica ferre debet, quatenus salus & utilitas Reip. id exigit … Cum autem Reipublicae ut omnium humanarum rerum non eadem semper facies sit, Majestas solum, quia nemini nisi illi & qui jura analoga, vel ab eam facultatem habent haec potestas competit, jus abrogare, mutare, dispensare & corrigere potest', Blume (1683), p. A2r.

[30] Blume (1683), pp. A2r–v.

[31] Blume (1683), pp. A2r–v.

[32] 'In nostro Imperio universo tales sunt Imperator & status Imperii simul sumti, qui conjuntim in comitiis leges universales condunt, nec Imperator citra Electorum & reliquorum statuum consensum legem, quae omnes Imperii cives obligat, ferre potest, uti apparet ex formula in Recessibus & Constitutionibus Imperii recepta … Tales leges universales sunt Constitutiones Politicae Pax publica & Religiosa de Anno 1552 & 1555', Blume (1683), p. A4v. See Padoa Schioppa (2017), pp. 248–249.

[33] Blume (1683), pp. Br–v.

to enact laws that may deviate from the common law (*ius commune*). Critically, such territorial laws are deemed to 'oblige in conscience' (*in conscientia*), meaning they carry a moral imperative for obedience.[34] Finally, the author furnishes the reader with a final, yet pivotal, distinction: an individual can be either a 'public person' (*persona publica*), acting on behalf of the prince (such as a magistrate), or a 'private person' (*persona privata*), who may be either a layperson or a clergyman.

After establishing the broader legal framework, the author proceeds to delineate the specific actions a magistrate (*magistratus*) can undertake during times of pandemic to prevent the spread of the plague. As a fundamental principle, the magistrate is bound to do everything necessary to keep the pestilence under control. This duty extends even to acting against imperial laws if required, demonstrating the extreme urgency and overriding importance of public health. The magistrate must act promptly, emphasizing prevention over belated remedies after the plague has already begun to spread. This proactive stance might even involve the drastic measure of burning a private house (*domus privata*). In such dire circumstances, the inherent 'sacrality' of a home as its owner's refuge becomes irrelevant when weighed against the paramount importance of the people's health. The inhabitants of such a house, forcibly displaced for the greater good, must then be accommodated, either in a hospital or in another dwelling situated distinctly apart from the main city.[35] Furthermore, the magistrate bears the responsibility for addressing the religious needs of those confined to hospitals. This is achieved by appointing a dedicated 'plague clergyman' (*Pestilenz Pfarr-herrn*, or *Pestprediger*) to the facility.[36] This measure is crucial to prevent extraneous clergymen from entering or exiting the hospital to offer assistance to the sick, thereby curbing the dangerous potential for further plague dissemination. This appointed clergyman's duties extend beyond the spiritual dimension, particularly for those nearing death, involving the celebration of the Eucharist. Crucially, the minister must also address the psychological dimension for individuals deprived of their freedom due to isolation. Beyond caring for the souls and minds of the sick, the magistrate must also ensure their physical well-being by appointing surgeons (*chirurgi*) and other personnel responsible for patient care, ensuring that nothing appears to be lacking for those residing in the hospitals.[37]

---

[34] 'Quaeritur hic 1. an status Imperii leges & privilegia contra jus commune concedere possint? & an leges principum obligent in conscientia? Quod ad priorem attinet quaestionem, affirmandum hoc est, quia constitutiones provinciales obtinent vim legis in territoriis, leges vero posteriores prioribus derogant.... Quod posteriorem quaestionem concernit, affirmatur has leges in conscientia obligare', Blume (1683), p. Bv. See Padoa Schioppa (2017), pp. 375–377.

[35] Blume (1683), p. Bv

[36] In the Holy Roman Empire, the term *parochus* in Latin and its German translation *Pfarr* could refer to both a Catholic parish priest and a Lutheran pastor who headed a parish. Therefore, *parochus* and *pfarr* function as a *vox media*–a neutral or mediating term. This broad applicability across confessions highlights Blume's aim to provide instructions relevant to all parts of the Empire. Throughout the work, Blume's detailed attention to both Catholic practices (e.g., Extreme Unction) and Lutheran contexts (e.g., Helmstedt University) further underscores his intention to create a universally applicable treatise.

[37] 'Praeterea Magistratus in tali nosocomio parochum, ein Pestilenz Pfarr–herrn/ Pestprediger constituere debet, ne reliqui pastores opus habeant, ut infectos visitent, atque adeo contagionem,

Following the requisition and subsequent burning of an infected house and its contents, a thorough investigation is mandated. This inquiry aims to determine whether the infection was a deliberate act (*culpa*) or occurred by accident (*fortuito*). In the former instance, legal action must be initiated: the householder cannot expect any compensation for their destroyed goods, and they will, moreover, incur a punishment (*poena*). In the latter scenario, however, as it was beyond the holder's power to prevent the contagion, and their property was sacrificed for the paramount public health, they are entitled to receive compensation from the administration.[38]

Another possible scenario arises if the householders refuse to leave their property and relocate to a hospital. In such a case, they are permitted to remain in their home, but they must be excluded from social life, thereby forfeiting the right to attend churches or engage in other public activities to prevent any potential contagion. Furthermore, their house must be marked with a cross or another clear symbol indicating the presence of the plague within, ensuring that anyone passing by is fully aware of the danger of death should they dare to enter the property.[39]

In times of famine, also serving as a preventative measure against the onset of pandemics, the magistrate possesses the authority to distribute 'public wheat' (*publica annona*). This supply is drawn from public granaries (*granaria publica*), which store grain either produced on 'public fields' (*in publicis praedis*) or purchased with 'public money' (*publica pecunia*).[40] Nonetheless, the magistrate can only provide this assistance as a loan (*mutuum*), with interest (*usura*) applied. Blume specifies that this interest cannot be high or 'lucrative'; rather, it must be understood as simple compensation for the state's organizational effort in aiding the community. Importantly, Blume clarifies that the interest applied must be proportionate to the individual's income. Society is therefore categorized into three groups regarding this assistance: poor people (*pauperes*), to whom the magistrate—acting as the 'protector of miserable people' (*protector miserabilium*)—shall distribute food for free, as an

dum sanos iterum adeunt, disseminant, Et saluti aeternae aegrotantium prospiciendum: possunt enim a parocho constituto admoneri ut ad mortem se praeparent & sacram coenam accipiant, alias enim effent derelicti in summis angustiis quod nimis crudele & inhumanum foret et. Chirurgi itidem ut & aliae personae, quae curam aegrotantium habent, a Magistratu hic sunt constituendae, ut nihil personis in noscomiis existentibus deesse videatur', Blume (1683), p. B3v.

38 Blume (1683), p. B4v.

39 'Ob eandem causam Magistratus subditos peste infectos, si in nosocomium te recipere nolint, domibus propriis indulos tenere potest, ac ab omni conversatione, imo & frequentatione templorum, quod alias Magistratus non prohibebit, neque ipsi licitum erit excludere potest, quia metuendum ne contagio hoc modo disseminetur, ac transportetur. Solet itaque eorum domus cruce aliqua vel alio signo notari, ut praetereuntes sani eo melius infectas domus a nondum infectis dignoscere queant, ille enim qui ejusmodi aedes ingreditur, periculum mortis fubire dicitur', Blume (1683), p. B4v.

40 'Accidit autem saepius, ut caritas & penuria annonae tempore pestis in loco aliquo existat, tum succurrendum illis, quibus aliquid deest, & publica & privata annona. Publica annona est, quae vel ex publicis praediis fuit percepta, vel publica pecunia comparata. Si jam Respublica ejusmodi publica praedia non habeat, tum confugiendum ad granaria publica, inquibus frumentum asservatur. Et tum Magistratus frumetum civibus id desiderantibus mutuo dare potest, ut certo tempore restituatur cum usuris... Illae usurae autem non sint lucratoriae aut mordaces, quae illicitae & inhonestae J.Civ. habentur, sed compensatoriae', Blume (1683), p. C2r.

act of charity; the 'middle' people (*medii*), who may receive wheat as a loan but without any interest being charged—though even in this case, the restitution of the loan cannot always be guaranteed, and while the magistrate has the right to be severe, in such instances, he shall ultimately renounce the collection of the money –; and rich people (*divites*), who must fully repay the debt contracted with the state. Of course, to avoid repayment, some individuals might falsely declare themselves to be poor or even sick. In such cases, the magistrate has the right to issue an 'extraordinary penalty' (*extraordinaria poena*), also referred to as an 'arbitrary penalty' (*arbitraria poena*). Blume clarifies that 'arbitrary' here does not imply that the magistrate can apply the measure according to his personal will (*arbitrium*). Instead, a punishment is defined as 'extraordinary' or 'arbitrary' to indicate that a specific case is not covered by a specific law, but the magistrate must, in any circumstance, act with moderation, even though such moderation does not preclude the application of the death penalty.[41]

While trade typically falls under international law (*ius gentium*), the magistrate retains the authority to alter market conditions during a pandemic, as commerce can serve as a significant vector for the plague's propagation. Consequently, the magistrate may opt to grant a monopoly to a specific individual, especially when the pestilence is imminent, while simultaneously prohibiting competitors from trading goods. This measure aims to reduce the overall possibilities of disease spread. In implementing such a policy, the magistrate must exercise prudent judgment in selecting the beneficiary of the monopoly to ensure that the populace does not face a scarcity of goods. Furthermore, the chosen monopolist must sell the goods at a proper price, thereby avoiding the induction of famine due to people's inability to afford food. Finally, the magistrate must be prepared to withdraw the monopoly as soon as the plague subsides.[42] The magistrate is obligated to encourage people to purchase essential provisions, such as wood, wheat, salt, and flour, 'in time.' Furthermore, he must implement rationing of goods through formal 'ordnung,' explicitly declaring that only vital necessities are permitted for sale. It falls upon each citizen to secure their own food supplies promptly, and likewise, the magistrate bears the responsibility to do the same for the city as a whole, in preparation for any unforeseen event.

The author even argues that if someone is found stealing food due to their impoverished condition, they cannot be considered guilty of thieving. The rationale behind this perspective is that the sole purpose of such an act is mere subsistence, whereas, in scholastic terms, the illicit gain constitutes the formal cause (*ratio formalis*) of stealing goods, which is demonstrably absent in cases of extreme necessity. Interestingly, the Lutheran author here references Leonard Lessius, an early seventeenth century Flemish Jesuit theologian, and his work *De iustitia et iure*.[43] This reference is used to assert, against Hobbes, that solidarity is an intrinsic part of human nature, thus obligating people to provide aid to those in need.[44]

---

41 Blume (1683), p. C2v.

42 Blume (1683), p. C3r.

43 Rai (2020).

44 Blume (1683), p. C4v.

Another critical issue addressed is the management of bodily fluids, faeces, and other substances that may emit a strong odour—and which were traditionally linked to the spread of the plague.[45] These waste materials are strictly prohibited from being discarded onto the street; instead, they must be contained within a dunghill (*sterquilinium*). It is explicitly stated that this *sterquilinium* must in no way be placed close to a neighbour's wall, specifically to prevent any substance from passing through it and potentially contaminating adjacent properties. Furthermore, certain professions, such as skinners (*pelliparii*) and sulphur manufacturers (*sulphurarii*) and similar workers, are forbidden from carrying out their 'fetid works' (*foetida ars*). The underlying reason for this prohibition is consistent: smelling air was widely considered a favourable element for the propagation of contagion. Hence, the magistrate possessed the authority to suspend any type of activity that could produce such an effect, prioritizing public health over specific trades.[46]

In cases of illegal acts punishable by the death penalty, the magistrate should preferably imprison the condemned. Their capital sentence must only be executed after the plague has subsided: the magistrate may therefore choose to alter or even dismiss the penalty, unless the offense is subject to divine law.[47] Indeed, public executions, by their very nature, could become focal points for the spread of contagion. However, this postponement or dismissal must be considered an extreme solution, as the public execution of one person can instil the fear of law in many.[48]

Concerning burials, Blume specifies that, according to canon law, they can take place both inside and outside the city. However, civil law mandates that burials occur only in cemeteries located outside the city, to prevent the—contagious—'smell of death' from spreading among the living.[49] During a plague, the magistrate possesses the power to derogate from canon law, compelling the burial of people in deep mass graves (*outside the city*), where the corpses are covered with quicklime (*calx viva*). There is a clear necessity for corpses to dissolve rapidly and for beasts to be denied access to them, thus preventing the further spread of the plague. These mass graves should be situated close to hospitals, given the high number of deaths the plague causes. Those who possess family chapels may opt to bury the corpse there, provided that the body is deeply interred and that all family members agree to this arrangement.[50]

Before burial, it is imperative to verify that the person is indeed deceased, given the fear of apparent death. Burial expenses are the responsibility of the heirs, but if

---

45 Cole (2016), pp. 25–48.

46 Blume (1683), pp. D1r–v.

47 'Magistratus... in carcere detinere potest... poterit poenam mutare, dispensare, nisi poena capitalis de eo crimine sit constituta in jure divino, aut executio fieri potest in occulto ad evitandum majus malum, quod ex congregatione hominum, si pestis in illo loco sit, est metuendum', Blume (1683), p. D1v.

48 'Princeps non debet permittere, ut justitia fiat in occulto, nisi gravibus de causis: interest enim Reipublicae fontes poenas publice luere... ut scilicet poena unius sit metus multorum', Blume (1683), p. D1v–D2r.

49 Blume (1683), pp. D2r–v.

50 Blume (1683), pp. D2v.

they are poor, the state must cover the costs. Undertakers are typically tasked with burials, but in times of plague, they might be unavailable. Hence, the deceased's familiars must undertake the task of inhuming the dead. However, if there are no survivors, the magistrate can compel any citizen to perform this duty, as it would be considered 'inhuman' not to bury the dead. In this context, the magistrate's most practical choice is to employ prisoners condemned to the deadly penalty for this high-risk task of interring bodies.[51] As a proactive measure to prevent any possible spread of the plague, cities must share information about outbreaks. Furthermore, the magistrate must actively eradicate any means of contagion: this includes stagnant backwater, accumulated dirt, and even prostitution (*coitus immoderatus*)—which the author connects to the alternating conditions of poverty and abundance.

Once an outbreak begins, the magistrate must address sacred and ecclesiastical matters, arranging for subjects to be seriously admonished by divine words through ministers to undergo genuine penance. In this context, Blume stressed that hospitals must be erected and founded, and 'plague clergyman' must be appointed. They are often granted a certain expectation of the next vacant parish, meaning they should occupy the first parish that becomes available. This incentive is established because few individuals are willing to undertake such a perilous duty and office, given the great danger involved.[52]

Blume underlines a challenging procedural issue here: generally, clergymen—who might also receive a prebend in relation to their office—are not appointed by secular authorities. On the other hand, to prevent the spread of the plague, 'ordinary' clergymen cannot be in contact with sick people. Blume clarifies that while the magistrate does not hold a *ius patronatus*, – the right to provide a prebend –, he retains the right to appoint plague clergymen, not as substitutes, but in addition to 'ordinary' clergymen, viz., priests or pastors. The ordinary parish priest, however, might not be enthusiastic about the arrival of new colleagues—and perceived competitors. In such a case, the magistrate may even take money from their tithes and annuities.[53] This reference to the parish priest's potential reluctance, although not explicitly tied by Blume to the question of penance in this specific passage, provides a crucial insight. It suggests an underlying tension that connects to the broader mandate since Lateran IV[54]—a source he mentioned elsewhere in the text: at least once per year, any

[51] Blume (1683), pp. D3v–4r.

[52] 'Circa sacra et ecclesiastica, magistratus enim disponit, dum subditi per ministros verbis divini ad veram poenitentiam agenda serio admonetur, feriae repentinae die Pest–Betstunden/ singulis septimanis semel vel bis habendae instituuntur, hospitalia eriguntur ac conduntur, pastores pestilentiales constituuntur, quibus plerumque certa exspectativa in proximam vacantiam conceditur, das die erste Pfarre so ledig wird/ sie wiederum bekleiden sollen / & hoc ideo constitutum, quia non multi reperiuntur, qui huic muneri & officio praeesse velint, ingensque periculum hi homines subire teneantur', Blume (1683), pp. D4r–v.

[53] 'Nunquam igitur in bene constituta Republica permittendum, ut ordinarii parochi & sanos & infectos visitent, sed hoc Pastoribus pestilentialibus permittendum, qui quandoque ordinariis adjunguntur, & licet parochus ordinarius sibi adjungi aliquem recusaret, Magistratus tamen in hac flagrante necessitate, licet jus Patronatus non habeat, quendam constituere potest, ex decimis & reditibus parochi recusantis alendum', Blume (1683), p. D4v.

[54] Larson (2018).

citizen must be heard in confession by the parish priest. This confessional practice aimed to maintain control over the flock and prevent the spread of another kind of 'pestilence'—heresy—a very real possibility in a multi-confessional empire. To anchor his explanation of the magistrate's power, Blume referred to the Silesian *Pest-Ordnung* (1680), showing that these edicts were contributing to developing a coherent system of plague law.

Moreover, the magistrate must appoint a Council of Public Health (*collegium sanitatis*), chaired by a prefect (*praefectus sanitatis*). This council can even include Jewish doctors in the absence of available Christian ones (whether Catholic or Lutheran).[55] Contrary to Grotius' openness, Blume rejected the idea that the magistrate could provide doctors with the license to euthanize individuals whose fate was sealed by the pestilence, being gravely affected and close to death, simply due to the fear of contagion. He argued that other measures could be taken, such as enclosing the sick within the hospital or plague shelters.[56]

In case of an outbreak into a close city, the magistrate must inhibit the arrival of people from that city, and impede any travel to that city, but no one can impede the use of public ways (*via publica*) and public rivers (*flumen publicum*), connecting cities. But again, and on the basis of concrete examples, such as the legal case by the city of Aachen to William Duke of Jülich-Cleves-Berge on 27th October 1586, in case of possible contagion, the cities keep the power to put incoming people, either by land or river, in quarantine, in a specific place, close to the city, where a custodian must keep a watchful eye on them. Such control must be severe, without exception and it may even include the holder of power in the region, like a Prince, who can be even excluded by his subjects from the city. That was Ripa's opinion, but Blume is not really in line with such interpretation, even sustaining that such a severe control must not to be necessarily applied also to the neighbouring territories.[57]

A journey can only be undertaken after receiving approval from the local authority, formalised through a document, the *littera dimissoria* also known as *bullettinum*—Blume affirms it derived from the Italian word 'bullettino' –, designed to ensure trustworthiness and prevent deceit. For this *bullettinum* to be fully valid and accepted, the following requirements must be met: 1. It must be issued by a Magistrate or other designated authorities; 2. The public seal must be properly affixed and clearly imprinted. Without this, the *bullettinum* is not valid. The document must specify these key elements: (*a*) how long the individual stayed in the place from which he or she is departing; (*b*) It must clearly state the destination to which the traveller

[55] 'Quandoque etiam certum collegium instituitur, quod vocatur Collegium sanitatis, cui praeest praefectus sanitatis, in quod etiam recipi potest Judaeus, si alius Medicus Christianus haberi nequit. Quemadmodum enim salva conscientia alias, ita multo magis quis tempore pestis a Judaeo medicinam accipere potest', Blume (1683), p. E1r.

[56] 'Quaeritur hic an Magistratus medicis facultatem dare possit, occidendi hominem infectum, si sanari nequit & ex ipso contagium toti Reipublicae immineat? H. Grotius... hoc affirmat... recedo. Non enim statim ob metum contagionis occidendus est, cum alia adsint remedia, v. g. intra aedes pestilentiarias & nosocomia occludi, per personas specialiter ad id destinatas custodiri & curari possit', Blume (1683), p. E1v.

[57] Blume (1683), p. E2r.

intends to go; (*c*) the date of departure must be included. This is crucial because even if one is presumed free from plague: the lack of a departure date could mean they have since entered a contagious area; (*d*) finally, the document should include a description of the person regarding their stature, age, face, hair, and clothing. While not always precisely observed, this was intended to prevent unauthorized individuals from associating themselves with a valid *bullettinum* thereby curbing potential malice and opportunities for wrongdoing. It specifically states that if multiple people are using one *bullettinum*, each must be individually described.[58]

To maintain strict control over incoming people (*peregrini*), the magistrate must opt for closing the city gates, with only a few designated entrances remaining open. Here, guardians (*custodes*) and appointed officials must register all incoming individuals, verify their *bullettinum*, and confirm the correspondence between the document's information and its holder's identity, paying particular attention to surname and name.[59] People are obligated to use the major roads (*ordinaria via*). Should individuals arrive via other routes, they may be suspected of attempting to defraud the *ius viarum*. In such a case, the punishment is 'arbitrary'—in accordance with the above definition and reflecting the extraordinary nature of plague time—and can range from flogging to even the death penalty. Furthermore, for those transporting goods by means of transportation like wagons, their goods can be confiscated and burnt as a punitive measure.[60] Similarly, also the postal service officer (*cursor publicus*)—who generally deviates from major roads to swift their journey—might be a way of contagion, hence letters must be collected in a specific and isolated place of the city.[61]

Specific categories, such as the clergy, may benefit from *iura singularia* because of their special status. If a parish priest/pastor (*parochus*) dies, a closer colleague cannot be forced to move into the infected area. Instead, a new one must be appointed. Then, in the absence of *parochus*, the sacristan (*æditaus*) or another person can read the Holy Scripture, Psalms, and Postils for as long as necessary. Moreover, as regards Catholics, if the danger of contagion is imminent, the priest, in administering extreme unction, must use only what is essential to the rite, such as the holy anointing oil. Furthermore, in times of plague, the parish priest can avoid solemn rites. Canons may abandon the city, though at least two or three of them must remain to maintain the college. Nuns may also receive a license to relocate to another monastery. Finally, a clergyman required to attend a synod is permitted to be absent, but only if the plague is severe (*magna pestis*).[62] Other categories may benefit from specific rights, due to

---

[58] Blume (1683), pp. E2v–E3r.

[59] Blume (1683), pp. E2v–E3r.

[60] 'Si jam quis viam ordinariam non sequitur, incurrit suspicionem, quod voluerit fraudare jus viarum … puniendus est, poena autem solet esse arbitraria, quae ratione circumstantiarum tempore pestis ad fustigationem & capitalem usque paenam extendi potest. Si aurigae vehiculis vias inusitatas transeant ac ita gebellas telonia & vectigalia defraudent, pignorari possunt, donec vectigalia solvant, praetereaque puniri solent … Quandoque etiam vehicula mercibus onusta pestis tempore in poenam comburuntur uti', Blume (1683), p. E4r.

[61] Blume (1683), p. E4v.

[62] Blume (1683), p. Fv.

the contingency of the pandemic, in which law may follow the war law—as Ripa had already stated (*a bello ad pestem argumentum valet*): for instance, (1) vassals who did not ask the investiture to their lord within a year, in case of pestilence they do not lose their fief; (2) University personnel (*tota Academia*) can leave the city, without losing privileges (and salaries), and if a professor dies, the salary of the entire year is to be given to his heirs; (3) a lease-holder (*emphyteuta*) can avoid paying the canon in case of pandemic, without incurring penalties, since he could not benefit from the leasing (as it happens in war time); (4) newborns outside the city retain their citizenship: in case of necessity, the law allows a legal fiction (*ubi enim necessitas postulat, lex fictionem admittit*) in order that anyone who is born outside the city may keep all the rights granted by the citizenship; (5) no one can be obliged to receive sick people or any person in general.[63]

Only before the arrival of the pandemic, any person has the right to flee the city, with some important exceptions. Those who hold a public office essential for the city itself cannot abandon it, such as the magistrate, who must coordinate the actions to be taken during the pandemic. Similarly, parish priests/pastors must remain in the city to provide spiritual assistance. Husband and wife cannot separate from each other: Blume explicitly states that it is forbidden for spouses to flee from one another 'because they are one flesh (*una caro*) and maintain an indivisible custom of life'. In this context, Blume seems to implicitly refer to specific Biblical passages. The concept of *una caro* is a clear reference to Genesis 2:24 and Matthew 19:5,[64] underscoring the profound bond of marriage. Moreover, consistent with Pauline teachings (Ephesians 5), in case of plague, the husband must take care of his sick wife. Analogously, just as Paul claims that from a spiritual point of view the husband must 'make her holy by cleansing her with the washing of water by the word' (Ephesians 5:26), so in case of disease, the husband must call a doctor—otherwise, he would lose the dowry. Furthermore, the wife cannot seek a divorce from her sick husband, reflecting principles akin to Paul's admonition: 'wives, be subject to your husbands as to the Lord' (Ephesians 5:22).[65]

At the end of his *Discursum*, Blume addresses various categories of legal acts, which he divides into extra-judicial acts, such as testaments, and judicial acts, such as legal proceedings. First, he explained that legal acts need not be celebrated with solemnity during a plague (*negotia non opus est, ut tempore pestis solenniter celebrentur*), primarily to avoid the gathering of people. Such a principle, however, is in contrast with others. Among the most interesting examples Blume focused on was the necessity of having witnesses during the drafting of a last will. As Blume maintains, scholars hold divergent opinions on what to do in times of pandemics. Even the required number of witnesses is a matter of controversy—whether two, three,

---

[63] Blume (1683), pp. Fv–F2v.

[64] 'Therefore, a man leaves his father and his mother and clings to his wife, and they become one flesh'. Cf '[coniuges] sunt una caro', Blume (1683), p. F3v.

[65] 'Quod si tamen conjux maritum peste laborantem deserit, successionis commodo ex pacto, statuto, consuetudine & jure communi debito privari potest ... Si maritus uxori peste laboranti medicum non adhibuerit, lucro dotis privatur ... Nunquam igitur uxor divortium ob pestem petere potest', Blume (1683), p. F3v.

five, or seven—also in relation to the type of plague, whether *magna* or *exigua*. After presenting these various opinions, Blume proposes a possible procedure, one not necessarily shared among all scholars. According to Blume, witnesses should not be close to the testator or directly in front of him, but rather to the side. They may not see him, but they must clearly hear him. For the validity of such a last will, the testator must die as a result of the disease, while the witnesses must be alive when the last will is opened: if only one witness is alive, the document is not valid. Concerning legal proceedings, among the most interesting aspects, Blume explains that if the summoned party is required to appear in a place deemed unsafe due to the plague, they are permitted not to appear and cannot incur into a conviction in absentia.

Blume's assertions are consistently corroborated by legal sources, including references to specific legal cases—particularly those in German—that established precedents.[66] While this approach can make it challenging for today's readers to follow the entire line of reasoning, it simultaneously demonstrates Blume's considerable competence in navigating these sources. Moreover, it underscores how crucial it was for him to establish objective legal anchors to validate the indications he proposed, especially given that contemporary legal literature often lacked a common direction.

4 Conclusion

This chapter has provided the very first in-depth analysis of Christian Ulrich Blume's *Discursum Juridicum de Peste et Juribus circa Tempus Pestis*, revealing it as a unique and largely unexplored primary source for understanding 'plague law' (*pestis ius*) in the late 17th century Holy Roman Empire. Blume's treatise emerges not merely as a legal compilation but as a comprehensive, pragmatic, and contextually rich response to the multifaceted challenges posed by pandemics. By drawing extensively from juridical-philosophical sources (like Aristotle, Grotius, and Pufendorf), Civil and Canon Law, and practical-juridical treatises (including the *Pest-Ordnungen* and specific legal cases), Blume meticulously constructed a framework for action. His work notably navigated the complex landscape of a multi-confessional Empire, striving for a broad applicability that addressed concerns pertinent to both Lutheran and Roman Catholic practices, and even including provisions for Jewish doctors. The recurring invocation of the legal principle *a bello ad pestem argumentum valet* underscores the extraordinary nature of plague jurisprudence, allowing for deviations from 'normal' legal practices. This principle reveals a foundational connection between public health law and the state of exception, a conceptual link that represents a core characteristic of public intervention in public health already consolidated in the Early Modern Era.

Blume's *Discursum* thus offers invaluable insights into the intellectual and administrative efforts to maintain order, health, and spiritual welfare amidst the chaos of epidemic disease. His meticulous attention to objective legal anchors, even in the

[66] Blume (1683), pp. G1r–H2r.

face of contemporary scholarly divergence, highlights the urgent need for clarity and authority when society's very fabric was threatened. Ultimately, this analysis of Blume's work enriches our understanding of Early Modern pandemic responses, demonstrating how jurists grappled with unprecedented circumstances by adapting existing legal traditions, developing specific *iura singularia*, and forging practical guidance for officials. The *Discursum* serves as a powerful testament to the era's attempts to impose legal and moral order on the terrifying randomness of plague, a historical experience that resonates even in contemporary reflections on global health crises.

References

Ascheri M (2020) Rimedi contro le epidemie. I consigli di diritto europeo dei giuristi (secoli XIV–XVI). Aracne, Roma

Bartolus de Saxoferrato (1505) Super prima [−secunda] Digesti novi. Cum additionibus antea positis additis etiam apostillis Andree Barbatie. Battista Torti, Venezia

Blume CU (1683) Discursum iuridicum de peste et iuribus circa tempus pestis. Hammi, Helmstedt

Boccaccio G (1956) Decamerone. Einaudi, Torino

Cerrito A (2020) Leprosy and inherited diseases in 13th century discussions on original sin. In: Palazzo A, Bonini F (eds) Medical and philosophical perspectives on illness and disease in the middle ages. E-theca OnLineOpenAccess Edizioni, Firenze–Parma, pp 187–217

Cole L (2016) Imperfect creatures: vermin, literature, and the science of life, 1600–1700. University of Michigan Press, Ann Arbor, MI

Crawshaw JS (2013) The renaissance invention of quarantine. In: Clark L et al (eds) The fifteenth century XII: society in an age of plague. Boydell and Brewer, Martlesham, pp 161–174

de Vries F (1682) Disputatio juridica inauguralis de peste. Elzevier Lyons

Drage W (1665) Daimonomageia. In: A small treatise of sicknesses and diseases from witchcraft, and supernatural causes. J. Dover, London

Eckert EA (1996) The structure of plagues and pestilences in early modern Europe: Central Europe, 1560–1640. Karger, Basel

Eckert EA (2020) The retreat of plague from Central Europe, 1640–1720: a geomedical approach. Bull Hist Med 74:1–28

Episcopius (1652) Disputatio juridica de peste … quoad ultimas voluntates. Hackius, Leiden

Flamm H (2008) Die ersten Infektions– oder Pest–Ordnungen in den österreichischen Erblanden, im Fürstlichen Erzstift Salzburg und im Innviertel im 16. Verlag der Österreichischen Akademie der Wissenschaften, Vienna, Jahrhundert

Forster VW (1598) Disputatio Iuridica de peste. Gronenberg, Wittenberg

French RK (2001) Canonical medicine: gentile da Foligno and scholasticism. Brill, Leiden

Gensini GF et al (2004) The concept of quarantine in history: from plague to SARS. J Infect 49:257–261

Justinian (1575) Authenticae seu novellae constitutiones. Plantin, Antwerpen

Larson AA (2018) Lateran IV's decree on confession, Gratian's De poenitentia, and confession to one's sacerdos proprius: a re-evaluation of Omnis utriusque in its canonistic context. Cathol Hist Rev 104:415–437

Lee ARA (2022) Plague and popular revival: ecclesiastical authorities, civic religion and the Bianchi devotions in 1399. Stud Church Hist 58:68–90

Leipzig (1680) Der Stadt Leipzig verneuerte und verbesserte Pest–Ordnung. https://gdz.sub.uni–goettingen.de/id/PPN591084767?tify=%7B%22pages%22%3A%5B3%5D%2C%22view%22%3A%22%22%7D

Levack BP (2016) The witch-hunt in early modern Europe, 4th edn. Longman, London
Limborch R (1652) Disputatio juridica de peste … quoad actus inter vivos. Maire, Leiden
Mannagetta JW (1680) Pest-Ordnung oder der gantzen Gemein nutzlicher Bericht und Gutacht von der Eigenschafft und Ursachen der Pestilentz in Genere. Mair, Wien. https://www.digitale-sammlungen.de/de/view/bsb11062356?page=,1
Meyer W (1894) Verzeichniss der Handschriften im Preussischen Staate. I Hannover, 3 Göttingen. Verlag von A. Bath, Berlin
Mordechai L et al (2019) The Justinianic plague: an inconsequential pandemic. Proc Natl Acad Sci USA 116(51):25546–25554
Padoa Schioppa A (2017) A history of law in Europe from the early middle ages to the twentieth century. Cambridge University Press, Cambridge
Pastore A (1991) Crimine e giustizia in tempo di peste nell'Europa moderna. Laterza, Roma–Bari
Rai E (2020) 'Ex meritis praevisis': predestination, grace, and free will in intra-Jesuit controversies (1587–1613). J Early Mod Christ 7(1):111–150
Richter AL (ed) (1959) Corpus iuris canonici. Akademische Druck- u. Verlagsanstalt, Graz
Riva GF (1598) Illustris de peste tractatus iuridicus ac politicus. Apelli, Leipzig
Römer ZJ (2004) I lazzaretti di Dubrovnik (Ragusa). In: Vanzan Marchini NE (ed) Rotte mediterranee e baluardi di sanità. Venezia e i lazzaretti mediterranei, Skira, Milano, pp 246–250
Schlesische (1710) Schlesische Infections-Ordnung Vom 14. Febr. 1680. Heinichen, Cüstrin. https://digital.staatsbibliothek-berlin.de/werkansicht?PPN=PPN665808526&PHYSID=PHYS_0001&DMDID=
Suevus G (1653) Disputatio Iuridica de Peste. Fincelius, Wittenberg
Žepič V (2022) 'Pandemic criminal law' in continental European legal history. J Eur Hist Law 13(2):50–63

Antonio Gerace holds a PhD in Religious Studies from KU Leuven. In Belgium, his research focused on the development of Biblical studies in the Early Modern Low Countries. He has co-authored numerous publications, spanning from medieval philosophy to early modern history, including his first monograph, Biblical Scholarship in Leuven in the Golden Sixteenth Century (V&R, 2019). From 2018 to 2023, he was a postdoctoral fellow at FSciRe in Bologna, where he focused on the education of the clergy before the Council of Trent, publishing a second monograph titled Un manuale per il clero (Marietti, 2024). In 2024–25, he was a postdoctoral researcher at the University of Bologna, working on the political theology of Renaissance Rome. During this time, he co-edited The Renaissance Papacy's Projects of Religious Reform between Ancient Christianity and 'Catholic Orientalism' (V&R, 2025).

Moving on the Latitude of Health and Disease. Some Remarks on the Galenic Concept of *Neutrum* from the 16th to the 18th Centuries

Simone Guidi and Luca Tonetti

Abstract This article examines how Italian physicians between the sixteenth and eighteenth centuries developed a logic of 'intermediate states' between health and disease. Moving from late Scholastic Galenism to early mechanistic medicine, it shows how a dynamic view of the body allowed physicians to describe overlapping configurations of healthy and morbid states. Particular attention is given to the concept of neutrum, which helps to frame processes such as falling ill and convalescence. In both qualitative and mechanistic paradigms, medical art emerges as primarily concerned with processes and transitions rather than fixed conditions: health appears as a contingent, time-bound relation (ut nunc), modulated by age, constitution, environment, and the biographical history of alternating episodes of illness and recovery.

1 Introduction: Galen's *Neutrum* in its Context

Since 1948, the World Health Organization has defined health as 'a state of complete physical, mental, and social well-being and not merely the absence of disease or infirmity'.[1] This notion seems to take health as a fixed and ideal status, which one

[1] World Health Organization (1946), p. 1

Although this work has been conceived and written by both authors in all its parts, sections 1–3 are to be attributed to Simone Guidi, section 4 to Luca Tonetti. We wrote the conclusion together.

S. Guidi (✉)
Institute for the European Intellectual Lexicon and History of Ideas (CNR-ILIESI), Italian National Research Council, Rome, Italy
e-mail: simone.guidi@cnr.it

L. Tonetti
Department of Historical and Geographic Sciences and the Ancient World (DiSSGeA), University of Padua, Padua, Italy
e-mail: luca.tonetti@unipd.it

M. Balestrieri and A. Cauduro (eds.), *The Legal Anatomy of the Body*, Ius Gentium: Comparative Perspectives on Law and Justice 142,
https://doi.org/10.1007/978-3-032-26434-3_3

can achieve completely and positively, acquiring the qualitative condition of health, and not via the decrease or negation of infirmity.

Such a definition would have probably captured the attention of the early modern physicians we address in this chapter, used to regarding health and disease in more dynamic and complex terms. It would suffice to recall that, still in the mid-eighteenth century, Diderot and d'Alembert's *Encyclopédie* defined *santé* in a much more complex manner; as 'the most perfect state of life', but especially as the

> natural accord, the reasonable arrangement of the parts of the living body, from which it follows that the exercise of all its functions is done, or can be done in a sustainable manner, with ease, freedom, and to the extent which each of its organs is susceptible, according to its purpose, and relative to the actual situation, to the different needs, age, sex, temperament of the individual who is in this position, and to the climate in which he lives.[2]

Here, health is not conceived as a stable and 'complete' well-being, but rather as the relative state of well-being resulting from the mediation of a number of contrasting forces, which push and vibrate inside and outside the organic body and constantly carry it back and forth from health to illness and from illness to health. In this constant contrast, health ultimately results from the balance between these factors and so includes illness and its causes as components of health itself.

This dynamic definition of health and disease dates back a very long time in Western medical and philosophical culture. However, it took its modern shape mostly via some crucial debates generated by the practice to comment on Galen's works from the sixteenth to the seventeenth century, and then in the subsequent discussions aroused in eighteenth century medicine, which, still in the age of the Scientific Revolution, embodied substantial elements from Galenism.

In this paper, we aim to address some significant episodes in these debates, in order not only to revisit early modern medicine's dynamic conception of health, but also to point out some important shifts in the conceptions of health, illness, their co-presence in the body, and the processes that lead a living organism from one to another. We do so by analysing a number of case-studies in Italian early modern medicine, having chosen the specific context of Italy for its influential and long-standing medical tradition, which starts already in the Middle Ages and culminates in the seventeenth century.

In effect, via the notions of *oudéteron* (literally 'neither')[3] and *ygeías platos* ('latitude of health'), then translated into Latin respectively as *neutrum* and *latitudo sanitatis*, for centuries Galenic medicine carried on a complex relative conception of health and disease which is very far from that presented by the WHO. The origins of this idea are found in Galen's *Ars medica* (*Techné Iatriké*), also known in the Middle Ages as *Tegni* or *Microtegni*, one of the most commented Galenic works, and a

[2] Jaucourt (1765/2013), p. 628.

[3] As noted by van der Lugt (2011), p. 15, 'Galen did not invent this tripartite division of medicine *ex nihilo*. In the 3rd century BCE, the Alexandrian physician Herophilus had already proposed a similar classificatory scheme. However, Herophilus applied the categories healthy, unhealthy and neutral not to the objects of medicine (bodies, signs, causes), but to the main branches of the medical art.' See Von Staden (1989), pp. 89–114. On Galen's neutry see also Kaye (2014), pp. 141–144.

crucial one for the education of physicians throughout the medieval and early modern period.[4] In particular, Galen presented his understanding of health and disease in the first section of *Tegni*, where he defined medicine as 'the knowledge of what is healthy, what is morbid, and what is neither',[5] just before his treatment of semeiology and aetiology, two fundamental parts of medical reasoning.

Famously, Galen understood health in terms of *complexio*,[6] the 'proper balance of primary qualities'—a fundamental mixture of the Aristotelian four elements[7]—and conceived disease as 'a disturbance of it'.[8] Such a peculiar notion of health and disease led Galen to understand *complexio* as a 'relative conception',[9] in the sense that *complexio* is a particular balance[10] of elements, proper to each living species, and even to specific categories of individuals. Each was hence given an ideal *complexio*, the *eukraton haplōs*.[11] Importantly, for Galen, as with Aristotle, health and disease are opposite and contrary qualitative states.

A crucial element in our story is that, in this conceptual context, Galen introduced the—likely Stoic[12]—idea of *neutrum*: a third, intermediate, and neutral state placed halfway between health and disease. Famously, this notion is presented in *Tegni* by the following words, which identify three possible meanings of *oudéteron*:

> The 'neither,' as cause, sign, and body, both generally and with application to the present, has three subdivisions in each case. The first is the sense of having no part in either of the opposites; the second that of participating in both; the third that of participating sometimes in one, sometimes in the other. And of these, too, the second admits of a distinction; for it may participate in both equally, or in one more than the other.[13]

Note that, for Galen, what is 'neither' is not only a body, but also a cause of either health or disease, and a sign of them. All these things can be 'neither,' healthy, or ill, in three senses:

(a) Being neither of the two opposites, healthy and ill, and so being perfectly in the middle of these two states.

---

[4] See Palmieri (2006), Pesenti (2000), and McVaugh (2019). See also Joutsivuo (1999), pp. 18–42 and (2002), p. 290. On the circulation of Galenic texts in the Middle Ages see Green (2019). See also Agrimi and Crisciani (1988).

[5] Galen (1821–1833), vol. 1, p. 307. English translation from Galen (1997), p. 345.

[6] On this important notion see in particular the recent Beneduce (2023). See also Kaye (2014), pp. 141–144. For the medieval and Renaissance tradition see Siraisi (1990), pp. 101–106 and Chandelier and Robert (2013).

[7] Ottosson (1984), pp. 129–136.

[8] Ottosson (1984), p. 131. For Galen there are eight kinds of 'imbalances': four simple ones (hot, cold, wet, dry) and four composite (hot-dry, hot-wet, cold-dry, cold-wet).

[9] Ottosson (1984), p. 133.

[10] On the notion of balance, particularly in the scholastic medieval context, see Kaye (2014), pp. 128–240.

[11] Ottosson (1984), p. 134.

[12] Ottosson (1984), pp. 166–167; van der Lugt (2011), pp. 15–16. Galen's primary source seem to be, however, Herophilus. See Von Staden (1989), pp. 82–83.

[13] Galen (1821–1833), vol. 1, pp. 308–309. English translation from Galen (1997), p. 346.

(b) Being at the same time healthy and ill, for instance, when one is healthy in some physiological aspects, but ill in others—this allows for different proportions of this status.
(c) Participating partially in health and partially in illness.

As we shall see, this notion, and its definition in *Tegni*, theoretically challenged Galenic physicians, especially due to the fact that it can either be applied to the constitution of a body or to its current condition. However, in their respective ways, all these notions of *neutrum* could surely be interpreted in light of Galen's relative conception of health and disease. These are not fixed and univocal categories, but two poles, connected to each other by a gradient, through which they partially merge and converge. This gradient is the so-called 'latitude' of health (and illness), a notion that describes health and disease as the conditions of a dynamic subject, which *moves* over the entire magnitude of health and can draw any possible trajectory on it. Here, thus, the same body can be—and very often is—simultaneously healthy and ill, and health and disease are understood more in terms of direction than in terms of fixed statuses. Interpreting signs and reasoning of the causes, semeiology and aetiology help the physician to understand in real time where an individual living body is located on the map of health and illness, and what is happening in its physiology that causes certain motions, from health to disease, or from illness to health.

To understand the early modern reception of Galen's theory in particular, a further and important point lies then in a twofold distinction that Galen himself proposed for these three states—the health, the morbid, and the neutral state. Indeed, for Galen, these can be.

(α) 'in the general sense' (*haplōs*, in Latin: *simpliciter*), or

(β) 'with application to the present' (*en tō nūn*, in Latin: *ut nunc*).

We will see later how 16th and seventeenth century physicians in particular would interpret this distinction. For now, let us note that, for Galen, a sign, a cause, or a body taken *simpliciter* (α) can be considered—the expression is now obviously Aristotelian—either:

(α_1) 'always' (*diapantos*, in Latin: *semper*) healthy or morbid or neutral *simpliciter*; or.

(α_2) 'for the most part' (*os epi to polu*, in Latin: *ut multum*) healthy or morbid or neutral *simpliciter*.

2 Medieval Philosophical Problems and Solutions Related to the Latitude of Health

By these wide conceptual tools, Galen introduced a notion of health and disease that could hardly be framed within philosophical categories dominating ancient and medieval philosophy. In particular, the notion of *neutrum*[14] raised three relevant and

[14] On the notion of *neutrum* in medieval scholastic medicine see in particular Joutsivuo (1999) and van der Lugt (2011).

interdependent issues that would have worried physicians and philosophers from the thirteenth century up to the late Renaissance at least.

The first issue is that conceptions (B) and (C) of the 'neither', as participating simultaneously in health and disease, two qualitative contraries, were not compatible with Aristotle's logical notion of contrariety, as presented in the *Categories*.[15] Indeed, for Aristotle, if health and disease are contraries, they cannot persist in the same moment in the same subject, and hence there cannot be any neutral state that simultaneously takes both together.[16] Vice versa, a neutral state represents an impossible (for Aristotelian logic) overlap of two contrary qualities. Hereafter, we shall call this the 'transition problem'.

The second problem was about the true nature of neutral bodies—an aspect left ambiguous within the Galenic tradition. Physicians were particularly puzzled by the problem of whether neutral bodies tend towards health or disease, and how their nature conditions medical intervention. Moreover, they wondered whether they should be regarded as the object of preventive care or of therapeutic treatment.

The third problem—which we could not delve into sufficiently here—is that Galen's understanding of health and disease required a dynamic conception of the form-matter relationship that dominated Aristotelian and scholastic theories of the living body and vital functions. In particular, it involved the consequence that qualitatively different forms constantly coexist or push each other away in the same substantial subject, and that—according to Galen's conception—forms such as health and disease are structured by degrees. This point especially intersects the issue of the measurability of qualities and their degrees, launched by Arnaldus de Villa Nova in the fourteenth century and later developed by the so-called *Calculatores*.[17]

These issues connected with the notions of 'neither' and latitude of health were well-known by medieval and Renaissance physicians, who would have elaborated complex solutions in order to save the notion of *neutrum* from unavoidable critiques due to its inconsistency with Aristotle's logic; above all Haly (Ali ibn Ridwan)[18]

---

[15] Aristotle, (1991) *Categories*, 10, 11b38–12a2: 'If contraries are such that it is necessary for one or the other of them to belong to the things they naturally occur in or are predicated of, there is nothing intermediate between them. For example, sickness and health naturally occur in animals' bodies and it is indeed necessary for one or the other to belong to an animal's body, either sickness or health' (translation from Barnes's edition).

[16] Besides Ottosson, on this specific issue see Joutsivuo (1999), pp. 45–53 and Joutsivuo (2002).

[17] See especially Sylla (1971–1972, 1973), Roudaut (2021, 2022). About the medical context see Bigotti (2019), pp. 233–248; Bigotti (2022) and Bigotti (2023).

[18] Se Joutsivuo (1999), p. 54 and van der Lugt (2011), pp. 23–24, who notes that 'In order to bring Galen and Aristotle into accordance, Haly reinterpreted the first sense of *neutrum* in his own way, by saying that Galen meant that in that state of the true medium, health and disease are not absent but mixed, as in the mixture of water and oil, in which both ingredients can still be distinguished'.

and Avicenna's[19] critique or dismissal of this concept.[20] However, medieval and early modern physicians found in Galen a set of conceptual tools to engage with the 'transition problem', namely, to conceive individual movements on the latitude of health as logically consistent with a logic of contrary qualities.

In the first place, as said, they could count on a very dynamic conception of health and disease. In the specific case of medieval and Renaissance Galenism, the organism is a closed system, and life is a constant fight and opposition between health and disease. Health instantiates in particular in the notion of 'resistance to disease' (*resistentia*, or *potentia resistiva*, or *potentia resistendi*), a cardinal concept for medieval medicine since the fourteenth century at least,[21] and still a pivotal notion among early modern philosophers[22] and physicians. A healthy body is hence one which is structurally capable of resisting illness, and the latter is always the result of a deflection in this capacity, or the sign of a lack in it; or, finally, the effect of the victory of disease on resistance. This unavoidable interplay between opposite forces constantly moves the body over the latitude of health and disease, dynamically generating health and illness that are expressed by symptoms.

In the second place, they could use Galen's distinction between *simpliciter* (α) and *ut nunc* (β)[23] in order to create different conceptual levels for health, disease and the neutral state, in the main complexion of a body (what we might call a healthy, morbid or neutral constitution), or in its current condition (what we might call a health, morbid, or neutral current condition). By means of this distinction, one

---

[19] See van der Lugt (2011), pp. 27–28, who notes how, in *Canon*, 'he claimed that it is futile to fight the *neutrum*, since the physician has no need for it. The categories of health and disease are sufficient'. On Avicenna's impact on the Italian Renaissance medical context, see especially Siraisi (1987). See also Strohmaier (2019).

[20] One popular solution to the 'transition problem', still topical in the sixteenth century, was that of Taddeo Alderotti (1215–1295), later followed by his pupil Pietro Torrigiano (d. ≃1320). Both Alderotti and Torrigiano accepted the *neutrum* as just a theoretical possibility without accepting that it could be physically and really possible. See Ottosson (1984), pp. 171–172. On Alderotti—a very major figure in these debates—see Siraisi (1981), Joutsivuo (2002), pp. 292–295, and van der Lugt (2011).

[21] See Caroti (1989), Caroti (1995) and Roudaut (2025).

[22] See Des Chene (1996), p. 46 ff.

[23] As aptly noted by Joutsivuo (1999), pp. 127–128, 'The terms *simpliciter* and *ut nunc* were used in scholastic logic as early as the thirteenth century, and can be traced, for example, in Albert the Great's confused theory of the distinction between 'simple assertoric statements (*de inesse simpliciter*) and assertoric statements as of now (*de inesse ut nunc*)'. Torrigiano, however, as well as other scholastic physicians, relied on Aristotle's logical works in interpreting the difference between *simpliciter* and *ut nunc* more directly'. Torrigiano drew on Aristotle's *Sophistical Refutations* where Aristotle distinguished between 'unqualified (*simpliciter*)' propositions or those which 'have some qualification of respect, place, time, or relation (*secunduni quid*)'. This separation 'between 'something without qualification' and 'something with qualification' definitely had an impact on Pietro Torrigiano's formulations. *Simpliciter* was for him something without qualification, something in itself. It indicated lasting existence or existence without reference to any particular time. The term *ut nunc* referred to some qualification in relation to the present time'. Furthermore (p. 130), 'In Torrigiano's view, the term *simpliciter* principally denoted the ability to remain in a certain state. For example, a healthy body *simpliciter semper* was characterized by the ability to remain in good health always, not that a person with this kind of ability was necessarily in good health'.

could argue that, while a body remains *simpliciter* healthy, morbid, or neutral, as its steady natural status (and so its quality as health, morbid or neutral are fixed and not compatible with their opposites), it can also travel in different regions of the latitude of health, where it 'accidentally' (so to speak) participates in mixed forms of health and illness. So, the *simpliciter* and *ut nunc* distinction, opposing what is stable and structural in an organism from the in-time transition of the map of health and disease, provided important epistemological and logical elements to reconcile Aristotelian logic and Galenic methodology in medicine.[24]

Finally, a connection between 'resistance to disease' and the *simpliciter/ut nunc* distinction could easily be obtained by understanding the latter in act-potency terms. As Ottosson aptly noted, especially in Italian medieval medicine, the *simpliciter/ ut nunc* distinction ultimately came to be understood as the opposition between a *potential* capacity of the body and its *actual* condition. In this specific interpretation, a body is 'structurally' and *simpliciter* healthy when it has and maintains a constant potential for health, namely the natural capacity to remain healthy or to recover after a disease. The *ut nunc* condition regards the present moment and the way this potentiality persists or deflects in time. So, a healthy body *simpliciter* decreases this potentiality *ut nunc* during an illness and retrieves it in convalescence.[25] Exactly the same logic applies to the *simpliciter/ut nunc* morbid body, as well as to the *simpliciter/ ut nunc* neutral state, creating a very complex ensemble of possible combinations. Furthermore, in the Italian medical environment, more than one version of this interpretation circulated. Taddeo Alderotti, for instance, interpreted the *simpliciter* state of health, morbid condition, and neutrality, as a steady feature received from birth (*ex generatione*), while the *ut nunc* condition developed in life.[26] Pietro Torrigiano, by contrast, considered *simpliciter* (healthy, morbid, or neutral) as what is true unconditionally, thus independently of any relation with external causes.[27] At the same time, he regarded *ut nunc* as the characteristic domain, which runs in time, of the variable state of alteration in the *simpliciter* state.[28]

[24] In connection to this, it is worth pointing out an additional and less problematic epistemological point related to the latitude of health, one that would be particularly important for early modern philosophers. If health and disease are magnitudes that can increase or decrease, they metaphysically depend on Aristotle's category of *poson*, namely quantity. Since they are not discrete statuses—that is, their parts are not separated from each other and are indeed organized in a continuity, in which one can go from health to disease and from disease to health, they are continuous quantities. As such, health and illness can be represented and understood in terms of space and time, two continuous quantities. For instance, they can be represented in spatial diagrams as things that qualitatively move not only in space, but also in time. On this point see Maclean (2001), in particular pp. 171–188.

[25] Ottosson (1984), p. 180.

[26] Ottosson (1984), p. 183.

[27] Ottosson (1984), pp. 182–183.

[28] Ottosson (1984), p. 183. On Torrigiano's conception of *ut nunc* and *simpliciter*, see Joutsivuo (1999), pp. 127–133.

3 The Dynamics of *Neutrum* and *Latitudo Sanitatis* in the Sixteenth Century: Exploring the Cases of Sclano and Santorio

Before delving more in detail into the seventeenth-and eighteenth-century conceptions of latitude of health, neutral state and convalescence, in the present section we examine two significant moments in the debate on these notions in the sixteenth century, showcased in the views of Salvo Sclano and Santorio Santorio. Indeed, these two important physicians very clearly represent the main tendency of their age, which still remains within the conceptual predominance of Galenism, but is already embarking on the path of an experimental practice of medicine.[29]

More in detail, by analysing these two case-studies, we wish to show how early modern physicians elaborated a complex conceptual framework in order to understand the constant interplay in the body of health and illness, their structural coexistence in the same complexion, and the expression over time of their effective opposition. What stems from this is a very dynamic and processual conception of health, which, as of the eighteenth century, would result in a re-understanding of the latter as a balance of different states of matter contrasting each other.

3.1 Salvo Sclano

In his commentary on *Tegni*, Sclano presents a very complex account of Galen's thesis, mainly realized by commenting the positions of Giovanni Manardo (1463–1536),[30] Giovanni Battista Monte (1489–1552),[31] Giovanni Argenterio (1513–1572),[32] and his preceptor Giovanni Filippo Ingrassia (1510–1580). The result is a full-fledged theory of health, disease, and the neutral state.

Like his medieval predecessors, and in an overt attempt to reconcile Galen and Aristotle, Sclano rejects an immediate equivalence of *simpliciter-ut nunc* with potentiality and actuality. More originally, reprising Ingrassia,[33] he also denies that health is immediately the same as *potentia resistendi*. Indeed, these are for Sclano two different features of the same healthy (*salubre*) body: on the one hand, we have health as a 'categorical' quality, and the healthy body is the one which benefits in act from it; on the other hand, we have *potentia resistendi*, which is the specific capacity to preserve or retrieve health against the causes of illness, a capacity that is however

[29] On Renaissance Galenism see in particular Ward (1981). For an overview on Galenism in early modern culture, specifically in connection with philosophy, see Favaretti Camposampiero and Scribano (2022). On *methodus medendi* in sixteenth and seventeenth centuries, see Boss (1979).

[30] On his position see Joutsivuo (1999), pp. 143–144.

[31] On his view see Joutsivuo (1999), pp. 150–152.

[32] On his position see Joutsivuo (1999), pp. 152–153.

[33] See Joutsivuo (1999), pp. 140–142.

structurally 'included' in actual health.[34] So, while a healthy body is actually such, it also has, in act, the capacity/potency to resist illness.

From this definition, it follows that the morbid condition is what is contrary to the healthy condition, namely what has no health in act (and so is ill in act) and/or what has no *potentia perseverandi* (capacity to persist) in health and so can easily be defeated by illnesses.[35] The neutral state is, for Sclano, equally twofold, but in an even more complex way. Indeed, it can be an intermediate state between a healthy and a morbid condition in two ways:

- between what is healthy, and the morbid condition taken as what has no *vis resistendi* ('power to resist') against illness;
- between what is healthy, and the morbid condition taken as what is ill in act.[36]

These definitions are strongly related to Sclano's understanding of the *simpliciter/ut nunc* distinction. Blending Alderotti and Torrigiano's positions, to him, something is *simpliciter* healthy, morbid, or neutral, when it is such 'absolutely and by nature', and so in a 'perfect' way.[37] The expression 'absolutely and by nature' seems to mean here that something is healthy, morbid or neutral 'in the general sense' when such a condition is unconditional and structural, and so from birth. Instead, something is healthy, morbid, or neutral *ut nunc*, when it is such 'with respect to the possessing subject' (*respectu habentis*), and not 'absolutely and by nature'. This means that in *ut nunc* health, illness, or neutrality, these states are taken only insofar as they are currently present in a specific body, and not insofar as they are structural features of it. They are rather the effect of other emergent causes which can be opposed and contrasted or increased and facilitated, by the *simpliciter* healthy, morbid, or neutral complexion of the body.

One important point that Sclano does not explicitly cover is whether *ut nunc* statuses should be considered natural or not. As mentioned, he defines *ut nunc* as not 'absolutely and by nature'—does this mean that *ut nunc* situations are generated by Galen's *res non naturales*[38] and never by nature? This interpretation—which marks an important point of departure from Santorio—might fit well with Sclano's conception of health, illness, and the 'neither' as *actual* states determined *simpliciter* by nature, such that they could not convert into their opposite, not even *ut nunc*.

Hence, while healthy subjects *simpliciter* are those who are such absolutely/ unconditionally and by nature, and have the capacity to resist illness, the *simpliciter* morbid organism is what is unconditionally morbid and has no resistance to disease. As a consequence, however, Sclano accepts that some morbid bodies can be *ut nunc* healthy (not showing any particular current symptom of illness), but remain *simpliciter* morbid insofar as they are disposed to illness by their lack of a capacity

[34] Sclano (1597), p. 58.

[35] Sclano (1597), pp. 58–59.

[36] Sclano (1597), p. 59.

[37] Sclano (1597), pp. 66 and 68.

[38] Namely, food and drink, exercise and rest, air, sleep, evacuation and repletion, and strong emotions.

to resist, and can be easily defeated by a disease.[39] In sum, health does not equate to being healthy at a given moment, but rather possessing in act health structurally and, with it, the capacity to remain in such a condition (which in the normal state is accompanied by health *ut nunc*). However, when speaking in absolute terms, that is *simpliciter*, all healthy bodies have this capacity. By contrast, a morbid complexion implies that an organism can easily be surmounted by the progression of an illness, thus being unable to resist it.

Another peculiar aspect of Sclano's position regards the distinction between Galen's (α_1) *diapantos* and (α_2) *os epi to polu*, formulated in *Tegni*. Unlike most of his colleagues, Sclano does not understand these terms as temporal expressions, so that *diapantos* would mean *semper* ('always'), and *os epi to polu* would mean *ut multum* ('for the most part [of time]'). For Sclano this translation is a blatant mistake,[40] since these two expressions indicate, instead, different degrees of health and disease or healthy and morbid constitution. It follows that *diapantos* should be translated into Latin as *omnino* ('altogether') and *os epi to polu* as *ex magna parte* ('mostly').[41] This distinction adds to the *simpliciter/ut nunc* one and to the three states of causes, signs, and bodies, creating a very complex vocabulary and conceptual framework. However, Sclano maintains that *omnino* indicates a perfectly good or a perfectly bad natural constitution of the organism, and so coincides with the highest degree of the *simpliciter* healthy or morbid constitution; whereas, *ex magna parte* indicates an intermediate state between the healthy/ill condition and the neutral state, brought about by falling ill or by convalescence.[42]

Let us now consider Sclano's understanding of the neutral state. It must be noted that he provides a quite tangled explanation of Galen's threefold 'neither' theory, mentioned above as (A), (B), and (C). The first 'meaning' of the neutral state (A)—which describes it as non-participation, either to health, or to morbid complexion or illness—concerns, for Sclano, both the *simpliciter* and *ut nunc* senses of 'neither'. Instead, the second and the third 'meaning' (B) and (C)—which describe the 'neither' as a simultaneous participation to both the extremes (in different proportions, or partially)—regard only the neutral state taken *simpliciter*.

Having established these premises, Sclano argues that *simpliciter* neutral subjects, according to the meaning (A), are those who are constituted in a middle state between these two: 'neither good', as healthy *simpliciter* bodies, 'nor bad' as morbid *simpliciter* ones, Sclano states.[43] Hence, the *simpliciter neutrum* organism is what is halfway between the 'altogether' (*omnino*) and 'perfectly' healthy organism and the 'altogether' (*omnino*) morbid one.[44] Accordingly, it coincides with the 'altogether' state of neutrality, characterized not by the simple 'neutral and intermediate disposition between health and disease', but by 'being constituted by nature in an

---

[39] Sclano (1597), p. 67.
[40] Sclano (1597), p. 138.
[41] Sclano (1597), pp. 138–142.
[42] Sclano (1597), pp. 140–142.
[43] Sclano (1597), p. 67.
[44] Sclano (1597), p. 149.

intermediate way'. This constitution bestows on the *neutrum* the 'act of health, and not that of neutrality', if we read Sclano's argument correctly, to a lesser extent than in *simpliciter* healthy bodies. So, the 'neither' in the sense of (A) (hence non-participation in both health and morbid complexion) has vital operations that are in-between perfect and imperfect operations, and just an intermediate capacity to resist the causes of illness.[45]

As regards, instead, the *simpliciter* 'neither' in the sense (B), Sclano postulates its simultaneous participation in both healthy and morbid complexion, if we mean that certain parts of the *simpliciter* 'neither' organism are well-constituted and healthy, whereas other parts are not. This disparity is due to different mixtures of the four elements that form the human body.[46] Finally, Sclano considers the (C) meaning of *simpliciter* 'neither' as possible only in the sense that, by nature (and by nature only), certain bodies are constituted in such a way that they waver in time between healthy and morbid status, or change from one to another.[47] For instance, this is the case when a bad complexion (dominated by heat and humidity) in youth is replaced by a healthier constitution.[48] These bodies are *omnino* 'neither' *simpliciter* in the sense (C) if this oscillation is constant during their life or proportional between the permanence in the two states, and *ex magna parte* in the case it is not exactly proportional.[49]

But what about the neutral status *ut nunc*, which explains the intermediate condition generated by the 'movement' over the latitude of health? For Sclano, unlike the *neutra simpliciter*, 'neither' organisms *ut nunc* are those that have an intermediate disposition in act—that is, currently (*actu*)—but which are not such by reason of their absolute or natural state.[50] Neutral state *ut nunc*, indeed, is due to acquired (*ascititijs*, from *ascisco*, 'to acquire') causes like illness; in particular, neutral bodies are those bodies which tend to health as the good of the organism itself, but do not have sufficient capacity to persist in the same state. So, if we read Sclano's tangled arguments correctly, while the neutral state *simpliciter* is an absolute condition determined by the nature of a given subject, the neutral state *ut nunc* comes always as an 'accidental' (so to speak) deviation from an absolute state of health or illness; this deviation is due to the (metaphorical) 'motion' on the latitude of health from one pole to another, generated by the progress of an illness or its remission.

The aforementioned points are, however, strictly connected with a further one, which is particularly important in the present reconstruction, namely the issue of falling ill (*decidentia*) and convalescence (*convalescentia*).[51] Galenic physicians agree that both these processes belong to the *neutrum simpliciter*: but do they belong to the 'neither' *simpliciter* in the sense (A) or in the sense (B)? With respect to his

---

45 Sclano (1597), p. 148.

46 Sclano (1597), p. 152.

47 Sclano (1597), p. 157.

48 Sclano (1597), pp. 157–158.

49 Sclano (1597), pp. 158–159.

50 Sclano (1597), pp. 67 and 68.

51 For an overview on this problem see again Joutsivuo (1999).

interlocutors, Sclano takes an intermediate position and maintains that, while falling ill occurs within the sense (B) of the 'neither', convalescence brings about a neutral state in the sense (A). Indeed, in falling ill, a body participates in both extremes (health and morbid condition), since—as Galen himself noted—it simultaneously shows signs that could indicate both.[52] Conversely, convalescence results from the mediation between health in act and 'a very bad ongoing illness'. In this way, convalescence consists of the non-participation in health and morbid condition: on the one hand, indeed, the convalescing body is not morbid, but healthy; on the other hand, though, it is not actually a healthy body, but one in which a severe illness is still ongoing.[53]

3.2 *Santorio Santorio*

In his corresponding treatment of the problem,[54] included in his commentary on *Tegni*, Santorio, the ancestor of the seventeenth century experimental revolution in medicine,[55] shapes his position in a constant dialogue with Sclano's, besides many others—the aforementioned Manardi, Monte, Argenterio, and his mentor Bernardino Paterno (d. 1592).

In the first place, Santorio also clarifies the meaning of the *simpliciter/ut nunc* distinction. As with Sclano, to him, healthy, morbid, or neutral states of causes, signs, and body are called *simpliciter* to describe a structural and permanent state of the organism, and its capacity or incapacity to resist illness (*potentia resistendi*).[56] Significantly, Santorio qualifies the *simpliciter* state not only as 'absolute', but also as 'exact'.[57] Instead, the *ut nunc* qualification indicates an equally natural feature,[58] albeit temporary; a movement on the latitude of health and disease that can be intensified or reversed, and which—being in transition—is never absolute nor exact.

However, unlike Sclano—who, as seen, conceived of healthy and morbid complexion *simpliciter* as having health in act, including the actual possession of the capacity to resist—Santorio follows Manardi and Paterno[59] in conceiving healthy status *simpliciter* as the pure 'aptitude and potency to resist',[60] and morbid

---

[52] Sclano (1597), p. 155 ff.

[53] Sclano (1597), p. 156.

[54] On Santorio's view of the *neutrum* see already Joutsivuo (1999) and Joutsivuo (2002), pp. 302–304. On his conception of the latitude of health and gradual intension/remission of health, see Hollerbach (2023), pp. 149–150.

[55] For a general overview on Santorio, see in particular the several essays in Barry and Bigotti (2022). See also Hollerbach (2023) and Wear (1981), pp. 250–256.

[56] Santorio (1612), p. 78.

[57] Santorio (1612), p. 79.

[58] Santorio (1612), p. 111.

[59] Santorio (1612), p. 72.

[60] Santorio (1612), p. 72.

status *simpliciter* as the absence thereof—what Santorio calls 'non resisting potency' (*potentia non resistens*).[61] In sum, for Santorio, a healthy body *simpliciter* is one which by nature has the potency to resist illness, and not—as with Sclano—one which has health in act, and in addition, the potency to resist. As regards the *neutrum*, Santorio defines the neutral state *simpliciter* as what is halfway between the *simpliciter* healthy constitution and the *simpliciter* morbid one. Hence, the neutral is not what simultaneously (i.e., in time) participates in health and illness, but is 'absolutely and exactly' an intermediate between a healthy constitution, which possesses *potentia resistendi,* and the morbid one characterized by *potentia non resistens.*

In addressing the *ut nunc* problem, Santorio devotes the three states individual attention. As said, to him, the *ut nunc* is directly opposed to *simpliciter* as a potential state, so the former is understood here as the health or illness or neutrality in act in a certain body. For Santorio, every *ut nunc* status can be reversed or increased by *potentia resistendi* or *potentia non resistens*, which opposes it by being the body *simpliciter* healthy or morbid, or neutral.[62] The healthy status of a body *ut nunc* is, however, a natural state (*ab ortu naturae*) caused by natural combinations of elements.[63] As such, it can be introduced in a morbid body *simpliciter*, or persist in a healthy body *simpliciter*, without contradicting this structural state, which, as said, is the cause of resistance or non-resistance to illness, and so it can be the cause of health *ut nunc* by rejecting the illness or by triggering healing.[64] Exactly the opposite applies for the ill status of a body *ut nunc*, which, according to Santorio, can be caused by the presence of a current disease in any form of *simpliciter* healthy, morbid, or neutral bodies, or by the aptitude or potency of the morbid body *simpliciter*.[65]

Consequently, the neutral state *ut nunc* is a relevant concern. Santorio is particularly interested in the second Galenic sense of the 'neither' (B), meaning being at the same time healthy and ill, since he reckons that the neutral state *ut nunc* coincides with this second sense of the neutral state. In this sense, hence, the *neutrum* is what simultaneously has healthy and unhealthy dispositions in different parts of the body and so at the same time participates in health and illness *ut nunc*.[66] Not by accident, and unlike Sclano's solution, the second sense (B) of the 'neither' state is also involved in convalescence and aging. In contradiction with Avicenna in particular, Santorio denies that convalescence and aging coincide with the neutral state in the first sense (A), as a non-participation in healthy and morbid statuses *simpliciter*. For him, convalescence is rather the simultaneous participation in health and illness *ut nunc*. Santorio, thus, conceives of convalescence as a neutral state deriving from movement process over the latitude of health and disease in time, in which the body participates at the same time and with its different parts, or in different proportions, in health and illness.

---

[61] Santorio (1612), p. 128.
[62] Santorio (1612), p. 129.
[63] Santorio (1612), p. 111.
[64] Santorio (1612), pp. 128–129.
[65] Santorio (1612), p. 131.
[66] Santorio (1612), p. 150.

Some important further remarks about the issue at stake here can be found, however, in a more famous work by Santorio, his *De statica medicina* (1614). Although the notion of *latitudo* is not explicitly addressed here, this concise yet influential collection of aphorisms, which achieved international renown, offers valuable insights to reflect on the continuous movement between health and illness. In this work, Santorio investigates the measurement of the body's *perspiratio insensibilis* (insensible perspiration) in relation to the six non-naturals: air, exercise, sleep, food, excretion, and the passions of the soul. *Insensible perspiration* refers to the imperceptible emission of matter (for example, through the pores of the skin), whose quantitative variations can affect the equilibrium between what the body takes in and what it expels. This balance, in turn, determines each individual's state of health or disease.[67]

The Hippocratic concept of *additio et ablatio*—the restoration of humoral balance through the addition of what is lacking and the removal of what is excessive—was no longer sufficient to guarantee the recovery of health once the unnoticed losses of the body, through insensible perspiration, had been brought to light. According to Santorio, these excretions, though subtle, can indeed be measured and quantified. What was once, in Hippocratic medicine, a purely qualitative notion of balance is thus reinterpreted through a quantitative lens. Moreover, in Santorio's thought, the idea emerges that it is the body's solids and fluids themselves that must be held in proportion—an insight that would become increasingly central to medical theory in the centuries that followed, as we shall see in the following section.

4 The Quest for Equilibrium: The Dynamics of Health and Disease in Seventeenth-and Eighteenth-Century Medicine

As seen, until the sixteenth century, Galenic physicians understood health as the visible outcome of a complex process of contrast between illness and a healthy constitution. Accordingly, they interpreted in this sense the Hippocratic-Galenic idea of *krasis*, as well as the role of the physician in moving the body onto the latitude of health, constantly passing through the middle-land of the 'neither' in the (A) sense—the only meaning compatible with Aristotle's logic of contrariety. At the same time—and this is specifically the case with Santorio—they departed from a purely Hippocratic conception of health and paved the way for an influential conception of the body as a system of solids and fluids, and medicine as a quantitative and exact science.

But how does this notion further evolve after the mechanist turn of seventeenth century medicine? For sure, the rise of new medical approaches entailed the dismissal

[67] On the notion of insensible perspiration, see Renbourn (1960), Bylebyl (1977), several essays in Barry and Bigotti (2022), and Purnis (2023). On Santorio's legacy in eighteenth century medical practice and the development of 'systematic weighing', see Dacome (2001), and Dacome (2012).

of the logic of movement over the latitude of health, and in particular of the set of conceptual tools provided by *Tegni*: the distinction between *simpliciter* and *ut nunc* statuses, as well as that of the different forms of neutrality.[68] However, through the study of the specific cases of Giorgio Baglivi (1668–1707), Niccolò Graniti, and Giovan Battista Mazini (1677–1743), in this section we endeavour to weigh the persistence of the general idea of health as 'balance' within the new mechanical paradigm, and to point out the 'translation' into mechanical terms of the traditional 'dynamic' conception of health and disease, as resulting from the interplay between forces and resistances, here understood anew in terms of solids and fluids.

4.1 Giorgio Baglivi

It is no coincidence that Santorio's *De statica medicina* achieved remarkable success, as evidenced by its many re-editions, translations, and commentaries between the 17th and 18th centuries—the text receiving comments from Giorgio Baglivi, Martin Lister, Denis Dodart, and James Keill, mostly from a mechanistic and 'solidistic' perspective.[69] Santorio's theory of insensible perspiration fit seamlessly into the physiological framework of the time. The equilibrium pursued through Santorio's 'statics' served as a key to predicting health and disease, as well as guiding our understanding of the transitions between these two states of the body, thus inviting a reinterpretation of the ancient notion of balance.[70]

The Hippocratic concept of humoral equilibrium thus became just one aspect of a more complex interpretation of the living organism, in which the bodily fluids—with their forces and resistances—had to counterbalance the forces and resistances of the solids. Health and disease were seen as the result of 'dynamic' interactions between these opposing forces, with the heart acting as the body system's driving mechanism. This view is aptly exemplified by Baglivi, who dedicated a commentary to Santorio's work, titled *Canones de medicina solidorum*, adopting the same aphoristic style. His goal was to employ Santorio's theory of statics—enriched by new physiological

[68] Considerable attention was given, especially between the 18th and 19th centuries, to the nature of *convalescence*. See, among others, Adolphi (1732), Struve (1735), Bidischini (1783) and De Vering (1816). Is it truly an intermediate state between health and illness? Does it tend more toward health or toward disease? Some authors, such as Friedrich Hoffmann, regarded it as belonging to the realm of illness; for others, it represented an 'opportunity' for health. For Struve (1735), the state of convalescence coincides with that of the decline of illness. A substantial body of literature reflects on how one might precisely determine the onset of convalescence, as well as the moment when health is fully restored. Some attempted—albeit unsuccessfully—to classify the various states of convalescence, even recognizing the existence of doubtful forms (*convalescentia lenta, vel difficilis, vel dubia*) and even false ones (*convalescentia spuria*): cf. Delius (1773). On recovery from illness in early modern medicine, see Newton (2018).

[69] On Santorio's legacy, see Barry and Bigotti (2022). On the category of 'iatromechanics' and the role of quantification in early modern medicine, see the overview provided by Guidi (2023).

[70] See Bigotti (2019), pp. 226–233.

discoveries such as blood circulation—as a framework to reinterpret the Hippocratic legacy in a mechanistic light.[71]

Baglivi conceives of the body as a *fasciculum fibrarum*—a bundle of fibres interwoven and in continual correspondence, animated by a flow of oscillations and vibrations originating from the meninges of the brain.[72] These cerebral coverings function as a kind of 'second heart', exerting a regulatory influence on the solid and fluid parts of the body. The fibres are thus not isolated entities but form a complex network. Moreover, they are not static but 'elastic', endowed with the capacity to contract and relax. Life itself, ultimately, depends on the continuous and balanced movement among these parts. 'He who well understands the balance between the oscillating solids [i.e. the fibres and the parts composed of them] and the fluids that flow', Baglivi writes in aphorism XI, 'knows how to rightly treat many diseases'.[73] 'And he who can compare the manner and quantity of insensible perspiration with the flow and amount of the other excretions, and rediscover the balance and proportion, will confidently prescribe remedies even for the most difficult illnesses'.[74] And again: 'Whosoever knows the statics of the oscillating solids and the flowing fluids, because he learned it from others, or from us through our books *On the Medicine of Solids* or *On the Motor and Morbid Fiber*, masters Santorio's very statics and thus the key to disclosing and removing the nature of many difficult diseases'.[75] Baglivi was referring to his own work on motor and morbid fibres, *De fibra motrice et morbosa* (1702), which was unfortunately only partially completed. In this earlier treatise, he sought to articulate his theory of fibres and to examine the connection between the brain's meninges and the heart, exploring the principle that claims balance between the body's solid and fluid components—a balance that he regarded as fundamental to distinguishing between states of health and disease. What, then, is this kind of equilibrium? Baglivi wrote:

> In these matters, we shall not interpret equilibrium according to its strictest laws, as in mechanics or hydraulics. Rather, we shall define equilibrium as a certain proportion between the motion of the dura mater and that of the heart; between the oscillatory motion of the villi, or membranous solids, of one part and those of another; between the successive or oscillatory motion of the membranous villi and the motion of the fleshy villi; between the fibres that contract perpetually and the fluids that flow in contact with them; and, finally, between the fluids themselves, and those fluids – both homogeneous and heterogeneous – that flow through different channels with various inclinations of motion.[76]

It is, therefore, a *proportion* among the parts of the body—one that cannot be the same for all, but necessarily varies from individual to individual according to

---

[71] See Tonetti (2016), and Tonetti (2022). On Baglivi and the early modern reception of Hippocrates, see Maclean (2021). A general overview on Baglivi's clinical methodology is provided by Andrault (2018).

[72] See Vidal (1990), Tonetti (2016).

[73] Baglivi (1704a), pp. 168–169 (aph. XI). All translations of quotations are our own.

[74] Baglivi (1704a), pp. 168–169 (aph. XI).

[75] Baglivi (1704a), p. 183 (aph. XXXI).

[76] Baglivi (1704b), p. 297.

multiple factors. It is within this proportion, Baglivi claims, that our vital being resides, together with the diversity of temperaments, complexions, and natures.[77] 'Perfect health' is attained when all our operations—animal, vital, and natural—are performed with motion and resistance between the *dura mater* and the heart in proper proportion, both acting as regulators of the body's solid and fluid components, and among the bodily parts themselves. This reinterpretation of the notion of equilibrium enables Baglivi to question earlier theories and remedies, including the long-standing belief that abstinence and moderation could ensure the body's *resistance* against any diseases—a notion perpetuated by a long tradition of texts on the preservation and prolongation of life, beginning with Luigi Cornaro's *Della vita sobria* (On a Sober Life)[78]:

> Many are astonished that sober and temperate men do not live longer than others, nor are they healthier; indeed, they often die suddenly. They are ignorant of Santorio's statics, nor do they, by his sound precepts, rightly govern and steer the ship of health, constantly shaken by the six non-natural things; hence their premature death or sickly life. Physicians are less susceptible to this because they are skilled in statics.[79]

However, proportion can only be discerned through direct experience with patients. It is a notion that resists precise definition, for it cannot easily be formalized or translated into a truly measurable quantity. In this sense, disease is not merely the malfunction of a machine, but rather the disturbance of a delicate, living balance—the 'rhythm' of life.[80]

4.2 *Niccolò Graniti and Giovan Battista Mazini*

An attempt to visualize this notion of equilibrium comes from the lesser-known Salernitan physician Niccolò Graniti, author of a compilatory work titled *Dell'antica, e moderna medicina teorica, e pratica meccanicamente illustrata* (Of Ancient and Modern Theoretical and Practical Medicine, Mechanically Explained) (1739).[81] He provides a 'symbolic representation' of the health-disease transition: an algebraic tool, the so-called 'chiave logistico-medico-meccanica', designed to express in formulas the relationship between the solid and fluid parts of the body. His goal is strictly practical—to establish rational therapeutics and formalize the choice of remedies to restore health.[82]

Graniti shares many aspects of Baglivi's theory (except for the role attributed to the cerebral meninges) as well as those of related authors such as Giovanni Alfonso Borelli and Lorenzo Bellini:

[77] Baglivi (1704b), p. 297.

[78] On Cornaro's work, see Bellini (2018), and Madella (2023).

[79] Baglivi (1704a), pp. 166–167 (aph. 6).

[80] On Baglivi's concept of disease, cf. Tonetti (2023).

[81] On Graniti, see De Renzi (1852), pp. 410–411.

[82] Graniti (1739), pp. 227–254.

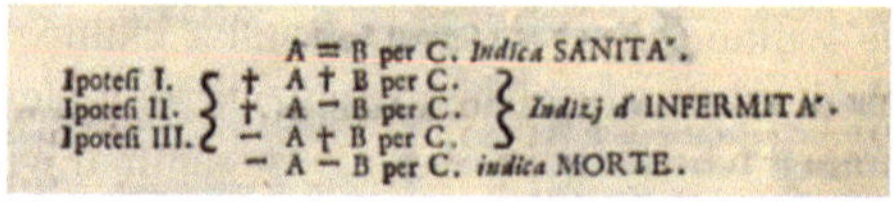

Fig. 1 Medical diagram by Graniti illustrating, through formulas, the balance between solids and fluids in the body as the basis for understanding health (*sanità*), illness (*infermità*), and death (*morte*). From Graniti (1739)

> [...] in the human body, strictly speaking from a medical perspective, nothing is observed except solids and fluids; that is to say, the former *ratione potentiae* and the latter *ratione resistentiae* are reciprocally the cause of the systole and diastole of the heart (from Baglivi, Borelli, and Bellini's *De fibra motrice*).[83]

Both solids and fluids, with their respective forces and resistances, thus work together to sustain the rhythm of the heart; taken together, the three constitute the variables that determine the state of health or disease. Echoing Baglivi's aphorisms almost *verbatim*, Graniti maintains that the physician's main task is to 'understand the equilibrium between the oscillating solids and the flowing fluids' (§103) and that 'the diseases of the human body cannot be properly treated without a precise knowledge of the statics of the solids, and especially without a full inspection of their equilibrium, forces, and reciprocal resistances' (§106).[84]

On one hand, healthy life consists in the proper equilibrium between the force of the solids and the resistance of the fluids, maintained through the natural rhythm of the heart; on the other hand, all possible illnesses arise from the greater or lesser oscillatory motion of the solids and the greater or lesser flow of the fluids. Death occurs, however, when the movements of both solids and fluids come to a complete halt.[85] Using algebraic symbols, Graniti visualizes these relationships in five different formulas, where A stands for solids, B for fluids, and C for the rhythm of the heart, + or – indicates a greater or lesser quantity than necessary, and = signifies equilibrium (see Fig. 1)[86]:

$$A = B \times C \, \text{indicates health}$$

This represents perfect health, which occurs when the movement of the solids (A) is in balance with the movement of the fluids (B) through the well-ordered systoles and diastoles of the heart (C).

$$+A + B \times C$$

[83] Graniti (1739), p. 227.

[84] Graniti (1739), p. 239.

[85] Graniti (1739), p. 242.

[86] Graniti (1739), p. 244.

$$+A - B \times C$$

$$-A + B \times C$$

These three formulas represent the different states of illness that the body can experience when A and B are either above or below the necessary degree. In the order presented, they correspond to the most severe, acute and chronic diseases, reflecting the long-standing medical distinction between acute and chronic conditions.

$$-A - B \times C \text{ indicates death}$$

If both A and B fail, then the conditions necessary for the heart's natural rhythm—an essential requirement for life—will also fail.

The physician should therefore intervene by selecting remedies that can affect the individual variables, sometimes increasing and sometimes reducing the movement of solids or fluids, or both. In fact, as acknowledged by Graniti, this scheme is merely a formalization of the Hippocratic principle of *additio et ablatio*:

> As you have already seen, A denotes the solid, B the fluid. These two lines = thus signify equality, or the balance between the two. This single line alone – denotes less. Likewise + denotes more, etc. [...] I have derived this diagram from Hippocrates, the Prince of Medicine, who described it succinctly: *Additio seu Adiectio eorum* (here is the 'more') *quae deficiunt* (here is the 'less') and *Subtractio eorum* (here is the 'less') *quae supersunt* (here is the 'more'). For who does not know that equality (=) is composed between the more and the less?[87]

A similar approach is found in the work of the physician Giovan Battista Mazini, a pupil of Domenico Guglielmini and Antonio Vallisneri, who was among the leading interpreters of medical mechanism in Padua.[88] In the first two parts of his *Mechanices morborum* (Brescia, 1723–1725)—a work that earned him an appointment to the chair of *medicina practica* at the *Studium* of Padua—Mazini set out a mechanistic theory of disease based on the movement of fluids and solids (the third part, published in 1727, being devoted instead to the mechanics of fever). In the *Mechanica medicamentorum* (Brescia, 1734)—perhaps his most accomplished attempt to develop a pharmacology grounded in mechanical principles—Mazini not only seeks to explain the elastic and oscillatory motion of the fibres (drawing on the works of Borelli, Bernoulli, and Baglivi), but also reflects on the very definition of health and disease.

Since Nature is like a wise geometer (*sapientissima geometra*), arranging all things according to number, weight, mass, shape, motion, and time, one must assume that some form of proportion is necessarily required in all the physical operations of the animal body. Yet, as in Baglivi's case, Mazini admits to distancing himself from the strictness of geometrical proportion, viewing instead *proportion* as that balance among the parts which preserves—*aliqua latitudine*—the unity and cohesion

---

[87] Graniti (1739), p. 254.

[88] Ongaro (2008).

of the whole.[89] His aim is to show physicians how such connection, unity, order, or equilibrium (and, interestingly, a kind of *quasi-equilibrium*) can be achieved in both fluids and solids, so that an 'appropriate health' (*opportuna sanitas*) may be obtained and maintained within the living machine. Mazini begins by analysing the blood fluid—'[starting] from which all the actions of the body, whether healthy or diseased, are chiefly to be understood'—and then turns to 'the nutrition, forces, motions, and movements of all the solids'.[90]

In this system, health can be easily altered or destroyed. When the components of the blood and other fluids have deviated considerably from their reciprocal proportion (*proportio reciproca*), owing to a defect in the number, mass, weight, or shape of the elements composing the fluids, or to a defect in their density, looseness, or roughness—or when the homologous proportion (*homologa proportio*) between fluids and solids has been notably disturbed—then diseases and disorders must necessarily follow; for in such a condition the elements of the blood fluid are no longer perfectly mixed with one another.[91] The same applies to the solids.[92]

Hence, Mazini offers two, in a sense, operative definitions of the states of health and disease, grounded in the body's own sensations. A body in a full state of health—in which fluids and solids are in equilibrium (or nearly so) and proportional to one another—should feel in all its parts equally light, equally strong, equally steady, equally mobile, and so forth.[93] Conversely, a body in a state of illness, where everything is *sine aequilibrio*, should perceive, either in part or as a whole, something heavier, or unnaturally lighter, softer, harder, warmer, or colder.[94]

Interestingly, none of these three perspectives makes an explicit reference to an intermediate state between health and illness. For instance, Baglivi never mentions convalescence or considers the condition of the body during this transition from illness to health. However, he acknowledges that relapses and transformations of one disease into another can occur during the recovery process, according to mechanisms that are yet to be explored.[95] Nevertheless, the notion of proportion enables them to provide a more nuanced representation of health and illness states, recognising a gradation in illness depending on the extent to which the balance between solids and fluids is disturbed. This also implies that there is no fixed definition of illness, as it is always situated within a variable *continuum* that is never identical from one person to another.

[89] Mazini (1743), pp. 278–279.

[90] Mazini (1743), p. 279.

[91] Mazini (1743), pp. 284–285.

[92] Mazini (1743), p. 285.

[93] Mazini (1743), p. 285.

[94] Mazini (1743), p. 285.

[95] See the section *De morborum successionibus* in Baglivi (1704b), pp. 367–376.

5 Conclusion

Summarizing its historical premises, we have followed a path through Italian medical tradition between the 16th and 18th centuries. It reveals, in early modern physicians, the need to shape a logic of intermediate states of health between healthy and unhealthy constitution, health and disease. Their attempts drew especially on the originally Galenic idea that these states are always and necessarily the result of dynamic processes.

In late sixteenth century Galenic medicine, still characterized by a qualitative view of nature, and therefore of physiology, the balance between these different dimensions is rendered through a network of conceptual and terminological distinctions, inherited from Medieval scholastic medicine. They allow one to think of the same organism as a closed system, simultaneously endowed with a healthy constitution and disease, as well as an unhealthy constitution and health. In particular, the concept of *neutrum* allows us to address the issue of the intermediate state and the processes of falling ill and convalescence.

Starting with the emergence of a mechanistic perspective, this dynamic conception remains essentially unchanged, despite undergoing a readjustment in the conception of the elements involved in the constitution of the body—now seen as composed of solids and fluids interacting with each other in a closed system. In this specific context, however, the notion of equilibrium involves a multiplicity of factors and a physical-chemical conception of forces and resistances that generate such states by counteracting each other.

Throughout this tradition spanning three centuries, there is a general focus in medical art on the process and transition rather than on the actual state, to the point that the physician's task is clearly defined as accompanying this transition. However, the possibility of recurrence and 'conversion' of the disease into other morbid states remains open and, in some ways, constitutive of the very nature of health. Medical action, therefore, takes place primarily in the dimension of time (*kairos oxys*, in Latin *occasio praeceps*) in the space between these moments. Although somehow measurable, and even if it depends on structural, absolute elements of a body's constitution, health—in the *ut nunc* sense—is therefore a contingent relationship. It is expressed in proportions and balances of an individual and relative nature, encompassing a wide range of elements such as age, constitution, and environment, including the *history* that has shaped and reshaped the individual body through alternating states of health and illness over time.

Acknowledgments We are grateful to Fabrizio Bigotti for his comments on an earlier version of this chapter. Any inaccuracies are ours alone.

References

Adolphi M (praes.) (1732) De statu convalescentiae. Ex officina Langenhemiana, Leipzig

Agrimi J, Crisciani C (1988) Edocere medicos. In: Medicina scolastica nei secoli XIII–XV. Guerini e associati, Milan

Andrault R (2018) What does it mean to be an empiricist in medicine? Baglivi's De praxi medica (1696). In: Rey A-L, Bodenmann S (eds) What does it mean to be an 18th century empiricist? Construction and circulation of a pluralistic concept. Springer, Cham, pp 169–188

Aristotle (1991) Categories. In: Barnes J (ed) Selected works. Princeton University Press, Princeton

Baglivi G (1704a) Canones de medicina solidorum ad rectum Statices usum. In: Santorio S (ed) De medicina statica libri octo. Typis Berbabò, Sumpt. Haered, L'Hulliè, Rome

Baglivi G (1704b) Opera omnia medico-practica et anatomica..., 6th edn. Sumptibus Anisson & Joannis Posuel, Lyon

Barry J, Bigotti F (2022) Santorio Santori and the emergence of quantified medicine, 1614–1790: Corpuscularianism, technology and experimentation. Palgrave Macmillan, Cham

Bellini F (2018) Diet and hygiene between ethics and medicine: evidence and the reception of Alvise Cornaro's La vita sobria in early seventeenth-century England. In: Lancaster JAT, Raiswell R (eds) Evidence in the age of the new sciences. Springer, Cham, pp 251–268

Beneduce C (2023) Complexio. Across disciplines. Early Sci Med 28(3–5):1

Bidischini F (1783) Dissertatio inauguralis medico-practica de reconvalescentia.... Typis Mathiae Andreae Schmidt, Vienna

Bigotti F (2019) Mind, body, and matter in the Galenic tradition of the late renaissance (1550–1630). Brepols, Turnhout

Bigotti F (2022) Gradus dimetiri: intensity and classification of complexions in 14th-century Italian medicine. Ann Sci 79(4):419–441

Bigotti F (2023) Intensity meters: new notes and discoveries on the invention of early modern precision instruments. Early Sci Med 28(6):597–630

Boss J (1979) The methodus medendi as an index of change in the philosophy of medical science in the sixteenth and seventeenth centuries. Hist Philos Life Sci 1(1):13–42

Bylebyl JJ (1977) Nutrition, quantification and circulation. Bull Hist Med 51(3):369–385

Caroti S (1989) Da Buridano a Marsilio di Inghen: la tradizione parigina della discussione "De reactione". Medioevo 15:173–233

Caroti S (1995) Da Walter Burley al Tractatus de sex inconvenientibus. La tradizione inglese della discussione medievale 'De reactione'. Medioevo 21:257–374

Chandelier J, Robert A (2013) Nature humaine et complexion du corps chez les médecins italiens de la fin du Moyen Âge. Rev Synth 134(4):473–510

Dacome L (2001) Living with the chair: private excreta, collective health and medical authority in the eighteenth century. Hist Sci 39(4):467–500

Dacome L (2012) Balancing acts: picturing perspiration in the long eighteenth century. Stud Hist Philos Sci Part C 43(2):379–391

De Renzi S (ed) (1852) Collectio Salernitana, ossia documenti inediti, e trattati di medicina appartenente alla scuola medica salernitana. Dalla tipografia del Filiatre-Sebezio, Naples

De Vering JE (1816) Dissertatio inauguralis medica de convalescentia eiusque cura. Typis Caroli Gerold, Vienna

Delius H F (praes.) (1773) Dissertatio inauguralis medica de convalescentia vera et spuria. Ex officina Viduae Camerariae, Erlangen

Des Chene D (1996) Physiologia: natural philosophy in late Aristotelian and Cartesian thought. Cornell University Press, Ithaca–London

Favaretti Camposampiero M, Scribano E (eds) (2022) Galen and the early moderns. Springer, Cham

Galen (1821–1833) Opera omnia Claudii Galeni, edited by K. G. Kuhn. Cnobloch, Leipzig

Galen (1997) Selected works, translated with an introduction and notes by P. N. Singer. Oxford University Press, Oxford

Graniti N (1739) Dell'antica, e moderna medicina teorica, e pratica meccanicamente illustrata. Domenico Occhi, Venice

Green MH (2019) Gloriosissimus Galienus: Galen and Galenic writings in the eleventh-and twelfth-century Latin west. In: Vallianatos PB, Zipser B (eds) Brill's companion to the reception of Galen. Brill, Leiden, pp 319–342

Guidi S (2023) Data vs. mathesis. Contrasting epistemologies in some mechanizations and quantifications of medicine. In: Guidi S, Braga J (eds) The quantification of life and health from the sixteenth to the nineteenth century: intersections of medicine and philosophy. Palgrave Macmillan, Cham, pp 201–240

Hollerbach T (2023) Sanctorius Sanctorius and the origins of health measurement. Springer, Cham

Jaucourt L (1765/2013) Santé. In: Encyclopédie ou Dictionnaire raisonné des sciences, des arts et des métiers, vol 14, p 628. Translated in: Meyer V (ed) The encyclopedia of Diderot & d'Alembert. Collaborative translation project. Michigan Publishing, University of Michigan Library, Ann Arbor

Joutsivuo T (1999) Scholastic tradition and humanist innovation: the concept of neutrum in renaissance medicine. The Finnish Academy of Science and Letters, Helsinki

Joutsivuo T (2002) Aristotle and Galen on neutral bodies: perspectives on Aristotle's and Galen's auctoritates in late medieval and renaissance medicine. In: Leijenhorst C, Lüthy C, Thijssen H (eds) Dynamics of Aristotelian natural philosophy from antiquity to the seventeenth century. Brill, Leiden, pp 289–306

Kaye J (2014) A history of balance, 1250–1375: the emergence of a new model of equilibrium and its impact on thought. Cambridge University Press, New York

Maclean I (2001) Logic, signs and nature in the renaissance: the case of learned medicine. Cambridge University Press, Cambridge

Maclean I (2021) The reception of Hippocrates by physicians at the end of the seventeenth century: a comparative study. In: Levitin D, Maclean I (eds) The worlds of knowledge and the classical tradition in the early modern age. Brill, Leiden–Boston, pp 217–274

Madella L (2023) The more the years the less the food: Alvise Cornaro on the sober life (1558). In: Guidi S, Braga J (eds) The quantification of life and health from the sixteenth to the nineteenth century: intersections of medicine and philosophy. Palgrave Macmillan, Cham, pp 62–78

Mazini GB (1743) Opera omnia… tomus secundus Mechanicam tum Morborum, tum Medicamentorum continens. Excudebat Joannes-Maria Rizzardi, Brescia

McVaugh M (2019) Galen in the medieval universities, 1200–1400. In: Vallianatos PB, Zipser B (eds) Brill's companion to the reception of Galen. Brill, Leiden, pp 381–392

Newton H (2018) Misery to mirth: recovery from illness in early modern England. Oxford University Press, Oxford

Ottosson P-G (1984) Scholastic medicine and philosophy: A study of commentaries on Galen's Tegni (ca. 1300–1450). Bibliopolis, Naples

Palmieri N (2006) L'Ars Medica (Tegni) de Galien: lectures antiques et médiévales: actes de la journée d'étude internationale, Saint-Étienne, 26 juin 2006. Publications de l'Université de Saint-Étienne, Saint-Étienne

Pesenti T (2000) The teachings of the Tegni in Italian universities in the second half of the fourteenth century. Dynamis 20:159–208

Purnis J (2023) Sanctorius's weighing chair: measurement, metabolism, and mind. In: Guidi S, Braga J (eds) The quantification of life and health from the sixteenth to the nineteenth century: intersections of medicine and philosophy. Palgrave Macmillan, Cham, pp 111–132

Renbourn ET (1960) The natural history of insensible perspiration: a forgotten doctrine of health and disease. Med Hist 4(2):135–152

Roudaut S (2021) La mesure de l'être. Le problème de la quantification des formes au Moyen Âge (ca. 1250–1370). Brill, Leiden–Boston

Roudaut S (2022) Paul of Venice's theory of quantification and measurement of properties. Noctua 9(2):104–158

Roudaut S (2025) Heat, coldness, and contrariety in late scholastic philosophy. Aristotelica 7:61–88

Santorio S (1612) Commentaria in Artem Medicinalem Galeni. Apud Iacobum Antonium Somaschum, Venice
Sclano S (1597) Commentaria præclarissima in tres libros artis medicinalis Galeni. Apud Ioannem Guerilium, Venice
Siraisi N (1981) Taddeo Alderotti and his pupils: two generations of Italian medical learning. Princeton University Press, Princeton
Siraisi N (1987) Avicenna in renaissance Italy: the canon and medical teaching in Italian universities after 1500. Princeton University Press, Princeton
Siraisi N (1990) Medieval and early renaissance medicine: an introduction to knowledge and practice. University of Chicago Press, Chicago
Strohmaier G (2019) Avicenna between Galen and Aristotle. In: Vallianatos PB, Zipser B (eds) Brill's companion to the reception of Galen. Brill, Leiden, pp 215–226
Struve E G (1735) Dissertatio inauguralis medica de convalescentiae statu eius impedimentis et praesidiis. Typis Joh. Christiani Hilligeri, Halle in Magdeburg
Sylla E D (1971–1972) Medieval quantifications of qualities: the 'Merton school'. Arch Hist Exact Sci 8:9–39
Sylla ED (1973) Medieval concepts of the latitude of forms: the Oxford calculators. Archives d'histoire doctrinale et littéraire du Moyen Âge 40:223–283
Tonetti L (2016) Corpus fasciculus fibrarum: teoria della fibra e pratica medica nel De praxi medica di Giorgio Baglivi. Physis 51(1–2):379–392
Tonetti L (2022) Bodies in balance: Santorio's legacy in Baglivi's medicine. In: Barry J, Bigotti F (eds) Santorio Santori and the emergence of quantified medicine, 1614–1790. Corpuscularianism, technology and experimentation. Palgrave Macmillan, Cham, pp 289–315
Tonetti L (2023) 'Nature is more subtle than any mathematician': Giorgio Baglivi on fluids in the human body. In: Guidi S, Braga J (eds) The quantification of life and health from the sixteenth to the nineteenth century: intersections of medicine and philosophy. Palgrave Macmillan, Cham, pp 157–174
van der Lugt M (2011) Neither ill nor healthy: the intermediate state between health and disease in medieval medicine. Quad Stor 46(1):13–46
Vidal M (1990) Giorgio Baglivi tra osservazione clinica e speculazioni iatromeccaniche. Atti del centro ricerche storiche di Rovigno 20:133–214
Von Staden H (1989) Herophilus. The art of medicine in early Alexandria. Cambridge University Press, Cambridge
Wear A (1981) Galen in the renaissance. In: Nutton V (ed) Galen: problems and retrospects. The Wellcome Institute for the History of Medicine, London, pp 229–262
World Health Organization (1946) Constitution of the WHO. WHO, Geneva. https://apps.who.int/gb/bd/PDF/bd47/EN/constitution-en.pdf?ua=1

Simone Guidi is a Senior Researcher in the Institute for the European Intellectual Lexicon and History of Ideas (CNR-ILIESI) at the Italian National Research Council. He teaches History of Modern Philosophy at the Sapienza University in Italy. Previously, he was Assistant Professor of Philosophy in the University of Coimbra's Faculty of Arts and Humanities, Portugal. Simone's work focuses on the history of early modern philosophy, with special attention to the thought of Descartes, his sources and legacy.

Luca Tonetti is a Researcher in the History of Science at the Department of Historical and Geographic Sciences and the Ancient World (DiSSGeA), University of Padua. He also serves as Book Review Editor of *Nuncius: Journal of the Material and Visual History of Science* (Brill). His research delves into the history of early modern science and medicine, with a specific focus on Marcello Malpighi's unpublished manuscripts housed at the Bologna University Library and the Royal Society.

Governing the Experimental Body: Codification, Delegation, and the Economy of Practice in the Early Modern Period

Marco Storni

Abstract This chapter examines the relationship between practical rationalities and systematic modes of reasoning in the early modern period, focusing on the codification of practical knowledge. Given the entangled nature of scientific thought and technical practice, codification reveals a fundamental tension between two movements. On the one hand is the effort to identify and generalize the contingent regularities that emerge from the situated manipulation of nature; on the other hand is the transformation of these regularities into abstract norms of reason. To explore this tension, I examine the functions and motivations of codification. Codification responds to the need to recognize and articulate the internal logic of practical operations, but also to the imperative to govern them by establishing procedural norms that future practitioners are expected to follow. Among the tools used to codify practical knowledge, I emphasize quantification. Quantification is a powerful instrument of standardization as it also introduces forms of delegation: measuring devices assume the authority to regulate technical procedures and shape the practitioner's embodied engagement with materiality. Regarding the motivations behind codification, I turn to the notion of economy and identify three interrelated dimensions that this notion had in the early modern age: the management of resources, the optimization of technical operations, and the reduction of risk, understood in moral terms. These layered meanings suggest that, while the early modern codification of practical knowledge prepared the ground for the rise of technoscience and the logic of industrial capitalism, it also conveyed values such as frugality, care, and bodily stewardship, which point in a fundamentally different direction.

M. Storni (✉)
Centre de recherche en philosophie (PHI), Université libre de Bruxelles, Bruxelles, Belgium
e-mail: marco.storni@ulb.be

M. Balestrieri and A. Cauduro (eds.), *The Legal Anatomy of the Body*, Ius Gentium: Comparative Perspectives on Law and Justice 142,
https://doi.org/10.1007/978-3-032-26434-3_4

1 Introduction

Simply put, practical knowledge can be defined as 'the knowledge needed to obtain a certain product [...] that follows a defined workflow'.[1] The workflow consists in a series of actions or transformations, either manual or mental, that generally fall within the domain of a *techne*. Historians have emphasized the complex ways in which this type of knowledge developed from the Renaissance to the dawn of the Industrial Age. One of the main concerns of twenty-first century interpreters has actually been to unravel a deeply rooted cliché, namely, that practical knowledge, reduced to the mere execution of predetermined directives, is radically different from theoretical knowledge, and somewhat inferior to it.

Traces of this conception can already be found in early nineteenth century texts, such as the introductory essay of the *Encyclopaedia Metropolitana*, published in 1818 under the title *Treatise on Method* by the poet and philosopher Samuel Taylor Coleridge. Adopting a Kantian approach, Coleridge distinguishes the 'pure sciences', that 'represent pure acts of the mind', from the 'mixed or applied sciences', meaning disciplines where 'certain ideas of the mind are applied to general properties of bodies, solid, fluid, aerial'.[2] The same distinction was appropriated by later writers of political economy and industrial management, such as the British polymath Charles Babbage. In the treatise *On the Economy of Machinery and Manufactures* (1832), Babbage stresses that 'the applied sciences derive their facts from experiment; but the reasonings, on which their chief utility depends, are the province of what is called abstract science'.[3]

It would be redundant to list the many other authors who repeated the same idea. It is more interesting to notice the pervasiveness of this view, which remained vital well into the contemporary age.[4] A notable example is the work of Joel Mokyr, an influential historian of economy. In *The Gifts of Athena* (2002), Mokyr defines prescriptive knowledge—or 'knowledge how' (*techne*)—as a set of 'executable instructions or recipes for how to manipulate nature', which, once 'carried out in practice, [is] no longer knowledge but action'.[5] Prescriptive knowledge is opposed to propositional knowledge, or 'knowledge what', to which Mokyr attributes a foundational role in the process of industrialization and economic growth.

---

[1] Valleriani (2017), p. 1.

[2] Coleridge (1818), pp. 35–38. On technology as 'applied science', see Bud (2012).

[3] Babbage (1832), pp. 379–380.

[4] Michael Polanyi represents an interesting and peculiar case. In his influential work *Personal Knowledge: Towards a Post-Critical Philosophy* (1958), he also emphasized the alleged lack of communication between science and technology in the eighteenth century. However, his purpose was to highlight the independence of technological development and the fact that science remained largely speculative until the mid-nineteenth century. He writes: 'Actually, up to that time [1846] natural science had made no major contribution to technology. The industrial revolution had been achieved without scientific aid. [...] The appreciation of science was still almost free from utilitarian motives' (Polanyi 1998), p. 193.

[5] Mokyr (2002), p. 10.

The renewed scholarly interest in practical knowledge has been driven by a critical reassessment of the traditional opposition between *episteme* and *techne*. Recent studies have highlighted that practical knowledge, far from being a merely mechanical or subordinate form of knowing, operates according to its own rationality—one that evolves over time, is subject to revision, and generates debate within communities of practitioners.[6] More generally, historians have challenged the validity of this dichotomy altogether, emphasizing instead the fluidity of the boundaries that separated epistemic regimes during the early modern period.[7] Increasing attention has been given to actors and forms of knowledge that bridged the divide between theory and practice. Notable among these are the 'hybrid experts' described by Ursula Klein in her work on eighteenth century chemistry: figures who embodied a 'combination of technical work, technological research and learned natural inquiry'.[8] Klein argues that the 'interconnection of chemical science and technology' can be considered as 'an early form of technoscience', namely 'a hybrid scientific-technological endeavor'.[9]

The aim of this essay is to explore the relationship between practical rationalities and systematic modes of reasoning in the early modern period. Given their entanglement, what power dynamics arise between the embodied knowledge of practice—analytical yet dispersive, often marked by a certain inertia—and the synthetic drive of scientific reasoning, with its emphasis on abstraction? At the heart of this inquiry lies the problem of the codification of practical knowledge. Codification reveals a fundamental tension between two movements: on the one hand, the endeavor to identify and generalize the contingent regularities emerging from a situated manipulation of nature; on the other, the transfiguration of these regularities into abstract norms of reason. In what follows, I will not only discuss how practical knowledge has been codified in the early modern age, but also its underlying motivations. In particular, I will reflect on the notion of 'economy' and distinguish its various meanings to explain one of the main causes that triggered the process of codification in the 17th and 18th centuries.

2 Codification and Governance

The early modern renewal of European science, known under the contested label of the 'Scientific Revolution', involved an increasing codification of practical knowledge.[10] This codification was primarily a process of abstraction and generalization. The gestures, the operations, the implicit and verbalized knowledge involved in experimental and practical work became the subject of critical and philosophical

[6] See Garçon and Hilaire-Pérez (2002) and Bertucci (2017).

[7] See Roberts et al. (2007).

[8] Klein (2017), p. 288.

[9] Klein (2005), p. 227.

[10] For critical perspectives on the Scientific Revolution, see Merchant (1980) and Secord (2023).

reflection. The goal was to define the rules of practice and make them more rational, and thus communicable.

One key example is the emergence, from the sixteenth century onward, of a literature devoted to the 'reduction into art' of various disciplines and techniques, from fortification to dance and fencing. The reduction into art consisted in the translation of actions and events into a rational sequence of operations, designed to achieve predictable results.[11] It is no coincidence that this movement coincided chronologically with the emergence of theoretical reflections on method and the critique of traditional knowledge by authors such as Francis Bacon and René Descartes.[12]

The *Encyclopédie* (1751-1772), edited by Denis Diderot and Jean d'Alembert, is a canonical example of a sustained effort to codify practical knowledge during the *Ancien Régime*. Ordering the arts and crafts required addressing the limitations of artisanal language. This language was characterized by two major issues: scarcity and proliferation. There was a lack of accurate, standardized terms and an overabundance of synonyms. In the language of the workshop, for example, every tool and gesture might have a different name depending on the group of practitioners or the community of reference, and thus have no official name at all. The challenge for the encyclopaedists was to bring the *arts et métiers* into the realm of articulated language by unifying the fragmented, vernacular vocabularies in which they had traditionally been expressed. In the article *Art*, Diderot states that 'the most singular operations and the most complex machines could be explained by a small number of familiar and well-known terms', and that ultimately, 'it is the lack of precise definitions and the great number, not the diversity, of movements in various operations that makes it difficult to speak clearly about the arts'.[13] Diderot concludes that the only way to achieve this clarity is 'to familiarize oneself with the objects'.[14]

The common thread among the articles dedicated by the encyclopaedists to arts and crafts is an emphasis on the manual processes underlying material production. These articles explore how manual processes are combined to form technical operations, and how these operations are arranged according to a logic reflecting collective procedures, governed by a division of labour. Both the written texts and the illustrated plates of the *Encyclopédie* are meant to represent this order of practice, as a form of knowledge materialized through organized, controlled actions. Consider, for instance, the plates dedicated to soap manufacturing: they depict not only the successive stages of production—from heating olive oil with sodium carbonate, to the solidification of the mixture in moulds, and the cutting of soap bars—but also the tools involved, each drawn in detail, as well as the architectural layout of a soap factory (Fig. 1). It is important to emphasize that the encyclopaedists were not just imagining such technical procedures and manufacturing plants: they were directly

---

[11] See the contributions gathered in Dubourg Glatigny and Vérin (2008).

[12] Bacon is also one of the protagonists of the early modern debate on the reduction into art. See Vérin (2008), pp. 17–58.

[13] Diderot (1751), p. 716b.

[14] Diderot (1751), p. 716b.

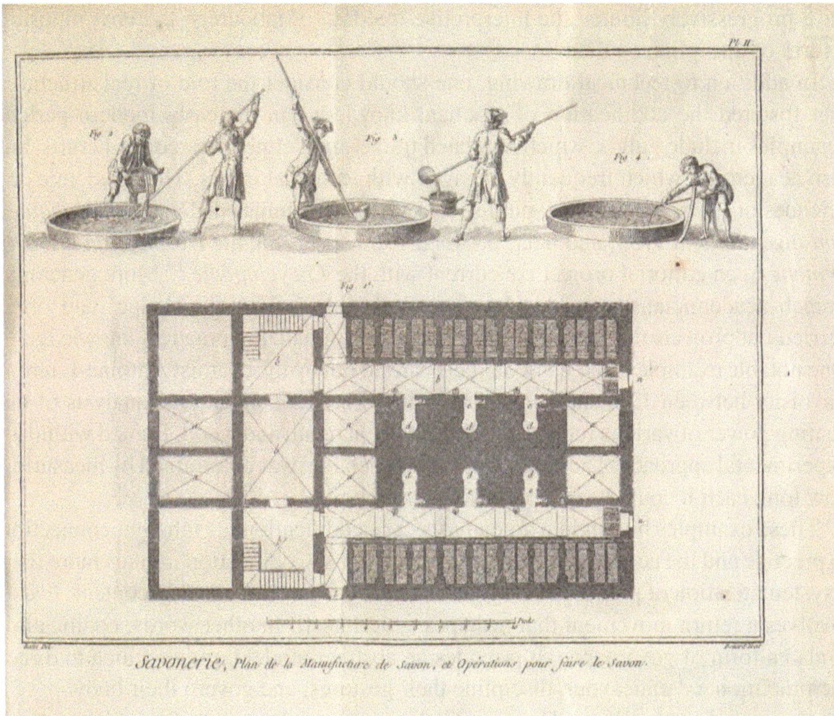

Fig. 1 *Recueil de planches, sur les sciences, les arts libéraux, et les arts mécaniques, avec leur explication*, vol. 9, Briasson, Paris, 1771. Planche 2: Plan d'une manufacture de savon, et opérations pour faire le savon. Bibliothèque Mazarine (2° 3442-3), Paris, France. Public domain mark. https://bibnum.institutdefrance.fr/ark:/61562/mz2141

familiar with them. One notable example is Diderot's interest in tapestry and his acquaintance with the Gobelins manufactory in Paris.[15]

The reference to graphic representations suggests that codification should not only be understood as a discursive process, but that its material dimension should also be considered. Drawing, especially in its technical function, is not merely representational; it can also function as a means of controlling the knowledge it conveys or the actions it prescribes.[16] As transnational studies of modernity have shown, a hierarchy often emerges between image-makers and object-makers, specifically between engineers and artisans, where schematic drawing plays a central role in mediating that divide. By making technical designs more geometric and objective, engineers

[15] The Royal Manufactory of the Gobelins primarily produced tapestries for royal residences. However, the Gobelins also functioned as a workshop where cutting-edge chemical research, particularly in the field of dyeing, was conducted. See Belhoste (2019), pp. 160–167.

[16] See Baudry and Nègre (2024), pp. 9–13.

have progressively limited the interpretive freedom of labourers, thereby imposing a form of discipline on them.[17]

In addition to technical drawing, one should consider the role of real structures that fostered the codification of practical knowledge in the early modern period. Examples include guilds, which regulated trades and defined the scope of crafts, but also academies, which frequently engaged with technical issues. The Académie des sciences of Paris, for instance, published a series of volumes dedicated to *Machines and inventions* in 1735, and later, between 1760 and 1788, the *Description des arts et métiers*, an editorial project concurrent with the *Encyclopédie*.[18] More generally, French academicians were deeply concerned with 'useful knowledge' and often carried out projects that aimed at codifying and rationalizing practical knowledge.[19] One notable example is the work on fuels carried out by the chemist Antoine-Laurent Lavoisier between 1779 and 1781. Lavoisier offered a comparative analysis of the heating power of various fuels, including coal, charcoal, and wood, framed within an experimental approach. The heating power of each fuel was determined by measuring how long each it could keep a pot of water at a boil.[20]

These examples highlight a crucial aspect of codification: its inherent connection to practice and the active, generative power it entails. Codification implies more than a systematization of practices through abstraction from their sensory content. It also involves a return movement that reshapes action itself. In other words, codification is also a form of governance. It provides an abstract model through which to direct the practitioners' endeavour, discipline their gestures, and govern their body.

As pointed out by Pascal Dubourg Glatigny, a useful category for understanding the productive nature of codification is that of *Erkenntnissteuerung* (cognitive control).[21] Originally coined in the context of literary studies, it was, like the reduction into art, applied first and foremost to the textual and discursive dimension. When examining the transition from manuscripts to printed books in the early modern period, theorists of *Erkenntnissteuerung* argued that the formal structures of a book—frontispiece, chapter segmentation, indexes, etc.—not only codified information, but also reshaped it. This made knowledge more widely disseminated and easier for authors and editors to handle, allowing for 'new possibilities of knowledge management and reader control'.[22] Applying this insight to the codification of practical knowledge allows us to recover the etymological meaning of *Erkenntnissteuerung*

---

[17] See Ferguson (1992).

[18] On technology at the Paris Academy, see Delaunay (2018).

[19] On the notion of 'useful knowledge' in academic debates in Paris, see Oki (2011).

[20] Lavoisier (1781), pp. 379–395. This approach was fairly common among eighteenth-century French chemists involved in research for public use. One example is the *Instructions sur l'usage de la houille, plus connue sous le nom impropre de charbon de terre, pour faire du feu*, published by the chemist Gabriel-François Venel in 1775. This work, which adopts a comparative approach to different types of fuel, was published '*par ordre des États de la province de Languedoc*' as part of a broader program in political economy. See Bernasconi (2025), pp. 154–155.

[21] See Dubourg Glatigny (2017).

[22] Enenkel and Neuber (2005), p. 2.

as the 'steering of knowledge'. This term is in fact borrowed from maritime navigation and evokes the piloting of ships.[23] In this sense, codification reconfigures practical knowledge in order to direct it and achieve specific goals, bridging the rational systematization of action and its embodied governance.

What does the governance implied by codification actually entail? What are its methods and instruments? And how does it affect practical activity?

3 Quantification and Delegation

In experimental practices, codification is approached through both empirical and rational methods. Empirical methods are emblematically illustrated by Francis Bacon's *tabulae praesentiae, absentiae in proximitate* and *graduum.* In the *Novum Organum* (1620), Bacon devised an inductive procedure that involves collecting instances (*instantiae*) and organizing them into tables, designed to reveal the manifestations of a natural principle. The 'tables of presence' collect known instances, namely, cases in which a particular nature (such as heat, in Bacon's canonical example) is clearly present. 'Tables of absence' gather instances that lack this nature, even though they are closely related to or associated with instances that possess it. Finally, the 'tables of degrees' record and compare cases in which the target nature appears with varying intensity, such as an increase or decrease of a property within the same subject. Based on these tables, the actual work of induction begins. An initial hypothesis about the nature of the phenomenon is formulated, which Bacon calls the 'first vintage (*vindemiatio prima*)', namely, the first version of the interpretation of nature. With respect to heat, he suggests that it might be 'an expansive motion which is checked and struggling through the particles'.[24]

Alongside these empirical methods of codification, the early modern period also saw the emergence of rational methods, one of which was quantification.[25] As scholars such as Alistair C. Crombie and, more recently, Edward Grant have shown, meaningful attempts to quantify natural phenomena, such as motion, were already present in the Middle Ages. However, it was during the early modern era that the concept of quantification became more precisely articulated and widely applied. It evolved from a localized analytical tool into a comprehensive framework for interpreting natural reality.

---

[23] Dubourg Glatigny (2017), p. 36.

[24] *Novum Organum*, II, XX; in Bacon ([1857] 2011), p. 266: '*Calor est motus expansivus, cohibitus, et nitens per partes minores*'. For the English translation see Bacon (2000), p. 135. The Baconian method does not stop at the 'first vintage', but continues with further work of exclusion based on 27 instances that include experiments, refinements, and possible exceptions to the formulated hypothesis. Bacon aims to understand the structure (*latens schematismus*) and modes of generation (*latens processus*) of things, as these two aspects define the form of a natural object.

[25] The distinction between empirical and rational methods is a simplification. Quantification has also an enacted and practical element, and conversely, methods such as Baconian tables are embedded within an abstract, speculative discourse.

Although the well-worn historiographical narrative of a shift from the 'world of approximation' to the 'universe of precision', made possible by the mathematical exploration of nature, requires some qualification, it nonetheless reflects a genuine historical development—or at least an intellectual agenda shared by many key figures in the rise of modern science.[26] One could trace a trajectory stretching from Galileo, who famously argued in the *Saggiatore* (1623) that the book of nature is written in mathematical language, to William Thomson—best known as Lord Kelvin—who synthesized the positivist view of the centrality of quantification for doing science. Kelvin writes: 'I often say that when you can measure what you are speaking about and express it in numbers you know something about it; but when you cannot measure it [...] your knowledge is of a meagre and unsatisfactory kind'.[27]

The nature of quantification is a controversial subject among present-day commentators. Some emphasize its epistemic dimension, while others highlight the social aspect of mathematical representations of nature.[28] One particularly delicate topic is the relationship between three key concepts that are closely connected, yet the exact nature of this connection is rarely clarified in the literature: measurement, mathematization, and quantification. I define measurement as the process of comparing a natural phenomenon to a standard and assigning it a position on a pre-determined scale. By contrast, mathematization refers to translating one or more natural phenomena into numerical or geometrical language. Although mathematization typically presupposes measurement, since location on a scale is often expressed mathematically, the two should not be conflated. Quantification is the general consideration of natural reality in terms of measurable quantities that can, at least in principle, be expressed mathematically. Quantification emerges as a response to qualitative, everyday perception of nature, which is considered too unstable or imprecise to serve as a foundation for scientific understanding.

My reflection on the importance of quantification in the early modern codification of practical knowledge begins with a classic work of twentieth century philosophy: *Die Krisis der europäischen Wissenschaften und die transzendentale Phänomenologie* by Edmund Husserl (1936). In this work, Husserl offers a well-known critique of 'Galileo's mathematization of nature.' At the heart of this critique is the idea that applying mathematics to the study of nature necessarily involves an

---

[26] The reference is to Alexandre Koyré's well-known text *Du monde de l'à peu près à l'univers de la précision* (1948). Koyré argues that what was lacking in pre-modern times—or in pre-modern disciplines—was not primarily the material instruments or intellectual capacity to quantify nature, but rather the very notion that nature could be subjected to precise measurement. A key example is alchemy: what the alchemist lacked was not the thermometer, but the idea that heat might be susceptible to exact quantification. Lucien Febvre offered a corrective to Koyré's thesis in his 1950 article *De l'à peu près à la précision en passant par ouï-dire*, in which he underscores the role of interpersonal networks and the often fragmented or informal transmission of knowledge in the gradual formalization of modern scientific practice. See Koyré (1948) and Febvre (1950).

[27] Thomson (1891), p. 80.

[28] For a historical and philosophical perspective, see Daston (1995) and Roux (2010); for a sociological perspective, see Henneguelle and Jatteau (2021).

idealization, namely a reduction of physical reality to geometrical coordinates and series of numbers. Husserl writes:

> Mathematics […] showed that one can universally obtain objectively true knowledge of a completely new sort about the things of the intuitively actual world, in respect to that aspect of them (which all things necessarily share) which alone interests the mathematics of shapes, i.e., a [type of] knowledge related in an approximating fashion to its own idealities.[29]

According to this view, the *Lebenswelt* ('lifeworld', or the lived world) is reduced by early modern natural philosophers to an ideal network of quantitative magnitudes that lend themselves well to calculation. Notably, Husserl highlights another essential component of this codification of experience: 'the practical art of measuring'.[30] This suggests that, for Husserl, quantification is not only a mental act of excluding certain qualities (what John Locke would have called 'secondary') in favour of others (Locke's 'primary' qualities), but also a materially grounded operation, that is, a practice embedded in tools, techniques, and embodied procedures.[31]

Although the shift toward quantified knowledge was gradual, and modern scientific knowledge often maintained a qualitative and informal character, there are various examples that clearly demonstrate the profound impact of quantification on the codification of practical knowledge.[32] Consider a significant episode in the history of early modern medicine: pulse measurement.[33]

Since Greek antiquity, sphygmology, alongside uroscopy, had been one of the principal diagnostic techniques. Although this practice remained qualitative for a long time, the early modern period saw a new demand for rigor in pulse measurement emerge. Despite criticism from various schools, particularly Vitalist physicians who viewed the growing interest in pulse quantification as a prelude to the mechanistic reduction of the human body, advances in mechanical horology made the quantification of pulse rate an increasingly common practice.[34] In the work of English physician John Floyer, one of the first to advocate for the systematic integration of the mechanical watch into medical practice, we find a clear attempt to reduce diagnostic work to the quantitative assessment of the patient's pulse. In his treatise *The Physician's Pulse-Watch* (1707-10), Floyer explains that once a patient's 'natural pulse' is established through repeated measurements, it is possible to define illness in terms

[29] Husserl (1970), p. 32.

[30] Husserl (1970), p. 33.

[31] Primary qualities are the basic properties (e.g., bulk, figure, texture, motion) that Locke considers to be inseparable from bodies, regardless of their state. Secondary qualities, on the other hand, do not actually exist in objects themselves, but rather are powers determined by primary qualities that produce sensations in the perceiving subject (e.g., colour, warmth, pain). On Locke's distinction between primary and secondary qualities, see Wilson (2015).

[32] Thus, I would nuance Harald Witthöft's assertion that 'the ancient way of thinking was concrete, comparative and relative, not abstract, normative or absolute', in Witthöft (2008), p. 27.

[33] The discussion that follows builds upon the results presented in Storni (2023a).

[34] See Bernasconi (2019), p. 251–253.

of 'excesses and defects' of pulse rate, and draw from these data 'indications for the use of diet and medicines' aimed at restoring the pulse to its normative rhythm.[35]

A crucial aspect of Floyer's proposal is the technicization of the medical art. Codifying medicine through pulse measurement required physicians to rely less on their judgment and more on measuring instruments that replaced qualitative values with quantitative data, which only became meaningful against a reference scale. This shift had two consequences. First, the pulse watch was conceived as an extension of human sensibility. It could correct the vagueness and inconsistency of perceptual data, thereby imposing new standards on medical practice. Second, technology acquired normative value, replacing the physician's sensory judgment as the new gold standard. In fact, practitioners had to 'delegate' diagnostic authority—and, more broadly, experimental control—to the instrument.

Interestingly, the controversies surrounding the use of pocket watches in medicine, which persisted well into the nineteenth century, centered on the alleged loss of medical expertise in favour of a technical instrument whose reliability was questioned. As the physiologist Hermann von Helmholtz recalls in his 1877 discourse *Das Denken in der Medizin*, although at his time 'counting [the pulse] with the second watch was already common, the old gentlemen considered it to be a method of not very good taste', since it 'disparaged the patient, who is a human being, degrading them to a machine'.[36] Alongside the mechanical watch, other technical instruments generated suspicion, such as the ophthalmoscope, which a practitioner in conversation with Helmholtz declared 'useful for doctors with bad eyes, while he had very good eyes and did not need it'.[37]

The attempt to exert cognitive control over experimental matters through quantification, and the technical delegation that this process necessarily entails, was not uncommon among early modern practitioners, even in fields significantly different from medicine. A revealing example is offered by the 'arts of fire', namely a group of disciplines based on the transformation of matter through the action of flame and heat. In addition to applied chemistry, the arts of fire encompassed glassmaking, ceramics, and cooking, among others. A key aspect of the practical knowledge involved in the arts of fire was the ability to assess the intensity of heat.[38] This knowledge was crucial for gaining technical control over operations in both chemical laboratories and artisanal workshops. Between the 17th and 18th centuries, the practical knowledge of degrees of heat gradually became detached from immediate sensory experience and was increasingly subjected to measurement.[39] Although the thermometer is the most obvious instruments that prompted this development, indications derived from other

---

[35] Floyer (1707), p. 13. An analysis of Floyer's therapeutic ideas shows that he remained fairly close to the Galenic paradigm and to a qualitative conception of medicine. See Jenner (2010).

[36] Helmholtz (1896), p. 179.

[37] Helmholtz (1896), p. 179.

[38] I have discussed the quantification of heat in the arts of fire in Storni (2025). The analysis presented here builds on that essay, particularly on pp. 101–109.

[39] See Powers (2014).

technical tools and procedures also contributed significantly to the emerging culture of quantifying heat.

From an epistemic standpoint, we observe the development of a technical vocabulary of heat degrees that reflects a broader attempt to generalize and rationalize the physical sensations of heat and cold. In the *Lexicon alchemiae* (1612), the alchemist Martin Ruland the Younger offered an experimental codification of heat, abstracting from bodily sensation to define its different degrees:

> The first degree is very slow, such as the warmth of a small fire (*ignaviusculi*) [...]. The second degree is more intense, so much that it strikes the hand more evidently, although it does not affect the organ with much strength. [...] The third degree causes injuries if touched [...]. The fourth is the highest and most destructive degree.[40]

This same distinction was repeated multiple times throughout the seventeenth century. A few decades later, in 1661, Thomas Blount's *Glossographia*, a popular English dictionary, still described the standard method of distinguishing heat intensities as being based purely on bodily sensations: 'The first degree is so small, that it can scarce be perceived. The second, that which manifestly may be perceived without hurting the sense. The third, that which somewhat offends the sense. The fourth, which so much offends, that it may destroy the body'.[41] However, by the time an updated version of Blount's work was published, namely, the *Glossographia Anglicana Nova* of 1707, a new technical dimension had entered this classification system, reflecting a growing trend of objectification in the arts of fire:

> The first [degree of fire] is made by two or three coals, and is the most gentle of all; the second is made with four or five coals, or only just to warm the vessel, but so that you may endure your hand upon it for some time. The third degree is when there is heat to make a pot boil that contains five or six quarts of water. The fourth is as great a heat as can be made in the furnace.[42]

By the eighteenth century, practitioners were reflecting more explicitly on the shift from bodily knowledge—which is, by definition, private and incommunicable—to a more standardized technical framework for distinguishing heat intensities. For instance, the physician and chemist Johann Moritz Hoffmann, in his *Acta laboratorii chemici altdorfini* (1719), acknowledges that degrees of heat could still only be distinguished by the senses, particularly by how long one's hand could tolerate fire.[43] However, Hoffmann emphasizes that, by his time, this sensory classification was 'rarely used in practice (*rarius in usum vocatur*)'.[44] Instead, artisans typically gauged heat intensity by controlling the fire based on the configuration of the furnace's air fans: 'If only one register or fan (*registrum sive ventilabrum*) is open, the fire is of

---

[40] Ruland (1612), p. 261–262.

[41] Blount (1661), unnumbered page [*Degree*].

[42] Blount (1707), unnumbered page [*Degree of Fire in Chymistry*].

[43] Hoffmann (1719), p. 18: 'The first degree is characterized by the mild and moderate heat which never harms the hand; the second by a sharper heat that the hand can endure only with difficulty; the third is more intense and causes injury; the fourth appears entirely destructive'.

[44] Hoffmann (1719), p. 18.

the first degree; if two are open, it is the second degree; three, the third; and four, the fourth'.[45]

Over time, the task of quantifying heat intensity became increasingly delegated to the thermometer, which emerged as a pivotal instrument in the arts of fire. There was no longer a need to rely on the ingenuity traditionally required to master technical processes in artisanal work. In other words, heat no longer needed to be evaluated from within the processes themselves, but could be measured with an external tool. This shift gave the thermometer a powerful unifying role in practical knowledge of heat: it enabled precise determinations and made it possible to think differently about the various fire-related arts and their emerging distinctions. In fact, these disciplines gradually moved toward separation and specialization. For instance, fewer chemists would simultaneously develop theories of chemical elements and manage porcelain manufactories, engaging directly with arcanists or common workers.[46] Likewise, cooking became confined to kitchens or food processing laboratories, where chemical knowledge was still sometimes foundational but no longer considered an integral part of culinary techniques.

As the practical knowledge related to the arts of fire became increasingly codified, the thermometer was soon joined by a wide array of instruments designed to quantify technical processes, often leading to radical rationalization of production. A compelling example of this can be found in developments in the culinary arts at the turn of the nineteenth century. In an article of Alexandre Grimod de la Reynière's *Almanach des gourmands* (1807), one of the first gastronomic guides and an early example of culinary popularization, we read that:

> Of all the professions in this world, that of the cook (litt. *gourmand*) is the only one that demands the most rigorous precision in the calculation of minutes and hours; the only one where it is essential to coordinate time with the most scrupulous accuracy; where delays bring about the most disastrous consequences […]. Everything in the kitchen is regulated by the pendulum of the clock. A good cook knows, within two minutes, the time it takes to roast a sirloin, a truffled turkey, or even a chicken […]. At that precise moment, they act without delay, and the dish is instantly paraded onto the kitchen table […]. There may also be a discrepancy between the dining room clock and the kitchen clock, and from that difference can arise serious inconveniences every day.[47]

Grimod acknowledges the importance of innate artistic talent, particularly taste and visual intuition, but he also emphasizes the need for discipline in service coordination and precise timing. The rigor of time quantification is essential to avoid culinary failure, which Grimod describes in dramatic, catastrophic terms. Grimod even offers advice on which instruments to use and how to maintain them, revealing the increasingly authority of measuring instruments—in this case, the clock—over kitchen work.

---

[45] Hoffmann (1719), p. 18.

[46] An emblematic case is that of the French chemist Pierre-Joseph Macquer. See Lehman (2019).

[47] Grimod de la Reynière (1807), pp. 163–169. I wish to thank Gianenrico Bernasconi for pointing out this reference to me.

> It is essential that every dining room be equipped with an equation clock from the finest makers; and that another, less magnificent but equally good, be installed in a prominent spot in the kitchen, protected from greasy vapours that might interfere with its precision by soiling its springs.[48]

In Grimod's work, the systematization of culinary knowledge into recipes and codified instructions is accompanied by a strong normative impulse that subjects culinary practices to the rule of measurement. Quantifying processes makes these practices not only more widely intelligible and standardized, but also transforms them into *exempla* that should be imposed as norms for future practices, thereby disciplining the actions of those who will replicate the codified procedures. In fact, Grimod's recommendations border on the logic of industrial labour or military discipline.

The emphasis on the clock is no coincidence. One might recall Edward Thompson's seminal article *Time, Work-Discipline, and Industrial Capitalism* (1967), in which he argues that the regulation of working hours was a form of discipline imposed on labourers by capitalists from the earliest stages of industrialization. The goal was to enhance productivity and reduce wasted time, which was increasingly equated with financial loss.[49] This observation brings us directly to the final issue explored in this essay: the reasons behind the early modern drive to codify practical knowledge, particularly through quantification. I identify a compelling explanation in the domain of economics—though the term must be carefully qualified here, as the framework I propose diverges in key respects from those of Thompson and other historians.

4 The Economies of Codification

Why was practical knowledge increasingly codified during the early modern period? There are many possible answers, including references to pure contingency, or a collective need for the rational organization of knowledge, prompted by the invention of printing and shaped by the new social structures that emerged after 1500. As indicated above, I will here focus on a different explanation, that centres on the notion of 'economy' and the various meanings subsumed under this label.

The early modern ideas and practices of economy differs from the ones that developed in connection with industrial capitalism and the rise of a free market. The current understanding of the economy as a self-regulating system with an inherent tendency

---

[48] Grimod de la Reynière (1807), p. 169.

[49] Thompson's definition echoed the classical appraisal of time economy provided by Benjamin Franklin in the famous piece of *Advice to a Young Tradesman, Written by an Old One* (1748): 'In short, the way to wealth [...] depends chiefly on two words, industry and frugality; i.e., waste neither time not money, but make the best use of both', reprinted in Fisher (1753), p. 388. However, there is an important difference between Franklin's and Thompson's ideas of time economy. While the Founding Father considered it a positive entrepreneurial quality, the twentieth century Marxist historian regarded it as a typical feature of 'mature industrial societies of all varieties', driven by a desire for domination and profit, in Thompson (1967), p. 93.

toward growth is in fact historically specific. According to some commentators, this understanding is opposed to, or only loosely compatible with, the conceptions and practices of the economy during the *Ancien Régime*. As Ann Firth notes:

> Current conceptions of 'the economy' date from late in the 18th century and are based on the idea of a self-regulating unity or system with a natural tendency to growth. In the absence of such a conception, 18th century writers discuss trade, agriculture and manufacturing as distinct entities and there is no sense in which these entities spontaneously combine to form a self-regulating system.[50]

Other scholars offer even more radical perspectives, placing the emergence of the contemporary notion of 'the economy' at a much later time. According to Margaret Schabas, the concept of the economy did not exist before the nineteenth century.[51] Historian and political theorist Timothy Mitchell takes this idea even further, treating the concept as a twentieth century invention.[52] In light of this, recent scholarship has proposed the use of the term 'oeconomy' to refer to early modern economic practices.[53] This term explicitly recalls the Greek *oikonomia*, which literally means 'household management', and contrasts with the market-based, exchange-oriented logic that would define post-Restoration economic thought.

In what ways did early modern conceptions of the economy differ from our own? How do they offer valuable insight into the reasons for the codification of practical knowledge? Here, I will distinguish three ways in which the term 'economy' was understood in the early modern times.

In the first sense, economy referred to the careful management of domestic and material resources. As Simon Werrett has argued, early economic practices were grounded in finding a 'balance between buying new and using old things, between spending and saving and making the most of the resources you already had'.[54] For example, the agronomist Louis Liger, in his *Œconomie générale de la campagne, ou nouvelle maison rustique* (1700), defined economy as 'the art of prescribing order for oneself, in such a way that nothing, if properly managed, fails to yield great benefit'.[55] The idea of economy as an order implies a form of discipline, governed by precise rules aimed at optimizing the use of material goods.

---

[50] Firth (1998), p. 21.

[51] Schabas (2005), especially Chapter 1.

[52] Mitchell (2002), p. 4: 'The idea of economy in its contemporary sense did not emerge until the middle decades of the twentieth century. Between the 1930s and 1950s, economists, sociologists, national statistical agencies, international and corporate organizations, and government programs formulated the concept of the economy, meaning the totality of monetarized exchanges within a defined space. The economy came into being as a self-contained, internally dynamic, and statistically measurable sphere of social action, scientific analysis, and political regulation'.

[53] See Roberts (2014).

[54] Werrett (2019), p. 6.

[55] Liger (1700), p. 2.

While this notion certainly applies to everyday practical knowledge, it also extends to technical and scientific domains, as illustrated by various sources. Consider handbooks of domestic economy such as John Perkins's *Every Woman Her Own Housekeeper*, originally published in 1696, and reprinted multiple times during the eighteenth century. This text compiles common household knowledge and supplements it with conceptual tools and updated household management strategies.[56] In the preface to the 1796 edition, the editor explains: 'the intention of the following work is to present the female sex with a complete body of information, respecting the conduct and arrangement of their domestic concerns'.[57] In addition to providing practical instructions, such as a 'practical system of cookery' with recipes for 'pickling, preserving, and distilling', Perkins includes scientific knowledge relevant to domestic life: the culinary and medicinal properties of fruits and vegetables, as well as the 'first rules of arithmetic'.[58] The work is presented as an act of codification, offering a 'practical system' synthesized from nearly thirty authors. The guiding principles of this compilation are 'frugality and elegance', and the stated aim is to promote 'the frugal management of family expenses'.[59]

Economic concerns about material resources are also evident in scientific textbooks from the early modern period, which often offered advice on repurposing or conserving equipment. One notable example is William Henry's *Epitome of Chemistry* (1801). When discussing the necessary chemical apparatus for experiments, Henry observes: 'some of the most interesting chemical facts may be exhibited with the aid merely of Florence flasks, of common vials, and of wine glasses. In converting these to the purposes of apparatus, a considerable saving of expense will accrue to the experimentalist'.[60] Henry emphasizes that significant scientific work can be accomplished with ordinary objects that are adapted for experimental purposes. The economic practice considerably reduces resource consumption and waste.

As these examples suggest, the early modern period witnessed a growing concern for finding a balance between income and expenditure, reflecting what might be called an 'ecology of practice': a set of behaviors and principles by which practitioners—learned experimenters, artisans, or household practitioners—sought to manage resources, tools, and techniques in a way that did not compromise the welfare of their households or communities.[61]

Second, the idea of 'economy' could also refer to the optimization of technical operations. In the context of production, this involves increased mechanization and simplifying the workers' tasks by codifying them into precise protocols. The goal of this approach is to improve the efficiency of the technical procedures that connect

[56] This body of literature was widespread in the 17th and 18th centuries, particularly in Great Britain. See Werrett (2018), pp. 37–41.

[57] Perkins (1796), p. iii.

[58] Perkins (1796), pp. iv–vi.

[59] Perkins (1796), pp. iv, vii.

[60] Henry (1801), pp. 12–13. Cited in Werrett (2018), p. 39.

[61] For a more thorough discussion of these issues, and of the lemma 'ecology of practice', see Storni (2023b).

humans and machines, thereby optimizing the entire production process. A telling example is the digester, a machine invented by Robert Boyle's laboratory assistant Denis Papin in the late 1670s.[62] The digester was an early pressure cooker designed to extract an edible jelly from the leftovers of butchered animals, primarily beef bones. This jelly served as the base for a nutritious and inexpensive soup. During the eighteenth century, philanthropists across Europe adopted this '*marmite économique*' to prepare large quantities of food, in the context of institutional programs aimed at poverty relief.[63] Many users of the digester observed that it enabled a dual form of economy: to save of material resources, but also to make cooking itself faster and easier.

After a journey to France, the Dutch natural philosopher Martinus van Marum began investigating the digester as a potential solution for feeding the poor of Haarlem, near Amsterdam. His interest was spurred by an invitation from the Haarlem municipality to improve an existing poverty-relief program. The need for large-scale food production was driven by demographic pressures: in March 1799, the Amsterdam area had a population of 215,000, of whom 80,000 depended on public assistance; 10 years later, that number had grown to 110,000.[64] As van Marum writes in a journal article dated 9 December 1800:

> Seeing that the Municipality have planned to distribute an inexpensive soup among the destitute, I thought of employing a closed cooker, usually called Papin's digester after its inventor Papin, in order to obtain readily, and in an economic way, strong decoctions of bones and to make the soup more nourishing and at the same time more savory by this means.[65]

In his accounts of the experiments, which continued until 1818, van Marum adopted a quantifying approach: he meticulously recorded the weight of the ingredients and the jelly produced, as well as the duration of cooking. The idea was to demonstrate how delegating significant parts of the transformation process to a machine could make it more efficient, reducing both material consumption and human effort. For instance, in his report on a public demonstration held on 26 December 1800, van Marum notes: '15 pounds of beef bones were boiled with 15 ounces of salt in 40 pounds of water for 2 hours; the jelly obtained from this weighed 36¼ pounds'.[66] In an extended version of this report, he also described in detail the entire productive process of the soup:

> The jelly from beef bones is previously cooked for a thousand portions. 100 buckets of water are then placed in a copper boiler, and 250 pounds of the best barley are poured into it. After it has soaked in there for 3 hours, the fire is started and the water is brought to boil while stirring steadily. It is left to boil for 3 hours and then the fire is removed from the stove, but stirring can continue for half an hour afterwards to prevent any burning. Half an hour before

[62] On Papin's digester, see Storni (2021). The following discussion is based on that paper, particularly pp. 459–462.

[63] The digester is described as an 'economic pot' in multiple French sources. On the 'economic use' of the digester, see in particular Quériau (1761).

[64] See Forbes (1971), p. 290.

[65] van Marum (1800), pp. 194a–196b. English translation in Forbes (1971), p. 292.

[66] van Marum (1801), p. 27.

> the end of the cooking, 20 pounds of salt are poured into it, and then one begins to put the jelly in the boiler by portions from time to time, and the fat obtained from cooking the bones is mixed with it. It is customary to start this cooking about seven o'clock, and the food is left in the boiler at night; the barley then expands more and more in the warm moisture, and the food retains enough heat in the closed kettle to be distributed still moderately warm the next day at eleven o'clock: this quantity is divided into 1000 portions of more than 2 and a half pounds each.[67]

In this passage, Van Marum does not present the digester within the aseptic environment of a chemical laboratory, but in the real conditions of large-scale kitchens, where food was prepared for the destitute. His detailed quantification is paired with the description of cooking phases, each corresponding to a specific time of day. As he emphasizes, these procedures did not require specialized expertise. The digester could be operated by virtually anyone: 'The Papinian pot, as it is now configured, can be easily operated by ordinary workmen.'[68]

Even when not explicitly structured around the digester, we can discern the same type of rational organization in many philanthropic kitchens of the nineteenth century. Count Rumford, a physicist and philanthropist who experimented with the digester, invented a soup that was widely promoted in nineteenth century England as a response to poverty and widespread hunger.[69] Collective kitchens were established around it, and despite the scarcity of detailed records concerning their material organization, from paintings and engravings we know that these kitchens were organized as workshops of collective labor, efficiently coordinated. One notable example is scenes representing the Society of Friends (Quakers) preparing and distributing soup to the poor in Manchester in 1862 (Fig. 2).

The example of the digester and of collective kitchens leads us to a third meaning of the term 'economy': managing the risks inherent in practical operations and, more broadly, to economy in a moral sense.[70] The digester was a dangerous device that required careful handling. The high pressure it generated could easily lead to explosions, posing a real threat to operators. Historical sources regularly highlighted this danger and often included discussions about how to resolve the machine's material instability to ensure the safety of its operators.[71]

However, the digester is not the only relevant example. The moral economy of codification can be observed in other areas as well. Consider, for instance, the philanthropic dissemination of chemical knowledge. In the eighteenth century, free chemistry courses were held in public institutions, such as the Jardin du Roi and the Jardin des apothicaires in Paris, as well as in private workshops. These courses were

---

[67] van Marum (1818), pp. 13–15.

[68] van Marum (1801), p. 27.

[69] On Rumford's philanthropic activities, and on his 'economic soup', see Redlich (1971).

[70] I am not referring to a third use of the term 'economy', which is rare in this sense, but to an idea that is sometimes included in reflections on the economy, and includes references to safety and health preservation.

[71] See for example the discussion proposed by Girolamo Ottolini in his paper *Il digestore di Papino ridotto ad uso di cucina*: Ottolini (1783).

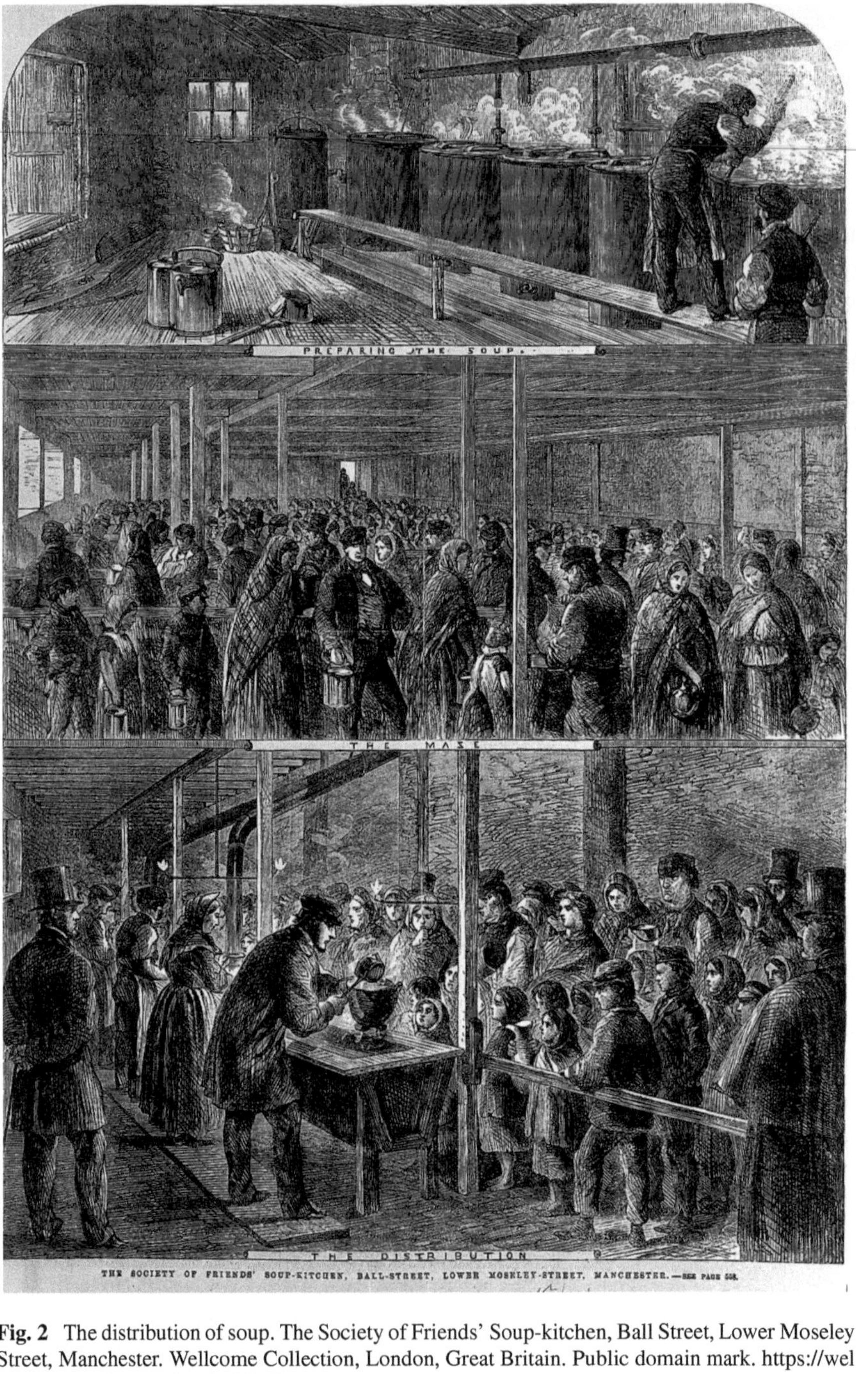

Fig. 2 The distribution of soup. The Society of Friends' Soup-kitchen, Ball Street, Lower Moseley Street, Manchester. Wellcome Collection, London, Great Britain. Public domain mark. https://wellcomecollection.org/works/b8p5nwna

attended by many individuals who were not necessarily trained in chemistry, pharmacy, or medicine.[72] They introduced students to the fundamentals of chemistry, often combined with the basic principles of physics, botany, and related disciplines. In this context, the goal was not to manage the physical dangers of a specific practice, such as handling fire. Rather, the goal was to make basic scientific knowledge accessible so that it could be applied in practical pharmaceutical operations or serve as a foundation for amateur experimentation. This reveals a pedagogical form of economy that sought to mitigate epistemic risks and provide knowledge that could improve one's quality of life.

The three meanings of the notion of economy discussed above correspond to the distinct motivations behind the codification of practical knowledge: resource management, technical improvement, and enhancing human welfare. In all three cases, however, we can clearly see the two sides of codification: on the one hand, it organizes the current practices in a rational way, and on the other, it establishes new rules and standards that affect any future use of codified practical knowledge.

Before concluding, it is interesting to briefly examine the broader picture that emerges from this analysis of economic motivations as a driving force behind codification. What seems to emerge is a particular feature of the early modern period, characterized by a tension between two opposing poles. On the one hand, we find a form of prudence or care for life—not only human life but also that of things.[73] This relationship can be interpreted, in Latourian terms, as a lost sensibility that perceives 'actants' everywhere, or as an early form of ecological awareness.[74] More simply, it may be understood within the framework of two strong imperatives that consolidated between the sixteenth and eighteenth centuries: philanthropy as a philosophical value, and the response to resource scarcity through technical ingenuity.[75]

This prudence, however, stands in stark contrast to the acceleration that characterizes the sphere of production, and acts as the incubator of the capitalist market and industry. Already in the *Ancien Régime*, we can detect a drive toward increased production and technical optimization, emerging as markers of excellence increasingly evaluated in relation to competitors. This perspective introduces a contradictory impulse with respect to the former: namely, a commodification of nature and the human. From there, this tension has shaped the history of Western societies until the present day.

---

[72] See Lehman (2011).

[73] Simon Werrett has recently proposed the category of 'emoterial' to highlight the connection between materials and emotions in the early modern period. According to Werrett, 'an emoterial is a process rather than a thing and it refers to the unfolding emotional relationship that bodies have with one another when they interact together, being co-constitutive of identities, feelings, experiences and physicality', in Werrett (2025), p. 333.

[74] An actant is defined as the source of an action, but it is not necessarily a human agent. Bruno Latour introduced this concept to challenge traditional notions of agency and propose that all social phenomena are the result of intricate networks of human and non-human actors, which he treats as equivalent in their ability to shape action. See Latour (1987), pp. 83–84.

[75] On early modern philanthropy, see Duprat (1993). On the role of dearth in the elaboration of early modern knowledge, see Mukherjee (2015).

5 Conclusion

This essay has examined the codification of practical knowledge in the early modern period. Drawing on recent scholarship, I have challenged reductive narratives of top-down rationalization. Instead of viewing codification as the imposition of abstract scientific norms on unthinking practices, I approached it as an ongoing, dynamic negotiation, marked by the persistent tension between practical rationalities and the drive toward abstraction characteristic of philosophy and the hard sciences.

Within this framework, I have proposed two lines of reflection on the purposes and the reasons for codification. Codification responds to the need to recognize and articulate the underlying order of practical operations, but also functions as a mechanism of control. It brings order to material processes and, at the same time, imposes a form of governance on the experimental bodies that carry them out. Codification establishes procedural norms that future practitioners are expected to follow, thereby transforming savoir-faire into a series of standardized, repeatable actions.

Of the tools that helped codify practical knowledge, I have emphasized quantification, namely, the analysis of natural reality in terms of measurable quantities that can be expressed mathematically. Quantification is interesting because it is a powerful means of standardization but also introduces forms of delegation. Measuring instruments assume the authority to regulate technical procedures, shaping—and sometimes constraining—the practitioner's bodily engagement with materiality.

In answering the question 'Why codify?' I turned to the notion of economy, identifying three dimensions it had in the early modern age. First, economy referred to the careful management of domestic and material resources. Second, it related to the optimization of technical operations. Third, it was a mode of risk management and moral reflection on practice. These dimensions reveal that the development of industrialization and technoscience, beginning in the late eighteenth century, was not a linear, uncontroversial process but rather one traversed by various tensions. We often forget the importance, up until the early nineteenth century—and perhaps even later—of cultures of technical ingenuity, attention to waste reduction, knowledge of repair, and care for the integrity of practitioners' bodies. This complex interplay demonstrates that codification was never a unidirectional process. While it undoubtedly laid the groundwork for the logic of industrial capitalism, it also preserved and conveyed values that resisted pure commodification.

References

Babbage C (1832) On the economy of machinery and manufactures. Charles Knight, London

Bacon F (2000) The new organon. Ed. Silverthorne M, Jardine L. Cambridge University Press, Cambridge

Bacon F ([1857] 2011) Philosophical works, vol. 1. Cambridge University Press, Cambridge

Baudry J, Nègre V (2024) Dessiner la technique. Pensée et discours visuels (XVIe-XXe siècles). Presses des Mines, Paris

Belhoste B (2019) Paris savant: capital of science in the age of Enlightenment. Oxford University Press, Oxford
Bernasconi G (2019) Pour une archéologie des pratiques. Socio-anthropologie 40:247–262
Bernasconi G (2025) The kitchen fire (eighteenth and early nineteenth century). In: Bernasconi G, Storni M (eds) Early modern fire. Science, technology, and the urban space. Brill, Leiden, pp 147–171
Bertucci P (2017) Artisanal Enlightenment: science and the mechanical arts in old regime France. Yale University Press, New Haven (CT)
Blount T (1661) Glossographia: or a dictionary interpreting all such hard words of whatsoever language, now used in our refined English tongue. T. Newcomb for G. Sawbridge, London
Blount T (1707) Glossographia anglicana nova: or, a dictionary, interpreting such hard words of whatever language, as are at present used in the English tongue. D. Brown et al, London
Bud R (2012) 'Applied science': a phrase in search of a meaning. Isis 103(3):537–545
Coleridge ST (1818) General introduction; or, preliminary treatise on method. In: Encyclopaedia Metropolitana, vol 1. B. Fellowes, London
Daston L (1995) The moral economy of science. Osiris 10:3–24
Delaunay B (2018) Penser la technique à l'Académie royale des sciences (1699–1750). Honoré Champion, Paris
Diderot D (1751) Art. In: d'Alembert J, Diderot D (eds) Encyclopédie ou Dictionnaire raisonné des sciences, des arts et des métiers, vol 1. Briasson et al, Paris, pp 713–717
Dubourg Glatigny P (2017) Réduction en art et *Erkenntnissteuerung*. Deux tendances historiographiques actuelles sur l'écriture des savoirs à l'époque moderne. In: Carvais R et al (eds) Penser la technique autrement. En hommage à l'œuvre d'Hélène Vérin. Classiques Garnier, Paris, pp 31–41
Dubourg Glatigny P, Vérin H (2008) Réduire en art: la technologie de la Renaissance aux Lumières. Éditions de la Maison des sciences de l'homme, Paris
Duprat C (1993) Pour l'amour de l'humanité. Le temps des philanthropes: La philanthropie parisienne des Lumières à la monarchie de Juillet. In: Editions du Comité des Travaux historiques et scientifiques, Paris
Enenkel KAE, Neuber W (2005) Einleitung. In: Enenkel KAE, Neuber W (eds) Cognition and the book: typologies of formal organisation of knowledge in the printed book of the early modern period. Brill, Leiden
Febvre L (1950) De l'à peu près à la précision en passant par ouï-dire. Annales 5(1):25–31
Ferguson ES (1992) Engineering and the mind's eye. MIT Press, Cambridge (MA)
Firth A (1998) From oeconomy to 'the economy': population and self-interest in discourses on government. Hist Hum Sci 11(3):19–35
Fisher G (1753) The American instructor: or, young man's best companion. Containing spelling, reading, writing, and arithmetick, in an easier way than any yet published; and how to qualify any person for business, without the help of a master. B. Franklin and D. Hall, Philadelphia, PA
Floyer (1707) The physician's pulse-watch, vol 1. Printed for Samuel Smith and Benjamin Walford, London
Forbes (1971) Martinus van Marum: life and work, vol 3. Tjeenk Willink, Haarlem
Garçon A-F, Hilaire-Pérez L (2002) Open technique between community and individuality in the eighteenth-century France. In: De Goey F, Veluwenkamp JW (eds) Entrepreneurs and institutions in Europe and Asia, 1500-2000. Aksant, Amsterdam, pp 237–256
Grimod de la Reynière A (1807) Almanach des gourmands, 5e année. Cellot, Paris
Helmholtz H (1896) Vorträge und Reden, vol 2. Friedrich Vieweg und Sohn, Braunschweig
Henneguelle A, Jatteau A (2021) Sociologie de la quantification. La Découverte, Paris
Henry (1801) An epitome of chemistry. Collins & Perkins, New York
Hoffmann JM (1719) Acta laboratorii chemici altdorfini, chemiae fundamenta, operations praecipuas et tentamina curiosa, ratione et experientia suffulta, complectentia. Apud haeredes J.D, Tauberi, Nuremberg-Altdorf

Husserl E (1970) The crisis of European sciences and transcendental phenomenology. ed. Carr D. Northwestern University Press, Evanston, IL
Jenner MS (2010) Tasting Lichfield, touching China: sir John Floyer's senses. Hist J 53(3):647–670
Klein U (2005) Technoscience avant la lettre. Perspect Sci 13(2):226–266
Klein U (2017) Hybrid experts. In: Valleriani M (ed) The structures of practical knowledge. Springer, Cham, pp 287–306
Koyré A (1948) Du monde de l'à peu près à l'univers de la précision. Critique 28:806–823
Latour B (1987) Science in action: how to follow scientists and engineers through society. Harvard University Press, Cambridge (MA)
Lavoisier AL (1781) Expériences sur l'effet comparé de différents combustibles. Mémoires de l'Académie Royale des Sciences:379–395
Lehman C (2011) Les multiples facettes des cours de chimie en France au milieu du XVIIIe siècle. Histoire de l'éducation 130:31–56
Lehman C (2019) Les lieux d'activité du chimiste Pierre-Joseph Macquer (1718-1784): Laboratoires et instruments. Revue d'histoire des sciences 72(2):221–254
Liger L (1700) Œconomie générale de la campagne, ou nouvelle maison rustique, vol 1. Charles De Sercy, Paris
Merchant C (1980) The death of nature: women, ecology and the scientific revolution. Harper & Row, New York
Mitchell T (2002) Rule of experts: Egypt, techno-politics, modernity. University of California Press, Berkeley, CA
Mokyr J (2002) The gifts of Athena: historical origins of the knowledge economy. Princeton University Press, Princeton, NJ
Mukherjee A (2015) Penury into plenty: dearth and the making of knowledge in early modern England. Routledge, New York
Oki S (2011) L'utilité des sciences d'après les discours des secrétaires perpétuels de l'Académie royale des sciences de Paris au XVIIIe siècle. In: Salaün F, Schandeler JP (eds) Entre belles-lettres et disciplines: les savoirs au XVIIIe siècle. Centre International d'Étude du XVIIIe siècle, Ferney-Voltaire, pp 77–88
Ottolini G (1783) Il digestore di Papino ridotto ad uso di cucina. Marelli, Milan
Perkins J (1796) Every woman her own house-keeper; or, the ladies' library. J. Ridgway, London
Polanyi M (1998) Personal knowledge: towards a post-critical philosophy. The University of Chicago Press, Chicago
Powers JC (2014) Measuring fire: Herman Boerhaave and the introduction of thermometry into chemistry. Osiris 29(1):158–177
Quériau FG (1761) Mémoire sur l'usage œconomique du digesteur de Papin. P. Viallanes, Clermont-Ferrand
Redlich F (1971) Science and charity: count Rumford and his followers. Int Rev Soc Hist 16(2):184–216
Roberts L (2014) Practicing oeconomy during the second half of the long eighteenth century: an introduction. Hist Technol 30(3):133–148
Roberts L, Schaffer S, Dear P (2007) The mindful hand: inquiry and invention from the late renaissance to early industrialisation. Royal Netherlands Academy of Arts and Sciences, Amsterdam
Roux S (2010) Forms of Mathematization: (14th-17th centuries). Early Sci Med 15(4-5):319–337
Ruland M (1612) Lexicon alchemiae sive dictionarium alchemisticum. Z. Palthenius, Frankfurt
Schabas M (2005) The natural origins of economics. The University of Chicago Press, Chicago
Secord JA (2023) Inventing the scientific revolution. Isis 114(1):50–76
Storni M (2021) Denis Papin's digester and its eighteenth-century European circulation. Br J Hist Sci 54(4):443–463
Storni M (2023a) The pulse watch and the physician's senses: John Floyer on the quantification of the body. In: Guidi S, Braga J (eds) The quantification of life and health from the sixteenth to

the nineteenth century: intersections of medicine and philosophy. Palgrave Macmillan [Springer Nature], Cham, pp 241–263
Storni M (2023b) Time thrift and economic science in the eighteenth century. Science in Context 36(2):175–191 https://doi.org/10.1017/S0269889725000468
Storni M (2025) Without a thermometer: the technical knowledge of heat in the early modern age. In: Bernasconi G, Storni M (eds) Early modern fire. Science, technology, and the urban space. Brill, Leiden, pp 90–116
Thompson EP (1967) Time, work-discipline, and industrial capitalism. Past Present 38(1):56–97
Valleriani M (2017) The epistemology of practical knowledge. In: Valleriani M (ed) The structures of practical knowledge. Springer, Cham, pp 1–19
van Marum M (1800) Bericht omtrent zyne proefneemingen ter bereiding van mee versterkende soupe voor behoeftigen, op de minst kostbare wyze, door middle van een digtgeslotene of Papiniaansche pot. Nieuwe Algemene Konst-en Letterbode 14:194–196
van Marum M (1801) Beschryving der verbeeterde papiniaansche pot. Algemene Konst-en Letterbode 1:24–30
van Marum M (1818) Beschrijving van den Papiniaanschen pot of dampketel. [Haarlem]
Vérin H (2008) Rédiger et réduire en art: un projet de rationalisation des pratiques. In: Dubourg Glatigny P, Vérin H (eds) Réduire en art: la technologie de la Renaissance aux Lumières. Éditions de la Maison des sciences de l'homme, Paris, pp 17–58
Werrett S (2018) Household oeconomy and chemical inquiry. In: Roberts L, Werrett S (eds) Compound histories: materials, governance and production, 1760–1840. Brill, Leiden, pp 35–56
Werrett S (2019) Thrifty science: making the most of materials in the history of experiment. The University of Chicago Press, Chicago
Werrett S (2025) Spectacle, enthusiasm, objectivity—managing fire as an emoterial. In: Bernasconi G, Storni M (eds) Early modern fire. Science, technology, and the urban space. Brill, Leiden, pp 329–344
Wilson R (2015) Primary and secondary qualities. In: Stuart M (ed) A companion to Locke. Wiley Blackwell, Oxford, pp 193–211
Witthöft H (2008) Ökonomie, Währung und Zahl—Wirtschaftgeschichte und historische Metrologie. Ein Literatur-und Forschungsbericht 1980 bis 2007. Viereljahrschrift für Sozial und Wirtschaftgeschichte 95(1):25–40

Marco Storni , Ph.D. (2018, ENS Paris-Università di Bologna) is a postdoctoral fellow at the Université libre de Bruxelles. He is the author of *Maupertuis. Le philosophe, l'académicien, le polémiste* (Honoré Champion, 2022; prize of the Fondation Del Duca-Institut de France 2023). He recently co-edited *Early Modern Fire. Science, Technology, and the Urban Space* (Brill, 2025).

Philosophies of the Body and Legal Responses to Health Emergencies

Why the Body Matters. Sovereignty, Control, and Individual Freedom

Giovanni Leghissa

Abstract Since the inception of the state as the institution that limits the room of manoeuvre for human action, the individual body has been the target of specific sets of intervention aimed at controlling what is and what is not allowed. In the contemporary age the range of governmental intervention in the sphere within which the individual is supposed to be granted a relative sovereignty has grown exponentially. Both legal and extra-normative forms of control undermine the property of one's own body that the classical liberal tradition intended to grant, at least partially, to individuals. The present contribution aims at exploring the philosophical, political and legal frameworks that authorizes and executes the current forms of restrictions of individual freedom.

1 Foucault's Notion of Biopolitics

Foucault's theory offers a valuable framework to scholars seeking to examine how institutional devices are committed to directing the interactions among individuals. For decades now, there has been broad consensus regarding the relevance of Foucault's contribution in this field. Foucault's concern with processes of subjectivation through the history of Western civilization led him to elaborate a conceptual framework whose relevance become particularly evident whenever the question of power arise. Yet, it would be misleading to reduce Foucault's philosophy solely to a description of how power mechanisms work and reproduce. He devoted such careful attention to these mechanisms because, in his view, only a proper understanding of how power devices operate can illuminate the emergence of specific forms of subjectivity within particular historical contexts of action. This point is essential in order to make appropriate use of Foucauldian terminology within any analysis that aims to investigate the relationship between the sphere within which law is supposed to rule and the other domains of individual action.

G. Leghissa (✉)
Department of Philosophy, University of Turin, Torino, Italy
e-mail: giovanni.leghissa@unito.it

M. Balestrieri and A. Cauduro (eds.), *The Legal Anatomy of the Body*, Ius Gentium: Comparative Perspectives on Law and Justice 142,
https://doi.org/10.1007/978-3-032-26434-3_5

In Foucault's toolbox, one finds—perhaps as a primary instance—the notion of biopolitics, among many conceptual devices that help usefully elucidate how the system of law shape human interaction. The first observation to be made here is that Foucault introduces this notion within a deliberately limited context—namely, within his analysis of how the modern Western nation-state began to acquire the structure and function that it still retains. A second observation concerns the intertwinement between biopolitics and governmentality. Foucault developed these two notions simultaneously, around the mid-1970s, when he deemed it necessary to expand the scope of his analysis of power relations.[1] Until that time, his work had largely concentrated on power structures best described in terms of discipline. While the latter helps clarify how a set of coded and well-defined rules shape individual conducts by restraint and constraint, the realm to which governmentality refers is more opaque, ambiguous, and fluid. With this notion, Foucault sought to capture the fact that power relations are not only constituted by disciplinary interventions issuing from the top of social and political hierarchies, but also operate within the interstices of social networks. The theoretical yield from this shift is considerable—and it may be one of the reasons why Foucault's late work found such wide acceptance even far beyond the disciplinary boundary of philosophy. This shift consists in a reconfiguration of the locus of power: no longer power is regarded as a singular, solid, and easily identifiable site situated atop a political system. What now comes to the fore is the impersonal and anonymous character of various practices that target individual conduct in order to embed it within specific sets of procedures and apparatuses. What is most important is that these procedures and apparatuses can include rules, laws and norms but cannot be reduced to them. Consequently, the very image of a 'source' meant to convey the generative force of social hierarchies becomes obsolete. Foucault's concept of governmentality paved the way for a metaphoric domain inspired more by the image of social relations held together by assemblages of human and non-human agents, which constitute the condition of possibility for human action. Here, one might cite Bruno Latour's or Katherine Hayles' works as prominent examples of how the image of a network can fruitfully serve to describe human interaction.[2] Governmental interventions function as anonymous networks of discourses, institutional practices, and spatial arrangements that together constitute the architecture of choice within which individuals make the decisions they need in order to pursue their goals or achieve self-fulfilment.

> By this world 'governmentality' I mean three things. First, by 'governmentality' I understand the ensemble formed by institutions, procedure, analysis and reflections, calculations, and tactics that allow the exercise of this very specific, albeit very complex, power that has the population as its target, political economy as its major form of knowledge, and apparatuses of security as its essential technical instrument. Second, by 'governmentality' I understand the tendency, the line of force, that for a long time, and throughout the West, has constantly led towards the pre-eminence over all type of power – sovereignty, discipline, and so on – of the type of power that we can all 'government' and which has led to the development of a series of specific governmental apparatuses (*appareils*) on the one hand, [and on the other] to

[1] See at least Foucault (1978), (2003), (1982), and (2008).

[2] See Latour (2005) and Hayles (2017).

> the development of a series of knowledges. Finally, by 'governmentality' I think we should understand the process, or rather, the result of the process by which the state of justice of the Middle Ages became the administrative state in the fifteenth and sixteenth century and was gradually 'governamentalized'.[3]

Foucault's primary objective is to challenge the conventional and widely accepted concept of the state, according to which the state is presumed to function as a monolithic entity that stands above both those who govern and those who are governed, and is therefore regarded as the exclusive bearer of power. Foucault's effort to de-substantialise the state is not entirely new—Max Weber's analysis of the role of bureaucratic power in Modernity yielded to similar conclusions. What is undoubtedly novel in Foucault's account is the shift towards the idea that power relations are responsible for producing all the positions that can be occupied by participants in collective life. The opposition between the two extreme poles of a given hierarchy, the one at the top and the one at the bottom, is only one among a multiplicity of differentiations that characterise all the possible processes of subjectivation within which individuals are involved. This system of differences is linked both to physical elements—such as a given territory with defined boundaries, which allows for the spatial arrangement of a particular collective—and to discursive elements—such as various forms of knowledge, that underpin the management of social life. Albeit one may still refer to this system by the name 'state', it is important to stress that the state should not be regarded as the centre or matrix of this system. Rather, according to Foucault, the state both produces and is produced by this network of differences.

Foucault' second objective is to demonstrate how, and to what extent, governmental interventions are directed towards the body of individuals who are part of the collective. It is within this framework that the concept of biopolitics acquires its full heuristic value.[4] To govern a collective means to gather a particular set of data concerning the condition of individuals, in order to manage their conduct appropriately. On the one hand, such data are made intelligible by using a grid of intelligibility that new forms of knowledge, whose emergence is coalescent with the self-fashioning of the European nation-state, have the task to produce.[5] Foucault paid specific attention to the group of disciplines that took form within the *Polizeywissenschaft* along the eighteenth century and later acquired autonomy as independent disciplines.[6] This list includes political economics, law, statistics, administrative science, public health, criminology—and to these one might now add informatics, as

---

[3] Foucault (2009), p. 108 ff.

[4] See, among others, Leghissa (2020).

[5] In this regard, Foucault's genealogical stance shares the idea of many other constructivist positions according to which knowing something does not coincide with a direct access to what is perceived, studied, analysed or described, which does not mean, however, that the 'world outside there' is a sheer product of the knowing subject. Foucault's constructivism is perhaps the major cause of the prejudice according to which his philosophy is to be inserted in the stream of postmodern theories—a prejudice that not an inconsistent part of the scholarship has been holding for decades.

[6] It is worth noting that, if one excludes Schiera (1968) and Oestreich (1969), scholars were not so prompt in paying attention to the *Polizeiwissenschaften* when Foucault held his courses at the Collège de France.

it is the science responsible for the production and implementation of algorithms that govern contemporary life through the management of LLM and AI devices. On the other hand, what is explained, studied or analysed through the conceptual tools developed by each of these disciplines gains its consistency not only as an object that is worth being known, but more crucially as an object of governmental intervention. The body of individuals—or the population, understood as the collective living under the sovereignty of a state within a definite territory—existed long before the emergence of modern disciplines such as medicine or statistics. Yet, once these disciplines were integrated into the administrative apparatus as essential instrument of governance, both individual bodies and populations began to acquire visibility as variants within a broader system of coordinates. Thus, the deployment of an array of disciplines, each tasked with producing the data necessary for tailoring governmental interventions, contributes to the construction of the individual body as an asset, whose value may increase or decrease depending on the governmental objectives pursued at any given time. Individuals become subjects—that is autonomous agents—only to the extent that they are capable of negotiating their room of manoeuvre within institutional spaces, power relations, and hegemonic narratives embedded in the collective imaginary. The terms of this negotiation are, of course, prescribed, but this does not imply that individuals are not free. On the contrary, one of Foucault's fundamental claim is that human behaviour is grounded in both the capacity for choice and the desire to shape one's own life according to autonomously adopted models and narratives. What cannot be chosen, however, is the general framework within which such choices are made. This framework defines the range of conduct deemed intelligible or possible within a particular social context.

When Foucault introduced the notion of biopolitics into his conceptual toolbox, he significantly expanded the scope of his analysis of the relationship between power and knowledge. From the outset of his philosophical career Foucault—deeply influenced by Nietzsche's thought—focused not on what makes it possible for a statement to be considered true, but rather on why the existence of statements supposed to be true is necessary for guiding specific courses of action. This line of inquiry famously led him to explore the genealogy of discourses concerning the exclusion of the mad and the criminal from societal life—exclusion that, paradoxically, helped constitute the norms of what is considered as 'normal' within a given historical framework. It is crucial to emphasise the continuity that runs throughout the various phases of Foucault's inquiry into power relations. He never abandoned the view that, in order to be effective, power must be supported by a grid of discourses whose function is not merely to distinguish between what is true and what is false, but more fundamentally to define what a given collective is able to accept as true, effective, reasonable, and so forth—and, conversely, what lies beyond the limits of what can be said or thought.[7] The analysis of biopolitical interventions continues Foucault's overarching

[7] Here I am suggesting, contrary to the position of some interpreters of Foucault's philosophy, that Foucault (1972) should be read as a sort of research program, to which he held on along the whole of his philosophical career.

project: to demonstrate the intrinsic connection between the production of truth and the efficacy of power.

Nonetheless, the emphasis placed on the individual body as the pivotal site around which governmental actions revolve makes a significant expansion of his previous approach. Biopolitical governance not only structures the discursive space in which knowledge is produced, but also enhances the capacity to control what can actually be done in order to produce, maintain, or curtain life. This development signals the shift, in Foucault's view, from pre-modern to modern forms of sovereignty. In early regimes, sovereignty was defined by the power to decide between life and death; more precisely, by the right to take life or to let live. In contrast, modern sovereignty, as exercised by the administrative state, encompasses a broader range of functions, all oriented towards the production of the forces that sustain life within a population.[8] Both individual bodies and the population—which may be regarded as an artificial body constituted by the sovereign's gaze—must be produced, in the sense that their existence and function depend on the performativity of various institutional arrangements. In order to clarify how biopolitical measures operate to enhance life by means of devices that pervade the entire field of social interactions, Foucault introduces another concept that has had a notable influence in contemporary scholarship: the notion of 'apparatus' ('*dispositiv*' in French). This term is intended to highlight the material specificity of the configuration within which governmental interventions are enacted. These apparatuses include norms, laws, administrative measures, architectural forms, scientific statements, moral and philosophical discourses, and they became effective not by coercing or compelling, but rather as forces that nudge individuals to assume a specific behaviour. The discursive level within which norms and rules are created and expressed can acquire, thus, the same consistency—better: the same thickness—that marks the performative power of apparatuses whose materiality is more evident, like, for example, the architectural and urban devices that frame the flow of individual bodies within the boundaries of any given political system. Since the beginning of his activity at the Collège de France, namely since the inaugural address delivered on December 2, 1970,[9] Foucault has been always pleading for a 'incorporeal materialism', whose scope is to confer visibility on the apparatuses that collect, direct and produce the paths along which flows the existence of individuals. It might be interesting to follow the line that connects Foucault's 'incorporeal materialism' to the 'new materialisms' that permeate part of the contemporary debate within the Humanities. It is enough, however, to point to its heuristic power: blurring the boundary between the discourses that shape the space of the imaginary and the devices that shape the interactions among individual bodies allows for an analysis that conflates different modes of production of subjectivity within only one gaze.

Finally, it is important to understand the neutral character of the notion of biopolitics. Biopolitical interventions can be referred, in fact, both to practices that imply the use of violence against individuals and to practices that aim at improving their

[8] Foucault (1978), p. 135 ff.

[9] This speech, *The Discourse of Language* (or.: *L'ordre du discours*), can be found as Appendix in Foucault (1972), pp. 215–237.

welfare. The vast array of racist policies that scattered among western countries from the end of the 19th to the first half of the twentieth century and found their peak with the extermination of Jews in Nazi Germany is a good example of the first case. Racism and antisemitism made it possible to turn the administrative organization of the German state into a killing machine; such a result could be obtained only by putting the health of the nation at the top of the value system: the murderous undertaking, in which Hitler's willing executioners took part, has been accomplished in order to preserve the 'purity' of the German blood—a 'purity' whose function was to represent symbolically the perfect condition of public health.[10] The policies that contemporary Western states adopt in order to improve the collective welfare is, conversely, a good example of the second case. Governmental apparatuses of various kind—from health care and educational systems to support services for migrants, unemployed or disabled people, just to mention some examples—are deployed in order to allow for the creation of a sphere within which individuals can pursue their objectives of well-being. This kind of biopolitical interventions do not amount to the empowerment of those rights of third generation that Marshall, among others, considered to be the accomplishment of a mature democratic state.[11] The enhancement of the collective welfare is to be considered, rather, as the result of the governmentalization that the state is undergoing in the present era.[12]

2 Modernity and the System of Law

Foucault's contribution to the contemporary debate about how to frame the relationship among power relations, processes of subjectivation and the production of knowledge remains unique—this fact is worth repeating once again. And the core of his contribution concerns precisely the main issue that comes to the fore when the theoretical interest focuses on how the body becomes the target of governmental interventions. If one draws all the consequences from the whole of Foucauldian analysis of biopolitical power, it seems to be persuasive to argue that the body intervenes within the processes of subjectivation both as a construct and as the most immediate instantiation of individual self-presence. The body, on the one hand, outreaches the individual self-mastery because of its exposure to various power apparatuses; but, on the other hand, it constitutes the sole entry both into every possible social game and into the source of self-consciousness. Within such a theoretical framework the body loses the concreteness that the common sense usually ascribes to it and becomes the crossing point of various forces whose function is to shape the space of social interactions. Thus, becoming a subject means to perceive one's own corporeality as an unstable element that fluctuates between immediacy and mediation; it means, more precisely, to identify with oneself by passing through the different images of the self

[10] On this, see Foucault (2003).

[11] See Marshall (1950).

[12] See Dean (1999).

that are made available within the different contexts of action in which subjects are involved.

Foucault's proposal, according to which the body is to be put in the point of intersection between processes of subjectivation and the capability an individual has to establish its own identity, invites us to compare his stance with other important philosophical traditions within which the reflection upon the subject is strictly tied with the acknowledgment that the individual body matters as a condition of possibility for the constitution of the subject. Husserl's phenomenology on the one hand, and Freud's psychoanalysis on the other are the examples that come immediately to our mind—despite the fact that Foucault has always emphasized the distance he meant to keep toward both the first and the second. Further, if we approach the present time, it seems to be unavoidable to perceive the similarity between Foucault's biopolitics and Peter Sloterdijk's anthropotechnic. According to Sloterdijk, in fact, the subject is not a substance, but is the result of a series of repeated exercises that shape the process of self-constitution. The various anthropotechnical arrangements that characterize a historical period, or a geographical area, give to individuals the opportunity to choose the best way to achieve the desired form of self-fulfilment, but individuals are only partially in the position of choosing the exercises that lead to the accomplishment of an autonomous life; some anthropotechnics are, in fact, other-directed and thus amount to a reduction, and not to an increase, of freedom. However, instead of following the suggestion to compare Foucault' theory of subjectivity in general with similar position held by other authors, in the present context it is surely much more fruitful to continue along the path opened by the concept of biopolitics in order to investigate the specific relationship between the system of rules and the constitution of subjectivity.

According to the results obtained above, it can be assumed that the system of law can operate only as a part of a broader network of apparatuses, which also include informal norms and forms of tacit knowledge. This does not mean, however, that the law loses its autonomy, or, to say it better, its ontological status as a system characterized by a constitutive self-sufficiency. The point is, rather, that a correct assessment of its function requires an understanding of how porous the boundary between the system of law and the whole of the societal system is, and against which law is supposed to work as a regulatory device.

The autonomy of the law can be at best perceived if one looks at the form of a legal statement. The latter floats—this metaphor may not sound inappropriate—within a realm where the temporality that gives order and consistency to our everyday experience does not hold. If a court delivers a ruling, which ascertains, for example, that 'X has done Y', this statement can be considered as true not because it refers to something that happened somewhere, someday, namely in a place where X was present and busy in doing Y, but because it refers to facts and events that have been constructed during the trial. The members of the court might be variously biased, the judge might be drunken, or—which would be even worse—X is not at all the one who committed Y: all these circumstances do not disprove the truth of the statement 'X has done Y', if this statement has the form of a pronouncement issued by a court. In sum, it is the procedure that underpins the trial that which produces the truth of a legal statement.[13] The same line of reasoning is valid if one takes into consideration the status of the laws promulgated by a Parliament. They do not refer to the fact that 'X' can happen or not—whereas 'X' means an action, or a courses of actions, that an agent could perform—but they establish the boundaries within which an action, or a course of actions, can be defined as legal or illegal. The system of law does not work according to the couple true/false, but, rather, according to the couple legal/illegal.

The matter of fact that law has an autonomy that assures its self-consistency and its detachment from other spheres of human action does not imply, however, that it has no relation at all with what humans do when they work within a scientific research program, when they create an artwork, when they fight for the accomplishment of a reform within the public domain, when they worship a deity through a specific ritual, or, lastly, when they make love in a bush or in a bedroom. In Luhmann's term, the system of law is a closed system in the environment of which all the other systems operate—namely the systems of science, art, politics, religion and love. The system of modern society encompasses all these sub-systems, each of which operates thanks to its own autopoietic closure, whereas the latter is the condition of its openness. The closure Luhmann refers to is to be understood as the fact that a system can reproduce—or better: can produce its own maintenance—only recursively, i.e. only by producing its own elements. These elements have the function to link closure and openness. In the case of biological systems, an awareness of, or knowledge about, the environment is not required. On the contrary, social and psychic systems are aware of the environment, and this is possible because in both cases meaning is the component of the system—and meaning allows for a re-entry of the difference between the system and the environment within the system. In other words, each system is a source of irritations for the other, and it must continuously process these irritations. The fact that this operation of processing takes place within the system rests on its closure, whereas the modifications that result from it speaks to its openness. The joint presence of closure and openness that characterized systems is particularly useful if the issue to be clarified is how the system of law acts not only as a sub-system within the social system, but, above all, upon it. The conceptual tools offered by Luhmann's theory, in fact, help frame law within the broader context of the social system without undermining its autonomy.

More precisely, there are two reasons why I suggest to take the theoretical contribution of Luhmann's thought into consideration. First, Luhmann's thought is thoroughly based on a strong commitment to a process ontology that aims at accounting for how an observer does not simply see 'what exists in the world out there', but rather sees which differences among elements of a system produce metastable structures that can, on their part, be rearranged as soon as there emerge events capable to cause any kind of modifications. Such a commitment, that exclude the displacement of the epistemological dimension when discussing ontological issues, has not

[13] See Hart (1948–1949).

only a broader metaphysical relevance,[14] but it is precisely what one needs when the theoretical gaze is directed to that complex system that we keep on calling 'Modern society'. The second, and more relevant reason refers to how Luhmann's theory helps explain why the degree of complexity that affects modern societies requires the presence of the system of law in order to develop their autopoiesis. This point deserves a more detailed examination. Values of different nature and provenance, and with different degrees of justification, continue to circulate and spread within the totality of the various communicative domains, as it was the case before the inception of the modern age. At first glance, the function of the system of shared values does not differ from the function of the system of law: both values and juridical norms attain socially stabilised expectations. In the name of values one establishes what is wrong and what is correct, and the validity of what a value helps define as correct or not does not depend on the consequences of the actions undertaken in their name, as well as it does not depend on the fact that there is a concrete actor willing to behave in conformity to them. The same is true for juridical norms. But there is an enormous difference between norms and values: legal norms imply a clear-cut distinction between lawfulness and its contrary, whereas it is impossible to manage the system of values by introducing in it such a structure of alternatives. Values are essentially contested, and their validity is always tied to each of the idiosyncratic contexts within which they are recognised as valid. A hierarchy of values that can put an end to disputes concerning values does not exist—more precisely: it cannot exist within modernity. In fact, in a pre-modern era the system of values rested upon a set of universally accepted truths, which allowed for a consensus on what is to be taken for universally valid within the realm of values. A sort of nostalgia, tinged with mythical elements, for a world resting on universally shared values keeps on creeping in the mindset of men and women living in the present day; this is due to the fact that arguments feeding off their persuasive power from values give the illusion that the complexity of the social system can be reduced cheap (and this fact alone should invite us to keep away from values as such). In other worlds, values amount to a closure of the infinitely open horizon of possible human actions. By contrast, quite the opposite can be stated if one looks at the function of the system of law. The latter is the condition of possibility of all the conceivable courses of action within the different sub-systems of modernity.[15]

If considered within this perspective, the relationship between governmentality and the law can be much better understood. The action of governmental interventions can be put in question in the name of the law, since the regime of governmentality does not coincide with the regime of the law. This does not change, or alter significantly, the biopolitical structure of power that characterizes contemporary societies, but can offer a frame to its various effects. Such a frame, which has been heavily underestimate within the reception of Foucault's theory of biopolitics, is important in order to better understand why laws are norms of specific nature—albeit Foucault

[14] On the intertwinement of ontology and epistemology within Luhmann's theory, see Luhmann (2002).

[15] See Luhmann (1999).

is not wrong, it must be added, when he put norms and laws under the encompassing ensemble of governmental apparatuses. Legal norms, and the system of law in general, have its origin in a discursive regime deeply rooted in the traditions—both ancient and Christian—that preceded the modern age. The rule of law had the function to limit, at least to a certain extent, the power of the sovereign.[16] After the inception of modernity, law began to establish itself as an autonomous domain—more precisely: as a sub-system of the modern system, to put it in Luhmann's term. The result of this self-establishment is that law finds in itself what can or may create a limit to its own enforcement, and, at the same time, law works as a powerful device that restrict other devices whose function is to exert power within the social system. If we take as our point of departure the Hobbesian framework through which modernity finds its conceptual coherence, the issue may be articulated in the following terms: the legal system provides individuals with the assurance that sovereign power will remain constrained within certain limits in its exercise over human lives. Yet, more significantly, law constitutes the very condition that enables the state to act upon individuals; they function as the mediating space between the domain of the governmental intervention and that of individual liberties. Absent the legal system—and, in particular, the so-called fundamental rights (such as the right to vote, freedom of speech, and equality before the law)—state action upon individual existence would lack any form of legitimacy. Law thus emerges, ultimately, as the medium through which individuals and institutions of power are brought into communicative relation.

3 The Legal Construction of a Healthy Body

If we accept Luhmann's theory as valid—namely, if we regard system theory as a useful tool for pursuing the objectives at hand—then we yield a clearer understanding of the role of law within the system of modernity. The latter is characterized by what Luhmann terms 'functional differentiation', which entails the autonomy of each of the subsystems comprising the social system. This autonomy, as previously noted, is marked by operational closure, which enables interdependence among the various subsystems. Now, for modernity to exist at all—modernity meant as an anthropologically significant project—it is essential that the subsystems of society remain available to one another, for only in this way can mutual interdependence be realized. The system of law is precisely what activates the flexibility of the boundaries that unite and separate the various subsystems. It is the subsystem that, more than any other, serves to ensure that the social system preserves its intrinsic rationality. For Luhmann, a system is rational when it is capable of maintaining a less

[16] After Octavian's takeover—the expression may not sound as an exaggeration—it was surely true that, as Ulpianus put it, '*quod principi placuit, legis habet vigorem*'; nevertheless, even after the establishment of the *principatus*, the rule of law could buffer autocratic expressions of the Emperor's sovereignty. On this, see, among others, Lucrezi (1995) and Straumann (2016); for the Middle Age, see Calasso (1954).

complex order—that is, a higher and more intelligible one—by excluding alternative possibilities.

This also clarify the role played by the individuals' capability to take care of themselves. Individuals must be understood as geometric and cognitive sites of the constitution of social reality. They are geometrical points where the interplay of security and freedom takes place. The governmental regimes that Foucault taught us to identify are responsible both for the intensification of control and for the enhancement of individuals' ability to take care of themselves. This self-care should not be linked to a universal human vulnerability, but rather seen as the sign of a possible individual autonomy. Such autonomy may indeed be externally directed, or steered—that is, conditioned and constrained—but it can nonetheless be actively exercised insofar as it responds to the universally human need to have mastery over oneself and one's own body.

The following question now arises: to what extent can a demand for autonomy of this kind—one that is closely tied to the body, to its potentialities, to its capacity to define autonomous spaces of action—be brought into relation with the domain of the law? To what extent, in other words, can the reach of law over the body be extended? It is true that law enhances individuals' capacity to act, insofar as it renders more flexible the boundaries between the various subsystems that constitute the social system. It is true that law can protect individuals from intrusive governmental interventions aimed at delineating too precisely the limits of individual action. But it is also true—and this is the question I am raising now—that it can be not desirable for the reach of law to be extended to the point where it encompasses every sphere of human action.

Every governmental intervention aimed at safeguarding individual life, for example, entails a non-negligible trade-off. As the concept of biopolitics suggests, even those measures intended to ensure all individuals a decent standard in terms of bodily health are inextricably linked to forms of control. Such control is not exerted externally with respect to medical practice, but operates directly through the construction of clinical protocols that govern the trajectory of individuals' pathways within healthcare institutions. To provide care, in other words, is also to act upon individuals on the basis of normative models that they have rarely the opportunity to negotiate. This becomes particularly evident in matters involving mental health, reproductive health (especially in the case of women), or decisions concerning the permissibility of ending one's own life—domains where the biopolitical governance intersects most intensively with both ethical and legal boundaries.

Even beyond the specific domains just mentioned, the issue of control over bodies constitutes a crucial aspect of the relationship between processes of subjectivation and biomedical practices, one that now deeply permeates all regions of the world marked by what Nikolas Rose refers to as advanced liberal democracies. In such contexts, the body is embedded within hybrid assemblages composed both of machines and discursive networks. The former aim to render visible the molecular dimension of the organism; the latter govern the production of a new conception of biomedical corporeality that no longer centres on the traditional distinction between health and illness. From the integration of the body into these hybrid assemblages arises the possibility of constructing a subject oriented towards self-optimisation, and it is here that a crucial element of novelty can be distinguished—namely, in the changing modalities of the relationship between individuals and biomedical apparatuses. If the primary objective is to combat illness, understood as a disruptive element capable of undermining one's state of health, then one will relate to the biomedical sphere only in situations of necessity or need. If, by contrast, the goal is the continuous enhancement of bodily performance and organ function, then the exposure to the biomedical sphere becomes constant and enduring. In this context, becoming a subject—that is, constructing one's individuality through a set of practices and narratives—entails allowing biomedical intervention to play a non-marginal role in shaping the characteristics of one's personal identity. More importantly, it means accepting the insertion of one's somatic condition into contexts where aspects of individual life can be rendered productive of value. Biopolitics, in the perspective outlined by Rose, is thus transformed into bio-economics: the biomedical apparatuses with which bodies interact, while enhancing individual performance, simultaneously feed bodily data into chains of value production. Those who allow biomedical apparatuses to intervene in their lives thereby consent to making available the data concerning their somatic condition to a range of actors whose aim is to capitalize the meaning of such data. In this way, the distinction between a healthy and an ill body gives way to a new binary: that between a marketable body and one that resists commodification. The transformation of the relationship between bodies and biomedical institutions entails the emergence of a novel attitude within individual life. Individuals are no longer encouraged merely to remain healthy, but are instead invited to manage the risks they incur should they fail to pay sufficient attention to the possible consequences of, for instance, the development of specific pathologies inscribed in their genetic code.[17]

This critical perspective on healthcare policies within advanced liberal democracies effectively captures certain salient features of contemporary governmentality. It rightly draws attention to the models of rationality—grounded in a neoliberal *Weltanschauung*[18]—that shape the very meaning of life and death. These models of rationality tend to integrate the value of life within a broader economic discourse, whereby health becomes a good to be preserved as part of an overarching investment in the self. Within such a framework, individuals are encouraged to assume responsibility for their health only insofar as it is conceived as an asset to be managed and optimized. As a result, the principle of individual autonomy risks being substantially undermined: healthcare ceases to be a means toward good life and instead becomes part of a broader logic of human capital maximization, where the body itself is rendered an object of strategic investment. Nevertheless, this analytical framework—while illuminating in certain respects—risks being both short-sighted and reductive. The lived realities of individuals in many parts of the world diverge sharply from those presupposed by critiques of Western liberal biopolitics. In contexts where access to even basic healthcare is lacking, and where life expectancy falls well below global averages, the concern is not the excess of regulatory intervention but the absence of

[17] Rose (2007).

[18] On the relationship between the performativity of economics and the establishment of shared mental models, see Becchio and Leghissa (2017).

meaningful protections. In such situations, the emphasis on the limitations of individual freedoms by healthcare policies appears misplaced. What characterizes these settings is not a regime of life-maximising biopolitics, but rather one in which life is reduced to exploitable material. This is particularly evident in certain African countries, where the extraction of national and local resources is controlled by political and economic élites who are not committed to advancing equity or public welfare.[19] In such contexts, individual paths are constrained by structural conditions of such severity that the question of the right to health—enshrined in instruments such as the International Covenant on Economic, Social and Cultural Rights—emerges as a matter of urgent global concern. A genuinely critical engagement with biopolitics must therefore remain attentive not only to the excesses of medical governance in affluent societies but also to the absence of care, infrastructure, and legal recognition in those regions where the very condition for life remains structurally unfulfilled.

It is therefore necessary to ask in what sense the right to health may be defined—a right that is intended to guarantee everyone the possibility of taking care of their own body in view of a good life. This right could easily be included among the list of universal human rights. Thomas Pogge, for example, in his reflections on the responsibility borne by humanity as a whole towards its poorest and most disadvantaged members, suggests precisely this inclusion.[20] Those who are poor have no access to the essential services that enable them to take adequate care of themselves. Pogge's arguments rest on an ethical universalism aimed at defining the ways in which the scope of human rights should ideally be extended—rights which must include the right to health. This universalism entails a substantial and original extension of Rawls' philosophical and political project, and prescribes the establishment of a human right to basic necessities. More precisely, it ought to be the duty of all citizens to ensure that any coercive social order they collectively impose upon themselves be one in which, as far as reasonably possible, everyone has secure access to primary goods.

Here, however, at least two problems may be identified. First, such a conception of universal human rights rests upon moral assumptions. In other words, this form of universalism frames human rights as moral claims concerning the organization of society. What is at stake here is not a theory of distributive justice that seeks to allocate a given quantity of resources or to improve an existing distribution; rather, it concerns the design of the basic rules governing property, cooperation, and exchange—rules which, in turn, shape both production and distribution. Such design becomes conceivable only insofar as a shift in mentality occurs that is profound enough to bring about a substantial transformation of the legal and political structures of a state, in accordance with moral principles presumed to be universally shared. And this is highly problematic: as noted above, the entanglement of the legal and moral spheres does not appear to be easily compatible with the complexity that characterizes modern social systems.

Secondly, such universalism acquires a degree of plausibility only if it is capable of operating on a global scale. In concrete terms, this would entail a transformation

---

[19] A classical study concerning Africa remains Bayart (2009).

[20] See Pogge (2008).

of the political and legal structure of all states—or at least of the majority of them. The problem is akin to the one addressed by Kant in his 1795 essay *Perpetual Peace* (*Zum ewigen Frieden*). According to Kant, lasting world peace—as opposed to a mere truce between successive wars—will be achieved only if all states adopt a republican constitution, defined by three key elements: guarantees of freedom for all members of society insofar as they belong the human species; the subjection of all members to a common system of legislation; and equality of all before the law. Furthermore, such a regime ensures full transparency and public scrutiny of decisions concerning collective life. This is not the place to present Kant's entire argument in detail; nevertheless, in relation to it, I wish to emphasise just one point: Kant's project stands if and only if all states are governed by a republican regime—it being undesirable that perpetual peace be achieved through the imposition of a world government capable of abolishing the sovereignty of individual states. If we accept the logic underpinning Kant's argument and apply it to the context in which global justice is discussed, we must draw the following conclusion: global justice will be attainable if and only if all states agree to adopt legal systems that promote the pursuit of a good life for all members of society, while ruling out the possibility that such system might be imposed by a world government that would undermine the sovereignty of each individual state. Yet here too, it is clear how difficult it would be to achieve such an outcome.

It does not seem out of place at this juncture to introduce the question of sovereignty. Sovereignty must remain the point of departure whenever notions are discussed which, for one reason or another, refer to the concrete realisation of projects with global ambitions. Without a state-based legal order that enacts laws and ensure their enforcement it makes no sense to speak meaningfully of law at all. And unless proven otherwise, every sovereign state asserts—and proves—its sovereignty precisely by promulgating laws and securing their observance. In relation to the issue at stake here, it is reasonable to suppose that significant shifts in collective attitudes within certain states may lead to the establishment of legal frameworks that provide explicit guarantees regarding the right to health—guarantees that enable access to medical care even for the truly disadvantaged. Such a situation cannot be observed in the United States, whereas it is present, for instance, in a country like Italy. Be that as it may, the relationship between the ethically grounded imperative to ensure universal access to basic healthcare services, and the construction of suitable legislative measures capable of realizing such access, remains a question that only makes sense within the boundaries of a nation-state. It is a question that gives rise to a number of dilemmas, both ethical and legal—dilemmas which, as Jon Elster among others has shown, can at best be met with provisional solutions, that rarely allow for an appeal to universally applicable principles of justice.[21]

---

[21] See Elster (1992).

4 The Capability Approach and the Pre-Political Meaning of Universal Rights

In order to avoid the difficulties that arise when the domain of universal rights clashes with the domain of law, I propose that the definition of the right to health ought to be situated within the bounds of a pre-political and pre-juridical domain. By this I refer to that domain which precedes the enactment of laws and norms. This sphere undoubtedly encompasses the formulation of ethical principles, which, as previously noted, maintain a fraught relationship with the domain of law. Yet it is also within this domain that the foundational principles to which a prospective legislator might appeal—prior to the establishment of any specific norm—are to be discerned. These are principles to which a rational agent may give their assent, having weighed their reasonableness. In other words, they are principles that remain closely tied to the anthropological dimension, insofar as they concern the way in which human beings typically and characteristically function. On the basis of such principles, one may construct a theoretical framework centred on the notion of the good life—that is, a life which may reasonably be regarded as choice worthy by any agent endowed with our general human characteristics. From such a framework, it becomes possible to formulate evaluative judgements concerning a given political or legal system. Yet it is important to stress that such judgements are not intended to subject law to moral adjudication; rather, their aim is to assess the extent to which a given institutional order enables those under its jurisdiction to choose and pursue a good life.

A theoretical approach of this kind is exemplified in the capability approach developed by Amartya Sen and Martha Nussbaum. As Sen puts it, the capability approach to a person's advantage is concerned 'with evaluating it in terms of his or her actual ability to achieve various valuable functionings as a part of living'.[22] This approach begins with the observation that there are certain functionings intrinsic to human beings, which underpin the capability of individuals to choose how to relate them to their own conception of a flourishing life. It stands in contrast to utilitarianism, which centres on happiness and pleasure—since human beings are not mere utility-maximising machines, the utilitarian approach overlooks the circumstances within which individuals make their choices. The capability approach thus emphasises the interdependence between freedom and economic situation: what matters is not the goods an individual possesses, but whether, through those goods, the individual is genuinely able to pursue a particular course of action conductive to his or her well-being. Likewise, it diverges from relativist perspectives, which overstate the dependence of individual life plans on the specific historical and cultural contexts in which persons act. It is certainly true that individuals choices are shaped by the environments to which people belong—environments governed by shared values and belief systems. Within such environments, individuals encounter readily available narratives that make certain life projects intelligible and conceivable; for instance, in order to desire a given thing, one must be able to conceptualise it as

[22] Sen (1993), p. 30.

a real possibility. Nevertheless, Nussbaum—drawing on an explicitly Aristotelian anthropology—argues for the identification of a set of capabilities that are universally human, and thus independent of historical and cultural variability. The list of capabilities is not derived by asking people what they happen to prefer; rather, it is grounded in an observation of what is universally human, with a view to the goal of leading a good life. In this list, Nussbaum refers to various aspects of human conduct, encompassing both one's relationship with oneself and with others. The purpose of the list is to provide legislators with the normative guidance necessary to ensure that all individuals are afforded genuine capabilities. That is, the legislator should not concern themselves with whether or how a person chooses to act with regard to the pursuing of a good life; what matters is, rather, that the individual is presented with the opportunity to make such a choice. If this possibility is denied, one may rightly say that the individual has been deprived of the opportunity to lead a fully human life.

As one might expect, the capability to enjoy good health occupies a central position in this framework, alongside the capability to be adequately nourished, to live in dignified housing, to satisfy one's sexual needs, to choose freely in matters of reproduction. Other important capabilities—related with what Foucault would term as the 'care of the self'—are the following: being able to live to the end of a human life of normal length, not dying prematurely, or before one's life is so reduced as to be not worth living. Other capabilities required in order to size up the boundaries within which a good life concern the possibility to be secure against violent assault; to be able to use the senses to imagine, think and reason; to have attachments to things and people outside ourselves, to love those who love us and care for us; to be able to form a conception of the good and to engage in critical reflection about the planning of one's life; to be able to live with and toward others, to recognize and show concern for other human beings, to engage in various forms of social interaction; to have the social bases of self-respect and non-humiliation; to be able to live with concern for and in relation to animals, plants, and the world of nature; to be able to laugh and play; to be able to participate effectively in political choices that govern one's life; to be able to hold property and to have the right to employment.

It should be clear that this list is aimed at providing the image of a relationship between individuals and the broader context within which they live that does not underestimate the differences that exists among humans, but is concerned, at the same time, with the necessity of smoothing the effects of the inequalities that may derive from those differences. In other words, Nussbaum's principal philosophical concern lies in whether and how the capabilities approach can inform the design of political and legal systems that may be deemed just by a reasonable observer—that is, systems that respect human dignity. Since her Aristotelian framework is explicitly interwoven with elements drawn from the Marxian tradition,[23] her position displays a radicalism that is absent from both classical liberalism and the Rawlsian model, despite her profound intellectual debt to the latter. This orientation also brings her close to positions such as that of Thomas Pogge, in the sense that Nussbaum, too,

[23] See Nussbaum (1990).

raises the question of how the international order must be structured if all human beings are to have genuine access to fundamental entitlements[24]—among which the right to health must undoubtedly be included. The distinctive strength of the capability approach, however, lies in its capacity to offer a theoretical framework that makes possible a principled distinction between the domain of law and that of morality. This aspect makes the capability approach particularly fruitful within debates concerning the right to health. That there are compelling reasons to regard this right as a fundamental entitlement is, indeed, one of the principal contributions of Nussbaum's account. At the same time, her philosophical framework makes clear that such a discussion cannot take place within the political and legal domain. The most that the philosopher—together, of course, with all other members of the *res publica*—can do is to remind the legislator of what Aristotle already affirmed in a well-known passage of his *Politics*, where he states: 'it is evident that the best constitution is necessarily the one under which anyone might live in the best way and live happily' (Arst. *Pol.* 1324a 23–25).[25]

References

Aristotle (1995) Politics. Translated by Barker E, revised with an introduction and notes by Stalley RF. Oxford University Press, Oxford

Bayart JF (2009) The state in Africa: the politics of the belly. Polity, Cambridge

Becchio G, Leghissa G (2017) The origins of neoliberalism. Insights from economics and philosophy. Routledge, New York

Calasso F (1954) Medio Evo del diritto. Giuffré, Milano

Dean M (1999) Governmentality. Power and rule in modern society. Sage, London

Elster J (1992) Local justice. How institutions allocate scarce goods and necessary burdens. Russell Sage Foundation, New York

Foucault M (1972) The archaeology of knowledge. Pantheon Books, New York

Foucault M (1978) The history of sexuality, vol 1: An introduction. Pantheon Books, New York

Foucault M (1982) The subject and power. In: Dreyfus HL, Rabinow P (eds) Michel Foucault: beyond structuralism and hermeneutics. University of Chicago Press, Chicago, pp 208–226

Foucault M (2003) 'Society must be defended': lectures at the Collège de France, 1975–1976. Picador, New York

Foucault M (2008) The birth of biopolitics. Lectures at the Collège de France, 1978–1979. Palgrave Macmillan, New York

Foucault M (2009) Security, territory, population. Lectures at the Collège de France, 1977–1978. Palgrave Macmillan, New York

Hart HLA (1948–1949) The ascription of responsibility and right. Proc Aristot Soc 49:171–194

Hayles NK (2017) Unthought. The power of the cognitive unconscious. University of Chicago Press, Chicago

Latour B (2005) Reassembling the social. An introduction to actor-network-theory. Oxford University Press, Oxford

Leghissa G (2020) Biopolitics. In: Vercellone F, Tedesco S (eds) Glossary of morphology. Springer, Cham, pp 55–59

[24] See Nussbaum (2006), especially chapter 5.

[25] Aristotle (1995), p. 255.

Lucrezi F (1995) Aspetti giuridici del principato di Vespasiano. Jovene, Napoli
Luhmann N (1999) Grundrechte als Institution. Ein Beitrag zur politischen Soziologie. Duncker & Humblot, Berlin
Luhmann N (2002) The cognitive program of constructivism and the reality that remains unknown. In: Theories of distinction. Stanford University Press, Stanford, pp 128–152
Marshall TH (1950) Citizenship and social class. Cambridge University Press, Cambridge
Nussbaum M (1990) Aristotelian social democracy. In: Douglass B, Mara GM, Richardson HS (eds) Liberalism and the good. Routledge, New York
Nussbaum M (2006) Frontiers of justice. Disability, nationality, species membership. Belknap Press of Harvard University Press, Cambridge, MA
Oestreich G (1969) Geist und Gestalt des frühmodernen Staates. Ausgewählte Aufsätze. Duncker & Humblot, Berlin
Pogge T (2008) World poverty and human rights. In: Cosmopolitan responsibility and reforms. Polity Press, Cambridge
Rose N (2007) The politics of life itself. Biomedicine, power, and subjectivity in the twenty-first century. Princeton University Press, Princeton
Schiera P (1968) Dall'arte di governo alle scienze dello stato. Il cameralismo e l'assolutismo prussiano, Giuffré, Milano
Sen A (1993) Capability and well-being. In: Sen A, Nussbaum M (eds) The quality of life. Clarendon Press, Oxford, pp 30–53

Giovanni Leghissa is Associate Professor at the Department of Philosophy and Educational Sciences, University of Turin; editor of *Aut aut*; and editor-in-chief of the online philosophy journal *Philosophy Kitchen.* He has published widely in Italian and English. His recent publications include *Per la critica della ragione europea. Riflessioni sulla spiritualità illuminista* (Orthotes, 2019); G. Becchio, G. Leghissa, *The Origins of Neoliberalism* (Routledge, 2016); *Postumani per scelta. Verso un'ecosofia dei collettivi* (Mimesis, 2015); *Neoliberalismo. Un'introduzione critica* (Mimesis, 2012).

What Is a Body? Law, Health, and Well-being in Times of Emergency

Mauro Balestrieri

Abstract This chapter addresses the foundational question 'What is a body?' from the perspective of legal epistemology, focusing on how the law conceptualizes, regulates, and transforms the human body in times of emergency, particularly during health crises. In these exceptional contexts, the body becomes both hyper-visible and structurally vulnerable, turning into a site of intervention, data extraction, and political scrutiny. Drawing on critical legal theory, Foucauldian biopolitics, and quantitative methodology, the chapter argues that the legal conception of the body is not fixed or universal but deeply shaped by the historical and technological conditions under which law operates. Emergency measures (such as lockdowns, biometric surveillance, and digital health tracking) disrupt the conventional distinction between public and private, rendering bodily autonomy increasingly contingent on collective imperatives and narratives. Particular attention will also be devoted to the concepts of 'medicalisation' and 'healthism', along with the political agendas they embody. Finally, through a specific focus on the 'quantitative turn' in health law and the rise of new digital technologies, the chapter demonstrates how moments of crisis tend to accelerate pre-existing trends toward the medicalisation and datafication of life, making the body the central axis around which legal and political transformations revolve.

1 Introduction

In times of global crisis, the human body emerges as an 'essentially contested concept' where legal, political, medical, and symbolic discourses intersect and clash.[1] Legal scholars, sociologists, and philosophers have long grappled with the 'problem'

[1] The expression 'essentially contested concept' is used here with reference to the well-known article by Gallie (1955), p. 170.

M. Balestrieri (✉)
Department of Law, University of Turin, Torino, Italy
e-mail: mauro.balestrieri@unito.it

M. Balestrieri and A. Cauduro (eds.), *The Legal Anatomy of the Body*, Ius Gentium: Comparative Perspectives on Law and Justice 142,
https://doi.org/10.1007/978-3-032-26434-3_6

of the body, that is, its undeniable biological reality on the one hand, and, on the other, the persistent difficulty of conceptualizing it within coherent cultural and juridical frameworks, including its ambiguous oscillation between life and death.[2] The body, as revealed by these diverse fields, is far more than a physiological organism; it is a deeply *politicized* and *regulated* entity, shaped by institutional practices and discursive formations. In a sense, the body may also be described as a porous concept, constantly awaiting to be shaped and subsumed within specific categories, in which the distinction between health and illness becomes increasingly subtle, intangible, and almost impossible to disentangle.[3]

This chapter proposes to explore the body through the epistemological lens of *legal anatomy*, that is, a framework that interrogates how emergency contexts—such as pandemics, environmental disasters, and systemic healthcare breakdowns—transform the meanings of health, rights, and political agency. By focusing on how these exceptional circumstances affect our understanding of bodily integrity and human vulnerability, legal anatomy invites us to rethink conventional notions of personhood and autonomy. Drawing especially on Michel Foucault's seminal analyses of the medical gaze and biopolitical governance, we will examine how the body is rendered passive, monitored, and reconstituted under the pretence of care, security, or optimization. The body becomes then a target of institutional attention: objectified, quantified, categorized.

In the course of the present analysis, however, it is essential to bear in mind a crucial point. What is termed an 'emergency' is not only, or even primarily, the extraordinary event but, on the contrary, is often revealed to be entirely ordinary and routine. Paradoxically, the most significant political categories of our contemporary world 'are losing their meaning', and what is frequently taken to denote novelty or exceptionality rests upon phenomena that are widespread, systemic, and yet—precisely for that reason—substantially beyond control.[4] Emergency contexts magnify and accelerate the ongoing processes of medicalization, bringing into sharper relief the fragile boundaries between treatment and control, care and coercion. The body becomes then a site of contestation, repurposed into medical data, the object of public health interventions, and a resource within the political economy of healthcare systems. Cities and liminal zones, populated by subjects who are neither fully healthy nor overtly ill but in a condition of 'quasi-health' or 'semi-illness', constitute the new habitats in which the human body is subjected to constant monitoring, categorisation, and potential exclusion.[5]

---

[2] See Machado (1998), p. 120. As Machado observes, within medical science no concept exists that does not, by necessity, engender specific practices.

[3] See e.g. the global emergence of the notion of 'body burden', denoting the progressive accumulation in our bodies of potentially persistent pollutants (such as microplastics, PFOA, and other similar chemical compounds) capable, over the medium to long term, of reshaping physiological processes and reframing the very parameters by which health and illness are defined.

[4] On the collapse of meaning in words fundamental to modern legal-political theory, see the provocative essay by White (1984).

[5] On the medical concept of 'semi-illness' in contemporary societies, see Bronzini (2013), p. 51.

Yet the issue at stake is not only how the body is classified in legal terms, but how it is understood at a deeper, ontological level. How, indeed, can we truly govern our bodies in times of emergency? What changes when rights are suspended, norms are tightened, and the law turns its gaze to the most microscopic, intangible, and almost invisible elements of ourselves? States of emergency bring the body into focus in ways that are both urgent and disquieting: the very notions of health and well-being, oscillating between the public sphere and private life, are redefined under pressure, thereby becoming the object of reconsideration or of a different regulatory framework. In such moments, the body is no longer simply *our own*: rather, it becomes a site of scrutiny and intervention, where scientific, legal, and economic forces intersect. Its meaning is shaped by conflicting demands: the protection of society, the defence of individual rights, the pursuit of efficiency. This chapter seeks to trace those tensions, to explore how emergency governance reshapes the space between biology and law, and to ask what kind of democracy is possible when our bodies themselves are drawn into the calculus of risk and necessity.

2 The Body Between Person and Thing

In a series of lectures delivered between 1980 and 1981, the French philosopher Gilles Deleuze, reflecting on the legacy of Spinoza's thought, posed the question: *What can a body do?*[6] At stake, in that context, was the power of affects, the expressivity of life, the becoming sensible of emotions. Deleuze could scarcely have anticipated that, some years later, we would no longer be asking what a body can *do*, but, more fundamentally, what a body *is*, that is, what its very essence might be. This fragile, precarious, malleable substance, assailed and continually challenged by pathological agents, unfamiliar substances, and resistant viruses and bacteria; this centre of gravitation for everything that happens around us: not only our feelings and passions, but also the rules that govern our civic life, our rights, our obligations, and our hopes for the future. In some sense, everything seems to oscillate around the body; and when questions risk becoming too abstract, it is precisely our sensory experience of the world that brings them back to immediate reality. The body is both the site of our actions and thoughts and the primary recipient of external forces including, above all, the law. Always situated at the crossroads of competing forces, the body emerges as a central stake in legal theory.[7] Contemporary thought, we might say, is nothing other than a juridical reflection on the body: on what it is, on what defines it, on its constant capture by law and regulation.

[6] Deleuze (2007), p. 43.

[7] For a discussion on the role of the body at the intersection of philosophical, legal, and anthropological thought, see Esposito (2014). For a specifically legal analysis on the 'discipline' of the body, see Hyde (1997).

This awareness of the body's fundamental significance stands at the heart of Maurice Merleau-Ponty's philosophical enterprise.[8] Although legal scholarship has rarely engaged with Merleau-Ponty's work, in one of his most important writings—*Phenomenology of Perception* (1945)—the French philosophers offers a profoundly original account of the body and its ontological status that implicitly suggests a specific legal conception of corporeality.[9] As Merleau-Ponty argues, no strict ontological separation can be maintained between the 'I' and the 'body' we inhabit.[10] Rather, the body appears as an opening onto the world, as the gateway to all the experiences it undergoes: it shapes our very way of living, how we visualize and fashion our lives, how we identify with ourselves.[11] Described as 'pre-philosophical' and 'pre-theoretical', this dimension is also, in a deeper sense, 'pre-legal': it arises *before* the law, constituting a raw form of worldly experience beyond political, juridical, or social frameworks. The body, we might say following Merleau-Ponty's thought, escapes the classic 'subject-object' divide, occupying a threshold that challenges traditional thought.[12] Illness, for example, offers a clear and compelling illustration of this primal experience: in the act of diagnosing a disease, it is not only the body that changes in appearance or function, but our *entire understanding* of the world, including our sense of possibility and our future plans.

To suggest that the body lies outside conventional philosophical categories, that it occupies an 'exceptional space' resistant to reductive objectification, is also to recognise that it inhabits a distinct legal sphere, one endowed with its own legality.[13] This might be described as the body's *internal normativity*: a domain of juridical force that resists straightforward subsumption under the standard categories of philosophy and law. The stark, oppositional divide between persons and things—between 'subjects' and 'objects'—which Merleau-Ponty so incisively interrogated through his phenomenological approach, has nonetheless long been taken for granted in legal thought.

As is well known, Roman law presents a famous classification of the entities that populate the world, theorized by Gaius and set out in his *Institutes* (1, 2, 8), which rests on the tripartition of 'persons' (*personae*), 'things' (*res*), and 'actions' (*actiones*).[14] This scheme distinguishes between individuals who possess legal capacity (persons), objects that may be owned or controlled (things), and the legal remedies or procedures available to enforce rights (actions). By allocating distinct functions to each of these categories, Roman jurists could delineate who or what could be subjected

---

[8] Shusterman (2005), p. 151.

[9] A remarkable exception to the indifference of legal scholars towards the thought of Merleau-Ponty is the excellent and inspiring volume by Hamrick (1987).

[10] Merleau-Ponty (2012), p. 73 ff.

[11] Ibid., p. 94: 'The body is the vehicle of being in the world, and having a body is, for a living creature, to be intervolved in a definite environment, to identify oneself with certain projects and be continually committed to them'.

[12] Morris (2008), p. 113.

[13] A dimension evoked also by Nussbaum (1995).

[14] See Gaius (1904), p. 13: 'Omne autem ius quo utimur vel ad personas pertinet vel ad res vel ad actiones'.

to ownership, by whom, and how rights might be affirmed or contested. Within that framework, the separation between those *sui iuris* ('of one's own right') and those *alieni iuris* ('under the control of another') hinges upon the legal availability of one's own body, that is, the capacity to distinguish between individuals who possess and directly administer their bodies, and those who on the contrary remain subject to decisions taken by others. In other words, the body itself functions as the *legal threshold* marking the presence of a life (*bios*) capable of legal and political self-determination, as opposed to a form of existence (*zoē*) which, though undeniably alive (as in the case of slaves), nonetheless remains restricted and subordinate.[15] In Roman law categories, in other words, life attains its highest legal standing only when it transcends mere matter and rises to a status of dignity and legal autonomy, what we call legal personality. Many commentators have challenged this strict tripartition, noting that even within Roman law there were grey areas, points of intersection where the boundaries between these categories appeared less clear-cut or direct.[16] Nevertheless, this framework was successfully transmitted through generations of Western legal culture, from Justinian's *Corpus Iuris Civilis* to the modern codifications, ultimately shaping the very core of private law reasoning.[17]

This amphibology, which situates the body midway between person and thing, has paradoxically led legal thought to overlook it as a distinct object of regulation. Strikingly, the body has never been addressed as an autonomous 'legal concept'.[18] Precisely because it straddles the boundary between the personal and the material, it has remained in the obscurity of an ill-defined domain, a state of ontological fluctuation in which a range of actors, from the Church and other religious authorities to the modern State and even the individual's own will, have contended for absolute ownership.[19] At times, therefore, attempts have been made to define the body at a 'zero degree', in terms that stand beyond any cultural context, and grounding its reality solely in scientific or biological knowledge.[20] Yet this approach does not truly resolve the issues; rather, it defers them, leading into an even more pressing tangle of problems. Without any apparent contradiction, thus, the body can be regarded as something sacred or something purely profane, as subject to an individual's absolute control or as a common possession shared by humanity at large. Similarly, the mere fact—so profoundly private and personal—that the body is capable of experiencing pain may be understood as the foundation of a universal ideal: that of fundamental rights, insofar as it acknowledges the one thing that unites us all, that is, our capacity as living beings to suffer both physically and emotionally.[21]

---

[15] This distinction became well known after the work of Agamben (1998), p. 8.

[16] Trahan (2008), p. 9; Kurki (2019), p. 31 ff.

[17] Watson (1974), p. 179 ff.

[18] Byk (1999), p. 265.

[19] See the fascinating historical analysis provided by Baud (1993).

[20] As attempted by Dierkens (1966), p. 27: 'each product of conception reaching a certain degree of development is a body. This body is neither a man nor a person because the body is not an abstract philosophical or legal concept. It is essentially an anatomical and biological reality'.

[21] Hunt (2007), Phillips (2013).

These issues are further intensified by biomedical and scientific advances, which increasingly challenge the very idea of body in several forms. Blood, organs, cells, gametes, and genes can now move beyond and between bodies, charting a largely unexplored and often highly contested terrain, wherein an individual's physical existence intertwines with the possibility of transcending the very boundaries of corporeality.[22] In some of these cases, the unexpected outcome of this persistent ambiguity surrounding certain essential components of the body emerges in the declaration of their partial inalienability, which leads them—once again invoking a category of Roman law—to be classified among the *res extra commercium.* The human body, thus, remains within the realm of 'things', and yet, for reasons of public policy, is withdrawn from economic or commercial exploitation.

Even the term 'property' becomes problematic when we speak of the body.[23] One of the principal objections to its use lies in the fact that it is things—chattels—that may be owned, not organs or the human body as a whole. This objection essentially restates Kant's warning that trafficking in one's bodily parts is aberrant as it negates human dignity and the right to bodily integrity.[24] It is also a way of arguing that 'subject' and 'object' cannot be separated, because to do so would be to concede the possibility of intermediate states that divide persons from things.[25]

This set of moral, philosophical, and medical issues have posed a considerable challenge to legal doctrine and courts. Historically, particularly in the common law world, there was a widespread tendency to classify the human body as *res nullius*: an entity that could not be acquired.[26] This notion, commonly referred to as the 'no property rule', initially arose in the context of cadavers but was soon extended to the living body, albeit with notable exceptions. Today, technological advances make it possible to dispose of bodily parts in ways once unimaginable, leading to a growing number of cases in which the assertion of property rights over biomaterials has been recognised, particularly when these serve a specific purpose (most often, in medical research).[27] All this is especially intriguing because it demonstrates how the body can be individually 'owned' by each person while also oriented toward collective purposes, assuming the shape of an 'intangible good', yet at the same time open to social uses. In this context, biomaterials, having moved beyond the taboo of property and into a nexus of relationships that expand the scope of possible uses, acquire a special legal status—one that increasingly points toward a broad

---

[22] The topic is now the subject of growing attention throughout legal scholarship. See at least Skegg (1976), Matthews (1983), Grubb (1998), Hardcastle (2007) and Smith and Deazley (2009).

[23] Herring and Chau (2007), p. 34.

[24] Kant (1963), p. 165: 'Man cannot dispose over himself because he is not a thing; he is not his own property; to say that he is would be self-contradictory; for in so far as he is a person he is a Subject in whom the ownership of things can be vested, and if he were his own property, he would be a thing over which he could have ownership. But a person cannot be a property and so cannot be a thing which can be owned, for it is impossible to be a person and a thing, the proprietor and the property'.

[25] Munzer (1993). For a critical view on this point, see Gerrand (1999), p. 60.

[26] Quigley (2018), p. 55.

[27] Quigley (2012), p. 661.

'governance strategy' aimed at regulating bodily resources in accordance with public interests, market demands, and ethical imperatives.[28]

These examples illustrate just how contested the very nature of the body can be from a legal perspective, that is, from its 'legal anatomy', as we have defined our approach. Every organ that composes our body, every tissue that covers it, and every cell that gives it structure ceases to be a mere 'private matter', becoming instead a political and juridical criterion for determining the nature of the person, a decisive point for future judicial rulings, or the proclamation of fundamental rights and statements. As in Kafka's famous short story, the law is *inscribed* on our bodies, marking them, shaping them, and altering their status and meaning.[29] In this 'second birth' of the body within the categories and practice of law, legal thought lends it a new physiognomy, artificially re-creating what nature had already brought into being.

We may then ask where contemporary reflection on the body stands, both from a legal perspective and from philosophical and political standpoints. As Kafka's final reference reminds us, the relationship between law and the body warrants renewed scrutiny. In the Western legal tradition, this centrality is most vividly exemplified by the writ of *habeas corpus*, where physical presence (being seen, touched, and presented) serves as a critical safeguard for the accused, almost as if to counterbalance the dissonant vision that Kafka himself presents.[30] *Habeas corpus* is the most essential legal vehicle through which individuals subject to the State's disciplinary power can seek a review of the legitimacy of their detention by demonstrating the very fact of their being 'naked life', that is, a life worthy of defence just because of its physical corporeality. The body—a category long overlooked—re-emerges in legal theory as if, paradoxically, only the concreteness of physical existence could lend substance to the edifice of conceptual thought and provide the ultimate line of resistance against arbitrary power.[31] In this sense, throughout the following pages, we must remain acutely aware of the central role of corporeality in the development of modern and contemporary conceptuality: despite its definitional undecidability, its conceptual complexities, and its status as a terrain of conflict and contestation, the human body remains the law's ultimate and inescapable stake.

---

[28] Wall (2015), p. 145.

[29] Kafka (1995), p. 140. On this point, see also McNally (2001), p. 229.

[30] Federman (2006), p. 4.

[31] As Halliday (2010) writes, *habeas corpus* is the legal measure that allows the judiciary branch to 'hear the sighs of prisoners'.

3 Biopolitics, Governmentality, and Their Legal Consequences

As we have seen, the body (and with it the very notion of life) occupies a central place in the history of legal thought. Indeed, we might contend that law, the body, and life form a triadic constellation through which modern legal thought has evolved and continues to define itself.[32] Within this constellation lie many of the most contested questions in contemporary legal theory and practice: from abortion and euthanasia to informed consent and the administration of medical treatment, from the financial governance of healthcare to the regulation of reproductive technologies, vaccination policies, performance-enhancing substances, and genetic engineering.[33] Each of these domains reveals the persistent tension between personal autonomy, collective interests, and the law's biopolitical reach.[34] In this sense, legal thought has always been, since its early beginnings, a 'biopower', that is, a way of intertwining life with its juridical regulation and with the discipline of its potentialities.[35] In this vein, to inquire into the body is to illuminate both the biological and the legal substance of the living being. As anticipated in the previous paragraph, what the Greeks called *zoē* (mere natural life) marks the threshold at which *bios* (political life) comes into being, signalling the processes through which individuals become objects of interest, care, and governance within the political-legal apparatus.[36] It is within this terrain that Michel Foucault's influence on modern legal scholarship has been most profoundly felt.[37]

Although Foucault never produced a monograph explicitly devoted to law or its institutional forms, he did not consider it either theoretically marginal or empirically insignificant. On the contrary, he recognised law as a central actor in shaping the very terms, models, and conceptual frameworks that underpinned his inquiries.[38] As we shall see, his theories have been particularly consequential for the history of medicine, for the relationship between health and political authority, and, most of all, for the *legal* implications these have had in contemporary social science. Briefly stated, the chief merit of Foucault's work does not lie in providing a *positivist* definition of the law (that is, what it appears to be or what it 'is'), but rather in tracing the successive stages of its *evolution*: how it originated, how it developed, and how it ultimately transformed.[39] His approach was less concerned with the thing in itself than with the

---

[32] Lindholm (2024).

[33] For a fascinating journey into the politics of life, the economics of population, and the practices of modern medical science, see Murphy (2017), p. 6 ff.

[34] Esposito (2008), p. 13.

[35] Ojakangas (2016), p. 6.

[36] See again Agamben (1998).

[37] For a brief account on the legal aspects of Foucault's theories, see Golder and Fitzpatrick (2009), p. 4, and Golder (2013), p. 1.

[38] Lawlor and Nale (2014), p. 243.

[39] Sullivan (2012), p. 106.

process by which it came into being, the transformations that shaped it, and, finally, the effects it produced.

This processual dimension of Foucault's methodology is particularly significant for the reconstruction of the power/knowledge dynamics that underpin these phenomena and, ultimately, drive their legal emergence. As we have noted, the body (and with it the concepts of health, well-being, and bodily integrity) has undergone a process of transformation that profoundly altered its very physiognomy. When applied to the question of corporeality, Foucault's method proves indeed both valuable and revealing: as he suggested, the body does not endure as a rigid entity fixed in time and space; rather, it is the product of power dynamics that modify our vision and practice of medicine.[40] The body, understood as the very idea of a continually 'becoming' body, is therefore always in flux, rendered porous to the power relations that traverse it, and finding crystallisation within different forms of knowledge, such as demography, statistics, health law, and medicine itself.[41] Yet in Foucault's own vocabulary, 'power' likewise lacks any inherent rigidity. Much like the body, it is composed of relationships ('microphysical' logics) that dispel an absolutist nature, yielding instead a more fragmented, relational, and open reality.[42] We should not, however, be misled by the notion of fluidity. While power relations and historical–political circumstances remain in perpetual flux, material conditions can—and often do—play a decisive role in processes of subjectification, sometimes in the starkest possible terms. These processes, in turn, generate a distinct juridical identity that serves as the fulcrum of normative discipline. This leads directly to two of the most significant concepts in Foucault's thought: first, the 'microphysics of power', a critical analysis of relations of dependency and control as they unfold in everyday settings, from the workplace to the doctor–patient encounter; and second, the emergence of a 'governmentality' of subjects, produced through the combined operation of sovereignty, disciplinary mechanisms, and the regulation of bodies.[43]

One of the key works in which Foucault undertakes his ambitious project of charting a political and legal history of the body is undoubtedly the first volume of *The History of Sexuality* (1976).[44] Here, rather than investigating the metaphysical essence of power, Foucault traced its historical expressions identifying two distinct 'technologies' of governmental control. The older variant—the *sovereign power*—was characteristic of medieval and early modern rulers who exercised near-absolute authority, grounded in the capacity to kill those who defied their dominance. By contrast, the newer technology—*biopower*—aims to optimize life, treating individuals and populations as objects of meticulous political administration.[45] Under

[40] Foucault (1995), p. 167, and Potte-Bonneville (2012), p. 36.

[41] Turner (1997), p. xi.

[42] Foucault (1980), p. 198.

[43] Tadros (1998), pp. 77–78.

[44] Foucault (1978), p. 135 ff.

[45] Rentea (2016), p. 5.

sovereign power, the central act was punishment: transgressing the law was tantamount to a personal affront against the ruler, often met with severe or public chastisement. Biopower, on the contrary, centres on fostering the well-being of citizens and ensuring their productivity, security, and happiness.[46]

But what, then, is the significance of this shift in sovereign power from an intrinsically punitive dimension to one that is, we might say, supportive and care-oriented? Foucault argued that this contemporary configuration started emerging in the eighteenth century with the rise of the 'human sciences', such as biology, political economy, and statistics, all of which offered innovative insights into human life. Biopower considers the population a *resource* that can be shaped through policies regulating birth rates, life expectancy, and other public health measures. This marked a stark break from the indifference that once characterized sovereign power, whose subjects were little more than taxpayers or conscripts. Now, Foucault argues, governments are often judged by how effectively they *manage* citizens' health and prosperity, employing measures like screenings, immunization campaigns, and socialized medicine.[47] Rather than wielding the sword to enforce obedience through fear and capital punishment, power assumes a more expansive and insidious form, wherein subtle processes of normalisation operate to shape and regulate conduct.

In mapping this cartography of the body between law and politics at the dawn of the modern era, Foucault's analysis highlights the interplay between two dimensions: the *micro* (individual bodies) and the *macro* (the population as a whole).[48] On the *micro* level, biopower manifests as a technology for guiding personal behaviour and bodily practices. Through health campaigns, compulsory education, medical oversight, and other 'normalizing' procedures, States and institutions subtly direct how individuals live, shaping everything from hygiene habits to fertility decisions. Rather than relying on the threat of physical punishment, such measures secure compliance through the production and dissemination of knowledge, reinforced by prevailing social norms and expectations. The individual body becomes then the focus of meticulous observation, categorization, and management, giving rise to what Foucault famously labels 'the medical gaze'.[49] At the same time, according to Foucault, biopower started operating on a *macro* level by treating the population as a strategic resource with an entire network of disciplinary practices. National governments, aided by biology, statistics, political economy, and management studies, endeavoured to track birth rates, life expectancies, morbidity trends, and general well-being to maximize productivity and minimize risk. Administrations implemented a variety of health practices, such as immunization programs or social welfare policies, that gained success not by the subjugation of individuals but by the overall enhancement of public health, security, and prosperity. According to Foucault, by making the collective body a focal point of governance, authorities effectively *reshaped* social priorities, basing legitimacy on how effectively they safeguarded and improved the population's welfare. This

[46] Dreyfus and Rabinow (1982), p. 168.

[47] Rose (1994), p. 53 ff.

[48] Foucault (1978), p. 139.

[49] Armstrong (1983), pp. 1–6; Gutting (1989), p. 120.

two-tiered system, operating both on individual and collective bodies, revealed a transformation in the nature of power itself: while sovereign rule was largely *reactive* (exacting taxes, inflicting punishment, and enforcing loyalty), biopower started functioning more *proactively*, that is, striving to mould behaviour pre-emptively and guide citizens to become healthier, more compliant, and thus more productive.[50]

We are thus brought back to the question posed at the outset of this study: through which practices has the body transformed into a substance malleable to power, and what medical-legal implications might this entail? Both the private politics of the human body and the public mechanisms of regulatory control converge upon a common objective: the governance of human life, a project that Foucault famously encapsulated in the notion of 'governmentality'.[51] He explained this idea through three related components. First, governmentality refers to the collection of institutions, procedures, calculations, and strategies that allow for a particular yet intricate form of power to function. This form of power specifically targets entire populations, uses political economy as its core body of knowledge, and implements security measures as its main technical framework. Second, governmentality captures a historical process in Western societies in which the governmental mode of power gradually gained primacy. Through this ascendancy, specialised administrative bodies, together with a host of new forms of knowledge, emerged and gained institutional recognition. Finally, Foucault understood governmentality as both a process and a result: the historical transformation of the medieval 'state of justice' into an administrative state beginning in the fifteenth and sixteenth centuries, which in turn progressively developed into what he called a 'governmentalized' state.[52]

Paradoxically, it is perhaps the least frequently noted dimension that here emerges as the most consequential. What, then, is the role of law within such a configuration, and what specific juridical consequences flow from this logic? A form of power aimed at disciplining individual life at the most granular level (measuring it, organising it, and integrating it into the bureaucratic machinery of the modern administrative State), inevitably demands a pervasive and continuous regulatory mechanism designed to shape practices and behaviour.[53] In this framework, law no longer merely punishes or sanctions; rather, it *conducts*, steering individuals toward collective aims such as prosperity and health, supported by normative framework and scientific tools designed to measure, quantify, and rank.[54] Far from sidelining legal authority, Foucault instead underscores how its meaning and functions inevitably expanded, revealing the profound interconnection between judicial institutions and a constellation of knowledge–power dynamics such as economics, statistics, medicine, and bureaucracy.[55] In short, the 'Foucauldian method' may be regarded as an essentially juridico-medical model, situated precisely at the intersection of modern political

[50] Rabinow and Rose (2006), p. 196.

[51] Foucault (1991), pp. 102–103.

[52] Lorenzini (2023), p. 25.

[53] Foucault (2003), p. 242.

[54] Gordon (1991), p. 19.

[55] Foucault (1978), p. 144.

technologies and the erosion of the rule of law, which illuminates how the strategies and mechanisms of power have found (and continue to find) their locus both around and within the body.[56] The body thus becomes the unceasing focal point of power's interventions: constantly shaped, standardized, disciplined, and directed toward specific managerial objectives. Within this genealogy of modern power, the technologies that converge upon the corporeal dimension stand as a critical proving ground for evaluating the resilience of the rule of law and the capacity of legal systems to safeguard fundamental rights.[57]

4 Medicalisation, Healthism, and the 'Docile Body'

There are strong grounds for arguing that the Foucauldian vision is anything but optimistic and, indeed, harbours a tendency that might almost be described as dystopian, particularly in its account of the enveloping and suffocating reach of institutional power.[58] At the same time, however, there are equally compelling reasons to note that the themes of the body, health, and well-being constitute a privileged object of power, which, perhaps even beyond Foucault's own anticipations, are only now beginning to attain full visibility. At key moments in European cultural history, prevailing philosophies of medicine played a decisive role in shaping conceptions of the human body and its defining characteristics. Conversely, the ways in which scientists have observed the body also reflects the cultural frameworks within which they themselves are embedded.[59] One way to define this approach is as 'constructivism', understood as the epistemological stance that regards knowledge as actively constructed through our cognitive and social frameworks. Although constructivism may risk oversimplifying the way in which medicine and law operate, it nonetheless emphasizes the body's malleability. Thinking along these lines entails envisaging the emergence of a specific paradigm which, in Foucauldian terms, may be defined as the 'docile body'.[60] Here, at the intersection of science and power, two distinct approaches to the study of the body have long been established: 'medicalisation' and 'healthism'.

In sociological literature, the term 'medicalisation' often bears a distinctly negative connotation. It is understood as a coercive process through which diverse aspects of life are subsumed under a rigid medico-scientific framework, typically maintained by an elite possessing specialised expertise, such as legal or medical professionals.[61]

---

[56] Driver (1994), p. 113.

[57] A theme that has assumed a central position in contemporary legal scholarship, and which has been incisively brought to the fore by Frankenberg (2014), p. 20.

[58] As noted, for instance, by Walzer (1986) and Taylor (1985), both however emphasising the 'unmasking' value of Foucault's work.

[59] Turner (2008), p. 11.

[60] Foucault (1984), pp. 180–182.

[61] Szasz (2007), p. xiii.

Influential voices in this debate, particularly in the 1970s, argued that medicine, understood as a system of knowledge and power, had come to dominate human life in a regulatory manner reminiscent of the role once played by religion, customary norms, or even tyrannical regimes.[62] Some scholars have gone further, arguing that medicalisation distances individuals from both awareness and responsibility for their own health, ultimately undermining, rather than improving, their overall well-being.[63] These perspectives emphasise the pervasive social control exerted by medicine and highlight the role of class struggle, where those with limited medical or scientific knowledge are placed at a clear disadvantage compared to individuals in higher socio-economic groups. From this perspective, medicalisation is viewed as a process that must be politically opposed and resisted, with the aim of safeguarding individual autonomy against the encroachment of expanding institutional and potentially despotic authority.

It is important to emphasise, however, that the term 'medicalisation' does not inherently bear a negative connotation. To 'medicalise' may simply mean framing a particular phenomenon in medical terms, without this necessarily amounting to *over*-medicalisation.[64] Today, for instance, we may speak of the medicalisation of life and death to denote those instances of medical intervention that accompany an individual from birth until death. Whereas birth is now increasingly conceived not as a domestic event as was often the case in the past, when women gave birth at home, but as one that takes place in hospital facilities, death too has ceased to be a 'private' matter.[65] The main issue arises, however, when the technical-scientific act of medicalisation is coupled with the *pathologisation* of the very phenomenon in question, thereby framing it as a potential disease. Consider, for instance, menopause, which, from a physiological stage of female ageing, can be reframed as a 'syndrome' to be treated through hormone therapy; the development of lively or restless behaviour in children, brought under the spectrum of ADHD and consequently treated pharmacologically; obesity, construed as a chronic disease; and even bereavement, regarded as a potential depressive disorder.[66] All of this echoes Foucault's insight that the categories of 'normal' and 'abnormal' are themselves social constructs. In this light, medical knowledge operates as a highly *disciplinary* force, establishing standards of behaviour, definitions, and classifications grounded in the very epistemological categories it produces.[67]

---

[62] Freidson (1970), and Zola (1972).

[63] Illich (1976).

[64] Conrad (2007), pp. 5–6.

[65] On the medicalisation of death and the possibilities for prolonging life—or, as some have suggested, for 'resisting death'—through the deployment of medical technologies situated outside the domestic sphere, see Hall (2019), pp. 14–15.

[66] For the debate on menopause, see Lock (1995); for ADHD in children and the expansion of diagnostic criteria, see Conrad and Potter (2000); on the myth of obesity as a chronic disease emphasised by health and cultural institutions, see Campos (2004); and on bereavement as a potential depressive disorder, see Horwitz and Wakefield (2007).

[67] Conrad and Schneider (1992), p. 8.

The centrality of medicalisation to our discussion lies precisely in its capacity to bring the body back into focus, a dynamic rendered especially visible in the movements that have sought to *resist* it.[68] First, for example, among homosexual movements, which have asserted that their sexual orientation should not be viewed as a 'pathological deviation' but rather as an expression of the sexual freedom of their own bodies. Equally, feminist approaches have strongly championed the 'right to choose' (as in the case of the right of abortion) in accordance with a woman's own will and without surrendering to hetero-direction imposed by a male-dominated or patriarchal power. These approaches may thus be described as instances of '*de*-medicalisation', in which the body emerges as both a mechanism of resistance and a means of contesting power. Once again, the 'medical gaze' operates as a mechanism of control, demarcating the boundaries between the regular and the irregular, the healthy and the pathological; and in so doing, it positions the human body at the nexus of a struggle that is simultaneously political, legal, and medical.[69]

If medicalisation represents the theoretical framework underpinning the indefinite expansion of medicine into every sphere of life, the concept of 'healthism' constitutes, from the other side, its most immediate practical and political declination.[70] According to some scholars, healthism indeed marks the ultimate culmination of medicine, a form that, in many respects, embodies its most problematic and perhaps most extreme consequences.[71] Traditionally, healthism is defined as 'the government's promotion of coercive health norms, and its attempts is to impose lifestyle choices deemed healthy on its citizens'.[72] As is evident, what characterises this definition is its direct reference to State practices, that is, to a legislative, normative, and above all disciplinary dimension whose true locus resides in the sphere of public intervention. Healthism articulates a worldview in which the attainment of 'perfect health' is construed not only as a personal responsibility but equally as a *civic duty*, thereby imposing obligations on both the individual body and the society as a whole. Being consistently healthy is regarded as something both patriotic and morally commendable, whereas falling into 'poor health' is tacitly conceived as a personal fault. Evidently, healthism—like all ideologies ending in '-ism'—can harbour troubling traces of discrimination and exclusion, which become particularly apparent in the workplace, where employers, whether in the private or public sector, may engage in differential treatment of individuals based on their perceived health status. Tobacco use, excess weight, and sedentary lifestyles are, for instance, often framed as matters of personal culpability. This framing calls for radical changes in individual habits but also, more radically, legitimises political measures aimed at discouraging such behaviours.[73] Additionally, as will be discussed in the following section, the rapid circulation of health-related data, facilitated by advanced tracking

[68] Williams (2001), p. 148.

[69] Lupton (1997), p. 96.

[70] Roberts and Weeks (2018).

[71] Crawford (1980).

[72] Roberts (2012), p. 1159.

[73] A perfect example of that is the famous analysis provided by Thaler and Sunstein (2021).

and monitoring technologies such as mobile applications, smartwatches, and other surveillance devices, highlights the problematic nature of attributing responsibility exclusively to the individual. Health outcomes are frequently shaped by aggregated and complex determinants (many of them systemic and structural, such as socioeconomic inequality, environmental conditions, and access to healthcare) over which individuals have only minimal control.[74] In this context, the pursuit of a 'healthy life' presupposes access to adequate resources and supportive infrastructures. If such discourses are not supported by public policies designed to improve living conditions, particularly for the most disadvantaged and economically marginalised segments of the population, the risk inherent in healthism is that it will reproduce, rather than eliminate, the very disparities it seeks to address, further compounding them through social and moral censure.[75]

We thus find ourselves within a highly intricate web of legal and moral obligations, at the centre of which the body, together with its health and well-being, becomes the focus of continual inquiry. As is well known, the existence of a specific normative dimension to the concept of health is made vividly clear by the guidelines issued by the World Health Organization (WHO).[76] According to its famous definition, health is '[a] state of complete physical, mental and social well-being and not merely the absence of disease or infirmity'. This definition has been subject to criticism from medical, legal, and philosophical perspectives, and it is not difficult to see that a state of *complete* well-being, encompassing the physical, the mental, and the social, is, in practice, an unattainable condition for any human being.[77] Furthermore, if we take seriously the scope of this definition and its implications for health policy, it becomes evident that the idea of health shared by the WHO is not merely descriptive but normative: the attainment of such objectives can be realised, indeed, only through the implementation of targeted practices, the imposition of regulatory policies, and the establishment of statistical and surveillance systems designed to manage populations and to channel them towards prescribed ways of life.

The historical context in which the WHO framed its now-canonical definition of health is well established. Firstly, it emerged from an atmosphere of growing optimism regarding progress in medical sciences and scientific research, coupled with the ambition to establish a truly universal right, equally extended to all citizens of the world. In this light, health was viewed as something intrinsically *positive*, a state toward which everyone naturally strives, and consequently as an element that governments are obliged to guarantee, promote, and ultimately achieve. A corollary of this logic, however, was the tendency to transpose all political and social issues, which unquestionably affect health, into a framework shaped and constrained by medical discourse. As it has been observed, the WHO has progressively reflected a broader cultural tendency to recast social problems in the language of science, thereby medicalising issues that might otherwise be more appropriately addressed

[74] Roberts and Fowler (2017).

[75] Schmidt et al. (2010).

[76] WHO (1948).

[77] Nobile (2014); Bickenbach (2017).

through economic policy.[78] Moreover, the conflation of health with well-being has proven to be one of the most contentious aspects of this definition, precisely because it blurred the boundary between scientific terminology and the language of political responsibility. This issue has recently been addressed by the WHO itself, which has now explicitly separated 'well-being' from 'health'.[79] Equally significant is the strengthened imperative to quantify health and to compare its varying levels, thereby enabling more direct forms of political intervention. As we can read:

1. Health is a separate concept from well-being, and is of intrinsic value to human beings as well as being instrumental for other components of well-being;
2. Health is comprised of states or conditions of functioning of the human body and mind, and therefore any attempts to measure health must include measures of body and mind function; and
3. Health is an attribute of an individual person, although aggregate measures of health may be used to describe populations.[80]

In other words, a *quantitative turn* in the concept of health has now powerfully emerged, reflecting a logic oriented towards the establishment of indicators, statistical indexes, and empirical measurements.[81] To see the body, to understand its functioning, and to treat it is, in effect, to *measure* it. From this perspective, medical science is inseparable from the measurement of health, and from the classification and hierarchical ordering of bodies. A close reading of the WHO's definition reveals that medical jurisdiction extends, thus, well beyond the treatment of disease: it encompasses a wide spectrum of ancillary practices, from the management of severe pathologies to the mitigation of risks associated with their emergence, and from preventive measures to the continual optimisation of the body's physical and psychological dimensions in everyday life.[82]

Surely, as the recent pandemic has shown, the concept of health occupies a central place on the political agendas of States.[83] It operates as a formative force, shaping individual choices, structuring our very sense of identity, and facilitating what Foucault aptly described as the 'technologies of the self'.[84] What is most significant, however, is that both at national and international levels, the body remains the central legal-political axis around which contemporary societies, now more than ever, continue to evolve. Human bodies become, again in Foucault's sense, 'docile': shaped, regulated, and redefined by prevailing medical paradigms. What is at stake, then, is understanding the extent of agency we still possess to avoid taking them, too often, 'for granted'.[85]

---

[78] Callahan (1973).

[79] Salomon et al. (2003).

[80] Salomon et al. (2003), p. 303.

[81] Davis et al. (2012).

[82] Rose (2007), p. 10.

[83] Coggon (2012), p. 22.

[84] Allen (2008), p. 1.

[85] On the strong idea of reclaiming and re-experiencing our own bodies, see Lupton (2012), p. 32.

5 Embodied Futures: Privacy, Digital Technologies, and the Quantitative Paradigm

As we have seen in the previous section, to speak of the legal status of the body is, unavoidably, to enter a domain in which political, legal, medical, and economic forces converge to construct the very notion of corporeality itself. The WHO has progressively embraced a model of health governance based on the quantification of populations, reinforcing neoliberal logics of control and optimization.[86] This is neither exceptional nor anomalous. Rather, it is a phenomenon of far broader scope, which has now acquired a systemic and structural morphology. According to leading scholars, we now inhabit a society markedly different from that of even two decades ago: a 'metric society', as it has been named, in which virtually every dimension of individual and collective life is subject to precise measurement and systematically transformed into data.[87] Data surrounds us, forms part of us, and, at times, constitutes the very core of our being. Even in the micro-practices of everyday life, where the development of digital tracking and measurement technologies (from smartwatches and mobile devices, to apps, cameras, and sensors) has created an environment of constant surveillance, we manifest ourselves through the measurable traces we leave behind. Running, for example, is no longer merely the act of running; it has become the measurement of the steps, the tracking of our route, the calories burned, and the heart rate maintained. Almost ironically, we have become the subject of our own quantification, that is, a 'quantified self'.[88] A question of great significance concerns, thus, the impact of such epistemological, political, and legal revolution, particularly as it bears on the body and on the rights to health in the digital age.

If the body is always something constructed and assembled, then the environment in which this anthropological transformation takes place becomes particularly significant. In the specialist literature, the term 'assemblage' is frequently employed to denote the complex of elements and instruments (comprising software, hardware, algorithms, servers, cloud storage systems, mobile devices, and other components) that work in concert to configure a sophisticated system of observation and tracking.[89] Our everyday, professional, and healthcare environments are, in effect, *assemblages* designed to extract information deemed relevant for the management of our bodies. The interweaving of human and non-human elements, of life and machine, gives rise to a distinctive mode of engaging with the body, in which the data extracted from such measurements becomes what might be termed 'lively data': personal information that, when aggregated on a vast scale, encompasses every aspect of bodily existence. This may include height, weight, blood pressure, lifestyle, sleep–wake cycles, and caloric intake and expenditure, as well as more sensitive indicators derived from continuous medical monitoring, ranging from insulin levels to the functioning of

[86] Kenny (2015).
[87] Mau (2019), p. 67.
[88] Lupton (2016), p. 16.
[89] Marcus (2006).

the lymphatic, nervous, or immune systems.[90] In short, the body in its entirety is reduced to a number, and this number, in turn, can be assembled, sorted, exploited, and commercialised in countless ways that render life itself intangible, fluid, and hybrid.

This scenario might easily be cast as a dystopian world, meticulously designed and regulated. Yet, paradoxically, it is our own everyday practices that remain the primary agents in moulding and reshaping our bodies. In this entanglement of the human body within new technological frontiers, these newer forms of 'technologies of the self' shift from instruments of governance to means of bodily experimentation, almost becoming, at times, a form of play.[91] Indeed, the term *gamification* is often used in this context to describe the process by which individuals actively participate in the collection and profiling of their own personal data, engaging in a large-scale digital competition that ranks daily lives according to measurable metrics.[92] Every app offers goals, milestones, rankings, and rewards; we are in competition with ourselves, with a model of health that is presented to us, and that becomes attractive because it is embedded in a routine of which we are both passive recipients and primary architects. This constitutes, we may argue, a newer form of 'self-care' in which the subject's active and autonomous agency becomes the principal instrument for a broader, cross-cutting surveillance cooperation. The body is part of a game in which the stakes extend beyond mere health, aiming instead at its maximisation, that is, the continual drive toward an optimal and absolute state aligned with the parameters set forth in the WHO's original definition of health. In this technocratic utopia, where health, happiness, and well-being converge in the fabrication of the 'perfect individual', the body emerges as the principal locus of biometric surveillance, while life, numerical data, and digital substance coalesce to the point of becoming almost indistinguishable.[93]

For some critics, this erosion of the line between 'offline' and 'online' signals an anthropological shift, redefining the very terms of human existence. In this regard, according to the Italian philosopher Luciano Floridi, the term *onlife* refers precisely to the complex, hybrid technological environment in which analogic and digital experiences coincide, intertwine, and overlap, creating trajectories that essentially alter the very substance of our daily existence.[94] The (somehow outdated) concept of privacy, traditionally understood as non-interference in one's personal sphere, has become the subject of profound rethinking, revealing its porous nature and the need for fundamental change. We are, in a sense, facing a 'privacy dilemma', exceedingly difficult to fully delineate in all its consequences.[95] While a vast body of critical literature underscores the risks to personal identity posed by the massive influx of data into

[90] Savage (2013).

[91] Braga (2021).

[92] For an insightful discussion on the political and philosophical implications of 'gamification' applied to health, see Ajana (2018), and De Cesaris (2021).

[93] Ajana (2013).

[94] Floridi (2014).

[95] Lupton (2017), p. 22.

platforms that operate within a capitalist logic, others argue that the dissemination and use of such information do not inflict real harm on the individual, but rather lead to an exponential increase in the possibilities for treatment and diagnosis of diseases, particularly as manifested through predictive technologies.[96] Artificial intelligence, by virtue of its capacity to analyse, compare, and yield insights from an extraordinarily vast corpus of data, can facilitate the detection of diseases at remarkably early stages (such as the onset of tumours, or acute neurodegenerative conditions that leave distinct traces in our DNA).[97] According to this view, the potential harm that big data may inflict on privacy should be carefully weighed against the advantages that might originate from the full sharing of information.

But perhaps, more than the focus on digital or tracking devices, it is the quantitative paradigm itself that marks the true epistemological turning point both in our conception of the body and in the theoretical foundations of health law. While surveillance systems have always existed and operated under different political regimes, it is the very idea of transforming something into a number that engenders an entirely new vision of the world. There can be no 'privacy dilemma' without acknowledging the quantitative transformation in how health is measured.[98] Similar to the language of competitive sports, what we now confront are scores, classifications, and rankings. Yet here, the decisive contest takes place not on the playing field but in the legal arena, where the stakes lie in how we define the boundaries of our own bodies and those of others.

References

Agamben G (1998) Homo sacer: sovereign power and bare life. Heller-Roazen D (trans). Stanford University Press, Stanford

Ajana B (2013) Governing through biometrics: the biopolitics of identity. Palgrave Macmillan, Basingstoke

Ajana B (ed) (2018) Self-tracking: empirical and philosophical investigations. Palgrave Macmillan, Cham

Allen A (2008) The politics of our selves: power, autonomy, and gender in contemporary critical theory. Columbia University Press, New York

Armstrong D (1983) Political anatomy of the body: medical knowledge in Britain in the twentieth century. Cambridge University Press, Cambridge

Baud J-P (1993) L'affaire de la main volée: une histoire juridique du corps. Seuil, Paris

Bickenbach J (2017) WHO's definition of health: philosophical analysis. In: Schramme T, Edwards S (eds) Handbook of the philosophy of medicine. Springer, Dordrecht, pp 961–974

Braga J (2021) Body, media and quantification. In: Ajana B, Braga J, Guidi S (eds) The quantification of bodies in health: multidisciplinary perspectives. Emerald Publishing Limited, Bingley, pp 15–28

[96] On the potential benefits that these technologies and the dissemination of data generate in the field of medical prognosis, see Skopek (2018), p. 30.

[97] Yang (2022).

[98] Southwood (2019), p. 167.

Bronzini M (2013) Le frontiere indefinite della medicina e la medicalizzazione del vivere. In: Vicarelli G (ed) Cura e salute. Prospettive sociologiche, Carocci, Rome, pp 51–85
Byk C (1999) The impact of biomedical developments on the legal theory of the mind-body relationship. In: Cherry MJ (ed) Persons and their bodies: rights, responsibilities, relationships, Philosophy and medicine, vol 60. Springer, Dordrecht, pp 265–274
Callahan D (1973) The WHO definition of 'health'. Stud Hastings Cent 1(3):77–87
Campos P (2004) The obesity myth: why America's obsession with weight is hazardous to your health. Gotham Books, New York
Coggon J (2012) What makes health public? A critical evaluation of moral, legal, and political claims in public health. Cambridge University Press, Cambridge
Conrad P (2007) The medicalization of society: on the transformation of human conditions into treatable disorders. Johns Hopkins University Press, Baltimore
Conrad P, Potter D (2000) From hyperactive children to ADHD adults: observations on the expansion of medical categories. Soc Probl 47(4):559–582
Conrad P, Schneider JW (1992) Deviance and medicalization: from badness to sickness, expanded edn. Temple University Press, Philadelphia
Crawford R (1980) Healthism and the medicalization of everyday life. Int J Health Serv 10:365–388
Davis K, Fisher A, Kingsbury B, Merry SE (eds) (2012) Governance by indicators: global power through classification and rankings. Oxford University Press, Oxford
De Cesaris A (2021) Quantified care: self-tracking as a technology of the subject. In: Ajana B, Braga J, Guidi S (eds) The quantification of bodies in health: multidisciplinary perspectives. Emerald Publishing Limited, Bingley, pp 49–67
Deleuze G (2007) Cosa può un corpo? Lezioni su Spinoza, edited by Pardi A. Ombre Corte, Verona
Dierkens R (1966) Les droits sur le corps et le cadavre de l'homme. Masson, Paris
Dreyfus HL, Rabinow P (1982) Michel Foucault: beyond structuralism and hermeneutics. University of Chicago Press, Chicago
Driver F (1994) Bodies in space: Foucault's account of disciplinary power. In: Jones C, Porter R (eds) Reassessing Foucault: power, medicine and the body. Routledge, London, pp 113–131
Esposito R (2008) Bíos: biopolitics and philosophy. Campbell T (trans). University of Minnesota Press, Minneapolis
Esposito R (2014) Le persone e le cose. Einaudi, Torino
Federman C (2006) The body and the state: habeas corpus and American jurisprudence. State University of New York Press, Albany
Floridi L (2014) The 4th revolution: how the infosphere is reshaping human reality. Oxford University Press, Oxford
Foucault M (1978) The history of sexuality, vol 1: an introduction. Hurley R (trans). Pantheon Books, New York
Foucault M (1980) The confession of the flesh. In: Gordon C (ed) Power/knowledge: selected interviews and writings 1972–1977. Pantheon Books, New York, pp 194–228
Foucault M (1984) In: Rabinow P (ed) The Foucault reader. Pantheon Books, New York
Foucault M (1991) Governmentality. In: Burchell G, Gordon C, Miller P (eds) The Foucault effect: studies in governmentality. University of Chicago Press, Chicago, pp 87–104
Foucault M (1995) Discipline and punish: the birth of the prison. Sheridan A (trans). Vintage Books, New York
Foucault M (2003) In: Bertani M, Fontana A (eds) "Society must be defended": lectures at the Collège de France, 1975–1976. Picador, New York. Macey D (trans)
Frankenberg G (2014) Political technology and the erosion of the rule of law: normalizing the state of exception. Edward Elgar Publishing, Cheltenham
Freidson E (1970) Profession of medicine. Dodd, Mead, New York
Gaius (1904) Institutiones or Institutes of Roman law. Poste E (trans),, 4th edn. Clarendon Press, Oxford
Gallie WB (1955) Essentially contested concepts. Proc Aristot Soc 56:167–198

Gerrand N (1999) The misuse of Kant in the debate about a market for human body parts. J Appl Philos 16(1):59–67
Golder B (2013) Introduction. Re-reading Foucault on law, power and rights. In: Golder B (ed) Re-reading Foucault: on law, power and rights. Routledge, London, pp 1–9
Golder B, Fitzpatrick P (2009) Foucault's law. Routledge, Abingdon
Gordon C (1991) Governmental rationality: an introduction. In: Burchell G, Gordon C, Miller P (eds) The Foucault effect: studies in governmentality. University of Chicago Press, Chicago, pp 1–52
Grubb A (1998) "I, me, mine": bodies, parts and property. Med Law Int 3:299–325
Gutting G (1989) Michel Foucault's archaeology of scientific reason: science and the history of reason. Cambridge University Press, Cambridge
Hall LK (2019) The medicalization of birth and death. Johns Hopkins University Press, Baltimore
Halliday PD (2010) Habeas corpus: from England to empire. Harvard University Press, Cambridge
Hamrick WS (1987) An existential phenomenology of law: Maurice Merleau-Ponty. Springer, Dordrecht
Hardcastle R (2007) Law and the human body: property rights, ownership and control. Hart Publishing, Oxford
Herring J, Chau P-L (2007) My body, your body, our bodies. Med Law Rev 15(1):34–61
Horwitz AV, Wakefield JC (2007) The loss of sadness: how psychiatry transformed normal sorrow into depressive disorder. Oxford University Press, New York
Hunt L (2007) Inventing human rights. W.W. Norton, New York
Hyde A (1997) Bodies of law. Princeton University Press, Princeton
Illich I (1976) Medical nemesis. Pantheon Books, New York
Kafka F (1995) In the penal colony. In: Glatzer N (ed) The complete stories. Muir W, Muir E (trans). Schocken Books, New York, pp 140–167
Kant I (1963) Lectures on ethics. Infield L (trans). Hackett, Indianapolis
Kenny KE (2015) The biopolitics of global health: life and death in neoliberal time. J Sociol 51(1):9–27
Kurki VAJ (2019) A theory of legal personhood. Oxford University Press, Oxford
Lawlor L, Nale J (2014) Law. In: The Cambridge Foucault lexicon. Cambridge University Press, Cambridge, pp 243–250
Lindholm S (2024) Jean Bodin and biopolitics before the biopolitical era. Routledge, Abingdon
Lock M (1995) Encounters with aging: mythologies of menopause in Japan and North America. University of California Press, Berkeley, Los Angeles
Lorenzini D (2023) Foucault, governmentality, and the techniques of the self. In: Walters W, Tazzioli M (eds) Handbook on governmentality. Edward Elgar Publishing, Cheltenham, pp 8–27
Lupton D (1997) Foucault and the medicalisation critique. In: Petersen A, Bunton R (eds) Foucault, health and medicine. Routledge, London, pp 94–110
Lupton D (2012) Medicine as culture: illness, disease and the body, 3rd edn. SAGE Publications, London
Lupton D (2016) The quantified self: a sociology of self-tracking. Polity Press, Cambridge
Lupton D (2017) Digital health: critical and cross-disciplinary perspectives. Routledge, London
Machado N (1998) Using the bodies of the dead: legal, ethical and organisational dimensions of organ transplantation. Routledge, London
Marcus G (2006) Assemblage theory. Cult Soc 23(2–3):101–106
Matthews P (1983) Whose body? People as property. Curr Legal Probl 36:193–221
Mau S (2019) The metric society: on the quantification of the social. Polity Press, Cambridge
McNally D (2001) Bodies of meaning: studies on language, labor, and liberation. State University of New York Press, Albany
Merleau-Ponty M (2012) Phenomenology of perception. Routledge, London
Morris D (2008) Body. In: Diprose R, Reynolds J (eds) Merleau-Ponty—key concepts. Acumen, Stocksfield, pp 111–120
Munzer SR (1993) Kant and property rights in body parts. Can J Law Jurisprud 6(2):319–341

Murphy M (2017) The economization of life. Duke University Press, Durham
Nobile M (2014) The WHO definition of health: a critical reading. Med Law 33(2):33–40
Nussbaum MC (1995) Objectification. Philos Public Aff 24(4):249–291
Ojakangas M (2016) On the Greek origins of biopolitics: a reinterpretation of the history of biopower. Routledge, London
Phillips A (2013) Our bodies, whose property? Princeton University Press, Princeton
Potte-Bonneville M (2012) Michel Foucault's bodies. J Br Soc Phenomenol 43(1):1–32
Quigley M (2012) Property in human biomaterials—separating persons and things? Oxford J Legal Stud 32(4):659–683
Quigley M (2018) Self-ownership, property rights, and the human body: a legal and philosophical analysis. Cambridge University Press, Cambridge
Rabinow P, Rose N (2006) Biopower today. BioSocieties 1:195–217
Rentea S (2016) Introduction. In: Prozorov S, Rentea S (eds) The Routledge handbook of biopolitics. Routledge, London, pp 1–10
Roberts JL (2012) "Healthism": a critique of the antidiscrimination approach to health insurance and health-care reform. Univ Ill Law Rev 2012:1159–1171
Roberts JL, Fowler LR (2017) How assuming autonomy may undermine wellness programs. Health Matrix 27:101–146
Roberts JL, Weeks E (2018) Healthism: health-status discrimination and the law. Cambridge University Press, Cambridge
Rose N (1994) Medicine, history and the present. In: Jones C, Porter R (eds) Reassessing Foucault: power, medicine and the body. Routledge, London, pp 48–72
Rose N (2007) The politics of life itself: biomedicine, power, and subjectivity in the twenty-first century. Princeton University Press, Princeton
Salomon J, Mathers C, Chatterji S, Sadana R, Üstün TB et al (2003) Quantifying individual levels of health: definitions, concepts, and measurement issues. In: Murray CJL, Evans CJL (eds) Health systems performance assessment: debates, methods and empiricism. World Health Organization, Geneva, pp 301–318
Savage M (2013) The 'social life of methods': a critical introduction. Theory Cult Soc 30(4):3–21
Schmidt H, Voigt K, Wikler D (2010) Carrots, sticks, and health care reform—problems with wellness incentives. N Engl J Med 362:e3
Shusterman R (2005) The silent, limping body of philosophy. In: Carman T, Hansen M (eds) The Cambridge companion to Merleau-Ponty. Cambridge University Press, Cambridge, pp 151–180
Skegg PDG (1976) Human corpses, medical specimens and the law of property. Anglo-Am Law Rev 4:412–442
Skopek JM (2018) Big data's epistemology and its implications for precision medicine and privacy. In: Cohen IG, Lynch HF, Vayena E, Gasser U (eds) Big data, health law, and bioethics. Cambridge University Press, Cambridge, pp 30–41
Smith SW, Deazley R (eds) (2009) The legal, medical and cultural regulation of the body: transformation and transgression. Ashgate, Aldershot
Southwood D (2019) In genes we trust: genetic privacy in the age of precision medicine. In: de Leeuw M, van Wichelen S (eds) Personhood in the age of biolegality: brave new law. Palgrave Macmillan, Cham, pp 167–183
Sullivan N (2012) Foucault's body. In: Turner BS (ed) Routledge handbook of the body. Routledge, London, pp 106–116
Szasz T (2007) The medicalization of everyday life: selected essays. Syracuse University Press, Syracuse
Tadros V (1998) Between governance and discipline: the law and Michel Foucault. Oxford J Legal Stud 18(1):75–103
Taylor C (1985) Foucault on freedom and truth. In: Philosophical papers. Cambridge University Press, Cambridge, pp 152–184
Thaler RH, Sunstein CR (2021) Nudge: the final edition. Penguin Books, London

Trahan J-R (2008) The distinction between persons & things: an historical perspective. J Civ L Stud 1(1):9–20
Turner BS (1997) Foreword: from governmentality to risk, some reflections on Foucault's contribution to medical sociology. In: Petersen A, Bunton R (eds) Foucault, health and medicine. Routledge, London, pp ix–xxi
Turner BS (2008) The body and society: explorations in social theory, 3rd edn. SAGE Publications, London
Wall J (2015) Being and owning: the body, bodily material, and the law. Oxford University Press, Oxford
Walzer M (1986) The politics of Michel Foucault. In: Hoy DC (ed) Foucault: a critical reader. Blackwell, New York, pp 51–69
Watson A (1974) Law making in the later Roman Republic. Clarendon Press, Oxford
White JB (1984) When words lose their meaning: constitutions and reconstitutions of language, character, and community. University of Chicago Press, Chicago
WHO (1948) Constitution. World Health Organization, Geneva
Williams SJ (2001) Sociological imperialism and the profession of medicine revisited: where are we now? Sociol Health Illn 23(2):135–158
Yang CC (2022) Explainable artificial intelligence for predictive modelling in healthcare. J Healthc Inform Res 6:228–239
Zola IK (1972) Medicine as an institution of social control. In: Conrad P (ed) The sociology of health and illness: critical perspectives, 6th edn. Worth, New York, pp 404–414

Bodies of Risk. Medicine, Law, and the Paradox of Decision-Making in Health Crises Analysed Through Social Systems Theory

Alberto Giustiniano

Abstract In early societies, disease was often perceived as a random, natural phenomenon tied to moral transgressions. Modern societies, however, frame illness through the lens of medical science, emphasizing risk management and decision-making. This shift has redefined the understanding of health, moving from a deterministic view of nature to one of human intervention, particularly through medicine. The distinction between risk and danger becomes pivotal: risk emerges internally, as a product of decisions, while danger is seen as an external threat. The COVID-19 pandemic highlights this complexity, where decisions by authorities about prevention and treatment produced divergent perceptions—what decision-makers saw as necessary risks, the public often experienced as dangers. Through the theoretical framework of Niklas Luhmann, we can analyse this tension between risk and observation, focusing on how different actors perceive responsibility. The body becomes a site of this legal-sociological negotiation, as decisions about medical treatment, quarantine, and public health measures reshape how we understand both personal and collective safety. Consensus, then, is less about aligning interests and more about managing the inevitable dissent that emerges in crisis.

1 Introduction

Any onset of disease in early human societies was seen as an apparently random event produced by ungovernable and mysterious 'Nature'. Given the limited options available to control any such event, solutions to attribute some form of responsibility and causality was found by duplicating natural order in a different and 'socially-manageable' type of order: morality. There needed to be a way to trace illness and disease back to a negative form of moral behaviour. Doing so could help justify

A. Giustiniano (✉)
Department of Philosophy, University of Turin, Torino, Italy
e-mail: alberto.giustiniano@unito.it

M. Balestrieri and A. Cauduro (eds.), *The Legal Anatomy of the Body*, Ius Gentium: Comparative Perspectives on Law and Justice 142,
https://doi.org/10.1007/978-3-032-26434-3_7

the manifestation of disease in a way that went beyond a purely ever-present potential 'divine whim', and thereby counterbalance this perception of 'randomness' by linking it to the natural order of things. Individuals were an integral part of this order and could therefore count on a certain margin of manoeuvre, at least in terms of their independent freedom to adapt, or suffer the consequences.

The early modern age saw the beginning of a long process that led to today's technologically-developed societies where disease definitively lost these theological and moral connotations. It has now come to be identified with abnormal organic or psychological physical states that can only be effectively treated with the help of science, especially physics, chemistry, biology, and certain specific techniques. The connection is no longer to a harmonious relationship with the natural order of things but to medicine. In terms of the evolution of social semantics, this shift also witnesses a restructuring of the temporal dimension, and a corresponding increase in contingency attributed to actions or experiences undergone by individuals. In other words, there are different connotations to how we portray uncertainty in contemporary society, and these are linked to the fact that we conceive the past and the future as 'open horizons' separated by an elusive and somewhat ambiguous midpoint; the observer's present.

With these presuppositions in mind, the concept of time becomes a reason for reflection: the future is created by observers on the basis of their present expectations regarding continuity and discontinuity they have experienced in the past, so that even those events that are considered to be constant each time they occur, may actually be subject to change.[1] Therefore, if we wish to understand how diseases nowadays come into existence and then begin to spread, it is not sufficient to simply, and conveniently, accept some kind of supposed natural order. On the contrary, we must turn to doctors and their knowledge—a knowledge based on statistical-causal correlations, and a knowledge that legitimises the expectation that we can always intervene to a certain extent. The effect is that of building a multidimensional future where we can not only distinguish between a multitude of causes and recurring events, but also between a multitude of ways to attribute a range of causes and responsibilities. The focus shifts from a generally standardized arrangement of things, defined as 'Nature', to medical intervention, and this shift redefines the entire 'constellation of attributions' on the basis of the distinction between risk and danger. Everything now depends on what decisions will be made both in order to prevent disease and regarding the type of treatment.

Research into the concept of risk over the last few decades has clearly demonstrated that in this situation the idea of health, or safety, loses any plausible empirical correlation. It is no longer a question of seeking to guarantee and maintain ideal conditions, but rather, creating different forms of uncertainty that are more or less sustainable.[2] This in turn leads to the paradoxical conclusion that in order to achieve certain benefits in terms of health and safety, it is necessary to accept the possibility

---

[1] See Koselleck (1979).

[2] Discussion on this issue has reached uncontrollable proportions. We limit ourselves to citing three classics on the matter: Douglas and Wildavsky (1982), Beck (1986) and Luhmann (1991b).

of harm. This generates a 'loop' in which decision-making and forms of uncertainty are inevitably linked, with problematic legal issues as an inevitable consequence of this. We need no better, or more dramatic, example than events during the recent COVID-19 pandemic.

Our essay aims to use Niklas Luhmann's theory of social systems to explore this issue. In particular, we will focus on the relationship between observation and risk. If external dangers are always accompanied by risks that we generate internally by reason of our own independent decisions, what then happens when these external dangers coincide with the potential consequences of decisions taken by another person which also involve us? These two perspectives exist in apparent irreconcilability, given that the risk taken by the decision-maker is perceived as a danger by the observer involved in that decision. Within this structure of incompatible expectations, we are able to recognise the conflict matrix that arises during health crises when we attempt to govern by means of prevention and containment measures. The question then is whether, and how, we can create agreement, i.e. consensus, based on dissent.

Our discussion of this topic and relative considerations will be outlined below and divided into three parts.

Section one will introduce some core concepts involving the theory of social systems: the difference between system and environment, the individual as a structure comprising three distinct systems—the organism, mind and social status (in this theoretical context, hereby referred to as a 'person').

Section two will introduce social system concepts, where this system is understood as consisting of operations whose ultimate elements are communication and functional differentiation. Medicine, and specific characteristics and features of medicine, will then be collocated and examined as a specific subsystem within this more generalised view of 'society'.

Finally, the third and final section will explore one aspect of how disease is treated in a public 'domain', or namely, the role of collectively-binding decision-making in preventing health risks, i.e. its relationship with other society subsystems such as politics and law.

2 Health and Disease in Systems Theory

The theory of social systems uses a complex concept map, or framework, to study its subject of interest. However, unlike other paradigms, this framework consists of dissimilarities between the interconnected elements. The main difference that guides and shapes the entire matter is that between 'system' and 'environment'. A system can only exist in an environment to which it must relate, in order to constantly produce those operations that define it, and distinguish it from the environment itself. In order to continue to 'be' itself, the system must continue to refer to itself, and to the network of its own interconnected operations in order to 'reproduce' itself, or rather, regenerate that specific set of relationships that cannot be confused with the environment. Were that not to happen, the system would dissolve and cease to be. However, if this is the case, then it is also true that the system must continually use the environment to redefine its distinction from that same environment, while, at the same time, internally regulating the issue of how it 'closes' and 'opens' this relationship. In this sense, Luhmann defines the system as being autopoietic and self-referential; in order to preserve its identity within the environment, it must be able to incorporate into itself the difference system/environment and use it to guide its operations and continue to exist. In other words, the system is both 'closed' and 'open' because its ability to regenerate depends not only on the 'history' of its connections between operations, but also on disturbance from the external environment that contributes to producing the conditions for how it chooses to select these connections.[3]

This conceptual model has been used and further developed to understand the dynamics that lead to the reproduction of health and the onset of disease in living systems, and also to develop strategies to deal with, and influence, system reproduction (treatment or therapy).[4] Health and disease can be interpreted as the potential outcomes of the reproduction of living systems. In the first case, it is a positive outcome. The system shows an improved capacity to function (well-being), and this over the long-term translates into longevity, i.e. the expected length of survival measured as 'life expectancy', and the expected 'quality of (future) life'. In the second case, the outcome is negative (unhealthiness) and we witness a malfunction, or disability, of the living system, which, in some cases, may well be fatal.[5]

The system-oriented approach therefore suggests focusing on the fact that health and disease are strictly linked to the outcome of a living system's continuous reproduction in its environment. Their alternation gives rise to fluid and remarkably malleable dynamics, since systems use structures and processes to reproduce their own operations. Structures can be described as being defined environments where operations and processes connect. Processes, on the other hand, can be considered as sequences of irreversible operations. The difference between the two, if we consider them on a temporal scale, is somewhat blurred and indistinct. Processes and structures interpenetrate in every system, including living organisms. The anatomy of an organism undoubtedly determines its processes. However, it is also true to say that these processes, observed as behaviours, also modify to a certain extent the anatomy itself. Without diving too deeply into the technicalities of the theory, it can still be seen that the processes and structures that govern how system operations are reproduced act as enablers or inhibitors of effects—both in relation to their environment and themselves—according to a cybernetic logic.[6] A living system reproduces itself within its environment, and thanks to its environment. Doing so, the specific outcome of its actions generates results that have an impact both on itself and its

[3] Luhmann (1984), pp. 34 ff, (1991b), pp. 66 ff, (1997), pp. 60 ff.

[4] See Simon (1993), Simon (1995), Bauch (1996), Bauch (2000), Pelikan (2007a), Röthlin (2007) and contributions collected under Bauch (2017). For a detailed overview of the available bibliography, see Pelikan (2007b).

[5] Pelikan (2007a), pp. 75–76.

[6] Pelikan (2007a), pp. 76–78. See Luhmann (1984), chap. 8.

environment. However, it also generates a series of unforeseen internal and external effects as a simple consequence of its actions. This means that the reproduction of the living system over time can act as a catalyst for the creation of both salutogenic and pathogenic internal or external processes and structures in a constant state of renewal and with limited options as regards their control.[7]

The emphasis placed on the ways in which system and environment interrelate reciprocally clearly demonstrates the circular nature of this phenomenon. In fact, the conditions that enable the system to function well (namely, resources) or poorly (namely, risk factors) can be found equally in both the system and the environment as a metastable product of their interaction.[8] On a practical level, an observer is therefore in a position to decide in any given situation which of the two sides to act on in order to take corrective action. However, more importantly, this interrelationship makes any difference between health and disease conceptually much more complex. Thanks to the reproduction of the system's operations, health and disease are two interconnected conditions which coexist along a temporal continuum. The correct functioning of an organism will generate a new state of health but, inevitably, also age and, therefore, potentially generate disease.

This dichotomous alternative between the two conditions is not negated by theory but rather set within a broader framework in which it manifests solely as a subset in instances of particular prominence. Moreover, this is demonstrated by the possibility of recovery. If illness totally excluded health, it would not be possible for the organism to activate the resources needed to overcome it and, conversely, if health completely excluded any possibility of becoming ill, we would achieve an ideal state far removed from the biophysical conditions typical of organisms.[9]

We will discuss the social consequences of this model later on. However, for now, it is suffice to highlight that, for practical reasons, and from a medical-health point of view, it is undoubtedly useful to once again distinguish between health and disease, in a (so-to-speak) 'ideal' sense. In other words, how these two opposites effectively merge, especially on a practical level, within the perspective of their impact on resources in relation to health, and risk factors in relation to illness. Work in this context will show how health and disease influence each other directly and independently, but how interactive processes also have an indirect effect on each other.

There are four social strategies for managing these potential variations[10]:

1. Reactive treatment to the onset of disease.
2. Prophylaxis based on risk factor control.

[7] See Antonovsky (1996) and Hafen (2007).

[8] 'Within the ecological discourse oriented at sustainability, the effects of the reproduction of a system on its environment are observed: the relevant distinction here is whether these effects of system reproduction are making this environment more or less salutogenic or pathogenic for the quantity and quality of survival of this or similar kinds of living systems in the future', Pelikan (2007a), p. 77.

[9] Pelikan (2007a), pp. 78–79.

[10] Pelikan (2007a), pp. 80–82.

3. Proactive health care by monitoring functions, providing the organism with adequate resources and taking specific protective measures.
4. Implementing and supporting practices to become, and stay, heathy by training, exercising and doing rehabilitation.

This is by no means a hard and fast division. The boundaries between the different strategies are hazy and the four are often used in combination. However, in the context of what we will go on to discuss, the aspect to emphasise is that these strategies always have a dual effect that impact on both the system and its environment. This is regardless of whether they are directly aimed at changing how the system functions, or the relative conditions of possibility that surround it. Indeed, if we consider the fact that each system is located in other systems' environments, we realise that any action—obviously, with significant differences in terms of impact and visibility—has a certain repercussion on the environment and therefore on all the other systems involved. Actions and investments in salutogenesis that target the system or its environment can have positive effects on many organisms simultaneously, and can improve resistance to other potential diseases in the long term. The problem is that the opposite is also true. Any action carries with it the chance that risk factors may emerge that are unforeseen, limited to specific targets, or due to other factors such as the impact on the availability of limited resources, etc. Therefore, the option to intervene, regardless of how, is never risk-free if seen in terms of scale or time. The 'neutrality' of action is no longer conceivable.[11]

The conceptual framework we have presented up to now becomes even more sophisticated by the involvement of the systemic approach when it comes to identifying the recipient of these conditions of well-being or ill-health, i.e. the human being. In line with how WHO[12] defines health, the subject of a health-related condition, and therefore the subject upon which any health-related actions will focus, enjoys certain characteristics that do not allow it to be treated as a single autopoietic system. According to Luhmann's definition, we find ourselves dealing with a system solely when we are in the presence of 'operational closure', i.e. when we can identify a specific operation that occurs exclusively within itself—thus distinguishing it from an 'environment'.[13]

If we apply this definition to human beings, we immediately realise that it is extremely complicated and controversial to identify a single characteristic operation whose action distinguishes it from its environment—unless we admit the presence

[11] Michel Foucault understood the structure and importance of this new interpretative model. In his writings, it is referred to as 'safety mechanism', as opposed to 'law' and 'discipline'. As with Luhmann, he generalised it as a characteristic form of modern Western rationality, albeit with different objectives and awareness. See, for example, Foucault (2005), pp. 32–48, pp. 51ss.

[12] 'Health is a state of complete physical, mental and social well-being and not merely the absence of disease or infirmity', WHO (1946), p. 1.

[13] Luhmann (1986a).

of concepts dating back to metaphysical traditions (e.g. the soul or the transcendental subject). By using expressions such as 'soul' or 'subject', traditional European thinking has primarily sought to cover up this difficulty.[14]

The conceptual nature of the systems theory offers the opportunity to develop an alternative description of a human individual bearer of health—and a description that is both more comprehensive, and in line with experience. This approach sees the individual as the result of a set of three separate, yet interdependent, autopoietic systems: the organic system, the psychic system and social status. The organic system corresponds to the living organism, and its autopoiesis is characterised by the metabolism's biochemical operations which maintains what a person calls the 'body'. The psychic system involves consciousness, and its operations are perception and thoughts that occur recursively over and over again. While this division may seem initially disconcerting, closer analysis shows that it is simply based on the somewhat banal observation that even if the organism and consciousness operate on two different media—one matter, and the other through the senses—they cannot in any way determine each other directly, even while remaining mutually open at a causal level. The flow of thoughts with its changing contents is in no way dependent on the body, even though the body is able to provide stimuli which consciousness is able to grasp—thanks to its structures—and use for its own purposes. Similarly, the body's biochemical reactions cannot be directly produced by thought, even though the perceptions of consciousness allow the body to be guided towards its maintenance (but also hinder it). Therefore, support for this idea does not mean supporting the possibility that a mind may exist in the absence of a living organic substrate that supports at a 'material' level, but, rather, means focusing on how two systems, which are simultaneously both autonomous and interdependent, can co-evolve.

To describe this situation in systems theory, we talk about structural coupling or interpenetration: each of the systems involved acts as a necessary environmental prerequisite (which therefore cannot be produced or guaranteed) for the other's operations to be reproduced. The psychic system is coupled to the organism's neurophysiological structures, but this does not mean that its thoughts must reflect the behaviour of the body. If anything, one's 'own body', with which consciousness identifies, allows it to understand the difference between 'itself' and something 'other than itself' to the extent that its 'own' body is perceived as the only thing that can be felt simultaneously from both the outside and the inside, for example in the form of weight or pain. It is precisely because of the uniqueness of this experience that consciousness is able to distinguish other bodies and other objects respectively as things that, while recognisable as bodies, are positively presented as 'bodies-that-are-not-mine' or as things that are neither 'my-own-body' nor 'another's body'. The psychic system therefore operates on the basis of complex premises that are guaranteed by another system in an environment, without these premises being included in the system. The resulting effect is that of a high level of internal operational autonomy.[15]

---

[14] See Luhmann (1989).

[15] See Luhmann (1984), pp. 346 ff., and Luhmann (1995a).

As regards social status, we need to remember that here we are not talking about a system in itself, but rather a communicative structure that communication uses to refer to stable identities known as 'people'. The concept of 'person' in this context, therefore, does not refer to an individual's body or consciousness, but to a social structure that allows us to find an orientation for the production of communications, i.e. to assign responsibility, such as decisions, and to identify opportunities to understand communications by others, i.e. expectations.[16] Status is a social artefact and essentially pinpoints those contexts in which a person might be expected to behave in a relatively defined way; what we can call 'roles'. When we enter a doctor's office, we do not expect to have to sing, but we would not be surprised if we were asked to undress.

This brings us to the third system that contributes to creating the human individual bearer of health, namely, the social system, and its specific operations, the communications.

Luhmann saw communications as a complex operation. He considered it to be the result of the synthesis of three selections: the act of communicating (or, utterance), information, and understanding the difference between utterance and information. In short, communication does not consist in transmitting information from one consciousness to another (impossible in itself due to the autopoietic closed nature of each consciousness). Communication occurs when Ego understands that Alter has uttered information; solely in this case. The emphasis is on understanding. This is what distinguishes the scope of communication from that of perception, and consequently marks the difference between psychic systems and social systems. Moreover, a consciousness that simply perceives something, such as the sound of water or the distant light from a star, is not automatically communicating, because it is not necessarily possible to distinguish between an act of utterance and the uttered information.[17] In other words, from the point of view of consciousness, communicating means attributing selections to another consciousness in conditions of mutual intransparency (black box). Since—due to its inaccessibility—Alter's selections are always unpredictable and contingent for Ego, a situation of double contingency arises between the two. In this situation of social contingency, any chance to mutually coordinate take the form of a dual horizon of interwoven perspectives, such as: 'I will do what you want if you do what I want'.[18]

A new autonomous systemic order—the social system—emerges from this tautological circularity. This system produces interruptions and asymmetries and generates how we coordinate selections—what we call communication. This coordination continuously creates new information, or rather, specific selections that are capable of restructuring expectations. Therefore, specific communications are not created by consciousness, but are, instead, the product of a recursive network of further communications that defines the autopoietic unity of a social system. Indeed, understanding does not only act in its psychic quality as the genesis of thought, but also

[16] Luhmann (1995b).

[17] Luhmann (1995c).

[18] Luhmann (1984), pp. 148 ff.

as a selection for future communication. In this latter case, it takes on the role of a premise for potential new communication that may potentially be connected to the previous communication, regardless of the thought it produces on a psychic level. In other words, the event of understanding structurally couples consciousness and communication. Everything that is communicated must necessarily pass through the filter of consciousness while being, at the same time, completely excluded from it. This condition allows communication to be remarkably autonomous from the material substrate of living systems. It only depends on this substrate indirectly through consciousness. Consciousness, in turn, depends on the brain and the proper functioning of the entire organism, and is independent from communication as regards how it reproduces thought.[19]

The conceptual framework proposed by Luhmann is complex and abstract. However, it has the advantage of being able to provide a sufficiently flexible notion of the individual to be able to deal with extreme cases (typically the prerogative of medicine) with scientific precision. Consider, for example, the case of a body kept alive in the absence of a functioning mind and the need to continue to treat it as a person, not only from a medical point of view but also from a legal and economic point of view, etc. Even without having to resort to such extreme examples, the effectiveness of conceiving the individual in this way is also evident if we take into account the analytical possibilities created by causal circularity involving these three systems when taking decisions involving the choice of treatment, therapy or health prevention strategies. Mind, body and social status have only a causal impact on each other indirectly within the framework of their respective environments; environments which primarily impact on their opportunities to develop, and flexibility to change. A biochemical environment will be relevant for the body, a structured learning context with a reference culture as its foundation, for the mind, and a social environment comprising legal, political, economic, romantic, religious prerogatives, etc., to reproduce social status. Some interpreters of Luhmann's thinking believe that these premises provide the chance to create a framework of salutogenic and pathogenic factors that can, in turn, provide a multifactorial model that takes all levels of interrelation between the three systems into account. All the above is geared towards two main objectives. First of all, to analyse the specific semantic and structural features of modern societies and their consequences on how society manages health. Secondly, to introduce social systems theory into health promotion practices to improve the effectiveness and efficiency of professional public health practice and promote health through targeted actions and activities.[20]

---

[19] See Luhmann (1991a), pp. 218–230.

[20] For an analytical discussion of options as to how to develop this theory, see Pelikan (2007a), pp. 83 ff.

3 The System to Treat Disease

However, as has been pointed out,[21] the central issue raised by Luhmann's theory is most likely found elsewhere. The most important consequence (in terms of interpretation) of accepting the conceptual framework he presents,[22] relates to the possibility, and nature, of *treating* disease. It is certainly true that modern medical treatment involves measures primarily aimed at the body, using the tools from biology, chemistry and physics. However, it is equally indisputable that the massive deployment of organisational, technical, administrative, scientific and infrastructural resources (central to achieving results) is created through communication. As we have said, mind, body and social status only have a causal impact on each other indirectly through their respective environmental contexts, and this is exactly what happens when activities to safeguard our health take place. Communication is the point of departure to attempt to motivate people to focus their attention on specific perceptions (symptoms) with a view to changing a set of behaviours which we presume can help the organism function well. Medicine is therefore structured according to a logic that is exclusively social. Above all, the doctor and the patient must be able to meet. For this to happen, a whole host of conditions must be in place. Firstly, those to motivate the doctor to examine a particular body and produce all the necessary documentation required by medical procedure. Secondly, those to motivate the patient to attend the appointment and describe their symptoms. In order for the expectations of both parties to be sufficiently guaranteed within an established routine, organisations such as clinics, hospitals, medical departments, etc. are necessary to monitor protocols, accreditations and service quality. These organisations that make up the healthcare system normalise communications and behaviour that otherwise could not occur with any frequency due to their high degree of improbability. For example, only in a dental practice would we accept having a stranger put their hands and various tools in our mouths without our protesting too much![23]

Although the current state of medical development would be unthinkable without differentiating between modern science and monetary economics, it is essential to highlight that the structural importance of this dynamic lies upstream of any specific 'form' that knowledge takes on at any given moment in history, and upon which medicine is consequently based. As such, medicine (taken in its larger sense as a system for the treatment of diseases) cannot really be described as a science as such, but rather as a set of scientific, technical and consuetudinary knowledge based on statistics and the experience of the doctor, where the primary function is not to produce 'true' knowledge but to identify and understand diseases with a view to their

---

[21] Corsi (2015).

[22] Unlike the extensive analyses of other society subsystems, Luhmann deals with medicine only in a limited manner. The entire discussion is reduced to four articles in which certain characteristic elements are set out but not followed by a complete integration into the conceptual framework of the theory. See Luhmann (1983a, 1983b, 1990a, 1990b). In the case of Luhmann (1983a), the Italian edition contained in Corsi (2015) was consulted; the pages indicated refer to that edition.

[23] Corsi (2015), pp. 14–15.

treatment. Indeed, if no cure is available, the patient is not asked to wait, as would be the case if knowledge was missing in the field of science. On the contrary, the best job is done with what is available at the time.[24]

Medicine is an organised communication system and therefore exists within the social system as a specific subsystem. Its function as a subsystem—and this is the main point put forward by Luhmann—is to bring about change to bodies without being able to do so directly through communication.[25] In other words, it is a system focused on its environment; its communications deal with the organic or psychic conditions of individuals who (as we have seen) organise and regenerate themselves autopoietically through various actions and operations that are incommensurable with communication. If we look at it from this angle, we see that medicine intervenes when a person demonstrates that they are no longer in a position to guarantee the necessary organic or psychological 'conditions' to communicate. However, to do so, medicine must rely on the conscience and understanding of doctors and patients and their ability to conform to the demands of the organisation; doctors and patients who are, in turn, driven by the need to maintain their own organic substrate, and address the issues that impact on this substrate—the most obvious of these being pain.[26] Of course, the threshold required to activate the use of medicine cannot be reduced solely to the onset of pain—after all, we do not automatically go to the doctor when we feel pain. Furthermore, this threshold also depends on the historical context of society and its evolution. So not only is this threshold variable, but also determined by many other factors related to other social subsystems and how they are regulated, such as economic costs, political obligations with consequent legal sanctions established by law in the event of non-compliance, and so on.

Despite this, medicine retains a monopoly on the treatment of diseases functionally speaking, and all the communication it produces and focuses on (medical knowledge, interaction, procedures, etc.) only makes sense in view of carrying out and fulfilling this function. In systemic terms, this means that medicine is separated into an autonomous subsystem of a modern, functionally-differentiated society, i.e., a society that no longer addresses problems by segmenting or classifying into strata, but by creating a separate specific subsystem for each problem.[27] The various subsystems enjoy functional primacy for their reference problem but consider their environment (which is composed of all the other subsystems) useless and ineffectual when it comes to resolving the problem. Medicine intervenes precisely because it knows that organic systems (bodies) left to their own devices cannot heal themselves, and that neither politics, law, economics nor religion can replace it (even if they can indirectly help by promoting or hindering certain significant conditions by performing their specific functions).[28]

---

[24] Luhmann (1983a), pp. 57–61; Corsi (2015), p. 13.

[25] Luhmann (1983b).

[26] Luhmann (1990a), p. 189.

[27] Luhmann (1997), pp. 743 ff.

[28] Luhmann (1990a), pp. 183–184; Luhmann (1983a), pp. 59–62.

Based on this functional primacy, medicine achieves operational closure and acts as an autopoietic system within the autopoietic system of society. In order to do so, each functional system links all communication produced within it to a specific binary code in order to make it unmistakable and free from any uncertainty as to how it has been assigned. The code is two-sided, and this differentiation not only guides all the system's operations, but also distinguishes it on a practical level from everything else and thereby defines its autopoiesis. In the case of medicine, the code corresponds to the distinction between disease and health. The communication between doctors and patients is therefore oriented towards this differentiation in a way that has no equivalent in other subsystems in society.[29] The binary nature of the code is central to how the function performs because its two sides are not taken as indicating objective states of reality, i.e. as particular physical or mental states. If this were the case, we would not be dealing with a function but with a goal, the achievement of which would cause the system to dissolve. Instead, healing does not bring about the end of medicine because medicine is not a teleological system. On the contrary, medicine is a system oriented towards a function which, if anything, makes use of different purposes from time to time to address a problem that continues to persist at the level of communication.[30]

The codes should therefore be considered as regulatory models for duplication that allow a negative correlation to be provided for everything that falls within their scope of application. At a linguistic level, this corresponds to the ever-present possibility of transforming any positive statement into its negative form. The two sides of the code therefore follow a positive value/negative value pattern in a strict binary system that does not allow for any third alternative. In other words, the condition allowing for the positive side to be given is that its opposite, the negative side, can also be given. Starting from this point of reference, each subsystem can use this binary pattern to construct structures by reducing the infinite possibilities associated with each case to two alternatives, provided that these always occur together. Luhmann defines this feature of the codes as 'Technicisation'—using Husserl's term to emphasise how subsystems use this approach to gain a series of advantages in ensuring the connectivity of their particular communication structures. Connecting the two sides of the code through simple negation makes the connection between them much more direct, because any other option is excluded, which ensures the 'exhaustiveness' of the code itself. The system will always be able to find a connection for new communication since the scope of application for any differentiation that functions as a code is universal. Every potential communication becomes a potential field of application for the differentiation, and can be evaluated according to its positive or negative value. The subsystems therefore operate differentially, and amplify both sides of their code. Science is oriented towards a true/untrue code, thereby producing new knowledge, and its related new 'non-knowledge'. The economy, where the orientation is towards a solvent/insolvent code, produces a constant stream of new wealth, and seeks to meet market needs, together with a related scarcity of goods and

[29] Luhmann (1990a), pp. 184–186.

[30] See Luhmann (1968).

the creation of new market demand. The legal system is obviously oriented towards the wrong/right code, and resolves litigation and disputes on the basis of current legislation while, at the same time, producing new legislation, as it is only by the law and legislation that we create the conditions to challenge an injunction or court order. Therefore, by reproducing both the positive and negative sides in every operation, subsystems can orient their operations by using these uninterrupted 'horizons for possibilities' and, as a result, cater to the paradoxical need for specification and generalization that is a key feature of modern society's functions.[31]

In the case of medicine, the code is naturally the distinction between sick and healthy and, as with other society subsystems, the two values do not correspond to specific tangible states but to alternatives to connect communications that serve to orient medical communication. This means that each subsystem, including medicine, builds its own objects and, at the same time, emphasizes the importance of the positive value of the code, since the positive code encompasses the value of connection, while the negative side encompasses the value of reflection, i.e., it allows us to reflect on the eventuality of the positive value. Positive values of individual subsystems, such as truth in the case of science, wealth in economics, and justice in legal systems, tend to be aligned, and thereby consolidate communications in that particular field. For example, scientific truths are aligned with previous truths, and a 'right' decision is integrated into the existing system of rules and regulations. On the other hand, when negative values are imposed, they lead communication to modify system structures. The discovery of a non-truth puts previous truths under discussion, and the potential emergence of some new previously undebated controversy can lead to the development of new rules and regulations. According to Luhmann, this mechanism demonstrates the empirical connection between the social differentiation of functional systems and binary codification. This is because this is the only way potential way to imagine our own behaviour as absolutely contingent, and, at the same time, think of ourselves as capable of conditioning our behaviour based on the history of previous connections.[32]

The peculiarity of medicine is seen precisely in relation to the way its code is built in view of this function. Counterintuitively, the positive value transmitted by the connectivity of the system operations is disease, while the negative value transmitted by the reflection of contingency, is health. This does not mean that disease is assigned a 'value' at the expense of health. It simply means that, in practical terms, only diseases inform and 'support' doctors; doctors cannot literally operate on health. Health has the sole function of indicating what is missing when disease arises. Furthermore, this should not be underestimated as it allows us to focus on the fact that we cannot know with certainty what diseases will arise in the future, but, regardless, their discovery and treatment will depend on medicine and no other subsystem. The effect is a sudden and in-depth growth in technical terminology associated with diseases, while the concept of health remains unique, empty, and

[31] On the notion of 'code' see Luhmann (1986b), pp. 75 ff.

[32] Luhmann (1990a), pp. 185–188.

constantly problematic.[33] For these reasons, medicine can only view individuals as potential patients and act accordingly, whereas it has no role with healthy individuals. It is true, medicine is sometimes called upon to ascertain particular health conditions in view of specific needs. However, these cases are always demanded by other functional systems.[34] On the other hand, the fact that health cannot be identified with any specific medical form allows the system not to give up on this eventuality, thereby avoiding any 'fanatical' behaviour that fails to take into account the variability and complexity of the environment.

Given the above, we should highlight once again that the structure of the code poses an operational problem as it does not allow us to specify the conditions under which the two values should be allocated during its use. Knowing that health is preferable to disease does not provide any indication as to what should actually be done to identify diseases and design the appropriate therapy and treatment. Similarly, the right/wrong or true/untrue codes do not, in themselves, provide guidance to the judge or scientist on how to reach a verdict in a trial or prove the validity of a hypothesis. To do this, additional supplementary organizations are needed, which Luhmann defines as programs, i.e., general 'conditions of correctness' to attribute code values so that the system can orient itself and control its progress over time. Since programs determine the circumstances that must occur for a system operation to take place, they compensate for the rigid closure produced by the binary nature of the code, making it possible—despite this closure—for the system to open up to criteria that are extraneous to those of the system itself. In other words, although system programs are oriented towards its code, they allow valid criteria and conditions in other social environments to be taken into account. For example, economic, political, religious, and other conditions will also be taken into account when applying laws and drafting regulations. Similarly, political expediency and economic costs will be taken into account in the case of scientific research programs. However, having said this, these external influences can never determine the legality or legitimacy of how we behave, or the truth of some item of knowledge, as these depend exclusively on the system codes of law and science.[35]

Therefore, codes remain fixed, but programs change continuously based on a system's ability to construct programs capable of giving shape and form to plausible expectations that provide a means of orientation. The individual values of the code cannot therefore assume the function of a program. Any attempt to do so, quickly leads to the realisation that all we are doing is simply indicating ideal guidelines or stating principles referring to universally shared values. This is evident in the case of health, where the need to promote and protect health is agreed upon by all, until it comes to defining specifically what actions need to be taken to make this happen. This is where the discontinuity between different social systems becomes apparent. Politics can take appropriate measures in terms of legislation or allocating resources,

[33] Luhmann (1990a), p. 187.

[34] For example, in the case of enlistment in the army or forensic expertise in criminal proceedings. On the latter case, see Lottenbach (2015).

[35] See Luhmann (1986b), pp. 40 ff, pp. 89 ff.

but how all this translates into practice depends on doctors and the healthcare system. The same applies to the right to health. Health can continue to be an ideal to be defended, but any action aimed at having an effect on the system of treating the disease can only be considered—in terms of how it relates to the ill/healthy code—a tangible plan aimed at allocating the two values, and will therefore always be contingent and subject to debate and discussion.[36]

The peculiarity of medical programs aimed at treating disease lies in their need to deal primarily with the social system environment, i.e., the organic system, the sick body. This aspect makes the system for treating disease somewhat different from other social systems as its goal does not lie directly in mitigating the improbability of treatment-oriented communication. The success of communication is, in a certain way, guaranteed by the urgency resulting from a body that suffers as a result of the consciousness perceiving it. Structural coupling between mind and body allows the mind to experience a synchrony with the external world that has no equivalent. Pain and illness cause temporal order, 'before' and 'after', the hierarchy of values, and social strata to collapse. The person's entire world retreats into their body, clouding any distinction between internal and external. The only thing that matters is the urgent intervention of the doctor, who can obviously take time to alleviate the pain in order to develop a future cure, but with the knowledge that everything that happens to the body happens concurrently, always in the present, and without the possibility of deferral.[37]

This condition naturally impacts on medical communication. The successful outcome of medical communication depends, on the one hand, on the willingness of doctors and patients to cooperate, together with symbolic 'apparatus' (i.e. the accuracy of prescriptions and the technical nature of the language employed) and, on the other hand, the establishment of formal organisations such as hospitals, clinics, medical institutes, etc. Organisations are essential in enabling patients to agree to undergo certain treatment, sometimes invasive, despite the unlikelihood of this happening. Unable, as it is, to persuade the body not to resist doctors on a communicative level—even by appealing to money or truth—medicine is able to make use of organisations to repeat and intensify certain relations over time that would otherwise be impossible to produce on a continuous basis, despite their being considered useful. From a patient's perspective, this apparatus provides guarantees in terms of the quality of procedures, information detailing acceptable standards of practice, success expectancy, potential rehabilitation and recovery, and, in general, the potential to declare both wanted and unwanted expectations in the face of institutionalised decision-making programmes.[38]

---

[36] See Corsi (2015) pp. 19–20: 'The meaning of a prohibition or regulation inevitably differs in different subsystems'.

[37] Luhmann (1990a) pp. 188–190.

[38] On the role of organisations in the treatment of disease, see Vogd (2005).

4 Body of Risk

This rather general overview of the relationship between functional differentiation and medicine highlights how illness and disease in today's society ends up becoming a condition that encompasses all areas of an individual's life. Medicine no longer intervenes solely when someone falls ill. The globality of its code, and the variability of the conditions governing how it is applied (programmes), lead us to consider everything possible—even diseases that result from lifestyle choices and no longer simply those diseases caused by external factors. As if to say, 'Everyone is ill because everyone must die'.[39] Faced with this remarkable extension in how the scope of the medical code is applied, health becomes fundamental; the only indisputable value capable of rising above any controversy. This occurs precisely because, in this context, the social system must not simply reproduce medical communication but communicate in order to influence change in its environment. Disease occurs in bodies, i.e. in organic systems that are not part of the social system but upon which the social system depends. For this reason, the body represents a real window of opportunity for medicine. It is the insuperable horizon where every action acquires meaning. It is the definitive and undisputable foundation underpinning every claim, and attracting ever more attention: 'the body, today, is the last remaining thing that makes sense, when nothing else does'.[40] On the other hand, even if social system communications cannot help but take into account the problems of their environment, such as diseases in the body, this does not mean that the same priority is automatically transmitted to individual behaviour regarding other values. This prioritizing is essentially abstract, and of even lesser importance when it comes to the daily life of the individual—both in relation to their own health (we continue to smoke even though we know it will harm us) and to that of others (towards whom we are less inclined to make sacrifices and change our habits).

Despite this, the need to delay death as long as possible, avoid pain, and cure disease are obligations that, in a social context, can no longer be avoided for functional reasons: 'as long as their fulfilment is deemed feasible, failing to fulfil them cannot be contemplated or justified'.[41] The effect boils down to what Luhmann refers to as 'the inflation of the demands' on functional systems, resulting from the ever-increasing importance they gain from this unlimited capacity to apply their code. It is a typical consequence of a functionally differentiated society, where the political management of modern welfare systems is its most conspicuous testing ground. All aspects regarding the conduct of an individual's life are therefore potentially relevant and capable of stimulating the healthcare system and how we treat disease. This also has consequences in terms of social evolution because the same applies to all other social systems (economy, law, politics, etc.). We therefore witness a gradual increase in mutual interdependence between the various functional systems. These systems are required to operate autonomously and exclusively within their own sphere, while

[39] Luhmann (1990a), p. 190.

[40] Luhmann (1983a), p. 67. See Baecker (2007).

[41] Luhmann (1983a), p. 69.

at the same time having to take into account an ever-increasing number of constraints, i.e. environmental constraints represented by the operational requirements of other inter-linking systems. In other words, there is an ever increasing likelihood that so-called 'hypostasised' functions belonging to different social subsystems, end up generating unsolvable problems due to the fact that they must be pursued simultaneously and interdependently. This mix of functional differentiation interdependence creates the paradoxical structure typical of the most pressing problems of modern society where each binary code lays claim to universal validity but only from its own perspective.[42] An example of a problem with this structure is the difficulty in making available a scientific result which, if implemented, could guarantee a cure for a terminal illness but only at financially unsustainable costs. The 'reasons' underpinning individual functional systems—science, medicine, economics—represent a constraint for all the others, and generate a complex set of interdependencies from which it is well-nigh impossible to escape with an optimal solution (i.e. maximum knowledge, better care, lower costs) due to these structural reasons.

It might therefore be worth bringing the issues raised by 'safeguarding the right to health' back into this complex theoretical framework. This would avoid, on the one hand, bringing the whole question down to a statement of principle in the face of what seem to be insurmountable difficulties, and, on the other, providing simplistic explanations for these difficulties by attributing a single aspect of society to them, such as capitalism or bureaucracy. If we come back to the example, and bear in mind the premises from which the entire line of reasoning began, we realise that any condition that might act as an obstacle to satisfying expectations will immediately seem scandalous, regardless of any reasonable feasibility analysis, since the right to health remains both a priority and urgent. Appealing to politics and its capacity to make binding decisions to solve issues, simply exposes us to further disappointments. Rather than satisfying demands by solving the problem, a political system in such cases ends up transferring incompatible demands from one system to another in the hope that something will somehow happen. Pharmaceutical and medical equipment manufacturers can be forced to cap prices by threatening them with higher taxes or promising them public investment, but there is no political way of eliminating the costs associated with the technical and industrial production of drugs and equipment. Alternatively, we can try to gain a result through science by encouraging further research, but without any guarantees in terms of timeframes or, once again, achieving cost savings. On the other hand, the close interdependence of systems can have repercussions. If we achieve the results we aim for in terms of costs, and if the treatment of disease becomes simpler and easily accessible, the system governing the treatment of disease could react by reducing prevention and lengthening treatment timeframes, thereby contributing to an increased risk of infection, etc.

Since we cannot fully resolve the problem by coordinating and reconciling functions, the only viable alternative seems to be to leave how we regulate expectations and, therefore, deal with disappointment, to the individual. This trend is increasingly evident in the complex organisations now responsible for public health and

[42] Luhmann (1983a), pp. 70–72.

can already be seen in the way doctor-patient interaction occurs. Doctors are no longer able to use their authority, professional code, social status, etc. to safeguard their control over decisions on limiting expectations, as they did in the past. So now doctors tend to be more accommodating towards patients' expectations, shifting the burden and disappointment to the more objective (and less open to contestation) nature of the drug treatment and equipment required. The patient is reassured, but also warned of the 'depersonalised' risks they face in one situation or another, with the final decision being theirs and theirs alone.[43] In the face of this new condition, potential disappointments can once again be de-individualized, i.e. assimilated more effectively through the legal system, which assumes the burden of deciding whether the accusations and claims of an individual, whose expectations have not been met, are legitimate or unfounded. However, the transformation of medical expectations into legal expectations through rules and procedures can only work up to a certain point, beyond which the legal 'apparatus' itself weakens to the point of becoming ineffective.[44] It is also clear that this is purely a substitute solution, since a victory in court cannot translate into successful medical treatment.

This weakening of rights is caused by limitations imposed by other systems. If the economy is unable to provide the necessary means to guarantee these rights, measures must be taken (cuts, rationalisation of expenditure, redistribution). However, in doing so, we create detachment and distance from the right by reinterpreting the issue in terms of energy supply and resource procurement. In turn, we accept the fact that this is a different 'reality' (determined on a global scale by consumption and investment) and that it is unwise to expect much in terms of any financial regulation of legal claims relating to health problems and their urgency. The focus therefore returns to the political system. This system will find itself obliged to solve the problem of distributing insufficient resources equitably, and ending up opting for wise 'Solomonic' across-the-board divisions that have the effect of dissatisfying everyone. After all, such an outcome is foreseeable, since the political reasoning behind the division is foreign to those other functional systems that are looking to those resources in order to operate better. And it cannot be otherwise.[45]

Given this, Luhmann suggests changing perspective: to stop treating society as something that can be planned and start observing it as an evolving system that is subject to time, to the history of its past operations, and oriented towards a future that remains uncertain. Doing so makes it far less unreasonable to imagine the possibility of carrying out exploratory actions, and admitting a high degree of uncertainty about the potential results. This change in perspective would put us in a position to capitalise on self-generated uncertainty by analysing the consequences of our actions retrospectively, thus generating a form of adaptive self-orientation. Obviously, embracing this strategy means facing new difficulties; both politically in terms of maintaining overall consensus, and legally in terms of justifying the legitimacy of such an approach. However, the price to pay from choosing this strategy would be offset empirically by

[43] Luhmann (1983a), p. 70. See Corti (2015).

[44] See Luhmann (1975) and Romano (1996).

[45] Luhmann (1983a), pp. 72–75.

a greater capacity to analyse the situation. We could take into account the progressive shift in medical semantics towards contingency—demonstrated by a public discourse that is increasingly oriented towards distinguishing between risk and danger.[46] The recent breakthrough in this field in genetic engineering has made this particularly evident.

This change in perspective leads to at least two striking conclusions. Firstly, in the medical field, no decision is free from potentially-negative consequences, so safety is no longer an achievable condition to aspire to. Secondly, forms of uncertainty about the future change depending on how damage is attributed. Consequently, awareness grows of the close relationship between decisions taken in the present and the possibility of a negative future scenario occurring. In short, everything is reinterpreted in terms of calculating risk: to obtain a certain advantage, you must also accept potential damages. The effect of all this is a widespread change in the way we relate to forms of uncertainty. Since the onset of a disease can always be a present consequence of a past decision attributable to the disease treatment system itself (lack of prevention or information, mistakes in therapy or procedures, quality standards not met, poorly used or insufficient resources, etc.), how we determine responsibility becomes increasingly urgent and justifiable. However, the burden on the system becomes difficult to bear because it ends up being passed on to the doctor-patient interaction, making the two perspectives increasingly irreconcilable and conflictual. Indeed, from the point of view of the patient involved in this interaction, the external danger represented by the disease will increasingly tend to coincide with the decision-making process implemented by the doctor or team; a process over which the patient has very limited understanding or control. Conversely, the doctor or team will tend to interpret the potentially negative scenarios resulting from their decisions as being calculable risks and therefore almost never as danger, as danger will always be traced back to procedures and it is within this context that it assumes its meaning. The two perspectives are therefore mutually irreconcilable, since the risk for the decision-maker is perceived as a danger for the individual involved.[47]

The root of the conflict lies in our tendency nowadays to view ourselves and others essentially as observers. Doctors and patients are now observers who observe each other, each of them aware of being observed but unable to know how, and conscious that the way they are being observed will impact them in the course of the interaction—thus obliging them to try to take this fact into account. This results in communication overload due to the fact that this 'observation of observations' catches us in a web of ever-new 'distinctions of distinctions' and the world becomes intransparent. Each observer behaves like a 'black box' for all the others, and although this form of communication is now completely indispensable, it is also possible to envisage ways of reducing the complexity involved. This happens when the two observers cease to engage in direct mutual observation aimed at ascertaining why the observer observes the way they do, thereby realising that this way can only lead them to build theories

[46] Luhmann (1991a), pp. 9 ff.

[47] Luhmann (1991a), pp. 111 ff.

of risky behaviour without being able to reach a consensus. When both parties understand this and are able to assume that the other has reached a similar conclusion, then they potentially create the right conditions for a regulatory negotiation where it suits both of them to make certain interactive structures transparent—or available—and agree to be content to observe them as facts. Medical prescriptions, understood as communications, could then be interpreted as forms of temporary 'agreement' where doctors and patients find common ground to continue their interaction, starting from their mutual disagreement.[48]

Attempts to control the inflation of demands on the healthcare system through prevention and containment measures (during a health crisis for example) may find that this way of managing the paradox does not necessarily offer a definitive solution, but at least provides an opportunity to draw conclusions as to how to 'manage and tend the path to agreement'.[49]

References

Antonovsky A (1996) The salutogenic model as a theory to guide health promotion. Health Promot Int 11:11–18

Baecker D (2007) Zur Krankenbehandlung ins Krankenhaus. In: Saake I, Vogd W (eds) Moderne Mythen der Medizin. Studien zur organisierten Krankenbehandlung. VS Verlag für Sozialwissenschaften, Wiesbaden, pp 39–62

Bauch J (2000) Selbst-und Fremdbeschreibung des Gesundheitswesens. In: de Berg H, JFK S (eds) Rezeption und Reflexion. Zur Resonanz der Systemtheorie Niklas Luhmanns außerhalb der Soziologie. Suhrkamp, Frankfurt a.M, pp 387–410

Bauch J (2017) Gesundheit als System. In: Systemtheoretische Beobachtungen des Gesundheitswesens. Hartung-Gorre, Konstanz

Beck U (1986) Risikogesellschaft—Auf dem Weg in eine andere Moderne. Suhrkamp, Frankfurt a.M

Corsi G (2015) Introduzione. Malattia e salute: il contributo della teoria dei sistemi. In: Corsi G (ed) Salute e malattia nella teoria dei sistemi. A partire da Niklas Luhmann. Franco Angeli, Milano, pp 9–41

Corti A (2015) La medicina cambia. Il rapporto medico–paziente in prospettiva storica. In: Corsi G (ed) Salute e malattia nella teoria dei sistemi. A partire da Niklas Luhmann. Franco Angeli, Milano, pp 129–148

Douglas M, Wildavsky A (1982) Risk and culture. University of California Press, Berkeley

Foucault M (2005) In: Ewald F, Fontana A, Senellart M (eds) Sicurezza, territorio, popolazione. Corso al Collège de France (1977–1978). Feltrinelli, Milano

Glanville R (2012) The form of cybernetics: whitening the black box. In: Glanville R (ed) The black B∞x, vol 1: cybernetic circles. Echoraum, Wien, pp 425–437

Hafen M (2007) Mythologie der Gesundheit. In: Zur Integration von Salutogenese und Pathogenese. Carl-Auer, Heidelberg

Koselleck R (1979) Vergangene Zukunft. In: Zur Semantik geschichtlicher Zeiten. Suhrkamp, Frankfurt a.M.

[48] Luhmann (1991a), pp. 242–247. See Glanville (2012).

[49] Luhmann (1991a), p. 247.

Lottenbach SF (2015) Giudice in camice bianco o medico in toga nera? Le perizie forensi nel processo penale. In: Corsi G (ed) Salute e malattia nella teoria dei sistemi. A partire da Niklas Luhmann. Franco Angeli, Milano, pp 149–166

Luhmann N (1968) Zweckbegriff und Systemrationalität. In: Über die Funktion von Zwecken in sozialen Systemen. Suhrkamp, Frankfurt a.M

Luhmann N (1975) Legitimation durch Verfahren. Luchterhand, Darmstadt–Neuwied

Luhmann N (1983a) Anspruchsinflation im Krankheitssystem. Eine Stellungnahme aus gesellschaftstheoretischer Sicht. In: Herder-Dorneich P, Schuller A (eds) Die Anspruchsspirale: Schicksal oder Systemdefekt? 3. Kölner Kolloquium. Kohlhammer, Stuttgart, pp 28–49 [ed it.: Inflazione di pretese nel sistema delle malattie: una presa di posizione dal punto di vista della teoria della società. In: Corsi G (ed) Salute e malattia nella teoria dei sistemi. A partire da Niklas Luhmann. Franco Angeli, Milano, pp 57–76]

Luhmann N (1983b) Medizin und Gesellschaftstheorie. Medizin Mensch Gesellschaft 8:168–175

Luhmann N (1984) Soziale Systeme. Grundriss einer allgemeinen Theorie. Suhrkamp, Frankfurt a.M

Luhmann N (1986a) The autopoiesis of social systems. In: Geyer F, van der Zouwen J (eds) Sociocybernetic paradoxes: observation, control and evolution of self-steering systems. Sage, London–Beverly Hills, CA–New Delhi, pp 172–192

Luhmann N (1986b) Ökologische Kommunikation. Kann die moderne Gesellschaft sich auf ökologische Gefährdungen einstellen? Westdeutscher, Opladen

Luhmann N (1989) Individuum, Individualität, Individualismus. In: Luhmann N Gesellschaftsstruktur und Semantik. Studien zur Wissenssoziologie der modernen Gesellschaft, Band 3. Suhrkamp, Frankfurt a.M., pp 149–258

Luhmann N (1990a) Der medizinische Code. In: Luhmann N (ed) Soziologische Aufklärung 5. Konstruktivistische Perspektiven. Westdeutscher, Opladen, pp 183–195

Luhmann N (1990b) Glück und Unglück der Kommunikation in Familien. Zur Genese von Pathologien. In: Luhmann N (ed) Soziologische Aufklärung 5. Konstruktivistische Perspektiven. Westdeutscher, Opladen, pp 218–227

Luhmann N (1991a) Soziologie des Risikos. de Gruyter, Berlin–New York

Luhmann N (1991b) Einführung in die Systemtheorie. Carl-Auer, Heidelberg

Luhmann N (1995a) Die Autopoiesis des Bewußtseins. In: Luhmann N Soziologische Aufklärung 6. Die Soziologie und der Mensch. Westdeutscher, Opladen, pp 55–112

Luhmann N (1995b) Die Form "Person". In: Luhmann N Soziologische Aufklärung 6. Die Soziologie und der Mensch. Westdeutscher, Opladen, pp 142–154

Luhmann N (1995c) Was ist Kommunikation? In: Luhmann N Soziologische Aufklärung 6. Die Soziologie und der Mensch. Westdeutscher, Opladen, pp 113–124

Luhmann N (1997) Die Gesellschaft der Gesellschaft. Suhrkamp, Frankfurt a.M

Pelikan J (2007a) Understanding differentiation of health in late modernity by use of sociological system theory. In: McQueen DV, Kickbusch I (eds) Health and modernity: the role of theory in health promotion. Springer, New York, pp 74–102

Pelikan J (2007b) Zur Rekonstruktion und Rehabilitation eines absonderlichen Funktionssystems—Medizin und Krankenbehandlung bei Niklas Luhmann und in der Folgerezeption. Soziale Systeme 13(1–2):290–303

Romano B (1996) Filosofia e diritto dopo Luhmann. Il "tragico" del moderno, Bulzoni, Roma

Röthlin F (2007) Binäre Codes in der Systemtheorie: Entwicklung, logische Grundlagen und Anwendungen in der Gesundheitssystemforschung. Wien

Simon FB (1993) Die andere Seite der Krankheit. In: Baecker D (ed) Probleme der Form. Suhrkamp, Frankfurt a.M., pp 266–289

Simon FB (1995) Die andere Seite der Gesundheit. Ansätze einer systemischen Krankheits-und Therapietheorie. Carl-Auer, Heidelberg

Vogd W (2005) Medizinsystem und Gesundheitswissenschaften—Rekonstruktion einer schwierigen Beziehung. Soziale Systeme 11(2):236–270

World Health Organization (1946) Constitution of the World Health Organization. Basic documents. World Health Organization, Geneva. https://apps.who.int/gb/bd/PDF/bd47/EN/constitution-en.pdf

Alberto Giustiniano , PhD in Theoretical Philosophy from the University of Padua, is Teaching Assistant at the University of Turin. His research focuses on the history and epistemology of cybernetics and systems theory, with particular emphasis on the influence of these research programmes on philosophical thought in the second half of the twentieth century. He is the author of several papers on the genealogy of cybernetic thought and the formal structure of Niklas Luhmann's theory of self-referential social systems. He is co-editor of the BIT series dedicated to the classics of cybernetic thought for the publisher Orthotes, where he edited the Italian edition of *Das Bewusstsein der Maschinen. Eine Metaphysik der Kybernetik* by Gotthard Günther. He is editor-in-chief of the contemporary philosophy journal *Philosophy Kitchen.*

The Body and the Punishment: The Ideology of Cure Between Past and Present

Dario Ippolito and Matija Žgur

Abstract This chapter explores the return of the punished body to the public stage, situating the imaginaries produced by contemporary populism against the backdrop of a deep and ramified cultural genealogy. The study of (self-legitimising) representations of the power to punish leads us to focus on the ideology of punishment as a therapy to combat the disease of crime. In detail, sections 2–5 outline the archetypes, topoi, and trajectories of this protean ideology, while sections 6–9 show how these archaic imaginaries re-emerge in contemporary populist and securitarian politics, where processes of othering converge in the spectacle of punished bodies, revealing the persistence of the ideology of cure within modern practices of exclusion.

1 Introduction

Alex's body is forced into immobility. Weakened by a subcutaneous injection, he is tied to an armchair (whose shape resembles that of a dentist's). His arms and legs are restrained by straps. His head is secured to a helmet connected to an electrical device. Two clamps applied to his forehead lift his eyelids, preventing both spontaneous blinking and voluntary closure. This is how, in *A Clockwork Orange* (1962), British writer Anthony Burgess describes the setting of the 'Reclamation Treatment',[1] designed to effectively replace prison: a medical-scientific technique

[1] Burgess (1968), p. 96.

These pages are the result of a collaborative process between the two authors. Nevertheless, we specify that Dario Ippolito wrote Sections 2–5, while Matija Žgur wrote Sections 6–9. Matija Žgur wishes to thank Federica Borlizzi for her attentive reading of his parts and her help with the more technical aspects of the treated subject matter.

D. Ippolito (✉) · M. Žgur
Department of Law, University Roma Tre, Rome, Italy
e-mail: dario.ippolito@uniroma3.it

M. Žgur
e-mail: matija.zgur@uniroma3.it

M. Balestrieri and A. Cauduro (eds.), *The Legal Anatomy of the Body*, Ius Gentium: Comparative Perspectives on Law and Justice 142,
https://doi.org/10.1007/978-3-032-26434-3_8

aimed at rehabilitating criminals. The men in white coats begin the therapy session. The patient's hearing is assaulted by the extremely loud volume of dissonant music. His gaze is directed at a screen projecting images of brutal violence. Alex begins to suffer from induced discomfort that pervades his entire body, from his stomach to his head. He needs to vomit, to free himself from his restraints, to stop watching. He begs the doctors to stop the projection. In vain. Later, Dr. Branom explains to him: 'We have to be hard on you, you have to be cured. [...] Violence is a very horrible thing. [...] Your body is learning it.'[2]

A year after the publication of Burgess' dystopic novel, Spanish director Luis García Berlanga brings to the screen another story that prompts reflection on the relationship between the state, society, and the individual, looking at the body as an object of domination and penal reaction. A black comedy set in Franco's Spain, *El Verdugo* (1963) is one of the most incisive cinematic denunciations of the death penalty. The moment of execution is narrated from the perspective of the one who is required to kill in order to punish: a naive and disoriented executioner, completely unprepared to end the life of the condemned man. The emotional turmoil of this reluctant executor of public will echoes the psychological suffering of the man who awaits death at his hands (by means of *garrote vil*). In the symbolic mirroring of the final scene, we recognize the identity of the inhuman condition in which both are thrown. The executioner and the condemned man—reduced to bodies expropriated of two souls in torment—are dragged by force of arms toward the inevitable appointment to which criminal justice has destined them. 'It is society that demands this trial,' resonates the exhortation that preludes the conclusion.

In different ways, Burgess and Berlanga contribute to activating the power of empathy among readers and viewers: a cultural factor that has been historically significant in the transformation of the penal system.[3] Through artistic invention (of characters, situations, interactions), the director and the writer share a feeling of revulsion for the despotic excesses of punitive power and produce an effect of identification with the suffering of those who endure its violence. Obviously, along with the narrative forms, the strategies and targets of delegitimization change. While Berlanga challenges the criminal barbarism of a real dictatorial regime, Burgess condemns the correctionist ideology of clinical treatment, proposing a paroxysmal representation of it (depicted by Kubrick in a film sequence of rare power). Both, however, lead us to a critique of punitive reason, showing us the human faces of the dominated subjects and the physical dimension of the power exercised over bodies.

Empathy, therefore, passes through knowledge, recognition and understanding of others. In this sense, Vittorio Foa offers a penetrating reflection on the invisibility of modern punishment and its socio-political implications:

> When I was young, I used to believe that the walls of a prison existed to shield civilized life from the impure, physical contact of criminals. [...] I later realized that [...] the architecture of prisons is not only meant to keep offenders apart from the outside world, but is designed to stifle any moral concern the public might feel for what goes on within – built to lull, in

[2] Burgess (1968), pp. 109–110.

[3] See Hunt (2007).

> total indifference, the consciences that might otherwise be disturbed […] The prison repels free men.[4]

However, by going beyond the prison walls, by shining a light on the cells and by making the conditions of the inmates visible—through the testimonies of those who, like Foa, have experienced imprisonment—it is possible to transform indifference into indignation, ignorance into awareness, and apathy into empathy. If punitive power is exercised invisibly, exposing its violence becomes an act of protest.

From this perspective, it might seem paradoxical that today it is the power itself that vindicates its punitive ferocity by exhibiting and asserting it. Videos and photos, accompanied by propaganda messages, thrust images of punished bodies before our eyes. Bodies bent over, bodies piled up, bodies caged, bodies kneeling, stripped naked, shaved, depersonalized, degraded. It is a political phenomenon that shakes and undermines the legal foundations of civil coexistence. A worrying phenomenon that brings to mind images from the past and raises questions about the future of constitutional democracy. To what end does this penal spectacle serve? Whence the 'ostentatious inhumanity at the top of the state'?[5] How should we interpret the rhetoric of dehumanization that accompanies securitization policies?

In the following pages, we reflected on the return of the body at the center of the criminal scene, placing the semantics and pragmatics of the punitive discourse that characterizes contemporary populism against the backdrop of a deep and ramified cultural genealogy. The study of (self-legitimizing) representations of the power to punish has led us to focus our attention on the ideology of punishment as a therapy to combat the disease of crime. In the first part of the essay (§§ 2–5), we outlined the archetypes, topoi and itineraries of this protean ideology. In the second (§§ 6–9) we explored how these archaic imaginaries re-emerge in contemporary populist and securitarian politics, where processes of othering converge in the spectacle of punished bodies—revealing the persistence of the ideology of cure within modern practices of exclusion.

2 The Body of the Patient

The current use of the noun 'patient' obscures its origins and enduring polysemy (which the adjective still carries). According to the established meaning in contemporary English, a 'patient' is a person who receives medical cure (for example, during a hospital stay) or who is regularly treated by a trusted doctor (who might say, for example, 'Jannik Sinner is my patient', even if the Wimbledon winner is in perfect

---

[4] Foa (1949), p. 302 (translation is ours). It should not be lost on us that Foa's text is part of a monographic issue of the magazine *Il Ponte* (The Bridge), dedicated to the prison problem, and whose introductory text, written by the editor Piero Calamandrei is entitled *Bisogna aver visto* (Eng. 'You have to have seen it').

[5] Ferrajoli (2025), p. 47.

health).[6] Those who provide cure are the active participants in the clinical relationship (the agents), while those who are cured undergo the therapeutic action: they are the patients ('I was a patient of Dr. Freud,' Ida Bauer might have said).

The etymology is well known but evoking it helps us to grasp ambiguities and semantic shifts. The term 'patient' (noun and adjective) derives from the present participle *patiens* of the Latin verb *patior*, whose meaning—active, despite the passive grammatical form—can be translated into the Italian verb *patire*, the Spanish *padecer*, and the French *pâtir*: to suffer, to endure, to bear. Before being the one who undergoes the doctor's cures, the patient is the one who suffers from the illness. The doctor intervenes because there is a *patiens*. One is not a patient because one is being cured, one is being cured because one is a patient (i.e., suffering, as one is ill).

'Who is affected by an illness': this is the primary meaning of the noun *paziente* recorded in the most authoritative dictionary of the Italian language (which obviously does not neglect to refer the term 'also' to 'those that are being cured by a doctor').[7] Similarly, the dimension of suffering is highlighted in the connotative definition of *paciente* proposed by the *Diccionario de la lengua española* of the *Real Academia*: 'A person who suffers physically and bodily [*física y corporalmente*], and especially one who is under medical care'.[8] The *Trésor de la langue française*, on the other hand, uses a synonymous definition: *patient* means, before being a medically assisted subject, *malade*.

The semantic equivalence between 'patient' and 'person diseased' is also registered by the English dictionaries from past centuries.[9] A disease, however, is only one specific form of the vast and diverse range of ills that humans can suffer (*patire*, *padecer*, *pâtir*). It belongs to the class of natural ills: those not inflicted on humans by humans. However dissimilar social and institutional ills may be, the vocabulary of suffering often unites them. It is not surprising, therefore, that in languages derived from (or permeated by) Latin, the word 'patient' has also been widely used in the field of criminal justice: where suffering, produced by the force of the Leviathan, is willed, justified, and organized.

In the middle centuries of the modern age, jurists, theologians, chroniclers, memoirists, etc. describe (when they do not prescribe) practices of torture and punitive treatments (*supplices*, executions) using the word 'patient' (*paziente, paciente, patient*) in reference to the subjects on whose bodies the agents of power wreak havoc. The patient is the defendant induced to confess through traction, suspension, tearing, pressure, burns, and suffocation. The patient is the condemned person receiving his punishment. The patient is the executed person: the hanged, the beheaded, the quartered, etc. If in the operating room the patient's life is in the saving hands of the doctor, on the scaffold the 'patient' is the one who suffers, in the flesh, the bloody operations of the executioner.

---

[6] See Merriam-Webster (2025), Cambridge Dictionary (2025) and Oxford Learner's Dictionaries (2025).

[7] Battaglia (1984) (translation is ours).

[8] Translation is ours.

[9] For instance, 'a person diseased' is the *definiens* of the noun 'patient' in Scheridan (1780).

In English, occurrences of the term in the criminal context are rare (so much so that they are generally overlooked by lexicographers). In Romance languages, however, they abound. Although it seems completely foreign to the contemporary ear, this obsolete meaning is not at all archaic. It touches on the semantic fields of the twentieth century, deposited in the viscous customs of technical language and transported by the vivid pages of nineteenth-century novels. When Victor Hugo, in *The Hunchback of Notre Dame*, shows us Quasimodo being dragged and hoisted onto the wheel of the sedan chair—chained, stripped naked, mocked, flogged—he accompanies him to the Place de Greve, describing him as *le patient*.[10] For much less, in *The Betrothed*, Manzoni uses the word *paziente*, describing Renzo's arrest and the 'instruments' ('*ruffles*') used to bind his wrists.[11]

The semantic history of the term, therefore, seems to evoke the association between punishment and illness. However, it is possible to adopt a different perspective: *ex parte agentis*, rather than *ex parte patientis*. In the medical field, the patient is the one who—because they are sick—is cured. In the legal field, the patient is the one who—guilty (or presumed so)—undergoes criminal intervention. In the first case, the agent is the one who treats; in the second case, the agent is the one who punishes. This gives rise to a connection opposite to the previous one: between punishment and cure; a parallelism that can be pushed to the point of assimilation and valorization of punishment as cure.

3 Punishments and Healings

What can punishment heal? How can punishment heal? Who can be healed by punishment? In the ancient and evergreen tradition of doctrines that represent and justify punishment as a cure, the answers to these questions are many and varied: sometimes they recur, sometimes they are renewed; some combine, others diverge. The fundamental alternative would seem to concern the determination of 'who' (i.e., the subject benefiting from the penal cure). Is punishment administered to heal the guilty party, whose conduct is a diagnostic symptom of a pathology, or to defend the health of the social body in response to criminal infection? When the question mark is missing, the query becomes an inclusive disjunction.[12]

The repertoire of metaphors and analogies on which the discourse of therapeutic punishment is structured and developed originated, already robust, in the cradle of Western philosophy: Greece.[13] The most profound footprint is that of Plato,[14] who spread the idea that punishment should not look to the past but to the future, aiming to

---

[10] Hugo (2008), VI, IV, p. 131.

[11] Manzoni (1900), XV, p. 227.

[12] See Ferrajoli (1989), pp. 251–262.

[13] See Cohen (2005).

[14] See Saunders (1991), Mackenzie (1981).

prevent the repetition of evil through moral correction.[15] Since virtue can be taught, those who punish according to reason act so that the punished, and others, may act according to justice.[16]

Those who commit injustices are afflicted by an immaterial but very serious evil: injustice (or wickedness). Worse than poverty (which is the evil in terms of possessions), worse even than illness (which is the evil in terms of the body), injustice is an evil that disfigures the soul, produces unhappiness and, therefore, requires a remedy. If the remedy for poverty is the art of business and the remedy for illness is medicine, the remedy for injustice is a just punishment. Like the sick person, the unjust person can only return to happiness by overcoming the evil that afflicts them. Therefore, like the sick person, who accepts treatment even if it is painful, the unjust person—in order to heal—must accept the pain of punishment. They must become the patient, we might say (playing on the ambiguities we have noted).[17]

Thus, the metaphor of punishment as cure leads to the analogy between the doctor and the judge. The morally ill must turn to the latter 'of his own free will' to prevent 'the ailment which is immorality does not become entrenched, rot his mind, and make it incurable':[18]

> We should require ourselves and everyone else not to flinch, but to put a brave face on it and submit courageously and fearlessly to the cautery and surgery of the doctor … [taking] no account of the pain. We should submit to the lash, if that's what the crime warrants, or to imprisonment, if that's what we deserve. If we're fined, we should pay up; if we've earned exile, we must go; if the penalty is death, we should let ourselves be executed.[19]

In this passage from *Gorgias*, which is openly paradoxical and deliberately provocative, the healing of the unjust person's sick soul comes through the violence of the punishments inflicted on the body. The foundation of the paradigm of penal medicine, therefore, does not correspond to the renewal of pharmacopoeia: the punitive methods evoked and legitimized are the usual ones. In Plato's dialogue on the *Laws*, however, the answer to the question 'how to punish in order to heal?' begins to change: moral therapy is not limited to physical punishment.[20]

The analogy with medicine now extends to legislation. Rules and sanctions cannot be imposed on citizens like the prescriptions of a hasty and uneducated doctor who does not bother to give explanations to his patients. The legislator, in his nomothetic activity, must follow the example of those attentive and knowledgeable doctors who prescribe treatment while explaining the reasons for it. Rationality and authority; persuasion and force: imperative norms must rest on this double pedestal. In the perspective of this pedagogy of law, Plato entrusts the justification of laws to the preludes and the correction of non-compliers to penalties.[21]

---

[15] See Stalley (1995).

[16] See Plato (2005), 324a–b.

[17] See Plato (2008), 472e–479c.

[18] Plato (2008), 480b.

[19] Plato (2008), 480c–d.

[20] See Stalley (1995a), Jinek (2021) and Adams (2019).

[21] Plato (1980), IV, 718a–724b.

The scope of the discourse is framed by the axiomatic thesis that punishment 'that takes places according to law […] makes the one who receives the judicial punishment either better or less wicked'.[22] In the catalogue of penalties associated with different classes of offences, we still find flogging, humiliation, expulsion and capital punishment. However, Plato's political imagination devises two new penal institutions to save the city from the dangerous contagion of impiety. The wicked and harmful impious—'like beasts'[23]—are destined for perpetual imprisonment in a prison inaccessible to free men, located 'in some spot that is deserted and as wild as possible'.[24] The impious who are not evil—that is, those who do not believe in the gods due to a lack of intellect—are instead imprisoned for at least 5 years in a different type of prison, created not to guard or afflict, but to reform.[25] The name chosen by Plato makes clear the pedagogical-correctional function of the new place of detention: *sofronisterion* (from the verb *sophronizo*: to restore to one's senses, to moderate, to discipline).[26]

The valorization of punishment as a means of rehabilitation is therefore deeply rooted, not only in philosophy, but also in religion.[27] In the branches of a cultural genealogy that spans our entire history, one can discern the Christian doctrines of *poena medicinalis*, the disciplinary models characteristic of utopian thought (beginning with Thomas More's eponymous work[28]), the modern ideologies of the penitentiary,[29] as well as the multiple variants (moralistic, authoritarian, therapeutic, charitable or orthopedic) of contemporary correctionalism.[30] Alex's body is tied to a history.

In the evolution of this kind of doctrine, the relationship between medical science and criminal justice moves from theory to practice, from analogy to synergy, from rhetorical figures to professional figures. Those who do not go as far as anatomical observation of patients' bodies bet on the scientific possibility of classifying their personalities. From this perspective, the objectivity of the actions performed matters less than the subjectivity of the guilty actors. The differentiation of penalties depends not so much on the type of crime as on the type of offender. The fundamental distinction is binary (since Platonic doctrine): correctable and incorrigible. The criminal treatment of the former serves to readjust them to society. The criminal treatment of the latter serves to defend society. The health of the body politic also depends on the death of human beings.

[22] Plato (1980), IX, 854e.
[23] Plato (1980), X, 909b.
[24] Plato (1980), X, 908a.
[25] Plato (1980), X, 909a.
[26] Plato (1980), X, 908a.
[27] See Ricœur (1960), (1995), (2012).
[28] Besides More (2012), see also, for example, Campanella (1981), Mercier (1772).
[29] See Beaumont and Tocqueville (2018), Foucault (1995), Ignatieff (1978).
[30] See Garland (1985), Garland (1990), Pifferi (2016).

4 Human Beings and the Political Body

'Remedy for a sick society':[31] this is how Montesquieu represents capital punishment in *The Spirit of Laws* (1748).[32] In the rhetoric of punishment as cure, the metaphor is ancient and long-standing. If moral therapy heals the soul of the offender, social prophylaxis reacts to the criminal virus. The perpetrator of the crime is the pathogen; the sick patient is the body politic.[33]

Salus rei publicae suprema lex esto[34]: evoking the specter of Catiline's conspiracy, Cicero urges Roman senators to purge the state of the vectors of disease: 'if this man alone is executed, I know that this disease in the state can be checked for a little time, but it cannot be completely crushed.'[35] The vocabulary of anatomy (*viscera, venae*) accompanies that of pathology (*pestis, morbum, febris*). The prescription for therapeutic intervention is based on the similarity with the human body, in which extreme punishment is confused with war: 'so this disease in the state, though relieved by the punishment of this man, will grow much worse so long as the rest remain alive.'[36]

The medical-penal topic also owes to Cicero's flowery oratory the most vivid and crude analogy: that of the surgical solution to social pathology.[37] Here it is in the formulation of the eighth Philippic: 'If something in the body is causing harm to the rest, we allow it to be cauterized and cut so that this or that member may perish rather than the whole body. Likewise in the body politic: let whatever is noxious be amputated so that the whole may be saved.'[38] Even those who are not familiar with Latin literature will probably find the image behind this warning familiar. It is a recurring theme that is widely used in the apologetics of the death penalty.

A paradigmatic confirmation of the dual nature of discourses that accredit punishment as a cure can be found in Thomas Aquinas' *Summa Theologiae*.[39] The most influential theologian of medieval Europe discusses the relationship between punishment and correction.[40] In assimilating punishments (including corporal punishment) to *medicinae* (or *rimedia*), he considers their function in relation to the soul and its healing (*sanatio, salus*).[41] But the benefit of penal treatment also extends to the ills of the body politic. Thus, the *Doctor Angelicus* authorizes and recommends surgical intervention:

---

[31] Montesquieu (1989), XII, IV, p. 191.

[32] See Ippolito (2019).

[33] See Helmers (2016).

[34] See Mebane (2024).

[35] Cicero (1964), I, XII, 30.

[36] Cicero (1964), I, XIII, 31. In this rhetorical perspective, the legitimisation of capital punishment reappears in the fourth Catiline Oration, on which see Cape Jr (1995) and Woodman (2021).

[37] See Walters (2020).

[38] Cicero (2007), 8, 15.

[39] See Koritansky (2012).

[40] See Gardner (2023).

[41] See Aquinas (1947), I–II, q. 87, a. 6–a. 8.

> […] if the health of the whole body demands the excision of a member, through its being decayed or infectious to the other members, it will be both praiseworthy and advantageous to have it cut away. Now every individual person is compared to the whole community, as part to whole. Therefore if a man be dangerous and infectious to the community … it is praiseworthy and advantageous that he be killed in order to safeguard the common good.[42]

Taken as *argumentum ex autoritate* in the treatises of modern criminal law scholars (Carpzov, Farinaccio, etc.), this passage is quoted *in extenso* in the report to the King of Italy in which the fascist minister Rocco—'grand Solon of the regime'[43]—presents the penal code (1930) and defends the decision to reinstate capital punishment. The data is significant. The convergence, in the affirmation of the *ius necandi*, between the traditional doctrine of the Catholic Church[44] (only archived by Pope Francis[45]) and the totalitarian doctrine of fascism is part of the organicist conception of society, according to which the whole is superior to the parts.

In the metaphor of the body politic, society is to individuals as the physical body is to its limbs. Just as the body is more important than the individual limbs that compose it, society is more important than individuals. The relevance of the parts of the body depends on the function they perform in its overall physiology. Similarly, individuals are subordinate to the functions of the social organism.[46] As an 'organism that is at once economic and social, political and legal, ethical and religious,'[47] the fascist state celebrates and imposes its axiological primacy over the individual, who, as an 'infinitesimal and transitory element' of the 'indefinite series of generations,' is degraded to a 'means to social ends that far exceed his life.'[48] Thus, death as punishment regains its millennial legitimacy.

Emancipation from the political imagery of organicism is one of the cultural prerequisites for the rejection of capital punishment.[49] Only by escaping the normative logic of the corporatist metaphor—thus denying the superiority of the whole over the parts—is it possible to affirm the intangibility of life as an individual good.[50] But there is more. Overcoming organicist axioms leads to the valorization of the person as an end in itself; to the recognition of their ethical priority in social and institutional

[42] Aquinas (1947), II–II, q. 64, a. 2

[43] This is how he is described—with polemical sarcasm—by the antifascist lawyer Trentin (1983), p. 332 (translation is ours).

[44] See Brugger (2003).

[45] See the new revision of number 2267 of the Catechism of the Catholic Church on the death penalty—Rescriptum 'ex Audentia SS.mi', 02.08.2018 (where we read that the Church teaches, in the light of the Gospel, that 'the death penalty is inadmissible because it is an attack on the inviolability and dignity of the person', and she works with determination for its abolition worldwide).

[46] See Briguglia (2006).

[47] Rocco (1930), p. 11 (translation is ours).

[48] Rocco (1930), p. 16 (translation is ours).

[49] See Bobbio (1990), Audegean and Ippolito (2023).

[50] See Costa (2005).

life; to the affirmation of their centrality in the legal construction of the political universe.[51]

This 'Copernican revolution'[52] in the configuration of relations between authority and the individual gives rise to the humanistic conception of punishment, which takes root in constitutional law and is nourished by the awareness that there are no good powers (let alone salvific ones).[53] However necessary, the power to punish represents a constant and terrible threat: a danger to be contained. Punishment is not a cure: it is an evil, justifiable only as a means of preventing greater evils. It serves civil coexistence, not moral correction. It aims to reduce social violence, but is always exposed to the risk of degenerating into institutional violence. For this reason, the exercise of punitive power must be regulated and limited by the legal system in accordance with and in respect of subjective rights.[54]

By shaping criminal law as a system of guarantees, constitutionalism tends to remove the human body from public claims of criminal affliction. The rights of immunity and the principle of dignity raise a barrier to protect the individual.[55] Today—but not only today—the Europe of law prohibits the tampering with the body by those in power. Human life is placed above and outside the domain of criminal law.[56] The intentional infliction of physical pain as a form of punishment is condemned as a violation of the prohibition of inhuman or degrading treatment or punishment, established by Article 3 of the ECHR (which allows no exceptions or balancing).[57]

At the level of the legal 'ought', the power to inflict pain is banished even from the institutional space in which the time of the punishment unfolds. Penal humanism demands a prison system that is worthy of the rule of law: a prison of law (which is no longer—as it has always been—a repository of arbitrary and violent punishment).[58] A person sentenced to prison remains a person. Their human dignity is not diminished by the conduct of which they are guilty.[59] Their punishment consists of and is limited

---

[51] See Tuck (1979); Bobbio (1999).

[52] This is the expression used by Bobbio (1990a), p. 56.

[53] See Ippolito (2025).

[54] See Ferrajoli (2014), Audegean (2023), Ippolito (2025a).

[55] See Ferrajoli (1989).

[56] See Bessler (2022).

[57] See *Ireland v UK* (1979–80) 2 EHRR 25, par. 163, where the Court first established that '[t]he Convention prohibits in absolute terms torture and inhuman or degrading treatment or punishment, irrespective of the victim's conduct. Unlike most of the substantive clauses of the Convention [...] Article 3 (art. 3) makes no provision for exceptions and, under Article 15 para. 2 (art. 15-2), there can be no derogation therefrom even in the event of a public emergency threatening the life of the nation.' On the absolute nature of the rights enshrined in Art. 3 ECHR, see, above all, Mavranicola (2021).

[58] In this regard, it is worth noting, for their importance and rigour, the reports to the Italian Parliament, drafted between 2017 and 2023, by the National Guarantor for the Rights of Persons Detained or Deprived of Liberty (an Authority chaired at the time by Mauro Palma).

[59] See Gonnella (2014), Ruotolo (2014) and Anastasia (2022).

to the deprivation of personal liberty.[60] The integrity of their body is protected by law against the agents of power.[61] Actions that were once accepted as punishment are now called crimes.

5 Cared-for Bodies and Punished Bodies

In the constitutional paradigm, therefore, the terms of the relationship between the human body and political authority change. The body of the legal subject is not an object of domination. It participates fully in the value of the person. It contributes to defining the normative implications of the principle of dignity.[62] It is an individual body, not part of a body that reduces it to a member. The legal system correlates negative and positive expectations in the form of fundamental rights with this body, which is valued as a very personal asset. These rights correspond to prohibitions on injury and obligations to provide services. On the one hand, the body-person is, in principle, immunized from the evil of painful punishment[63]; on the other hand, its needs form the basis of the legal claim to care in terms of the right to health. Therefore, the state—stripped of the ideological trappings of the surgeon of society and/or the penal therapist of the soul—is charged with the duty of creating the public structures necessary to ensure the care of persons in the flesh.[64]

The universality of fundamental rights and the personalist principle also lead to the deconstruction of the relationship of special supremacy between the prison administration and prisoners.[65] Even in the context of criminal enforcement, care is distinct from punishment. Persons deprived of their liberty retain the right to health.[66] Just as the integrity of their bodies constitutes a limit to disciplinary sanctions, their

---

[60] See *Hirst v UK (No 2)* (ECtHR, 6 October 2005) App No 74025/01, par. 69 and 70 ('There is no question, therefore, that a prisoner forfeits his Convention rights merely because of his status as a person detained following conviction.') and *Khodorkovskiy and Lebedev v Russia* (ECtHR, 31 May 2013) Apps Nos 11,082/06 and 13,772/05, par. 836.

[61] See, in particular, *Bouyid v Belgium* (ECtHR, 28 September 2015) App No 23380/09, par. 90. For a comprehensive presentation of the relevant case-law on the rights of prisoners, see European Court of Human Rights (2025).

[62] See Kateb (2011), Rosen (2012) and Dupré (2015); Daly (2021).

[63] See United Nations, *Standard Minimum Rules for the Treatment of Prisoners (the Nelson Mandela Rules)*, UN Doc A/RES/70/175 (17 December 2015), Rules 1, 43 (prohibition of corporal punishment and prolonged or indefinite solitary confinement). For the ECtHR case-law on the subject, see European Court of Human Rights (2025), IV.

[64] See Ferrajoli (2007), (2021).

[65] See Buffa (2015).

[66] United Nations, *Standard Minimum Rules for the Treatment of Prisoners (the Nelson Mandela Rules)*, UN Doc A/RES/70/175 (17 December 2015), Rules 1, 24–35 (equivalence of care; professional independence of health-care staff; continuity of treatment), 43 (prohibition of corporal punishment and of prolonged or indefinite solitary confinement); Council of Europe, *European Prison Rules* (Rec(2006)2-rev, consolidated text 2020), Rules 39–48 (prison health services: equivalence of care; clinical independence; consent and confidentiality).

physical and mental well-being imposes obligations on the public administration to take responsibility for them and provide them with healthcare.[67] Ultimately, the legitimacy of the prison institution is measured against constitutional principles.[68] It fails when the prison system does not respect or ensure the guarantees of fundamental rights: of all rights whose restriction is not part of the punishment.

Obviously, there are no 'deontically perfect worlds'.[69] The effectiveness of legal norms depends on a variety of factors (social, political, economic, and cultural). The nature of power is never reflected in the mirror of the law. The gap between the levels of 'ought' and of the actual reality can be reduced, but not eliminated. Generally, it is greater where power escapes control (as is the case in the opacity of the prison system). And it tends to widen when the law imposes costly decisions (as is the case in relation to the satisfaction of rights to benefits). Thus, in a context of crisis (axiological and institutional) of constitutional democracy, the welfare state retreats and the space of the criminal system expands.[70]

The ideological union between neoliberalism and populism, reshaping the political imagination, produces a hegemonic discourse that changes the semantics of security, conditions the social demand for state intervention, and renews the techniques of producing democratic consensus.[71] While public health care wastes away in a vicious circle of 'discredit-disinvest-discredit' (which is, in fact, very virtuous for the profits of insurance companies and businesses), the propaganda effectiveness of securitarianism grows. In the privatization of care, the patient's body is identified with the figure of the customer. In the political use of punishment,[72] the body of the offender is torn from the personal sphere of dignity/immunity and thrown back into the public arena.

When not blatantly displayed, the punished body is evoked, imagined, visualized. In November 2024, during the presentation of a new armored vehicle for transporting prisoners in maximum security, Italian Undersecretary of Justice Andrea Delmastro stated: 'It gives me great joy to let citizens know how we are pressing forward and not letting those behind that tinted glass breathe'.[73] In August 2019, in Brazil, Jair Bolsonaro (then President of the Republic), promoting a legislative reform aimed at empowering the lethal use of force by agents and private individuals against criminals, declared: 'They will die on the streets just like cockroaches. And it must be that way'.[74] In 2017, in Brentwood (Long Island), US President Donald Trump, speaking in front of hundreds of police officers, mocked the caution with which arrestees are

---

67 The reality of prison life in this regard is examined in an exemplary manner by Gonin (1991).

68 See Ruotolo (2002).

69 Ferrajoli (2011), p. 289.

70 See Actes de la recherche en sciences sociales (1998); see also Wacquant (1999), Wacquant (2004), Anastasia (2012), Fassin (2017) and Ferrajoli (2024).

71 See Garland (2001), Ferrajoli (2025).

72 See Pratt (2007), Anastasia et al. (2015).

73 Il fatto quotidiano (2024).

74 Ying (2019).

treated: 'Please, don't be too nice,' he said while recommending rougher methods.[75] These are just a few very telling examples of how the discourse on security breaks down the barriers of legal civilization, overwhelming personal dignity. The body subjected to criminal law is assumed to be the visible seat of power that generates order: the harshness of treatment becomes a political message.

This is not, of course, a return to the punitive spectacle of the *ancien régime*. The display of force and control over the body now serve a completely different function. In the absolute monarchies of modern Europe, the penal system was based on the objectives of general prevention.[76] Punishment (threatened or imposed) was conceived as a deterrent to non-compliance with prohibitive rules. From the height of royal sovereignty, the *Ordonnance criminelle* (1670) of Louis XIV illuminates the meaning of capital punishment: 'those who do not restrain themselves out of respect for their duty' must be kept within the bounds of the law 'through fear of punishment'.[77] Behind the burnings, the wheels, the quarterings, and the hangings, there is a firm conviction: the intimidating effect of punishment depends on its severity. The fight against crime, through the spectacular affliction of bodies, also requires 'tortures capable of instilling more terror than simple death'.[78]

In the punitive phenomenology of contemporary populism, the suffering body is not used to deter potential criminals, but to reassure the governed and legitimize the rulers. The agent uses the patient to build loyalty and expand his political clientele. Emblematic in this sense is the video shot and released by the Secretary of State for Homeland Security of the current US administration, Kristi Noem. The setting is the well-known Salvadoran prison CECOT. The images are taken from a cell phone camera. Noem appears in front of a cell crowded with men of Latin American appearance, standing in front of the bars or sitting on metal bunks. Her speech—posted on social network X—has two layers of meaning. On the surface, it exploits the spectacle of punished bodies to instill fear: 'President Trump and I have a clear message to criminal illegal immigrants: leave now. If you do not leave, we will hunt you down, arrest you, and you could end up in this El Salvadorian prison.'[79] The ideal viewer, however, is the American voter: images and words are chosen with the aim of satisfying their need for security. Through the display of repressive force, the government celebrates its ability to eradicate evil from society.

The punished body is the body of others.

[75] ABC News (2017).

[76] See Carbasse (2000), Sbriccoli (2002).

[77] *Ordonnance criminelle du mois d'août 1670*, in: Isambert and Decrusy (1829), p. 372 (translation is ours).

[78] Domat (1701), V, III, p. 174 (translation is ours).

[79] Arulanantham (2025).

6 Other(Ed) Bodies

The body of others is a foreign body. Its removal benefits the health of the political body. Its display is a powerful anxiolytic. The punishment becomes visible (and visibly corporeal) again, not to instil fear, but to alleviate it. The deterrent effect of the penal spectacle presupposes that the spectator imagines herself in the position of the patient. The prerequisite for the reassuring function, on the other hand, is the separation between subjects integrated into the order and subjects of disorder. When the former identify themselves as others with respect to the latter, the punitive act takes the form of a collective ritual: a ritual of cohesion that confirms the separation.

The ritual of punitive reassurance necessitates the identification of a collective self and, conversely, the designation of those who stand outside it. The cohesion of the political body requires a visible object of exclusion—a body that can be marked as foreign to the collective organism. In contemporary societies, such figures of exclusion are not given but produced through discursive and symbolic processes of 'othering'.[80] Considering that 'the nation' is still today one of the most relevant forms of collective identification,[81] it comes as no surprise that immigrants are a prime candidate for becoming the other in today's societies. The construction of the other is, in fact, seen as a necessary element of national self-identification.[82] In this sense, Triandafyllidou's notion of the 'significant other' seems particularly insightful. It refers 'to another nation or ethnic group that is territorially close to, or indeed within, the national community and threatens, or rather is perceived to threaten, its ethnic and/or cultural purity and/or its independence'.[83]

A paradigm of such a construction of the significant other is Donald Trump's long-standing rhetoric in relation to the Latin American immigrants, both within the country and at its borders. Ever since becoming a presidential candidate in 2015, Trump has targeted Mexicans and other Latin American immigrants in his exclusionary nation-building exercise.[84] While it is true that anti-Latin American sentiment is nothing new in the US, the exclusionary discourse that targets these immigrants has been radicalized and normalized in the Trumpian era. Notably, his early campaign statements depicted Mexicans as 'bad hombres' and rapists,[85] a pledge to build a wall on the Southern border,[86] and a promise to deport every one of almost

---

[80] Othering is defined by Brons (2015), p. 70, as 'the simultaneous construction of the self or in-group and the other or out-group in mutual and unequal opposition through identification of some desirable characteristic that the self/in-group has and the other/out-group lacks and/or some undesirable characteristic that the other/out-group has and the self/in-group lacks'.

[81] See Triandafyllidou (1998), p. 593.

[82] See Triandafyllidou (1998), p. 599: '[N]ational identity implies difference. Its existence presupposes the existence of 'others', other nations or other individuals, who do not belong to the ingroup and from which the ingroup must be distinguished.'

[83] Triandafyllidou (1998), p. 600.

[84] See Ellis (2025).

[85] See Tennery (2016).

[86] See The American Presidency Project (2015).

11 million undocumented immigrants in the US.[87] In his second presidential term, we have witnessed an intensification of border enforcement and immigration restrictions,[88] the introduction of retaliatory tariffs on imports from specific Latina American countries,[89] and the massive nationwide arrests and deportations of presumed undocumented immigrants with criminal record by ICE agents.[90]

Such radical policies and actions, however, could not have been implemented overnight in a community that has been built by immigrants and is generally open to welcoming those seeking a better life in their midst. The public's receptiveness to at least a passive acceptance of exclusionary policies, if not outright hostility toward immigrants, typically grows slowly and must therefore be built patiently and systematically. Hence, the othering is not a singular discursive act, but rather operates as a multi-layered constellation of rhetorical, visual, and symbolic mechanisms.

If we closely examine Trump's speeches on the topic, we realize that (at least) two different, albeit intertwined, rhetorical strategies are typically employed by the US President to achieve his goal. We shall call them the 'contamination' strategy and the 'securitization' strategy, respectively, and examine them separately.

7 The Contamination Threat

As we have seen, throughout history, the language of cure and affliction has provided the political imagination with a grammar for legitimizing exclusion. When disorder is framed as disease, the act of punishment becomes a therapeutic intervention meant to defend the collective body from infection. This same symbolic logic resurfaces in contemporary populist discourse, where metaphors of purity and pollution translate the old vocabulary of penal medicine into a rhetoric of national hygiene. The contamination strategy thus recasts the punitive treatment of deviance as a campaign against foreignness, shifting the site of correction from the criminal's body to the body politic itself.

In this sense, Mary Douglas argued that metaphors of purity and danger function as symbolic devices for boundary-making. Her evocative definition of dirt as 'matter out of place' illustrates how labelling something as dirt invokes a dualistic, exclusionary logic. 'Dirt,' she says, 'is the by-product of a systematic ordering and classification of matter, in so far as ordering involves rejecting inappropriate elements'.[91] Dirt 'appears as a residual category, rejected from our normal scheme of classifications', adds the British anthropologist.[92] Importantly, something is not dirt due to some

[87] See BBC (2015).

[88] For an analysis of the immigration policies in the first 6 months of Trump's second presidential term, see American Immigration Council (2025).

[89] See Leme (2025).

[90] See Bier (2025).

[91] Douglas (1966), p. 36.

[92] Douglas (1966), p. 37.

objective, inherent characteristic, but is rather socially constructed as such only in relation to a particular thing (in our case: the ingroup or the nation).[93] To understand the force such rhetoric carries, we need only to think how heavily twentieth century totalitarian regimes relied on the contamination discourse—portraying Jews, Roma, and other minorities as parasites or infections—to justify widespread radical exclusion and extermination.[94]

Although never absent from public discourse, the contamination strategy has in recent years gained renewed prominence, largely due to the rise of right-wing illiberal politicians such as Viktor Orban in Hungary, Matteo Salvini in Italy or Marine Le-Pen in France. These leaders have developed a nuanced vocabulary that includes depicting immigrants as invaders,[95] blaming them for the spread of diseases in the country,[96] or outright calling them a poison.[97]

Such communicative devices often find their way into Donald Trump's political speeches, as well. For instance, in a public appearance on 16 May 2018, the first-time President said: 'We have people coming into the country, or trying to come in, we're stopping a lot of them. And we're taking people out of the country you wouldn't believe how bad these people are. These aren't people, these are animals'.[98] An examination of his later comments reveals an escalating biologistic rhetoric. In a radio show appearance during his third election campaign, Trump argued that his opponent Kamala Harris, at the time the Vice President of the USA, was responsible for letting masses of murderous immigrants into the country: 'Many of them murdered far more than one person, and they're now happily living in the United States. You know, now, a murderer, I believe this, it's in their genes. And we've got a lot of bad genes in our country right now'.[99] Finally, in what is arguably his most extreme declaration on the topic to date, Trump, in a campaign rally in Waterloo, Iowa, on 19 December 2023, explicitly depicted immigrants as pathogenic elements.[100] Criticizing the Biden administration for their 'open borders' policy, he was explicit: 'They're destroying the blood of our country. That's what they're doing. They're destroying our country'. Despite the evident similarities between this rhetoric and that of Hitler's in *Mein Kampf*, Trump appeared untroubled and fully embraced the language when he continued: 'They're coming from all over the world. They could be healthy. They could be very unhealthy. They could bring in disease that's going to catch on in our country, but they do bring in crime, but they have them coming from all over the world and they're destroying the blood of our country'.

---

[93] Douglas (1966), p. 9: 'What is clean in relation to one thing may be unclean in relation to another, and vice versa'.

[94] See, for example, Bauman (1989), p. 66 ff.; Perry (1983), Cassata (2011).

[95] See De Boni (2015).

[96] See Euronews (2018).

[97] See AFP (2016).

[98] See Abramson (2018).

[99] See Roll Call (2024).

[100] See Roll Call (2023).

In Trump's populist discourse, the contamination metaphor is employed strategically as a nation-building device that strengthens the in-group by excluding a designated other. By portraying migrants as pathogenic agents, Trump seeks to activate deep-seated cultural anxieties about purity, health, and collective survival. At this point, a crucial new discursive element is introduced, when Trump argues:

> On my first day back in the White House, I will terminate every open border policy … stop the invasion on our southern border and begin the largest domestic deportation operation in American history. We have no choice. No country can sustain this. We will restore law and order to our communities.[101]

Here, the language of contamination becomes inseparable from the logic of *securitization*: besides being outsiders immigrants are now also existential threats whose presence endangers the health and life of the nation itself. To protect the body politic from this threat thus becomes imperative. Extraordinary measures to achieve this goal acquire a new aura of legitimacy.

8 The Security Threat

To 'securitize' a given issue—be it terrorism, environmental change, a pandemic or organized crime—is to frame it as an emergency, a crisis or, most decisively, as *an existential threat*. The strategic function of such dramatization is to enable and justify the resort to extraordinary measures, exceeding ordinary political procedures, to promptly resolve the matter.[102] Securitization operates above all as a rhetorical practice[103]: an issue is not inherently a security threat but becomes one when a securitizing agent successfully persuades an audience to recognize it as such.[104] In the last few decades, a substantial body of scholarship has emerged demonstrating how immigration is increasingly being conceived through the lens of security as reflected in progressively othering political discourses, policies and executive action.[105]

A paradigmatic case is provided by Donald Trump's repeated declarations on the matter. The first example comes from his first major political speech, that is, the announcement of his first presidential bid on 16 June 2015. At the very outset of

---

[101] Roll Call (2023).

[102] See Buzan et al. (1998), p. 23–24.

[103] A prominent current within the field of security studies, led by the Copenhagen School, perceives security (securitization) in terms of speech acts. See, for instance, Waever (1995), Balzacq (2005).

[104] Securitizing agents may include political leaders, executive agencies or the government as such. Their privileged status as securitizing actors is usually due to the superior knowledge of issues of public importance that government actors possess over other actors, as well as their *a priori* position of power (See Balzacq (2005), p. 191). However, as Buzan et al. (1998), p. 32, claim, '[n]o one is guaranteed the ability to make people accept a claim for necessary security action [...], nor is anyone excluded from attempts to articulate alternative interpretations of security'.

[105] This is evidenced in the extensive literature on the matter, particularly within security studies. See, for instance, Huysmans (2000), Bigo (2002), Green and Grewcock (2002), Huysmans (2006), in particular ch. 4; Messina (2014) and Vigneswaran and Bourbeau (2023) and others.

a speech whose leitmotif was depicting the US as being in crisis and under threat from different elements during the Democrats' reign in the White House, one of his very first concerns referred to the Southern border and the nature of the people entering the US through it. He asserted: 'When Mexico sends its people, they're not sending their best. They're not sending you. They're sending people that have lots of problems, and they're bringing those problems with [them]. They're bringing drugs. They're bringing crime. They're rapists'.[106] The statements seem to come directly out from a securitization playbook ('First, establish the other as a security threat for your community').

The second example is even more indicative in this sense—his 8 January 2019 public speech was entitled Oval Office Address on Immigration and Border Security.[107] With the very first sentence—'Tonight I am speaking to you because there is a growing humanitarian and security crisis at our southern border'—the speaker overtly and unequivocally framed immigration as a threat for national security. With the next sentence—'Patrol agents encounter thousands of illegal immigrants trying to enter our country'—he slightly yet importantly shifted the focus from the general phenomenon to the immigrants themselves. Perhaps the clearest reference to the presumed security threat posed by these individuals comes soon thereafter when Trump employs distorted criminal statistics to argue that between 2017 and 2019, 'ICE officers made 266,000 arrests of aliens with criminal records, including those charged of 100,000 assaults, 30,000 sex crimes, and 4000 violent killings.' He finally reaffirmed his fabrication with a deceitful and fearmongering claim that 'thousands of Americans have been brutally killed by those who illegally entered our country and thousands more lives will be lost if we don't act right now'.

Two crucial observations can be deducted from these two examples. First, a subtle yet significant shift in the target of securitization is performed. What is framed as a policy of 'border protection' no longer targets immigration as a process to be regulated but immigrants *as persons* to be contained. The focus moves from controlling movement to controlling bodies, from managing flows to neutralizing presences. In this sense, securitization ceases to concern a social phenomenon and becomes embodied: it is the immigrant who is securitized.

Second, there emerges a new rhetorical approach in the treatment of the issue at hand: besides being 'a potential risk', the foreigner now also becomes 'an existential threat'. The language of infection and danger is complemented with the vocabulary of warfare and defense. The immigrant is not only imagined as a contaminant to be removed for the nation's health, but also as an adversary whose very existence threatens its survival.

The latter approach appears emblematic of the transition in state governance from welfare to risk management. In what Ulrich Beck called 'risk society',[108] potential threats are now more often than not socially constructed and, ideally, acted upon before they even materialize. In this mind-set, a willful escalation of conflictual

[106] See Washington Post (2015).

[107] See American Rhetoric (2019).

[108] Beck (1992).

rhetoric increasingly transforms the immigrant other into *the enemy* of the society, its values and collective way of life.[109] While a total annihilation of the immigrant body is today beyond the pale of actions available to States, militarized language ('the war on [insert the purported threat here]') and the idea that pathogenic immigrants must somehow be physically eliminated from endangering the body politic are very much at the core of securitization practices.

Within this symbolic framework, *deportations* and *detentions* of immigrants in offshore centers are presented as a necessary, but also the only possible solution to the problem they pose. These formally administrative measures, increasingly acquire the moral, political and even legal meaning of punishment[110]—a punishment that does not seek to respond to a particular criminal offence by the immigrant but instead pre-emptively seeks to neutralize the danger that the immigrant herself poses for the community. Reminiscent of the Italian Positivist School of Criminology's shift from responsibility to dangerousness,[111] this erosion of fundamental legal (penal) guarantees is justified precisely by the logic of securitization, which invokes a state of emergency, a crisis, even war with the enemy.[112] In supposedly exceptional circumstances, such draconian actions against the immigrants are presented as extraordinary, yes, but necessary and legitimate nevertheless. The disposal of the pathogenic immigrant body for the protection of the health of the body politic is now perceived less as a matter of political opportunity than as a necessity. It is perceived as a ritual cleansing of the body politic through which the latter reaffirms its integrity.

9 Beyond the Spectacle

What are the reasons for the perceived necessity to parade the dehumanized immigrant bodies before the world? How can we make sense of the recent reappearance of the punitive spectacle and its new function?

First of all, the importance of the gradual and systematic nature of the process of othering (dehumanization) should be stressed once again.[113] In fact, the ultimate success of exclusionary discourses and practices, i.e. their ability to facilitate the efficient disposal of immigrants in some extra-territorial site, depriving them of fundamental legal protections, and leaving them there indefinitely, crucially relies on the ability to gradually transform them, in the eyes of the public, from people with

---

109 It seems that in his 1932 *The Concept of the Political*, Schmitt (2007), p. 27, anticipated contemporary securitization debates, when he argued that the enemy needn't be considered morally evil, aesthetically ugly or an economic competitor—'But he is, nevertheless, the other, the stranger; and it is sufficient for his nature that he is, in a specially intense way, existentially something different and alien, so that in the extreme case conflicts with him are possible'.

110 On the blurring between administrative and penal elements in deportations see Spalding (2024).

111 See Ferrajoli (1989), p 497 ff.

112 See Hallsworth and Lea (2011).

113 For a comprehensive socio-psychological analysis of dehumanization, see Volpato (2011); in the same vain, see also Bandura (1999) and Zimbardo (2007).

hopes, ideals and dignity into dirt, refuse, or dangerous pathogens. The necessity to proceed in a rational and methodical manner was not lost even on the Nazi regime in its genocidal project against European Jews. The awful logic of their reasoning was masterfully captured by Hannah Arendt in *The Origins of Totalitarianism.* In the second part of Chap. 9, where she discusses the perplexities related to the discovery of the inefficiency of supposedly universal human rights, once confronted with people who lost their status of members of political communities, she lucidly exposes the fundamentally procedural nature of 'the final solution':

> The calamity of the rightless is not that they are deprived of life, liberty, and the pursuit of happiness, or of equality before the law and freedom of opinion [...] but that they no longer belong to any community whatsoever. Their plight is not that they are no longer equal before the law, but that no law exists for them [...] Only in the last stage of a rather lengthy process is their right to live threatened; only if they remain perfectly 'superfluous,' if nobody can be found to 'claim' them, may their lives be in danger. Even the Nazis started their extermination of Jews by first depriving them of all legal status (the status of second-class citizenship) and cutting them off from the world of the living by herding them into ghettos and concentration camps; and before they set the gas chambers into motion they had carefully tested the ground and found out to their satisfaction that no country would claim these people. The point is that a condition of complete rightlessness was created before the right to live was challenged.[114]

Arendt's analysis reminds us that even one of the most heinous crimes in human history did not occur over night, but with slow, systematic erosion of legal and political belonging. In the same way, today's deportation and detention practices rely on a progressive dehumanization of migrants that are ultimately rendered superfluous bodies that can be displaced and confined with little resistance by anyone.

The question, however, remains: why do such dehumanizing practices require public visibility?[115] Any plausible explanation for this phenomenon seems to require of us to delve into developments—or rather, the devolutions—in the juridico-political, social and economic situation of the past decade or so.[116] Economic stagnation, growing inequality, and the perception of globalized markets benefiting elites have fuelled widespread discontent, thus opening the doors for the rise of leaders with illiberal and populist tendencies.[117] Socially, rapid demographic shifts, cultural anxieties, and the spread of polarized media have amplified feelings of marginalization and distrust.[118] Legally and politically, transformations in institutional norms, e.g. the weakening of checks and balances, eroding judicial independence, and the reinterpretation of constitutional principles, have created opportunities for leaders to consolidate power disregarding established constitutional limits and procedures.[119]

---

[114] Arendt (1973), p. 295–6.

[115] This need for publicity is even more striking if we consider how just twenty years ago leaders of the same superpower sought to conceal the deportations and degrading interrogation techniques conducted on suspected terrorists in their 'war on terror'. What has so drastically changed in the meantime?

[116] See Garland (2001) and Lacey (2008).

[117] See Guiso et al. (2024), Scheiring et al. (2024).

[118] See Tucker et al. (2018).

[119] See Blokker (2019), Pozsár-Szentmiklósy (2024).

With regard to immigration, the policies introduced by emboldened populist leaders mark a clear schism with the liberal culture of open borders and acceptance of diversity. In reference to criminal justice, these developments mark a specific revival of the therapeutic conception of punishment.

When all of these phenomena and practices converge—the pathologization and securitization of the immigrant; the rise of illiberal polities; the populist revival of the organicist conception of society; the return of the therapeutic conception of punishment—a new narrative emerges: protecting the health of the body politic requires not only the prevention of intrusion of the pathogenic other (or, if it is already inside, its excision). Instead, the vulnerable social body requires a medicine that it can see having an effect. Thus, reminiscent of the famous aphorism '*Not only must Justice be done; it must also be seen to be done*', the pathology must now also be seen to be removed efficiently. As Pratt lucidly observes in his study of penal populism, the populist leader 'seeks opportunities to turn the punishment of offenders into a symbolic spectacle of reassurance and vengeance for an onlooking public, humiliation and debasement for its criminal recipients.'[120] Thus, it is only by making a public spectacle of the entire process of othering and of disposing of the immigrant-criminal-pathogen that the body politic can be reassured that the danger has actually been dealt with.

However, as any other performance, the contemporary punitive spectacle must also come to an end: once the immigrant bodies have been shown to be disposed of far from our communities, the prison doors are closed, the camera lights are turned off and the viewing public is cathartically liberated of their anxieties and reassured of their safety. Yet, the objects of the spectacle remain. The public's relation to their fate resembles its relation to waste disposal: the interest lies, above all, in their removal, not in their afterlife.[121] What we are left with are bodies that are confined in these off-shore detention centers which function as true concentration camps. Agamben portrays them as spaces where law is suspended and individuals, deprived of any meaningful legal and political status, are reduced to *bare life*.[122] In these camps, the paradigm of modern state sovereignty, a paradoxical situation is produced in which individuals are simultaneously included and excluded: included as living bodies under state control, yet excluded from the domain of rights and political agency.

In these circumstances, the immigrant body becomes a modern-day *homo sacer*, compelled to live yet left to die: its body is constantly monitored, regulated, and preserved at the most minimal threshold of survival, while at the same time exposed to abandonment and disposal.[123] Its is simultaneously kept alive and politically dead, managed as a risk rather than recognized as a person. Like the rightless pariahs of the twentieth century, today's immigrants are rendered disposable, inhabiting zones where law has abdicated and only the management of bare life remains.

---

[120] Pratt (2007), p. 30.

[121] On the (in)visibility of securitized migrants, see Mountz (2015).

[122] See Agamben (1998).

[123] See Agamben (1999), p. 82 ff.

Their condition demonstrates the continuity between the older medical-political analogies of punishment and cure, and contemporary punitive practices of exclusion and disposal. If, as Agamben contends, the camp is the *nomos* of modernity, then the immigrant's bare life in these sites is not a peripheral tragedy but a central symptom of our political present.

References

ABC News (2017) Trump to police: 'please don't be too nice' to suspects. https://abcnews.go.com/Politics/trump-police-nice-suspects/story?id=48914504
Abramson A (2018) 'They aren't people.' President Trump calls deported gang members 'animals'. Time, 16 May 2018. https://time.com/5279995/they-arent-people-president-trump-calls-deported-gang-members-animals/
Actes de la recherche en sciences sociales (1998) Special Issue De l'État social à l'État pénal", 124
Adams M (2019) Plato's theory of punishment and penal code in the laws. Australas J Philos 97(1):1–14
AFP (2016) Migration is 'poison' for Europe, says Hungary PM. RFI, 26 Jul 2016 https://www.rfi.fr/en/contenu/20160726-migration-poison-europe-says-hungary-pm
Agamben G (1998) Homo sacer. Sovereign power and bare life. Stanford University Press, Stanford
Agamben G (1999) Remnants of Auschwitz. The witness and the archive. Zone Books, New York
American Immigration Council (2025) Mass deportation: analyzing the Trump administration's attacks on immigrants, democracy, and America. Special report. https://www.americanimmigrationcouncil.org/report/mass-deportation-trump-democracy/
American Rhetoric (2019) Donald J. Trump Oval Office address on immigration and border security.https://www.americanrhetoric.com/speeches/donaldjtrumpovalofficebordersecurity.htm
Anastasia S (2012) Metamorfosi penitenziarie. Carcere, pena e mutamento sociale. Ediesse, Roma
Anastasia S (2022) Le pene e il carcere. Mondadori, Milano
Anastasia S, Anselmi M, Falcinelli D (2015) Populismo penale: una prospettiva italiana. Wolters Kluwer, Trento
Aquinas T (1947) Summa Theologica II-II (literally translated by the fathers of the English Dominican province). Benziger Brothers, Inc., New York
Arendt H (1973) The origins of totalitarianism (1951). Meridian Books, Cleveland–New York
Arulanantham A (2025) Deportation to CECOT: hte constitutional prohibition on punishment without charge or trial. Just Security. https://www.justsecurity.org/110679/deportation-cecot-punishment/
Audegean P (2023) Violenza e giustizia. Beccaria e la questione penale. Il Mulino, Bologna
Audegean P, Ippolito D (2023) 'La peine de mort n'est donc pas un droit'. La décision abolitionniste de Beccaria. Histoire de la justice 34:31–42
Balzacq T (2005) The three faces of securitization: political agency, audience and context. Eur J Int Relat 11(2):171–201
Bandura A (1999) Moral disengagement in the perpetuation of inhumanities. Personal Soc Psychol Rev 3(3):193–209
Battaglia S (1984) Grande dizionario della lingua italiana, vol XII. UTET, Torino
Bauman Z (1989) Modernity and the holocaust. Polity Press, Cambridge
BBC (2015) Donald Trump wants to deport every single illegal immigrant—could he? https://www.bbc.com/news/world-us-canada-34789502
Beaumont G, Tocqueville A (2018) On the penitentiary system in the United States and its application to France (1833). Palgrave Macmillan, Springer, Cham
Beck U (1992) Risk society. Towards a new modernity. SAGE, London

Bessler JD (2022) The death penalty's denial of fundamental human rights. Cambridge University Press, Cambridge
Bier DJ (2025) 65 percent of people taken by ICE had no convictions, 93 percent no violent convictions. https://www.cato.org/blog/65-people-taken-ice-had-no-convictions-93-no-violent-convictions
Bigo D (2002) Security and immigration: towards a critique of the governmentality of unease. Alternatives 27:63–92
Blokker P (2019) Populis as a constitutional project. Int J Const Law 17(2):536–553
Bobbio N (1990) Contro la pena di morte (1981). In: L'età dei diritti. Einaudi, Torino, pp 189–204
Bobbio N (1990a) L'età dei diritti (1987). In: L'età dei diritti. Einaudi, Torino, pp 45–65
Bobbio N (1999) In: Bovero M (ed) Teoria generale della politica. Einaudi, Torino
Briguglia C (2006) Il corpo vivente dello stato. Una metafora politica. Mondadori, Milano
Brons L (2015) Othering an analysis. Transcience 6:69–90
Brugger C (2003) Capital punishment and roman catholic moral tradition. University of Notre Dame Press, Notre Dame
Buffa P (2015) Umanizzare il carcere. Laurus Robuffo, Roma
Burgess A (1968) A clockwork orange (1962). In: A clockwork orange and honey for the bears. The Modern Library, New York
Buzan B, Waever O, De Wilde J (1998) Security: a new framework for analysis. Lynne Rienner Publishers, London
Cambridge Dictionary (2025) 'Patient'. https://dictionary.cambridge.org/us/dictionary/
Campanella T (1981) The city of the sun: a poetical dialogue (1623). University of California Press, Berkeley–Los Angeles–London
Cape RW Jr (1995) The rhetoric of politics in Cicero's fourth Catilinarian. Am J Philol:255–277
Carbasse JM (2000) Histoire du droit pénale et de la justice criminelle. PUF, Paris
Cassata F (2011) Building the new man. Eugenics, racial science and genetics in twentieth-century Italy. Central European University Press, Budapest
Cicero (1964) In: Catilinam I-IV, Lord LE (eds) The speeches (with an English translation). Harvard University Press, Cambridge (Mass.), pp 3–144
Cicero (2007) Philippics 3–9 (Vol 1: introduction, text and translation, references and indexes). Walter de Gruyter, Berlin–New York
Cohen D (2005) Theories of punishments. In: Cohen D, Gagarin M (eds) The Cambridge companion to ancient Greek law. Cambridge University Press, Cambridge, pp 170–190
Costa P (2005) Cittadinanza. Laterza, Roma–Bari
Daly E (2021) Dignity rights. Courts, constitutions, and the worth of the human person, updated edn. University of Pennsylvania Press, Philadelphia
De Boni M (2015) Marine Le Pen compare la crise des migrants à la chute de l'empire romain. Le Figaro, 15 Sept 2015. https://www.lefigaro.fr/politique/le-scan/citations/2015/09/15/25002-20150915ARTFIG00111-marine-le-pen-compare-la-crise-des-migrants-a-la-chute-de-l-empire-romain.php
Domat J (1701) Le droit public, suite des loix civiles dans leur ordre naturel (1697). Pierre Emery, Paris
Douglas M (1966) Purity and danger. An analysis of concepts of pollution and taboo. Routledge, New York
Dupré C (2015) The age of dignity. Human rights and constitutionalism in Europe. Hart Publishing, Oxford
Ellis J (2025) The media construction of a threat: scapegoating the Latinx community to 'Make America Great Again'. https://www.ifimes.org/en/researches/the-media-construction-of-a-threat-scapegoating-the-latinx-community-to-make-america-great-again/5545
Euronews (2018) Is Salvini right to claim tuberculosis is spreading in Italy and blame immigration? https://www.euronews.com/2018/09/13/is-salvini-right-to-claim-tuberculosis-is-spreading-in-italy-and-blame-immigration-thecube

European Court of Human Rights (2025) Guide on the case–law of the European convention on human rights: prisoners' rights. Council of Europe/European Court of Human Rights, Strasbourg. https://www.echr.coe.int
Fassin D (2017) Punir. Une passion contemporaine. Seuil, Paris
Ferrajoli L (1989) Diritto e ragione. Teoria del garantismo penale. Laterza, Roma–Bari, Laterza
Ferrajoli L (2007) Principia iuris. Teoria del diritto e della democrazia. Laterza, Roma–Bari
Ferrajoli L (2011) Intorno a principia iuris. Questioni epistemologiche e questioni teoriche. In: Di Lucia P (ed) Assiomatica del normativo. Filosofia critica del diritto in Luigi Ferrajoli. Edizioni Universitarie di Lettere Economia Diritto (LED), Milano, pp 235–292
Ferrajoli L (2014) In: Ippolito D, Spina S (eds) Il paradigma garantista. Filosofia e critica del diritto penale. Editoriale Scientifica, Napoli
Ferrajoli L (2021) La costruzione della democrazia. Teoria del garantismo costituzionale. Laterza, Roma–Bari
Ferrajoli L (2024) Giustizia e politica. Crisi e rifondazione del garantismo penale. Laterza, Roma–Bari
Ferrajoli (2025) Progettare il futuro. Per un costituzionalismo globale. Feltrinelli, Milano
Foa V (1949) Psicologia carceraria. Il Ponte Rivista mensile di politica e letteratura V(3):299–304
Foucault M (1995) Discipline and punish: the birth of the prison (1975). Vintage Books, New York
Gardner E (2023) Punishment as medicine in the thought of St. Thomas Aquinas The Thomist 87(1):1–42
Garland D (1985) Punishment and welfare: a history of penal strategies. Gower, Aldershot
Garland D (1990) Punishment and modern society: a study in social theory. Oxford University Press, Oxford
Garland D (2001) The culture of control: crime and social order in contemporary society. University of Chicago Press, Chicago
Gonin D (1991) La santé incarcérée; médecine et conditions de vie en detention. l'Archipel, Paris
Gonnella P (2014) Carcere. I confini della dignità. Jaca Book, Milano
Green P, Grewcock M (2002) The war against illegal immigration: state crime and the construction of a european identity. Curr Issues Crim Justice 14(1)1:87–101
Guiso L, Herrera H, Murelli M, Sonno T (2024) Economic insecurity and the demand for populism in Europe. Economica 91(362):588–620
Hallsworth S, Lea J (2011) Reconstructing leviathan: emerging contours of the security state. Theor Criminol 15(2):141–157
Helmers H (2016) Illness as metaphor: the sick body politic and its cures. In: Grave J, Honings R, Noak B (eds) Illness and literature in the low countries. From the middle age until the 21 century. V&B Academic, Göttingen, pp 97–120
Hugo V (2008) The hunchback of Notre-dame (1831). In: Three novels (complete and unabridged). Barnes & Noble, New York, pp 1–288
Hunt L (2007) Inventing human rights. A history. Norton & Company, New York–London
Huysmans J (2000) The European Union and the securitization of migration. J Common Mark Stud 38(5):751–777
Huysmans J (2006) The politics of insecurity. Fear, migration and asylum in the EU. Routledge, Abingdon
Ignatieff M (1978) A just measure of pain: the penitentiary in the industrial revolution, 1750–1850. Pantheon Books, New York
Il fatto quotidiano (2024) Delmastro: 'un'intima gioia far sapere che non lasciamo respirare chi sta dietro il vetro oscurato nell'auto della penitenziaria'. https://www.ilfattoquotidiano.it/2024/11/15/polizia-penitenziaria-delmastro-video/7769041/
Ippolito D (2019) L'esprit des droits. In: Montesquieu et le pouvoir de punir. École Normale Supérieure Éditions, Lyon
Ippolito D (2025) El humanismo penal entre pasado y presente. Jueces para la democracia 113:91–101
Ippolito D (2025a) Génesis del garantismo penal. Zela, Puno–Buenos Aires

Isambert FA, Decrusy TA-H (eds) (1829) Recueil général des anciennes lois françaises: depuis l'an 420 jusqu'à la révolution de 1789. Belin-Le-Prieur, Verdiere, Paris
Jinek J (2021) Pleasure and pain and the penal theory in Plato's laws. Etica & Politica / Ethics & Politics 23(3):425–442
Kateb G (2011) Human dignity. The Belknap Press of Harvard University Press, Cambridge (Mass)
Koritansky PF (2012) Thomas Aquinas and the philosophy of punishment. The Catholic University of America Press, Washington, DC
Lacey N (2008) The prisoners' dilemma: political economy and punishment in contemporary democracies. Cambridge University Press, Cambridge
Leme L (2025) LatAm in focus: navigating Trump's tariff tests—The Brazil edition. https://www.as-coa.org/articles/latam-focus-navigating-trumps-tariff-tests-brazil-edition
Mackenzie MM (1981) Plato on punishment. University of California Press, Berkeley–Los Angeles
Manzoni A (1900) The betrothed (1830). D. Appleton and Company, New York
Mebane J (2024) The body politic in Roman political thought. Cambridge University Press, Cambridge
Mercier LS (1772) Memoirs of the year two thousand five hundred (1771). G. Robinson, London
Merriam-Webster (2025) 'Patient'. https://www.merriam-webster.com/dictionary/patient
Messina A (2014) Securitizing immigration in the age of terror. World Polit 66(3):530–559
Montesquieu C (1989) The spirit of the laws (1748). Cambridge University Press, Cambridge
More T (2012) Utopia (1516). Penguin Classics, London
Mountz A (2015) In/visibilty and the securitization of migration. Shaping publics through border enforcement on islands. Cult Politics 11(2):184–200
Oxford Learner's Dictionaries (2025) 'Patient'. https://www.oxfordlearnersdictionaries.com/definition/english/
Perry S (1983) Rhetorical functions of the infestation metaphor in Hitler's rhetoric. Cent States Speech J 34(4):229–235
Pifferi M (2016) Reinventing punishment: a comparative history of criminology and penology in the nineteenth and twentieth centuries. Oxford University Press, Oxford
Plato (1980) The laws. Basic Books, New York
Plato (2005) Protagoras. Penguin Classics, London
Plato (2008) Gorgias. Oxford World Classics, Oxford
Pozsár-Szentmiklósy Z (2024) Informal concentration of powers in illiberal constitutionalism: the case of Hungary. Hague J Rule Law 16:289–314
Pratt J (2007) Penal populism. Routledge, London–New York
Ricœur P (1960) Finitude et culpabilité. II. La symbolique du mal, Aubier–Montaigne, Paris
Ricœur P (1995) Le Juste. Éditions Esprit, Paris
Ricœur P (2012) Il diritto di punire (eds Alici L). Morcelliana, Brescia
Rocco A (1930) Relazione a S.M. il re del ministro guardasigilli. In: Lavori preparatori del codice penale e del codice di procedura penale. Tipografia delle Mantellate, Roma
Roll Call (2023) Speech: Donald Trump holds a campaign rally in Waterloo, Iowa - December 19, 2023. https://rollcall.com/factbase/trump/transcript/donald-trump-speech-campaign-rally-waterloo-iowa-december-19-2023/
Roll Call (2024) Interview: Hugh Hewitt interviews Donald Trump on his radio and podcast show—October 7, 2024. https://rollcall.com/factbase/trump/transcript/donald-trump-interview-hugh-hewitt-radio-october-7-2024/
Rosen M (2012) Dignity: its history and meaning. Harvard University Press, Cambridge, MA
Ruotolo M (2002) Diritti dei detenuti e costituzione. Giappichelli, Torino
Ruotolo M (2014) Dignità e carcere. Editoriale Scientifica, Napoli
Saunders TJ (1991) Plato's penal code: tradition, controversy, and reform in Greek penology. Clarendon Press, Oxford
Sbriccoli M (2002) Giustizia criminale. In: Fioravanti M (ed) Lo Stato moderno in Europa. Istituzioni e diritto. Laterza, Roma–Bari, pp 163–205

Scheiring G, Serrano-Alarcón M, Moise A, McNamara C, Stuckler D (2024) The populist backlash against globalization: a meta-analysis of the causal evidence. Br J Political Sci 54(3):892–916
Scheridan T (1780) A general dictionary of the English language. Dodsley-Dilly-Wilkie, London
Schmitt C (2007) The concept of the political (1932). The University of Chicago Press, Chicago–London
Spalding A (2024) Revisiting the punitiveness of deportation. Leg Stud 44:369–384
Stalley RF (1995) Punishment in Plato's Protagoras. Phronesis 40(1):1–19
Stalley RF (1995a) Punishment in Plato's laws. Hist Political Thought 16(4):469–487
Tennery A (2016) Trump's 'bad hombres' and 'nasty women' remarks stoke online outrage. https://www.reuters.com/article/world/trump-s-bad-hombres-and-nasty-woman-remarks-stoke-online-outrage-idUSKCN12K0HL/
The American Presidency Project (2015) Trump campaign press release—Donald Trump: I would build a great, great wall on our southern border and make Mexico pay for it. https://www.presidency.ucsb.edu/documents/trump-campaign-press-release-donald-trump-i-would-build-great-great-wall-our-southern
Trentin S (1983) Dallo statuto albertino al regime fascista (1929). Marsilio, Venezia
Triandafyllidou A (1998) National identity and the 'other'. Ethn Racial Stud 21(4):593–612
Tuck R (1979) Natural rights theories: their origin and development. Cambridge University Press, Cambridge
Tucker JA, Guess A, Barberá P, Vaccari C, Siegel A, Sanovich S, Stukal D, Nyhan B (2018) Social media, political polarization and political disinformation: a review of the scientific literature. The Hewlett Foundation. https://hewlett.org/wp-content/uploads/2018/03/Social-Media-Political-Polarization-and-Political-Disinformation-Literature-Review.pdf
Vigneswaran D, Bourbeau P (2023) Special issue on insecurity, deportability and authority. Secur Dialogue 54(6):517–638
Volpato C (2011) Deumanizzazione. Come si legittima la violenza. Laterza, Roma–Bari
Wacquant L (1999) Les prisons de la misère. Raisons d'agir, Paris
Wacquant L (2004) Punir les pauvres. Le nouveau gouvernement de l'insécurité sociale. Agone, Marseille
Wæver O (1995) Securitization and desecuritization. In: Lipschutz R (ed) On security. Columbia University Press, New York, pp 46–86
Walters B (2020) The deaths of the republic: imagery of the body politic in ciceronian Rome. Oxford University Press, Oxford
Washington Post (2015) Full text: Donald Trump announces a presidential bid. https://www.washingtonpost.com/news/post-politics/wp/2015/06/16/full-text-donald-trump-announces-a-presidential-bid
Woodman AJ (2021) Cicero and Sallust: debating death. Histos 15:1–21
Ying X (2019) Bolsonaro says in interview, 'criminals should die on the streets like cockroaches'. https://www.riotimesonline.com/brazil-news/rio-de-janeiro/bolsonaro-says-in-interview-criminals-must-die-on-the-streets-like-cockroaches
Zimbardo P (2007) The Lucifer effect. Understanding how good people turn evil. Random House, New York

Dario Ippolito , PhD, is a Full Professor at the Department of Law, University Roma Tre, where he teaches Philosophy of Law, Logic and Legal Argumentation and legal writing. He has been a visiting professor and lecturer at numerous European and Latin American universities. He has published several books and essays that have been translated into different languages, among them, *L'Esprit des droits. Montesquieu et le pouvoir de punir (École Normale Supérieure Éditions, 2019)* and *Génesis del garantismo penal* (Zela, 2025). His work explores themes such as constitutional garantism, the limits of punitive power, and the relationship between law and freedom.

Matija Žgur , PhD, is currently a Researcher (*contrattista di ricerca*) at the Department of Law, University Roma Tre. He serves as co-Editor of *Revus. Journal for Constitutional Theory and Philosophy of Law* as well as the head of the drafting committee at *Diritto & Questioni Pubbliche.* He has published in different peer-reviewed journals and is the author of a monograph *Legal exclusionism: the de-personifying power of law (Klub Revus, 2023).* His main research interests are related to topics in the general theory of law and, more recently, to the psychology of decision-making in public administration.

Global Health Governance Between Access, Innovation, and Regulatory Challenges

Strengthening Legal Preparedness in the European Union After the Pandemic: Law, Policy, and Parliamentary Accountability

Mirko Djukovic and Tamara Hervey

Abstract This chapter considers the European Union's legal preparedness: 'the capability to map, develop, refine, and utilize legal instruments across sectors that enable the implementation of capacities to prevent, detect, and respond to infectious disease threats'. Legal preparedness—both an outcome and a process—includes paying attention to inequalities. Legal frameworks have the potential to create an enabling environment for effective and timely prevention, preparedness for, response to, and recovery from public health emergencies, ensuring that no one is left behind. Strengthening legal preparedness in the EU should involve a process of reviewing and reforming legal instruments to establish a set of well-designed, well-understood, and well-implemented laws in advance of any public health emergency that may arise. The law should address common legal issues that occur during a public health emergency. The law must be inclusive, in the sense of taking into account the unequal effects that public health emergencies have on the most vulnerable, both within the EU and globally. A common legal issue is the insufficient attention to human rights, as well as issues of inequality and discrimination.

1 Introduction

The COVID-19 pandemic exposed major gaps in healthcare system capacities worldwide. Even in the wealthy parts of the global North, including the North and West of Europe, healthcare systems were, or almost became, overwhelmed by the challenge posed by the novel pathogen, to which humans have very little natural immunity. What we observed was—despite international law obligations—the widespread lack of sufficient planning, investment priorities, capacity, and extra resources needed

M. Djukovic (✉)
Centre for Fundamental Rights, Hertie School, Berlin, Germany
e-mail: m.dukovic@hertie-school.org

T. Hervey
City St George's, University of London, London, UK
e-mail: tamara.hervey@citystgeorges.ac.uk

M. Balestrieri and A. Cauduro (eds.), *The Legal Anatomy of the Body*, Ius Gentium: Comparative Perspectives on Law and Justice 142,
https://doi.org/10.1007/978-3-032-26434-3_9

to protect populations and individuals against illness and serious health threats—precisely what nationally funded and organized healthcare systems should safeguard against. Whether or not another pandemic occurs soon, Europe continues to face uncertainties regarding its healthcare system capacity and its ability to protect public health from geopolitical threats (such as the China/U.S. trade tensions), war, oppression, and civil unrest (like in Ukraine, Syria, Afghanistan, Gaza), resulting mass displacement, cyber-attacks, misinformation campaigns, and the climate crisis. In this chapter we treat these concurrent threats as an integrated policy challenge: each may trigger or exacerbate a public-health emergency, and each places distinctive stress on decision-making procedures that must, at once, remain transparent, proportionate and attentive to human-rights obligations.

In the European Union, health is in effect a shared competence between the Union and its Member States. While Member States are primarily responsible for organizing and delivering healthcare, the EU has a shared competence in public health, particularly concerning issues that have cross-border implications. The Union thus has a role to play in pandemic/health crisis preparedness, alongside its Member States, and also alongside international organizations, such as the OECD and the World Health Organization. This chapter is focused on the legal and policy dimensions of the Union's preparedness for future health crises. It asks two questions: to what extent is the Union's pandemic preparedness (i) consistent with basic principles of legal preparedness, and focusing on the principle that legal preparedness involves inclusivity (ii) sufficiently 'outward facing' or globally open? By addressing these questions, the chapter aims to clarify how far current reforms move the Union toward a resilient, rights-sensitive framework and where further adjustment is required for the benefit of both European and global public health.

Our response to these two guiding questions is deliberately staged. Section 2 frames the concept of *legal preparedness* in the public-health domain, distilling from the literature four benchmarks: anticipatory scope, cross-sectoral reach, procedural legitimacy and external solidarity. These benchmarks supply the analytic grid against which the rest of the chapter is read. Section 3 then situates the inquiry within the Union's constitutional order. By distinguishing treaty-based public-health competences from ancillary powers in the internal-market, security-and-defence and research fields, the chapter clarifies both the legal opportunities and the constraints that shape preparedness initiatives.

Section 4 presents three case studies: the Union-level emergency declaration mechanism (Regulation 2022/2371), the European Preparedness Union Strategy and the emerging package on supply-chain resilience, to illustrate how different instrument types (hard law, soft law and contractual models) map onto the preparedness benchmarks. Section 5 draws the comparative strands together, evaluating transparency, parliamentary oversight. A concluding Sect. 6 synthesizes the findings into some concrete recommendations for legislators and policy-makers. In this way, the chapter moves from definition to constitutional setting, to case analysis, and finally to normative appraisal, providing a coherent route through which the initial questions on adequacy and inclusivity are answered.

Throughout this volume, the Union's current responses to COVID-19, such as the National Recovery and Resilience Plans, are read not merely as budgetary blueprints but as windows onto the re-ordering of European power. Our chapter complements that ambition by asking how the *legal* infrastructures that sprang up between 2020 and 2024 expose the Union's underlying constitutional grammar. Public-health emergencies, to borrow Isaac Weldon's language, 'unsettle the normalcy' of governance and render visible the discretionary levers that usually stay hidden. What becomes thinkable in the *state of exception*—as one of the contributors to this volume, Giovanni Leghissa, discusses—and who is authorised to decide to provide a stress-test for both the rule of law and the embodied subjects it is meant to protect.[1]

Weldon's research on antimicrobial resistance demonstrates how framing a threat as an 'emergency' activates exceptional legal powers while muting the deliberative grammar of ordinary politics.[2] The Commission's 2020 Guidance on procurement, for example, invited contracting authorities to invoke *extreme-urgency* clauses almost by default—a discursive move that normalised suspension of competition rules.[3] This chapter traces this same rhetorical pattern in the move from ad hoc derogations to the codified trigger in Regulation 2022/2371, underscoring how narrative choices condition the legal architecture that follows.

2 Conceptual Framework: 'Legal Preparedness'

Public health legal preparedness was defined in the 1980s as the attainment by a public health system of legal benchmarks essential to the preparedness of the public health system.[4] Even at this early stage, note that the question of legal preparedness is nested within a multi-level system: preparedness can be of 'a community, a state, the nation, the world community'.[5] This list also includes regional organisations like the European Union.

But this early definition is rather static. Legal preparedness is not just about being prepared, it's an ongoing state of being. As the Global Health Security *Legal Preparedness Action Package* 2021 tells us, 'legal preparedness is the capability to map, develop, refine, and utilize legal instruments across sectors that enable the implementation of capacities to prevent, detect, and respond to infectious disease threats'.[6] This active definition has been highlighted in recent academic publications, notably the publication in the inaugural issue of the *Journal of Global Health Law*,

[1] See the chapter by Leghissa in this volume.

[2] See the chapter by Weldon in this volume.

[3] Telles (2022).

[4] Institute of Medicine (1988) and Moulton (2003), p. 673.

[5] Institute of Medicine (1988), p. 673.

[6] Global Health Security Agenda (2021), Ayala et al. (2022), pp. 200–203 and Negri et al. (2024), pp. 88–105.

by Negri and colleagues. Legal preparedness, then, is not so much a state of being, as an ongoing process. And it is a process that takes place 'across sectors'.[7]

The idea of legal preparedness as an ongoing process is also present in The International Federation of Red Cross and Red Crescent Societies, *World Disasters Report 2022* and the accompanying *Guidance on law and public health emergency preparedness and response.*[8] This confirms that legal preparedness is both an outcome and a process. The process involves 'reviewing and strengthening legal instruments so that they (i) provide an enabling environment for effective and efficient disaster risk management; and (ii) mitigate the common legal problems that arise during disasters and emergencies'.[9] The outcome means 'having in place well-designed, well-understood and well-implemented laws, regulations, procedures and plans relating to disasters and emergencies'.[10]

Furthermore, legal preparedness refers to an *inclusive* process: it is the job of legal frameworks 'to create an enabling environment for effective and timely prevention, preparedness for, response to, and recovery from public health emergencies that ensures that no-one is left behind'.[11] The need for pandemic preparedness to pay special attention to the inequalities that flow from pandemics has been highlighted widely, including in the Lancet Commission on *Lessons from the Future from the COVID-19 pandemic*.[12]

Putting those together, strengthening legal preparedness in the European Union after the pandemic should involve a process of review and strengthening of legal and policy instruments, so that the Union has in place a set of well-designed, well-understood and well-implemented laws and policies in advance of any public health emergency that arises. These aspects of legal preparedness relate to fundamental 'rule of law' obligations: law should be knowable, known, and consistent. The law should address common legal issues that arise during a public health emergency. These include giving more discretionary power than is strictly necessary to executive or administrative authorities; law becoming *de facto* non-transparent because it is poorly drafted (often because it is drafted quickly), or because it changes too frequently, without clear indications of a set of non-discretionary criteria on which legal changes are based, which can be understood in advance; insufficient attention to incursion on fundamental human rights, and on non-discrimination. The law should be inclusive, in the sense of taking into account the unequal effects that public health emergencies have on the most vulnerable, both within the Union and globally.

[7] Global Health Security Agenda (2021).

[8] IFRC (2022), p. 66.

[9] IFRC (2022), p. 6.

[10] IFRC (2022), p. 6.

[11] Granger (2023) and Sachs et al. (2022).

[12] Sachs et al. (2022).

3 EU Constitutional Setting for Health Emergencies

3.1 Competence and Legal Bases

The European Union operates under certain constitutional or quasi-constitutional constraints. In this chapter we treat these as fixed, although of course they are not, as the Union's constitutionalised legal order changes over time. Whether the Union needs more formal legal competence in this domain is not the focus of this paper. Existing scholarship already demonstrates that the Union possesses ample legal competence to pursue progressive measures in public health—and indeed in the wider health domain.[13] It is not the formal legal position that usually impedes Union action in health, it is usually political will. However, that said, Union competence is limited, and in keeping with the rule of law principle that the law should be known, knowable, and consistent, effective legal preparedness will be based on a sound legal basis in Union law that respects the competences of the Member States.

The primary-law anchors for such action include Articles 168, 114, 122 and, residually, 352 of the Treaty on the Functioning of the European Union (TFEU), together with Articles 35 and 21 of the EU Charter of Fundamental Rights. These provisions form the 'constitutional floor' on which secondary legislation, soft-law measures and contractual techniques must stand if they are to survive judicial scrutiny. Because most pandemic-related measures are adopted through the ordinary legislative procedure, the roles of the European Parliament and the Council are symmetrical; nevertheless, emergency clauses (e.g. Art. 122 TFEU) and the solidarity clause (Art. 222 TFEU) allow the Council to act more swiftly when circumstances so require. This will be discussed later in the chapter.

Legal preparedness needs to consider every level or type of Union legal and policy instrument, starting from the 'constitutional' provisions in the Treaties and especially the EU Charter of Fundamental Rights, which includes Article 21 on equality, for instance. The TFEU itself also includes the 'mainstreaming' obligation in Article 9, obliging the Union to consider health in all policies. Of course, primary legislation should be considered; and delegated legislation. Also administrative decisions taken by the European Commission, or other Union bodies. It is important to have a wide frame: Union health preparedness law and policy may be found in many different domains of Union law and policy, with various legal bases providing Union competence to act.

In terms of the institutional dimensions, we should also acknowledge that many Union institutions will need to be engaged in legal preparedness, if it is to be effective. The obligation to ensure the Union is legally prepared does not sit just with the legal departments of DG Santé, or HERA, or ECDC, but is dispersed across almost everything the Union does. That includes both the Union's 'inward facing' law and

---

[13] See, e.g., Hervey and McHale (2015), Hervey and de Ruijter (2020), Purnhagen et al. (2020), and Hervey (2008).

policy and its 'outward facing' external relations law and policy. It includes the central 'pillar' of Union law and the Union's common foreign and security policy.

The other important constitutional dimension of post-pandemic preparedness is the 'transversal' nature of Union health law.[14] Union health law is not just the law that flows from Article 168 TFEU, and involves DG Santé, HERA and ECDC. Union health law cuts across the 'established categories' of Union law: internal market law, including consumer protection law and public procurement law; competition law; Union law on free movement of people within the Union and Union migration law; Union environmental law; Union external trade and development law, and so on.

Further—in terms of constitutional dimensions, an effective legal preparedness process and outcome will take account of the constitutional obligations of the Union's institutions and Member States when implementing Union law, to respect general principles of Union law and fundamental human rights. And, as noted above, they will ensure key legitimacy mechanisms, especially respecting rules on transparency; accountability; and subsidiarity.

Taken together, the competence provisions, horizontal obligations and legitimacy safeguards indicate that preparedness is as much about respecting the existing rule-of-law architecture as about mobilising new powers.

3.2 *Hard, Soft and Contractual Instruments*

Other parameters that surround the Union's legal preparedness processes are the range of types and forms of legal and policy instruments available to the Union institutions. In addition to the 'classical Union method' of 'hard law' harmonising national law, the Union has a number of other types of legal instruments available. 'Hard law' can, for example, mandate information gathering in certain forms and information sharing by Member States with a central Union institution, usually the European Commission, but could also be a body like the European Centre for Disease Prevention and Control (ECDC). Hard law can mandate coordination, for example, of social security systems, including providing state health care for migrants. Hard law can provide funding or other resources for desired activities or outcomes, be that critical disaster response, biomedical research, education, or infrastructure building. Examples include uniform formats for epidemiological reporting to the ECDC adopted under Decision 1082/2013/EU,[15] the 2022 revision of Regulation 2019/6, obliging Member States to notify disruptions to veterinary-medicine supplies[16] and earmarked preparedness funding within Horizon Europe's 'Health' cluster.

[14] See e.g., Hervey (2023) and Hervey and McHale (2015).

[15] European Parliament and Council (2013) Decision No 1082/2013/EU on serious cross-border threats to health. Official Journal of the European Union L 293:1–15.

[16] European Parliament and Council (2019) Regulation (EU) 2019/6 on veterinary medicinal products. Official Journal of the European Union L 4:43–109, as amended by Regulation (EU) 2022/132 of 28 January 2022.

Then there is the persuasive power of 'soft law', which builds up expectations of what is 'the norm' among Member States, or a desired end point towards which Member States are encouraged to converge, without having the difficult purchase of hard law. Soft law can be beneficial for managing both political differences and unclear science;[17] and different political interpretations of science; but also, for dealing with the wide range of stages of economic development of the EU-27, and the consequent available resources from GDP for national healthcare and public health systems. Recent illustrations are the Council Recommendation on a coordinated approach to travel restrictions (2020/1475)[18] and the 2020 Toolbox on contact-tracing apps, which provided non-binding technical benchmarks yet rapidly shaped national practice.[19]

Beyond regulatory and persuasive law, legal preparedness should encompass contractual legal provisions, such as the power of Member States to utilize the Union to enter into joint contractual obligations, as seen in vaccine purchases during the COVID-19 pandemic. These Advance Purchase Agreements, concluded on the basis of Article 122(1) TFEU and financed through the Emergency Support Instrument, combined public funding with contractual liability shields to de-risk rapid manufacturing. At each rung of the regulatory ladder—hard, soft and contractual—the Commission's Better Regulation Toolbox requires an impact assessment, an often-overlooked yet indispensable element of preparedness because it documents evidence gaps and downstream distributional effects.[20]

The typology sketched above constitutes the organizing lens for Sect. 5, where each case study will be evaluated against four benchmarks of legal preparedness: anticipatory scope, cross-sectoral reach, procedural legitimacy and external solidarity.

---

[17] See e.g., Delhomme and Hervey (2022) and Hervey and Michalak (2025).

[18] Council of the European Union (2020) Council Recommendation (EU) 2020/1475 on a coordinated approach to the restriction of free movement in response to the COVID-19 pandemic. Official Journal of the European Union L 337:3–9.

[19] European Commission (2020).

[20] European Commission (2023c), p. 5.

4 Case Studies of Crisis Instruments

4.1 *Governance Trigger: Public Health Emergency Declaration*

Regulation 2022/2371/EU on serious cross-border threats to health now includes the formal legal power to declare a public health emergency,[21] which, once declared, has clearly delineated (though also non-exhaustive) legal effects for the European Union institutions. This provision meets legal preparedness principles in that it provides a legal basis for what has previously been a political act, offering legal clarity and transparency.

First, a declaration under Regulation 2022/2371/EU enables Regulation 2022/123/EU on the European Medicines Agency's role in crisis preparedness and management for medicinal products and medical devices, to respond to critical medicines shortages. The Commission is empowered to 'take all necessary action within the limits of the powers conferred on the Commission with a view to mitigating actual or potential shortages of medicinal products included on the critical medicines lists'.[22]

Second, such a declaration enables Union law to monitor shortages of, and to develop, procure, manage, and deploy medical countermeasures.[23]

Third, the declaration activates the EU Health Emergency Task Force,[24] part of the work of the ECDC. The Task Force cooperates with Member States and the WHO and assists when asked to respond to outbreaks of communicable diseases, both within the Union and beyond. This aspect of the power to declare a public health emergency enables the Union to develop an inclusive response to a public health crisis like a pandemic, not only considering the effects of the crisis within the Union, but also beyond its borders.

And fourth, a declaration under Regulation 2022/237/EU activates the Union's Integrated Political Crisis Response arrangements, as outlined in Council Decision 2014/415/EU on the arrangements for implementing the Union's solidarity clause. All of these measures are legally determined and thus transparent.

However, note that this power to declare a public health emergency does not impose any direct obligations—neither procedural nor substantive—on Member States, nor does it have any effect at the national level. Yet in a pandemic, responses need to be coordinated between different levels. If the Union is declaring a public

---

[21] European Parliament and Council (2022) Regulation (EU) 2022/2371 *on serious cross-border threats to health* and repealing Decision No 1082/2013/EU. Official Journal of the European Union L 314, 6 December 2022, p. 55, art 23.

[22] Regulation (EU) 2022/2371 art 12, 28.

[23] Regulation (EU) 2022/2371 art 12, 28, 'in accordance with Decision No 1082/2013/EU and other applicable Union law'.

[24] Regulation (EU) 2022/2371 art 15.

health emergency, it is difficult to imagine that its Member States are not also experiencing such an emergency. One possibility, therefore, to strengthen legal preparedness, would be to oblige Member States that do not also declare a public health emergency at the same time (say within 1 week) to give a reasoned opinion to the European Commission as to why they do not believe they need to do so. Such an obligation would respect national competences but also respond to the practical reality of communicable diseases not stopping at borders.

4.2 Health Dimensions of the European Preparedness Union Strategy

Regulation 2022/2371 obliges the Commission to develop a prevention, preparedness and response plan for the European Union.[25] There is no direct reference to 'legal preparedness', but it is implicit in the obligation to include provisions on the governance arrangements for the various items listed.[26] The plan must be published,[27] complying with principles of transparency. There is no corresponding obligation in Union law for transparency of national plans.[28] Such national plans must be assessed by the ECDC.[29] This power has been described by Eerens et al.[30] as very positive, as it fills a gap of non-compliance with the International Health Regulations and significant variance between Member States in terms of preparedness. Assessment is subject to pre-determined criteria,[31] which is legally appropriate. The legal obligation to continually update the plans is a good feature of legal preparedness. The Commission must also report on the state of play of prevention, preparedness and response planning, to the European Parliament and Council.[32] This report is to be 'at Union level' but it has to take into account the national reporting and assessment cycle, so it is multilevel in effect,[33] compensating to some extent for the lack of transparency obligations for the national plans.

The Union published its plan on 26 March 2025.[34] Called the *European Preparedness Union Strategy*, this is a multidimensional ('integrated all-hazards approach')

---

[25] Regulation (EU) 2022/2371 art 5 (1).

[26] Regulation (EU) 2022/2371 art 3 (a)–(j).

[27] Regulation (EU) 2022/2371 art 5 (7).

[28] Member States must have plans, notified by December 2023, and every 3 years thereafter.

[29] Regulation (EU) 2022/2371 art 8.

[30] Eerens et al. (2023), pp. 42–48.

[31] Set out in Commission Delegated Regulation (EU) 2024/1232 Official Journal of the European Union L 1232, 8 May 2024.

[32] By 27 December 2023 and every 3 years thereafter, Regulation 2022/2371/EU, Article 9.

[33] The first such report was issued in late 2023. Obviously it had no data from a cycle of reporting yet, so it is quite bland, mainly listing preparedness activities. The report does not address legal preparedness. See European Commission (2023a).

[34] European Commission (2025) Joint Communication to the European Parliament, the European Council, the Council, the European Economic and Social Committee and the Committee of the

strategic plan, integrating crisis preparedness in a wide range of security threats, not only those flowing from public health emergencies. Its legal form is a Joint Communication from the European Commission and the High Representative of the Union for Foreign Affairs and Security Policy, reflecting the range of policy areas covered, and that some are part of Union common foreign and security policy, rather than Union law. The *Preparedness Union Strategy* flows from the recommendations of the Niinistö Report on Preparedness and Readiness of the EU,[35] the EU Strategic Agenda 2024–2029 and the European Council conclusions of June 2023, March 2024, and December 2024, the Commission Political Guidelines 2024–2029.

The *Preparedness Union Strategy* claims that the existing framework of Union law, including 'cross-cutting crisis legislation and sectoral contingency plans and legislation that increase[s] resilience of [European] societies' covers most areas ensuring 'vital societal functions'. The Critical Entities Resilience Directive 2022/2557 includes healthcare systems within its list of 'essential services', to which the Strategy refers when defining 'vital societal functions'.[36] This list of essential services has been elaborated in delegated legislation,[37] and includes not only providers of healthcare services, but also entities carrying out research and development activities of medicines; manufacturing of basic pharmaceutical products, basic pharmaceutical preparations, and medical devices considered as critical during a public health emergency; and medicines distribution. The Strategy cites 'the European Health Union' as the general source of relevant Union legislation, although the European Health Union is not itself a legislative act, but more like a policy aspiration and collection of current and proposed legislation.[38] This aspect of the Strategy is weak in terms of legal preparedness, as it bases its claims—and therefore recommended actions—on an insufficiently accurate account of Union law.

Key strategic actions to reduce vulnerabilities in areas including essential services in health domains are, according to the *Preparedness Union Strategy*:

> Enhance[d] circularity, long-term supply chain security, and resilience to external coercion, ensuring access to raw materials, essential goods, and critical supplies, and optimise the use of space assets and services, while investing in research and innovation to sustain industrial competitiveness and technological leadership.

Regions on the European Preparedness Union Strategy. JOIN(2025) 130 final, Brussels, 26 March 2025.

[35] Niinistö (2024).

[36] Directive (EU) 2022/2557 of 14 December 2022 on the resilience of critical entities and repealing Council Directive 2008/114/EC. Official Journal of the European Union L 333:169–191, 27 December 2022.

[37] Commission Delegated Regulation (EU) 2023/2450 of 25 July 2023 supplementing Directive (EU) 2022/2557 of the European Parliament and of the Council by establishing a list of essential services. Official Journal of the European Union L 2450, 30 October 2023, art 2(5).

[38] European Commission (2024) Communication from the Commission to the European Parliament, the Council, the European Economic and Social Committee and the Committee of the Regions: The European Health Union: acting together for people's health. COM(2024)206 final, Brussels, 22 May 2024.

Here, the Union can draw on 'reshoring' of healthcare system capacities (see further below). Stockpiling of critical medicines is to be supported by a proposed Critical Medicines Act,[39] which, if adopted in its current form, will draw on the Union List of Critical Medicinal Products which is established in the proposed revision to the Union's Pharmaceutical Regulation.[40] On the supply side, the proposed Critical Medicines Act will empower the financing of strategic investment projects that address a critical medicine supply chain vulnerability. On the demand side, the proposed Act envisages, where duly justified by such vulnerability, changes to the Union's general procurement law, to the effect of favouring suppliers who manufacture a significant portion of critical medicines in the Union. Requests for joint procurement supported by the European Commission are also envisaged. Part of the approach of the Strategy is to build public-private partnerships, among other things to 'to secure critical supplies and services through strategic stockpiles, joint procurement, framework contracts, diversification of sources and circular solutions, reducing risks from global market disruptions and shocks'.[41] A full revision of the Union's public procurement law and policy is envisaged,[42] drawing on lessons from the COVID-19 pandemic, despite the considerable existing flexibilities in Union procurement law that were deployed at that time.[43] The Act's provisions will be supported by a Critical Medicines Coordination Group, made up of national and European Commission officials.

Further, enhancing civil/military cooperation is an aspect of the *Preparedness Union Strategy* relevant to future health crises.[44] One health-specific proposal is to boost rescEU, the Union's reserve of response capacities. Among other areas (aerial firefighting, shelters, transport, energy), the Strategy proposes that the Commission at least maintains, and possibly scales up, capacity to respond to cross-border health threats, including chemical, biological, radiological and nuclear threats, and medical capabilities, including setting up a European field hospital.[45] Again, this aspect of the Strategy is relatively thinly justified in terms of allocation of competences in Union law.

Most of the *Preparedness Union Strategy* concerns internal-facing resilience. It is about *European* supply chains, *European* societies, *European* critical sectors, and so on. A short section of the Strategy—just eight paragraphs[46]—covers 'Resilience

---

[39] European Commission (2025) Proposal for a Regulation of the European Parliament and of the Council laying a framework for strengthening the availability and security of supply of critical medicinal products as well as the availability of, and accessibility of, medicinal products of common interest, and amending Regulation (EU) 2024/795. COM(2025)102 final, Brussels, 11 March 2025.

[40] Regulation (EC) No 726/2004 of 31 March 2004 laying down Community procedures for the authorisation and supervision of medicinal products for human and veterinary use and establishing a European Medicines Agency. Official Journal L 136:1–33, 30 April 2004.

[41] European Commission (2025), p. 11.

[42] European Commission (2025), p. 12.

[43] Delhomme and Hervey (2022), Telles (2022), McEvoy (2022) and Petti (2022).

[44] European Commission (2025), p. 12.

[45] European Commission (2025), p. 15.

[46] European Commission (2025), pp. 15–17.

through External Partnerships'. These include some health-related aspects, specifically 'health security and pandemic preparedness'. The Strategy's external-facing aspects focus on the Union's 'partners', particularly on the one hand neighbour and especially candidate countries, and on the other hand international organisations. Preparedness and resilience is to be integrated into Union cooperation with the UN and NATO.[47] Candidate countries are to be fully associated with relevant Union preparedness initiatives.[48] In focusing more efforts on partnerships with candidate and neighbour countries, this aspect of the Strategy is insufficiently attentive to the unequal effects of public health emergencies like pandemics on the most vulnerable globally.

For the rest of the world, the Union's external economic (note, not 'trade') and development policies are fleetingly mentioned as a vector to 'develop mutual resilience with partners and reduce over-dependencies'. It is not clear whose over-dependencies are meant here: it is possible to interpret this as the Union's dependency on countries elsewhere in the world. Such an interpretation is also supported by the Strategy's statement that 'diversifying and strengthening the integration of supply and value chains in partner countries through Free Trade Agreements, Clean Trade and Investment Partnerships, Strategic Partnerships on raw materials, and Digital Partnerships, will also contribute to this effort'.[49] Focusing on *the Union's* 'over-dependencies' again underplays the effects of pandemics on the most vulnerable globally speaking: it is not in the Global North that the worst impacts of COVID-19 were felt, and this will also be the case for a future pandemic or other public health crises such as those from climate crisis. The Union's development policy instrument—Global Europe: the Neighbourhood, Development and International Cooperation Instrument—is mentioned, but alongside Union neighbour-focused policies, in particular the Instrument for Pre-Accession III, and the forthcoming New Pact for the Mediterranean.

There is absolutely no explicit mention in the *Preparedness Union Strategy* of parts of the world most vulnerable to future health crises like pandemics. There is no sense of 'no one is safe until everyone is safe'. Although the Strategy begins with assertions of the interconnected nature of preparedness, when it comes to the proposed policy strands flowing from the strategy, there is almost nothing about One Health or planetary security. Even the small aspects of the Strategy that are outward-facing are focused mainly on Union neighbours, and on using external policy to protect the immediate interests of the Union's population(s), rather than the Union's interests in global solutions to what are fundamentally global problems.

---

[47] European Commission (2025), p. 16.

[48] European Commission (2025), p. 16.

[49] European Commission (2025), p. 17.

4.3 Supply Chain Resilience and Reshoring

The above-described exclusionary and discriminatory aspect of Union preparedness is especially evident in the Union's preparedness law and policy that is focused on 'reshoring' of healthcare system capacities.

Before exploring Union's 'reshoring' of healthcare system capacities, we need to acknowledge that there are some legal challenges associated with Union's reshoring policies. The Union's economic policy framework, especially as embedded in the semester system of economic governance and the Union's international trade law, traditionally focuses on free trade, market competition and fiscal discipline.[50] The Union does not enjoy the macroeconomic or fiscal competencies necessary for massive redistributive industrial policies. Indeed, the Union's internal market law treats aspects of industrial policy as 'suspect': the Union's state aids rules, for example, prohibit 'inefficient' governmental propping up of national champion industries. These 'constitutional' limitations are enshrined in the Union's founding treaties: they are legally binding. However, this traditional interpretation of the Treaty rules has been challenged and has changed since the COVID-19 pandemic. 'Next Generation EU', the Union's pandemic recovery plan, departs from the traditional approach to Union economic governance. In Next Generation EU, health and healthcare systems are conceptualised as a productive economic factor, to be invested in, rather than a drain on public finances. Other aspects of Union law and policy, like the 'EU Green Deal', also do so. So the starting point for the legal frameworks here departs from earlier assumptions about what is 'legally feasible' for the European Union to do.[51]

An initial scoping exercise has found two main approaches in European law and policy to 're-shoring' of healthcare system capacities in the context of product supply. The first focuses on national capacity building, using European level institutions to support such efforts. The second focuses on building capacity at the European level.

First, the Union is supporting national capacity building. Much of this is taking place through Next Generation EU funding and the semester system. Every Member State includes healthcare system capacity building in its annual plans. This type of capacity building is not about *European Union level* reshoring, but about using the power of the Union to leverage resources through borrowing, and reinvest them in *national* healthcare systems. Other European-level institutions are also taking action to support national capacity building in healthcare systems. For example, the Council of Europe is focused on helping national healthcare systems better manage supply chain fragilities. One example is the work of the European Directorate for the Quality of Medicines & HealthCare (EDQM), working to tackle medicines supply chain issues through enabling short (and potentially medium) term preparation of 'off-label' medicines in hospital and/or community pharmacies.[52]

---

[50] Noted above that the Preparedness Union Strategy does not mention Union external 'trade' policy, but rather external 'economic' policy.

[51] See Hervey and McHale (2015).

[52] European Directorate for the Quality of Medicines & HealthCare (EDQM) (n.d.).

Second, European-level capacity building is incidental to some of the Union's key regulatory instruments in the healthcare domain: the EU's pharmaceuticals legislation.[53] The main aims of this legislation are to ensure quality and safety of medicines within the European Union. But it also has incidental effects, especially seeking to steer industry behaviours, and one relatively new aspect of this is a move in the direction of incentivising re-shoring.

The new pharmaceuticals legislation package includes a new Regulation and a new Directive. Currently, the proposals have been approved, with amendments, by the European Parliament, and are being discussed by the Council. We are still quite far from having a final legal text, so the analysis here is perforce provisional. One of the main changes in the legislation is a shift from a focus only on quality, safety and efficacy towards also covering access to medicines. This is challenging within the limits of Union competences, because questions of financing of healthcare systems—which include deciding which medicines will be covered in the 'basket of care' within the national system—are a national competence. The proposed new legislation takes some tentative steps in this direction, and some of them also relate to incentivising 'reshoring'.

For example, Article 56 of the proposed new Directive imposes obligations on the holders of marketing authorisations of medicines placed on the market in a Member State, to 'ensure appropriate and continued supplies of that medicinal product … so that the needs of patients in the Member State in question are covered'. The European Parliament text strengthens this obligation, with a proposed new Article 58a, requiring holders of marketing authorisations to apply for pricing and reimbursement of the medicine, within 12 months, and to negotiate that pricing. If a Member State brings the medicine within its reimbursed 'basket of care', then the obligation to 'ensure appropriate and continued supply to cover the needs of patients in that Member State' applies. If adopted, these provisions would have the effect of requiring the holders of Union marketing authorisations for medicines to consider the whole of the Union, rather than 'cherry picking' which Member States they wanted to supply. The provision thus seeks to promote greater equity of access to medicines across the Union, while respecting the authority of Member States to determine which medicines are reimbursed in their national healthcare systems. Marketing authorisation holders would also need to pay attention to how their products are supplied to Europe, otherwise they would run the risk of breaching obligations under the legislation. This would potentially incentivise pharmaceutical companies to invest in European-based manufacturing capacity. This aspect of the Union's preparedness work fosters greater inclusivity *within* the Union.

Further, the new Directive includes several provisions designed to ease production of generic medicines in the Union and make these more profitable. Union

[53] It is also incidental to the EU's legislation on substances of human origin (SoHO). The SoHO legislation has always involved a stated aim of 'European self-sufficiency' which is quite at odds with the practical reality on the ground especially for supply of plasma and blood products, which is still heavily reliant on supply from outside of the European Union.

law currently provides significant protection to branded medicines. The companies involved (the branded pharma industry)—traditionally companies which have invested significantly in the research necessary to invent a new medicine—hold patents to protect the patent holders from the generics industry using data from their product (the 'reference medicinal product') to easily generate marketing authorisations for generic forms of the product. The Directive proposes an exception to the 'regulatory data protection period':[54] the period of time during which other market actors may not rely on the market authorisation dataset to create a generic product and enter the Union market. In the proposal, this is set at 6 years (Commission text)/seven and a half years (Parliament text) from the date of the Union marketing authorisation, with a further 2 years (Commission text)/1 year (Parliament text) before the generic medicine may be placed on the market.[55] However, Article 80 (4) proposes that, in the context of a public health emergency (Commission text) or 'under conditions laid down in Union law and in compliance with international agreements' (Parliament text), where a compulsory licence has been granted to address that public health emergency, the regulatory data protection period is to be suspended as long as the compulsory licence is in place. This would make it easier for generics companies to respond to medicinal needs during a public health emergency, and would potentially reduce reliance on only branded medicines, thus enhancing the robustness of supply-chains, especially if accompanied by greater investment in European-based generics manufacturers. There is also a proposed exception to patent rights and rights given by 'supplementary protection certificates' under (current) Regulation 469/2009/EC.[56] A supplementary protection certificate extends the period of patent protection (at present in the Union for up to 5 years, for most medicines), to compensate for the loss of patent protection because of the time it takes to secure marketing authorisations. The new Directive proposes that patent protection should not extend to 'studies, trials and other activities conducted to generate data for an application for (i) a marketing authorisation of generic, biosimilar, hybrid or bio-hybrid medicinal products and for subsequent variations'.[57] Furthermore, patent protection would not cover use of a reference medicinal product for health technology assessment (determining whether the new medicine represents 'value for money' for a national healthcare system) or pricing and reimbursement. These proposed new rules are designed to make it easier for generic medicines to become part of the 'basket of care' available to patients in the Union Member States, not just in public health emergency situations. Again, potentially these provisions could incentivise investment in generics manufacturing in the European Union.

---

[54] European Commission (2023) Proposal for a Directive of the European Parliament and of the Council on the Union code relating to medicinal products for human use, and repealing Directive 2001/83/EC and Directive 2009/35/EC. COM(2023)192 final, Brussels, 26 April 2023, art 80 and 81.

[55] European Commission (2023) COM(2023)192 final art 80 (1) and (2).

[56] European Parliament and Council (2009) Regulation (EC) No 469/2009 of 6 May 2009 concerning the supplementary protection certificate for medicinal products. Official Journal of the European Union L 152:1–9, 16 June 2009.

[57] European Commission (2023) COM(2023)192 final art 85.

Finally, the pharmaceuticals legislative package includes new rules on coordinated EU-level management of shortages and supply of all medicines, and particular rules on 'critical medicines', to seek to secure security of supply. This is part of proposed Union law to which the *Preparedness Union Strategy* refers—and essentially refers as if the proposed new Union law had already been adopted. There is some Union law on critical strategic supply, specifically Regulation 2024/795/EU on the Strategic Technologies for Europe Platform (STEP), which aims to support critical and emerging strategic technologies and their respective value chains in relevant sectors.[58] This is an enabling Regulation, setting the parameters by which projects of 'important common European interest' may be enabled by Union funding and support from existing Union programmes.[59] One of the areas of critical strategic supply covered is 'biotechnologies, including medicinal products on the Union list of critical medicines and their components'.[60] The STEP is managed through Commission Guidance. This Regulation interacts with Regulation 2024/1252/EU (the 'Critical Raw Materials Act'), which provides that a project which makes a 'meaningful contribution' to the security of the Union's supply of strategic raw materials can be recognised as a strategic project.[61] The Commission (through a 'Critical Materials Board' comprised of national representatives) is also required to take on a coordinating role in monitoring national information—for which there is a national reporting requirement[62]—on stocks of critical raw materials.[63] The lists of strategic and critical raw materials in the Act includes several raw materials used in manufacture of medicines and medical devices or equipment, such as bauxite, bismuth, boron, cobalt, copper, gallium and titanium.[64]

The new pharmaceuticals Regulation proposes that shortages of medicines be monitored by national authorities in the Union Member States and by the European Medicines Agency, through a 'structured dialogue' with the industry, at all stages of

[58] Regulation (EU) 2024/795 of the European Parliament and of the Council of 29 February 2024 establishing the Strategic Technologies for Europe Platform (STEP), and amending Directive 2003/87/EC and Regulations (EU) 2021/1058, (EU) 2021/1056, (EU) 2021/1057, (EU) No 1303/2013, (EU) No 223/2014, (EU) 2021/1060, (EU) 2021/523, (EU) 2021/695, (EU) 2021/697 and (EU) 2021/241. Official Journal of the European Union L 795, 29 February 2024.

[59] Eleven Union programmes, listed in the Commission Guidance of May 2024 as relevant to the implementation of STEP, are the Digital Europe Programme, the European Defence Fund, EU4Health, Horizon Europe, the Innovation Fund, InvestEU, the Recovery and Resilience Facility, as well as the Cohesion Fund, the European Regional Development Fund, the European Social Fund Plus (ESF+), and the Just Transition Fund.

[60] Regulation (EU) 2024/795, art 1 (a) (iii).

[61] Regulation (EU) 2024/1252 of the European Parliament and of the Council of 11 April 2024 establishing a framework for ensuring a secure and sustainable supply of critical raw materials and amending Regulations (EU) No 168/2013, (EU) 2018/858, (EU) 2018/1724 and (EU) 2019/1020. Official Journal of the European Union L 1252, 3 May 2024 art 6.

[62] Regulation (EU) 2024/1252 art 22.

[63] Regulation (EU) 2024/1252 art 23.

[64] Regulation (EU) 2024/1252 Annex I and II.

the manufacturing chain. Marketing authorisation holders will be under new obligations to notify either national authorities or the EMA 12 months before withdrawal of a medicine from the Union, and 6 months before temporarily suspending marketing, or a disruption in supply of more than 2 weeks.[65] Marketing authorisation holders will also be required to have in place a shortage prevention plan.[66] National authorities and the EMA will monitor shortages, and share information about actual shortages on a publicly available website, having removed commercially confidential information.[67]

The proposed new Regulation defines a 'critical medicinal product' as one 'for which insufficient supply result in serious harm or risk of serious harm to patients'.[68] A methodology for determining the list of critical medicines is set out in the proposed Regulation.[69] Where there is a 'critical shortage' of a medicine, national authorities are to be obliged to notify the EMA.[70] The Medicines Shortages Steering Group—which was established within the EMA in 2022[71]—is to be empowered to make recommendations on how to resolve or mitigate the critical shortage. These recommendations may be addressed to Member States, the Commission, healthcare professionals, or holders of marketing authorisations for medicines.[72] Although the Steering Group's recommendations are soft law, the proposed Regulation would give the European Commission power to adopt implementing acts—that is, binding law—'to improve security of supply', having taken those recommendations into account.[73] Implementing acts may impose obligations on 'marketing authorisation holders, wholesale distributors or other relevant entities', and those obligations may be to require contingency stock of active pharmaceutical ingredients, or finished dosage forms, 'or other relevant measures required to improve security of supply'.[74] The proposed Regulation also provides that if a company wants to withdraw a critical

65 European Commission (2023) Proposal for a Regulation of the European Parliament and of the Council laying down Union procedures for the authorisation and supervision of medicinal products for human use and establishing rules governing the European Medicines Agency, amending Regulation (EC) No 1394/2007 and Regulation (EU) No 536/2014 and repealing Regulation (EC) No 726/2004, Regulation (EC) No 141/2000 and Regulation (EC) No 1901/2006. COM(2023)193 final, Brussels, 26 April 2023, art 116.

66 European Commission (2023) COM(2023)193 final art 117.

67 European Commission (2023) COM(2023)193 final art 121.

68 European Commission (2023) COM(2023)193 final art 2(13).

69 European Commission (2023) COM(2023)193 final art 130.

70 European Commission (2023) COM(2023)193 final art 121 (1) (c).

71 See European Parliament and Council (2022) Regulation (EU) 2022/123 of 25 January 2022 on a reinforced role for the European Medicines Agency in crisis preparedness and management for medicinal products and medical devices. Official Journal of the European Union L 20:1–37, 31 January 2022.

72 European Commission (2023) COM(2023)193 final art 123 (4).

73 European Commission (2023) COM(2023)193 final art 134.

74 European Commission (2023) COM(2023)193 final art 134.

medicine from the Union market, they would be obliged to offer the transfer of the marketing authorisation of that product 'on reasonable terms' to another entity.[75]

If the proposal is adopted, it would therefore significantly enhance the European Union's powers to mandate behaviours from the pharmaceutical industry that are aimed to secure supply of critical medicines to the EU. These new obligations would incentivise the industry towards behaviours that enhance security of supply, and one of those behaviours is likely to be to at least consider 'reshoring' of at least some manufacturing capacity.

In terms of legal preparedness norms, the provisions of the new pharmaceuticals legislation package, if adopted, would provide transparency, and more legal clarity and certainty. They would make obligations on the industry during a health crisis like a pandemic more explicit, and would provide a legal basis for governmental acts requiring the industry to hold and make available contingency stock of pharmaceuticals themselves, or raw materials.

However, other legal preparedness norms are either missing or are in the background. The reasoning behind a move towards EU-level reshoring for medicines—especially essential medicines—is most commonly articulated as concerns about self-sufficiency, and EU-level security. Human rights protection is very much secondary in the relevant legal and policy discourses.

For example, the European Parliament's Policy Department for External Relations report from 2021 assesses the pros and cons of reshoring as policy tool.[76] The report notes that reshoring is not a policy objective in itself, but should always be at the service of other policy objectives. It stresses that the exogenous shocks caused by 'pandemics, extreme weather events, political conflict and cyber-attacks' expose global value chain-based production. The report implicitly contrasts the 'more progressive version' of global governance supporting free trade (on which global value chain production is based), which involves requiring human rights and democracy conditionality in return for market access, with a more (large) nation-state-based securitised closure of economies, within which larger states and satellite smaller states form regional blocs. The latter model considers the social costs of trade, but (implicitly) not through human rights frames. In so far as the European Parliament report considers human rights, they are seen as a cost (to offshored industry), not an obligation with any other relevance to reshoring.

Another example is the European Commission's April 2023 press announcement summarising its proposed revision of the Union's pharmaceutical legislation.[77] The European Commission acknowledges that, although 'strategic autonomy and reshoring are not directly addressed in the proposal', there is in fact scope in what is proposed to address some 'specific vulnerabilities, including problematic dependencies'. This—if adopted in its current form—would provide new rules on coordinated

[75] European Commission (2023) COM(2023)193 final art 24 (4).

[76] European Parliament DG External Relations (2021) Post-Covid value chains: opportunities for reshoring production back to Europe in a globalised economy (EP/EXPO/INTA/FWC/2019-01/LOT5/R/07 EN, PE 653.626, March 2021).

[77] European Commission (2023b).

Union-level management of critical shortages and supply of critical medicines, to seek to secure security of supply. The underlying ideas include offering greater incentives to pharmaceutical companies who supply the Union Member States' national healthcare systems to ensure security of supply, and access to medicines—especially essential medicines—in all Member States. The proposed new arrangements are modulated to incentivise and support also the generics and biosimilars industry, in practice critical for ensuring access to medicines at prices that state healthcare systems in Europe can bear. Again, human rights narratives are largely invisible.

The proposed legislative texts themselves refer to human rights protection only very fleetingly. The rationale for the new Regulation and Directive both cite Article 35 of the EU Charter of Fundamental Rights on the right to health. But they do not cite the 'right to health' aspect of that provision; instead they refer to the obligation it imposes on the EU to 'achieve a high level of human health protection'. The proposal for a new Regulation links medicines shortages with 'the right of patients to access medical treatment';[78] and states that it 'respects the fundamental rights' in the EU Charter of Fundamental Rights, 'notably human dignity, the integrity of the person, the rights of the child, respect for private and family life, the protection of personal data and the freedom of art and science'.[79] The proposal for the Directive refers in the preamble to the UN Convention on the Rights of Persons with Disabilities, Article 25, on the right to health without discrimination on the basis of disability.[80] The proposal also states that it 'seeks to enable the right to access preventive healthcare and to benefit from medical treatment under the conditions established by national laws and practices'.[81] The former is only one aspect of the right to access essential medicines, itself just one aspect of the right to healthcare. The latter is not formulated as a human right per se. But most importantly, none of these statements are linked with the detailed provisions in the proposal, or stated as justifying or animating them, or the need for legislative change.

What about inclusion and attention to the unequal effects of public health crises on the most vulnerable? Reshoring of human and product capacities would come at a cost. To understand this for medicines, we need to take into account the different types of medicines supplied globally. The Union (especially Austria, France, Germany, Ireland and Italy) and Switzerland already make significant contributions to the global market in branded and on-patent products, with large firms having manufacturing units located there. Expanding that capacity would mean European national health systems paying the costs associated with high Union labour standards.

Making high value generic medicines available to national health systems would ease costs, but the research-intensive side of the industry is reluctant to see the significant legal changes to their intellectual property rights that such a change would entail. This is one of the key questions driving the new Union pharmaceuticals legislation

[78] European Commission (2023) COM(2023)193 final recital 136.

[79] European Commission (2023) COM(2023)193 final recital 155.

[80] European Commission (2023) COM(2023)192 final recital 7.

[81] European Commission (2023) COM(2023)192 final recital 150.

package.[82] The Union hosts some contributors to the global generics industry, in the countries listed above, but also elsewhere including in Central European Member States, such as Czechia, Hungary and Poland.[83] Some smaller or less developed Union Member States do not have any medicine production facilities at all. Balancing all of this points to expanding the Union's high value generics manufacturing capabilities. Even if the capacity expansion took place in Central or Eastern Europe, moving more production to Union-based manufacturing would undoubtedly involve greater costs than the current reliance on generics supplies from India, Taiwan, China and Korea, given the differential production costs, particularly associated with labour standards and pay.

Furthermore, to incentivise pharmaceutical companies to de-risk their supply chains, by moving manufacture away from offshored mass production suppliers to more local suppliers, guaranteed governmental purchases would be required. Again, this would involve an increase in the cost of medicines. As the European Parliament's 2021 report notes:

> while the existence of trade-offs between the goals of increasing economic efficiency and security of supply is widely recognised, the question of whether reshoring is both an effective and efficient policy for increasing the security of supply is still highly contested.[84]

An increase in costs is not a reason to avoid a policy *per se*, but costs and benefits do need to be balanced. Protecting and promoting human rights is never cost-free; that does not mean that it is not a valid aim. It is about the balance between the benefit from the outcome (protecting human rights) and the cost. It is a political choice, not a legal question, but framing it as a human rights or equality and inclusion issue increases the (moral) obligation to make a change.

Reshoring medicine manufacturing in Europe would not only involve costs for European healthcare systems. Healthcare systems and the patients within them do not exist in atomised spaces co-terminous with nation states. Products move around the globe. And so do infectious diseases. As was noted repeatedly during the COVID-19 pandemic, 'no one is safe until everyone is safe', but the response was a retreat to the 'my nation state first' position.[85] While re-shoring healthcare system capacities might have a positive effect on the rights and inclusion of *some* humans (those within Europe, or European healthcare systems, for example), it may have a significantly negative effect on the rights of other humans.

For example, the independent non-profit Access to Medicine Foundation's *Access to Medicine Index* (2022) points out that none of the world's largest pharmaceutical companies are targeting emerging infectious diseases other than COVID-19 with pipeline projects, despite the evident need to be prepared for the next epidemic or pandemic.[86] Further, the populations of low- and middle income countries are already

[82] Sokol (2024).

[83] See e.g. BiopharmGuy (n.d.).

[84] European Parliament DG External Relations (2021).

[85] Gostin (2023).

[86] Access to Medicine Foundation (2022).

facing threats from Ebola, Marburg virus, and Lassa Fever, with widespread lack of access to vaccines or treatments. Of course, access to medicines is not all that is needed: the broader contexts of climate crisis, urbanisation and migration exacerbate vulnerabilities to human rights violations and exclusion. However, a widespread reshoring of healthcare system capacities to Europe through active reshoring policies and legal obligations that incentivize reshoring would do very little to rectify this situation. Arguably, it would focus energy in the pharmaceutical industry in Europe, rather than seeking to create incentives to ensure that everyone in the world has the right to healthcare (and especially access to essential medicines).

The outward-facing aspects of the Union's 'reshoring' law and policy—like the Strategy—are based on the idea of 'strategic partnerships' with third countries. For example, the Critical Raw Materials Act's first concern for such strategic partnerships is to improve *Union* security of supply.[87]

5 Parliamentary Invisibility and the Rule-of-Law Deficit

Article 10(3) TEU affirms that 'decisions shall be taken as openly and as closely as possible to the citizen', locating the European Parliament and national parliaments at the heart of Union accountability. Building on this premise, chapter already showed that the Union's public-health competences rest on a 'constitutional floor' of Articles 168, 114 and 122 TFEU (supra). Yet the pandemic toolbox adopted since 2022 progressively detaches emergency decision-making from the legislature, threatening the very democratic principle the Treaties proclaim.

Under the ordinary legislative procedure the European Parliament co-decides statutes and controls the EU budget; national parliaments meanwhile enjoy an ex-ante subsidiarity review under Protocol No 2 with an 8-week window.[88] These mechanisms presuppose sufficient time and transparency. Pandemic governance reverses that logic: once an EU-level emergency is declared, critical acts migrate to executive procedures where parliaments hold, at best, residual scrutiny rights (to borrow from the English law). In this context we refer to the limited power that the European Parliament (and the Council) retain once a measure is relegated to an implementing act under the Comitology Regulation. Article 11 of Regulation (EU) 182/2011 allows either chamber, at any time, to notify the Commission that in its view a draft implementing act exceeds the powers conferred in the basic statute; the Commission must 'review' the draft and inform the legislature of the outcome, but it is under no legal duty to amend or withdraw the act, and the adoption timetable is not suspended.[89] Unlike the ordinary legislative procedure, where the European Parliament may veto,

[87] Regulation (EU) 2024/1252 art. 37 (1) (a) (i).

[88] Protocol (No 2) on the application of the principles of subsidiarity and proportionality. Consolidated version of the Treaty on European Union. Official Journal of the European Union C 115:206–209, 9 May 2008.

[89] Regulation (EU, Euratom) No 182/2011 of 16 February 2011 of the European Parliament and of the Council laying down the rules and general principles concerning mechanisms for control

amend, or delay legislation, this mechanism offers only an *ex-post*, non-binding signal confined to ultra-vires concerns. It thus amounts to a residual, largely symbolic safeguard; effective control must then be sought either politically (through resolutions or budget leverage) or judicially (by an annulment action), neither of which provides real-time democratic scrutiny during a fast-moving public-health emergency.

A Union health emergency is now recognised by Commission implementing act (Article 23 §1–4). Because that act follows the examination procedure of Regulation 182/2011, the EP's role is reduced to a generic 'right of scrutiny' under Article 11 of that framework. The Parliament may pass a resolution asking the Commission to reconsider, but it cannot veto. The choice to locate the decisive moment in tertiary legislation therefore substitutes administrative speed for democratic deliberation, in tension with Article 290(1) TFEU's requirement that delegated powers exclude 'essential elements' of the field. Activation of the emergency framework for medical countermeasures occurs by Council regulation on a Commission proposal (Article 3 §1), with the European Parliament sidelined from co-decision and admitted only as an observer on the Health Crisis Board, an arrangement the Parliament criticised in its 12 July 2023 resolution.[90] Concentrating procurement powers in an inter-governmental body not only curtails legislative oversight, but also blurs accountability between Member-State executives and the Commission.

Unlike EMA or ECDC, the Health Emergency Preparedness and Response Authority was created by Commission Decision 2021/576 under Article 17 TEU and Article 122 TFEU, bypassing the ordinary agency-founding regulation that would have required European Parliament approval. A 2023 CEPS in-depth analysis labels this design an 'accountability gap', noting that HERA commands multi-billion budgets without ex-ante parliamentary mandate.[91] Budget discharge powers remain, but they operate *post factum* and cannot re-shape HERA's crisis posture.

When the Council Presidency activates the Integrated Political Crisis Response (IPCR) arrangements, Article 14 of Decision 2018/1993 merely obliges it to 'inform' the European Parliament.[92] No access to situational-awareness reports is guaranteed, and national parliaments are entirely absent. By contrast, in police cooperation the Joint Parliamentary Scrutiny Group for Europol provides a model of continuous bicameral oversight,[93] which underscores how health security lags behind comparable domains.

Protocol No 2 is ill-suited to crisis governance: technical draft acts arrive late, and the eight-week deadline often expires before an emergency instrument is even

---

by Member States of the Commission's exercise of implementing powers. Official Journal of the European Union L 55:13–18, 28 February 2011.

[90] European Parliament (2024) Resolution (EU) P9_TA(2023)0282 of 12 July 2023 on the COVID-19 pandemic: lessons learned and recommendations for the future. Official Journal of the European Union C 4003, 17 July 2024.

[91] CEPS (2023).

[92] Council of the European Union (2018) Council Implementing Decision (EU) 2018/1993 of 11 December 2018 on the EU Integrated Political Crisis Response Arrangements. Official Journal of the European Union L 320:28–34, 17 December 2018.

[93] Cooper (2018).

published for scrutiny. Nor is there a standing inter-parliamentary forum for health security, unlike the COSAC model that meets for justice and home-affairs questions.[94] The result is a democratic blind spot at the very moment when executive discretion peaks.

The Court of Justice has shown its willingness to annul Commission tertiary acts for procedural overreach in fields as diverse as data protection (*Schrems I*, C-362/14)[95] and chemicals regulation (*Commission v Sweden*, C-389/19 P).[96] Reliance on ex-post litigation, however, is no substitute for legislative control: judgments arrive years after the fact and cannot remedy democratic exclusion during a fast-moving crisis.

In our view, to realign emergency governance with Article 10 TEU the Union should (i) insert a *sunset clause* in Regulation 2022/2371 requiring European Parliament and Council consent to prolong emergencies; (ii) transform HERA into an independent agency under the common-agency template, ensuring co-legislative input into its mandate; (iii) grant the European Parliament and national parliaments observer status, including access to classified documents, on the IPCR round-tables and the Health Crisis Board; and (iv) establish a permanent Health-Security Scrutiny Sub-committee in the European Parliament.

6 Conclusions

From this initial overview of the Union's pandemic preparedness law and policy we can draw together some preliminary conclusions about the extent to which the relevant law and policy is (i) consistent with basic principles of legal preparedness; and—focusing on the principle that legal preparedness involves inclusivity—(ii) sufficiently 'outward facing' or globally open.

Legal preparedness should be process-based, aiming to have in place in advance of a public health emergency like a pandemic, the legal and policy instruments necessary to respond. Consistent with basic 'rule of law' norms, law should be knowable, known and consistent. Several elements of the Union's pandemic preparedness as it is unfolding are process-based. There are obligations to make and review plans, at both Union and national level. New institutional arrangements, drawing on comitology and other existing Union institutions such as the ECDC, are involved in processes of review. Arguably, the review of legislation such as the Union's pharmaceuticals package could count as part of the process of legal preparedness. In terms of the law being knowable, known and consistent, here we can point to an unfolding density of overlapping legal instruments, supported by policy documents such as guidance.

[94] Pinheiro Dias (2018).

[95] Schrems v Data Protection Commissioner (2015) Case C-362/14, ECLI:EU:C:2015:650. Judgment of the Court (Grand Chamber) of 6 October 2015.

[96] Commission v Kingdom of Sweden (2021) Case C-389/19 P, Judgment of the Court (First Chamber) of 25 February 2021, ECLI:EU:C:2021:131.

The embedding of preparedness activity in formal laws, adopted long before a health crisis emerges, is consistent with basic principles of legal preparedness, including transparency. But the sheer numbers of overlapping legal documents, emanating from different Union processes, different legal bases, and different parts of the European Commission, does run the risk of fostering inconsistencies, and making the law less knowable than if it were contained in a single set of legal instruments. There is also a tendency of policy documents to overstate the legal position, for example, to refer to proposed legislation as if it had already been adopted or was definitely going to be adopted.

Whether the Union's pandemic preparedness law and policies pay sufficient attention to the tendency to grant too much discretionary power to executive or administrative authorities is a topic that should be explored in greater detail than what this chapter is able to offer. Our rule of law concerns rest uneasily with the current modus operandi. One thing is crystal clear for the authors: pandemic preparedness should not be built on executive prowess alone. By marginalizing parliaments, the EU forfeits the deliberative legitimacy that underpins citizen compliance and risks exposing its emergency acts to annulment for procedural defects. Re-embedding the European Parliament and national elected parliamentary chambers at each stage of the crisis cycle is therefore not a luxury but a constitutional necessity if the Union's next response is to be both effective and lawful.

In terms of incursion on fundamental human rights, this question is rather invisible in the law and policy discourses discussed in this preliminary review. It may be that a deeper dive would reveal more attention to human rights questions, but this chapter suggests that human rights are almost entirely missing from the Union's reshoring law and policy, which is a key plank of its pandemic preparedness work. Other elements of the Union's preparedness planning, such as Regulation 2022/2371/EU on serious cross-border threats to health, do refer to some human rights protection, for instance data protection in the context of contact tracing.

By far the weakest aspects of the Union's pandemic preparedness law and policy, in terms of legal preparedness norms, are its 'outward facing' aspects. There is very little attention—especially when focusing at a global level—which, after all, is how a pandemic is experienced, by definition—to the unequal effects that a pandemic or other public health emergency has on the most vulnerable. The Union's *Preparedness Union Strategy* 2025 notes that 'the connection between internal and external Union action needs to be strengthened',[97] and resilience through external partnerships is one of the seven areas of actions envisaged.[98] But the actual content of these external partnerships is all about *Union* resilience, and the effects of a future health crisis on the *Union* population. The Union's reshoring law and policy pays almost no attention to the notion that, in a pandemic, 'no one is safe until everyone is safe'. By implication, it values the human rights (and lives) of European citizens and residents more highly, leaving the rest of the world to fend for itself.

[97] European Commission (2025), p. 2.

[98] European Commission (2025), p. 3.

In light of the preceding analysis, particularly the instrument-mapping in Sect. 4 and the democratic-oversight critique in Sect. 5, the Union should adopt a concise 'Pandemic Preparedness Checklist' for the 2024–2029 institutional cycle that tackles three residual deficits simultaneously. First, the legal maze identified in Sect. 4.2 would benefit from codification: a digitally accessible *Pandemic Code*, updated at fixed intervals, would consolidate scattered acts and supply an authoritative point of reference for national administrations. Second, to correct the executive-legislative asymmetry exposed in Sect. 5, a *Pandemic Urgency Procedure* should be grafted onto Regulation 182/2011, granting the European Parliament and national chambers time-bound veto opportunities whenever the Commission triggers emergency implementing powers. Third, consistent with the external-solidarity benchmark, future subsidies and joint-procurement contracts ought to be conditioned on verifiable global-access clauses, ensuring that Union capacity translates into affordable counter-measures beyond its borders. Addressing complexity, accountability, and outward justice in one integrated checklist would position the Union not only to manage the next outbreak more coherently but also to demonstrate that multilevel crisis governance can remain rights-respecting, democratically legitimate, and globally responsible and show that Article 3(5) TEU has an actual meaning in reality and is not just ink pressed on the paper.

Antonio Gerace's reconstruction of early-modern *Pest-ordnungen* reminds us that law has long served as the thin line between civic survival and collapse: '*Quemadmodum homo absque anima rationali non potest consistere, ita etiam societas absque jure est peritura*'.[99] Girolamo Gastaldi's 1656 *Tractatus de Avertenda et Profliganda Peste*—a handbook prescribing movement bans, price controls and compulsory burial rites—illustrates how magistrates asserted *strict yet limited* authority to contain contagion. The analogy to contemporary Union health law is instructive: just as early-modern rulers were confined to *ius territoriale*, today's Union acts under a *supporting* competence (Art 168 TFEU), its reach defined as much by political consent as by formal powers (Sect. 4.1 supra). Gerace's historical insistence on *limited magistracy* finds a modern counterpart in the Union's duty to respect proportionality and subsidiarity even under duress. Section 4.2 catalogued the Union's expansive menu of hard, soft and contractual tools; what is missing is not competence but a parliament(s)-centred *Pandemic Urgency Procedure* that could discipline those tools in real time. Anticipatory law-making, in other words, must be matched by anticipatory democracy.

Giovanni Leghissa has argued that every apparatus devised 'to measure, govern and protect the body' is simultaneously a dispositif that *produces* the very population it claims only to record.[100] Section 4's case studies—on emergency declarations, supply-chain reshoring and HERA—show precisely this dynamic: epidemiological dashboards and stockpile algorithms translate biological vulnerability into governable risk categories, enabling what Foucault called the 'biopolitical take-over of life'. Yet they do so without systematic parliamentary mediation (Sect. 5 supra), confirming

---

[99] See the chapter by Gerace in this volume.

[100] See the chapter by Leghissa in this volume.

Leghissa's caution that technocratic sovereignty thrives where democratic oversight recedes.

Taken together, the historical, theoretical and doctrinal strands sketched above support the volume's claim that emergencies reveal latent power structures. By foregrounding how legal technique, political narrative and ethical judgment converge on the vulnerable body, the chapter turns European Union preparedness into what we can call a *'space of critical enquiry'*, inviting readers to query not only what the Union *can* do in the next outbreak but what it *ought* to do if it is to recover resilience without forfeiting democratic and human-rights-regarding soul.

References

Access to Medicine Foundation (2022) Access to medicine index 2022. Access to Medicine Foundation, Amsterdam. https://accesstomedicinefoundation.org/medialibrary/2022-access-to-medicine-index-1668514482.pdf

Ayala A, Brush A, Chai S, Fernandez J, Ginsbach K, Gottschalk K, Halabi S, Hosangadi D, Mapatano D, Monahan J, Moretti C, Pillinger M, Ramirez GS, Rosenfeld E (2022) Advancing legal preparedness through the global health security agenda. J Law Med Ethics 50(1):200–203

CEPS (2023) Mission governance and operations of the EU HERA: CEPS in-depth analysis 2023/01. Centre for European Policy Studies, Brussels

Cooper I (2018) A new form of democratic oversight in the EU: the joint parliamentary scrutiny group for Europol. Perspect Fed 10(3):184–213

Delhomme V, Hervey T (2022) The European Union's response to the Covid-19 crisis and the legitimacy of the Union's legal order. Yearbook Eur Law 41:48–82

Eerens D, Hrzic R, Clemens T (2023) The architecture of the European Union's pandemic preparedness and response policy framework. Eur J Public Health 33(1):42–48

European Commission (2020) Common EU toolbox for Member States on mobile applications to support contact tracing in the EU's fight against COVID-19. Publications Office of the European Union, Luxembourg. https://health.ec.europa.eu/document/download/70c9e921-4930-4dbc-925e-d5a38ec393b8_en

European Commission (2023a) State of health preparedness report 2023. Publications office of the European Union, Luxembourg. https://health.ec.europa.eu/publications/state-health-preparedness-report-2023_en

European Commission (2023b) Frequently asked questions—revision of the EU pharmaceutical legislation. Press release Q&A_23_1844, Brussels. https://ec.europa.eu/commission/presscorner/detail/en/qanda_23_1844

European Commission (2023c) Better regulation toolbox. Publications Office of the European Union, Luxembourg. https://commission.europa.eu/system/files/2023-09/BR%20toolbox%20-%20Jul%202023%20-%20FINAL.pdf

European Commission (2025) European preparedness Union strategy. https://commission.europa.eu/topics/preparedness_en

European Directorate for the Quality of Medicines & HealthCare (n.d.) EDQM Initiatives on medicine shortages. https://www.edqm.eu/en/edqm-initiatives-on-medicine-shortages

European Parliament DG External Policies (2021) Post-COVID value chains: opportunities for reshoring production back to Europe in a globalised economy. EP/EXPO/INTA/FWC/2019-01/LOT5/R/07 EN, PE 653.626, March 2021. https://www.europarl.europa.eu/RegData/etudes/STUD/2021/653626/EXPO_STU(2021)653626_EN.pdf

Global Health Security Agenda (2021) Global health security legal preparedness action package. https://globalhealthsecurityagenda.org/legal-preparedness/

Gostin L (2023) The great coronavirus pandemic: an unparalleled collapse in global solidarity. In: Wilkinson D, Savulescu J (eds) Pandemic ethics: from COVID-19 to disease X. Oxford University Press, Oxford, pp 15–47
Granger I (2023) Launching the world disasters report 2022. In: International Federation of Red Cross and Red Crescent Societies (eds) World disasters report 2022. IFRC, Geneva, emphasis added
Hervey T (2008) The European Union's governance of health care and the welfare modernisation agenda. Cambridge Yearb Eur Leg Stud 10:1–32
Hervey T (2023) EU health law. In: Barnard C, Peers S (eds) European Union law. Oxford University Press, Oxford
Hervey T, de Ruijter A (2020) The dynamic potential of European Union health law. Eur J Risk Regul 11(4):726–735
Hervey TK, McHale JV (2015) European Union health law: themes and implications. Cambridge University Press, Cambridge
Hervey T, Michalak M (2025) European Union border law during the COVID-19 pandemic. Common Mark Law Rev 62(3):747–796
IFRC (2022) Guidance on law and public health emergency preparedness and response. International Federation of Red Cross and Red Crescent Societies, Geneva
Institute of Medicine (1988) The future of public health. National Academy Press, Washington, DC
McEvoy E (2022) Procuring in a pandemic: assessing the use of the EU public-procurement directives, the joint procurement agreement and advance purchase agreements. Northern Ireland Leg Q 73(2):260–282
Moulton AD, Gottfried RN, Goodman RA, Murphy AM, Rawson RD (2003) What is public health legal preparedness? J Law Med Ethics 31:672–683
Negri S, Bonfigli S, Cesta E, Di Federico G (2024) Strengthening legal preparedness and response within the global health emergency framework: the role of the GHSA legal preparedness action package. J Glob Health Law 1(1):88–105
Niinistö S (2024) Safer together—strengthening Europe's civilian and military preparedness and readiness. Office of the special adviser to the president of the European Commission, Brussels
Petti A (2022) EU COVID-19 purchase and export mechanism: a framework for EU operational autonomy. Common Mark Law Rev 59(5):1333–1370
Pinheiro Dias B (2018) The contribution of COSAC to joint parliamentary scrutiny in the EU: a practitioner's view. Perspect Fed 10(3)
Purnhagen KP, Flear ML, Hervey TK, Herwig A, de Ruijter A (2020) More competences than you knew? The web of health competences for Union action in response to the COVID-19 outbreak. Eur J Risk Regul 11:1–14
Sachs JD, Abdool Karim SS, Aknin L, Allen J, Brosbøl K, Colombo F, Cuevas Barron G, Espinosa MF, Gaspar V, Gaviria A, Haines A, Hotez PJ, Koundouri P, Larraín Bascuñán F, Lee J-K, Pate MA, Ramos G, Reddy KS, Serageldin I, Thwaites J, Vike-Freiberga V, Wang C, Were MK, Xue L, Bahadur C, Bottazzi ME, Bullen C, Laryea-Adjei G, Ben Amor Y, Karadag O, Lafortune G, Torres E, Barredo L, Bartels JGE, Joshi N, Hellard M, Huynh UK, Khandelwal S, Lazarus JV, Michie S (2022) The Lancet Commission on lessons for the future from the COVID-19 pandemic. Lancet 400(10359):1224–1280
Sokol T (2024) European health data space, use of data and data subjects' control over their own health data: can an opt-out restore the balance? Eur J Health Law 31(4):365–388
Telles P (2022) Extremely urgent public procurement under Directive 2014/24/EU and the COVID-19 pandemic. Maastricht J Eur Comp Law 29(2):215–228

Mirko Djukovic , LLB, LLM, SJD, is a postdoctoral researcher at the Hertie School's Centre for Fundamental Rights and a former CIVICA postdoctoral fellow at the EUI Department of Law. He holds a law degree from the University of Montenegro and L.L.M. degrees in European Integration Law from the University of Belgrade and in International Economic and Business Law from Kyushu University. He defended his thesis, 'Regulating Biomedicine: The Case of Human Tissues Bioprinting', at the Central European University. He has taught EU law, human rights and new technologies, and non-discrimination law, law and public policy, and international law at universities in Montenegro, Hungary, Austria, China and Germany; held research fellowships at the Max Planck Institute for Comparative Public Law and International Law in Heidelberg, at Kyushu University on regulatory approaches to new technologies, and at CEU CELAB on the ethical, legal, and social impact of new technologies. Mirko consulted for the EU, the CoE, the WHO, and the UNDP. His research focuses on human rights, health rights, technology regulation, ethics, and EU law. He is co-chair of the Young Scholars Research Group of the European Association of Health Law.

Tamara Hervey , LLB, PhD, FAcSS, PFHEA, MFPH (known as Tammy) is Jean Monnet Professor of EU Law ad personam at The St. George's City Law School, which she joined in 2021 after academic posts at the law schools of Durham, Manchester, Nottingham, and Sheffield; she holds visiting positions at the Universities of Vienna and Amsterdam. Her work lies in transnational, global, and comparative health law, especially EU health and medicines law, as well as equality and diversity and legal education. She leads the EU health law entries for the OUP Online Encyclopaedia of EU Law, convenes annual author workshops. She co-led an AHRC-funded project that produced Research Methodologies in EU and International Law (Hart, 2011), co-edited the Research Handbook on Comparative Health Law (OUP), and was Principal Investigator of the ESRC project Health Governance after Brexit, whose major output is Not What the Bus Promised (Hart/Bloomsbury, 2023). Her contributions include the Covid Lex-Atlas and articles on EU 'Covid law' in the Yearbook of European Law and the Common Market Law Review; she has advised the House of Lords and the House of Commons on cross-border care and health policy after Brexit.

Pharmaceutical Citizenship in the Pandemic: What Does the English Experience with 'COVID Passports' Reveal?

Keith Syrett

Abstract This chapter examines the short-lived English policy requiring certification of COVID-19 immunisation status for entry to certain venues, assessing its relevance to the concept of pharmaceutical citizenship. While the policy reflects aspects of that framework—particularly the restriction of freedoms based on pharmacological status—other core dimensions, such as access to treatment and marginalisation, are less prominent here. The analysis highlights the need to refine the concept when used to describe government strategies that purposefully shape individual rights through law. It also underscores the complicating role of personal autonomy, as the absence of pharmaceutical citizenship may result from freely made treatment choices. The chapter ultimately situates these issues within the enduring dilemma of public health law: balancing individual liberty with the state's responsibility to protect population health.

1 Introduction

Citizenship is fundamentally a legal construct (albeit one which possesses highly significant and controversial political dimensions), but to date the literature engaging with the concept of pharmaceutical citizenship, first formulated in 2005,[1] has focused mainly on its social aspects. Nevertheless, there is a fundamental, if overlooked, synergy at play here. In particular, the substantial body of advocacy, litigation and academic research work undertaken in recent years on access to medicines as a human right reflects an acknowledgement that there may be a facilitative role for law as a mechanism through which individuals may bring about the 'demarginalisation' central to pharmaceutical citizenship through the conferral of rights which enable

[1] See Ecks (2005), p. 239.

K. Syrett (✉)
University of Bristol Law School, Bristol, UK
e-mail: Keith.Syrett@bristol.ac.uk

M. Balestrieri and A. Cauduro (eds.), *The Legal Anatomy of the Body*, Ius Gentium: Comparative Perspectives on Law and Justice 142,
https://doi.org/10.1007/978-3-032-26434-3_10

them to recapture full membership of the community.[2] Yet, what is missing from this ever expanding oeuvre is a conceptualisation in the terms outlined in the article by Stefan Ecks which originated the pharmaceutical citizenship discourse. In short, it is as if the disciplines of medical anthropology and sociology on the one hand, and law on the other, are operating in different spheres with no points of commonality between them.[3]

This chapter seeks to offer a preliminary response to this lacuna through a brief analysis of the relationship between law and pharmaceutical citizenship in the context of particular responses to the COVID pandemic in England. This example provides an instructive framing for two related reasons. First, notions of citizenship were central to discourse concerning the appropriate public response to the threat presented by the pandemic, that is compliance with governmental demands vis-à-vis COVID vaccination was portrayed as a dimension of 'good citizenship'. Secondly, and conversely, policy was framed in such a way that failure to comply, i.e. COVID vaccine refusal, would carry negative implications for aspects of an individual's membership of the community: their 'citizenship rights' broadly understood. Arguably, the state could be said to be deliberately effecting a degree of marginalisation through the triggering of negative sanctions—effectively, utilising restrictions on citizenship as a means of coercion—although, as will be seen, the picture was in fact rather more nuanced than this.

It should be emphasised that the ambition of this chapter is strictly limited. My objective is not to offer a comprehensive analysis of the ways in which various states utilised potential or actual legal measures to penalise, or threaten to penalise, those who refused to participate in COVID vaccination programmes. Such would be an extremely onerous, and possibly tedious, task. Rather, my much more modest goals are to explicate and demystify the notion of pharmaceutical citizenship for those working in the legal field (albeit not necessarily restricted to that audience alone); and to consider its salience as an analytical tool which can help us to further comprehend certain exercises of authority—in Foucauldian terms, instances of 'biopower'[4]—prevalent in the contemporary state and exemplified by the COVID case. It is my hope that this will stimulate readers to develop a much fuller and richer research agenda than space permits me here.

I seek, first of all, to explore the meaning of the concept.

---

[2] For a comprehensive survey of access to medicines as an aspect of international human rights law, see Syrett (forthcoming).

[3] For a brief discussion of the value of sociological theory in the legal sphere, see e.g. Syrett (2019), pp. 112–113.

[4] See Foucault (1998, 2020) and Cisney and Morar (2015).

2 Understanding Pharmaceutical Citizenship

The notion of pharmaceutical citizenship has its genesis in the related but broader concept of biological citizenship, which refers to modes of belonging, conferral of rights and claims for access to resources which turn upon the biological status of the individual as distinct from other (politico-legal) forms of categorisation, such as national identity.[5] As a subset of this analytical insight, pharmaceutical citizenship is reflective of the contemporary salience of *pharmaceuticalisation*, a social phenomenon which has been described as the 'translation or transformation of human conditions, capabilities and capacities into opportunities for pharmaceutical intervention'.[6] It is explained by its originator as revolving around two forms of inquiry:

> Firstly, how does legal citizenship determine rights of access to pharmaceuticals? This includes, for example, the issue if equality between citizens also means equal entitlement to receive drugs. Secondly, what implications does the taking of pharmaceuticals have for a person's status as a citizen? Questions here include whether the taking of certain pharmaceuticals, such as various psychotropics, impairs one's rights as a fully responsible citizen, or whether patients can only regain full citizenship rights if they undergo pharmacological treatment.[7]

As can be seen from this extract, there is a innate connection between this form of citizenship and the contentious issue of access, which has emerged as a central dimension of global health policy in recent decades.[8] Pharmaceutical citizenship entails a right of access to medicinal substances that can enable one to function on full and equal terms with other members of society; in contrast, lack of access can deprive an individual of the opportunity to live one's life in the manner enjoyed by others. Hence, in addition to likely negative health consequences stemming from a lack of access, the 'pharmaceutical non-citizen' is one who experiences *social marginalisation.*[9] Conversely, and in keeping with the transformative power of pharmaceuticals,[10] provision or restoration of access can effect a reintegration of the individual into society, 'reinstat[ing] citizenship to individuals and communities that have been excluded by virtue of their biological... condition'.[11] Biomedical intervention by means of pharmaceutical therapy is thus characterised by 'promissory discourses of normalisation and demarginalisation'.[12]

[5] See Rose (2007), Chap. 5. Other terms used to capture similar ideas include 'biocitizenship', 'medical citizenship', and 'therapeutic citizenship'.

[6] Williams et al. (2011), p. 711. See also Biehl (2007), p. 1083.

[7] Ecks (2005), p. 241.

[8] See Syrett (forthcoming), especially Chap. 1.

[9] See Ecks (2005) and Ogunrotifa (2020).

[10] On the transformative nature of pharmaceuticals, see Whyte et al. (2002), pp. 5–6.

[11] Persson et al. (2016), p. 371.

[12] Persson et al. (2016), p. 359. See also Ecks (2005), p. 241.

What Ecks and other authors present is a deeper conception of a 'complex process of overlapping "citizenship projects" that is not limited to the politico-legal sphere'.[13] However, this endeavour may serve to somewhat camouflage the continued salience of law's role in structuring citizenship, even if we choose to view this concept through a biomedical lens. Notably, the conferral of rights of access as a dimension of pharmaceutical citizenship can be viewed as a matter of law since a right is fundamentally a legally enforceable claim,[14] albeit one which simultaneously sounds potently in the political realm as is the case with human rights. Similarly, the phenomenon of marginalisation which lies at the heart of the discourse may be underpinned by legal provisions which restrict or remove access to pharmaceuticals. Indeed, denial of pharmaceutical citizenship may be an intentional strategy on the part of government, mediated through legal mechanisms. This brings me to the COVID case, to which I now turn.

3 COVID and Citizenship

An admittedly crude means of partitioning the timeframe of the COVID pandemic is to divide it into the period before a vaccine had been developed and the subsequent phase of mass public immunisation, while of course being cognisant of the differential pace and reach of the vaccine rollout across nations. Notions of citizenship played an important part in both phases, to the extent that pandemic citizenship has been mooted as a valuable analytical category.[15]

One significant dimension of the pre-vaccination period was deployment of citizenship discourse to incentivise public compliance with the (onerous) requirements imposed by government. The virtuous, self-disciplined and other-regarding individual was cast as a citizen, in contrast to the selfish and irresponsible 'covidiot'.[16] Moreover, measures taken to combat the COVID pandemic also functioned to disrupt and recast contemporary understandings of citizenship. The dominant neoliberal model of the self-interested individual operating on the basis of a rational calculation of the costs and benefits of actions selected as an exercise of free choice—a *homo economicus*—was replaced (at least temporarily) by that of a constrained and unfree, passive but responsible individual prepared to make personal sacrifices for the collective good of population health,[17] such as restrictions on movement or gatherings with others.

The sacrifices demanded of an individual included, but were certainly not restricted to, those relating to bodily integrity, in that a 'good citizen' was expected to comply with recommendations to receive the COVID vaccine, once this had

[13] Ecks (2005), p. 241.

[14] See White (1982).

[15] See Hollings (2020), p. 81 and Piccoli (2024), p. 443.

[16] See Lim (2020), p. 78.

[17] See Andreouli and Brice (2022), p. 555.

been developed and made publicly available. This was the case notwithstanding the priority accorded to the principle of individual autonomy in many (especially Western) systems of bioethics and law.[18] Autonomy, which may be defined most straightforwardly as self-government,[19] entails that an individual has the freedom to make whatever choices they wish in respect of the receipt of medical treatment, including vaccination. This produces a strong presumption against mandatory vaccination programmes, often reinforced by widespread public opposition to these.[20] However, the public health case for high levels of vaccination against COVID was compelling, even if mandating immunisation for the public was thought to be too gross an infringement of the predominant principle of autonomy to be tolerated in most liberal societies.[21] In particular, the anticipated impact of vaccination on the severity of the disease promised to reduce the previously excessive strain on hospital resources, especially those allocated to critical care. It was therefore crucial for government to ensure as high a take-up of vaccine as was feasible. This would secure herd immunity within the population.[22]

4 The Potential of 'COVID Passports'

During both the pre- and post-immunisation phases of the COVID pandemic, state (and media) rhetoric therefore served to differentiate between the 'good' and 'bad' citizen according to the willingness to adhere to governmental requirements (or strong recommendations) as to the responsible mode of behaviour. There is an important connection here to the broader contemporary trend towards the 'securitisation of citizenship' wherein 'security concerns are used to legitimize a "politics of the exception" [and] it becomes more and more important to correctly "identify" individuals in order to distinguish between the "good" and the "bad", namely those considered as "normal" and those viewed as a "threat" to the polity'.[23] This is perhaps unsurprising, given the long-standing intersection between public health measures, including those pursued through legal mechanisms, and the security of the state.[24]

The discourse of good citizenship was reinforced by specific steps which served to distinguish the sick and the well in a manner which might be considered to be broadly comparable to those which differentiate citizens from others. Prominent amongst

---

[18] See Smith (1997), p. 182 and Herring (2025), p. 22.

[19] See Coggon and Miola (2011), pp. 524–525.

[20] For example, public unrest accompanied the various legislative attempts to mandate vaccination of children against smallpox in England in the second half of the nineteenth century. For discussion, see Coggon et al. (2017), pp. 42–43.

[21] For discussion of the incidence and nature of vaccine mandates worldwide, see Cameron-Blake et al. (2023), p. 1402.

[22] See Dong et al. (2021), p. 174.

[23] Frost and Winter (2017), p. 4. See generally Nyers (2009).

[24] For discussion, see Sidel and Levy (2002), Fidler (2007) and Aldis (2008).

these were measures which functioned to allowed individuals certain freedoms which were denied to other persons on the basis of COVID test or vaccination status. The close correlation to citizenship was evident here in the widely-used terminology of 'COVID passport' or 'vaccine passport' to label the documentation used to evidence status. In order to illustrate the nature of initiatives of this type, I shall briefly describe the position in England during the pandemic.

In the relatively early stages of the pandemic, proposals were floated by government for certification of immunity. This strategy was intended to assist in effecting some degree of rebalancing between freedom and economic imperatives on the one hand and public health goals on the other, by enabling lower-risk individuals to return to work and other facets of 'normal life' more quickly.[25] Such proposals raised awkward, but not insurmountable, ethical questions.[26] However, even more problematic were practical considerations including the doubtful accuracy of serological tests and, crucially, the evolving knowledge that the presence of antibodies as a consequence of previous infection did not confer immunity from reinfection.

Subsequently, in the wake of the programme of mass immunisation which followed administration of the first dose of the vaccine to a member of the public at University Hospital Coventry on 8 December 2020, certification became a more viable approach. Accordingly in April 2021—by which point more than 30 million people in the UK had received at least an initial vaccination—a series of events, including a comedy night, a snooker tournament and major football matches, were announced as venues for the trialling of 'COVID passports' for entry.[27] Documentation eventually took the form of an NHS COVID Pass available digitally or in paper format, which could also be used to fulfil international travel requirements. From 19 July 2021, as some restrictions eased, businesses such as nightclubs and large events were encouraged to use the Pass as a condition of entry.[28]

However, it was not until the emergence of the highly infectious Omicron variant, at a point when all those over 18 years of age had been offered two doses of the vaccine, that proof of status to gain access became mandatory, albeit only in certain high-risk instances. The Health Protection (Coronavirus, Restrictions) (Entry to Venues and Events) (England) Regulations 2021 came into effect on 15 December 2021.[29] These required mandatory certification of COVID status for entry to nightclubs, dance halls, discotheques and other late-night dance venues; indoor live music venues, theatres, concert halls, exhibition halls, conference centres and other public halls with 500 or more attendees expected to stand or move around; a sports stadium, arena, centre, pool, rink or sports ground with 500 or more indoor attendees or 4000 outdoor attendees expected to stand or move around; and any venue with a capacity of 10,000 where 10,000 or more were in attendance.[30] Certain exemptions applied,

---

[25] See e.g. Merrick (2020).

[26] For discussion, see Brown et al. (2020).

[27] See BBC News (2021a).

[28] See BBC News (2021b).

[29] SI 2021/1416, reg. 1(2)(b).

[30] SI 2021/1416, Schedule 1.

for example for weddings, funerals and communal worship.[31] ‘Responsible persons’ (such as event organisers and venue managers)[32] were required to take reasonable measures to ensure that only persons who could prove (via the NHS COVID Pass or equivalent, or proof of foreign vaccination)[33] that they had received a full course of COVID vaccines; or that they had tested negative within the preceding 48 h, or had participated in a clinical trial or were exempt from vaccination on clinical grounds.[34] Failure to meet the requirements constituted an offence punishable by a fine, with prosecution falling to the appropriate local authority or to the Crown Prosecution Service.[35] The local authority also had powers to issue notices requiring the making of improvements and ordering the closure of all or part of the premises.[36]

The provisions of the Regulations were temporary. They expired on 26 January 2022 and were not renewed by Parliament notwithstanding that the highest ever prevalence of COVID infections in England was recorded that month.[37] Voluntary use of the NHS COVID Pass for entry could continue, but government guidance relating to this was withdrawn from 1 April 2022, albeit that the Pass remained available digitally for a limited period to facilitate international travel.

5 ‘COVID Passports’: An Instance of Pharmaceutical Citizenship?

Does the analytical framework outlined previously in this chapter assist in building an enhanced understanding of the nature and effects of the policy on health certification pursued, by means of legal instrument, by the English government during the COVID pandemic? In this section, I offer some preliminary reflections on the value and applicability of the pharmaceutical citizenship concept in this particular context. Future researchers may wish to pursue these points, or others, in more depth than I have been able to do here.

A reading drawn from the literature on pharmaceutical citizenship appears apposite to this case because the ‘COVID passport’ policy functioned to confer (albeit only temporarily) certain rights which were denied to others based upon whether the recommended course of pharmacological treatment had been undertaken. Expressed in different terms, ‘full’ citizenship was available only to those who were able

[31] SI 2021/1416, Schedule 2.

[32] SI 2021/1416, reg. 5(7).

[33] SI 2021/1416, reg. 9.

[34] SI 2021/1416, reg. 8.

[35] SI 2021/1416, reg. 16.

[36] SI 2021/1416, regs. 12–14.

[37] See Elliott et al. (2022), p. 4500.

to evidence a particular immunisation status.[38] The scenario thus maps onto the second of the queries identified by Ecks.[39] Indeed, the connection to the conventional discourses and norms of citizenship is, arguably, even stronger in this instance than in those explored by Ecks and other authors, in that the status of the individual, and the consequent rights, are constructed and governed by law as is the case with citizenship as traditionally understood.

The 'COVID passport' example thus functions to demonstrate that conferral or removal of citizenship rights can be a tangible and deliberate strategy pursued by government through law rather than the much more nebulous reshaping of social relations which forms the subject-matter of much of the literature. Such a strategy forms a dimension of the state's exercise of public health powers: it is a vehicle by means of which the state seeks to better achieve protection and promotion of population health.[40] In this instance, government explicitly sought to reduce the risks of transmission of the virus in high-risk settings.[41] Less overtly, the policy had potential to incentivise vaccination—especially as it was most likely to impact a population cohort which might otherwise pass up the opportunity[42]—and thus contribute to the securing of herd immunity, while simultaneously minimising the economic and mental health harms associated with lockdown policies. However, this potential was far from fully realised given the relatively late stage at which the strategy was implemented, the short duration of its existence, and the acceptance of evidence other than vaccination status as the basis of grant of rights of entry.

The very limited duration of this policy also impacted upon the degree of marginalisation which was experienced by those affected by it. As noted previously, the dynamics of de/marginalisation are central to pharmaceutical citizenship, and marginalisation of those who had refused to undergo immunisation would assist in realising the aforementioned objective of incentivisation. There is, however, no particular evidence to prove or disprove the existence of this *social* effect in this instance, unsurprisingly so given that the policy was only in place for a little over 1 month. Furthermore, no marginalisation of vaccine refusers was effected *by law* since the sanctions for non-compliance with the Regulations were directed instead at 'responsible persons' i.e. those organising or managing the event or venue.

It might be inferred from this that the conceptual framing of pharmaceutical citizenship is, in fact, an imperfect fit for this case. This position is reinforced by the fact that access, which is a *leitmotif* of the work of Ecks and others, does not appear germane to the scenario discussed in this chapter. The suspension of certain 'citizenship rights' due to immunisation status did not stem from any inability to

---

[38] Although note that completion of a course of vaccines was not the only status which might entitle an individual to entry to the venues and events specified in the Regulation: see text accompanying n 34 above.

[39] See text accompanying n 7 above.

[40] For general discussion, see Coggon et al. (2017), *passim*.

[41] See DHSC (2021), paras 7.1, 7.5.

[42] Data demonstrates that vaccination rates decrease among younger population cohorts: see ONS (2023), Fig. 1.

access COVID vaccines[43]—that is, a systemic problem of health services—but rather from choices made freely by the individual in question.[44]

This is entirely consonant with the principle of autonomy, as outlined above. The weight attached to this principle may also be seen to underlie the approach taken towards sanctions in the Regulations. If refusal of the (freely available) course of vaccines was merely a matter of the expression of preference, imposition of penalties upon the individual would seem to be ethically impermissible. Hence, recipients and non-recipients of the vaccine should be accorded equal treatment by the law, with any legal sanctions instead being imposed upon those with some degree of control of the number of entrants to the venue or event.

6 Conclusion

This brief consideration of the short-lived English policy on certification of COVID immunisation status for entry to certain venues and events might leave readers in some doubt as to the usefulness of the concept of pharmaceutical citizenship. In some respects this framework is clearly pertinent, as reflected in the 'COVID passport' discourse and in the suspension of certain freedoms (notably those of movement, in the form of entry onto certain premises) as a consequence of, *inter alia*, status as an unvaccinated person (that is, one who has not undertaken a particular course of (preventative) pharmaceutical treatment). On the other hand, factors which are usually regarded as being of central significance to a proper understanding of the phenomenon, such as the question of access to pharmaceutical treatment or the dynamics of de/marginalisation, appear to be much less relevant to this case.

Such a summation prompts two final observations. The first of these is that there is clearly scope for further interrogation and refinement of the conceptual framework of pharmaceutical citizenship. In particular, future research would do well to focus upon the implications of its deployment as a dimension of a strategy adopted by government—that is: what is the character and effect of policies, realised through law, which purposely impinge upon (or, alternatively, confer) rights and freedoms of individual citizens with a particular pharmacological treatment status?

Second, and relatedly, the case study explored in this chapter serves as a valuable reminder that autonomy may function as a significant complicating factor. It is too simplistic to presume that all instances in which pharmaceutical citizenship is lost, or never secured, stem from systemic failure. Some, perhaps many, may arise as

[43] Of course, the situation was very different in the Global South, where inequitable access was a significant problem. For discussion, see Torreele and Amon (2021), p. 273 and Joseph and Dore (2021–22). Since a citizen of any country, including those with limited availability of vaccines, might be caught by the restrictions, there was the potential for lack of access to be a relevant factor in some cases. In practice, the brevity of the period during which the Regulations were in effect, coupled with travel restrictions, rendered this scenario unlikely.

[44] Except in the case of those who should not receive the vaccine on clinical grounds: see SI 2021/1416, reg. 8(2).

a consequence of treatment choices freely made by the individual.[45] The weight attached to autonomy—its status as a cardinal principle of medical ethics and law—would suggest that such choices should be respected. If that is so, is deprivation or suspension of certain of the rights and freedoms associated with citizenship (for example, because particular public health goals are valued) an acceptable strategy at all? In sum, we arrive back at what has been described as 'the central… dilemma' of public health ethics and law:[46] the difficulty of striking an appropriate balance between the freedom of the individual and the responsibility of the state to provide protection of the health of the population. This inherent tension was, of course, apparent in very many aspects of the COVID pandemic.

References

Aldis W (2008) Health security as a public health concept: a critical analysis. Health Policy Plan 23(6):369–375

Andreouli E, Brice E (2022) Citizenship under COVID-19: an analysis of UK political rhetoric during the first wave of the 2020 pandemic. J Community Appl Soc Psychol 32(3):555–572

BBC News (2021a) COVID: trials to begin for return of England mass events, 4 April 2021. https://www.bbc.co.uk/news/uk-56625307

BBC News (2021b) 19 July: England COVID restrictions ease as PM urges caution, 19 July 2021. https://www.bbc.co.uk/news/uk-57882029

Biehl J (2007) Pharmaceuticalization: AIDS treatment and global health politics. Anthropol Q 80(4):1083–1126

Brown RCH, Savulescu J, Williams B, Wilkinson D (2020) Passport to freedom? Immunity passports for COVID-19. J Med Ethics 46(10):652–659

Cameron-Blake E, Tatlow H, Andretti B, Boby T, Green K, Hale T, Petherick A, Phillips T, Pott A, Wade A, Zha H (2023) A panel dataset of COVID-19 vaccination policies in 185 countries. Nat Hum Behav 7(8):1402–1413

Cisney V, Morar N (eds) (2015) Biopower: Foucault and beyond. University of Chicago Press, Chicago

Coggon J, Miola J (2011) Autonomy, liberty and medical decision-making. Camb Law J 70(3):523–548

Coggon J, Syrett K, Viens AM (2017) Public health law: ethics, governance, and regulation. Routledge, Abingdon

Department of Health and Social Care (2021) Explanatory memorandum to the Health Protection (Coronavirus, Restrictions) (Entry to Venues and Events) (England) Regulations 2021

Dong M, He F, Deng Y (2021) How to understand herd immunity in the context of COVID-19. Viral Immunol 34(3):174–181

Ecks S (2005) Pharmaceutical citizenship: antidepressant marketing and the promise of demarginalization in India. Anthropol Med 12(3):239–254

Elliott P, Eales O, Bodinier B et al (2022) Dynamics of a national Omicron SARS-CoV-2 epidemic during January 2022 in England. Nat Commun 13:4500

Fidler DP (2007) A pathology of public health securitism: approaching pandemics as security threats. In: Cooper A, Kirton J, Schrecker T (eds) Governing global health: challenge, response, innovation. Routledge, Abingdon, pp 41–66

[45] This scenario is explored, in part, in Persson et al. (2016).

[46] Krebs (2008), p. 579.

Foucault M (1998) The history of sexuality, vol 1. Penguin, London
Foucault M (2020) Society must be defended: lectures at the Collège de France 1975–76. Penguin, London
Frost C, Winter E (2017) Making and authenticating the citizen: naturalisation and passport application in Canada. Rev Europ Russ Aff 11(1):1–23
Herring J (2025) Medical law and ethics, 10th edn. Oxford University Press, Oxford
Hollings S (2020) COVID-19: the changing face of global citizenship and the rise of pandemic citizenship. Knowl Cult 8:81
Joseph S, Dore G (2021–22) Vaccine apartheid: a human rights analysis of COVID-19 vaccine inequity. J Transnat Law Policy 31:145–172
Krebs J (2008) The importance of public-health ethics. Bull World Health Organ 86(8):579
Lim B (2020) Covidiots and the clamour of the virus-as-question: some reflections on biomedical culture, futurity and finitude. Anthropol Action 27(2):78–81
Merrick R (2020) Coronavirus: recovered patients to be given 'immunity certificates' to leave lockdown early. The Independent, 2 April 2020
Nyers P (ed) (2009) Securitizations of citizenship. Routledge, Abingdon
Office for National Statistics (2023) Coronavirus and vaccination rates in adults by socio-demographic characteristic and occupation, England: December 2020 to March 2023, 27 March 2023. https://www.ons.gov.uk/peoplepopulationandcommunity/healthandsocialcare/healthinequalities/bulletins/coronavirusandvaccinationratesinadultsbysociodemographiccharacteristicandoccupationengland/december2020tomarch2023
Ogunrotifa AB (2020) Expanding marginalisation in pharmaceutical citizenship: a case study of an antiretroviral therapy user. Int J Appl Sociol 10:13
Persson A, Newman C, Mao C et al (2016) On the margins of pharmaceutical citizenship: not taking HIV medication in the "treatment revolution" era. Med Anthropol Q 30(3):359–373
Piccoli L (2024) Pandemic citizenship. In: Cabeza M, Faist T (eds) Encyclopedia of citizenship studies. Edward Elgar, Cheltenham
Rose N (2007) The politics of life itself: biomedicine, power, and subjectivity in the twenty-first century. Princeton University Press, Princeton
Sidel VW, Levy B (2002) Security and public health. Soc Justice 29:108–126
Smith J (1997) The pre-eminence of autonomy in bioethics. In: Oderberg D, Laing J (eds) Human lives. Palgrave Macmillan, London, pp 182–195
Syrett K (2019) Healthcare resource allocation in the English courts: a systems theory perspective. N Irel Legal Q 70(1):111–129
Syrett K (forthcoming) Access to medicines and human rights at the UN. Edward Elgar, Cheltenham
Torreele E, Amon J (2021) Equitable COVID-19 vaccine access. Health Hum Rights J 23:273–281
White A (1982) Rights and claims. In: Stewart M (ed) Law, morality and rights. Springer, Dordrecht
Whyte SR, van der Geest S, Hardon A (2002) Social lives of medicines. Cambridge University Press, Cambridge
Williams SJ, Martin P, Gabe J (2011) The pharmaceuticalisation of society? A framework for analysis. Sociol Health Illn 33(5):710–725

Keith Syrett is Professor of Health Law and Policy in the *Centre for Health, Law, and Society* in the School of Law, University of Bristol, UK. He has written extensively on the legal regulation of resource allocation in healthcare, health technology assessment, and public health law. Among his most recent publications is the edited volume *NICE at 25: A Quarter-Century of Evidence, Values and Innovation in Health* (Routledge, 2025).

The Fundamental Right to Health and Its Universal Guarantees

Luigi Ferrajoli

Abstract This chapter examines the right to health through its *universal guarantees*, tracing a path from the national to the global level. From the perspective of social constitutionalism, national and global remedies for violations of the right to health—arising from the absence of *primary and secondary guarantees*—are identified, with the corresponding *guarantees institutions* envisaged. The project of a Constitution of the Earth is therefore situated within the broader framework of implementing the right to health, as well as other social rights, not only as a legal obligation but also as a necessary condition for the very survival of humankind.

1 Constitutionalisation and the Crisis of the Right to Health

The right to health is a logical corollary of the right to life. Until two centuries ago, human beings were essentially equal in the face of nature, not only in death but also in disease. Medicine witnessed extraordinary technological advances from the mid-nineteenth century onwards, including the discovery of antibiotics to combat infectious diseases, the development of anaesthesia that made surgical operations possible, and countless analytical tests enabling diagnoses and prognoses that would otherwise have been unthinkable. Serious illnesses were incurable and often fatal for everyone. At that time, therefore, it would have made little sense to establish a right to health.

Subsequently, technological progress in medicine made it possible—through the invention of ever-newer and more expensive therapies—to provide healthcare services that were previously impossible and that have allowed the defeat of diseases

This translation is by Alice Cauduro. It should be noted that many of the concepts used by the author in this chapter—such as *universal guarantees* and *guarantee institutions*—were introduced and subsequently developed in his works, contributing over time to the elaboration of his theory.

L. Ferrajoli (✉)
Department of Law, University Roma Tre, Rome, Italy
e-mail: luigi.ferrajoli@uniroma3.it

M. Balestrieri and A. Cauduro (eds.), *The Legal Anatomy of the Body*, Ius Gentium: Comparative Perspectives on Law and Justice 142,
https://doi.org/10.1007/978-3-032-26434-3_11

that would otherwise have been untreatable. For this reason, the right to health and the corresponding duty of care have become part of the social contract of coexistence, no less than the right to life as immunity from homicide.

Today, survival is no longer solely a natural matter, but also a social one, dependent on the existence of guarantees for health and subsistence. Moreover, the equal guarantee of the right to health and other social rights serves not only the well-being of individuals, but also the maintenance of peaceful coexistence and societal stability. Indeed, the equal guarantee of the right to health helps, at least in principle, to transform society into a community of equals. Due to medical and technological progress, access to healthcare has become increasingly costly. Hence, to guarantee life and equality, intervention by the public sphere is necessary; without it, health would remain an exclusive privilege of the wealthy.

As a result, the right to health has become part of contemporary democratic constitutionalism. Hence, for example, Article 32 of the Italian Constitution recognises the right to health 'as a fundamental right of the individual and as an interest of the community'. In implementing this right, Italy established one of the world's leading national healthcare systems in the 1980s. Indeed, Law No. 833 of 23 December 1978 abolished the various 'mutual funds' and introduced the Italian National Health Service (NHS) on the UK model, guided by the principles of universality and equality.[1] The NHS was designed to ensure equal access to healthcare services for all, funded through general taxation rather than insurance-based contributions.

In the 1990s, public, universal and free healthcare entered a period of crisis, not only in Italy. Following the neoliberal turn in global politics, Italy undertook a series of reforms through which the 'local health units' were first reorganised along corporate lines and subsequently regionalised.[2] This was followed by a gradual decline in healthcare provision, accompanied by the erosion of its universal and non-discriminatory character, driven by several factors. The erosion of healthcare universalism has been caused primarily by disparities in quality among the 20 regional systems, particularly between richer and poorer regions. Furthermore, it has contributed to arbitrariness, waste, and various forms of corruption, resulting from political party interference in the appointment of managers and the administration of local health units. Finally, cuts to public healthcare and the introduction of numerous co-payments have led to the monetisation of certain healthcare services, at the expense of the poorest, and imposed a heavy bureaucratic burden on both patients and physicians. The constitutional right to health, whose universal nature implies the free provision of its guarantees, has thus been downgraded—regarding medicines and medical examinations subject to co-payments—to a quasi-proprietary right, to the extent that millions of poor people forego healthcare. This co-payment by NHS users amounts effectively to a form of additional taxation. The absurdity of this

[1] The model—universal, free at the point of use, and entirely funded through general taxation—was conceived based on the Beveridge Report of 1942 and introduced throughout the United Kingdom with the establishment of the National Health Service on 5 July 1948, following the National Health Service Act of 1946.

[2] Legislative Decrees No. 502 of 1992, 517 of 1993, and 229 of 1999, followed in 2001 by the constitutional reform of regional system.

healthcare tax lies in the negligible revenue it generates: three or four billion euros, less than 3% of total healthcare expenditure, which has reached 130 billion. Added to this are the shortage of doctors and the reduction of healthcare facilities—despite the lessons of the COVID-19 pandemic—resulting in increasingly long waiting times for medical examinations, to the obvious benefit of private healthcare facilities.

This reduction in public healthcare services is not due to their excessive cost, but rather to a short-sighted view of the economy. Public healthcare expenditures are not merely costs, but productive investments that contribute decisively to economic and social development. European history bears this out. The period of economic growth during 'the thirty-five glorious years' of the early postwar era coincided with the expansion of social rights, whereas the subsequent 'inglorious' years of recession were marked by their erosion. Today, even in developed countries, the right to health is threatened by the progressive reduction of the public healthcare sector in favour of private sector.

The consequence is a loss of democratic legitimacy in political systems, since the weakening of equality in fundamental rights undermines the sense of belonging to the same community, which is based on the perception that everyone is endowed with the same fundamental rights and, therefore, the same dignity.

How can this regression be interpreted? One interpretation lies in the substantial disappearance of constitutional constraints from the political landscape. Due to the asymmetry between the global nature of markets and the local character of politics and law, the relationship between politics and the economy has been inverted. Indeed, it is no longer governments that guarantee competition among firms, but large corporations, which put governments into downward competition by leveraging their power to favour countries where they can pay lower taxes by reducing social expenditures, beginning with healthcare. This represents a concrete crisis of constitutional democracy. With the constitutional enshrinement of social rights, and particularly the right to health, the welfare state was effectively constitutionalised, so that its retrenchment in favour of the market constitutes a process of de-constitutionalisation.

2 The Theoretical and Institutional Underdevelopment of Social Constitutionalism

However, a deeper reason behind the current crisis of the right to health is the institutional weakness of its guarantees. Despite their constitutional recognition, social rights have not been supported by an institutional framework capable of guaranteeing them, comparable to that which, in a *state of law*, ensures the protection of freedom rights. Since no theory of *social constitutionalism* has been developed alongside that of 'liberal constitutionalism', no effective system of *social guarantees* has been established to complement the 'liberal guarantees' traditionally accorded to freedom rights.

Indeed, the structure of the old *state of law* has been preserved, based on the traditional tripartite division of powers conceived by Montesquieu, at a time when social rights and their corresponding institutions were inconceivable. Healthcare services, as well as those related to other social rights, have been assigned to the sphere of public administration rather than to independent *primary guarantee institutions*. Since they cannot be situated within the judiciary or the legislature, these services have in fact developed within and under the authority of the executive branch, taking the form of a bureaucratic welfare state rather than a *social state of law*, that is, one grounded in rights. Public services corresponding to social rights have thus been configured not as the fulfilment of obligations, but rather as measures entrusted to the discretion of politics or, worse, to the market economy. The crisis of the welfare state, and with it of the *constitutional state of law*, has thus unfolded, aided by triumphant liberal ideologies, through the discretionary reduction of public spending on social benefits, increasingly inadequate in relation to the growing demand. Certainly, this reduction in social spending has accentuated its selective and discriminatory character and has further encouraged degenerative processes within institutions, fostering clientelism and corporatism under the banner of inequality and privilege.

The constitutionalisation of the right to health and other social rights, if taken seriously, requires—in my view—a theoretical and institutional refoundation of constitutional democracy. It ought to have led to the construction of a *state of law* as a system not only of 'negative constraints'—that is, prohibitions on violations imposed on public authorities to safeguard fundamental freedoms—but also of 'positive obligations', namely duties of provision, equally imposed on the public sphere to guarantee social rights. To safeguard freedom rights, which are expectations of non-infringement, it suffices to have guarantees corresponding to the prohibitions imposed on the actions of public institutions, the violation of which can be challenged before the judiciary. The protection of the right to health—and more generally of social rights—which are expectations that instead require the creation of *erga omnes* obligations, demands complex and costly *primary guarantee institutions*: the establishment of a compulsory, universal, and free healthcare system, just as, to guarantee the right to education, the creation of free and universal schooling at the state's expense is required.

In Italy, for example, the absence of a theory of *social constitutionalism* and of corresponding obligations on the public sphere—mirroring the theory of liberal constitutionalism and limits on public powers—meant that the introduction of the Universal Health Service under Law No. 833 of 1978 was conceived as the product of progressive policy, revocable at the discretion of political authorities, rather than as a legally binding constitutional obligation.

The implications of guarantees for fundamental rights—duties of provision related to the right to health and, more generally, to social rights, no less binding than the non-infringement obligations corresponding to freedom rights[3]—require that public

[3] It is the logical implication, fundamental to the theory of guarantism—which I have set out in Volume I of my *Principia iuris. Teoria del diritto e della democrazia,* Ferrajoli (2007), p. 190, from the theses T3.28 and T3.29—among the passive expectations, positive or negative, in which all

healthcare, public education, social assistance, and social security be configured as *primary guarantee institutions* for the constitutionally established rights. From this perspective, their creation, implementation, and protection represent a constitutional obligation rather than a concession granted by political discretion.

With a further consequence arising from the very nature of guarantee institutions for healthcare services, as well as for educational and social assistance services: the source of legitimacy of these institutions (which I call *primary guarantee institutions*), like that of judicial institutions (which I describe as *secondary guarantee institutions*), does not lie in the principle of majority, but rather in subjection to the law and in the equality of individuals with respect to the rights guaranteed to them. Indeed, a judge is truly a judge only if, by virtue of their independence, they can acquit in the absence of evidence when everyone—the government, the press, public opinion—demands conviction, and convict when evidence exists—for instance, against a powerful individual—even when all are calling for acquittal. Likewise, a doctor or a teacher can be regarded as such only if they are able to perform their duties independently of the will of governments or majorities. It is on this difference in their sources of legitimacy that the separation of powers is based, which should therefore entail independence from governmental political powers not only for judicial functions of *secondary guarantee*, but also for administrative functions of *primary guarantee* over health and other social rights, equally legitimised by subjection to the law and by the principle of equality.[4] Such a system of social rights guarantees, based on obligation rather than the political discretion of their fulfilment, corresponds to a model of social democracy diametrically opposed to the policies pursued by current neoliberal strategies.

3 The Right to Health in International Charters: Towards Global Guarantees

The right to health is not only a constitutional right within national legal systems. It is also a right recognised under international law, as established by Article 12 of the International Covenant on Economic, Social and Cultural Rights, adopted on 16 December 1966.

Furthermore, in 1948 the Universal Declaration of Human Rights had already established that:

> Everyone, as a member of society, has the right to social security and is entitled to realization, through national effort and international co-operation and in accordance with the organization

individual rights consist, and the active modalities, that is, the duties or prohibitions that constitute their guarantees. This implication is an analytic truth, no different from the implications between 'permitted' and 'not prohibited' and vice versa, or between 'permitted not to' and 'not obligatory'.

[4] Regarding the distinction between governing institutions and guarantee institutions, and the consequent updating of the separation of powers theorised by Montesquieu, see Ferrajoli (2007), pp. 862–879 (vol I) and pp. 200–219 (vol. II); see also Ferrajoli (2021), pp. 254–264 and pp. 369–383.

> and resources of each State, of the economic, social and cultural rights indispensable for his dignity and the free development of his personality [Art. 22].

And:

> everyone has the right to a standard of living adequate for the health and well-being of himself and of his family, including food, clothing, housing and medical care and necessary social services, and the right to security in the event of unemployment, sickness, disability, widowhood, old age or other lack of livelihood in circumstances beyond his control [Art. 25 (1)].

Health, on the other hand, is not merely an individual concern. Nor is it a purely local or national matter. Today, health has become a global issue for two main reasons: the dependence of individual health on global health. Moreover the absence of universal health guarantees—even considering the speed with which contagions spread in an increasingly interconnected world—poses a general risk and leads to a widespread decline in the health of all human beings.[5] Hence the necessity of global vaccination, which, as was the case for smallpox, plague, and poliomyelitis, is capable, even to the benefit of wealthy countries, of eradicating and thereby suppressing the viruses that cause disease. We must indeed be aware that if a virus has not been completely eradicated, it can continue to spread worldwide. For this reason, it is also necessary to extend, beyond the state and within a possible Federation of the Earth, the guarantees of health, alongside other social rights such as education, subsistence, access to basic food, and housing.

The second reason for the global nature of the health issue lies precisely in this: conferred by the above-mentioned law to all human beings. This is a fundamental right, consisting in the positive expectation of healthcare services, which entails a universal guarantee obliging its fulfilment, by virtue of the logical implication connecting the first to the second—analogous to the logical implication linking negative expectations, which constitute freedom rights, to the guarantees provided through prohibitions against their limitation or violation.

This *universal guarantee* does not exist. Despite the proclamation of the right to health and the corresponding duties in the 1966 Covenant, the absence of any form of supranational guarantee is complete. This constitutes a blatant violation, with alarming consequences. Around 870 million people suffer from hunger and thirst. Every year, more than eight million people—24,000 per day—die, largely children, due to the lack of basic food and water. Many millions more, almost all in poor countries, die from infectious and tropical diseases, lacking access to essential or life-saving medicines, which in 1977 the World Health Organization declared must be universally accessible to all. At that time, there were just over 200 such medicines; today there are 460, yet they remain largely unavailable in much of the world, as the promise of their universal distribution—repeated several times since—has not been fulfilled.

[5] For an interesting pedagogical reading of One Health, see Schilkraut (2024), pp. 14–17. On the institutional definition of One Health, see the strategic document outlining a long-term framework for FAO-OIE-WHO collaboration to coordinate global activities addressing health risks at the human–animal–ecosystems interfaces: FAO et al. (2010).

We are therefore faced with a massive failure to provide aid, which compounds the policies of plunder and exploitation that have left hundreds of millions of people living and dying in conditions of extreme poverty. They are therefore more victims of the market than of disease: water is increasingly scarce and therefore subject to private appropriation; while essential medicines are either patented, or worse, neither distributed nor produced, despite costing almost nothing, because they concern infectious diseases—respiratory infections, tuberculosis, AIDS, malaria, and the like—that have been eradicated or disappeared in the wealthiest countries, and therefore generate no demand. Furthermore, in poor countries, there is virtually no hygienic or sanitary prevention, beginning with vaccinations.

The World Health Organization, the world's leading health institution, is largely powerless due to extremely limited financial resources, while also facing undue interference from contemporary global actors. Its financial constraints confine it to a mere role of studying and monitoring the most serious health emergencies. Moreover, it faces attacks from contemporary populist autarchies, which undermine even the fragile national public health institutions. One need only consider the tax law enacted in the United States by the current president, Donald Trump, which he described as 'great and beautiful'. This legislation reduces funding for the already meagre public healthcare system, leaving 12 million people without coverage, and transfers US$4 trillion from lower-income groups to wealthier ones through tax breaks.

The annual deaths of millions of people from hunger and untreated diseases constitute one of the most horrific crimes against humanity. It is the most serious of all humanitarian emergencies, the gravest of the four major social scourges: hunger, thirst, untreated diseases, and illiteracy. It results in a radical delegitimization of our political systems, which claim to be founded on the value of life and on the equality and dignity of all human beings as persons. Indeed, it amounts not only to the denial but also to the discrediting of these values, so frequently proclaimed yet conspicuously violated. The lack of guarantees for health and other social rights also undermines the economies of poor countries. The connection mentioned in the first paragraph between social guarantees and economic development—whereby the former constitutes a condition for the latter—applies at the international level no less than it does and has manifested itself at the national level.

4 What Alternatives Exist?

One must then ask whether any alternatives exist to these violations of the right to health, and if so, what they are. A common response is the claim that 'there are no alternatives', as if the absence of guarantees were a natural or inevitable phenomenon rather than an unlawful failure to fulfil them. This is the so-called realist thesis. In fact, it is the product of an ideological realism that naturalises what is artificial—politics, law, and the economy—while ignoring the natural reality of the ongoing health catastrophe. The alternative, however, does exist, and consists precisely in the introduction of universal guarantees for the fundamental right to health. This alternative is not only legally required, being implied by the right enshrined in all advanced Constitutions and in numerous human rights instruments but is also necessary in the vital interest of all. Here, I will distinguish rights-based responses to violations of the universal right to health, according to whether they are required at the national or supranational level.

4.1 The National-Level Alternative

At the national level, he reduction of healthcare guarantees and, more broadly, of social rights constitutes the most serious and dramatic aspect of the current crisis in our democracies. In response to governmental arbitrariness in reducing public healthcare funding, there exists, therefore, only one effective guarantee: the introduction, following the model established by the Brazilian Constitution, of a constitutional budgetary constraint that provides for the mandatory allocation of a rigidly predetermined fixed share—for example, 20%—to the functions and public healthcare institutions as guarantee institutions. Similar shares could be allocated to educational and welfare institutions to secure the right to education and to provide everyone with a basic income. This would thus guarantee the independence of such guarantee institutions from government functions and, thanks to their financial autonomy, enable the provision of fully free healthcare services.

The de-constitutionalising process of the welfare state, resulting from its tendency towards commodification and bureaucratisation, has moreover proven to be the most fertile ground for illegality and corruption. Its failure is a strikingly confirms of the juridical, economic, and political value of a general theoretical principle of social rights protection. Social rights can be guaranteed more fully, equally, simply, and effectively from a legal standpoint, less expensive from an economic standpoint, and more insulated from political-administrative discretion—and thus from the selectivity and corruption it fosters—the more bureaucratic or market-based intermediation required for their fulfilment is reduced, and ideally eliminated, through its equal and free provision ex lege, as free education and healthcare, a guaranteed minimum income for all, and free social services for all. However costly it may be, a *social state of law*—in addition to guaranteeing the highest degree of equality, transparency, automaticity, and therefore effectiveness—is certainly less costly than the same services when entrusted to the logic of the market or to the selective discretion of bureaucratic apparatuses. It should also be added that, once introduced in these forms, the guarantees of the right to health—and more generally of social rights—are even more certain and effective than those of the freedom rights.

The distinctive feature of the right to health, and more generally of constitutionally enshrined social rights, lies in the obligation they impose to adopt implementing legislation, which, *ope legis*, establishes the guarantee mechanisms necessary to ensure their fulfilment. It is evident that the social expenditures necessary to uphold the free guarantees of social rights—foremost among them the right to health—entail a redistribution of wealth that does not serve the interests of all. Unlike liberal guarantees, whose abstract introduction benefits everyone and is therefore determined by the 'veil of ignorance' described by John Rawls, *social guarantees* do not benefit from such a veil, since they require, to sustain public expenditure in favour of the poor, a progressive taxation system imposed primarily on the wealthy. This does not change the fact that the logical connection between the positive expectations embodied in the right to health and other social rights, and the corresponding obligations to fulfil them, is no less logically sound or legally binding than the connection between the negative expectations represented by freedom rights and the prohibitions against violating or limiting them.

The right to health can be guaranteed to all, in accordance with its universal nature, only insofar as its positive guarantees are entrusted to the public sphere. Only a public health service—which, as shown in § 2, should be independent of political power, as an *institution of guarantee* legitimised not by the principle of majority, but by the application of the law and the principle of equality—can, in fact, provide the positive guarantee of the right to health as a fundamental right for all. This unquestionably applies to the prevention of infectious diseases, which since the nineteenth century has constituted a typical function of the state and could not reliably be entrusted to private actors. In Italy, for example, consider the public health laws and consolidated codes—extended to the Italian legal system in 1865—aimed at combating the spread of smallpox, tuberculosis, trachoma, leprosy, typhus, diphtheria, venereal diseases, pellagra, tetanus, and poliomyelitis.[6] However, this principle applies to all diseases, by virtue of each individual's fundamental right to health, a right that today's neoliberal ideologies would seek to privatise.

Any form of privatisation of healthcare, beginning with that promoted through the replacement, in whole or in part, of the public service by private insurance schemes, effectively degrades the right to health from a fundamental right to a property right. We can measure the perverse effects of such a system by looking at the experience of those countries, such as the United States, where no adequate public guarantee of the right to health exists. Guaranteeing this right through sickness insurance undermines its universality, both objectively and subjectively. The level of health protection depends on the amount of the premium and on the contractual conditions, while those who are uninsured are, in any case, excluded. Furthermore, such a system is inevitably more costly for citizens than any public system, both because of the profits pursued by insurance companies and due to the considerable costs involved in assessing future disease risks prior to signing each policy and then verifying the conditions for disbursing insurance benefits. It is no coincidence that in the United States healthcare is among the most expensive and, at the same time, among the most inadequate in the advanced world, as well as the most scandalously unequal, since healthcare services are differentiated according to income.

The effect of healthcare privatisation is, in short, inevitably the nullification of the guarantee of the right to health as a fundamental right, because it is neither equal

[6] Rabaglietti (1969), pp. 488–496 and Rabaglietti (1964), pp. 59–63.

nor universal; because it is contingent, not compulsory; and because it is based not on general and abstract rules, but on negotiated contractual arrangements.

A full privatisation of healthcare would amount to a denial, even before it constitutes a violation, of the fundamental right to health. This does not, of course, preclude individuals from supplementing their health and welfare entitlements privately, alongside public services that are equal for all, by taking out health insurance or arranging annuities. However, such measures must remain supplementary and certainly cannot substitute for the public system.

4.2 The Global-Level Alternative

At the international level, as I have already noted, the absence of guarantees is total. The World Health Organization, established in 1948, is clearly incapable of ensuring health for all human beings. The funds it has at its disposal, mostly from private sources, amount to just under 5 billion dollars every 2 years, whereas some 5000 billion dollars—or perhaps more, would be required to provide everyone with the necessary healthcare services. The only viable way to implement of the right to health is therefore the transformation of the WHO into a genuine *global guarantee institution*, obliged to provide healthcare and medical services to all, by building hospitals and clinics worldwide and distributing medicines and vaccines to everyone.

This is what is envisaged by the project of a Constitution of the Earth in 100 articles,[7] promoted by the Constituent Earth association. There is, moreover, a measure capable of ensuring the effectiveness of the right to health while also guaranteeing the separation and independence of a global health service: the provision, in Article 99 of the project, of strict budgetary constraints on social expenditure, through the stipulation for each constitutionally established social right—following the model of the Brazilian Constitution—of a minimum share of the global budget that must be allocated to its guarantee; in the case of health, at least 10% of the budget.[8] Such a global guarantee of health, together with that of other social rights, would serve to ensure civil conditions of life and survival for the 8 billion human beings, promote social equality, and act as a driver of economic growth in poor countries, with beneficial effects not only for the direct recipients, but for all: from the reduction of migration flows to the limiting the recruitment capacities of terrorist and criminal

[7] I developed that project in Ferrajoli (2022, 2025).

[8] Regarding education art. 212 of the Brazilian Constitution provides that 'the Union shall annually apply no less than 18%, and the States, the Federal District and the Municipalities no less than 25% of the proceeds from taxes… to the maintenance and development of education'. With respect to health art. 198 (2) and (3) further provides, that 'the Union, the States, the Federal District and the Municipalities shall annually use, for public health actions and services, minimum resources derived from the application of certain percentages'; the complementary law No. 141 del 13.1.2012 established a rate of 12% for the States and 15% for the Municipalities and the Union, adding that these amounts must increase with GDP growth.

organisations, and even to the economic development of poor countries resulting from the increase in their productive capacities.

A dramatic confirmation of the necessity to expand the constitutional paradigm at the supranational level was provided by the COVID-19 pandemic, which is useful to recall here. It was not the objectively most serious emergency: one might consider the enormously more destructive effects, should nothing be done to prevent them, of the ecological crisis and the nuclear threat. Nor was it the only health catastrophe. Every year, in the world's peripheries, approximately eight million people die from untreated but treatable diseases, and an equal number from the lack of safe drinking water and basic nutrition.

However, what made the pandemic a global emergency, experienced more dramatically than any other, were certain of its specific characteristics. First, it affected the entire world, including wealthy individuals and countries, paralysing the economy and disrupting the daily life of all humanity. Second, it had spectacular visibility. Due to its terrible daily toll of infections and deaths, it highlighted, more than any other emergency, the absence of adequate supranational *guarantee institutions* that should nonetheless have been established to implement the right to health enshrined in numerous international human rights instruments. Third, the pandemic served as a warning signal about our future, as it proved to be a side effect of multiple ecological catastrophes—including climate change, deforestation, and intensive farming and livestock production—thus revealing the connections between human health and the health of the planet. Finally, a fourth tragically global aspect of the pandemic was the extremely high degree of planetary integration and interdependence it revealed among all human beings. The virus knows no borders, and the spread of infection in even the most distant countries cannot be indifferent to anyone, given its capacity to rapidly disseminate across the entire planet.

The pandemic thus revealed our shared human fragility and common destiny. It provided, to a limited extent, evidence of the total inadequacy of our institutions in facing even more serious global emergencies, such as ecological crises.

It also made glaringly evident the marked failure of policies implemented worldwide under two right-wing approaches—liberal and populist sovereigntist—which proved incapable of managing the crisis. In fact, they even exacerbated it through their opposition to measures aimed at limiting contagion, albeit motivated differently.

Two lessons can be drawn from this: one with an anti-liberalist character, relating to the public nature, and the other with an anti-sovereigntist character, relating to the global nature that guarantees should possess to prevent and limit the spread of viruses and, more generally, global emergencies. The first lesson concerns the vital role of the public sphere, which I have just discussed in § 4.1. By potentially affecting everyone, the pandemic demonstrated the value of public healthcare and its universal and free nature. No less important and vital is the second lesson: that of the global nature which, in the face of planetary phenomena such as the pandemic, but also peace, the protection of nature, and fundamental rights, guarantees and the corresponding institutions of guarantee should possess.

5 Towards a *Constitution of the Earth*

These are two lessons that apply to all contemporary global catastrophes that are endangering the future of humanity and require global responses such as climate change, the threat of nuclear war, the growth of inequalities and human rights violations worldwide, and the plight of migrants. Globalisation has, in fact, changed the geography of power: the political and economic powers that matter have moved beyond the borders of nation-states, escaping their political and legal control. Today, the political community is global. If humanity is to survive, a leap in civilisation is necessary: an expansion of constitutionalism beyond the state, commensurate with the global powers from which the threats to the future of the entire human race originate. Only a new global social contract among all the states and peoples of the planet can establish, in a binding form, the universal guarantees of peace, of the fundamental rights of all human beings, and of the vital resources of nature.

That contract was concluded in the aftermath of the Second World War through what can be seen as the embryonic Constitution of the world which is composed of the United Nations Charter and the many international charters of human rights. But it failed—and could not but fail—for two reasons. The first was the lack of rigidity of those charters, which were not placed above other sources, whether national or international, and the preservation within the United Nations Charter—contradicting the principles of peace and equality—of state sovereignty and of the different national citizenships. Peace and equality in fundamental rights, although proclaimed in numerous human rights charters, remain unfulfilled promises unless they are made effective and binding through their strict subordination of state sovereignties. The second and even more serious reason for the failure of these charters was the lack of provisions for the guarantees of freedom rights and for the institutions ensuring the protection of the social rights they established. Consequently, the principles of peace and equality, as well as the fundamental rights of individuals enshrined in the many human rights charters, have remained merely on paper for most of humankind.

For this reason, a refoundation of the pact of coexistence among all peoples and states is urgently needed, in order to give rise to a global constitutionalism capable of filling the vacuum of public law produced by the asymmetry between the planetary character of today's unrestrained powers of the markets and the most powerful states, and the still predominantly local character of politics and law.

Hence, the establishment of a *Constitution of the Earth* is both necessary and urgent. This is not a utopian proposal. It is the only rational and realistic response to the same dilemma that Thomas Hobbes faced almost four centuries ago: the general insecurity produced by the unrestrained freedom of the strongest, or the pact of peaceful coexistence founded on the prohibition of war and the guarantee of life.

Today's global arena of power is dominated not by natural predators, but by human-created entities—states and markets—which often operate beyond the control of their creators and possess a destructive capacity far exceeding that of historical weapons.

Secondly, unlike all previous catastrophes—world wars or the horrors of totalitarian regimes—the ecological and nuclear disasters are, to a large extent, irreversible, and we may not have time to formulate new 'never agains'. Indeed, there is the danger that awareness of the need for a new pact will come only when it is already too late.

Hence the need for a new social contract among all the states and peoples of the planet, one that can remedy the shortcomings of the UN Charter and of the many declarations of fundamental rights. It is not enough, in fact, merely to proclaim peace and human rights. It is necessary, in a Constitution of the Earth, to introduce their guarantees, without which peace and rights would remain mere rhetorical statements.

These include: the rigidity of the global Constitution, that is, its supremacy over all other sources, national and international; the guarantee of peace, through the criminalisation of the production and trade of all weapons as crimes against humanity; the guarantee of the vital resources of nature, by removing them from the market as assets of a planetary commons; the guarantees of social rights to health, education, and subsistence, through the transformation of the World Health Organization, UNESCO, and FAO into effective global institutions that ensure healthcare, education, and basic nutrition; a world labour organisation that provides broadly equal guarantees to all workers; a universal basic income that secures subsistence; a progressive global taxation system capable of financing the *global guarantee institutions*; and, finally, judicial guarantees, beginning with the establishment of a planetary Constitutional Court, capable of reviewing and redressing all violations of the Constitution of the Earth.

This should not be seen as a new legal order. It is the implementation of principles and rights, most of which are already enshrined in existing international charters: an implementation that is not only legally required, but also urgent and imperative, given that the survival of humanity depends upon it.

References

FAO, OIE, WHO (2010) The FAO-OIE-WHO collaboration: sharing responsibilities and coordinating global activities to address health risks at the animal-human-ecosystems interfaces. A tripartite concept note. https://www.who.int/publications/m/item/the-fao-oie-who-collaboration

Ferrajoli L (2007) Principia iuris. Teoria del diritto e della democrazia. Laterza, Roma–Bari

Ferrajoli L (2021) La costruzione della democrazia. Teoria del garantismo costituzionale. Laterza, Roma–Bari

Ferrajoli L (2022) Per una costituzione della terra. L'umanità al bivio. Feltrinelli, Milano

Ferrajoli L (2025) Progettare il futuro. Per un costituzionalismo globale. Feltrinelli, Milano

Rabaglietti G (1964) Malattie infettive. In: Azara A, Eula E (eds) Novissimo Digesto Italiano, vol X. Utet, Torino

Rabaglietti G (1969) Sanità pubblica. In: Azara A, Eula E (eds) Novissimo Digesto Italiano, vol XVI. Utet, Torino

Schilkraut P (2024) One Health. Fare l'insegnante 3. https://www.euroedizioni.it/198-notizie/698976-fare-l-insegnante-n-3-gennaio-2024

Luigi Ferrajoli is Emeritus Professor at the University Roma Tre where he taught Philosophy of Law and General Theory of Law. He is known for founding the theory of guarantees for fundamental rights, applicable to the entire legal system. Among his publications are *Diritto e ragione. Teoria del garantismo penale*, *Principia iuris. Teoria del diritto e della democrazia*, *Manifesto per l'uguaglianza* and *Per una costituzione della terra. L'umanità al bivio*. His works have been translated into several languages, and he has received numerous honorary doctorates from universities in Latin America and Spain. Prior to his academic career, he served as a judge.

Crisis as Usual: Antimicrobial Resistance and the Temporal Politics of Global Health

Isaac Weldon

Abstract Antimicrobial resistance (AMR) is often described as a defining challenge of our time. But what, exactly, is it defining? This chapter argues that AMR reconfigures the temporal foundations of the narratives through which global health governance organizes social and political relations. In addition to global rules, institutions, and laws, health governance unfolds through stories that make sense of uncertainty, justify intervention, and assign responsibility. The temporal assumptions contained within these narratives—about what counts as crisis, what progress looks like, and how time is experienced—shape who governs, how they govern, and toward what ends. They structure expectations of autonomy and care, delineate the boundaries of dignity and authority, and mediate obligations among individuals, states, and global bodies. As drug-resistant infections rise, AMR exposes fractures in three such temporal narratives. First, AMR blurs the boundary between normalcy and emergency, shifting governance from episodic interventions to continuous behavioural regulation. Second, AMR unsettles the myth of linear scientific progress. Antimicrobials, long celebrated as breakthroughs, contribute to their own obsolescence, revealing how innovation can generate progress and recursive vulnerabilities simultaneously. Third, AMR disrupts the fiction of universal time. While some benefit from effective treatments, others already face a post-antimicrobial future, and still others have yet to experience the antimicrobial present. By rupturing these three stories, AMR challenges how time itself is conceptualized in the narrative architecture of modern health governance.

I. Weldon (✉)
Centre for Advanced Studies in Bioscience Innovation Law, Faculty of Law, University of Copenhagen, Copenhagen, Denmark
e-mail: isaac.weldon@jur.ku.dk

Global Strategy Lab, York University, Toronto, Canada

M. Balestrieri and A. Cauduro (eds.), *The Legal Anatomy of the Body*, Ius Gentium: Comparative Perspectives on Law and Justice 142,
https://doi.org/10.1007/978-3-032-26434-3_12

1 Introduction

Antimicrobial resistance (AMR) is often framed as one of the most pressing public health challenges of the twenty-first century.[1] It emerges when microbes evolve to survive antimicrobial medicines, rendering essential life-saving drugs like antibiotics less effective or even completely ineffective for treatment.[2] Already, drug-resistant infections claim over a million lives annually, with millions more affected by complications from failing treatments.[3]At first glance, AMR appears to fit the mold of a modern health crisis. The failure of antimicrobials presents what the World Health Organization (WHO) has called a 'crisis that must be managed with the utmost urgency'.[4] Simultaneously, it has been described as: a 'silent',[5] 'slow-moving',[6] and 'grand pandemic';[7] an 'emergency'[8] demanding both 'immediate action'[9] as well as 'long-term management';[10] and a global threat that demands coordinated, evidence-driven action to prevent the world from sliding 'towards a post-antibiotic era'.[11]

Yet upon closer inspection, AMR unsettles the very narratives that make such framings possible. It does not erupt suddenly like a pandemic; rather, it creeps forward sporadically and unevenly with each antimicrobial use, blurring the line between routine and crisis.[12] It is not a failure of science *per se*, but rather a consequence of its own success—a byproduct of medical progress that simultaneously sows the seeds of its own demise.[13] Nor is it experienced uniformly.[14] Some populations benefit from reliable access to effective antimicrobials, others already face a post-antimicrobial future, while many remain in a pre-antimicrobial present, lacking access to even the most basic treatments. Thus, AMR is at once modern and archaic, urgent and protracted, and shared but deeply unequal.

This chapter takes these tensions seriously as windows into the evolving and unstable conceptual terrain upon which health governance is justified in today's world. It argues that AMR, in addition to challenging public health responses, destabilizes the foundational logics that have long structured global health governance: the binary between normalcy and emergency, the myth of linear progress, and

---

[1] WHO (2019a).
[2] O'Neill (2016).
[3] Naghavi et al. (2024).
[4] WHO (2015a), p. VII.
[5] European Commission Newsroom (2023).
[6] Davies and Oxlade (2021).
[7] Rupasinghe et al. (2024).
[8] The Lancet Respiratory Medicine (2024).
[9] WHO (2015a).
[10] WHO (2019b).
[11] WHO (2015a).
[12] Wilson et al. (2021).
[13] Fleming (1999).
[14] Mendelson et al. (2024).

the assumption of universal time. More than rhetorical tropes, these stories represent deep-seated and often taken-for-granted ideas that shape how health problems are conceptualized, how interventions are justified, and how individual rights are weighed against collective goals.[15] As pre-analytical commitments that influence recurring patterns of reasoning across global health, they structure the cultural, political, and legal grammars that underlie the design and uptake of norms across a spectrum of formal and informal governance instruments. From the binding obligations of global health law to the quasi-legal force of antimicrobial stewardship programs and international guidelines, AMR governance rests on institutional architectures that are entangled with these narratives. As these discursive foundations begin to fragment, so too do the normative and institutional grounds on which health governance has traditionally operated.

More specifically, narratives here function as implicit normative frameworks through which policy problems are interpreted and governance responses legitimized.[16] They operate as ideational substrates, or meta-formants in Rodolfo Sacco's sense, shaping what is thinkable, sayable, and doable in a given legal or political context.[17] They provide coherence and direction, organizing facts into cause-and-effect sequences, identifying threats and responsibilities, and framing what kinds of interventions are necessary or acceptable. In global health, such narratives construct the terrain of governance by reflecting and projecting embedded assumptions about the nature of the world, as well as the nature of crisis, progress, and time within it. They determine what counts as an emergency, who is authorized to act, and whose lives are prioritized. When AMR disrupts these governing stories, it provokes policy confusion.[18] But on a deeper register, it also reveals fractures in how we understand rights, responsibility, and the collective life public health is meant to protect.

This chapter shows how liberal democratic governance, especially in public health, is often justified through three narrative forms. *Emergency* provides the rationale for extraordinary interventions such as mandates, surveillance, or rationing. *Progress* legitimizes innovation-driven responses and defers questions about distribution or structural harm. *Universal time* underwrites synchronized global targets and strategies, masking the lived temporal disparities between and within countries.

The breakdown of these narratives complicates both the conception and governance of individual autonomy. It unsettles who is governed (whose behaviours are targeted), how they are governed (through what mechanisms of control or care), and to what end (for example, preserving population-level efficacy versus ensuring equitable access).

Ultimately, by tracing how AMR destabilizes these foundational stories of global health, the chapter shows how public health governance increasingly operates in a state of conceptual and temporal ambiguity. The management of individual bodies occurs amid fractured narratives, persistent emergencies, and uneven futures. My

---

15 Ney (2012).

16 Hall (1993).

17 Sacco (1991).

18 Mendelson et al. (2017).

aim is not to propose new narrative frameworks for governance. Instead, I aim to expose how autonomy is being reconfigured under pressure, and to raise critical questions about what is taken for granted in the stories we tell about health, time, and responsibility.

To be clear, the chapter does not argue against antimicrobial stewardship. Rather, it argues that the way stewardship is understood and implemented matters, not just for managing AMR, but for the political relationships it constructs. Throughout the chapter, I show how AMR governance is increasingly anticipatory, moralized, and indefinite. Autonomy, when viewed through the lens of AMR governance, is not an upheld or restricted entitlement; it is a contested political site of negotiation through contradiction, often appealed to rhetorically in the name of collective protection yet unequally granted and differentially enforced across space and time. By tracing how AMR unsettles the dominant stories of emergency, progress, and time, I show how health governance today is defined by three interdependent dynamics: a quiet normalization of exceptional authority in everyday life, a deferral and downward displacement of morality from the level of structure to everyday individuals, and the reproduction of temporal conditions that generate uneven vulnerability.

The following sections examine each of these three narrative ruptures in turn and reflect on how they reshape the relationship between public health authority and bodily autonomy. The reflections are brought together in a penultimate section that recasts autonomy in modern health governance as conditional, moralized, and stratified. A brief conclusion ends the chapter.

2 The Normal Emergency: AMR Blurs the Boundary Between Routine and Crisis

Public health governance has long relied on a conceptual and operational distinction between periods of normalcy and states of emergency. Indeed, this distinction underpins much of what we recognize as public health governance. Emergencies, whether pandemics, natural disasters, or wars, are treated as temporary disruptions that justify extraordinary interventions, such as lockdowns, border closures, surveillance, and rationing.[19] Measures that would be unacceptable infringements on autonomy during ordinary times become legitimate because they are exceptional, proportional, and time-bound. The logic is straightforward: in normal times, individual autonomy is protected; in emergencies, it may be provisionally curtailed to protect collective life.[20] Yet this binary is neither as stable nor as self-evident as it appears, especially in the context of AMR. Rather than existing as two distinct modes of governance, the boundary between normalcy and emergency is porous. As discussed below, AMR governance reveals how the exception increasingly permeates the everyday.

[19] Lipscy (2020).

[20] Hoffman et al. (2022).

Political thought has long wrestled with this fragile binary, with thinkers across traditions interrogating the dynamics of emergency and the authority they summon. From the Roman Republic's emergency dictatorships to modern statutes, moments of crisis let rulers suspend ordinary rules to preserve the polity.[21] Few theorists capture this tension more sharply than Carl Schmitt, who claimed that 'The sovereign is he who decides on the exception'.[22] He thus argued that true authority is not defined by compliance with law but by the power to set it aside. Declaring a crisis exposes the political foundation of social order that law normally conceals and shows who defines the limits of ordinary political life.

John Locke, writing from a liberal tradition, offered a more constrained view. Rulers may exercise prerogative power, acting outside the law when necessary for the public good, so long as that power remains accountable to the people.[23] Despite their ideological differences, both theorists grapple with an ancient and uncomfortable space where legal authority and political necessity collide, and both accept that emergencies create zones of temporary legal suspension, justified by threat and, in theory, constrained by time.

In global health law, this binary logic is formalized in the International Health Regulations (IHR),[24] which structure how the world responds to health threats through the mechanism of a Public Health Emergency of International Concern (PHEIC). Under the IHR, 'normal' time is defined by the absence of a declared emergency. That normalcy ends when specific thresholds are met (as outlined in IHR Annex 2), triggering an official declaration that enables an array of extraordinary measures.[25] These include mandatory reporting, cross-border coordination, trade and travel advisories, and in some cases, emergency use authorizations or quarantines. Measures that would provoke political resistance under ordinary circumstances become acceptable once a crisis is named. The PHEIC mechanism codifies the emergency/normalcy distinction in global health law, reinforcing the idea that extraordinary powers are permissible when necessary and temporally and materially bound.[26] Most national constitutions mirror this logic, enabling temporary expansions of executive authority during declared emergencies, often at the expense of civil liberties in the name of collective protection.[27]

Yet, this legalistic framing obscures a more diffuse and continuous form of governance. Public health governance is not only enforced through visible legal declarations or sovereign acts. It also operates beneath the surface through routines, norms, and infrastructures that shape how individuals perceive risk and regulate their own behaviour. Michel Foucault turns attention away from formal legal enactments and suspensions toward the subtler, more pervasive forms of power that govern everyday

---

[21] Drezner (2020) and Ridley (1979).

[22] Schmitt (2005), p. 5.

[23] Locke (1988).

[24] WHO (2006).

[25] Fidler and Gostin (2006).

[26] Wilson et al. (2021).

[27] Kipfer and Mohamud (2021).

life (i.e., the 'micro-physics of power'). In his account of biopolitics, power deals not 'simply with legal subjects over whom the ultimate dominion was death, but with living beings, and the mastery it would be able to exercise over them would have to be applied at the level of life itself'.[28] In public health, this shift is visible in how institutions increasingly aim not to punish wrongdoing but to manage risk and optimize vitality, governing populations by cultivating self-discipline and moral responsibility (e.g., by raising awareness through education and behaviour-changing campaigns).[29] In addition to being subjects of the law, individuals become active instruments of governance. As Foucault writes, 'the individual is no doubt the fictitious atom of an ideological representation of society; but he is also a reality fabricated by this specific technology of power that I have called *discipline*'.[30] Discipline, in this sense, does not operate through direct control and repression but through what Foucault calls 'governmentality', defined as 'the conduct of conduct'.[31] In the context of AMR, these modes of power are evident in everyday stewardship programs, antimicrobial prescribing dashboards, and clinical feedback mechanisms, which modify behaviour by embedding a logic of responsibility into routine care rather than through coercion or legal force alone. Rather than relying on the formal declaration of crisis, they enact a mode of anticipatory governance rooted in the possibility of future catastrophe carried out through the internalization of norms around responsible behaviour.

Where Foucault shows how governance becomes embedded through norms and expectations, Giorgio Agamben reveals how emergency governance becomes entrenched within legal and institutional frameworks. 'The state of exception', he writes, 'tends increasingly to appear as the dominant paradigm of government in contemporary politics'.[32] Unlike traditional legal modes that apply specific rules to specific circumstances, the state of exception functions not as 'a special kind of law (like the law of war); rather, insofar as it is a suspension of the juridical order itself, it defines law's threshold or limit concept'.[33] From this perspective, the law does not guarantee protection, it enables its own withdrawal, producing a legal grey zone in which individuals are governed but not fully protected. And over time, what begins as temporary coordination becomes the ordinary stuff of everyday life. During the COVID-19 pandemic, this dynamic became visible across liberal democracies, where rules and technologies of governance outlived the pandemic crisis, illustrating how emergency powers, once activated, can become self-perpetuating, extending far beyond their original justification. Australia, for instance, closed its international borders for nearly 2 years, preventing even its own citizens from returning.[34] Hong

[28] Foucault (1978), pp. 142–143.

[29] WHO (2015a).

[30] Foucault (1977), p. 194.

[31] Foucault (2009), p. 193.

[32] Agamben (2004), p. 2.

[33] Ibid., p. 4.

[34] Silva and Razum (2025).

Kong maintained compulsory isolation requirements into 2023, long after peak infection risk had passed.[35] In Canada, digital surveillance infrastructure, such as the ArriveCAN app, persisted beyond the formal emergency.[36]

Foucault and Agamben show how power operates, and emergencies becomes normalized, through discipline, legal suspension, and diffuse control; Bonnie Honig offers another way to view crisis. Rather than viewing emergencies solely as threats to law or tools of sovereign power, she insists that crises are not outside politics but intensely political events. They expose the background conditions of inclusion, vulnerability, and obligation that often go unacknowledged in ordinary times. Emergencies reveal whose suffering is recognized, whose freedoms are constrained, and what forms of political action are permitted. Thus, emergencies create openings. Honig cautions against the reflex to retreat into sovereign command or rigid legalism, arguing instead for the generative potential of emergency in their ability to surface new political claims, actors, and democratic possibilities. As she writes, 'The assumed antagonism between democracy and emergency is to some extent undone … The work of democratic politics can better be seen to entail not just rupture but maintenance, not just new beginnings but preparation, receptivity, and orientation'.[37] Honig's account reorients attention from exception to emergence, challenging governance systems to respond not just with control, but with openness to political renewal.

In other words, emergencies surface political dynamics that are often invisible, generating the potential for renewed negotiation. The COVID-19 pandemic, for example, revealed how emergency governance distributes risk unequally, exposing low-wage essential workers to disproportionate danger while shielding others. Vaccine nationalism revealed global hierarchies of protection. In rendering these dynamics visible, emergencies prompt important political questions that are otherwise deferred: Who is essential? Whose suffering counts? Who decides when normalcy returns, and what normalcy looks like? In these moments, governance is about recognition as well as control. However, in AMR governance, this democratic potential remains unrealized. Without a clear onset or endpoint, no 'day zero', no media spectacle, AMR governance unfolds through the quiet integration of anticipatory norms. Rather than catalysing democratic action, as many emergency events automatically do through mandatory inquiries and reviews, AMR governance relies on moralized expectations that individuals accept limited treatment, reduce antimicrobial use, and internalize a sense of responsibility for an uncertain global future.[38]

Taken together, these thinkers reveal both the power and fragility of the emergency/normalcy distinction. The authority to name a crisis shapes whose freedoms can be suspended, what interventions become legitimate, and how initially exceptional measures endure. Emergency governance often claims to be time-bound and

---

[35] Ho et al. (2025).

[36] Canada Border Services Agency (2024).

[37] Honig (2009), p. xvii.

[38] Kesten et al. (2018).

proportionate, yet its tools (surveillance, rationing, behavioural regulation) routinely outlast the threats they were meant to address. Crises redraw and intensify the lines of political life, deciding which lives are prioritized and which are governed through delay, denial, or discipline. Even without formal declarations, public health governance operates through norms that guide behaviour, assign moral responsibility, and make ongoing intervention feel routine. These dynamics help explain how emergency powers persist, and why public health authority so often expands through ambiguity rather than rupture.

AMR governance resembles this trajectory but in a different temporal register. It does not transition from normal to emergency to normal; rather, it begins as a condition of ongoing anticipation, with no promise of resolution.[39] It has prompted robust interventions, including global surveillance networks,[40] prescribing restrictions,[41] behavioural campaigns,[42] but without the rupture that typically justifies emergency powers. AMR lacks a single pathogen, a spike in deaths, or a defined start or endpoint.[43] Resistance accumulates irregularly, randomly, and potentially with every antimicrobial use across clinics, farms, wastewater systems, and microbial ecologies. WHO calls it a 'silent pandemic'.[44] Global leaders describe it as a 'slow tsunami'.[45] These evocative descriptions highlight the challenge of narrating a crisis that lacks clear boundaries.

This framing, in turn, enables emergency-style governance in the absence of a declared emergency. AMR governance becomes organized around the logic of pre-emptive, indefinite vigilance: crisis as usual. The UN Interagency Coordination Group frames AMR as a problem of 'urgent', 'coordinated', and 'sustained' action across sectors, invoking crisis language to justify indefinite intervention.[46] The WHO Global Action Plan calls for 'urgent' and 'sustained action', yet offers no temporal threshold for success.[47] Measures like prescription audits and international data reporting are not crisis responses, they are permanent.[48] In other words, the intervention occurs without the narrative justification. Governance is enacted without the familiar time- and materially-bound story.

This has implications for autonomy. When the distinction between emergency and normalcy collapses, so too does the temporal logic that once protected individual rights in ordinary times. People are not temporarily governed; they are continuously

[39] WHO (2015a).

[40] WHO (2022).

[41] Sharland et al. (2018).

[42] Huttner et al. (2019).

[43] Kirchhelle and Podolsky (2022).

[44] WHO (2023).

[45] WHO (2020).

[46] IACG (2019).

[47] WHO (2015a).

[48] WHO (2022).

enrolled in regimes of behavioural regulation. Patients are expected to avoid unnecessary antibiotics.[49] Providers are audited and compared.[50] Publics are asked to act responsibly and ration their expectations of care, not for immediate health gains, but to preserve a shared future.[51] The AMR subject is not only coerced through legal systems of recognition and denial, but is also disciplined, governed through behavioural campaigns, education, guidelines, dashboards, and appeals to global stewardship.

With no return to normal in sight, individuals are expected to internalize a new kind of norm: one where scarcity is permanent, and responsibility is personal. As Foucault might suggest, the 'responsible patient' becomes a central figure in this regime: an individual who self-disciplines in relation to global microbial risk. Autonomy here is not expressed through choice, but through restraint. Moral responsibility is displaced downward, yet the structural drivers of AMR, such as weak pharmaceutical regulation, inadequate sanitation, fragmented access to care, remain largely unchanged.[52] The responsible patient, in this configuration, is tasked with preserving a system that offers diminishing returns, managing a crisis they did not cause and cannot resolve.

One might argue that AMR governance has discursively evolved beyond the normal/emergency binary to a pragmatic shift centred around acting now to preserve a fragile future.[53] However, this perspective, while highlighting the anticipatory nature of the challenge, precisely illuminates how the traditional distinction collapses. The perceived imperative to 'preserve the future' effectively functions as a perpetual, indefinite emergency justification, enabling interventions and behavioural regulation that, in a classic emergency paradigm, would be time-bound and contingent on an acute, identifiable crisis. The absence of a discrete emergency *now* is replaced by the omnipresent threat of a *future* post-antimicrobial era, making the 'exception' a permanent feature of governance. Thus, the 'urgency' of 'preserving the future' becomes the very mechanism through which emergency powers are normalized and extended into routine life, reconfiguring individual autonomy in the process.

The instability of the emergency/normalcy distinction reveals a deeper shift in public health governance: from temporary exceptions to open-ended obligations, from collective mobilization to individualized discipline. Contained even within calls for acting now to preserve the future, time is central but redistributed. The present is governed through restraint while the future becomes a moral horizon. This redistribution raises pressing critical questions: whose futures are safeguarded? Whose presents are sacrificed? And how can autonomy be meaningfully exercised when governance unfolds in a continuous but uneven now?

These questions about the reconfiguration of time and authority set the stage for the next two narrative disruptions. As the following sections show, AMR unsettles not

[49] Kesten et al. (2018).

[50] WHO (2019b).

[51] Chandler (2019).

[52] Denyer Willis and Chandler (2019).

[53] IACG (2019).

only our understanding of emergency, but also how global health imagines progress, history, and shared planetary futures.

3 Recursive Progress: AMR Unravels Biomedical Advancement

Antimicrobials are among the most celebrated achievements of twentieth-century science.[54] Their discovery transformed clinical practice, drastically reduced mortality from once deadly infections, and helped anchor the legitimacy of modern biomedicine. In public health discourse, antimicrobials came to symbolize a technological breakthrough signalling a greater civilizational milestone: the triumph of reason over nature. Pharmaceutical advertisements from the 1940s and 50s captured this spirit vividly. Penicillin was hailed as a 'wonder drug',[55] streptomycin as a 'magic bullet',[56] and the future was imagined as one in which infectious disease had been permanently conquered. This narrative persists today, exemplified by Pfizer's 'Science Will Win' campaign,[57] which employs bold imagery and messaging to reaffirm faith in scientific innovation as the key to overcoming contemporary health crises like AMR.

Here, we can see the story of antimicrobials as a story of scientific progress—progress that is at once linear, cumulative, and universal. It rests on a belief that each generation will inherit a healthier world through the continuous application of reason and technology. Today, that same belief animates AMR governance. From push and pull incentives for reviving antimicrobial R&D,[58] to global calls for repairing innovation pipelines,[59] the solution to resistance is often imagined in terms of the next breakthrough rather than systemic reform. To fully understand the full force of this narrative and how it structures governance, we must turn to its deeper intellectual roots.

Enlightenment thinkers formalized the link between rational inquiry and humanity's collective destiny. Immanuel Kant, for example, envisioned human history as a teleological journey in which nature, through reason, pushes humanity toward a perfected civil condition. 'Nature has willed', Kant wrote, 'that man should produce everything that goes beyond the mechanical ordering of his animal existence entirely out of his own reason'.[60] This idea, that history and science unfold together, with progress being both rational and inevitable, still echoes in AMR policy. The

---

[54] Lightman (2005).

[55] Science Museum (n.d.).

[56] Gradmann (2011).

[57] Pfizer (2020).

[58] Simpkin et al. (2017) and Renwick et al. (2016).

[59] Årdal et al. (2018).

[60] Kant (1963), Third Thesis.

global ambitions to 'preserve modern medicine'[61] or to 'avoid a return to the pre-antibiotic era',[62] pragmatic as they may seem, express a Kantian belief in a shared, rational path forward, where science redeems vulnerability and secures the future.

Auguste Comte extended this logic by asserting that all societies progress through three inevitable stages: theological, metaphysical, and positive, with the last being the age of science.[63] In Comte's worldview, the authority of religion and metaphysics give way to empirical observation and technological mastery. This progression, he claimed, was as natural as it was desirable. In the context of AMR, this positivist legacy lives on in the conviction that scientific advancement, especially biomedical innovation, will solve resistance if we can just accelerate the timeline. The pipeline metaphor, used to describe the development of new drugs, echoes Comte's staged linearity: knowledge flows forward, and society is carried with it. It is no coincidence that AMR policy rarely questions the nature and direction of the pipeline itself, but instead reaffirms the belief that new technologies will keep us ahead of evolving microbes if only we could unlock the pipeline's full potential.

Long before Kant or Comte, Francis Bacon had already laid the foundations for viewing scientific knowledge as the rightful source of human power. For Bacon, science was not contemplative but interventionist. 'Human knowledge and human power meet in one',[64] Bacon wrote, proposing that understanding nature enabled its control. By the mid-twentieth century, the logic of Baconian mastery had entered the bloodstream of public imagination through antimicrobial marketing, with a 1950s Pfizer promotional film for Terramycin capturing this ethos with sweeping declarations: 'This is an age that men of the future looking back will call the age of promise', it announced. 'Terramycin… in less than a decade completely changed the course of medicine'. The film boasted that 'diseases are controlled which yesterday took an appalling toll', and that 'frontiers of health and well-being not even dreamed of a hundred years ago have already been surpassed'.[65] In selling a drug, these lines affirmed a worldview in which science was synonymous with progress, mastery, and salvation.

Governance logics mirror this message. Health authorities promise not just treatment, but control of nature, often cast as a battle against it. The microbial world is framed as an enemy, and the rise of antimicrobials narrated through the language of war. From 'magic bullets' to 'replenishing our medical arsenal' to 'fighting superbugs,' the dominant metaphor is militarized.[66] This framing does not so much 'securitize' AMR, but rather reinforces medicine's longstanding role as a mode of defence,[67] positioning scientific innovation as the front line in a perpetual conflict. War, after

[61] Davies and Oxlade (2021).

[62] WHO (2015a).

[63] Comte (1855).

[64] Bacon (1850).

[65] Pfizer Laboratories (1956).

[66] Wallinga et al. (2015).

[67] Howell (2014).

all, is also about control, justifying extraordinary measures, exceptional funding, and collateral sacrifice.

But today, that control is slipping. AMR threatens the Baconian dream of mastery through knowledge not because science has failed, but because it has succeeded too well. The effectiveness and ubiquity of antimicrobials have altered microbial ecologies and accelerated evolutionary pressures. Our greatest biomedical triumph has produced the conditions for its own undoing. The war-on-bugs metaphor, once a rallying cry for innovation, now reveals its limits. There is no final victory in this war, only a shifting front.[68] And the more it is pursued as war, the more it obscures the ecological entanglements that render resistance inevitable and governance far more complex than conquest.[69]

By the late twentieth century, the belief in the stabilizing power of science became deeply entangled with liberal political ideology. Francis Fukuyama's *The End of History and the Last Man* claimed that modern natural science had enabled prosperity and global political convergence.[70] Liberal democracy and capitalist economies, he argued, were the endpoint of humanity's rational development, made possible by the mastery of nature through technology. In AMR discourse, this logic remains latent. The stakes of AMR are framed as civilizational, not just clinical, with calls to preserve antimicrobials often framed as preserving modern medicine and agriculture themselves. As one OECD report warned, AMR threatens to reverse decades of medical progress and undermine the stability of healthcare systems.[71] In this framing, science anchors political and economic order, supporting both biological life and social life as we know it.

But what if this very vision of progress is the problem? Walter Benjamin offered a critique of Enlightenment teleology, arguing that what we call progress is often the piling of wreckage upon wreckage.[72] In his parable of the Angel of History, he describes a figure blown forward by the storm of progress, unable to repair the damage accumulating behind them. This image finds eerie resonance in the story of antimicrobials. Resistance is not the antithesis of progress; it is its consequence. The more widely we use antimicrobials, the faster resistance spreads. Each generation of new drugs arrives with greater promise, and each is eroded, sometimes within years, by microbial adaptation and overuse.[73] Benjamin's insight cuts to the core of AMR: perhaps we are not falling behind microbial evolution despite innovation, but because innovation is pursued without confronting the systemic logics of overuse, inequity, and short-termism that drive the crisis.

To put it in more concrete terms, health governance's deep entanglement with the narrative of scientific progress is most visible in global funding patterns. Innovation

---

[68] Wallinga et al. (2015).

[69] Weldon and Hoffman (2024).

[70] Fukuyama (2006).

[71] OECD (2018).

[72] Benjamin et al. (1973).

[73] Kirchhelle and Podolsky (2022).

and drug discovery command billions of dollars,[74] while less alluring—but arguably more essential—priorities like country-level implementation for infection prevention and basic water, sanitation, and hygiene measures remain underfunded. For example, the Multi-Partner Trust Fund for AMR, intended to support national action plans and systemic reforms, has raised only around $30 million to date.[75]

Emboldened by these funding patterns, institutional responses to AMR have overwhelmingly focused on accelerating biomedical research through push-and-pull incentives that fund early-stage discovery ('pull') and aim to make antimicrobial development financially viable ('push' such as market entry rewards, advance purchase agreements, and subscription models).[76] Various international organizations and public-private-partnerships coordinate these efforts, all emphasizing the urgent need to 'replenish the pipeline'. The dominant narrative is one of scarcity and rescue: we are 'running out' of antibiotics and must 'stimulate' innovation to stay ahead of microbial evolution.

Indeed, it is often put that research and development must be accelerated to stay ahead of evolving antimicrobial resistance.[77] We hear phrases like we must stimulate the development of new antibiotics to stay ahead in the arms race against resistance.[78] Both framings place governance itself as a race against biological time. Mission statements of global antimicrobial research programs reflect these sentiments, asserting that stimulating innovation and investment in new antibiotics and alternatives is essential to prevent a return to the pre-antibiotic era.[79] Here, history is imagined as linear and fragile. Absent continued technological breakthroughs, civilization risks collapse into a prior, more dangerous state. The solution to resistance, under this framing, lies in producing the next breakthrough—faster, smarter, better—thereby reaffirming the broader teleology of scientific progress that has shaped modern governance.

Yet the promise and appeal of innovation in addressing AMR shows visible fractures. The bankruptcy of Achaogen in 2019, after successfully developing the antibiotic plazomicin, highlights the structural fragility of the antimicrobial market: scientific success does not guarantee commercial survival.[80] No new major class of antibiotics targeting Gram-negative bacteria has been discovered since the 1960s.[81] Even when new drugs reach the market, they are often priced prohibitively high and reserved under stewardship protocols, resulting in low clinical uptake.[82] Products meant to rescue modern medicine thus circulate at the margins, caught between economic unviability and ecological precaution. The innovation pipeline,

---

[74] Global AMR R&D Hub (2023).

[75] UNDP (2024).

[76] Renwick et al. (2016).

[77] IACG (2019).

[78] Global AMR R&D Hub (2023).

[79] G20 (2017).

[80] Mullard (2019).

[81] Caceres et al. (2022).

[82] Yahav et al. (2021).

once imagined as a steady ascent, has proven vulnerable to forces that resist linear solutions.

But what is more troubling for the idea that 'Science Will Win' is that progress in this domain is recursive. As explained above, resistance has not accelerated despite antimicrobials, but because of them. The very success of these drugs, measured by their widespread effectiveness and adoption, creates the biological and ecological conditions for their undoing. Scientific advances thus produce their own horizon of failure. The progress narrative turns inward, caught in a loop where each solution hastens the next crisis.

This recursive logic challenges the belief that scientific advancement will necessarily yield lasting solutions. As Benjamin might suggests, what appears as forward movement may in fact be the accumulation of unresolved contradictions: technological fixes that deepen systemic vulnerabilities, innovations that perpetuate overuse, and governance frameworks that defer structural reform in favour of expedient solutions.

As cracks appear in the narrative of innovation-led progress, governance responses nonetheless double down on the same logic. New initiatives replicate the promise of technical salvation by funnelling more investment into R&D pipelines, designing new market incentives (e.g., transferable exclusivity vouchers), and urging faster scientific breakthroughs.[83] Yet the recursive structure remains. Rather than escaping the crisis, governance finds itself trapped in a cycle of deferral, treating innovation not as an uncertain intervention into a complex system, but as a ritual reaffirmation of the belief that progress remains possible. The result is the institutionalization of a permanent race against biological evolution, where solutions recede as efforts accelerate.

These contradictions have direct consequences for how individual autonomy is governed in the context of AMR. On one hand, individuals are encouraged to trust in biomedical progress, to believe that science will deliver new cures and preserve their health. On the other hand, they are expected to moderate their use of these very technologies, to avoid pressuring clinicians, to accept restricted access, and to act as stewards of collective efficacy. Autonomy, here, is governed through paradox: patients are positioned as both the beneficiaries of innovation and the potential threats to its sustainability. The individual right to access is reframed not as a guarantee, but as a privilege contingent on responsible behaviour.

Nowhere do these tensions surface more sharply than in the governance of last-line antibiotics. In many healthcare systems, reserve-group agents sit behind pre-authorisation gates released only when all other therapies have demonstrably failed.[84] In practice, clinicians must persuade stewardship teams that a patient is *sick enough*; otherwise, the ward's dwindling vials are saved for tomorrow's unknown catastrophe. When genuine shortages hit, or when a drug's price makes it effectively unavailable,

[83] Årdal et al. (2024).

[84] Sharland et al. (2018).

patients who might benefit can still go untreated due to supply shortages.[85] Professional guidelines, formulary restrictions, and tacit ward norms operate as quasi-legal instruments, translating conservation ethics into binding rules that carry the force of law without its formal trappings.[86] At the bedside, clinical judgment merges with resource accounting, redefining what counts as care. Health systems that once promised expanding access now operate through a logic of scarcity and triage, while each new 'breakthrough' molecule arrives already chained by usage caps. Innovation, once a tool to enable autonomy, becomes the basis for limiting it.

Ultimately, AMR reveals a structural instability in the progress narrative itself. Scientific advancement is not inherently linear, and its durability is never guaranteed. Resistance shows that progress can undo itself, and that governance models built to accelerate innovation may be ill-suited to manage ecological crises that are recursive, cumulative, and unevenly felt.

To be sure, I do not dismiss the importance of scientific research or the urgent need for new treatments. Rather, I ask whether we have mistaken the treadmill for the destination. Innovation promises salvation but also postpones structural reform. If the future of antimicrobial governance is to be more than a never-ending arms race against resistance, then recognizing the limits of progress as a guiding framework might enable a deeper grappling with the systemic changes that AMR demands.

If antimicrobials inaugurated a golden age for therapy, AMR forecasts its unravelling. This unravelling is not a return to premodern scarcity, but a perpetual crisis generated by the very logic of modernity itself, a logic grounded in the confidence of scientific power and the unlimitedness of human ingenuity. Yet the impacts of this crisis, including the benefits of 'world advancing science', are not experienced uniformly. While some systems grapple with how to restrict antimicrobial access, others have never fully achieved it. The assumption of a shared trajectory toward better care, which is central to the narrative of progress, obscures the vast disparities in how antimicrobials are accessed, regulated, and withheld across the globe. It is to this disruption of temporal universality, the belief that all societies move forward together, that the next section now turns.

4 Temporal Disparity: AMR Collapses Time

At this point, we can restate the central premise of the chapter. Modern global health governance rests on deep temporal assumptions built into the narratives that structure epistemic and ontological worldviews. These worldviews, in turn, govern people's lives through diffuse forms of power, shaping how individuals are seen, what responsibilities they bear, and how care and control are exercised. Among these temporal assumptions are: the belief that time can be divided (between normal and emergency); that time moves forward (through progress and science); and that time is singular,

---

[85] Fox and Wynia (2024).

[86] Karanika et al. (2016).

universal, and shared. The final narrative of universal time is, like the others, inherited from Enlightenment thought, where all peoples and places are imagined as travelling along the same developmental arc: from illness to health, from ignorance to science, and from the past through the present into the future. Time, in this framing, is both linear and unifying. It provides the basis against which progress is measured, interventions are sequenced, and futures synchronized. Temporal uniformity is treated as a technical baseline, enabling global goals, justifying targeted interventions, and organizing coordination around shared benchmarks.

We can trace these philosophical roots again to Kant, where history is cast as a rational unfolding toward a cosmopolitan end, where reason and freedom would be fully realized across humanity. Time, for Kant, was the unfolding of a universal condition of experience, and by extension, of human development.[87] Later thinkers extended this logic, presenting humanity's future as a collective destination.[88] Modernity was imagined as the horizon for all societies, led by Western achievement. Dipesh Chakrabarty offers a critique of this "developmental historicism" in which non-Western societies are not outside history, but behind in it, awaiting their turn.[89] Time, in this vision, becomes a political sorting mechanism: it places some lives ahead, others behind, and all in relation to a normative trajectory of advancement.

In global health, this temporal narrative is institutionalized at every level. The Sustainable Development Goals (SDGs), for example, establish targets to be met by fixed dates, assuming that all states can and should move toward shared outcomes on a common schedule.[90] Roadmaps, countdowns, and eradication timelines propose standardized futures against which performance is judged.[91] Countries are labelled 'on track' or 'lagging behind' by what they achieve and how closely their timelines align with those set by multilateral institutions. This transforms coordination into a form of governance through temporal discipline.[92] Time becomes a tool of authority: synchrony is valorised, deviation demands correction. Technical solutions, funding, and behaviour change programs are distributed according to perceived temporal positioning. Some are cast as temporally mature and capable ('developed'); others as delayed and in need of acceleration ('undeveloped' or 'developing').

This temporal ontology of global health reflects a shared calendar underwritten by a deeper belief in a singular developmental arc—a global clock to which all must eventually conform. When that belief holds, governance proceeds through standardization: of indicators, interventions, and imagined futures. But this logic conflates physical time with historical and social time, the latter of which are lived unevenly, shaped by political economy, infrastructure, and colonial legacies. When global health governance collapses this distinction, it casts asynchronous experiences of

[87] Kant (1963).

[88] Koselleck (2004).

[89] Chakrabarty (2000).

[90] United Nations (2015).

[91] WHO (2015b).

[92] Fukuda-Parr (2014) and Adams (2016).

health and development temporal failure (as lag, delay, or underperformance) rather than structural effects.

AMR unsettles this ontology. Resistance does not unfold according to a shared trajectory. It is recursive, ecological, and unevenly driven by microbial evolution, patterns of use, health systems, animal agriculture, and global trade. The result is a fragmentation of temporal experience that no universal schedule can contain. Some populations, particularly in high-income countries, continue to benefit from effective but strained antimicrobials. Others already face a post-antimicrobial future where treatable infections have once again become deadly and last-line drugs are ineffective or inaccessible.[93] Still others remain in a pre-antimicrobial present, where even basic antimicrobials are unreliable, unaffordable, or counterfeit.[94]

These disparate but simultaneously co-existing experiences complicate the alignment of past, present, and future in the universal temporal arc of humanity as imagined by Kant. As Anna Agathangelou and Kyle Killian argue, global governance regimes often rest on the fantasy of shared time while materially producing radically uneven temporal conditions.[95] Whose time counts? They prompt us to ask. Whose futures are imagined, and whose presents are suspended or sacrificed? These are not rhetorical questions. In AMR governance, they take concrete form. In high-income countries, stewardship campaigns encourage patients to decline antimicrobials to preserve future effectiveness.[96] But in many low- and middle-income settings, patients delay or forgo treatment because no antimicrobial is available. Waiting for some is responsibility; for others, it is imposed by necessity; put differently, what is framed as ethical restraint in one context becomes medical neglect in another.

To unravel these dynamics further, we return to the governance of last-line antimicrobials. This is an arena where temporal hierarchies are actively reinforced through systems of conditional access. Baked into the discourse around the introduction of these drugs is the demonstration 'readiness'—typically defined by the presence of stewardship infrastructure, diagnostic capacity, and professional compliance.[97] Although framed in terms of capacity-building, these assessments often carry implicit judgments about trustworthiness. Responsibility is treated as something to be proven before access is granted. Readiness becomes a temporal sorting mechanism, placing some health systems on the path to the antimicrobial future while holding others in prolonged preparation. Deviation from the master timeline is framed as a 'capacity gap', a technical flaw to be patched rather than evidence of structural exclusion. Like AMR governance writ large, the approach normalises unequal time by urging the 'laggards' to catch up instead of questioning who set the clock and whose futures get secured first. Scarcity is administered through technical protocols and institutional procedures as well as moralized deferral. Treatments that could save lives are held back until conditions are met, turning access into a reward for acceptable governance

[93] Naghavi et al. (2024).

[94] Mendelson et al. (2024).

[95] Agathangelou and Killian (2016).

[96] Charani and Holmes (2013).

[97] Pulcini et al. (2019).

behaviour. In this configuration, temporal legitimacy is granted unevenly. Some are welcomed into the future; others remain suspended, still expected to prove they belong. Achille Mbembe names this sorting of protection and exposure 'necropolitics'.[98] He shows that modern sovereignty reveals itself when it decides whose lives enjoy shelter from mortal danger and whose lives must unfold in zones of chronic threat, creating what he calls 'death-worlds'. When AMR governance withholds reserve antibiotics until health systems pass 'readiness' audits, it performs the same calculus, granting microbial safety to some populations while others remain exposed to rising, untreated risk.

This fractured temporal landscape also reshapes how autonomy is understood and governed. When time is implicitly imagined as universal and linear, autonomy becomes a matter of keeping pace, of making 'responsible' choices that align with global goals and predetermined timelines. Health interventions are then enabled or denied not only for individual health but for the health of a projected collective future. However, such appeals to 'responsible choice' presume inherent capacities that are far from universally distributed: the capacity to wait, to access care later, or to act with foresight. These appeals also naturalize the destination, assumed to be the universally desirable endpoint of progress (i.e., those ahead are 'developed', never 'overdeveloped'). Moreover, they subtly imply that those who cannot wait or plan ahead are somehow less rational or responsible. When access to care is uncertain or absent, the very idea of choice collapses. Autonomy therefore becomes conditional and stratified, constrained by unequal temporal positioning.

AMR reveals the fragility of the universal time narrative. It shows that global health does not operate in a single temporal register. It unfolds across multiple, intersecting timelines, each shaped by microbial evolution, social infrastructure, and the legacies of exploitation and neglect. This rupture is a challenge to the temporal grammar of global governance itself. At its worst, when governance proceeds as if the world moves in unison, it naturalizes uneven suffering, privileges certain futures, and obscures the structural conditions that produce delay. AMR exposes what global health prefers to deny: time itself is governed, and that governing it unequally is a political choice.

As with the breakdown of the emergency/normalcy distinction and the collapse of linear progress, the erosion of universal time complicates how governance structures justify their authority and how rights are distributed. The following section briefly summarizes the analysis thus far and turns to reflect and synthesize the consequences of these narrative ruptures.

[98] Mbembe (2003).

5 Governing Through Contradiction

The preceding sections have shown how AMR unsettles three dominant narratives that structure global health governance: the boundary between normalcy and emergency, the trajectory of linear progress, and the assumption of universal time. Together, these structural fractures reveal narratives of governance increasingly defined by contradiction rather than coherence. Public health institutions continue to function and intervene, but the conceptual foundations that once justified those interventions are eroding. The narratives have collapsed, but governance continues through ambivalence, improvisation, and disjuncture.

This adaptation is marked by three intersecting tensions analysed above. First, the crisis of AMR is both acute and persistent. Governance thus oscillates between urgency and routine, embedding exceptional measures into everyday practice without a clear endpoint or resolution. Second, innovation remains central to policy rhetoric, but its entanglement with its own undoing undermines its promise. Scientific breakthroughs are pursued not to expand access, but to manage scarcity, producing a recursive relationship between progress and restriction. Third, governance operates across radically uneven timelines. Global targets remain, but the lived experience of AMR diverges widely across contexts, eroding the premise of a synchronized global response.

Together, these tensions produce a fragmented logic of governance: continuous but exceptional, normative but unstable, structural but individual, globally ambitious but locally dissonant. The result is a patchwork of institutional responses trying to maintain legitimacy amid the erosion of shared narrative foundations.

The consequences for individual autonomy are quiet but profound. Autonomy is often imagined in liberal public health governance as a stable entitlement: protected in times of normalcy, suspended during emergencies, and ultimately expanded through scientific progress. It is exercised and enjoyed in a world where time advances linearly, where solutions accumulate, and where all are destined to arrive at a common destination. But under the contradictory governance of AMR, these assumptions no longer hold. Autonomy is not fixed. It is increasingly produced, conditioned, and distributed by systems of governance that reward alignment, moralize restraint, and replicate global inequities. Autonomy has become conditional, moralized, and stratified.

First, autonomy is conditional. As Foucault's account of governmentality suggests, autonomy is not an original entitlement but a capacity shaped through norms and expectations. It is fabricated through institutional techniques that train individuals to regulate themselves in alignment with broader logics of control. In the case of AMR, patients and practitioners alike are expected to internalize the logic of stewardship. This is not autonomy as freedom from interference, but autonomy as a product of discipline: something earned by conforming to the demands of risk management. Autonomy becomes less a right than a demonstration of governable subjecthood, calibrated through dashboards, audits, and the authority of clinical guidelines.

Second, autonomy is moralized. Individuals are called upon to act responsibly in the name of a shared microbial future. Appeals to restraint and responsibility ask individuals to manage the consequences of a crisis they did not cause, within systems they cannot control. Honig's reflections on crisis as a political moment are instructive here: instead of surfacing contestation or generating collective deliberation, AMR governance directs moral pressure downward. Responsibility becomes a private matter, decoupled from structural reform. The obligation to preserve antimicrobial efficacy is unevenly distributed, justified through the language of ethical action, but carried out through acts of denial, delay, and self-limitation.

Third, autonomy is stratified. As Mbembe's notion of necropolitics suggests, governance is not just about enabling life but managing who is exposed to risk, who is protected, and who is abandoned. In AMR governance, this stratification appears clearly. While patients in high-income settings may be asked to limit their antimicrobial use for the sake of future effectiveness, many in low- and middle-income countries still lack reliable access to even first-line treatments. Stewardship is imagined as a global ethic, but its obligations are felt unevenly, shaped by historical legacies. AMR governance allocates protection unevenly and obscures those who fall outside its normative gaze. Autonomy, in this context, is filtered through global asymmetries in access, risk, and legibility.

Together, these dynamics reveal how autonomy is no longer simply protected or suspended. It is governed: produced, rewarded, moralized, and withheld. People are asked to be self-regulating, forward-looking, and globally responsible, even as the material and institutional conditions for meaningful autonomy erode.

This raises a deeper question: what happens when the coherence that once underpinned global health governance gives way to fragmentation? Governance does not collapse, clearly, as we continue to grapple with AMR and similar threats like climate change. It persists. But its legitimacy has become increasingly contingent on moral appeals, institutional inertia, and ad hoc coordination rather than shared ethical or temporal frameworks. Rights and responsibilities are no longer anchored by stable narratives. They are negotiated in shifting, contested spaces.

AMR thus opens a conceptual space to reflect on the conditions under which governance itself is justified. When the organizing narratives of time, progress, and crisis no longer align with lived experience, but health governance continues, its claims to authority, fairness, and efficacy grow fragile. This shifts the question from 'how to craft policy responses to AMR' to 'what has global health governance become in the absence of its foundational certainties' and 'what must it become if it is to confront the inequalities of the past, respond to the challenges of the present, and build a more just and equitable future'.

This chapter does not offer easy answers. Instead, it invites reflection on what we mean by governance—not only in technical terms, but in conceptual, ethical, and political ones. What kinds of futures are being imagined? Whose pasts are being carried forward? And what forms of life, care, and responsibility are being quietly governed in the name of health? To meet the technical challenge of AMR is to respond to a medical crisis. But to confront its political nature is to interrogate whose lives are deemed to matter, whose time is counted, and what forms of governance are rendered thinkable in the world our actions continue to build.

6 Conclusion

Antimicrobial resistance produces a conceptual rupture. It exposes cracks in the stories that have long underpinned global health governance. As these narratives fray, governance adapts, not with clarity, but with contradiction. The result is a permanent mode of low-level control where individual autonomy is increasingly moralized and conditional, and dignity unevenly distributed.

What's needed may not be more action, but clearer thinking. When action now is no longer anchored in liberal promises of protection, progress, or parity, autonomy becomes a site of negotiation and dignity governed through temporal ambiguity, institutional drift, and moral appeal. People are called upon to self-regulate for futures they may not share, to defer access in the name of collective good, and to trust in systems that ration care while reproducing inequality.

The danger is not simply that autonomy is constrained, but that it is redefined without consent, reshaped by governance structures that continue to invoke broken narratives as if they still hold. AMR exposes a gap between the stories we tell and the world we inhabit. It forces us to confront the uneasy reality that governance persists even when its foundations erode.

What would it mean to take that erosion seriously? Not just as a problem to fix, but as a prompt to reimagine how we govern health, risk, and responsibility in the absence of coherence? If the promises of returning to normal, of accelerating progress, or of acting in global synchrony no longer hold, then perhaps the task is not to restore old certainties, but to learn how to govern with humility, attuned to uncertainty, complexity, asymmetry, and the uneven stakes of action.

This chapter has argued that AMR is a window into that challenge. It shows how individual autonomy and human dignity are being reshaped. Not by brute force, but by the slow grind of contradiction. And it suggests that the future of global health will depend not only on new drugs or stronger institutions, but on new ways of justifying action while living with ambiguity and risk.

Acknowledgement Preparation of this work was supported, in part, by a Novo Nordisk Foundation grant for a scientifically independent International Collaborative Bioscience Innovation & Law Programme (Inter-CeBIL) (#NNF23SA0087056 and #NNF17SA0027784), and benefited from insights generated through a Partnership Grant from the Social Sciences and Humanities Research Council (#895-2022-1015) hosted at the Global Strategy Lab, York University.

References

Adams V (2016) Metrics: what counts in global health. Duke University Press, Durham
Agamben G (2004) State of exception. University of Chicago Press, Chicago
Agathangelou AM, Killian KD (eds) (2016) Time, temporality and violence in international relations: (de)fatalizing the present, forging radical alternatives. Routledge, Abingdon/New York
Årdal C, Baraldi E, Busse R et al (2024) Transferable exclusivity voucher: a flawed incentive to stimulate antibiotic innovation. Lancet 403:e2–e4
Årdal C, Findlay D, Savic M, Carmeli Y, Gyssens I, Laxminarayan R, Outterson K, Rex JH (2018) DRIVE-AB final report: revitalizing the antibiotic pipeline: stimulating innovation while driving sustainable use and global access. Brussels: DRIVE-AB, 2018. available at: https://drive-ab.eu/wpcontent/uploads/2018/01/DRIVE-AB-Final-Report-Jan2018.pdf
Bacon F (1850) Novum organum. W. Pickering, London
Benjamin W, Arendt H, Zohn H (1973) Illuminations. Fontana, London
Caceres AM, Singh KK, Minssen T et al (2022) Using the international pandemic instrument to revitalize the innovation ecosystem for antimicrobial R&D. J Law Med Ethics 50:47–54
Canada Border Services Agency (2024) Use advance declaration to save time at the border. In: Government of Canada. https://www.canada.ca/en/border-services-agency/services/arrivecan.html
Chakrabarty D (2000) Provincializing Europe. Princeton University Press, Princeton
Chandler CIR (2019) Current accounts of antimicrobial resistance: stabilisation, individualisation and antibiotics as infrastructure. Palgrave Commun 5:53
Charani E, Holmes AH (2013) Antimicrobial stewardship programmes: the need for wider engagement. BMJ Qual Saf 22:885
Comte A (1855) The positive philosophy of Auguste Comte. Freely translated and condensed by Martineau H. Calvin Blanchard, New York
Davies SC, Oxlade C (2021) Innovate to secure the future: the future of modern medicine. Future Healthc J 8(2):e251–e256. https://doi.org/10.7861/fhj.2021-0087. PMID: 34286193; PMCID: PMC8285149
Denyer Willis L, Chandler C (2019) Quick fix for care, productivity, hygiene and inequality: reframing the entrenched problem of antibiotic overuse. BMJ Glob Health 4:e001590
Drezner DW (2020) The song remains the same: international relations after COVID-19. International Organization, Cambridge University Press 74(S1):E18–E35
European Commission Newsroom (2023) AMR: giving a voice to the fight against a silent pandemic. https://ec.europa.eu/newsroom/sante/items/788679/en
Fidler DP, Gostin LO (2006) The new international health regulations: an historic development for international law and public health. TJ Law Med Ethics 34:85–94
Fleming A (1999) Penicillin [Nobel Prize lecture, December 11, 1945]. Nobel lectures in physiology or medicine, 1942–1962. World Scientific Publishing Company, Singapore
Foucault M (1977) Discipline and punish: the birth of the prison, 1st American edn. Pantheon Books, New York
Foucault M (1978) The history of sexuality, 1st American edn. Pantheon Books, New York
Foucault M (2009) Security, territory, population. Palgrave Macmillan UK, London
Fox ER, Wynia MK (2024) How should critical medications be rationed during shortages? AMA J Ethics 26:E334–E340
Fukuda-Parr S (2014) Global goals as a policy tool: intended and unintended consequences. J Hum Dev Capab 15:118–131
Fukuyama F (2006) The end of history and the last man. Free Press, New York
G20 (2017) Berlin Declaration of the G20 Health Ministers. https://www.g20.utoronto.ca/2017/170520-health-en.html
Global AMR R&D Hub (2023) Investments in AMR R&D. https://dashboard.globalamrhub.org/reports/investments/overview

Gradmann C (2011) Magic bullets and moving targets: antibiotic resistance and experimental chemotherapy, 1900–1940. Dynamis 31:305–321
Hall PA (1993) Policy paradigms, social learning, and the state: the case of economic policymaking in Britain. Comp Polit 25:275–296
Ho GWK, Leung SF, Mak YW et al (2025) Social distancing and mental health two years into a global pandemic: a sequential exploratory mixed-methods investigation in Hong Kong. BMJ Open 15:e092160
Hoffman SJ, Weldon I, Habibi R (2022) A virus unites the world while national border closures divide it: epidemiologic, legal, and political analysis on border closures during COVID-19. Int J 22(2):188–215
Honig B (2009) Emergency politics: paradox, law, democracy. Princeton University Press, Princeton
Howell A (2014) The global politics of medicine: beyond global health, against securitisation theory. Rev Int Stud 40:961–987
Huttner B, Saam M, Moja L et al (2019) How to improve antibiotic awareness campaigns: findings of a WHO global survey. BMJ Glob Health 4:e001239
Interagency Coordination Group on Antimicrobial Resistance (IACG) (2019) No time to wait: securing the future from drug-resistant infections. Report to the secretary-general of the United Nations. https://www.who.int/publications/i/item/no-time-to-wait-securing-the-future-from-drug-resistant-infections
Kant I (1963) On history. Bobbs-Merrill, Indianapolis
Karanika S, Paudel S, Grigoras C et al (2016) Systematic review and meta-analysis of clinical and economic outcomes from the implementation of hospital-based antimicrobial stewardship programs. Antimicrob Agents Chemother 60:4840–4852
Kesten JM, Bhattacharya A, Ashiru-Oredope D et al (2018) The antibiotic guardian campaign: a qualitative evaluation of an online pledge-based system focused on making better use of antibiotics. BMC Public Health 18:5
Kipfer S, Mohamud J (2021) The pandemic as political emergency. Stud Polit Econ 102:268–288
Kirchhelle C, Podolsky SH (2022) An awkward fit: antimicrobial resistance and the evolution of international health politics (1945–2022). J Law Med Ethics 50:40–46
Koselleck R (2004) Futures past: on the semantics of historical time. Columbia University Press, New York
Lightman AP (2005) The discoveries: great breakthroughs in 20th century science, 1st edn. Pantheon Books, New York
Lipscy PY (2020) COVID-19 and the politics of crisis. Int Org:1–30
Locke J (1988) Locke: two treatises of government. Cambridge University Press, Cambridge
Mbembe A (2003) Necropolitics. Public Cult 15:11–40
Mendelson M, Balasegaram M, Jinks T et al (2017) Antibiotic resistance has a language problem. Nature 545:23–25
Mendelson M, Laxminarayan R, Limmathurotsakul D et al (2024) Antimicrobial resistance and the great divide: inequity in priorities and agendas between the global North and the global South threatens global mitigation of antimicrobial resistance. Lancet Glob Health 12:e516–e521
Mullard A (2019) Achaogen bankruptcy highlights antibacterial development woes. Nat Rev Drug Discov 18:411
Naghavi M, Vollset SE, Ikuta KS et al (2024) Global burden of bacterial antimicrobial resistance 1990–2021: a systematic analysis with forecasts to 2050. Lancet 404:1199–1226
Ney S (2012) Making sense of the global health crisis: policy narratives, conflict, and global health governance. J Health Polit Policy Law 37:253–295
O'Neill J (2016) Tackling drug-resistant infections globally: final report and recommendations. Review on antimicrobial resistance. Wellcome Trust and HM Government
OECD (2018) Stemming the superbug tide: just a few dollars more. OECD, Paris
Pfizer (2020) Science will win. In: Pfizer. https://www.pfizer.com/stories/podcasts/science-will-win
Pfizer Laboratories (1956) The age of promise [film]. Produced by Brandt Enos Associates, Inc., New York. Wellcome Collection: https://wellcomecollection.org/works/jkhgxzzj

Pulcini C, Binda F, Lamkang AS et al (2019) Developing core elements and checklist items for global hospital antimicrobial stewardship programmes: a consensus approach. Clin Microbiol Infect 25:20–25
Renwick MJ, Brogan DM, Mossialos E (2016) A systematic review and critical assessment of incentive strategies for discovery and development of novel antibiotics. J Antibiot 69:73–88
Ridley RT (1979) The origin of the roman dictatorship: an overlooked opinion. Rhein Mus Philol 122:303–309
Rupasinghe N, Machalaba C, Muthee T et al (2024) Stopping the grand pandemic: a framework for action–addressing antimicrobial resistance through World Bank Operations. The World Bank, Washington, DC. http://elibrary.worldbank.org/doi/book/10.1596/41533
Sacco R (1991) Legal formants: a dynamic approach to comparative law (Installment I of II). Am J Comp Law 39:1
Schmitt C (2005) Political theology: four chapters on the concept of sovereignty. University of Chicago Press, Chicago
Science Museum L (n.d.) Advertisement for penicillin production from life magazine, United States, August 14, 1944
Sharland M, Pulcini C, Harbarth S et al (2018) Classifying antibiotics in the WHO essential medicines list for optimal use–be aware. Lancet Infect Dis 18(1):18–20
Silva DS, Razum O (2025) COVID-19: border closures violate human rights. Lancet 405:1053–1054
Simpkin VL, Renwick MJ, Kelly R, Mossialos E (2017) Incentivising innovation in antibiotic drug discovery and development: progress, challenges and next steps. J Antibiot 70:1087–1096
The Lancet Respiratory Medicine (2024) Antimicrobial resistance: a global health emergency. Lancet Respir Med 12:837
UNDP (2024) Consolidated financial report of the antimicrobial resistance multi-party trust fund
United Nations (2015) Transforming our world: the 2030 agenda for sustainable development: A/RES/70/1
Wallinga D, Rayner G, Lang T (2015) Antimicrobial resistance and biological governance: explanations for policy failure. Public Health 129:1314–1325
Weldon I, Hoffman SJ (2024) 'Fit for purpose?' Assessing the ecological fit of the social institutions that globally govern antimicrobial resistance. Perspect Polit:1–22
Wilson LA, Van Katwyk SR, Weldon I, Hoffman SJ (2021) A global pandemic treaty must address antimicrobial resistance. J Law Med Ethics 49:688–691
World Health Organization (2006) International health regulations, 2. Geneva
World Health Organization (2015a) Global action plan on antimicrobial resistance. Geneva. https://www.who.int/publications/i/item/9789241509763
World Health Organization (2015b) The end TB strategy. Geneva. https://www.who.int/teams/global-programme-on-tuberculosis-and-lung-health/the-end-tb-strategy
World Health Organization (2019a) Antimicrobial resistance (AMR): a major public threat. Geneva WHO/UHC/IHS/2019.2
World Health Organization (2019b) Antimicrobial stewardship programmes in health-care facilities in low- and middle-income countries: a WHO practical toolkit. Geneva. https://www.who.int/publications/i/item/9789241515481
World Health Organization (2020) WHO director-general opening remarks at the AMR action fund launch. https://www.who.int/director-general/speeches/detail/who-director-general-opening-remarks-at-the-amr-action-fund-launch
World Health Organization (2022) Global antimicrobial resistance and use surveillance system (GLASS) report 2022. https://www.who.int/publications/i/item/9789240108127
World Health Organization (2023) Global antimicrobial resistance forum launched to help tackle common threat to planetary health. In: WHO. https://www.who.int/news-room/articles-detail/global-antimicrobial-resistance-forum-launched-to-help-tackle-common-threat-to-planetary-health
Yahav D, Shepshelovich D, Tau N (2021) Cost analysis of new antibiotics to treat multidrug-resistant bacterial infections: mind the gap. Infect Dis Ther 10:621–630

Isaac Weldon , PhD, is an Assistant Professor of Law at the Centre for Advanced Studies in Bioscience Innovation Law (CeBIL), University of Copenhagen, and an Investigator with the Global Strategy Lab, York University. A political scientist, he examines the intersections of law, global health, and international relations. He uses critical social science approaches to study global challenges, including antimicrobial resistance, pandemic preparedness, and planetary health. His work has appeared in *Perspectives on Politics*, *Policy Studies Journal*, and *The Milbank Quarterly*.

Access to Medicines as a Proxy for Universal Healthcare

Alice Cauduro

Abstract This chapter focuses on access to medicines as a key lens through which to evaluate the effectiveness of universal healthcare. The public governance of medicines exemplifies the tensions surrounding access to healthcare between universalist and market-oriented logics—tensions which have characterised the post-crisis period of welfare systems and persist in the context of health emergencies, which have become normalised. Reflection on universal access to medicines therefore unfolds through the examination of three main issues: medicine pricing, access to essential medicines, and the challenge of antimicrobial resistance. From the perspective of European policies and regulations, this chapter investigates how public institutions—particularly within universalist healthcare models—guarantee the right to health, taking this dimension as a paradigm for the future of universal healthcare.

1 Introduction

Pharmaceutical discoveries of the past century represented a groundbreaking turning point for contemporary medicine, making it possible to treat diseases that had previously been considered incurable. However, these extraordinary scientific advances have not been matched by a corresponding expansion in universal access to medicines. After the Second World War, healthcare models inspired by universalism were established. Yet, from the late 1990s onward, universalism has largely lost its practical effect, even in states where the founding norms of National Health Service (NHS) remain formally in force. This confirms how health increasingly tends to be framed as an 'economic variable' rather than as a fundamental right that, by its very nature, must be recognised and guaranteed to all.

From this perspective, medicines can be seen as a 'borderline good', situated at the crossroads of law and economics: an indicator through which the structural contradictions of contemporary health systems and the inequalities they generate become

A. Cauduro (✉)
Department of Law, University of Turin, Torino, Italy
e-mail: alice.cauduro@unito.it

M. Balestrieri and A. Cauduro (eds.), *The Legal Anatomy of the Body*, Ius Gentium: Comparative Perspectives on Law and Justice 142,
https://doi.org/10.1007/978-3-032-26434-3_13

visible. Indeed, the history of medicines exemplifies the evolution of the right to health, shifting from a central component in the construction of social rights to a commodity whose access is determined not only by the scarcity of public resources but also by the lack of allocation constraints. In this context, access to medicines governed by market rules exemplifies how the need for care is often subordinated to economic sustainability and determined by criteria for assessing needs that are unrelated to health. Thus, even in Europe, access to innovative medicines, which today play a central role in therapeutic management, is constrained by complex and weakly sustainable models of public healthcare expenditure governance. In other words, access to medicines highlights the unresolved tension between socio-economic determinants and equality, which should instead guide public healthcare systems in contemporary democracies. From this perspective, medicines function both as a testing ground and as an analytical lens through which to examine the tensions and challenges of contemporary health law.

2 Medicines at the Intersection of the Market and the Right to Health

The history of medicine is closely intertwined with the achievements of civil society in the second half of the twentieth century, when many countries experienced an expansion of the welfare state model, with the aim of rebuilding societies after the Second World War and ensuring universal social care.[1] During those years, the legal connection between health and rights was also established, particularly through the creation of health services based on universalist model. In many European countries, health policies were inspired by the British NHS, the paradigmatic expression of the Beveridge model.[2] As is well known, it is a system in which equality of access to healthcare for all—regardless of individual, economic, or social circumstances—gave practical expression to the concept of 'universalism', grounding it in the provision of essential care free of charge and access based on need.[3]

From that moment on, the evaluation of the effectiveness of medicines began to move beyond the empiricism that still prevailed, adopting more scientifically

[1] For an analysis of the origins and early development of the welfare state in the United Kingdom, as reflected in the policies implemented between the two world wars, see Bruce (1965), p. 197; also Pierson (2006), p. 243 particularly where he highlights that 'the welfare state will prove to be not just part of the problem, but part of the solution too'.

[2] See Jones and Lowe (2002), p. 82 where they highlight that 'since its establishment in 1948, the National Health Service has been so closely identified with the welfare state that the two terms have often been considered synonymous'.

[3] On the NHS model in the UK, which later served as an inspiration for other European countries, see Eckstein (1959), p. 268, where he identifies the two main objectives of the service: 'to remove all barriers between patient and treatment by the removal of economics barriers [and] to rationalize medical services'.

rigorous tools such as randomized population studies. The development of collaborative research networks contributed to making medicine a space of responsibility toward unmet needs. In this perspective, the World Health Organization (WHO) published the Essential Medicines List (1977), aimed at identifying the treatments to which everyone should have access. Shortly thereafter, the Alma-Ata Declaration (1978) established Health for All by the Year 2000 as a global goal.

With the emergence of the modern pharmaceutical industry in the second half of the twentieth century, medicines became industrial products with a distinct commercial identity. No longer merely symbols of medical and scientific progress, they became economic goods, patentable and tradable on a global scale. Thus, the pharmaceutical sector became fully embedded within market dynamics, where profit-driven logics influence research investment decisions, often misaligned with actual therapeutic needs. Even at that time, access to medicines began to reflect and amplify existing inequalities in healthcare, exemplifying, in an emblematic way, the retreat of the state and the dismantling of the NHS model founded on universalism.[4] During the 1980s and 1990s, the retrenchment of the state's role in the face of the global pharmaceutical market marked a phase of profound transformation.[5] In those years, the economic dimension of the pharmaceutical market was already evident, and access to medicines would soon become a key arena in which health inequalities were both manifested and deepened. Economic priorities began to prevail over individual rights, and health started to be regarded increasingly as a cost. Emblematic in this respect was the Global Burden of Disease (GBD) Report, prepared by the World Bank in collaboration with the WHO, which introduced a new approach to measuring health status based on the Disability-Adjusted Life Year (DALY) indicator and cost-effectiveness criteria.[6] This quantitative approach, though innovative, risked reducing health to a purely technical dimension, overlooking its social and political determinants (such as poverty, inequality, and privatisations).[7] Indeed, the seemingly objective metrics of the GBD may conceal political choices and conflicts of interest in the definition of health spending priorities.[8] From the perspective of 'health equity', however, health should be understood as a multidimensional concept, encompassing not only the distribution of healthcare services but also each individual's capability to achieve a good state of health.[9] The GBD approach claims universality, yet it overlooks local, cultural, and regulatory contexts, as well as the dimensions of health justice, the right to health, and structural inequalities—factors that over time have been recognised as essential, shifting the focus from the mere absence of disease to the promotion

---

[4] On the dismantling of the UK National Health Service, see Roderick and Pollock (2022).

[5] For an analysis of Sweden, Germany, the USA, and the UK see Ginsburg (1992), p. 193.

[6] See Murray and Lopez (1996), p. 2, who concluded stating that 'the study's impact will be judged in two ways: first, by the degree to which it stimulates other researchers to apply the same rigorous methods of measuring disease burden in all regions; and second, to the extent that it changes priorities for public health in the decades ahead'.

[7] About the 'social determinants of health, health equity, and human rights', see Chapman (2016), p. 248.

[8] See Adams (2016).

[9] See Sen (2002), pp. 659–666.

of individuals' capabilities to live a healthy life.[10] Furthermore, the GBD reflects a model of global health oriented toward cost-effectiveness and the containment of public expenditure, with DALYs often justifying low-cost, 'high-yield' interventions rather than the construction of equitable and universal public health systems. Since the data used to construct DALYs are frequently incomplete, heterogeneous, or estimated through complex, non-transparent statistical models that are difficult to verify, this can produce a false sense of objectivity, useful for legitimising political decisions already made.

At the same time, in the 1990s the concept of global health, already at the centre of legal debate, found fertile ground for interdisciplinary research aimed at defining the limits and potential of international law in global health governance.[11] Awareness grew of the need for a more equitable and inclusive governance, capable of integrating local and global dimensions, reducing social, economic, and environmental inequalities, promoting prevention and community-based care, and reaffirming the universalism of public health through global models that guarantee access to care.

3 Pharmaceutical Universalism Beyond the Crisis

In the global scenario, the debate on health as a human right has progressively given way to the issue of the 'costs' of illness. Thus, albeit in new forms, public authorities' attention has returned to the body as an object of quantification and control—a regression compared to the twentieth-century achievements that had shifted the focus 'from the body to the person'. Indeed today, the body has once again become a site for the extraction of economic value. In this context, health policies have progressively aligned with the neoliberal logic underpinning Reagan—and Thatcher—era policies, while the healthcare and pharmaceutical sectors have emerged as key drivers within the World Trade Organization (WTO). Whereas in the past the denial of access to medicines primarily affected poorer countries, the pharmaceutical sector has become a symbol of the denial of the right to health even in Europe.

Between the late 1990s and the first decade of the twenty-first century, an important reflection emerged on the role of medicines as a potential driver of global health policy. During this period, debate intensified over the difficulties faced by states in assessing the costs and benefits of new treatments, which were often unsustainable for public budgets without either increasing spending or reallocating resources. In this context, the retreat of the state from the governance of the pharmaceutical sector was facilitated by the broader deregulatory trends that affected the entire sphere of

[10] See Venkatapuram (2011).

[11] See Coggon (2024), pp. 150–176, who highlights that 'global health law has arisen as a critique of international health law'.

social rights.[12] It is well known that the patient-treatment cost can range from tens to hundreds of thousands of euros, pounds, or dollars. Today, the price of many reimbursed medicines is such that it challenges even health systems that remain formally universalist, compounded by the lack of transparency in pricing mechanisms—one of the clearest manifestations of the democratic deficit in this sector. Moreover, the market tends to arbitrarily favour certain medicines over others, thereby influencing the decisions of public policymakers.[13] The trend in the pharmaceutical sector fits within the broader context of the shift from public to private provision in healthcare, although there is 'evidence that overall efficiency increases with the public share of financing'.[14] In Europe, this was accompanied by the perspective of austerity, despite it having been clarified that the crises were not caused by excessive public debt or welfare state systems, but rather by the austerity measures themselves.[15]

Accordingly, the pharmaceutical sector has become one of the main items of health expenditure and a powerful driver of consumption. Numerous studies have shown how pharmaceutical companies influence the scientific and decision-making process, also through marketing strategies capable of creating new demand and new therapeutic needs.[16] The 'pharmaceuticalisation of society', understood as the translation of human and social problems into pharmaceutical terms, has been driven both by medicalization and by the push for consumption and deregulation.[17] Medicines are no longer merely goods of care but also of enhancement, as illustrated by the recent case of anti-obesity medicines and their ethical implications.[18]

The promises of future medicine stand in stark contrast to the persistent denial of access to essential medicines, even in states that formally uphold healthcare universalism. Indeed, the allure of therapeutic prospects through ever more sophisticated tools—such as artificial intelligence, robotics, and predictive algorithms—clashes with the systematic and structural denial of access to essential pharmaceutical care.

Certainly, the COVID-19 pandemic has highlighted the need to strengthen public healthcare and the universal protection of the right to health. However, the regulatory measures adopted in the post-pandemic period do not appear to represent a genuine paradigm shift, as not even the European Union (EU)—which enshrines a high level

---

[12] See Abraham and Lewis (2000), p. 78, where they argue that 'a crucial part of the establishment of drug regulatory agencies has been a neo-liberal political agenda aimed at increasing the responsiveness of regulators to industrial demands at minimal expense of the state'. On 'deregulation', see Stiglitz (2012).

[13] Regarding transparency in the medicines sector, Berne (2019), p. 44 clarified that 'pharmaceutical companies have dominated evidence generation in the pharmaceutical sector since the advent of randomized controlled clinical trials in the 1950s. This situation is gradually changing as health care systems begin to harness the potential of observational research based on data produced in routine clinical care'. See § 4 of this chapter for a detailed discussion.

[14] See Molander (2025), p. 1163.

[15] On this point see Stiglitz (2012), p. 220.

[16] See Fox and Ward (2008), pp. 856–868; also, Abraham (2010), pp. 603–622 and Busfield (2010), pp. 934–941.

[17] For a discussion of 'pharmacologisation', see Abraham (2010, 2011) and Williams et al. (2011).

[18] See Le Page (2025), pp. 30–38 and Cantor (2024).

of health protection (Article 168 TFEU)—has fully restored the central role of the public sector in guaranteeing the right to healthcare. The absence of a binding obligation to allocate adequate resources confirms that health is still perceived as a cost rather than as a necessary structural investment in contemporary democracies. This is observed across all EU Member States, despite the heterogeneity of the models employed.[19]

In this regard, medicines serve as a proxy of how health has progressively been interpreted as a 'chapter of economics' rather than as a fundamental right.[20] Although the pandemic has highlighted the value of local healthcare, no real strengthening of public health systems has taken place, not even in states with a tradition of universalism. This trend can also be explained by the higher profitability of sectors such as diagnostics, pharmaceuticals, and acute care, compared with essential but less remunerative community-based services.

Critical issues emerge on multiple fronts: from the lack of effective tools to assess the therapeutic and social value of treatments, to the opacity surrounding medicines price negotiations, and to the progressive medicalization of needs that would instead require structural responses. Moreover, even in systems funded through general taxation, cost-sharing mechanisms and long waiting lists undermine the principle of free access and push wealthier individuals toward the private sector, thereby exacerbating inequalities.

Only public funding grounded in the principle of fiscal democracy can ensure health services of equal quality for all, including individuals with chronic illnesses and those in socioeconomically vulnerable conditions.[21] These challenges undermine the foundations of the universalist model and the social contract that supports it, turning the right to health into an economically conditioned entitlement. The crisis of the universal health model thus reflects a broader crisis of social democracies, in which fundamental rights are progressively subordinated to market logics. In this regard, it is possible to emphasise the theoretical perspective that seeks to extend modern constitutionalism beyond the state, towards a form of global constitutionalism that envisages 'institutions of guarantee' at both global and national levels.[22] Indeed, global health law has long overlooked that perspective of social rights guarantees.

It has long been highlighted that global health law remains more a normative and moral project than an operational legal order, calling for stronger ethical and institutional foundations to make it effective.[23]

---

[19] On access to healthcare in Europe, see den Exter and Syrett (2020), p. 244, and on EU health law, see Hervey and McHale (2015).

[20] For an analysis of medicines regulation as a proxy for tracing the historical evolution of the NHS, see Tognoni and Cauduro (2018).

[21] See Liberati and Paradiso (2025), pp. 105–107.

[22] The reference is to Ferrajoli's theory, most recently developed in Ferrajoli (2022, 2025). It should be noted that Ferrajoli had already proposed the distinction between institutions of government and institutions of guarantee in Ferrajoli (2007). This theory was subsequently further developed in Ferrajoli (2021).

[23] See Smith (2014).

Nevertheless global health law does not consist solely in the regulation of infectious diseases or the management of health emergencies, but must engage states and other global actors to respect, protect, and fulfil the right to health.[24] In this regard, the COVID-19 pandemic has merely highlighted the structural shortcomings of global health law, emphasising the urgency of reforms that go beyond the emergency-based approach to public health management and address the weaknesses of existing public institutions.[25] There is now a growing recognition of the need for a permanent framework of health regulation that takes into account human rights, global solidarity, and the equitable distribution of the benefits of scientific discoveries, while also rethinking the renewed role of public institutions.[26]

4 The Hidden Cost of Medicines

In a global context characterized by insufficient public funding for healthcare systems, the issue of pharmaceutical expenditure governance within universal health systems acquires particular significance. While access to innovative medicines and their high costs are concerns shared across Europe, the debate over price governance is especially prominent in countries where NHS ensure equitable access through public financing and reimbursement mechanisms.[27] The issue of pharmaceutical reimbursement is often intertwined with the assessment of the genuine innovativeness of new medicines.[28] In such contexts, a strong public role in determining the price of reimbursable medicines is crucial for controlling pharmaceutical expenditure, ensuring the financial sustainability of NHS, and safeguarding equitable access to care. The high cost of innovative reimbursed medicines significantly impacts public pharmaceutical expenditure.

Challenges and solutions adopted by NHSs concern the governance of reimbursed medicine costs: institutional responsibilities, cost-effectiveness assessment, expenditure control, and price transparency. In the EU, pharmaceutical regulation has contributed significantly to improving access to new medicines through a network of European and national regulatory agencies. While the EU has improved access through pharmaceutical regulation, pricing remains a national competence, with each Member State retaining its own regulatory framework for determining the prices of reimbursed medicines. However, the notion that EU-level coordination could strengthen bargaining power with multinational pharmaceutical companies has long

[24] See Coggon (2024) and Gostin et al. (2020), p. 1618.

[25] See Burci (2024).

[26] In this regard, see Gross (2021).

[27] See Jackson (2022), Folino-Gallo et al. (2008), pp. 305–310 and Garattini et al. (2007).

[28] As is now widely acknowledged in the literature, and as highlighted by Jackson (2022), p. 610 ‘most new drugs do not offer patients significant benefit over existing ones’.

been recognised.[29] Greater European coordination on price-setting, would be necessary to strengthen bargaining power vis-à-vis pharmaceutical multinationals, while promoting tighter price control without undermining national competences.[30]

4.1 Low Transparency and High Prices

Even in the pharmaceutical sector, the regulatory issue is closely linked to the matter of transparency. Indeed, in addition to the lack of effective price coordination, fair price negotiation is undermined by the pervasive lack of transparency that affects the entire system at the global level.[31] Transparency is here understood as a systemic condition of openness, accessibility, clarity, and comprehensibility in the management of information over time, beyond the mere disclosure of data, essential for enabling participation in public decision-making processes.

The lack of transparency concerns both the assessment of the favourable risk–benefit ratio and the determination of medicine prices. Although the EU has recognised the importance of transparency in access to medicines,[32] greater transparency and information-sharing on medicine prices could help reduce costs across all EU countries. Price negotiations alone may not be sufficient to strike a balance between price and therapeutic value; this underlines the need for thorough evaluations in all countries with national price negotiation systems.[33] Furthermore, effective price governance is essential to healthcare policy, as it balances cost control with access and supports pharmaceutical innovation.[34] While mandatory disclosure in price negotiations is recognised as a way to reduce information asymmetry, it also raises concerns

[29] See Abraham and Lewis (2000), p. 78 where they highlight that 'a crucial part of the establishment of drug regulatory agencies has been a neo-liberal political agenda aimed at increasing the responsiveness of regulators to industrial demands at minimal expense of the state'; also Garattini et al. (2016), p. 425 who 'believe this European solution would constitute a step forward to make European prices (both inside and outside the EU) more transparent and reward companies that invest in research and provide innovative drugs, regardless of where the research is conducted'.

[30] According to Abraham and Lewis (2000), p. 33, 'European regulatory state must be understood as a network, including supranational and national bodies'.

[31] See Abraham and Lewis (2000), p. 33 where they highlight that the pharmaceutical market requires a 'regulatory state' to correct is 'information failures'. On the topic, see also Garattini et al. (2016), pp. 423–426 where they argue that 'the lack of transparency on many new drugs prices caused by the adoption of direct/indirect and public/confidential discounts has hidden the true prices of many of them in various EU countries and undermined their comparison among nations'.

[32] Council Directive 89/105/EEC of 21 December 1989 relating to the transparency of measures regulating the pricing of medicinal products for human use and their inclusion within the scope of national health insurance systems.

[33] European Parliament (2023), p. III where highlights that 'in the EU context, pricing and reimbursement decisions fall under the responsibility of national authorities. In contrast, most industry decisions are taken with a global perspective'.

[34] European Parliament (2023), p. 57: 'within the EU, the fact that Member States are responsible for market access procedures, including reimbursement and pricing decisions, leads to large disparities in access [...]'.

about potential market withdrawals by pharmaceutical companies seeking to protect their commercial interests.[35]

Establishing a 'fair price' for an innovative medicine presents significant challenges, both because the value attributed to the product follows market dynamics often disconnected from its therapeutic value, and because the final negotiated price is often not publicly disclosed. The lack of transparency in negotiations between the states and pharmaceutical companies does not ensure a fair price. In fact, reimbursed medicines in universal health systems operate in a market characterized by inelastic demand and the concentration of monopolistic power of manufacturing companies. In particular, the high cost of publicly reimbursed innovative medicines significantly impacts public pharmaceutical expenditure, which makes them the focus of this analysis rather than over-the-counter medicines.[36]

Public institutions exercise their bargaining power in the context of hospital procurement to negotiate confidential discounts, thereby enhancing access to costly treatments. However, these confidentiality clauses, while facilitating access, undermine transparency and obscure the fair cost and value of medicines within the healthcare system. The issue of transparency in high-cost medicine pricing is longstanding, particularly as discounts are negotiated after price and reimbursement determination. Such agreements are often deemed commercially sensitive, resulting in limited public disclosure and reduced transparency.

Numerous examples highlight the increasing impact of new medicines on healthcare system budgets and the lack of public transparency regarding the negotiated prices.[37] The price of new medicines is often not officially disclosed, but only reported through information portals, websites, or newspapers, even in countries where public institutions are responsible for price negotiations.

Among the most recent examples are *Kymriah* (a CAR-T therapy for leukemia and lymphoma), initially launched in the United States at 361 thousand dollars, a price slightly lower than its U.S. launch price by several European healthcare systems;[38] *Libmeldy*, a gene therapy for metachromatic leukodystrophy, launched in the United States at a price of approximately three million dollars, and slightly lower in Europe through confidential agreements; as well as *Zolgensma*, for spinal muscular atrophy, and *Hemgenix*, for hemophilia B, which represent additional examples of extremely costly therapies whose public reimbursement requires complex national negotiations.

[35] den Exter (2020), p. 80.

[36] Regarding the different kinds of medicines see López Vila et al. (2022), pp. 55–70.

[37] Berne (2019), p. 44 highlights that 'pharmaceutical companies have dominated evidence generation in the pharmaceutical sector since the advent of randomized controlled clinical trials in the 1950s. This situation is gradually changing as health care systems begin to harness the potential of observational research based on data produced in routine clinical care'.

[38] See Silbert et al. (2019) and Gonçalves (2025).

4.2 *The Governance of Pharmaceutical Expenditure*

The measures adopted to control pharmaceutical expenditure, such as spending caps, clawbacks on companies' profits, or reimbursements for budget overruns, are not accompanied by a broader vision capable of questioning the market logics that govern access to medicines. In this sense, the governance of public pharmaceutical expenditure is a central aspect of universalist healthcare systems, where essential medicines are accessible through reimbursement mechanisms.

Unlike standard consumer goods, medicines present complexities due to their inelastic public demand, limited public resources, and the inherent difficulty of assessing cost-effectiveness over time, further influenced by the emotional weight these products carry in public perception.[39] In the UK, the idea that medicines 'purchased by the NHS do not always have a price relative to their clinical value' is not new.[40] The issue of a medicine's value, even before its price, is closely linked to innovation and the tools public institutions have to assess it.[41] The cost-effectiveness ratio is among the parameters used in negotiating the price of reimbursable medicines in other states adopting a universal healthcare model, such as Italy, together with current prices in EU Member States, the prices of comparable products, and projected sales volumes.[42] The issue is particularly sensitive for high-cost essential medicines, such as anticancer drugs. In the EU, payers face public pressure against denying reimbursement due to high costs. Confidential discounts negotiated between Member States and companies lower medicine prices but do not improve the alignment between treatment costs and benefits.[43] It is therefore necessary to revise the evaluation framework to better reflect societal priorities and the implicit health trade-offs involved.[44]

Despite national differences, it is generally accepted that, for socially essential goods like affordable healthcare, there is a duty to protect public health to the extent that 'pricing of certain goods in certain markets displaying an unequal relationship between supply and demand has historically been deemed fit for a legal prohibition against unfair pricing'.[45]

In addition to evaluating the cost-effectiveness of medicines, some countries regulate NHS expenditure on reimbursed medicines through pharmaceutical governance models that include mechanisms for reimbursement assessment and public spending caps. However, these systems are currently under pressure and are unlikely to remain

---

[39] See Garattini et al. (2007), p. 333.

[40] Parliamentary Office of Science and Technology (2010), pp. 1–4; regarding the 'value-based price' see Danzon (2018).

[41] On the National Institute for Health and Care Excellence (NICE) in the United Kingdom, about the assessment of new medicines, see Littlejohns and Syrett (2025); see also Atkinson and Sheard (2025), p. 238 ff.

[42] Cauduro (2017), p. 89.

[43] See Trotta et al. (2019), p. 7.

[44] Naci et al. (2025), pp. 50–60.

[45] Kianzad (2022), p. 23.

sustainable in the long term.[46] A crucial area of research concerns the identification of models capable of protecting citizens from excessive healthcare costs and preserving the universalist character of the system, by distinguishing and safeguarding clinical needs and the real needs of patient populations from market preferences.

Public healthcare services should not be driven by the cost of medicines, but rather by the definition of the most appropriate therapeutic pathways. While it is essential to adopt effective and sustainable governance models for pharmaceutical expenditure, if the demand for medicines continues to respond to the logics of the pharmaceutical market, which in turn shapes public decision-making, attempts to control prices cannot ensure universal access to medicines.

Moreover it is evident that the control of medicine prices is undeniably a global issue, and that there is a need to find 'a more democratic way of governing pharmaceutical policies'.[47] In this regard, the recent reform of European pharmaceutical legislation has missed the opportunity to propose common pricing strategies,[48] although the objective of containing the cost of medicines should, by its very nature, include a global strategy as well as European policies.[49]

5 Essential Medicines for the Few

Access to essential medicines has long been central to debates on universalism in healthcare. The Declaration on the TRIPS Agreement and Public Health (2001), adopted within the WTO framework, marked a key recognition of the link between patent systems and medicine pricing. While acknowledging the importance of intellectual property for the development of new treatments, the Declaration also highlighted the resulting cost implications.[50] The TRIPS Agreement allowed Member

[46] Regarding the allowed growth rate and payment percentages in the UK, see Burstall (1997) and Shorthose et al. (2022). For a comparison of ICERs in the UK and Australia, see Wang et al. (2018), p. 939. See also Cauduro (2026).

[47] See Gautier and David (2022), where they highlight that 'since the 1980s, neoliberal policies and their implementation in health sector have shaped pharmaceutical policies, which would distinguish between those who could afford and those could not, leaving to the market the responsibility of weaving *Health for All*. As a result, and as revealed during the COVID19 pandemic, a more democratic way of governing pharmaceutical policies and shaping public health through pharmaceuticals remains to be instituted'.

[48] European Commission (2023) Proposal for a Directive of the European Parliament and of the Council on the Union code relating to medicinal products for human use, and repealing Directive 2001/83/EC and Directive 2009/35/EC, COM(2023) 193 final, 26 April 2023, art. 1 (9), which highlights that 'the provisions of this Directive shall not affect the powers of the Member States' authorities either as regards the setting of prices for medicinal products or their inclusion in the scope of national health insurance schemes, on the basis of health, economic and social conditions'.

[49] See Pogge et al. (2010), p. 21, where they highlight that: 'the aim of reducing the price of pharmaceutical drugs should be included in the global strategy'.

[50] World Trade Organization Doha Declaration on the TRIPS Agreement and Public Health, WT/MIN(01)/DEC/2, para 3, 14 November 2001.

States to grant compulsory licences for essential treatments; however, states with limited production capacity may face challenges in utilising this instrument.[51] In 2003, the WTO authorised the export of patented medicines to countries lacking manufacturing capacity through compulsory licences, a mechanism implemented in subsequent years.[52]

The denial of access to vital medicines has been a longstanding international concern, and a certain regulatory shortcoming in providing adequate medicines and healthcare has been acknowledged.[53] Compulsory licences for public health emergencies represent a mechanism to overcome patent monopolies, recognising the legitimacy of state action to protect collective health.[54] In recent decades, several countries have implemented strategies to contain medicine prices: Mexico introduced maximum price regulation to encourage generics;[55] South Africa promoted domestic production during the HIV/AIDS crisis; India became the 'pharmacy of the Third World' by supplying affordable medicines; Brazil locally produced Tenofovir and Kaletra by challenging patents and referencing lower international prices.[56]

Within the EU, Member States negotiate individually with pharmaceutical companies. However, patent exclusivities and information asymmetries highlight the need for coordinated European pharmaceutical governance. New medicines, protected by patents, carry high costs that strain public expenditure and limit equitable provision.[57] The monopoly created by intellectual property, especially in low-income countries, delays production and import of affordable generics, raising prices and restricting availability. Empirical evidence links stronger intellectual property rights to reduced access to prescribed medicines, even after accounting for income and socioeconomic factors.[58] The European framework on exporting medicines under compulsory license aims to 'improve access at affordable prices', particularly in less developed countries. This framework allows exceptions to patent rules in public health emergencies, which can also be interpreted as forms of restricted access due to excessive costs for public finances. This is a public intervention mechanism through which, for several years, European regulations have aimed to 'remedy public health problems'.[59] This mechanism for ensuring universal access to essential medicines

---

51 World Trade Organization, Doha Declaration on the TRIPS Agreement and Public Health, WT/MIN(01)/DEC/2, para 6, 14 November 2001.

52 World Trade Organization (2003) Implementation of paragraph 6 of the Doha Declaration on the TRIPS Agreement and public health: Decision of 30 August 2003. WTO document WT/L/540, 2 September 2003.

53 See Pogge et al. (2010), p. 38.

54 See Yamin (2003).

55 See Guzmàn (2011).

56 See Flynn (2011), pp. 169–170.

57 On this point, Abraham and Lewis (2000), p. 33 note that '[…] the pharmaceutical market requires a *regulatory state* to correct is *information failures*'.

58 See Jung and Kwon (2015), pp. 508 and 524.

59 In this regard European Parliament and Council (2006) Regulation (EC) No. 816/2006 of the European Parliament and of the Council of 17 May 2006 on compulsory licensing of patents relating to the manufacture of pharmaceutical products for export to countries with public health

can also be classified within the scope of European coordination achievable under the current legislation (Article 6 TFEU).[60] Even within the EU, access to truly innovative medicines is hindered by the weakness of public administration in price negotiations within a context of *de facto* oligopolies or monopolies. Even in small markets, such as in the case of 'orphan drugs', profits can be substantial, and the public role in supporting private enterprise development remains decisive.[61]

Failures in the pharmaceutical market, recently acknowledged by the European legislator, are closely tied to such monopolies and the lack of transparency. In particular:

> in addition to the growing threat of antimicrobial resistance, there are other market failures present in the pharmaceutical sector for which further action at Union level is required to meet the public health needs of Union citizens. In particular, there is misalignment between R&D priorities and the public health needs of Union citizens. The market failures in the Union have, in certain instances, resulted in no treatments being available for rare diseases and unequal access to medicinal products, and have led to shortages. This Regulation should therefore address those market failures through providing for a modulated approach to market exclusivities and increased transparency concerning R&D expenditure to better deliver on the objectives of affordability, accessibility and availability of medicinal products in the Union.[62]

The need for greater transparency between pharmaceutical companies and public authorities is emphasised, not only regarding the disclosure of required data, but also in the assessment of the true level of innovation and the determination of the 'fair price' of new medicines. Transparency should also extend to users of the public healthcare system, ensuring accessible and comprehensible information. Patent secrecy poses challenges for effective transparency in public administration, including in the negotiation and procurement of medicines. Both the WHO and the European Commission have emphasised that transparency in these negotiations is essential to secure affordable prices and ensure continuity of supply.[63]

---

problems, recital 5, states that it 'part of wider European and international action to address public health problems faced by least developed countries and other developing countries, and in particular to improve access to affordable medicines which are safe and effective, including fixed-dose combinations, and whose quality is guaranteed'.

[60] See Cauduro (2017), p. 159. Regarding the role of the EU in the field of public health, see Hervey and McHale (2015), pp. 535–550.

[61] See Mazzucato (2023), p. 89.

[62] European Parliament (2024) Legislative resolution of 10 April 2024 on the proposal for a regulation of the European Parliament and of the Council laying down Union procedures for the authorisation and supervision of medicinal products for human use and establishing rules governing the European Medicines Agency, amending Regulation (EC) No 1394/2007 and Regulation (EU) No 536/2014 and repealing Regulation (EC) No 726/2004, Regulation (EC) No 141/2000 and Regulation (EC) No 1901/2006 (COM(2023)0193—C9-0144/2023—2023/0131(COD)), P9_TA(2024)0221 art 78 b [Am. 50].

[63] The World Health Organization (2019) Improving the Transparency of Markets for Medicines, Vaccines, and Other Health Products, Resolution A72/A/CONF/2 Rev.1, adopted at the 72nd World Health Assembly, Geneva, 28 May 2019, identifies the following necessary actions: 'take appropriate measures to publicly share information on the net prices of health products. [...] Work

As noted earlier in this chapter, transparency in the pharmaceutical sector ensures access to medicines by sharing scientific knowledge and providing comprehensible information. Such transparency is essential for public authorities to make informed and accurate assessments of actual needs. In this context, the European Parliament highlights that guaranteeing patients' timely access to essential and innovative medicines, ensuring the sustainability of public healthcare systems, and fostering future pharmaceutical innovation are responsibilities shared by all actors within the healthcare system.[64]

Moreover, the European Commission has reaffirmed that 'everyone has the right to timely access to affordable, preventive, and curative healthcare of good quality'.[65] The EU expressed concern over medicine shortages during the COVID-19 crisis, including those affecting intensive care. In responding to such shortages, the EU emphasised the importance of ensuring the production, supply, distribution, development, and equitable access to high-quality medicines, coordinated by the European Medicines Agency (EMA). It also noted with concern the export bans imposed globally and welcomed the Commission's commitment to securing the supply of medicines, reaffirming that the experimental use of medicines to treat COVID-19 must not result in shortages for patients with other conditions.[66]

The issue of essential medicines shortages is not new. Indeed, in the context of treating rare and ultra-rare diseases, the absence of essential medicines has long been recognised. These are defined as 'orphan drugs' under European legislation, given that 'the pharmaceutical industry would not be willing to develop the medicine under normal market conditions'.[67] The regulation of 'orphan drugs' exemplifies the contradictions between the pharmaceutical market and universal health, exposing the limits of current public intervention and the need for coordinated European action. EU legislation presumes private 'parenthood' of producers, offering minimal public intervention through incentives rather than public production.

The denial of access to vaccines and essential medicines is a long-standing, systemic global issue. Since the early twentieth century, public intervention in Europe has been crucial for controlling diseases such as smallpox, cholera, malaria, and tuberculosis. Today, vaccines remain central to European prevention strategies, yet they are still inaccessible in many countries worldwide.

---

collaboratively to improve the reporting of information by suppliers on registered health products, such as reports on sales revenues, prices, units sold, marketing costs, and subsidies and incentives. [...] Improve national capacities, including through international cooperation'; see also the European Commission (2018), p. 40, where it is stated that 'there are several claims that price setting should be more transparent and should not be left to industry alone'.

[64] European Parliament (2017) European Parliament resolution of 2 March 2017 on EU options for improving access to medicines (2016/2057(INI)), P8_TA(2017)0061.

[65] European Commission (2017) European Pillar of Social Rights. Proclaimed 17 November 2017 in Gothenburg. Brussels.

[66] European Parliament (2020) European Parliament resolution of 17 September 2020 on the shortage of medicines—how to address an emerging problem (2020/2071(INI)), P9_TA(2020)0228.

[67] European Parliament and Council (2000) Regulation (EC) No 141/2000 of 16 December 1999 on orphan medicinal products.

The COVID-19 pandemic exposed deep contradictions in vaccine access, affecting even EU healthcare systems. In 2021, supply difficulties following European joint purchases and national acquisitions led to a 'vaccine war,' revealing the structural limits of market-driven dynamics on a global scale.

Within the EU, the main problem was not so much the price of vaccines, but the failure to deliver already negotiated doses, primarily attributable to the bargaining power of patent-holding companies. As recalled by the Commission, under EU vaccine strategy it has financed and secured the production of sufficient quantities of vaccines within the Union and concluded agreements with individual vaccine manufacturers on behalf of Member States, with the aim of ensuring that all Member States and their populations have timely and affordable access to COVID-19 vaccines, while also promoting global solidarity. The Commission emphasised that it is crucial for manufacturers to fulfil these supply commitments, given that vaccine production within the Union is concentrated in only a limited number of Member States.[68] To increase vaccine production capacity at the European level, public legal instruments, such as compulsory licences, could have been used. However, the political debate focused predominantly on emergency management measures, such as 'vaccine passports', 'prioritisation of the first dose', or 'export restrictions'. Ensuring universal access to COVID-19 vaccines would have required a more decisive use of compulsory licences, already provided for in cases of restricted access to patented medicines.

The EU, meanwhile, introduced a system of prior authorisation for the export of vaccines outside the Union to prioritise domestic supply. Considering the critical situation, the Commission deemed it necessary to implement immediate, temporary measures to ensure that COVID-19 vaccines covered by Advanced Purchase Agreements (APAs) with the Union were subject to prior authorisation, thereby securing adequate supplies to meet vital demand within the Union. At the same time, the Commission sought to uphold the Union's international commitments and to meet, as far as possible, the delivery expectations of third countries that had contracted APAs.[69]

However, this measure neither resolved production shortages nor ensured global vaccination coverage, and a 'patchwork' approach risked fostering new virus variants. The pandemic highlighted the inadequacy of regional responses and the dominance of market logic in healthcare, which structurally weakens public intervention. It also demonstrated the need for an integrated health approach, strengthening essential services such as clean water, education, and transport. A global response would require addressing regional vaccine disparities, temporarily suspending patents, and implementing social policies to mitigate the socioeconomic determinants of health crises.

---

[68] European Commission (2021) Commission Implementing Regulation (EU) 2021/111 of 29 January 2021 making the exportation of certain products subject to the production of an export authorisation, recital 2.

[69] European Commission (2021) Commission Implementing Regulation (EU) 2021/111 of 29 January 2021 making the exportation of certain products subject to the production of an export authorisation, recital 5.

In conclusion, access to 'orphan drugs' and vaccines underscores the need to prioritise people's actual needs over mere pharmaceutical production. Effective care demands sustained preventive measures and efforts to reduce socioeconomic inequalities in access to essential public services, including water and housing.

6 The 'Silent Pandemic'

The issues discussed thus far are exemplified by one of the most topical and widely debated concerns in pharmaceutical care: antimicrobial resistance (AMR). We now turn to an examination of this phenomenon, considering both its national and global dimensions, with particular attention to health policy within the EU. AMR has emerged as one of the most pressing challenges in contemporary pharmaceutical law. Often referred to as a 'silent pandemic', AMR poses a serious threat to global public health. It is estimated that over 35,000 people in the EU and more than 1.2 million worldwide die each year from infections caused by bacteria resistant to available antibiotics. In the absence of effective antibiotics, EU Member States could face a return to an era in which infections such as pneumonia, tuberculosis, gonorrhoea, and salmonellosis were difficult to treat. The reduced effectiveness of antibiotics also jeopardises chemotherapy and even routine surgical procedures. Consequently, there is ongoing debate regarding the need for a coordinated global public health strategy.[70]

Limited access to antibiotics has historically affected the poorest countries, where these medicines are still not guaranteed. In such contexts, the primary barrier is affordability. However, over time, misuse has compromised their effectiveness even in wealthier countries, including Europe, where access is generally ensured. Globally, this has led to a situation in which 'infections are increasingly difficult, if not impossible, to treat'.[71]

The phenomenon encompasses several interrelated aspects: from the public role in ensuring access to essential medicines, to the interaction between health protection and the environment, particularly concerning the environmental impact of medicines. Numerous interdisciplinary studies on AMR have highlighted not only the need to improve access to antimicrobials, diagnostic tools, and alternative therapies, but also the importance of robust stewardship programs to safeguard the efficacy of existing antimicrobials for both current and future generations.[72] Fighting AMR is widely recognised as one of the major challenges of our time, and reducing antibiotic use

[70] European Commission (2023) Communication from the Commission to the European Parliament, the Council, the European Economic and Social Committee and the Committee of the Regions: Reform of the pharmaceutical legislation and measures addressing antimicrobial resistance, COM(2023) 190 final, 26 April 2023, states that antibiotics (including antivirals, antifungals, and antiprotozoals) 'are among the most essential medicines'.

[71] European Commission (2023) COM(2023) 190 final.

[72] See Weldon et al. (2024), p. 836.

is a key global objective.[73] Public institutions themselves recommend moderate and prudent use of antibiotics to prevent progressive loss of efficacy and safeguard the health of future generations.[74]

The global and intergenerational dimensions of AMR require interventions at both local and international levels. In this regard, theoretical perspectives advocating for a rethinking of existing institutions as universal guarantors of fundamental rights are particularly pertinent.

6.1 Addressing Antimicrobial Resistance as a Paradigm for Patient Care

Access to effective antibiotics is addressed at the global, EU, and national levels. The EU has adopted regulations aimed at combating AMR by limiting the misuse of antibiotics in animals. These measures prohibit their use for growth promotion or routine, restrict their use in livestock farming,[75] promote research on new antimicrobial therapies,[76] and allocate significant resources to counter AMR and support initiatives under the 'One Health' approach.[77] For the containment of AMR, the 2023 EU Communication on the reform of pharmaceutical legislation and on measures to combat antibiotic resistance identifies the objective of improving the environmental sustainability of medicinal products and proposes strengthening the environmental risk assessment in the context of marketing authorisation, providing for the refusal of authorisation in the case of inadequate assessments and carefully considering the environmental risks arising from the manufacturing of antibiotics.[78]

The aim of the European legislator is to address emerging challenges, including the appropriate use of antibiotics, by recognising not only the need for research and development of new antibiotics, but also the promotion of proper use of existing

[73] See Denyer and Chandler (2019) and Opalska and Schmidt (2023), p. 73.

[74] European Parliament (2024) P9_TA(2024)0221 art. 77 [Am. 46]: 'the development of antimicrobial resistance is a growing concern and the pipeline of effective antimicrobials is obstructed due to a market failure whereby antimicrobial research and development (R&D) is hampered by the low commercial value of the antimicrobial medicinal product market. It is therefore necessary to maintain the efficacy of existing antimicrobials for as long as possible'.

[75] European Parliament and Council (2018) Regulation (EU) No 6/2019 on veterinary medicinal products and repealing Directive 2001/82/EC.

[76] European Parliament and Council (2014) Regulation (EU) No 536/2014 on clinical trials on medicinal products for human use, repealing Directive 2001/20/EC.

[77] European Parliament and Council (2021) Regulation (EU) 2021/522 establishing a Programme for the Union's action in the field of health for the period 2021–2027 (EU4Health Programme) and repealing Regulation (EU) No 282/2014.

[78] European Commission (2023) COM(2023) 190 final.

ones to ensure their effectiveness. Prudent use of antimicrobials is widely recognised as essential for maintaining access to effective antibiotics.[79] The EU proposes coordinated actions according to the One Health approach, focusing on prevention, reduction of environmental risks, awareness-raising, and responsible use throughout the entire supply chain.[80] The EU regulation emphasises that the limited research into new antimicrobials is largely due to their 'low commercial value'; it is therefore essential to preserve the efficacy of current antibiotics while simultaneously incentivising the development of new medicines, with targeted support for small and medium-sized enterprises and non-profit organisations; and appropriate use can be promoted through rapid diagnostic tools to support more precise and targeted prescriptions.[81] In designing European institutions to address AMR, the key priorities include prevention, the responsible use of existing medicines, development incentives, and measures to ensure responsible use. These priorities are integrated into the authorisation process, covering prescription regulation, packaging, and information management. They also strengthen surveillance and monitoring, and promote global initiatives and medical countermeasures, including vaccines and rapid diagnostic tools.[82]

EU legislation may appear contradictory for pharmaceutical companies, as it simultaneously encourages research into new antibiotics while restricting their use. This tension highlights that the public role cannot be confined to market regulation alone but would require coordinated public action at both local and global levels.

6.2 *The Challenges for Public Institutions*

From this perspective, the EU recognises the need for new institutions, and therefore the Health Emergency Preparedness and Response Authority (HERA) 'should primarily focus on the fight against the most urgent health threats, including AMR and shortages of medicinal products. However, in the future as its capacity increases, the Authority should expand the scope of its mission, specifically to tackle other areas of unmet medical need such as rare and neglected diseases. The Authority should have adequate resources to fulfil its mandate'.[83]

Interdisciplinary studies have considered not only how to improve access to antimicrobials and alternative therapies, but also how to preserve their effectiveness for future generations. From this perspective, the central question for global health challenges such as AMR should not be how to 'solve' the problem, but rather 'how do we create social systems that are better aligned with ecological and microbial

[79] European Parliament (2023) Resolution of 1 June 2023 on EU action to combat antimicrobial resistance (P9_TA(2023)0220; 2023/2703(RSP); C/2023/1227) art 15(a).

[80] European Parliament (2024) P9_TA(2024)0221 art 33a [Am. 25] and art 136 [Am. 79].

[81] European Parliament (2024) P9_TA(2024)0221 art. 77 [Am. 46].

[82] European Commission (2023) COM(2023) 190 final.

[83] European Parliament (2024) P9_TA(2024)0221 art 78a [Am. 49].

systems in a shared planetary environment'.[84] In this sense, 'the optimal relationship between human societies and microbial ecologies may require forms of social organization that transcend those currently in existence'.[85] The global dimension of AMR requires both local and global public intervention. It is therefore relevant to rethink institutions in light of the universal guarantee of fundamental rights, including vital and artificial goods such as life-saving medicines and vaccines.[86] The issue will continue to engage scholars from various disciplines, with particular attention to the role of public administrations.[87]

In the context of AMR, as well as of 'orphan drugs', the EU has recognised the existence of 'market failures',[88] acknowledging the risks and consequences associated with low profitability for companies and the absence of public production of these goods. Indeed, the EU has acknowledged that market failures have, in some cases, led to shortages of medicines and unequal access to treatments, particularly for rare diseases, and has therefore envisaged that the regulation should address these issues through a calibrated approach to market exclusivities and enhanced transparency of R&D expenditure in order to improve the affordability, accessibility, and availability of medicinal products across the EU.[89]

In conclusion, addressing antibiotic resistance from a universal healthcare perspective requires placing prevention and health education at the centre—historically core elements of the universalist healthcare model. The central question thus remains how universalism can guide strategies to tackle both present and future pandemics, including the widespread denials of access to care that are less 'visible' and therefore, in this sense, more 'silent', spanning essential, innovative, and 'orphan drugs' as well as vaccines.

---

[84] Weldon and Hoffman (2024), p. 17. See Weldon et al. (2024), p. 833 ff; and also the chapter by Weldon in this volume.

[85] Weldon and Hoffman (2024), p. 17.

[86] See Ferrajoli (2022); and also the chapter by Ferrajoli in this volume.

[87] See Pierre et al. (2023), p. 4111 where they argue that the AMR issue sheds light on the dynamics of contemporary European governance, showing how the administrative level of government can play a central role in shaping national policy.

[88] European Commission (2023) COM(2023) 192 final, on Explanatory Memorandum, 1. Context of the Proposal: Reasons for and objectives of the proposal, which states that 'there are market failures, especially in the development of priority antimicrobials that can help address antimicrobial resistance'; European Parliament (2024) P9_TA(2024)0221 art. 77a [Am. 47] which states that 'it is necessary to consider further Union level action to support the development of antimicrobials and address existing market failures'. For a discussion of 'market failures' in medical care, see Arrow (1963).

[89] European Parliament (2024) P9_TA(2024)0221 art. 78b [Am. 50].

7 Conclusions

An interdisciplinary approach to global health law encompasses not only international law, constitutional law, and human rights, but also public health and public administration, providing tools to rethink institutions and regulations in light of the planetary challenges posed by future pandemics and health inequalities. National health policies, shaped by supranational law (WHO, EU, and international treaties), require an intertwining of domestic powers and global constraints. However, the recent WHO pandemic document will need to contend concretely with the growing nationalist trend, which inevitably influences contemporary health governance.[90]

If economic and health crises raise questions about the survival and strengthening of universal healthcare systems, access to medicines—as a proxy for universalism—suggests structural solutions based on the global sharing of scientific knowledge, transparency in public health decision-making, earmarked resource allocation, and the rethinking of public institutions that effectively guarantee the right to health at both national and global levels.

The history of pharmaceutical law, even from a strictly European perspective, shows that the solution requires a viewpoint that unites the dimension of global health with that of universalism. Certainly, this perspective demands a political will that is currently difficult to discern; however, from a theoretical standpoint, there are no obstacles to achieving 'universalism in global health'.

This would imply taking local specificities and needs into account, while respecting universal principles: free access to essential care, shared contribution to public healthcare spending through general taxation, prevention, proximity of healthcare facilities to local communities, quality of care, and transparency in public decisions that respond to people's needs.

As demonstrated by the COVID-19 pandemic, a globalised society must necessarily be equipped with a 'global and universalist healthcare model'.

In conclusion, it is necessary to consider how to effectively address the underlying issues. Indeed, NHSs should not be driven by the cost of medicines but guided by the selection of the most appropriate care pathways. It is essential to distinguish between issues related to patient care and broader economic dynamics. If the future of global health is to be founded on renewed universalism, there is a need to rethink public healthcare from both a local and global perspective, as a space for person-centred care. However, this implies questioning the current relationship between law and the market, rethinking democratic institutions, and ensuring the effective transparency of their decisions and actions.

[90] European Commission (2025) Joint Communication to the European Parliament, the European Council, the Council, the European Economic and Social Committee and the Committee of the Regions on the European Preparedness Union Strategy, JOIN(2025) 130 final.

References

Abraham J (2010) Pharmaceuticalization of society in context: theoretical, empirical and health dimensions. Sociology 44(4):603–622

Abraham J (2011) Evolving sociological analyses of 'pharmaceuticalisation': a response to Williams, Martin and Gabe. Sociol Health Illn 33(5):726–728

Abraham J, Lewis G (2000) Regulating medicines in Europe: competition, expertise and public health, 1st edn. Routledge, London

Adams V (ed) (2016) Metrics: what counts in global health. Duke University Press, Durham–London

Arrow KJ (1963) Uncertainty and the welfare economics of medical care. Am Econ Rev LIII(5):941–973

Atkinson P, Sheard S (2025) NICE. A contemporary history of the national institute for health and care excellence, 1st edn. Routledge, London

Berne AS (2019) Big data in the pharmaceutical sector—between protection and transparency: opportunities and legal challenges. Eur Pharm Law Rev 3(1):37–45

Bruce M (1965) The coming of the welfare state, 2nd edn. B. T. Batsford Ltd, London

Burci GL (2024) The COVID-19 pandemic and the development of global health law: managing crises or achieving structural changes? J Glob Health Law 1(1):8–25

Burstall ML (1997) The management of the cost and utilisation of pharmaceuticals in the United Kingdom. Health Policy 41(Suppl):S27–S43

Busfield J (2010) 'A pill for every ill': explaining the expansion in medicine use. Soc Sci Med 70(6):934–941

Cantor C (2024) The rise of Ozempic for weight loss sparks ethical concerns. News October 16, 2024. https://www.columbiapsychiatry.org/news/rise-ozempic-sparks-ethical-concerns

Cauduro A (2017) L'accesso al farmaco. Ledizioni, Milano

Cauduro A (2026) Pharmaceutical expenditure governance in the UK and Italy. Eur J Health Law (published online ahead of print 2026)

Chapman AR (2016) Global health, human rights, and the challenge of neoliberal policies. Cambridge University Press, Cambridge

Coggon J (2024) Defining global health law. J Glob Health Law 1(2):150–176

Danzon PM (2018) Affordability challenges to value-based pricing: mass diseases, orphan diseases, and cures. Value Health 21(3):252–257

den Exter A (2020) Fighting excessive pharmaceutical prices: evaluating the options. Eur J Health Law 28(1):68–80

den Exter AP, Syrett K (2020) Access to healthcare in Europe. In: Orentlicher D, Hervey TK (eds) The oxford handbook of comparative health law. Oxford University Press, Oxford, pp 242–272

Denyer Willis L, Chandler C (2019) Quick fix for care, productivity, hygiene and inequality: reframing the entrenched problem of antibiotic overuse. BMJ Glob Health 4(4):e001590

Eckstein H (1959) The English health service. Its origins, structure and achievements. Harvard University Press, Cambridge

European Commission (2018) Innovative payment models for high-cost innovative. Report of the expert panel on effective ways of investing in health (EXPH). https://health.ec.europa.eu/publications/innovative-payment-models-high-cost-innovative-medicines_en

European Parliament (2023) Improving access to medicines and promoting pharmaceutical innovation. https://data.europa.eu/doi/10.2861/131056

Ferrajoli L (2007) Principia iuris. Teoria del diritto e della democrazia. Laterza, Roma–Bari

Ferrajoli L (2021) La costruzione della democrazia. Teoria del garantismo costituzionale. Laterza, Roma–Bari

Ferrajoli L (2022) Per una costituzione della terra. L'umanità al bivio. Feltrinelli, Milano

Ferrajoli L (2025) Progettare il futuro. Per un costituzionalismo globale. Feltrinelli, Milano

Flynn M (2011) Corporate power and state resistance: Brazil's use of TRIPS flexibilities for its National AIDS program. In: Shadlen KC, Guennif S, Guzman A, Lalitha N (eds) Intellectual

property, pharmaceuticals and public health. Access to drugs in developing countries. Edward Elgar, Northampton
Folino-Gallo P, Montilla S, Bruzzone M, Martini N (2008) Pricing and reimbursement of pharmaceuticals in Italy. Eur J Health Econ 9(3):305–310
Fox NJ, Ward KJ (2008) Pharma in the bedroom and the kitchen: the pharmaceuticalisation of daily life. Sociol Health Illn 30(6):856–868
Garattini L, Cornago D, De Compadri P (2007) Pricing and reimbursement of in-patent drugs in seven European countries: a comparative analysis. Health Policy 82(3):330–339
Garattini L, Curto A, Freemantle N (2016) Pharmaceutical price schemes in Europe: time for a 'continental' one? PharmacoEconomics 34(5):423–426
Gautier L, David P (2022) 'Health for all' and the challenges for pharmaceutical policies: a critical interpretive synthesis over 40 years. Soc Sci Humanit Open 5(1):100255
Ginsburg N (1992) Divisions of welfare state. A critical introduction to comparative social policy, 1st edn. SAGE Publications Ltd, London
Gonçalves E (2025) CAR-T cell therapies: patient access and affordability solutions. Future Sci OA 11(1):2483613
Gostin LO, Moon S, Meier BM (2020) Reimagining global health governance in the age of COVID-19. Am J Public Health 110(11):1615–1619
Gross A (2021) The past, present, and future of global health law beyond crisis. Am J Int Law 115(4):754–771
Guzmàn A (2011) The challenges of constructing pharmaceutical capabilities and promoting access to medicines in Mexico under TRIPS. In: Shadlen KC, Guennif S, Guzman A, Lalitha N (eds) Intellectual property, pharmaceuticals and public health. Access to drugs in developing countries. Edward Elgar, Northampton
Hervey TK, McHale JV (2015) European Union health law: themes and implications. Cambridge University Press, Cambridge
Jackson E (2022) Medical law: text, cases, and materials. Oxford University Press, Oxford
Jones M, Lowe R (2002) From Beveridge to Blair. The first fifty years of Britain's welfare state 1948–98. Manchester University Press, Manchester
Jung Y, Kwon S (2015) The effects of intellectual property rights on access to medicines and catastrophic expenditure. Int J Health Serv 45(3):507–529
Kianzad B (2022) Towards fair pricing of medicines? Lessons from the European Commission's Aspen decision. Eur Health Pharm Law Rev 6(1):3–23
Le Page M (2025) Living in an Ozempic world. New Scientist 29 March 2025, Volume 265, Issue 3536
Liberati P, Paradiso M (2025) Rebuilding fiscal democracy. How to bring the social contract back into economics. Palgrave Macmillan, Cham
Littlejohns P, Syrett K (eds) (2025) NICE at 25. A quarter-century of evidence, values, and innovation in health, 1st edn. Routledge, London
López Vila ED, Buts C, Jegers M (2022) An overview of the rules governing over-the-counter medicines in 30 European countries. Eur Health Pharm Law Rev 6(2):55–70
Mazzucato M (2023) The entrepreneurial state. Debunking public vs private sector myths, 5th edn. Penguin Books, New York
Molander P (2025) Public versus private healthcare systems in the OECD area—a broad evaluation of performance. Eur J Health Econ 26(7):1163–1173
Murray CJL, Lopez AD (eds) (1996) The global burden of disease: a comprehensive assessment of mortality and disability from diseases, injuries, and risk factors in 1990 and projected to 2020. Harvard School of Public Health, Cambridge (for WHO and the World Bank)
Naci H, Murphy P, Woods B, Lomas J, Papanicolas I (2025) Population-health impact of new drugs recommended by the national institute for health and care excellence in England during 2000–20: a retrospective analysis. Lancet 405(10472):50–60

Opalska A, Schmidt F (2023) Preserving our defences—prudent and appropriate use of antimicrobials. Legal and regulatory interventions on antimicrobial resistance in the recent commission proposal to review the EU pharmaceutical legislation. Eur Health Pharm Law Rev 7(2): 73–79
Parliamentary Office of Science and Technology (2010) Postnote 364: drug pricing, UK Parliament. https://www.parliament.uk/globalassets/documents/post/postpn_364_Drug_Pricing.pdf
Pierre J, Carelli D, Peters BG (2023) The four worlds of politics and administration in the EU: how institutional arrangements shape the struggle against antimicrobial resistance. J Eur Publ Policy 31(12):4088–4115
Pierson C (2006) Beyond the welfare state? The new political economy of welfare, 3rd edn. Polity, Cambridge
Pogge T, Rimmer M, Rubenstein K (2010) Introduction. Access to essential medicines, incentives for global public health. Patent law and access to essential medicines. Cambridge University Press, Cambridge
Roderick P, Pollock AM (2022) Dismantling the national health service in England. Int J Health Serv 52(4):470–479
Sen A (2002) Why health equity? Health Econ 11(8):659–666
Shorthose A, Willis P, de Maury C, Heenan B, Erasmus P (2022) United Kingdom. In: Kracov DA (ed) The pharmaceutical intellectual property and competition law review, 3rd edn. The Law Reviews, London
Silbert S, Yanik GA, Shuman AG (2019) How should we determine the value of CAR T-Cell therapy? AMA J Ethics 21(10):E844–E851
Smith GP (2014) Global health law: aspirational, paradoxical, or oxymoronic? In: Freeman M, Hawkes S, Bennett B (eds) Law and global health: current legal issues, volume 16. Oxford University Press, Oxford
Stiglitz JE (2012) The price of inequality. WW Norton & Company, New York
Tognoni G, Cauduro A (2018) Farmaci (e tecnologie) come indicatore, didattico e complessivo, della storia del Sistema sanitario nazionale. Polit Soc 2:157–172
Trotta F, Mayer F, Barone-Adesi F, Esposito I, Punreddy R, Da Cas R, Traversa G, Perrone F, Martini N, Gyawali B, Addis A (2019) Anticancer drug prices and clinical outcomes: a cross-sectional study in Italy. BMJ Open 9(12):1–9
Venkatapuram S (2011) Health justice: an argument from the capabilities approach. Polity, Cambridge
Wang S, Gum D, Merlin T (2018) Comparing the ICERs in medicine reimbursement submissions to NICE and PBAC—does the presence of an explicit threshold affect the ICER proposed? Value Health 21:938–943
Weldon I, Hoffman SJ (2024) 'Fit for purpose?' Assessing the ecological fit of the social institutions that globally govern antimicrobial resistance. Perspect Polit 22(4):1–22
Weldon I, Liddell K, Rogers Van Katwyk S, Hoffman SJ, Minssen T, Outterson K, Palmer S, Viens AM, Viñuales J (2024) Analyzing antimicrobial resistance as a series of collective action problems. Policy Stud J 52(4):833–856
Williams SJ, Martin P, Gabe J (2011) Evolving sociological analyses of 'pharmaceuticalisation': a reply to Abraham. Sociol Health Illn 33:729–730
Yamin AE (2003) Not just a tragedy: access to medications as a right under international law. Boston Univ Int Law J 21(2):325–327

Gender, Intersectionality, and Reproductive Rights in Health Crises

The Invisible Women: Gender in Global Legal Regimes of Health Emergencies

Mélanie Samson

Abstract Health emergencies constitute an amplifier of women's health issues. As attested by COVID-19, the impact of a pandemic on the health of women is unique in terms of exposure, access to care and social norms. Discourses on health emergencies, typically gender-blind, have made women's bodies largely invisible. Combining theoretical insights from gender studies, and empirically grounded in public health and international law, this contribution aims to deconstruct the legal anatomy of women's health in emergencies with a specific focus on the negotiations of the Pandemic Agreement, which offered the international community a unique opportunity to address the gendered impact of pandemics through law, and explores the question of how global health law can be leveraged to promote gender equality during health emergencies.

1 Introduction: Framing Gender in Global Health Emergencies

1.1 Biopower, Pandemics, and Gender at a Turning Point in Global Health

There is no doubt that global health is experiencing an existential turning point. An important part of that experience is the global backlash against women's right to health, along with 'new waves of resistance against gender equality'.[1] Indeed, despite remarkable progress achieved in the past decades, we are now observing widespread regression with the rollback on gender rights and the adoption of restrictive laws and policies on several fronts at the national, regional and national levels. As recently

[1] Brechenmacher (2025), p. 1.

M. Samson (✉)
Sciences Po, Paris, France
e-mail: melanie.samson@sciencespo.fr

M. Balestrieri and A. Cauduro (eds.), *The Legal Anatomy of the Body*, Ius Gentium: Comparative Perspectives on Law and Justice 142,
https://doi.org/10.1007/978-3-032-26434-3_14

highlighted by the Special Rapporteur on the Right to Health, 'the regression is widespread and strategic, part of a systematic effort to reassert control over sexuality and reproduction'.[2] What this phenomenon reflects, *inter alia*, is that women's bodies are highly political and that they are at the centre of complex systemic forces beyond public health. In situations of crisis, such as health emergencies, the *tyranny of the urgent*[3] amplifies such patterns, calling for an analysis of the body as an object which is not only cared for but is also politically contested,[4] specifically in the context of global health security approaches, defined as the 'activities focused on preventing, detecting and responding to infectious disease threats of international concern to limit the impact of transborder disease'.[5] In this sense, health emergencies reveal the deeply biopolitical nature of contemporary powers and forms of governmentality and show the importance of studying the interplay of global health security with other regimes and societal values.

The Foucauldian concept of biopolitics is particularly fruitful in this context, offering as it does the possibility to see how gender, norms and politics interact in public health policies and laws. Biopolitics 'deals with the population as a political problem, as a problem that is at once scientific and political, as a biological problem and as a power's problem'.[6] The link with public health is easy to see as biopolitics 'derive(s) its knowledge from, and define its power's field of intervention in terms of, the birth rate, the mortality rate, various biological disabilities, and the effects of the environment'.[7] In this sense, biopolitics refers to a set of strategies, policies, legal and regulatory discourses deployed to regulate life and health. Interestingly, Foucault deployed different models of management of health emergencies,[8] with the 'sovereignty' model for leprosy, which isolated vulnerable affected individuals,[9] the 'disciplinary' model for the plague,[10] with the establishment of the 'Magistrate' power and rules in the sixteenth century,[11] and the 'biopower' model for the management of smallpox, revealing the 'biological existence of a population'[12] through the 'administration of bodies and the management of life'.[13] This Foucauldian analytic grid sheds a great deal of light on how more recent 'public health emergencies of international concerns' (PHEIC)[14] have triggered different models of management and response, and how this divergence is reflected in normative approaches, specifically

[2] Mofokeng (2025), p. 91.

[3] Smith (2019).

[4] Harcourt (2022).

[5] Wenham (2021), p. 32.

[6] Foucault (2003), p. 245.

[7] Foucault (2003), p. 245.

[8] Mhazo and Maponga (2022), p. 7.

[9] Foucault (1965).

[10] Foucault (1975).

[11] See the contribution by Antonio Gerace in this volume.

[12] Foucault (1981), p. 137.

[13] Foucault (1981), p. 140.

[14] According to the IHR (2005), obligations are triggered by the declaration of a PHEIC.

for the coordination of different values in the management of health emergencies along the continuum from preparedness to resilience.

One of these highly politically contested values is the role of gender in global health security. This contribution aims to explore how gender, defined as 'the structure of social relations and practices that are organised in relation to reproductive bodies',[15] is made visible (or invisible) in the narrative and norm-settings in global health security. Indeed, health emergencies constitute an amplifier of the control and normalisation of women's health and bodies. In this sense, Foucault's framework offers a powerful tool for the analysis of the specific impact of pandemic responses systems on women during health emergencies such as Zika, Ebola and COVID-19 at the national and global levels.

1.2 *Beyond Gender Blindness in Normative Development in Global Health Law*

Global Health Security is historically linked with the emergence of international health law, with the sanitary conventions developed in the nineteenth century and later codified in the International Health Regulations (IHR) under the auspices of WHO. This unique regulatory instrument in international law, implemented under the auspices of the World Health Organization (WHO), establishes the functional rules governing the monitoring, the notification and the management of outbreaks. The IHR provides a guiding framework for the deployment of national legal regimes, from preparedness to response to health emergencies. Since its revision in 2005, the IHR (2005) has been applied in the context of nine public health emergencies of international concern (PHEIC), including H1N1, Zika, Ebola and the COVID-19 and more recently Mpox.

Due to its magnitude and impact, the COVID-19 pandemic exposed important flaws of the global legal regime, as the IHR (2005) did not contain any obligation of collaboration and solidarity between States to secure a global equitable response, so much so that the global response to the pandemic was described as 'the biggest moral failure of our times'.[16] In fact, the lack of efficiency in the implementation of the IHR (2005) revealed not only 'gaps in current disease detection, alert, and response mechanisms, but also plainly showed that a reset of the global health and health security system as a whole is required'.[17] This experience gave rise to calls for an in-depth revision of the global health security regime to ensure that global health security schemes are 'built on the base of equity, where rights and responsibilities are well coordinated, benefits and burdens are fairly distributed, national and global interests are carefully balanced, and short-term assistance and long-term capacity-building

[15] Hawkes (2025), p. 4.
[16] United Nations (2022).
[17] Singh (2021), p. 2121.

are provided with the intention of benefiting local populations in LMICs'.[18] Two parallel legal processes were initiated as a result in 2022. The first one consisted in the revision of the IHR (2005), with about 300 propositions of amendment submitted by Member States. The amended IHR entered into force in June 2024 in 196 States and is entering into force in September 2025. The equity problem that COVID-19 revealed also pushed the international community to elaborate a new treaty to set up the governance and modalities of collaboration for future pandemics. Initiated in December 2021, the negotiations led to the adoption of the Agreement in May 2025 subject to the finalisation of an annex.

Both processes attempted to build on the motto of 'building back better' based on the lessons of COVID-19 and a strong narrative on resilience, equity and solidarity. One of the well documented lessons was the invisibility of women in the pandemic response. How did the negotiations of the newly adopted Pandemic Agreement take into account and integrate the gendered impact of health emergencies? How can the mechanisms of compliance and transposition in national law make women visible in health legal regimes? These are the issues to which this chapter now turns. It builds on multidisciplinary perspectives on gendered impact, policies and regulations during health emergencies to enable a content analysis of all publicly available materials from the 13 negotiating rounds of the International Negotiating Body (INB) for the Pandemic Agreement from 2021 to 2025, draft texts, the transcripts of recordings of meetings of the INB, as well as other relevant legal and policy documents as part of the global health law and policies.

2 Making the Invisible Visible: Framing a Magnifying Glass on the Impact of Pandemics on Women

Global health security governs all policies, legislations and institutions involved in collective responses to epidemic outbreaks. The vast majority of these responses, at the national and global levels, are built on a gender-neutral way, rendering women invisible in the broader narrative. However, research has unveiled large inequities, based on structural determinants across countries but also across populations. This section aims to explore the gender blindness of epidemiological data as well as specific inequities in policies, access to key services such as sexual and reproductive services, and more broadly, women's right to health during health emergencies.

[18] The Lancet Global Health (2022), p. 927.

2.1 The Invisibility of Women in Health Emergencies

In her seminal book titled 'Invisible Women', Caroline Criado Perez demonstrates the impact of the gender data gap on the framing and implementation of policies.[19] This gender gap in data is particularly acute during health emergencies as exemplified during recent outbreaks: the 2014–2016 Ebola outbreak in West Africa, the 2019 Ebola outbreak in the Democratic Republic of the Congo, the 2015–2016 Zika virus outbreak in parts of Central and South America, and during the COVID-19 pandemic.

The absence of gendered data, leading to the *invisibilization* of women in the continuum of preparedness, response and resilience in health emergencies, can be illustrated in three representative areas. First, this invisibility exists in epidemiological surveillance with the absence of, or delays in collecting and disseminating, sex-disaggregated data during emergencies. According to a recent scoping review, less than 1% of studies on Ebola and Zika reported gender indicators.[20] During the Ebola outbreak, there were also significant delays in collecting sex-disaggregated data, with the impossibility of adapting the response to the specific needs of women during the health emergency, rendering women 'conspicuously invisible' in public health measures adopted to manage the outbreak.[21] In the context of the COVID-19 pandemic, the advocacy group Global 50/50 initiated the COVID-19 sex-disaggregated data tracker to build evidence on the availability of gendered data in countries, which highlighted that, in November 2021, only 41% of countries were reporting sex-disaggregated data on both incidence and mortality related to COVID-19.[22] Thus, women and gender remain invisible in comprehending the exposure to pathogens as well as in designing the countermeasures in policies. This invisibility has life-threatening consequences, as there is no data on the etiology of diseases specific to the woman body, which results in one-size-fits-all response schemes during health emergencies. As has been pointed out, 'evidence unequivocally illustrates that neglecting sex and gender dynamics during outbreaks yields adverse consequences, such as missed information, misguided actions across response phases and worse health outcomes for marginalised groups'.[23] In this sense, the lack of disaggregated data is the *original sin* of gender blindness in health emergencies, with little or no data of the epidemiological impact of major outbreaks on women.

Second, invisibility of women is also pervasive in clinical trials. The *male bias* in clinical research, which consists in not enrolling women and in not considering gender as a variable, has serious consequences in terms of health outcomes. In clinical research, based on fears of liability and on a cultural *male bias* in research, 'medicine has long treated women as 'smaller men' assuming that drugs tested on male bodies would work the same way in females'.[24] However, from a biological perspective,

[19] Criado Perez (2019).

[20] Gales et al. (2025).

[21] Harman (2016).

[22] Hawkes (2022).

[23] McKinzie (2025), p.14.

[24] Singh (2025).

women have very distinct and specific metabolic variables, with regard, among others, to hormonal cycles and immunities, affecting their responses to molecules. The lack of women-specific data can lead to detrimental consequences ranging from the absence of adapted treatments to disproportionate side effects. Studies have highlighted that women experience twice as many adverse drug reactions as men because of their invisibility in clinical trials.[25] This inequity is even more acute during health emergencies, as the *tyranny of the urgent* does not facilitate the identification of key intersectional determinants in the race towards the development of medical countermeasures. For example, in the case of COVID-19, a study highlighted that out of the 4420 registered clinical trials, only 178 studies (4%) mention sex/gender as a planned analytical variable.[26] Similarly, pregnant and lactating women have been historically excluded from clinical trials, leading to the uncertainty of effects of new pharmaceuticals on the health outcomes of this specific subpopulation. Overall, only 5% of available treatments have been tested and labelled with safety information for use in pregnant women, and more than 80% of pregnant women are prescribed treatments that have been never tested on their population.[27] The delays for the inclusion of pregnant women in the Ebola vaccine trials led to important debates from the ethical standpoint, between access and fear of teratogenic effects on women and foetuses.[28]

This dangerous invisibility in both vaccines and therapeutics developments triggered calls for making 'a general sex- and gender-sensitive approach' part of 'mandatory reporting requirements upon registration of clinical trials', including 'in times of crisis',[29] as illustrated in the US 1993 law that requires the NIH to enrol women in clinical trials. The implementation of the Sex and Gender Equity in Research guidelines (SAGER)[30] to stimulate a more systematic approach to sex and gender in research papers could also promote more inclusion. We will explore in the following sections how such considerations were reflected in the negotiations of the new global health security regime with the IHR and the Pandemic Agreement.

Third, this invisibility in data is pervasive regarding the socio-economic impact of outbreaks during health emergencies. In fact, during the COVID-19 outbreak, while it was clear that lockdowns and other societal disruptions had a gendered impact, policies were only 'based on a mix of anecdotal evidence, smaller case studies, and research from previous crises'.[31] In fact, during outbreaks, despite the growing recognition that gender-based indicators are essential in informing adapted policies, these indicators tend not to be prioritized in monitoring frameworks. Moreover, usual socio-economic monitoring systems are also disrupted and therefore streamlined, leaving 'non-essential' data collection and analysis behind. However, as it will be demonstrated in the following section, violations of women's rights and infringements of

[25] Zucker and Prendergast (2020).

[26] Brady (2021).

[27] World Economic Forum (2025).

[28] Grais (2025).

[29] Brady (2021), p. 4.

[30] Heidari (2016).

[31] ILO (2021a).

gender equality are exacerbated during health emergencies, as states of emergency regimes and measures relegate these values to the category of 'non-essential'.

2.2 *Gendered Impact of Pandemics: A Women's Rights Perspective*

Beyond the invisibility of women's vulnerabilities, there is no doubt that health emergencies have a disrupting effect on women's rights, by amplifying 'deep-seated inequalities within and between societies and magnify(ying) the suffering of those already marginalized, including women, girls and disadvantaged communities'.[32] While research remains limited for previous outbreaks (with the exception of Ebola and Zika), the gendered impact on women has been emphasised by several stakeholders, specifically by the gender community and women's rights advocacy organisations. These gendered impacts can be problematized from a human rights perspective, given the continuity of the obligation not to discriminate *de jure* or *de facto* during emergencies, in particular, pursuant to the Convention on the Elimination of Discrimination against Women (CEDAW). Discriminatory practices can be divided into three main categories: socio-economic discriminated impact, access to services and representation in decision-making.

First, health emergencies act as a magnifying glass, bringing to light gender norms that amplify socio-economic inequalities despite the fact that the health workforce is in majority composed of women. According to the World Health Organization, women healthcare workers represent more than 70% of the global health workforce and 90% of health workers in patient-facing roles.[33] This frontline role in the pandemic response leads to increased exposure to pathogens, as demonstrated during the Ebola outbreak.[34] The COVID-19 pandemic also revealed gender bias and inequalities in healthcare settings—traditionally in pay,[35] personal protective equipment (PPE), care burdens, and psychological challenges.[36] In response, the CEDAW Committee included a dedicated recommendation in its Guidance Note on CEDAW and COVID-19 stating that 'States parties should also protect women health workers and other frontline workers from contagion through measures such as the dissemination of necessary precautionary information and adequate provision of personal protective equipment as well as psychosocial support'.[37] The socio-economic impact is also exacerbated by the gendered norm that women act as unpaid carers in their families and communities, multiplying the 'care load' of women. For example, rapid gender impact assessments demonstrated that, in Cameroon, women's unpaid care

[32] Global Health Law Consortium, International Commission of Jurists (2024).

[33] World Health Organization (2019).

[34] WHO (2015).

[35] George (2007).

[36] Phillips et al. (2023).

[37] CEDAW Committee (2020), p. 1.

work has tripled and, and in Côte d'Ivoire, women's informal carer role increased by 25% during the pandemic.[38] This constitutes a specific stressor not necessarily recognized in economic response schemes and social security policies. Moreover, there is a clear gendered impact on employment and correlated risk of poverty amongst women during health emergencies. A higher rate of women loses their employment during health emergencies as they are representing the majority of workers in public-facing service or in the informal sector, which are strongly impacted by lockdowns and restrictions during health emergencies. For example, more than a year after the outbreak of Ebola in Sierra Leone, 17% of employed women returned to work, compared to 63% of men.[39] This disproportionate economic impact on women was also well documented during the COVID-19 pandemic, with the International Labor Organisation (ILO) estimating that, in the Americas, about 9.5% of women lost their employment as a result of the pandemic, compared to 7% of men.[40] This gendered impact remained after the pandemic as women recovered pre-pandemic employment levels in January 2023, almost a year after men.[41] The CEDAW Committee highlighted this discriminatory impact, pointing out that 'COVID-19 response and economic recovery plans should address gender inequalities in employment, promote transition of women from the informal economy to the formal economy and provide relevant social protection systems for them'.[42]

Another gendered impact of health emergencies comprises restrictions in terms of access to women's health services, at the intersection of the right to health and women's rights. With priorities centred on the pandemic response, overload of health systems and restrictions of movement, women are facing barriers in accessing services.[43] This is particularly acute in access to sexual and reproductive health services, with dire consequences in terms of access to gynaecological services, including contraception and safe abortion, which leads to a higher rate of unwanted pregnancies as well as morbidity and mortality.[44] For example, during the COVID-19, these barriers led to a 26% decrease in access to safe abortion in Nepal.[45] Restrictions on the reproductive choices of women can also result from the outbreak response management. As demonstrated by Wenham, the ultra-securized response to Zika, based on military models of management (disciplinary Foucauldian model), included official recommendations to delay or avoid pregnancies, targeting directly women's reproductive choices. In a nutshell, women were requested to 'clean your house and don't get pregnant'[46] in Brazil and several Latin American countries. Not only is the recommendation on avoiding pregnancy highly questionable from a women's rights

[38] CARE (2020).

[39] Bandiera (2019), cited by Davies and Wenham (2024).

[40] ILO (2021b).

[41] Institute for Women's Policy Research (2025).

[42] CEDAW Committee (2020), p. 2.

[43] Tam (2024).

[44] VanBenschoten (2022).

[45] Aryal (2021).

[46] Wenham (2021), p. 53.

perspective, invading a private sphere, it also ignores key determinants and structural causes that might not allow women to avoid pregnancies (Davies & Bennett 2016). Moreover, as emphasized by Wenham, this recommendation 'must be understood as embedded within a broader narrative of reproductive governance and stratified reproduction, whereby government regimes have sought to control reproductive behaviours'.[47]

The impact of de-prioritizing maternal health services during outbreaks is also considered as a direct violation of women's right to health. In the first months of the acute phase of the COVID-19 outbreak, the UN Working Group on Discrimination Against Women and Girls noted that 'the proliferation of barriers to healthcare, especially pregnancy-related healthcare, will profoundly jeopardize women's safety and well-being'.[48] Indeed, in the context of the Ebola outbreak, such barriers and access restrictions generated an increase of 36% of maternal mortality, leading to more deaths of women from this cause than of Ebola.[49] It is also crucial to consider women beyond their reproductive functions, as they were impacted in their right to health in all domains deemed as 'non-essential'. This de-prioritization of services such as preventative services for cancer and other non-communicable diseases as well as mental health services generated a long-term impact on women's health, beyond the emergency itself.[50]

Finally, from a gender equality perspective, the capital role of women at the frontline of health emergencies, as health workers and carers, leads to the question of the representation of women in decision-making processes. According to Sophie Harman, 'this is central paradox in global health: women are conspicuous in the delivery of care and thus the delivery of health, but are invisible to the institutions and policies that design and implement global health strategies'.[51] UN Women, in collaboration with UNDP, collected data on the representation of women in COVID-19 responses decision-making bodies in 187 countries, showcasing that less than 7% of these task forces were applying gender parity, and highlighting that the overall share of women in responses task forces was 24% worldwide with large variations across regions and countries.[52] This unequal representation is at odd with Article 7 of the CEDAW, which states that women 'on equal terms with men' have the right to 'participate in the formulation of government policy and the implementation thereof'. As highlighted by the CEDAW Committee, it is capital that women have 'meaningful participation and leadership in the formulation of COVID-19 response and recovery strategies, including social and economic recovery plans, at all levels and recognize

[47] Wenham (2021), p. 115.
[48] OHCHR (2020).
[49] Jones (2016).
[50] Shah (2025).
[51] Harman (2016), p. 526.
[52] UN Women, UNDP (2022).

women as significant agents for societal change in the present and post COVID-19 period'.[53] Indeed, in view of the broader human rights approaches to participation and the value of lived experience—'nothing about us, without us'—outbreak response and reconstruction policies have constantly failed to include women in their governance.

Overall, the gendered impact of pandemics is well documented, with many researchers and institutions rendering the issue visible globally, specifically with the COVID-19 pandemic. The latter also led to the realisation of the global moral failure in terms of equity between countries and of vulnerable populations, prompting an in-depth revision of global health security framework through international law. The question is whether these new norm-setting processes have considered the gender-specific impacts of pandemics.

3 Rethinking Global Health Security Legal Regimes Through the Gender Lens

In the context of COVID-19, inequities of access to vaccines and other social divides became increasingly visible with the response to the pandemic, a *moral failure* in terms of solidarity between States. In 2021, the Independent Panel for Pandemic Preparedness and Response underlined the inaptitude of the global health security architecture to manage such crises, and called the international community to engage in the normative development of a global framework convention for preparedness and response, grounded in human rights, equity and accountability.[54] This call for action confirm the pattern that governance crises in the context of outbreaks typically lead to a growing appetite for normative reform and development. For instance, the first revision of IHR in 2005 followed the SARS outbreak in 2002–2003. Similarly, the WHO Health Emergency Programme as well as monitoring bodies and mechanisms were established after the Ebola outbreak in 2014–2016.[55]

In the same vein, with the adoption in December 2021 of the resolution creating the International Negotiating Body (INB), States engaged in an in-depth reform of the global health security legal architecture in parallel to the revision of the IHR, to develop a new global treaty to coordinate the global response to pandemics. After more than 3 years of hard negotiations involving 13 formal rounds and constant informal discussions, the text of the Pandemic Agreement was finalized on 16 April 2025 and adopted at the World Health Assembly (WHA) on 20 May 2025. Celebrated as an historic moment for multilateralism, the adoption of the Pandemic Agreement marks the start of a potentially difficult negotiation of a contentious annex on the Pathogen Access and Benefit Sharing System (PABS) by the next WHA in

[53] CEDAW Committee (2020), p. 2.

[54] Independent Panel for Pandemic Preparedness and Response (2021).

[55] Clark and Johnson Sirleaf (2025).

2026, before the entry into force (after 60 ratifications) and the establishment of the Conference of Parties.

This new instrument was a unique opportunity to address the key gender gaps identified above. A textual analysis of all negotiation rounds, and draft texts is an effective way to see whether this was the case. After the adoption of the annex, states will need to ratify the Agreement and, in many cases, to transcribe it in their national laws. Therefore, compliance mechanisms can also be mobilized for mainstreaming gender in the implementation of the Pandemic Agreement.

3.1 Seizing the Momentum: Gender in Post-pandemic Negotiations

Launched in December 2021 with the creation of the INB, the negotiations 'to draft and negotiate a WHO convention, agreement or other international instrument on pandemic prevention, preparedness and response'[56] lasted more than 3 years (see Fig. 1), involving 13 rounds of negotiations and at least eight consecutive versions of the draft agreement and totalling a cost of more than 200 million USD.[57] These negotiations were innovative in terms of treaty-making processes in several respects, including participatory approaches through an initial consultative online survey to collect key substantive elements to be included in the treaty as well as an enhanced transparency with webcasts accessible online on WHO website. There were nonetheless critics as the participation of civil society was substantially limited and that a large part of the negotiations was informal, taking part behind closed doors.

There was an expectation that human rights, specifically gender and women's rights would be reflected in the negotiations and that gender sensitive approaches would be followed. To test this expectation, we engaged in a content analysis of the primary data available on the INB webpages, including consecutive draft texts of the agreement as well as the transcription of more than 60 h of webcast recordings of all INB rounds, from February 2022 to April 2025, to explore how the themes of gender and women were incorporated in the negotiations, identifying key narratives and variance. This analysis builds on the previous study conducted in 2024 by S. Davies and C. Wenham, which explored the evolution of gender-inclusive language in the former drafts of the treaty to issue recommendations to the INB. Unfortunately, it seems that the imperative of 'closing the deal' resulted in an increasingly diminished sensitivity to gender-related issues.[58]

Figure 2 below summarizes the evolution of the frequency of occurrences of 'gender' and 'women' in the texts.

It is interesting to observe an initial strong presence of key gender-related issues identified in the previous section in the conceptual and zero text, followed by a

[56] See WHO decision SSA2(5) (2021).

[57] Wenham and Potluru (2024).

[58] Davies and Wenham (2024), p. 13.

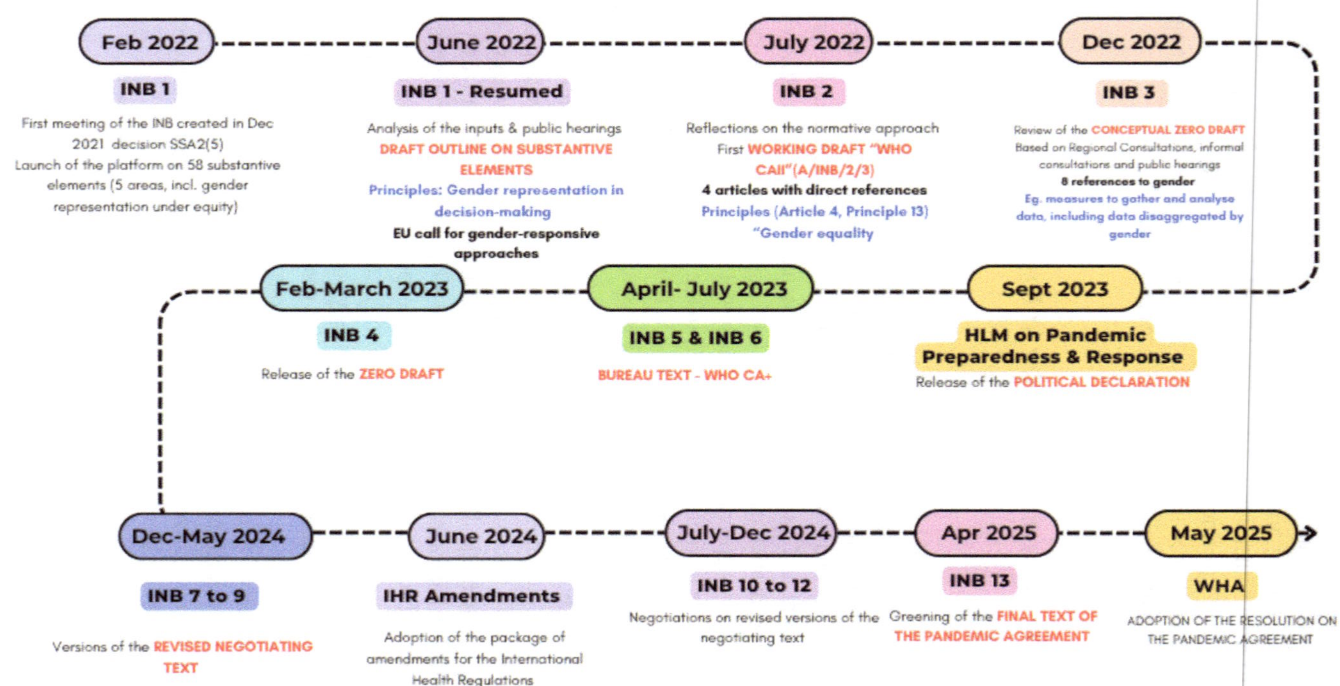

Fig. 1 Timeline of the main phases of the Pandemic Agreement

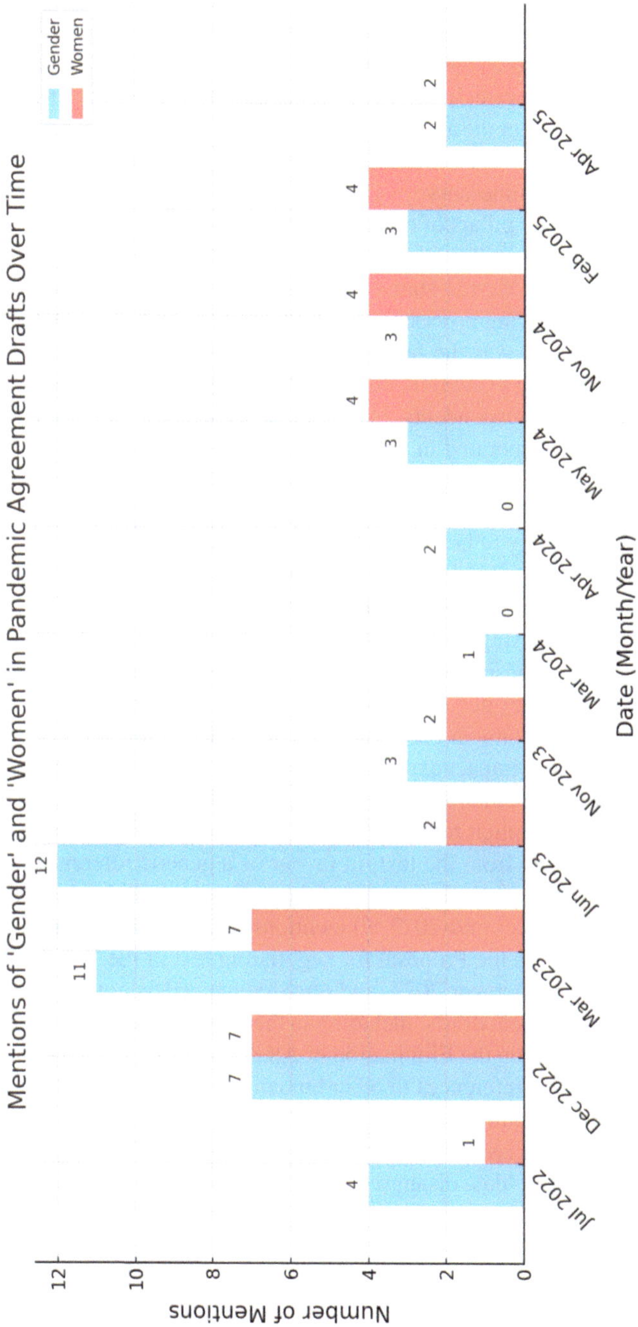

Fig. 2 Frequence of occurrences of gender and women in consecutive drafts of the Pandemic Agreement

progressive erosion, and almost a return to invisibility in the final text, which only contains one mention of the CEDAW, a mention of gender equality in the principles as well as a reference to unequal remuneration of women as health workers in a dedicated article.

Among the overarching principles, references to gender and women's rights can be found within the preamble or the article (now article 3) on Principles and Approaches. The first text, labelled the 2022 Draft Annotated text, was based on 58 substantive elements from an online survey. These substantive elements were classified according to four strategic pillars of equity, leadership and governance, systems and tools, as well as financing.[59] The Draft Principle 1.7. referred to 'Equitable gender, geographical and socioeconomic status representation and participation in global and regional decision-making processes'.[60] As pointed out by Davies and Wenham, this 'minimalist inclusion was the beginning of a trend that continued throughout negotiations'.[61] According to the INB summary report, this reference did not receive unanimous support from respondents. However, in subsequent drafts, the theme of gender equality was incorporated in the principles clauses, specifically in the 2023 Zero Draft, Article 4 of which included a comprehensive reference to gender mainstreaming in the agreement: '(11) Gender equality—Pandemic prevention, preparedness, response and recovery of health systems will be guided by and benefit from the goal of equal participation and leadership of men and women in decision-making with a particular focus on gender equality, taking into account the specific needs of all women and girls, using a country-driven, gender responsive/transformative, participatory and fully transparent approach'.[62] The overarching principles of the Zero Draft also referred to gender-balanced representation and described gender inequality as a socio-economic repercussion of pandemics, reflecting lessons learnt from the visible gendered impact experienced during the COVID-19 pandemic.

Starting from the end of 2023, as the initial May 2024 deadline to finalise the agreement was approaching, explicit references to various dimensions of gender equality progressively disappeared from the text, in favour of a generic reference to human rights principles and gender equality as one of those principles. Indeed, after a pause on negotiations on principles mid-2023, all mentions of gender disappeared from the preamble and principles in the Proposal for negotiating text of the WHO Pandemic Agreement discussed in October 2023, and only reappeared as a generic reference to the CEDAW in subsequent drafts, including in the final preambular paragraph: '5. Recalling the Convention on the Elimination of All Forms of Discrimination against Women (…)', along with references to other human rights treaties.

The same pattern of eroding frequency of references can also be seen in connection with other key gender issues. Initial drafts mentioned the gender data gap, highlighting the importance of 'data disaggregated by gender (…) to show the impact of

[59] WHO (2022c), UN Doc.A/INB/1/9.

[60] WHO (2022a), UN Doc. A/INB/1/12.

[61] Davies and Wenham (2024), p. 8.

[62] WHO (2023b), A/INB/4/3.

policies on different groups'[63] and of the disclosure of results from clinical trials.[64] However, such references to sex-disaggregated data disappeared in subsequent drafts. Gender responsive approaches to research and development (R&D) suffered a similar fate. Until November 2023, article 9 on R&D referred to the inclusion of 'gender diversity' in clinical trials. The reference to pregnant women in initial drafts was also an important step forward towards specific considerations in clinical trials. This shifted to a generic and gender-neutral mention of 'promoting representative trial populations' in the final text.

One of the most interesting trends towards *invisibilization* of women is observed in connection with healthcare workforce. The first drafts incorporated significant lessons learnt from past outbreaks. For example, the Zero Draft of February 2023 contained a dedicated paragraph addressing 'gender disparities and inequalities within the health and care workforce, to ensure meaningful representation, engagement, participation and empowerment of all health and care workers, while addressing discrimination, stigma and inequality and eliminating bias, including unequal remuneration, and noting that women still often face significant barriers to taking leadership and decision-making roles'.[65] Strong inclusion of gender-inclusive narrative for equity in the healthcare workforce disappeared in subsequent drafts in 2024, with the final text of the agreement only illustrating potential inequalities in article 7(b), which referred to 'unequal remuneration and barriers faced by women.' Finally, in a similar fashion, while gender-balanced representation in decision-making processes was referred to in initial drafts, both as a key principle and in articles covering coordination and whole-of-society approaches, there is no mention of it in the final text.

These findings show a considerable shift towards a minimization of gender-sensitive language in the text of the Agreement and in favour of gender-neutral references to human rights and representativity of vulnerable populations. The transcriptions of negotiations provide some insights into the reasons behind this shift. The need to include gender-specific language was stressed by some Member States and Stakeholders in the negotiations. For example, during the INB4, Costa Rica highlighted that 'the text needs to include specific language on a gender perspective, especially to raise awareness of this challenge in the health sector and to guarantee a greater representation of women in decision making processes, greater access to health services, as well as response and prevention efforts'.[66] Similarly, starting in November 2023, Canada constantly insisted on maintaining or reinstating specific gender-inclusive clauses in the text. As the initial May 2024 deadline approached and the efforts of negotiators focused on streamlining the text, Canada specifically highlighted that 'the new text misses opportunities to address gender-related issues'[67] and shared its disappointment 'to see that what appears to have been streamlined

[63] WHO (2023a), A/INB/5/6.

[64] WHO (2023b), A/INB/4/3.

[65] WHO (2023b), A/INB/4/3.

[66] Transcript of INB4, webcast of 27.02.2023.

[67] Transcript of INB7, webcast of 6.11.2023.

are some key provisions to advance health equity comprehensively' while 'pragmatically, this is too good and too rare of an opportunity to not take full advantage of' to anticipate key gendered impact issues in pandemics.[68] The Office of the High Commissioner on Human Rights (OHCHR) observed that the very reason for engaging in treaty-making was to prevent catastrophic consequences of pandemics, including the gendered impact of the COVID-19 along with other human right issues and insisted that 'if the right to health and human rights are meant to guide the implementation of this agreement, it will be important to see this in the text substantively and systematically, [...] and currently, this is not the case'.

Interestingly, during the INB9 discussions, the co-chair of the INB provided further explanation as to how streamlining led to the under-specification of key rights: 'what we try to do is come up with language that captures as much as possible the general concept of human rights without specifying to whom, in what situation and why is that because as soon as you start digging in, you start mentioning women or other specific groups or whomever, then you get a discussion on that. And we've seen that, we've tried that and that's what when we said let's just go back to the essence and say human rights in general for everybody'.[69] It seems, therefore, that in order to reach a broad consensus, specific references to gender were evacuated. As pointed out by some authors, 'gender-inclusive language is often considered as a 'trade-off' in the negotiations' discussions'[70] to ensure that other issues such as access to health products are prioritized in the text. Overall, it has been considered that this global health reform has 'retreated from rights-based frameworks'[71] and moved closer to a more technical perspective in managing health emergencies.

In sum, the final text does not properly address the gendered impact of pandemics. Dedicated legal obligations cannot be lightly assumed in the gender-neutral text when addressing specific issues faced by women during health emergencies. As highlighted by the sociologist E. Zerubavel, women are the 'unremarkable' in such a text, which leads to a cognitive bias consisting in assuming that the subject is 'presumably male unless specifically designated otherwise'.[72] This cognitive bias shows the link between global health security and military narrative, and accentuates the gender norms during health emergencies. Explicit legal norms are therefore critical during health emergencies as the *tyranny of the urgent* tends to exclude what is deemed as non-essential rights, a category to which women's rights are easily relegated.[73] It is not clear that the gendered impact of future health emergencies will be any different. As we experience a backlash on gender globally, with one out of four countries regressing on women's rights,[74] an important opportunity may have been

[68] Transcript of INB9, webcast of 9.03.2024.

[69] Transcript, INB9, Webcast of 21.03.2024, Open session with relevant stakeholders focusing on critical elements for a pandemic agreement.

[70] Davies and Wenham (2024), p. 13.

[71] Sircar (2025).

[72] Zerubavel (2018), p. 33.

[73] Smith (2019).

[74] UN Women (2025).

missed. That being said, the implementation of the Pandemic Agreement may still offer some potential to promote a greater gender sensitivity.

3.2 *Focusing on Implementation: Integrating Gender Through Monitoring Indicators and Interpretation*

The negotiation of the PABS annex to the Pandemic Agreement will likely be arduous, and securing 60 ratifications necessary for the entry into force of the Agreement might take some time. In the meantime, the amended IHR will enter into force in September 2025 and is expected to reshape the global health security legal architecture with its own set of implementation and accountability processes which are closely related to the Pandemic Agreement.[75]

Similarly to other regulatory treaty regimes, such as the Framework Convention on Tobacco Control (FCTC) and the UN Framework on Climate Change, the Pandemic Agreement will have its Conference of the Parties (COP) formally mandated 'to regularly take stock of the implementation of the WHO Pandemic Agreement, [...] review its functioning every five years, and [...] take the decisions necessary to promote its effective implementation.' (Article 19, para. 2). The experience of COP mechanisms in other areas of international cooperation shows that they 'can shape a treaty's identity over time'[76] and 'specify and develop the content of their parent treaties by setting out the standards that states parties must meet to comply with their obligations'.[77] Under the Pandemic Agreement, each party has the obligation to report periodically to the Conference of the Parties on its implementation (Article 21, para. 1). This review mechanism opens up new opportunities for reintegrating gender-transformative approaches to global and national pandemic laws. Two techniques can, in particular, be deployed to that effect: interpretations promoting consistency with women's rights as recognized in international human rights law and the use of global health indicators in monitoring mechanisms.

First, interpretation is a powerful way to give substance to vague clauses of the Pandemic Agreement. Article 26 of the latter explicitly introduces the principle of consistency with other relevant international legal regimes, providing that 'the WHO Pandemic Agreement and the International Health Regulations (2005) and other relevant international agreements should be interpreted so as to be compatible'. This is fully in line with the International Law Commission's views that '[i]n international law, there is a strong presumption against normative conflict'[78] and that 'when creating new obligations, States are assumed not to derogate from their existing obligations'.[79] The explicit preambular reference to the CEDAW reinforces

[75] Lee (2025).

[76] Sircar (2025).

[77] Rioseco (2023), p. 718.

[78] International Law Commission (2006), para. 37.

[79] International Law Commission (2006), para. 38.

the obligation of consistency and can be effectively deployed to promote a gender-sensitive reading of the Pandemic Agreement. For example, when a Member State designs its local pandemic response and recovery laws, it should do so in a way that is consistent with CEDAW Article 12 on access to sexual and reproductive health services during pandemics.

In a similar vein, the full realization of gender equality requires access to the array of services (and choices) regarding body autonomy and to adapted health services.[80] This obligations extend to non-state actors, as highlighted in the General Recommendation 24 of the CEDAW Committee: 'The obligation to protect rights relating to women's health requires States parties, their agents and officials to take action to prevent and impose sanctions for violations by private persons and organizations',[81] including during states of emergencies, as non-derogable and non-derogated human rights continue to be applicable.[82] Similarly, the CEDAW obligations regarding gender-balanced representation should influence recovery plans. For example, the Italian Recovery and Resilience Plan stimulated legislative measures on gender-equality, such as gender equality certifications and a strengthened gender equality machinery, with the launch in 2022 of the *Osservatorio nazionale per l'integrazione delle politiche per la parità di genere*.[83] In sum, a women rights-based interpretation of key articles of the Pandemic Agreement would allow gender mainstreaming to be reintegrated in the implementation of the Agreement, specifically as countries incorporate the Agreement into national laws and policies and as the COP is called to provide key authoritative interpretation in the future.[84]

The use of gender-sensitive indicators as part of the monitoring mechanism of the Pandemic Agreement can also significantly further gender mainstreaming. The resolution WHA78.1 adopting the Pandemic Agreement established an Intergovernmental Working Group (IGWG) charged with the task to negotiate the annex, and to conduct preparatory work on certain issues for consideration by the COP. One of the first agenda items in the future COP's order of business will be the matter of how States parties will report on the implementation of the Agreement as indicated in its Article 19. In the same vein, the IHR (2005) has developed monitoring mechanisms based on a holistic system of voluntary and external assessments of compliance with a long experience that can inform the future COP. In other words, a window of opportunity will present itself to ensure that monitoring mechanisms can be designed with a view to improving the integration of human rights, including women's rights in national legislations and policies. It is interesting to note in this regard the pervasive role of indicators as compliance tools in global health law, including for the IHR (2005), the FCTC as well as other WHO-led normative instruments such as the

[80] OHCHR (2021).

[81] CEDAW (1999).

[82] WHO (2007).

[83] Donà (2022).

[84] Correia (2025).

Global Code of Practice on the International Recruitment of Health Personnel and the International Code on the Marketing of Breastmilk Substitutes.[85]

Indicators have become increasingly important in gender mainstreaming, specifically in measuring progress towards the SDG 5—'achieve gender equality and empower all women and girls'—which comprises 9 targets and 14 indicators, including indicator 5.1.1. which measures 'whether or not legal frameworks are in place to promote, enforce and monitor equality and non-discrimination on the basis of sex'. Global policies and advocacy aiming to promote gender in all policies and legislations have influenced the design of monitoring mechanisms of instruments such as the IHR (2005). The IHR is equipped with a strong monitoring and evaluation framework composed of annual reporting, post-event reviews, simulation exercises and joint external evaluations (JEE). The JEE processes are multisectoral, led by experts to assess core capacities based on a set list of indicators for a harmonized assessment of countries capacities. Building on lessons learnt from the COVID-19 pandemic, WHO initiated an expert-led, technical process to update the JEE tool, in order to integrate 'equity considerations across various technical areas through technical questions aimed at identifying support for vulnerable populations, including through data collection and reporting'.[86] This new version of the tool, adopted in 2022, incorporates, for the first time, a dedicated indicator on gender mainstreaming to specifically measure, based on a scoring system, whether 'systematic gender analysis of IHR capacities is conducted, and action plans to address gender gaps and inequalities are developed, funded and operationalized in at least three IHR capacities, with mechanisms in place for monitoring, evaluation and reporting'. The tool also provides further guidance to experts on topics such as the availability of sex-disaggregated data, as well as all on key topics on gender mainstreaming in response plans. Since 2023, 55 countries have conducted JEEs, implementing the new edition of the tool with the gender indicator, with scores being made available online.[87]

The normative effect of such indicators should not be underestimated. Building on technical expertise and strongly influencing the adoption of new laws and regulations by countries, they benefit from the legitimacy of expert knowledge and indicate *how* treaty obligations are concretely implemented in practice in national jurisdictions. Moreover, while this was not the case before, all JEE reports are now available on the WHO website, increasing transparency and accountability at the implementation phase. Given their potential as monitoring mechanisms in the global health security legal regime, indicators can thus significantly contribute to gender mainstreaming in health emergency planning.

---

[85] Samson (2012).

[86] WHO (2022b).

[87] WHO IHR JEE Platform (2025).

4 Conclusion: Towards Gender-Integrated Approaches for Future Pandemics

Sitting at the intersection of biology, social norms, health determinants and human rights, women's rights in health emergencies are yet to be fully incorporated into global health security instruments. The recent developments through the amendments of the IHR (2005) as well as the adoption of the Pandemic Agreement have not taken onboard all the lessons learnt from previous pandemics in terms of gendered impact of the outbreaks in countries response and recovery planning. This might be seen as a missed opportunity to fully integrate women's rights-based approaches in the letter of the law in order to address similar experiences in future pandemics. However, other opportunities exist through systemic interpretation of the new instruments and the monitoring systems that will be established and nurtured by the COP, making the Pandemic Agreement a living instrument capable of integrating gender-transformative approaches into future responses to pandemic.

References

Aryal S, Nepal S, Ballav Pant S (2021) Safe abortion services during the COVID-19 pandemic: a cross-sectional study from a tertiary center in Nepal. F1000Res 10:112

Bandiera O et al (2019) The economic lives of young women in the time of Ebola: lessons from an empowerment program. World Bank Group, Washington, DC

Brady E, Nielsen MW, Andersen JP (2021) Lack of consideration of sex and gender in COVID-19 clinical studies. Nat Commun 12:4015

Brechenmacher S (2025) The new global struggles over gender, rights, and family values. Carnegie Endowment for International Peace, Washington, DC

CARE (2020) Building forward: creating a more equitable, gender-just, inclusive, and sustainable world. CARE International, Geneva

CEDAW (1999) General recommendation No. 24: Article 12 of the Convention (women and health). Adopted at the Twentieth Session of the Committee on the Elimination of Discrimination against Women. Contained in Document A/54/38/Rev.1, chap. I

CEDAW Committee (2020) Guidance note on CEDAW and COVID-19, para. 2

Clark H, Johnson Sirleaf E (2025) The pandemic agreement is a milestone: now it is time for action in national capitals. Lancet 405:2109–2111

Correia T (2025) The pandemic agreement: what's next? Int J Health Plann Manag 40:1029–1032

Criado Perez C (2019) Invisible women: data bias in a world designed for men. Abrams Press, New York, p 411

Davies SE, Bennett B (2016) A gendered human rights analysis of Ebola and Zika: locating gender in global health emergencies. Int Aff 92:1041–1060

Davies SE, Wenham C (2024) Gender inclusion in the pandemic agreement: a growing gap? International Peace Institute, New York

Donà A (2022) Gender equality in the Italian recovery and resilience plan: the depoliticizing effects of the technocratic Draghi government. Contemp Ital Polit 14(4):458–471

Foucault M (1965) Madness and civilisation: a history of insanity in the age of reason. Random House, New York

Foucault M (1975) Discipline and punish: the birth of the prison. Vintage Books, New York

Foucault M (1981) The history of sexuality, vol 1: an introduction. Vintage Books, New York

Foucault M (2003) 'Society must be defended': lectures at the Collège de France. Translated by D. Macey. Picador, New York
Gales MK, Yonally Phillips EL, Zilversmit Pao L et al (2025) Beyond COVID-19, the case for collecting, analysing and using sex-disaggregated data and gendered data to inform outbreak response: a scoping review. BMJ Global Health 10:e015900
George A (2007) Human resources for health: a gender analysis. Background paper prepared for the women and Gender Equity Knowledge Network and the Health Systems Knowledge Network of the WHO Commission on Social Determinants of Health. World Health Organization, Geneva
Global Health Law Consortium, International Commission of Jurists (2024) The principles and guidelines on human rights and public health emergencies. J Glob Health Law 1(1):122–143
Grais RF, Neuzil KM, Rees H, Toscano CM (2025) Protecting mother and baby: learnings from an Ebola vaccination campaign on the evolving landscape of vaccines and pregnancy. PLoS Med 22(2):e1004530
Harcourt W (2022) Body politics. In: Shepherd L, Hamilton C (eds) Gender matters in global body politics: a feminist introduction to international relations. Taylor & Francis, Abingdon
Harman S (2016) Ebola, gender and conspicuously invisible women in global health governance. Third World Q 37(3):524–541
Hawkes S et al (2022) Sex-disaggregated data matters: tracking the impact of COVID-19 on the health of women and men. Econ Polit (Bologna) 39(1):55–73
Hawkes S et al (2025) Achieving gender justice for global health equity: the Lancet Commission on gender and global health. Lancet 405(10487):1373–1438
Heidari S, Babor TF, De Castro P et al (2016) Sex and gender equity in research: rationale for the SAGER guidelines and recommended use. Res Integr Peer Rev 1:2
Independent Panel for Pandemic Preparedness and Response (2021) COVID-19: make it the last pandemic, Geneva
Institute for Women's Policy Research (2025) Women at work five years since the start of the COVID-19 pandemic: any progress?, March 2025
International Labour Organization (ILO) (2021a) Building forward fairer: women's rights to work and at work at the core of the COVID-19 recovery. Policy brief, July 2021
International Labour Organization (ILO) (2021b) Strengthening gender measures and data in the COVID-19 era: an urgent need for change. ILO, Geneva, p 11
International Law Commission (2006) Fragmentation of International Law, Report of the Study Group of the International Law Commission, finalized by Mr. Martti Koskenniemi, A/CN.4/L.682 and Add.1
Jones SA et al (2016) Women and babies are dying but not of Ebola: the effect of the Ebola virus epidemic on the availability, uptake and outcomes of maternal and newborn health services in Sierra Leone. BMJ Glob Health 1(3):e000065
Lee KW (2025) A blueprint or a band-aid? The promise and peril of the WHO pandemic agreement. J Public Health Policy 46(3):717–721
McKinzie M et al (2025) Beyond COVID-19: the case for collecting, analysing and using sex-disaggregated and gendered data to inform outbreak response—a scoping review. BMJ Glob Health 10:e015900
Mhazo AT, Maponga CC (2022) Governing a pandemic: biopower and the COVID-19 response in Zimbabwe. BMJ Glob Health 7:e009667
Mofokeng T (2025) Reclaiming sexual and reproductive rights through a decolonial lens. Health Hum Rights 27(1):91–94
OHCHR (2020) Statement by the UN Working Group on discrimination against women and girls: responses to the COVID-19 pandemic must not discount women and girls
OHCHR (2021) Report of the Special Rapporteur on the right of everyone to the enjoyment of the highest attainable standard of physical and mental health, Tlaleng Mofokeng, 'Sexual and reproductive health rights: challenges and opportunities during the COVID-19 pandemic.' UN Doc A/76/172, 16 July 2021

Phillips G et al (2023) Women on the frontline: exploring the gendered experience for Pacific healthcare workers during the COVID-19 pandemic. Lancet Reg Health West Pac 42:100961

Rioseco S (2023) Conferences of the parties beyond international environmental law: how COPs influence the content and implementation of their parent treaties. Leiden J Int Law 36:699–719

Samson M (2012) Indicators as a monitoring tool for the implementation of global health law. Global Administrative Law Working Papers, IRPA

Shah R, Hanna NM, Loo CE et al (2025) The global impact of the COVID-19 pandemic on delays and disruptions in cancer care services: a systematic review and meta-analysis. Nat Cancer 6:194–204

Singh K (2025) Women are poorly represented in clinical trials. That's problematic. Nature India

Singh S et al (2021) How an outbreak became a pandemic: a chronological analysis of crucial junctures and international obligations in the early months of the COVID-19 pandemic. Lancet 398(10316):2109–2124

Sircar NR et al (2025) Building rights-based implementation after the pandemic agreement. Health Hum Rights

Smith J (2019) Overcoming the 'tyranny of the urgent': integrating gender into disease outbreak preparedness and response. Gend Dev 27(2):355–369

Tam MW, Davis VH, Ahluwalia M, Lee RS, Ross LE (2024) Impact of COVID-19 on access to and delivery of sexual and reproductive healthcare services in countries with universal healthcare systems: a systematic review. PLoS One 19(2):e0294744

The Lancet Global Health (2022) The future of the international health regulations. Lancet Glob Health 10(7):e927

UN Women (2025) Women's rights in review 30 years after Beijing

UN Women, UNDP (2022) Government responses to COVID-19: lessons on gender equality for a world in turmoil

United Nations (2022) Calling vaccine inequity 'biggest moral failure of our times', Secretary-General says focus must be on fairness, in COVID-19 Tools Accelerator launch remarks. UN Doc SG/SM/21137

VanBenschoten H et al (2022) Impact of the COVID-19 pandemic on access to and utilisation of services for sexual and reproductive health: a scoping review. BMJ Glob Health 7:e009594

Wenham C (2021) Feminist global health security. Oxford University Press, Oxford

Wenham C, Potluru A (2024) Costing the intergovernmental negotiating body (INB) process. PLoS Glob Public Health 4(12):e0003978

World Economic Forum (2025) Prescription for change: policy recommendations for women's health research. White paper, June 2025

World Health Organization (WHO) (2007) Women's health and human rights: monitoring the implementation of CEDAW. WHO, Geneva

World Health Organisation, International Health Regulations (2005) Resolution WHA58.3, adopted on 23 May 2005; entered into force on 15 June 2007

World Health Organization (WHO) (2015) Health care workers infections in Guinea, Liberia and Sierra Leone: a preliminary report, 21 May 2015

World Health Organization (WHO) (2019) Delivered by women, led by men: a gender and equity analysis of the global health and social workforce. Human Resources for Health Observer Series No. 24, Geneva

World Health Organization (WHO) (2022a) Draft annotated outline of a WHO convention, agreement or other international instrument on pandemic prevention, preparedness and response. UN Doc A/INB/1/12, 14 June 2022

World Health Organization (WHO) (2022b) Joint external evaluation tool: International Health Regulations (2005), 3rd edn. WHO, Geneva

World Health Organization (WHO) (2022c) Summary report on the results of the INB digital platform. UN Doc A/INB/1/9, 3 June 2022

World Health Organization (WHO) (2023a) INB draft bureau text of WHO CA+. UN Doc A/INB/5/6, June 2023

World Health Organization (WHO) (2023b) Zero draft of the WHO CA+ for the consideration of the Intergovernmental Negotiating Body at its fourth meeting. UN Doc A/INB/4/3, 1 February 2023

World Health Organization (WHO) (2025) IHR Joint external evaluation (JEE) platform. https://extranet.who.int/sph/jee/

Zerubavel E (2018) Taken for granted: the remarkable power of the unremarkable. Princeton University Press, Princeton

Zucker I, Prendergast BJ (2020) Sex differences in pharmacokinetics predict adverse drug reactions in women. Biol Sex Differ 11:1–14

Mélanie Samson holds a Ph.D. in Global Health Law from the Geneva Graduate Institute and Panthéon-Sorbonne (Paris), as well as an MPH in Global Health Leadership from New York University. She completed a postdoctoral fellowship at NYU on global standards for health technologies and has published extensively on global health governance and access to care in low- and middle-income countries. She is currently Senior Technical Officer for Women's Health at the Global Surgery Foundation (Geneva, Switzerland). She has also been teaching global health law and regulation as a Lecturer at Sciences Po Paris for the past 10 years. Her career of over two decades has focused on rights-based approaches to public health, with expertise spanning global health governance, access to essential medicines, and the delivery of quality care. She has contributed to initiatives in cancer control, maternal and child health, and HIV, with a particular emphasis on vulnerable populations in resource-limited settings.

Women's Bodies, Abortion Law in the UK and the Right to Abortion in Emergencies

Stephanie Palmer

Abstract The COVID-19 pandemic raised specific problems for women seeking abortions in the UK. During the pandemic the Departments of Health in England, Scotland and Wales permitted telemedical abortion services with an online consultation and abortion pills sent by post. Such measures were not permitted in Northern Ireland. An unanticipated consequence of the telemedical service permitting at-home early medical abortion was a rise in the criminal law investigations and prosecutions for abortion-related offences across Great Britain. This was particularly evident in England and Wales but far fewer charges were initiated in Scotland. In Northern Ireland, the situation concerning abortion services was complex and difficult. Although abortion was decriminalised in Northern Ireland in 2019, pregnant women had restricted access to abortion procedures until December 2022. In addition to a lack of access to telemedical early abortion practices as in the rest of the UK, restricted services and travel difficulties further undermined the ability of pregnant women in Northern Ireland to obtain an abortion. Traditionally many women from Northern Ireland travelled to other parts of the United Kingdom to access an abortion.

1 Introduction

Law assigns meaning to bodies and significant political, social and legal consequences flow from these assignments. The legal person is conceptualised as a self-sufficient, self-directing agent whose relations with others are antagonistic. Thus, laws on abortion pose a challenge to these usually accepted assignations. The body and characteristics of the pregnant woman are measured against the unstated norm

S. Palmer (✉)
Faculty of Law, University of Cambridge, Cambridge, UK
e-mail: sp10002@cam.ac.uk

M. Balestrieri and A. Cauduro (eds.), *The Legal Anatomy of the Body*, Ius Gentium: Comparative Perspectives on Law and Justice 142,
https://doi.org/10.1007/978-3-032-26434-3_15

of the 'legal person' who is implicitly male. In some ways the legal person of criminal, tort and medical law are in tension with the pregnant person.[1] The law is very concerned with the choices that a pregnant woman makes and may place the pregnant woman and foetus in an antagonistic relationship.

Any analysis of abortion law is haunted by the decision of the Supreme Court of the USA to overturn *Roe v Wade* which had decided that the Constitution protected the right to have an abortion.[2] After standing as a precedent for 50 years, the decision in *Dobbs v Jackson Women's Health Organization* was the first time in its history that the Supreme Court has taken away a fundamental right.[3] Since the *Dobbs* judgment, control over abortion has been returned to each state and many of them have chosen to ban or severely limit abortion rights. The medical profession must navigate between criminal law prohibitions against terminating a pregnancy and the emergency care needed to save the patient's life or health.[4] The situation in the USA is not directly applicable to the UK but it does remind us that no gains in rights protection can be taken for granted. Abortion remains a contested subject in the UK.

This chapter explores the law on abortion and the disparities in abortion service provision which emerged during the COVID-19 pandemic and the consequences for the autonomy of women and pregnant persons. The interim provisions introduced in England, Wales and Scotland and designed to meet the challenge posed by the pandemic lockdown had unintended consequences for some women seeking abortion. The long-standing discrepancy between the provision of abortion services available in Northern Ireland as opposed to that in the rest of the UK became even more visible due to the pandemic travel restrictions. This chapter also considers the long-term consequences on abortion law which have evolved due to managing abortion services and women's health through the pandemic.

2 Abortion Law in England Wales and Scotland *Before the COVID-19 Pandemic*

Before the enactment of the Abortion Act 1967, illegal abortions were the leading cause of avoidable maternal mortality in the United Kingdom. The Abortion Act was a private member's Bill, introduced by Mr. David Steel MP, and it is one of a handful of examples where such legislation has been passed.[5] As abortion is considered a question of conscience there is a free vote and Members of Parliament decide how

[1] In this paper I primarily refer to pregnant girls and woman but it should be read as including transgender men who choose to bear a child.

[2] 410 U.S. 113 (1973).

[3] 597 U.S. 215 (2022).

[4] Fox (2023).

[5] As well as the Abortion Act 1967, other examples include Murder (Abolition of the Death Penalty) Act 1965; Sexual Offences Act 1967 (decriminalising homosexual acts in private between consenting men in England and Wales); Civil Partnerships, Marriages and Deaths Act 2019.

to vote without pressure from the party whips. Numerous factors led to the pressure to change abortion laws. Despite the legal prohibition in place, abortion was not unusual before 1967. Clandestine 'backstreet' abortionists and sympathetic doctors were prepared to risk prosecution and perform abortions. Thousands of women had an abortion each year and many of them died. It was usually the poorer more vulnerable members of society who paid the price with their lives. This transformative legislation ended 'the sordid injustice of well-to-do women paying for abortions on demand in private clinics and less fortunate souls risking life and limb in the hands of back-street abortionists'.[6]

The Abortion Act applied to England, Wales and Scotland.[7] It did not extend to Northern Ireland. Several rationales explain this omission. Health was a devolved matter and, at the time in Northern Ireland, an exclusion on matters of sexual morality was considered uncontroversial.[8] Perhaps even more telling was the fear that an attempt to extend this legislation to Northern Ireland would lead to the failure of the whole Bill.[9]

The new legislation permitted abortions in specified circumstances, but abortion was not decriminalised. In England, Wales and Northern Ireland, the criminal law still governed the provision of abortion through the Offences Against the Person Act 1861 (hereafter OAPA), ss 58 and 59 and the Infant Life Preservation Act 1929. In Scotland there are no equivalent underlying statutory criminal offences. However, abortion is potentially a criminal offence under the common law, unless carried out under the terms of the Abortion Act 1967. Under the Abortion Act, doctors authorising the performance of an abortion had a legal defence against its criminality. The law provided that in England, Scotland and Wales, there is no offence when a pregnancy is terminated by a registered medical practitioner 'if two medical practitioners are of the opinion formed in good faith' that one or more of the following conditions are met:

> (a) that the pregnancy has not exceeded its 24th week and that the continuance of the pregnancy would involve risk, greater than if the pregnancy were terminated, of injury to the physical or mental health of the pregnant woman or any existing children of her family; or
> (b) that the termination is necessary to prevent grave permanent injury to the physical or mental health of the pregnant woman; or
> (c) that the continuance of the pregnancy would involve risk to the life of the pregnant woman, greater than if the pregnancy were terminated; or
> (d) that there is a substantial risk that if the child were born it would suffer from such physical or mental abnormalities as to be seriously handicapped.[10]

---

[6] Boothroyd (2001), p. 196.

[7] In Scotland, control over abortion and the Abortion Act 1967 has been devolved to the Scottish Parliament since 2016.

[8] See Sheldon et al. (2022).

[9] Ibid, Chap. 6, The Battle for Northern Ireland.

[10] Abortion Act 1967, s.1.

The 1967 Act was revised in the Human Fertilisation and Embryology Act 1990 which specified an upper legal time limit for an abortion in some circumstances.[11] Currently the upper limit is 24 weeks but as the viability of a foetus is now below that limit, it remains a contentious issue. There is no time restriction applying to the abortion of a foetus which may be born with serious disabilities.[12]

Although hailed as a liberal landmark law, it did not reflect ideas about the rights over one's body. Women were given no right to abort a pregnancy. Rather the legislation protected doctors from the threat of criminal prosecution where it was believed that 'in good faith' an abortion should be performed in accordance with the prescribed grounds. Thus, in law, decision-making power in abortion lies with the medical profession. For some feminists, this medical model controlling abortion remains a key institutional site through which men control women's bodies. Sally Sheldon claims that far from being a liberalising measure, the Abortion Act was about putting in place a more rigorous and subtle system of medical control over women's fertility.[13]

Since 1967, clinical medicine has evolved substantially. Whereas in 1967 all abortions were carried out through surgical procedures, most are now medical abortions involving taking two different medicines to end the pregnancy. Since 2022, medical abortions are usually carried out in the home rather than in a clinical setting.[14] Despite this significant change, the legislation governing abortions has not been reviewed, and most abortions remain a criminal offence unless there is a statutory or common law defence.[15] While abortion is still governed by the criminal law, it is widely considered today to be a healthcare matter rather than an aspect of the criminal law.[16] The law does not formally acknowledge a women's right to abortion but the system primarily operates as though there is a right to an abortion, even if strictly this is not so.[17]

The European Convention on Human Rights has also influenced the law on abortion and Articles 2, 3, 8 and 14 ECHR have been considered by the courts. The Human

---

[11] The 1967 Act, as initially enacted, did not included a specific upper gestational time limit for abortions.

[12] Abortion Act 1967, s. 1(1) (d).

[13] Sheldon (1997), p. 30.

[14] The Abortion Act was amended by the Health and Care Act 2022. S. 3D Abortion Act now authorizes the woman's ordinary residence as a place where abortifacients can be self-administered, if the patient has had a prior in-person or telemedical consultation with a doctor, registered nurse, or registered midwife. See further details below.

[15] *R v. Bourne* [1939] 1 KB 687 found that there was a common law defence of necessity for a doctor facing a criminal law charge of procuring a miscarriage.

[16] The Scottish Government has commissioned an Expert Group in Scotland, chaired by Professor Anna Glasier, to review the law on abortion. The report, released on November 14, 2025, states that the law should be decriminalised and that access to abortion should be available up to 24 weeks. The group agreed unanimously that current Scottish abortion law is not fit for purpose and that alternative models should be considered. See the Scottish Legal News (2025).

[17] Romanis (2023).

Rights Act 1998 requires that a domestic UK court or tribunal, in determining a question that has arisen in connection with a Convention right, must take into account any 'judgment, decision, declaration or advisory opinion' of the European Court of Human Rights.[18] The European Court of Human Rights has considered abortion rights but it has not recognised a right to abortion. The European Court in *A, B and C v Ireland* held that 'legislation regulating the interruption of pregnancy touches upon the sphere of private life', which included 'the right to personal autonomy, personal development and to establish and develop relationships with other human beings and the outside world', as well as a 'person's physical and psychological integrity'.[19] Although the European Court found that Article 8 was engaged, it upheld the right of Irish law to prohibit abortion, stating 'that the impugned prohibition in Ireland struck a fair balance between the right….of the applicants to respect for their private lives and the rights invoked on behalf of the unborn'.[20] Nor has the European Court decided that a foetus is the subject of Convention rights.[21] The European Court has not found that the foetus has Article 2 (right to life) rights but nor has it ruled out the possibility that some 'safeguards may be extended to the unborn child'. Although some jurisdictions have recognised the foetus as rights bearing, to do so may lead to a challenge to the autonomy of the pregnant woman and potentially expose her to grave risks.[22] Catherine MacKinnon strongly asserts that 'the only point of recognizing fetal personhood, or a separate fetal entity, is to assert the interests of the fetus *against* the pregnant woman'.[23]

The competing rights of the unborn was one issue relied upon to challenge the compatibility of the Abortion Act with the Human Rights Act 1998 in *R (on the application of Crowter) v. Secretary of State.*[24] The case concerned a challenge by applicants with Down Syndrome, that an abortion after 24 weeks where there was a substantial risk that the child would be born with 'such physical or mental abnormalities as to be seriously handicapped' (the terminology used in the Act) would be a breach of Convention rights.[25] In the Divisional Court, an argument was made on the basis of Article 2 that the Abortion Act 'places in danger the life of a disabled unborn child….. at a time when it is both viable and sentient, by permitting

[18] Human Rights Act 1998 s.2(1).

[19] [2010] ECHR 2032, [106]-[107].

[20] Ibid. at [241]. The law in Ireland has been transformed by a constitutional amendment in 2018 which repealed the Eighth Amendment.

[21] For a discussion on the legal status of the foetus, see Herring (2025), pp. 418–422. Vo v France (2005) 40 EHRR 12.

[22] From 1983 to 2018 the Irish Constitution protected the right to life of the foetus. A system that permits abortion solely on the basis of a threat to life of the pregnant woman may expose the pregnant woman to very serious risks. See the case of Savita Halappanver who died in an Irish hospital following a miscarriage when she was 17 weeks pregnant. See Houston (2013).

[23] MacKinnon (1991), p. 131. See also RR v Poland (2011) 53 EHRR 31at [186].

[24] [2021] EWHC 2536 (Admin); [2022] 1 WLR 2513.

[25] Abortion Act 1967, s. (1)(d). In the Divisional Court, grounds relating to Articles 2 and 3 as well as Articles 8 and 14 were also considered. The case was dismissed. The Court of Appeal did not give permission to appeal relating to Articles 2 and 3.

abortion in circumstances where, and at a time at which, it would not be permitted in the case of a non-disabled child'. In rejecting the claim, the Divisional Court noted that the European Court has 'never decided that a foetus, even one post-viability, is the bearer of Convention rights, including Article 2'.[26] Permission to appeal to the Court of Appeal on this point was rejected, implicitly suggesting that the reasoning of the lower court was accepted. The arguments in the Court of Appeal concerned only Articles 8 and 14. The appellants claimed that the Abortion Act '*perpetuates and reinforces* negative cultural stereotypes about people with handicaps by sending a message that their lives are less valuable'.[27] They unsuccessfully sought a declaration of incompatibility under section 4 of Human Rights Act.[28] Interestingly, the Court of Appeal acknowledged that the effect of the Abortion Act is to provide a defence to an otherwise criminal action, but Lord Justice Underhill chose to characterise section 1 of the Abortion Act as conferring a 'right' to an abortion.[29]

The Abortion Act 1967 has created an 'abortion-permissive regime', a legal framework that enables the provision of abortion in some circumstances but restrictions remain.[30] This system has improved access but further legal reform is desirable. Recently, the Scottish government commissioned a report to review the existing abortion law.[31] The Abortion Law Expert Group reported in November 2025. One conclusion was that the current system requiring approval from two doctors was 'anachronistic, paternalistic and failed to reflect best modern practice'.[32] They also supported legal recognition of a woman's right to choose on request, at least within gestational limits. The report states that 'it is time for an abortion law that reflects the reality of current clinical practice where abortions are safely provided in the best interests of women'.[33]

3 The Law on Abortion in Northern Ireland

The Abortion Act 1967 has never applied in Northern Ireland. The devolution arrangements meant that Northern Ireland had competence to legislate on abortion and had done so 'in a far more restrictive manner than in the other parts of the United

[26] [2021] EWHC 2536 (Admin); [2022] 1 WLR 2513 at [62].

[27] [2022] EWCA Civ 1559 at [3]. See also Tongue (2022), pp. 177–187, Robinson (2024), pp. 218–230 and Sheldon (2023), p. 104.

[28] The Human Rights Act 1998 does not permit the courts to strike down legislation if there is inconsistency with primary legislation. Section 4 states that the courts can issue a declaration of incompatibility if they are unable to interpret legislation consistently with Convention rights. This a notice to the government and the legislature that there is an incompatibility with the law. These declarations have no legal effect.

[29] [2022] EWCA Civ 1559, [2023] WLR 989 at [1].

[30] Romanis (2023).

[31] Expert Group Report Scottish Government (2025).

[32] Ibid.

[33] Ibid.

Kingdom'.[34] Prior to 22 October 2019, abortion was only permissible in Northern Ireland if there was a risk to the pregnant woman's life or of serious long-term or permanent injury to their physical or mental health.[35] Procuring an abortion on other grounds was a criminal offence under the Offences Against the Person Act 1861 (OAPA). Women had to travel to Great Britain and fund the cost of travel and treatment themselves until in June 2017, the UK Department of Health and Social Care agreed to fund abortions.[36]

In 2010, an application was made under the Optional Protocol to the Committee on the Elimination of Discrimination Against Women (CEDAW) by Alliance for Choice, the Family Planning Association and Northern Ireland Women's European Platform alleging that the restrictive access to abortion in Northern Ireland was in violation of rights protected by the Convention. After an inquiry, the CEDAW Committee in 2018 published a highly critical report of the restrictive abortion laws in Northern Ireland.[37] It found that women and girls in Northern Ireland are subjected 'to grave and systematic violations of rights' through being compelled to either travel outside Northern Ireland to procure a legal abortion or to carry their pregnancy to term. Women who were denied access to safe abortion in Northern Ireland conveyed 'their experiences of extreme vulnerability, physical and psychological stress, mental anguish, desperation and isolation in seeking appropriate medical treatment to terminate their pregnancy'.[38] The Committee recommended that legislation should provide for expanded grounds to legalise abortion, at least in the following cases:

(i) Threat to the pregnant woman's physical or mental health without conditionality of 'long-term or permanent' effects;
(ii) Rape and incest; and
(iii) Severe foetal impairment, including FFA (Fatal Foetal Anomaly).[39]

The damming CEDAW report also prompted the Northern Ireland Human Rights Commission (NIHRC) to bring proceedings in Northern Ireland to challenge the compatibility of the law with the European Convention on Human Rights. The case eventually made its way to the Supreme Court of the United Kingdom. *In R v Northern Ireland Rights Commission's Application for Judicial Review* the Supreme Court had to consider the compatibility of the highly restrictive legislation in Northern Ireland with the Convention rights.[40] A majority of four (Lord Reed DPSC, Lady Black JSC, Lord Lloyd-Jones JSC and Lord Mance) decided that the Commission did not have standing to bring the proceedings and, accordingly, the Court had no jurisdiction to make a declaration of incompatibility. Nevertheless, a different majority of the Court (Lady Hale PSC, Lord Kerr JSC, Lord Wilson JSC and Lord Mance) were of the

[34] Hughes et al. (2025), p. 274.

[35] Limited exceptions to Abortion were set out in the Criminal Justice Act (NI) 1945 and the common law. See *R v Bourne* [1939] 1 KB 687.

[36] See BBC news (2017).

[37] UN. Committee on the Elimination of Discrimination against Women (2018).

[38] Ibid., [33].

[39] Ibid., [85]. See also Women and Equalities Committee (2019).

[40] [2018] UKSC 27; [2019] 1 All ER 173.

view that the Northern Ireland legislation was incompatible with the right to respect for private and family life, in Article 8 of the Convention, insofar as it prohibited abortion even in cases of rape, incest and (Lady Black concurring on this point) fatal foetal abnormality. The interference with a pregnant woman's Article 8 rights in those categories was not justified. The majority did not consider that the Northern Ireland legislation was incompatible with Article 8 insofar as it did not permit abortion on grounds of non-fatal foetal abnormalities. Lady Hale also stated:

But the community undoubtedly does have a moral interest in protecting the life, health and welfare of the unborn—it is that interest which underlies many areas of the law, including the regulation of assisted reproduction, and of the practice of midwifery, as well as of the termination of pregnancy. But the community also has an interest in protecting the life, health and welfare of the pregnant woman—that interest also underlies the regulation of assisted reproduction, of midwifery and of the termination of pregnancy. And pregnant women are undoubtedly rights-holders under the both the Convention and domestic law with autonomy as well as health and welfare rights. The question, therefore, is how the balance is to be struck between the two.[41]

The CEDAW Committee's report and the findings of the Supreme Court placed pressure on the UK Government to take steps to rectify this breach of human rights. The UK Government remained responsible for ensuring compliance with the UK's international obligations, but the situation was exacerbated by the absence of a functioning Northern Ireland government. The Northern Ireland government, known as the Stormont, had collapsed in January 2017 due to domestic political reasons. In July 2019, the UK Parliament passed the Northern Ireland (Executive Formation etc) Act 2019 ('the NIEF Act').[42] This Act placed a duty on the UK Government to introduce, by regulations, a new legal framework for abortion in Northern Ireland which ensured that the 'recommendations in paragraphs 85 and 86 of the CEDAW report are implemented in respect of Northern Ireland'.[43] This legislative change resulted in the immediate decriminalisation of abortion through the repeal of sections 58 and 59 of the OAPA, and came into effect on 22 October 2019.[44] It also introduced a moratorium on abortion-related criminal prosecutions.[45] Thus, no police investigations or prosecutions in respect of an offence under sections 58 and 59 of the OAPA (regardless of when an offence may have been committed) could be carried out, and no criminal proceedings could be brought or continued.

The Act also required the Secretary of State to make provision for the purposes of regulating abortions in Northern Ireland, including provision as to the circumstances

[41] Ibid., [21]. A further analysis of this case can be found in Hughes et al. (2025), pp. 275–276. See also *Re Ewart* [2019] NIQB 88 and *Re Ewart* [2020] NIQB 33.

[42] The NIEF Act provided for the extension of the period for forming a Northern Ireland executive until 13 January 2020. During the Committee stage of the Northern Ireland (Executive Formation) Bill 2017-19, the Labour MP, Stella Creasy tabled an amendment to change the law on abortion in Northern Ireland. HC Deb, 9 July 2019, c.232–234.

[43] NIEF Act, s.9(1).

[44] NIEF Act s.9(2).

[45] NIEF Act s.9(3).

in which an abortion may take place, to come into force by 31 March 2020.[46] The Abortion (Northern Ireland) (No. 2) Regulations 2020 permitted abortion in Northern Ireland in the following circumstances:

> Upon request in a pregnancy of up to twelve weeks gestation by a registered medical professional who is of the opinion 'formed in good faith' that the pregnancy has not exceeded twelve weeks;[47]
>
> In a pregnancy of up to twenty-four weeks gestation, where two registered medical practitioners are of the opinion 'formed in good faith' that 'the continuance of the pregnancy would involve risk of injury to the physical or mental health of the pregnant woman which is greater than if the pregnancy were terminated.' [48]
>
> In all cases regardless of the gestation weeks, where:
>
> 'a registered medical professional is of the opinion, formed in good faith, that the termination is immediately necessary to save the life, or to prevent grave permanent injury to the physical or mental health, of the pregnant woman.'[49]
>
> Or where:
>
> 'Two registered medical professionals are of the opinion, formed in good faith, that –
>
> (a) the termination is necessary to prevent grave permanent injury to the physical or mental health of the pregnant woman; or
> (b) the continuance of the pregnancy would involve risk to the life of the pregnant woman which is greater than if the pregnancy were terminated.'[50]
>
> There is also provision for a medical practitioner to terminate a pregnancy where two medical professionals are of the opinion formed in good faith that there is a substantial risk that the condition of the fetus is such that its death is 'likely before, during or shortly after birth; or if the child were born, it would suffer from such physical or mental impairment as to be seriously disabled.' [51]

These provisions are less restrictive than those under the Abortion Act that are in force in Britain. Considerable disquiet and anger in Northern Ireland were evident about the introduction of abortion law through legislation from the UK Parliament. Abortion law is a devolved matter and debates in the Stormont (after a 3-year suspension, the Northern Ireland Assembly reopened on January 11 2020) and an Urgent Question in the House of Commons questioned the legal basis for the UK Government's change to abortion law in Northern Ireland as well as the contents of the regulations.[52]

Despite the dramatic changes to the law on abortion in Northern Ireland, the UK government did not propose to decriminalise abortion in England and the OAPA remains in force in England, Scotland and Wales. As Northern Ireland's abortion

---

[46] NIEF Act s.9(4).

[47] Abortion (Northern Ireland) (No.2) Regulations 2020, 3.

[48] Ibid., 4.

[49] Ibid., 5.

[50] Ibid., 6.

[51] Ibid., at 7.

[52] See Northern Ireland Assembly, Abortion Legislation: Non-fatal Disabilities. 2 June 2020; HC Deb, 4 June, col. 1019. See also E. Rough, Abortion in Northern Ireland: Recent Changes to the Legal Framework, House of Commons Library, February 2025 https://commonslibrary.parliament.uk/research-briefings/cbp-8909/

provision implemented the CEDAW recommendations, it is more in line with human rights requirements than that operating elsewhere in the UK. However, in practice, difficulties arose as the responsibility for commissioning services rested with the Northern Ireland Health Minister and the associated Northern Ireland Departments. A further complexity was that the 2020 Regulations came into effect on 31 March 2020, just a few days after the UK lockdown due to the Covid-19 pandemic. The implications of the pandemic on abortion services in Northern Ireland are discussed in the next section.

4 Abortion Law and COVID-19

Circumstances during the pandemic forced some change to the operation of abortion law in the United Kingdom. Indeed, it has been the catalyst for a rethinking of access to abortion and reproductive health and the actual operation of the law itself. This section focusses on the changes to telemedical abortion services in parts of the UK, the increase in investigations and prosecutions in England, Wales and Scotland and finally the difficulty of access to abortion services in Northern Ireland which were further underlined during the pandemic.

4.1 Telemedical Abortion Services

During the pandemic changes were made to the law concerning early medical abortions. An 'early' medical abortion is defined as one where the pregnancy has not exceeded 9 weeks and 6 days.[53] A medical abortion involves taking two different medicines to terminate the pregnancy, usually at 1 or 2 days apart. Prior to the pandemic in the United Kingdom, an early medical abortion involved taking the first tablet at a hospital or a clinic thus ensuring medical control over the procedure, and the second tablet could then be taken at home. During the pandemic, changes were made to reduce the risk of Covid-19 transmission and to ensure continued access to medical abortion. In England, two temporary measures were approved by the Health Secretary on 30 March 2020.[54] The medical consultation requirements remained the same but there was provision for it to be provided via video link, over the telephone or by other electronic means. Doctors were also permitted to prescribe the medication from their homes rather than in a hospital or clinic. Importantly, for the pregnant woman, it enabled both tablets to be taken at home. Women's homes were made an 'approved place' for the purpose of the Abortion Act 1967. Pursuant to the Act,

[53] Rough (2025).

[54] See Department of Health and Social Care (2020a).

the Secretary of State has the power to approve places, for treatment of the termination of a pregnancy. Scotland[55] and Wales,[56] by their respective governments, also implemented temporary measures to provide for access to early medical abortion along the same lines as in England. In contrast to the rest of the United Kingdom, Northern Ireland made no changes. Under the Abortion (Northern Ireland) (No. 2) Regulations 2020, women in Northern Ireland must take the first tablet in Health and Social Care premises while the second tablet could be taken at home.

Apart from women in Northern Ireland, these measures enabled women to seek advice by telephone, be prescribed and take the drug, without the risks of visiting a hospital or clinic. The temporary measure in England was scheduled to expire on March 22, 2022 or when the Coronavirus Act 2020 provisions ended, whichever was earlier. From November to February 2021, the Department of Health and Social Care held a public consultation on whether to make this temporary measure for early medical abortion a permanent option.[57] A similar consultation was carried out in both Scotland and Wales.[58] In England, over 18,000 individual responses were received. Nearly half of the responses were from individuals affiliated with campaigns and the majority of these were associated with the 'Right to Life' campaign.[59] Unsurprisingly, a high number of these campaign responses said that the temporary measure should end immediately.[60]

In a statement to the House of Commons on 24 February 2022, the Government indicated that it would end the temporary approval put in place during the pandemic. The Minister stated: 'After careful consideration, the Government's view is that the provision of early medical abortion should return to pre-COVID arrangements'.[61] A short-term extension of 6 months to the temporary approval was made. This led to a flurry of statements. The Right to Life spokeswoman approved of the Government's decision to end 'DIY at home abortions' and that risks were linked to the removal of in-person consultation which allows medical practitioners 'to certify gestation and recognise potential coercion or abuse, 'at-home' abortion has presented serious risks to women and girls in abusive situations'.[62] Many medical practitioners reacted with dismay to the government's announcement. On 16 March 2022, Baroness Sug, in the House of Lords, tabled an amendment to the Health and Care Bill. The amendment's purpose was to amend the Abortion Act 1967 in order 'to maintain the existing provision of at-home early medical abortion following a telephone or video consultation

[55] Chief Medical Officer Directorate (2020).

[56] Minister for Health and Social Services (2020).

[57] Department of Health and Social Care (2020b).

[58] Director-General Health and Social Care (2020) and Women and Children's Health Branch (2020).
https://www.gov.wales/sites/default/files/consultations/2020-12/consultation-document.pdf

[59] Department of Health and Social Care (2022). See also Rough (2005) at 1.5.

[60] Ibid.

[61] UK Parliament Health (2022a).

[62] RightToLifenews (2025).

with a clinician'[63] and to reverse the government's original decision. Baroness Sug stated:

> There is overwhelming evidence that allowing women the option to access early medical abortion at home, where clinically appropriate, has created a safer and more effective service. During the pandemic, the largest ever study of UK abortion care, published by the *British Journal of Obstetrics and Gynaecology*, found that this service shortened waiting times and enabled women to receive care much earlier in their pregnancy. Some 150,000 women have received telemedical abortions since March 2020 and the data on the number of women presenting to NHS services with complications has shown a decrease.[64]

A free vote was held on the amendment which passed with a majority of 27 votes.[65]

The disruption to the settled system of early medical abortions caused by the pandemic led to a permanent change in the law. The Health and Care Act of 2022, amended the Abortion Act 1967 by adding sections 1(3B)-(3D).[66] These sections allow a medical practitioner to prescribe abortion medication over the phone or online.[67] A woman's ordinary residence is authorised as a place where abortifacients can be self-administered, if the patient has had a prior in-person or telemedical consultation with a doctor, registered nurse or midwife.[68] In February 2022, the Welsh Government made the temporary arrangements permanent.[69] Early medical abortions at home have also been confirmed in Scotland.[70] Consequently, access to early abortion across Britain has become more efficient and straightforward but these changes do not apply in Northern Ireland.

4.2 *Increased Investigations and Prosecutions*

Historically, there have been few prosecutions of women who have terminated their own pregnancies.[71] There has however been a recent and sharp increase in the number of investigations and prosecutions of offences around 'illegal abortions'.[72] In the period between December 2022 and November 2023, it was reported that one woman was convicted and six women were charged with offences.[73] There were further charges in 2024.[74] Stella Creasy, Labour MP and a campaigner on reproductive rights,

[63] HL Deb.16 March 2022 c. 407.

[64] HL Deb. 16 March 2022 c. 407–408.

[65] The government tabled 'an amendment in lieu'. HC Deb, 30 March 2022, c 898–900.

[66] Health and Care Act 2022, s.178.

[67] Wilson (2023), p. 158.

[68] Abortion Act 1967, s.1(3D).

[69] Morgan (2022).

[70] Scottish Government (2022).

[71] An example is *R v Catt* [2013] EWCA Crim 1187.

[72] Sheldon and Lord (2023).

[73] Williams (2023). See also Gibbons (2023).

[74] Royal College of Obstetricians and Gynaecologists (2024).

said: 'We cannot ignore the fact that hundreds of women are still being investigated in often the most gruelling circumstances, having had a late-term miscarriage, or not even knowing they were pregnant at all. Instead of a counsellor, they get a police officer visiting them'.[75] An explanation for the increase in investigations and prosecutions is not immediately clear. Sally Sheldon has suggested that the launch of telemedicine during the pandemic lockdown and greater awareness of abortion pills among health professionals and law officers 'fuelled suspicion regarding unexplained pregnancy loss, particularly when late in pregnancy…'.[76]

An infamous example is the case of Carla Foster who was charged with an offence of administering poison with intent to procure her own miscarriage contrary to s.58 OAPA. During the pandemic lockdown Ms. Foster, then aged 44, contacted the British Pregnancy Advisory Service by telephone and told them that she was approximately 7 weeks and 6 days pregnant. She was posted abortifacient medication. When it arrived, she took the medication and began labour. Paramedics unsuccessfully tried to resuscitate the foetus. Medical investigations estimated that the foetus (subsequently named Lily) was between 32- and 34-weeks gestation. Her cause of death was 'a combination of stillbirth and maternal use of abortifacients'.[77] The cause of Lily's death only became known because of subsequent admissions by Foster to medical staff and the police. The prosecution submitted evidence of internet searches which they claimed revealed that she was aware that her pregnancy was advanced and outside the permissions of the Abortion Act. She was convicted and sentenced to 28 months imprisonment. Foster successfully appealed her sentence. In reducing the sentence to 14 months, wholly suspended, the Court of Appeal emphasised mitigating factors; she had three children, including two who had special needs and during lockdown, she had been forced to live with her former partner who was not the father of the child that she was carrying. She was described as being in a state of emotional turmoil. The judge stated that this was 'a sad case that calls for compassion, not punishment, and it is one where no useful purpose is achieved by detaining Ms Foster in custody'.[78]

The case of Ms. Foster attracted considerable media attention in the UK and prompted new guidance for healthcare professionals when dealing with the police or other agencies following abortion, pregnancy loss and unexpected delivery. Concern at the increasing number of police investigations following later gestation abortion and pregnancy loss, The Royal College of Obstetricians and Gynaecologists (RCOG) published best practice guidelines for healthcare professionals unambiguously stating that it is never in the public interest to investigate a patient who is suspected of ending their own pregnancy.[79] It also confirms that healthcare professionals are under no legal obligation to contact the police following an abortion. In fact, the guidance states: 'Do not call the police or external agencies if a woman divulges, or you are

[75] Das (2025).

[76] Ibid. Sheldon and Lord (2023), p. 524.

[77] *Foster v R* [2023] EWCA Crim 1196 at [9]–[10].

[78] Ibid., at [11].

[79] Royal College of Obstetricians and Gynaecologists (2024).

suspicious, that she may have sought to end her own pregnancy unless she has given explicit consent to do so, or you consider it justified in her best interests'.[80] The President of the RCOG stated: 'We firmly believe it is never in the public interest to investigate and prosecute women who have sought to end their own pregnancy. These women should be treated with care and compassion, without judgement or fear of imprisonment'.[81]

In March 2025, the Labour Government introduced the Crime and Policing Bill dealing with, amongst other matters, anti-social behaviour, knife crime and sexual offenses. Tonia Antoniazzi MP introduced an amendment to the Bill which 'would disapply existing criminal law related to abortion from a woman acting in relation to her own pregnancy at any gestation, removing the threat of investigation, arrest, prosecution, or imprisonment'.[82] The change would decriminalize the woman's actions, but it would not alter the existing legal framework for healthcare provision, such as telemedicine, the time limits and grounds set out in the Abortion Act 1967. It would disapply section 58 (administering drugs or using instruments to procure an abortion) and section 59 (procuring drugs etc. to cause an abortion) OAPA 1861 and the Infant Life Preservation Act 1929. On June 17, MPs voted in favour of the amendment. In spite of pushback from members of the House of Lords who thought that abortion should remain a criminal offence, the amendment was passed and the Bill received Royal Assent on April 29, 2026. Section 241 of the Act removes women from the criminal law related to abortion in England and Wales. No criminal offence is committed by a woman acting in relation to her own pregnancy.

Telemedical abortion services were introduced in response to the pandemic but the unforeseen downside of this change was the increased vulnerability and surveillance of women seeking abortions which was exacerbated by the Covid lockdown. On the positive side the RCOG has clearly stated its position that healthcare professionals are under no legal obligation to contact the police. The decriminalising of abortion in the Crime and Policing Act 2026 is now law. Although this change is to be welcomed, it would be preferable for a more holistic look at the operation of the out-dated abortion law which continues to govern how and when abortions are provided.

4.3 Access to Abortion Services in Northern Ireland

The new legal framework on abortion was introduced into Northern Ireland by the UK Government. Since 22 October 2019, abortion has been legal in Northern Ireland. Although the Abortion (Northern Ireland) Regulations 2020 came into effect on 31

---

[80] Ibid.

[81] Ibid. See also Royal College of Obstetricians and Gynaecologists (2025a).

[82] Member's explanatory statement (2025). See also Royal College of Obstetricians and Gynaecologists (2025b).

March 2020, access to abortion services were not immediately commissioned.[83] The Executive and Assembly in Northern Ireland were restored in January 2020 and the Department of Health in Northern Ireland was responsible, in line with the Regulations, for the overseeing and implementing abortion services in Northern Ireland. Considerable reticence was displayed by the government departments responsible for implementing the changes to abortion law. In a debate in the Northern Ireland Assembly on 2 June 2020, Joanne Bunting MLA tabled a motion rejecting the imposition of abortion legislation that extends to all non-fatal disabilities and stated:

> You will be voting to reject the imposition of abortion legislation on Northern Ireland. Abortion is a devolved matter and we are responsible for reflecting our society's values in this area, not Great Britain. You will be voting for life.[84]

The amendment was carried and although this vote did not alter the Regulations, it was viewed by those opposed to the changes as a strong message that the Regulations were not supported by a majority in the Assembly.

A few days before the Regulations came into effect, the UK lockdown commenced because of the Covid-19 pandemic. It also coincided with the introduction of travel restrictions in the UK. Women who would previously have travelled to other parts of the UK for abortion services were unable to do so. One report suggested that two women attempted suicide after flights were cancelled and they were unable to travel.[85] As there were no flights, women wishing to access abortion services in England had to take an 8-hour ferry trip each way. Access to services continued to be limited as the Department of Health failed to commission the comprehensive service that was urgently needed. Some trusts (the statutory bodies responsible for integrating health and social care services across various regions in Northern Ireland) provided early medical abortion service but in many trusts, this was suspended. It was not possible to have a medical abortion at home, surgical options were not available and there was no service for women who were above 9 weeks and 6 days gestation.[86]

In response to the poor abortion services during the Covid pandemic, the Northern Ireland Human Rights Commission (NIHRC) initiated legal proceedings against the Department of Health, Secretary of State for Northern Ireland and the Northern Ireland Executive.[87] The NIHRC expressed deep concern at 'the lack of commissioned and funded abortion services in Northern Ireland leading to a vacuum for many women and girls seeking such services. Women and girls seeking an abortion then have to travel to England, elsewhere in Ireland and pay for a service or to use unregulated services.'[88] The headline challenge was that despite the obligation

[83] Drafting errors were noted in the first Regulations and they were rewritten as The Abortion (Northern Ireland) (No. 2) Regulations. They were laid before both Houses of the UK Parliament and came into force as law on the 14 May 2020. The Abortion Regulations 2 are materially identical to the Abortion Regulations 1.

[84] Northern Ireland Assembly (2020).

[85] Kirk et al. (2021), p. 293.

[86] Ibid., p. 295.

[87] [2021] NIQB 91.

[88] Northern Ireland Human Rights Commission (2021).

imposed on the Secretary of State by the 2019 Act and Article 8 ECHR, there is no State organised abortion services available to pregnant women and girls in May 2021. Any provision available is piecemeal, dependent on where a woman or girl may live and whether she is less than 10 weeks pregnant.[89] The Court identified the reasons for this situation. First, the Secretary of State had failed to ensure expeditiously that abortion services were available and had failed to comply with his duty. Second, the Northern Ireland Department's refusal to take steps to secure abortion services and finally, 'the point blank refusal' of the Executive to consider seeking agreement on commissioning abortion services.[90] The High Court found that the Secretary of State had breached section 9 of the 2019 Act which imposed a duty on him to ensure a human rights-compliant regime was '*implemented*' in Northern Ireland '*expeditiously*'. The then Secretary of State for Northern Ireland in the UK Parliament, Brandon Lewis, expressed disappointment with the verdict and stated that the 'Executive and Department of Health [in Northern Ireland] are continuing to seem to wilfully neglect the welfare and rights of women and girls in Northern Ireland'.[91]

While the power tussle between the UK and the Northern Ireland governments continued, women and girls in Northern Ireland had no access to high-quality abortion and post-abortion care in Northern Ireland. In March 2021, the UK Government laid the Abortion (Northern Ireland) Regulations 2021 to address the gaps in abortion services. The new regulations gave the Secretary of State 'a power to direct Northern Ireland Ministers and, departments or relevant agencies to implement all of the recommendations in paragraphs 85 and 86 of the CEDAW report, consistent with the conditions set out in the Abortion (Northern Ireland) (No. 2) Regulations 2020'.[92] The Secretary of State emphasised that it was his duty to ensure that the CEDAW recommendations were implemented but that the Government's 'strong preference is, and remains, for the [Northern Ireland] Minister of Health and his Department to take responsibility for upholding these rights…'.[93]

On 22 July, 2021 the Northern Ireland Secretary in the UK Parliament set out in a Statement that he had issued a direction to the Northern Ireland Department of Health and others to 'commission and make abortion services available in Northern Ireland as soon as possible, and no later than March 2022'. He also directed that 'there should be immediate support for interim services of early medical abortion, which are at risk of collapse'.[94] The Secretary acknowledged the strain that Covid had placed on healthcare but given that full commissioning proposals have not been put forward, he was under a legal and moral obligation to act so that women and girls could access abortion services.[95] He rightly stressed that women and girls in

---

89 [2021] NIQB 91 at [25].

90 Ibid., at [26].

91 Topping (2021).

92 UK Parliament (2021a).

93 HC Deb, 25 March 2021, c1072. See also UK Parliament (2022d).

94 UK Parliament (2021b).

95 Ibid.

Northern Ireland are denied the same reproductive rights as those in the rest of the UK.

The next move in this saga was that the Society for the Protection of Unborn Children (SPUC) was granted leave to bring judicial review proceedings against the Secretary of State for Northern Ireland.[96] The legality of both the Abortion (Northern Ireland) Regulations 2021 and Abortion Services Directions 2021 was challenged. The High Court dismissed this challenge to the lawfulness of the powers conferred on the Secretary of State to take the steps necessary to enable access to abortion services in Northern Ireland.

A week before the March 31 deadline set in the Abortion Services Directive, the Northern Ireland Secretary of State observed that as it was 'increasingly clear' that abortion services would not be secured by the deadline, he had no choice other than to prepare further Regulations to ensure abortion services are available.[97] These new powers to address the inertia of the Northern Ireland authorities were set out in the Abortion (Northern Ireland) Regulations 2022 which came into force on 20 May 2022. The Statement accompanying the Regulations stated that they removed the need for the Northern Ireland Executive Committee approval before services can be commissioned and confer on a Secretary of State the power to do anything that a Northern Ireland Minister or department could do to secure abortion services.[98]

Five months later, and 3 years after the decriminalisation of abortion in Northern Ireland, the UK Government took over the commissioning of abortion services and agreed to make funding available.[99] Abortion services in Northern Ireland were formally commissioned by the Secretary of State on December 2, 2022.[100]

5 Conclusions

The pandemic had a significant effect on the operation of abortion services in the United Kingdom. The position of women and girls in Northern Ireland during the Covid lockdown was extreme. Women and girls faced difficulties given the scarcity of abortion services in Northern Ireland but this was not new. The issue of lack of access services had been camouflaged by the fact that women could travel to Britain and obtain funded abortion services. The pandemic and the cancellation of flights meant that this safety net been removed. The CEDAW Report published before the pandemic also had a profound effect. It forced the UK Government to take responsibility for the lack of abortion services and overcame any reluctance to act because of cultural sensitivities or the fact that the provision of abortion services was a devolved issue. It is ironic that during the pandemic, Northern Ireland was the only part of the UK

[96] *Re SPUC Pro-Life Ltd's Application for Judicial Review* [2022] NIQB 9.

[97] UK Parliament (2022a).

[98] UK Parliament (2022b).

[99] UK Parliament (2022c).

[100] Northern Ireland Office (2022).

where abortion had been decriminalised and yet the provision for women and girls was largely limited to those whose pregnancies had not exceeded 9 weeks and 6 days. Although early medical abortion services were eventually widely available, after the deadline for early abortions had passed, the ability to access care in Northern Ireland was patchy. It depended on whether the woman lived at an address where a trust had commissioned services and was willing to assist. As the experience of Northern Ireland starkly illustrated, decriminalisation of abortion law alone is not enough to guarantee high-quality services.

In England, Scotland and Wales changes to the way early medical abortions are dealt with came about due to pandemic led shifts. These temporary changes have now become permanent. Nevertheless, the sudden increase in investigations and prosecutions was concerning. If the UK Government saw fit to abandon criminal law prosecutions in one part of the UK, it is hard to understand why the OAPA should not be repealed throughout the UK. Sally Sheldon argues that the legal framework of the OAPA is 'rooted in the punitive, conservative values of the mid-Victorian era' and requires reform.[101] The increase in prosecutions led to a vote in House of Commons in June 2025, to remove women acting in relation to their own pregnancy from the criminal law in England and Wales. It is hard to disagree that the retention of the criminal law to deal with abortion, even in a 'permissive-abortion regime', is to maintain the idea that abortion should be stigmatised. The Crime and Policing Act 2026 removes women from criminal liability related to abortion. In Scotland, the report by an Expert Group set up to review the law on abortion, was released on November 14, 2025 and recommended widespread reform. It states that the law should be decriminalised and that access to abortion should be available up to 24 weeks gestation without any specific grounds being required.[102] The report reflects the view that abortion is a healthcare issue. The initiative in Scotland may be the necessary catalyst for further change in England and Wales. The law indicates the attitude of society towards women and women should be given greater control over their reproductive choices. Nevertheless, it cannot be ignored that the constitutional changes to abortion law in the USA have emboldened anti-abortion activists in the UK. These activists endeavour to increase the political status of abortion law.

One further observation in relation to abortion law in the UK is that the important changes have come about due to the influence of individual politicians rather than broader governmental objectives or policies. The landmark Abortion Act 1967 was introduced into Parliament as a private members Bill by David Steel. The Labour MP, Stella Creasy tabled an amendment to the Northern Ireland (Executive Formation etc) Act 2019 which led to the implementation of the CEDAW recommendations into Northern Ireland and the duty imposed on the Secretary of State through section 9 of the Act. Baroness Sug, in the House of Lords, tabled an amendment to the Health and Care Bill with the aim of maintaining the at-home early medical abortion introduced in response to the pandemic. Finally, the amendment to the Crime and Policing Bill 2025, which seeks to decriminalise abortion law in relation to a woman's own

[101] Sheldon and Wellings (eds.) (2020).

[102] Expert Group (2025).

pregnancy, has been proposed by the Labour Party MP Tonia Antoniazzi. We must hope that the efforts of the Scottish Government will lead to a new governmental policy which takes a holistic view of abortion and the reproductive choices for women and this will lead to further change in the rest of the UK.

References

BBC news (2017) Northern Ireland women to get free abortions in England, 29 June 2017. https://www.bbc.co.uk/news/uk-politics-40438390

Boothroyd B (2001) Betty Boothroyd: the autobiography. Century, London

Chief Medical Officer Directorate (2020) Letter from the Chief Medical Officer (Scotland) abortion—Covid-19—approval for mifepristone to be taken at home and other contingency measures, 31 March 2020. https://www.publications.scot.nhs.uk/files/cmo-2020-09.pdf

Das S (2025) 'Unprecedented' rise in abortion prosecutions prompts calls for law change from medical leaders'. The Guardian, 12 January 2025. https://www.theguardian.com/society/2025/jan/12/unprecedented-rise-in-abortion-prosecutions-prompts-call-for-law-change-from-medical-leaders

Department of Health and Social Care (2020a) Temporary approval of home use for both stages of early medical abortion. https://www.gov.uk/government/publications/temporary-approval-of-home-use-for-both-stages-of-early-medical-abortion%2D%2D2?subject=

Department of Health and Social Care (2020b) Home use of both pills for early medical abortion. https://www.gov.uk/government/consultations/home-use-of-both-pills-for-early-medical-abortion

Department of Health and Social Care (2022) Consultation outcome: home use of both pills for early medical abortion (EMA) up to 10 weeks gestation: summary of consultation responses. https://www.gov.uk/government/consultations/home-use-of-both-pills-for-early-medical-abortion/outcome/home-use-of-both-pills-for-early-medical-abortion-ema-up-to-10-weeks-gestation-summary-of-consultation-responses

Director-General Health and Social Care (2020) Early medical abortion at home: consultation. https://www.gov.scot/publications/consultation-future-arrangements-early-medical-abortion-home/pages/2/

Expert Group Scottish Government (2025) Review of abortion law in Scotland Expert Group: report commissioned by the Scottish Government, 14 November 2025. https://www.gov.scot/publications/review-abortion-law-scotland-expert-group-report/pages/3/

Fox D (2023) The abortion double bind. Am J Public Health 113(10):1068–1073

Gibbons K (2023) 100 women and girls investigated over 'illegal abortions'. The Times, 10 December 2023. https://www.thetimes.com/uk/healthcare/article/100-women-and-girls-investigated-over-illegal-abortions-h6njmgwnf

Herring J (2025) Medical law and ethics, 10th edn. Oxford University Press, Oxford

Houston M (2013) Coroner identifies two failings in care of woman who died after being refused an abortion. BMJ 345:f2441

Hughes K, Martin S, Palmer S (2025) Human rights law in the United Kingdom: themes and principles. Cambridge University Press, Cambridge

Kirk S, Morgan L, McDermott S, McLaughlin L, Hunter C, Farrington T (2021) Introduction of the national health service early medical abortion service in Northern Ireland—an emergency response to the COVID-19 pandemic. BMJ Sex Reprod Health 47:293–295

MacKinnon C (1991) Towards a feminist theory of the state. Harvard University Press, Cambridge

Member's explanatory statement (2025) Crime and policing bill. Report stage, 19 May 2025. https://publications.parliament.uk/pa/bills/cbill/59-01/0235/amend/crime_policing_rm_rep_0519.pdf

Minister for Health and Social Services (Wales) (2020) The Abortion Act 1967—approval of a class of place for treatment for the termination of pregnancy (Wales), 31 March 2020. https://www.gov.wales/sites/default/files/publications/2020-04/approval-of-a-class-of-place-for-treatment-for-the-termination-of-pregnancy-wales-2020.pdf
Morgan E (2022) Minister for Health and Social Services. Written statement: arrangements for early medical abortion at home. https://www.gov.wales/written-statement-arrangements-early-medical-abortion-home
Northern Ireland Assembly (2020) Abortion legislation: non-fatal disabilities, 2 June 2020. https://www.youtube.com/watch?v=2aINiJQQrXk and https://aims.niassembly.gov.uk/officialreport/report.aspx?&eveDate=2020/06/02&docID=301413
Northern Ireland Human Rights Commission (2021) June 2021 fact sheet: human rights commission legal action on lack of abortion services in NI. https://nihrc.org/news/detail/june-2021-fact-sheet-human-rights-commission-legal-action-on-lack-of-abortion-services-in-ni
Northern Ireland Office (2022) Secretary of State for Northern Ireland instructs the Department of Health to commission abortion services. https://www.gov.uk/government/news/secretary-of-state-for-northern-ireland-instructs-the-department-of-health-to-commission-abortion-services
RightToLifenews (2025) Poll reveals more medical professionals oppose assisted suicide Bills in England and Wales, and Scotland than support. https://righttolife.org.uk/news/government-confirms-return-of-pre-pandemic-safeguards-for-abortion-provision
Robinson H (2024) Discrimination in abortion law and the message the law is sending: R (Crowter) v. secretary of state for health and social care. Mod Law Rev 87(1):218–230
Romanis EC (2023) Abortion access and the benefits and limitations of abortion-*permissive* legal frameworks: lessons from the United Kingdom. Camb Q Healthc Ethics 32(3):378–390
Rough E (2025) Abortion in Northern Ireland: recent changes to the legal framework. House of Commons Library. https://commonslibrary.parliament.uk/research-briefings/cbp-8909/
Royal College of Obstetricians and Gynaecologists (2024) Involvement of the police and external agencies following abortion, pregnancy loss and unexpected delivery guidance for health-care staff. https://www.rcog.org.uk/media/s3rf2brq/liaison-with-police-guideline-for-nhs-staff-in-womens-health-2.pdf
Royal College of Obstetricians and Gynaecologists (2025a) RCOG Issues guidance for health-care professional on involving the police following abortion and pregnancy loss, 22 January 2024. https://www.rcog.org.uk/news/rcog-issues-guidance-for-healthcare-professionals-on-involving-the-police-following-abortion-and-pregnancy-loss/
Royal College of Obstetricians and Gynaecologists (2025b) Call for urgent action by Parliament to protect women's essential reproductive rights. https://www.rcog.org.uk/media/00sjehln/multiagency-call-for-urgent-action-by-parliament-to-protect-women-s-essential-reproductive-rights.pdf
Scottish Government (2022) Early medical abortion at home. https://www.gov.scot/news/early-medical-abortion-at-home-1/
Scottish Legal News (2025) Scotland's abortion laws 'not fit for purpose', 17 November 2025. https://www.gov.scot/publications/review-abortion-law-scotland-expert-group-report/
Sheldon S (1997) Beyond control: medical power and abortion law. Pluto Press, London
Sheldon S (2023) Beyond the tram lines: disability discrimination, reproductive rights and anachronistic abortion law. Oxf J Leg Stud 44(1):104–132
Sheldon S, Lord J (2023) Guest editorial: care not criminalisation: reform of British abortion law is long overdue. J Med Ethics 49:523–524
Sheldon S, Wellings K (eds) (2020) Decriminalising abortion in the UK: what would it mean? Policy Press, Bristol
Sheldon S, Davis G, O'Neill J, Parker C (2022) Introduction. In: The Abortion Act 1967: a biography of a UK law. Cambridge University Press, Cambridge
Tongue ZL (2022) Crowter v Secretary of State for Health and Social Care [2021] EWHC 2536: discrimination, disability, and access to abortion. Med Law Rev 30(1):177–187

Topping A (2021) Northern Ireland Secretary failed to comply with abortion duty, judge rules. The Guardian, 14 October 2021. https://www.theguardian.com/uk-news/2021/oct/14/northern-ireland-secretary-failed-comply-abortion-duty-judge-rules

UK Parliament (2021a) Written Statement UIN HCWS875: The Abortion (Northern Ireland) Regulations 2021. Retrieved [data]. https://questions-statements.parliament.uk/written-statements/detail/2021-03-23/hcws875

UK Parliament (2021b) Written Statement UIN HCWS238). Retrieved [data]. https://questions-statements.parliament.uk/written-statements/detail/2021-07-22/hcws238

UK Parliament (2022a) Health Update Statement made on 24 February 2022. Statement UIN HCWS629. https://questions-statements.parliament.uk/written-statements/detail/2022-02-24/hcws629

UK Parliament (2022b) Written Statement UIN HCWS716. Retrieved [data]. https://questions-statements.parliament.uk/written-statements/detail/2022-03-24/hcws716

UK Parliament (2022c) Written Statement UIN HCWS39. Retrieved [data]. https://questions-statements.parliament.uk/written-statements/detail/2022-05-19/hcws39

UK Parliament (2022d) Written Statement UIN HCWS341. Retrieved [data]. https://questions-statements.parliament.uk/written-statements/detail/2022-10-24/hcws341

UN. Committee on the Elimination of Discrimination against Women (2018) Report of the inquiry concerning the United Kingdom of Great Britain and Northern Ireland under article 8 of the Optional Protocol to the convention on the elimination of all forms of discrimination against women, (CEDAW/C/OP.8/GBR/1), March 2018. https://digitallibrary.un.org/record/1480026?v=pdf

Williams Z (2023) The women being prosecuted in Great Britain for abortions: 'Her confidentiality was completely destroyed'. The Guardian, 10 November 2023. https://www.theguardian.com/world/2023/nov/10/the-women-being-prosecuted-in-great-britain-for-abortions-her-confidentiality-was-completely-destroyed

Wilson ALM (2023) The Health and Care Act 2022: inserting telemedicine into the Abortion Act 1967. Med Law Rev 31(1):158–166

Women and Children's Health Branch (2020) Termination of pregnancy arrangements in Wales. https://www.gov.wales/sites/default/files/consultations/2020-12/consultation-document.pdf

Women and Equalities Committee (2019) Abortion law in Northern Ireland. Eighth report of session 2017–19. Report, together with formal minutes relating to the report. Ordered by the House of Commons to be printed 3 April 2019 (HC 1584). https://publications.parliament.uk/pa/cm201719/cmselect/cmwomeq/1584/1584.pdf

Stephanie Palmer is a Professor at the Faculty of Law, University of Cambridge and a Life Fellow at Girton College, Cambridge. She is also a (joint) General Editor of the European Human Rights Law Review. Her latest publication is *Human Rights Law in the UK: Themes and Principles* with Kirsty Hughes and Stevie Martin and published by Cambridge University Press in October 2025.

The Legal Anatomy of Women's Bodies Beyond Emergency Times

Laurie Marguet

Abstract The COVID-19 crisis has highlighted the population's heavy dependence on so-called 'essential' jobs which were mainly care professions. However, the strong gender effects underlying this dependence was not showed nor raised. This paper proposes to show the role played by contemporary constitutions in the invisibilisation of these effects; and to underline the possible impacts of the constitutionalising of abortion (in France) on their attenuation.

1 The COVID Crisis: The Recognition of Care Work?

As we all remember it, most governments decided to confine their populations to limit the spread of the Coronavirus. They still had to determine which 'essential functions' would be maintained to ensure some continuation. The people in charge of these 'essential functions' were not, as a result, confined. We had to continue not only (obviously) to provide healthcare, but also to collect rubbish, make food available and deliver an astronomical number of packages.

In France, 17 professions were deemed, by the DARES (*Direction de l'animation de la recherche, des études et des Statistiques*, which is a French public administration of the labour ministry) 'essential',[1] representing some 4.6 million workers: vehicle drivers, maintenance workers, cashiers and self-service staff, dockers, forklift operators, warehousemen, construction workers, plumbers, carpenters, electricians, handymen and removal workers, home helps and housekeepers, security guards, bricklayers, roofers and carpenters, food sellers, butchers, butchers, bakers, market gardeners, gardeners, winegrowers, public works, concrete and quarry workers, farmers, livestock breeders, foresters, loggers.[2] These 'heroes of the shadows',[3] as the

[1] Amossé et al. (2021), p. 1.

[2] Amossé et al. (2021), pp. 14–15.

[3] Manelli (2021), para. 1.

L. Marguet (✉)
University of Rouen, Rouen, France

M. Balestrieri and A. Cauduro (eds.), *The Legal Anatomy of the Body*, Ius Gentium: Comparative Perspectives on Law and Justice 142,
https://doi.org/10.1007/978-3-032-26434-3_16

media presented them, ensured the minimum service to the country and the services essential to the daily life of the population.

As we know, these jobs have all in common that most of these people are poorly paid and have unfavourable employment conditions. Indeed, as the DARES study underlines, although these professions are very different from one another, a detailed analysis of their working and employment conditions in 2019 shows that they are often at a disadvantage in comparison with the average employee. In addition to sometimes very low pay (due in particular to short working hours), these are often arduous professions, marked by a high frequency of occupational accidents and illnesses. The opportunities for training and career advancement are generally limited. In some cases, working hours are fragmented, making it difficult to reconcile work and family life.[4]

For a moment, we pretended to be concerned about the exposure of these most vulnerable populations to an increased risk of contamination and about this bad works conditions. We saluted their courage; we even applauded the healthcare professionals;[5] we underlined their difficult working conditions and insisted on the changes that should take place next.

For a brief moment, but without explicitly saying so, we became more aware of our dependence and of the dependence of society as a whole on these professions and therefore on its people.[6] The pandemic crisis not only underlined the fragility of the human and social condition; more fundamentally, it demonstrated our dependence on others, particularly on the low-paid (economically vulnerable) workers. But even if our dependence has been exacerbated by the pandemic crisis, it is co-substantial with our social organisation. It is always there.

What the pandemic crisis has highlighted, among other things, is our entire social organisation, based in particular on a distinction between the public and private spheres, and on a sexual division of labour.[7] As proof of this, the pandemic crisis has also made care work more visible.

1.1 Clarification of the Sexual Division of Labour, Reproductive Work, and Care Work

1.1.1 Clarification of Concepts

According to feminist theories, societies are founded on a (virtual) division between two spheres, to which are attached tasks differentiated and distributed to people

[4] Amossé et al. (2021), p. 26.

[5] Renou (2020), para. 1.

[6] Pastier (2022), p. 155 and Guiraudon et al. (2024), p. 3.

[7] Hennette-Vauchez (2025), p. 85.

according to their gender.[8] Thus, the public sphere is the one of productive, economically prosperous work and 'politics' (i.e., where decisions are made); the private sphere is the one of reproductive work, not necessarily remunerated.

Here we take a broad view of reproductive work: The term 'reproductive labour' refers to both paid and unpaid activities that help to maintain and replenish the workforce. This encompasses a wide range of daily tasks, such as meal preparation, laundry, and child-rearing. The term 'reproductive labour' highlights the significance of certain activities in the production process, particularly the reproduction of the workforce. The focus of the debate on activities mainly carried out by women has shifted over the past years. Reproductive activities are no longer the main focus; the term "care" has taken over. Several aspects need to be taken into account to define the concept of 'reproduction'.[9] Firstly, reproduction should be understood, in the strict sense, as synonymous with procreation. Understood this way, reproduction is essential for the perpetuation of the human species.[10] Secondly, reproduction should be understood as 'procreative work': this includes pregnancy itself, medical monitoring of the pregnancy, compliance with social injunctions relating to the continuation of the pregnancy, as well as childbirth and postnatal care. This can also include caring for infants and educational tasks. Thirdly the notion of 'reproduction' encompasses, in the broad sense, reproduction in the sense of reproductive work. This includes both domestic work and care work.[11] Added to this is the emotional, affective and sexual work that binds family members together and contributes to their well-being.[12] Thus, 'reproduction' refers to the work involved in managing family relationships, friendships and daily life (shopping lists, meal menus, etc.).

1.1.2 Care Work and Inequalities

In all cases, this 'emotional and material'[13] work is carried out by women. As Nancy Fraser has theorised, this work is 'invisible', and because it is done out of love and self-sacrifice, this work is performed 'without financial counterpart'.[14]

Thus, care work encompasses care provided to dependent children, the elderly, the sick and the disabled in care institutions or in the home of the person requiring care. Care policies and the provision of care services are intrinsically related to the achievement of equality between women and men. The lack of affordable, accessible and high-quality care services and the fact that care work is not equally shared between

---

[8] Kergoat (2001), p. 78.

[9] For the following developments, see Hirata (2021), p. 62.

[10] On this point Federici (2014).

[11] Hirata and Zarifian (2000), p. 230.

[12] Hirata (2021), p. 62.

[13] Fraser (2020), p. 41.

[14] Fraser (2020), p. 41.

women and men have a direct negative impact on women's ability to participate in all aspects of social, economic, cultural and political life.[15]

Long before the COVID crisis, the feminist political theory shows how our social organisation builds on our dependence on reproductive work (i.e. care work) and how it entrenches a gender order, himself affected by class and racial inequalities.

The analysis about reproductive work, like the health crisis, 'brings us back to the need to see what is right before our eyes: the reality of inequality'.[16] These inequalities persist not only between men and women, but also between rich and poor. Indeed, as Sandra Laugier points out, the social division of care work leads to a distinction between 'emotional' care (attentive to the emotional needs of particular people) and 'service' care, which can be delegated and purchased.[17] 'Emotional care' would then be the prerogative of white bourgeois women, while service care could be delegated to others. That's why it's important to think together 'care' with the concept of delegation of 'service' (or 'servitude').[18]

According to Sandra Laugier, caregiving tasks, traditionally assigned to women, still exist, even if privileged Westerners are sometimes exempt from them when they have the means to do so. These tasks are then carried out by immigrant and marginalised populations. As Sandra Laugier reminds us, because women have historically been assigned to the domestic sphere, these domestic activities are discreetly devalued. The invisible work done by these people is also devalued. These people are not only women, but also those belonging to disadvantaged, ethicised and racialised social categories.[19] All these people, who carry out indispensable and vital work, are poorly paid, poorly considered, their needs ignored, their knowledge and know-how belittled and denied.[20] This encourages the moral and political devaluation of caregiving work. Care therefore raises many difficulties.

These difficulties were addressed, not long after Carol Gilligan[21] (who was one of the first to theorise the concept of care) by Carole Pateman in 'the sexual contract'.[22]

1.1.3 Care Work, Inequalities and Social Contract

In her book 'the sexual contract', Carole Pateman offers a fundamental re-reading of the work of Thomas Hobbes, John Locke and Jean Jacques Rousseau. She highlighted how their theorisations of the social contract are deeply rooted in the gendered division of labour and gender inequality.

---

15 Advisory Committee on Equal Opportunities for Women and Men (2021).

16 On this point, Fraisse (2010).

17 Laugier (2011), p. 138.

18 On this point, Fraisse (2010).

19 Laugier (2011), p. 138.

20 Laugier (2011), p. 138.

21 Gilligan (1982).

22 Pateman (1988), p. 36.

In classical theories of the social contract, the rational, autonomous individual renounces some of his natural rights to enter a social pact. In exchange, this rational and autonomous individual submits to a sovereign power (the 'Leviathan' for Hobbes, the 'civil government' for Locke, the 'general will' for Rousseau) capable of governing in the general interest. But, as Carole Pateman explains, the 'rational and autonomous' individual who enters the social contract is a man. More to the point, Carole Pateman argues that although women do not participate in the social contract, they nonetheless remain in the state of nature. While contractualist theories relating to the social contract claim that all subjects have the freedom to engage in productive and political labour, Pateman demonstrates that it is not true: 'the figure of the individual freed from all social, religious and other determinations stumbles over the difference between the sexes'.[23] According to her, those who can be active in the public sphere can only do so because the social contract presupposes and masks another contract: the sexual contract. This sexual contract underpins the distinction between a private sphere (where reproductive work takes place) and a public sphere (where productive and political work can take place).[24] Pateman's analysis showed that subjects who activate themselves in the public and political sphere enjoy the freedom to do so only because, upstream, everything that makes them dependent individuals (and in particular, reproduction) is managed by others: by women.[25]

For Sandra Laugier,

> Her theory is to take to its logical conclusion the critical and radical – feminist – idea that was already at the root of the ethic of care: that mainstream political and ethical conceptions, and in particular past and present theories of contract and justice, are the product and expression of 'patriarchy' and a tool for the subjugation of women.[26]

The COVID crisis has highlighted both this sexual contract and the inequalities inherent in care work.

1.2 COVID Crisis, Reproductive Work, and Care Work

As the COVID crisis showed, care work is not only made by women. It is however mostly done by women. Indeed, most of the trade's families 'in the second line' show a very high level of gender segregation: women are virtually absent from the building trades (their share rises to 2.8% for unskilled structural workers, for example), while they account for 95% of home helps and housekeepers. More than two-thirds of cashiers, self-service employees and food salespeople are also women, while over 80% of butchers, delicatessens and bakers are men. This very specific structure of employment by gender must be considered when analysing trades.[27]

---

[23] Pateman (1988), p. 36.

[24] Hennette-Vauchez (2025), p. 86.

[25] Hennette-Vauchez (2025), p. 86.

[26] Laugier (2011), p. 138.

[27] Amossé et al. (2021), p. 17.

The data produced by the DARES study show it: 67.6% of cashiers and self-service staff are women; 72% of food sellers are women; 65.8 of maintenance workers are women and 95.4% of home help and household help are women.[28]

While the COVID crisis has made care work more visible, it has largely continued to make invisible the special role played by women in the labour of reproduction and domesticity. For example, public discourse has failed to highlight the essential contribution made mostly by the mothers who looked after their children 7 days a week, 24 h a day, during the confinement period, carrying out (in addition to their professional activities) teaching duties.[29]

The French government only took seriously the access to abortion issue during confinement at a very late stage, which is an undeniable proof of the State invisibilising of reproductive work. The parliamentary debates relating to the enactment of the emergency law of March 23, 2020 (to deal with the COVID-19 epidemic) showed that, particularly in times of crisis, the issue of abortion was not seen as a priority.[30] Senator Laurence Rossignol's amendment to extend the legal time limit for abortion (from 12 to 14 weeks) during the state of health emergency was rejected. The senator pointed out that 'we know that confinement, the state of emergency, the disorganisation of hospitals and the concentration of work on intensive care have a deleterious effect on access to abortions.' However, the Minister of Health spoke out against the amendment. This rejection was supported by certain senators who were indignant that such a text could be

> voted through an amendment, when the National Assembly [...] will not have debated it [...]. Moving the abortion deadline from twelve to fourteen weeks of pregnancy is not a trivial decision, and it must be taken – if at all – within the framework of a democratic debate worthy of the name, and not by means of an amendment to an emergency bill aimed at making various provisions.[31]

This argument was not without irony, given the speed with which the laws relating to the state of health emergency were adopted. Much criticism has precisely focused on the anti-democratic nature of the adoption of these laws: lack of reinforced parliamentary control over measures taken by the government; suspension of the compulsory transfer of some constitutional controls, etc. It is also worthy to note that the Health Minister's argument about the link between the epidemic and the delay in access to abortion was unclear.[32] At a time when hospitals were fully saturated, when individuals were advised to go to a healthcare facility only in case of obvious emergency, and when women were confined to their homes, women cannot access abortion. Arguing that there is no obvious link between the COVID crisis and abortion clearly reveals that abortion was not fully perceived as a treatment in its own right in 2020.

However, although it did not 'spontaneously appear' to the Minister of Health at first, this link did become apparent to him later, when on April 14, 2020, he issued a

[28] Amossé et al. (2021), p. 17.

[29] Delhomme et al. (2022).

[30] Hennette-Vauchez (2020).

[31] Session at the National Assembly on May 28, 2020.

[32] Hennette-Vauchez (2020).

decree extending the time limit for abortion per medicine.[33] In this way, the government has ensured the continuity of abortion during the state of health emergency. Based on the state of emergency law, the Minister of Health was authorised to take all measures regulating the organisation and operation of the health system to put an end to the health crisis. These measures were justified by 'the strong mobilisation of health establishments in the crisis management and the need to limit consultations in hospitals' Therefore, both the conditions under which this decree was issued, and its justification clearly highlight the link between the health crisis and the access to abortion.[34]

If this is the example of how abortion was managed during the health crisis is mobilised, it is because everything is intertwined: while the health crisis has led to the recognition of certain forms of care work, it has continued to invisible reproductive work in its strict meaning (make children). It was not, and it is still not seen at all as 'work' and it is not always valued by the state. Generally speaking, it should be noted that contemporary societies dependence on reproductive/care work remains largely unacknowledged. Admittedly, the COVID crisis briefly brought it to light, but it was only partially (not all aspects of reproductive and care work) and temporary (just during the COVID crisis).

Even during the COVID crisis, the social contract still remains a sexual contract that excludes women and contributes to the invisibilisation of the reproductive work they perform.

Let us now change perspective and move on to a legal analysis of the issue, bearing in mind that the constitution is a form of 'legal transcriptions'[35] of this social/sexual contract. Considering such prospect, the analysis of the recent constitutional revision in France highlights the ambivalence of the State's position on the recognition issue of reproductive work.

[33] Decree of 14 April 2020 supplementing the decree of 23 March 2020 prescribing the organizational and operational measures required of the health system to deal with the COVID-19 epidemic in the context of the state of health emergency.

[34] This decree enables the use of telemedicine for mandatory consultations during medically induced abortion, the delivery of the drugs required for this abortion (mifepristone and misoprostol) directly to the patient, and the remote administration of the first drug (as part of a teleconsultation), the extension of the medical abortion deadline from 5 to 7 weeks, and the prescription of these drugs outside their marketing authorization (in terms of dosage, route of administration and implementation deadline, since precisely these three elements are modified by the aforementioned ruling of April 14, 2020), as well as an adjustment to pricing. This temporary change is justified by the French Ministry of Health as enabling, via telemedicine, both the provision of medical care at home for women wishing to have a voluntary interruption of pregnancy, and the protection of healthcare professionals from infection, as well as the other patients they care for.

[35] Hennette-Vauchez (2025), p. 87.

2 Constitutionalising Abortion: The Recognition of Reproductive Work?

If we consider in a very schematic way that constitutions are a form of legal translation of the social contract, it is possible to observe the invisibilisation of reproductive and care work; and in general, the strong invisibilisation of the sexual division of labour by these constitutions (and then by States).

At first glance, Constitutions start from and address this mythical figure of an autonomous, rational individual, ignoring the dependence and all the care work that enable men to be 'autonomous and rational' in the productive and public sphere.[36] 'From this point of view, the silence of constitutional texts on the question of reproduction, while it entrenches this assignment of women to the private sphere, is in reality only the expression of a much broader invisibilisation: that of the entire private sphere and of everything that takes place there (and more broadly: of all the forms of dependence that exist in a society)'.[37]

In reality, it is necessary to temper the purpose of the previous paragraph: in fact, not all textual constitutions make reproductive work invisible.

2.1 The Ambivalence of Recognising of Reproductive Work in Constitutional Texts

As Julie Suk has shown, the German Weimar constitution of 1919 was the first constitution in which 'the question of social reproduction explicitly became the subject of textual provisions'.[38] There is a few others examples from current constitutions.[39] The article 31 of the Italian Constitution states that 'the Republic assists the formation of the family and the fulfilment of its duties, with consideration for large families, through economic measures and other benefits. The Republic protects mothers, children and the young by adopting necessary provisions'. The article 6 paragraph 4 of the German Constitution states that 'Every mother shall be entitled to the protection and care of the community'. The §10 et 11 of the preamble to the constitution of 1946 in France (which has constitutional value) states that

> the Nation shall provide the individual and the family with the conditions necessary to their development. It shall guarantee to all, notably to children, mothers and elderly workers, protection of their health, material security, rest and leisure. All people who, by virtue of their age, physical or mental condition, or economic situation, are incapable of working, shall have to the right to receive suitable means of existence from society.

---

36 Hennette-Vauchez (2025), p. 86.
37 Hennette-Vauchez (2025), p. 88.
38 Suk (2018), p. 165.
39 Hennette-Vauchez (2025), p. 91.

But if these provisions—by granting mothers a special status or protection—do not make reproductive work invisible, they are no less problematic: they promote the confinement of women to the reproductive sphere, without giving them the possibility of extricating themselves from it. Let's take the example of article 6 paragraph 4 of the German Constitution: it alone reveals several ambiguities regarding maternity. On the one hand, the specific protection afforded to mothers is explained by the fact that their de facto social and economic situation is often less favourable than that of men. The precariousness of women and mothers is in fact greater than that of men and fathers, as the rate of professionalisation of mothers remains low in Germany. As such, they deserve special protection. This provision serves, for example, to guarantee the existence of maternity leave. Indeed, in 1972, the German Constitutional Court reiterated that Article 6 paragraph 4 of the Constitution provides specific protection for mothers.[40] But on the other hand, this provision tends to value the specific role of mothers over fathers. What is more, this provision could tend to reinforce the idea that mothers are more fragile than fathers and should therefore be given greater protection. The question then arises as to why the community should grant specific protection to women? Is it because they are de facto in a less advantageous situation than men? Does the provision seek to compensate for these inequalities, as do positive discrimination measures? Is it because they are more fragile than men that they deserve special protection? Is it because their role should be more highly valued in relation to the child than that of fathers? Or is it also because mothers are useful to the community, as they give birth to new citizens? Insofar as Article 6 paragraph 4 of the German Constitution was drafted in 1949, it seems difficult to consider that it was drafted to improve substantive gender equality. It seems difficult to consider that it was written to compensate de facto inequalities between the sexes. The wording of the article is not devoid of ambivalence: in particular, it tends to valorise maternity, and even to essentialise the fragility of women.[41]

Furthermore, these constitutions tend to invisibilise all procreational. In fact, procreative questions, and more generally reproductive questions, are readily presented as quintessentially belonging to the private, intimate sphere of individuals. They are therefore ignored. And when they are considered, it is often from the angle of privacy. The decision *Roe v. Wade* of the USA Supreme Court of the USA in 1973 is a good example of the exclusive linkage of these issues to the right to privacy.

In this decision, the Supreme Court decided that the *Due Process Clause* of the Fourteenth Amendment to the United States Constitution covers a fundamental 'right to privacy', which protects a pregnant woman's right to an abortion in the first pregnancy trimester.[42] This decision has long been a shining example of the constitutional recognition of abortion. Julie Suk points yet out that

---

[40] Decision of the German Constitutional Court of January 25, 1972 (BVerfGE 32, 273); Decision of the German Constitutional Court of November 13, 1979 (BVerfGE 52, 357).

[41] Suk (2010).

[42] Roe v. Wade, 410 U.S. 113 (1973).

> proponents of abortion rights in the legal academy have pointed to the inadequacies of the negative privacy right protected by *Roe*. This Subsection describes the critiques of Roe and its privacy logic by leading feminist legal theorists and Black feminists from the standpoint of reproductive justice and shows how similar ideas were invoked without being fully developed in *Roe* and *Casey*. Robin West has suggested that Roe's negative right to abortion has promoted an antigovernmental stance in matters of childbearing and childrearing. On her account, the right to abortion protected by *Roe v. Wade* is at odds with a capacious feminist understanding of reproductive justice. Roe's negative privacy right keeps the State out of family life, preventing both a robust role for government in childcare and heightened protections against domestic violence.[43]

Furthermore, the 'right of privacy' was unable to provide a solid enough basis for abortion rights to be definitively acquired. In 2022, the US Supreme Court in the *Dobbs v. Jackson* decision deleted this protection.[44]

Hence the need and the importance of recognising reproductive rights, and in particular the right not to have children (and therefore not to be forced into reproductive work), without linking this exclusively to the right to privacy Hence the necessity to analyse now the impact of the constitutionalisation of abortion in France.

2.2 *The Means of the Current Recognition of Abortion in the French Constitution*

2.2.1 The Recognition of Reproductive Work in Constitutions Around the World

By way of introduction, it should be pointed out that—while France is the only country to constitutionalise abortion—there are other countries whose constitutional texts protect reproductive rights.[45]

On the one hand, there is quite a bit of case law from constitutional courts around the world that have already granted praetorian protection to abortion,[46] such as in Colombia,[47] Canada,[48] Mexico,[49] Portugal,[50] Nepal,[51] and even South Korea.[52]

On the other hand, other texts, without mentioning the right to abortion, speak of reproductive rights. For example, the Bolivian constitution of 2009 states that 'men

43 Suk (2018) referring to West (2009).

44 Dobbs v. Jackson Women's Health Org., 597 U.S. 215 (2022).

45 Hennette-Vauchez (2025), p. 91.

46 Hennette-Vauchez (2025), p. 91.

47 Constitutional Court of Colombia May 10th, 2006, C-355/96

48 Supreme Court of Canada, R v. Morgentaler, 1988 1RC 30.

49 Supreme Court of Mexico, September 7th, 2021, n° 148/2017.

50 Constitutional Court of Portugal, n° 75/2010.

51 Supreme Court of Nepal, May 20th, 2009, Lakshmi v. Government of Nepal, n° 8464.

52 Constitutional Court of South Corea, April 11th, 2019, 2017 Hyn-Bal 27.

and women are guaranteed the exercise of their sexual and reproductive rights';[53] the Cuban constitution of 2019 contains a similar formula, but only applies to women.[54] In Ecuador, the constitution adopted in 2008 requires the State to promote reproductive health. This text protects 'the right to make free, responsible and informed decisions about one's health and reproductive life, and to decide on the number of children to have'.[55] The Kosovo's 2008 constitution also includes a provision on 'the right to make decisions related to reproduction in accordance with the laws and procedures in force'.[56] The Constitution of Fiji 2013 states that 'the State must take reasonable measures within its available resources to achieve the progressive realisation of the right of every person to health, and to the conditions and facilities necessary to good health, and to health care services, including reproductive health care'.[57] In Nepal, the constitution states that 'every woman shall have the right to safe motherhood and reproductive health',[58] and in South Africa, the article 12 of the constitution protects the 'right to bodily and psychological integrity, which includes the right to make decisions concerning reproduction (...)'; and in Zimbabwe, 'which includes the subject to any other provision of this constitution to make decisions concerning reproduction'.[59]

But France remains the only country to have explicitly used the word 'abortion' in its constitutional text for purposes other than simply banning abortion.

The context of constitutionalising is as follows. Affirming the importance of enshrining a right to abortion, the constitutional bill passed by the National Assembly in November 2022 provided for the insertion into the Constitution of the following phrase: 'the law guarantees effective and equal access to the right to abortion'.[60] But in February 2023, the Senat accepted the constitutionalising only on condition that this term did not appear. It thus voted the following terms: 'the law determines the conditions under which a woman's freedom to terminate her pregnancy is exercised'.[61] This lack of consensus brought the constitutionalising process to a halt. Several months later, the government tabled a bill providing for the constitutionalising of the phrase 'the law determines the conditions under which a woman's right to have a voluntary interruption of pregnancy is exercised'. This bill finally passed in congress on March 8, 2024. This wording, as we can see, is compromising: it deletes the term 'right' (present in the version voted by the National Assembly) and substitutes it with that of 'freedom' (absent from the version voted by the Senate). Furthermore, the law does not aim to *guarantee* access to abortion (as in the version proposed by the National Assembly), but must *determine* the conditions under which

[53] Article 66 of the Constitution of Bolivia 2009.

[54] Article 43 of the Constitution of Cuba 2019.

[55] Article 32 of the Constitution of Ecuador 2009.

[56] Article 26 §1 of the Constitution of Kosovo 2008.

[57] Article 38 of the Constitution of Fiji 2013.

[58] Article 38 of the Constitution of Nepal 2015.

[59] Article 52 of the Constitution of Zimbabwe 2013.

[60] Text no. 34 adopted by the National Assembly on November 24, 2022.

[61] Text no. 48 modified by the Senate on February 1, 2023.

it can be performed (as in the version proposed by the Senate). From now on, the law must determine the conditions under which this freedom *that is now guaranteed* may be exercised.

The debates surrounding the constitutionalisation of abortion, and more specifically the confrontations relating to its formulation, thus, suggest that the choice of words ('right' or 'freedom') matters.[62] Politically speaking, the choice of words unquestionably played an important role in the successful constitutionalising of abortion. Of course, words can carry important symbolic effects, and we must take seriously the political weight attached to the term 'right' ('*droit*'). Indeed, the failure of the constitutionalising process to register it shows that many members of parliament did not want constitutionalising to be accompanied by too much 'symbolic force'. Parliamentarians feared that constitutionalising the words 'right to abortion' would enshrine an enforceable right for women. They accepted a certain form of recognition of women's reproductive work, but on condition that the concrete legal effects of this recognition remain limited. This does not prevent this constitutionalisation of abortion from producing symbolic and legal effects nonetheless.

2.2.2 The Significant Effects of the Constitutionalising of Abortion in France

Symbolically, France is the only country whose current constitution explicitly refers to a (guaranteed) freedom to have an abortion. Constitutionalising the right of abortion may indeed be a way to preserve the constitutional valorisation of reproductive work and thus, to assert its social and political importance. It is also a way to recognise its nature as a common good or work of general interest, carried out for the benefit of all, while guaranteeing that women retain full control over it.[63]

In other words, making human and social reproduction a fully constitutional issue, not through maternity but through abortion, is of direct interest to full (and equal) citizenship. Recognising the reproductive autonomy and guaranteeing a socially equitable distribution of human reproduction at the same time, ensure that all men and women will be able to take an equal part in social, political, economic and civil life.[64] It is notably justified by the collective nature of the benefit derived from such recognition and guarantee.

Legally, the aim was to avoid a 'Dobbs effect' and a possible rollback of abortion rights. The aim was to constitutionalise abortion to prevent future legislation from reversing the possibility for women to terminate their pregnancies.

To what extent can this new constitutional provision prevent restrictions on access to abortion?

---

[62] Hennette-Vauchez (2023) and Beaud (2023).

[63] Hennette-Vauchez (2024).

[64] Hennette-Vauchez (2024).

We can assume that the Constitutional Council would now sanction a law that would penalise abortion.[65] It would probably also sanction a law that drastically restricts a woman's access to abortion (as is the case, for example, in Poland, where the conditions are so restrictive that abortion is de facto virtually impossible for most women). Such a drastic restriction would likely be interpreted as a breach of the legislator's obligation not to impede women's 'guaranteed freedom'.[66] During the parliamentary debates, there was, moreover, a consensus on the fact that the purpose of constitutionalising was to form a 'shield':[67] 'the essential contribution [of the constitutional draft] is the addition of the word 'guarantee' which clarifies the constituent's intention: it is a matter of framing the legislator's office so that he cannot prohibit recourse to abortion'.[68]

Could this new constitutional provision prevent any form of restriction on access to abortion?

The way section 34(18) is written makes it unclear how far the protections it offers in relation to abortion actually go. There are therefore arguments in favour of an extensive understanding of the constitutional revision of 2024, which could thus be read as requiring the legislator to guarantee the performance of abortions.

The first argument relates to the addition of the word 'guarantee' in the constitutional provision. Undoubtedly, the use of the verb 'to guarantee' is intended to 'give greater force to the statement':[69] to state a 'guaranteed freedom' is not only to impose an action on the legislator, but also a direction it must follow.[70] For example, the idea of a 'guarantee' was rejected in favour of 'encourage' during the 1999 constitutional amendment on gender parity because it was feared that it would place excessive constraints on the legislator.[71] According to some members of parliament at the time, the advantage of using the verb 'encourage' rather than 'guarantee' was that it only led to an obligation of means, rather than of results, being enshrined.[72] In the context of the 2024 constituent debates relating to abortion, advocates for the constitutionalisation of abortion argue that using the verb 'guarantee' would create a 'positive obligation' for the legislator to protect abortion:[73] the objective pursued was indeed to prevent the legislator from 'undermining its effectiveness'.[74]

---

[65] Marguet (2024).

[66] Marguet (2025).

[67] Session at the national assembly on January 16, 2024: Guillaume Gouffier Valente, discussions in the Law Commission.

[68] Marguet (2024).

[69] Hennette-Vauchez (2023).

[70] Hennette-Vauchez (2023).

[71] Thus, at the end, the wording finally adopted is 'the law promotes equal access for women and men to electoral mandates and elective functions', rather than 'the law guarantees access for women and men to electoral mandates and elective functions'.

[72] Session at the national assembly on December 15, 1998.

[73] Session at the national assembly on January 24, 2024: Eric Dupond-Moretti, discussions in the Law Commission.

[74] Session at the national assembly on January 16, 2024: Guillaume Gouffier Valente, discussions in the Law Commission.

The second relates to the arguments put forward during parliamentary debates. When the debate was ongoing about the constitutionalisation of abortion, those in favour of the bill said that it would stop the legislator from banning abortion completely. According to them, it should also stop the legislator from limiting the circumstances under which it can be performed to such an extent that this right would be rendered meaningless.

The second relates to the Constitutional Council's case law on the distortion of constitutional requirements, which in principle prohibits the legislature from 'distorting a constitutional requirement': that means that the legislature can't empty a constitutional provision it of its substance (or render a constitutional provision meaningless). For example, it is therefore not out of the question for the Constitutional Council to consider that a law removing the obligation for public health establishments to carry out abortions would undermine the new constitutional requirements. That the Constitutional Council considers that a law removing the obligation for healthcare establishments to perform abortions is unconstitutional, is all the more possible given that, in 2001, it had considered that this obligation contributes 'reinforces the constitutional principle of equality of users before the law and before the public service'.[75] It is, of course, equally possible that the *Conseil* might consider, for example, that abolishing the reimbursement of abortions would distort the constitutional requirements now laid down in article 34 (and all the more so as social security coverage also contributes 'to respect for the constitutional principle of equality of users before the law and before the public service').[76]

Beyond the possible effects of constitutionalisation on future laws, we can already observe certain indirect effects of constitutionalising. On April 23, 2024, the government issued a decree relaxing the conditions under which midwives can perform instrumental abortions.[77] In fact, a few months before constitutionalising, the decree of December 16, 2023 laid down conditions so drastic that it de facto annihilated the possibility offered to midwives to perform instrumental abortions.[78] However, in response to the outcry caused by this decree, a new decree dated April 23, 2024 authorises instrumental abortions to be performed by midwives if they can attest to having undergone appropriate training, including what to do in the event of complications.[79] The government has even gone so far as to raise the price of abortions (covered by the social security system) carried out in healthcare establishments.[80] These initiatives may well be seen as the first 'indirect effects' of the constitutionalising of abortion.[81]

---

[75] Decision of the Constitutional Council June 27, 2001, n° 2001-446 DC.

[76] Decision of the Constitutional Council June 27, 2001, n° 2001-446 DC.

[77] Decree No. 2023-1194 of December 13, 2023, on the practice of instrumental voluntary terminations of pregnancy by midwives in healthcare establishments.

[78] Marguet (2023).

[79] Section D. 2212-8 of the French Public Health Code.

[80] Decree of 1 March 2024 amending the decree of February 26, 2016, on flat-rate fees for abortion services.

[81] Carayon (2024).

2.2.3 The Limits of the Constitutionalisation of Abortion in France

However, it is important not to overestimate the concrete legal effects of this constitutionalising because the words 'guaranteed freedom' are indeterminate.

Let us imagine that, tomorrow, the Parliament were to reduce the legal time frame for abortion from 14 to 12 weeks. Is it certain that the French Constitutional Council would declare such a law unconstitutional? It is not certain at all: a legislative intervention could well be interpreted as fulfilling the constitutional mandate of 'determining the modalities' by which freedom to resort to abortion is exercised. It is not certain that the Constitutional Council would rule that a 2-week reduction of the legal time frame for abortion infringed the 'guarantee' requirement.[82] It is also conceivable that a legislative reform calling into question the Social Security coverage of abortion would be struck down—although here again, it is impossible to determine with certainty the delisting threshold at which the *Conseil constitutionnel* would place the cursor.

Certainly, during the debates on the constitutionalisation of abortion, the project's defenders assert that constitutionalising it would have the effect of preventing the legislature from prohibiting any recourse to abortion, and from 'restricting the conditions of exercise in such a way as to deprive this freedom of any scope'. Certainly, this formulation echoes the Constitutional Council's case law on the distortion of constitutional requirements. However, the Constitutional Council is flexible in its interpretation of this prohibition.[83] It generally considers that the law must be totally devoid of substance for it to be sanctioned. There is therefore no reason to believe that the Constitutional Council would consider a future law reintroducing dissuasive provisions such as a psychosocial consultation (abolished in 2001), as completely draining the substance of the 'guaranteed freedom to access abortion'. The Constitutional Council could however consider that such a potential law would limit the guaranteed freedom to access abortion but without completely draining it of its constitutional substance. The same concerns would exist if a future provision would restore the 'situation of distress' condition (abolished in 2014) or the 'cooling-off period' for abortion (abolished in 2016). Indeed, as the access to abortion would still be possible in fine, restoring dissuasive mechanisms would not be necessarily considered as a problem by the Constitutional Council.[84]

Furthermore, it should be emphasized that the Constitutional Council has always considered with regards to abortion, that 'it does not have a general power of assessment and decision of the same nature as that of Parliament, to call into question [...] the provisions thus adopted by the legislator'.[85] This means that the Constitutional

[82] Hennette-Vauchez (2024).

[83] Decision of the Constitutional Council, June 18, 2012, n° 2012-254 QPC.

[84] Some parliamentarians are concerned about the limited effects of constitutionalising. See, in particular, Paul Molac, debate at the National Assembly, January 24, 2024: 'It cannot be ruled out that, in the future, ordinary law will frame this right to the point of rendering it inapplicable'.

[85] Decision of the Constitutional Council, June 27, 2001, n° 2001-446 DC.

Council does not consider itself fully legitimate to question the choices made by the legislator on social issues.

Of course, the constitutionalising of abortion has undeniable symbolic effects: it contributes to the legal and social recognition of abortion; in short, it contributes to its legitimisation. This symbolic impact can have concrete effects: by helping to destigmatise the act, it creates a climate likely to make women (who are considering terminating their pregnancy) feel less guilty (and, consequently, to support them in their choice). It encourages them to find out more about this act. By enabling them to feel legitimate in terminating a pregnancy, it contributes to their psychological and physical well-being. Its political impact, particularly in terms of gender equality and the recognition of women as full citizens, has also been documented.[86] The fact remains, however, that its legal effects are more limited than suggested by the political rhetoric aimed at asserting the existence of a right to abortion.

Doubt is all the greater because the terms used by the constitutionalising in 2024 are indeterminate: it is not clear what is to be understood from the expression 'the freedom guaranteed to women to be able to interrupt her pregnancy'. For the guarantee to be called into question, the law would probably have to (more) drastically restrict the deadline—but then again, no one has any authority or mastery over the criteria that would allow the Constitutional Council to determine what threshold leads to violating the constitutional mandate.

In other words: only the future will endow this 25th amendment to the 1958 Constitution with its full and precise scope and meaning.[87] Of course, the constitutionalising of abortion is not a direct consequence of the COVID crisis. Of course, the constitutionalising of Abortion will not make instantly all the care and reproductive work made by all the women in France (or in the world) visible. Now that the pandemic crisis is over, the myth of autonomous, rational 'subject' can continue to live out his days in peace. But for now, the article 34 of the French constitution can be read as the first step in recognition of reproductive work and that is no mean feat.

References

Advisory Committee on Equal Opportunities for Women and Men (2021) Opinion on the care gap in the EU: a holistic and gender-transformative approach, p 3

Amossé T, Béatriz M, Erhel C, Koubi M, Mauroux A (2021) Les métiers de deuxième ligne de la crise Covid-19: Quelles conditions de travail et d'emploi dans le secteur privé? Étude de la DARES, Document d'études no 246:1–49

Beaud O (2023) Pour une interprétation raisonnable de la disposition votée par le Sénat sur la constitutionnalisation du droit à l'IVG. Blog Jus Politicum, 18 février 2023

Carayon L (2024) Modification du décret sur la pratique des IVG par les sages-femmes: Premier effet indirect de la constitutionnalisation de l'accès à l'avortement? Dalloz actualité

[86] Hennette-Vauchez (2025) and Froidevaux-Metterie (2025).

[87] Hennette-Vauchez (2024).

Delhomme I, Pétillon X, Rivillon Y (2022) Premier confinement et égalité femmes–hommes: une articulation des temps de vie plus difficile pour les femmes. Insee Analyses Pays de la Loire, no 103

Federici S (2014) Caliban et la sorcière. Femmes, corps et accumulation primitive. Entremonde, Montreuil

Fraisse G (2010) Femmes toutes mains. Essai sur le service domestique. Seuil, Paris

Fraser N (2020) Crise du care? Paradoxes socio-reproductifs du capitalisme contemporain. In: Bhattacharya T (ed) Avant 8 heures. Après 17 h. Capitalisme et reproduction sociale. Blast, Toulouse, pp 41–65

Froidevaux-Metterie C (2025) Le droit à l'avortement, socle démocratique. In: Hennette-Vauchez S, Marguet L (eds) De haute lutte. La révolution de l'avortement. CNRS Éditions, Paris

Gilligan C (1982) In a different voice: psychological theory and women's development. Harvard University Press, Cambridge

Guiraudon V, Ledoux C, Poblete L (2024) Perspectives comparées sur l'emploi et les services de care à domicile en temps de pandémie. Revue des politiques sociales et familiales 1:3–12

Hennette-Vauchez S (2020) L'urgence (pas) pour tou(te)s. La Revue des droits de l'homme, Actualités Droits-Libertés

Hennette-Vauchez S (2023) Raisons et déraison dans l'interprétation de la Constitution. Blog Jus Politicum

Hennette-Vauchez S (2024) The constitutionalization of abortion in France. In: ICON-S conference, Madrid

Hennette-Vauchez S (2025) L'avortement comme question constitutionnelle. In: Hennette-Vauchez S, Marguet L (eds) De haute lutte. La révolution de l'avortement. CNRS Éditions, Paris

Hirata H (2021) Travail productif, travail de care. Actuel Marx, Reproduction sociale 7:62–76

Hirata H, Zarifian P (2000) Travail. In: Hirata H, Laborie F, Le Doaré H, Senotier D (eds) Dictionnaire critique du féminisme. PUF, Paris, pp 230–235

Kergoat D (2001) Division sexuelle du travail et rapports sociaux de sexe. In: Bisilliat J, Verschuur C (eds) Genre et économie: Un premier éclairage. Graduate Institute Publications, Genève, pp 78–88

Laugier S (2011) Le care comme critique et comme féminisme. Travail, genre et société 2:183–188

Manelli S (2021) Coronavirus: Derniers de cordée, premiers face à la pandémie. La Provence

Marguet L (2023) Actualités choisies – Corps, santé, sexualité (janvier 2023 – décembre 2023). Intersection – revue semestrielle genre & droit, §5

Marguet L (2024) La constitutionnalisation de l'IVG: Deuxième round. Blog Jus Politicum

Marguet L (2025) De l'existence d'un droit à l'IVG en France. In: Hennette-Vauchez S, Marguet L (eds) De haute lutte. La révolution de l'avortement. CNRS Éditions, Paris

Pastier K (2022) La Covid-19: Un basculement vers une organisation par le care? Les cas d'EHPAD et d'établissements de travail social. Management & Avenir 1:155–178

Pateman C (1988) The sexual contract. Stanford University Press, Stanford

Renou A (2020) Coronavirus: À leurs fenêtres, de plus en plus de Français applaudissent les soignants. Le Parisien

Suk J (2010) Are gender stereotypes bad for women? Rethinking antidiscrimination law and work-family conflict. Colum L Rev 110(1):3–72

Suk J (2018) Gender equality and the protection of motherhood in global constitutionalism. Law Ethics Hum Rights 12:151–180

West R (2009) From choice to reproductive justice: de-constitutionalizing abortion rights. Yale Law J 118:1394–1432

Laurie Marguet is Professor of Public Law at the University of Rouen, specialising in the law of fundamental freedoms, bioethics, gender issues and the relationship between law, science and technology. She is recently co-author of *De haute lutte. La révolution de l'avortement* (CNRS Éditions 2025).

Governing AI in Public Health: Advancing the Right to Health Through an Intersectional Lens

Hannah van Kolfschooten

Abstract Governments across Europe are increasingly deploying artificial intelligence (AI) tools to fulfil their obligations under the right to health and advance the core functions of public health: prevention, promotion, and protection. Yet despite their promise, these technologies risk reinforcing health inequities, especially for those marginalized by intersecting forms of disadvantage such as race, gender, disability, migration status, and class. This chapter applies an intersectional lens to examine how AI-driven public health interventions affect states' legal duties under international and European human rights law. It analyses how AI is transforming public health governance and assesses whether current EU regulatory frameworks, particularly the Artificial Intelligence Act, can safeguard the right to health. Focusing on use cases such as population cancer screening, health chatbots, and epidemic surveillance, the chapter shows how algorithmic systems often replicate structural exclusions and undermine the principles of availability, accessibility, acceptability, and quality (AAAQ). It concludes by proposing legal and policy tools to align AI governance with intersectional health justice.

1 Introduction

In recent years, artificial intelligence (AI) has emerged as a powerful tool in the field of public health.[1] In the European Union (EU) and beyond, governments and public institutions increasingly rely on AI technologies to manage health systems more efficiently, monitor populations, and design interventions aimed at promoting healthier behaviours. From early warning systems that predict disease outbreaks[2] to

[1] del Castillo (2024), Bharel et al. (2024), Olawade et al. (2023) and Kamyabi et al. (2024).

[2] El Morr et al. (2024).

H. van Kolfschooten (✉)
Centre for Life Sciences Law, University of Basel, Basel, Switzerland
e-mail: hannah.vankolfschooten@unibas.ch

M. Balestrieri and A. Cauduro (eds.), *The Legal Anatomy of the Body*, Ius Gentium: Comparative Perspectives on Law and Justice 142,
https://doi.org/10.1007/978-3-032-26434-3_17

chatbots that personalize advice on healthy lifestyles,[3] AI is becoming embedded in the infrastructure of public health governance. These developments are often framed as efforts to fulfil state obligations under the right to health, enhancing the availability and accessibility of services, particularly in under-resourced or underserved areas.

Yet as AI systems assume a more prominent role in public health, they also raise fundamental questions about how bodies are known, governed, and acted upon. Public health has always treated the body not only as a subject of care but also as an object of intervention to protect the society at large.[4] AI technologies amplify this dynamic by transforming bodies into data points within systems of optimization, profiling, and behavioural influence.[5] In this context, the human body becomes both a source of information and a target of algorithmic action.[6]

This chapter examines the tension at the heart of AI-driven public health: while these technologies are deployed in the name of promoting the right to health, they may also undermine the very principles that this right is meant to protect. AI tools risk reinforcing existing inequities in access, autonomy, and dignity, especially for those already marginalized on the basis of race, gender, class, disability, or migration status.[7] They often rely on opaque decision-making processes, raise concerns about consent and manipulation, and may perpetuate biases embedded in the data and systems on which they depend.[8]

To understand how these harms arise and how they can be addressed, this chapter applies an intersectional lens to the legal framework of the right to health. Intersectionality, developed by Black feminist scholars and activists, provides a way of understanding how multiple and overlapping systems of disadvantage shape people's experiences of power and exclusion.[9] Rather than asking whether a given policy discriminates on the basis of gender or race, an intersectional approach asks how factors such as gender, disability, migration status, and language combine to structure who is visible in data, who defines risk, and who benefits or suffers from algorithmic interventions.[10] In the context of public health, where population-level decisions affect access to healthcare, this approach is especially urgent.[11]

While scholars have examined the human rights risks of AI in healthcare, the key literature tends to focus on clinical care settings[12] and less so on the domain of public health, particularly within the EU context. Although a growing body of legal scholarship addresses non-discrimination under the EU's main regulatory framework

---

[3] Abroms et al. (2025) and van Kolfschooten et al. (2025).

[4] Lupton (1995).

[5] Pedersen and Iliadis (2020).

[6] Ball et al. (2016).

[7] Leslie et al. (2021) and van Kolfschooten (2023).

[8] Bentley et al. (2023), Broussard (2023), Browne et al. (2023), Ciston (2019), Collett and Dillon (2019) and Toupin (2024).

[9] Crenshaw (1989).

[10] Crenshaw and HoSang (2023).

[11] Sekalala et al. (2021).

[12] See for example: van Kolfschooten (2025), Solaiman and Cohen (2024).

on AI—the EU AI Act—most analyses focus on isolated factors of discrimination, such as gender,[13] age,[14] and race.[15] One recent article has explored the EU AI Act through an intersectional lens,[16] yet the health-related implications remain significantly understudied. At the same time, the broader regulatory discourse surrounding AI in the EU often prioritizes innovation and economic competitiveness, while concerns about structural inequity remain underdeveloped.[17] This chapter contributes to bridging these gaps by focusing on AI in public health, a domain where individual and collective rights intersect. In particular, this chapter focuses on the EU as a key site for AI integration in public health governance.

The research question guiding this chapter is: How does the growing use of AI in public health affect states' obligations under the right to health, and how do current EU regulatory responses address these challenges? By foregrounding the right to health and applying an intersectional framework, the chapter offers a novel legal analysis of how AI is reshaping public health governance. Section 2 explores how AI is currently used across the three core functions of public health, promotion, prevention, and protection, and identifies emerging patterns of AI public health interventions. Section 3 examines why these developments matter from a human rights perspective, analysing how the deployment of AI in public health affects states' obligations under the right to health, particularly when viewed through an intersectional lens. Section 4 turns to the EU AI Act, critically assessing its capacity to safeguard the right to health in AI-driven public health systems. The chapter concludes by outlining three legal and policy pathways that can help align AI governance with the principles of intersectional health justice.

2 AI and the Three Ps of Public Health

AI is increasingly embedded in the infrastructure of public health, with governments and public bodies relying on algorithmic tools to enhance surveillance, tailor health interventions, and optimize resource distribution. While often framed as innovations that help fulfil the right to health, these technologies are transforming how health risks are assessed and managed at the population level. This section presents three key use cases of AI in public health, offering an overview of how these technologies are currently being deployed.

[13] Lütz (2024).

[14] van Kolfschooten (2023).

[15] Hupont et al. (2022).

[16] Karagianni (2025).

[17] Ulnicane (2024).

2.1 *Prevention: AI-Assisted Population Cancer Screening*

One of the most widespread preventive uses of AI in public health is its integration into population-level screening programs. In countries such as the United Kingdom, Sweden, and the Netherlands, AI models are increasingly used to assist in the early detection of diseases such as breast and cervical cancer.[18] These systems analyse large datasets, including imaging and clinical records, to stratify individuals by risk level and guide decisions about screening frequency or follow-up. Public health authorities often adopt such tools to improve accuracy, reduce the burden on human experts, and expand the reach of preventive care. By predicting who is most likely to develop the disease, AI systems promise to make screening more cost-effective and targeted. In public health settings, these tools do not merely assist clinical decision-making but shape who is selected for prevention in the first place.[19]

2.2 *Promotion: AI-Driven Healthy Lifestyle Chatbots*

Another significant use of AI in public health is the deployment of algorithmically tailored messaging to influence individual and collective behaviour. Governments and international organizations increasingly rely on AI-enhanced platforms to promote vaccination uptake, healthy eating, smoking cessation, and pandemic-related behavioural changes. These interventions use recommender systems, AI chatbots, and behavioural analytics to deliver personalized content across digital platforms. For example, during the COVID-19 pandemic, various countries employed AI tools to tailor vaccination messages on social media, using behavioural insights to increase uptake.[20] The World Health Organization's AI-powered chatbot S.A.R.A.H. and similar national initiatives illustrate the global shift toward digital health promotion via conversational agents. These tools are often designed to increase the reach and relevance of public health campaigns by adapting messages to individual users' preferences, behaviours, and concerns.[21] This use of AI promises to make public health messaging more engaging and effective, especially in large and diverse populations. It also reflects a broader trend of integrating behavioural science into public health strategies.

[18] Eisemann et al. (2025), Hernström et al. (2025) and Gentile and Malara (2024).

[19] Hernström et al. (2025).

[20] Aloise et al. (2024).

[21] van Kolfschooten et al. (2025).

2.3 *Protection: Predictive Analytics in Epidemic Control*

Another field of AI applications in public health is the use of predictive analytics to identify and monitor disease outbreaks. Governments have turned to AI systems to detect early warning signs of epidemics by analysing large volumes of data, including mobility patterns, climate conditions, social media activity, and health records.[22] Tools like BlueDot and HealthMap exemplify how AI is used to forecast virus spread and allocate public health resources. These systems are often developed in collaboration with private companies or academic institutions, and their data sources may include both traditional epidemiological data and more novel data streams.[23] The goal is to enable faster and more targeted interventions to control outbreaks and allocate resources more efficiently. In this way, predictive analytics serves the protective function of public health: guarding populations against emerging threats through early detection and rapid response.

These three use cases illustrate how AI is becoming integral to the practice of public health. From forecasting epidemics and targeting health communication to allocating scarce resources, AI technologies are reshaping how public health authorities understand and act upon population health needs. In the following sections, this chapter will analyse their implications for the protection and promotion of the right to health in the EU.

3 The Right to Health Through an Intersectional Lens

3.1 *The Right to Health and State Obligations*

The right to the highest attainable standard of physical and mental health is enshrined in international and regional human rights law.[24] Article 12 of the International Covenant on Economic, Social and Cultural Rights (ICESCR) recognizes 'the right of everyone to the enjoyment of the highest attainable standard of physical and mental health'. This right is elaborated in General Comment No. 14 of the UN Committee on Economic, Social and Cultural Rights, which outlines the core obligations of states to respect, protect, and fulfil the right to health. The World Health Organization (WHO) similarly defines health as 'not merely as the absence of disease, but as a state of complete physical, mental, and social well-being'. In light of this holistic understanding of health, the state's obligation to *respect*, *protect* and *fulfil* the right to health introduces a set of duties that extend well beyond healthcare to include the social, political, and environmental determinants of health.[25]

[22] El Morr et al. (2024).

[23] Tripathi and Rathore (2025) and Adeoye et al. (2025).

[24] Toebes (2001).

[25] Toebes and Stronks (2016).

The obligation to respect the right to health requires states to refrain from interfering with the enjoyment of health rights. The obligation to protect mandates that states prevent third parties, including private actors such as technology companies, from infringing on health rights.[26] The obligation to fulfil requires proactive measures to ensure access to healthcare, as well as the conditions necessary for good health, such as clean water, safe housing, adequate nutrition, and health-related education. Importantly, these obligations are both individual and collective in nature. States must ensure that health systems are responsive to the needs of diverse populations and address underlying inequalities that affect health outcomes.[27]

In the context of digital public health, these obligations take on new dimensions. States that use AI tools for public health surveillance, behavioural interventions, or resource allocation must ensure that such technologies do not undermine the availability, accessibility, acceptability, or quality (AAAQ) of health services. These four essential elements, articulated in General Comment No. 14, serve as a benchmark for evaluating public health systems. In a digital context, availability requires that technological health interventions are sufficiently resourced and functional. Accessibility entails both physical and digital access, including for persons with disabilities, linguistic minorities, and those in rural or low-income settings. Acceptability refers to the cultural and ethical appropriateness of digital interventions, including issues of consent, privacy, and trust. Quality demands that AI tools be evidence-based, reliable, and sensitive to social and cultural contexts.[28]

As AI-driven public health policy often operates at the level of populations rather than individuals, this creates tensions between collective goals and individual rights. For instance, AI systems that predict disease outbreaks or allocate health resources may optimize for efficiency at the expense of inclusivity or fairness. Such systems risk excluding or misrepresenting communities with limited digital access or historically underrepresented data profiles.[29] Public health interventions premised on algorithmic logics may also reshape understandings of responsibility and eligibility, shifting the focus from structural determinants of health to individualized risk scores and behavioural metrics. The shift toward algorithmic governance in public health thus raises critical questions about how state obligations under the right to health are being reshaped in practice, particularly in ways that are less transparent or accountable to those most affected.[30]

---

[26] Ó Cathaoir (2022).

[27] Toebes (2020).

[28] Ó Cathaoir (2022) and Murphy (2009).

[29] Fletcher et al. (2021).

[30] Cochlin et al. (2024).

3.2 Intersectionality and the Right to Health

An important aspect of the right to health is the objective of health equity.[31] The WHO defines health equity as 'the absence of unfair, avoidable or remediable [*health*] differences among groups of people, whether those groups are defined socially, economically, demographically, or geographically or by other dimensions of inequality (e.g. sex, gender, ethnicity, disability, or sexual orientation)'.[32] As explained by Amartya Sen, the concept of health equity has to be regarded as multidimensional. It extends much further than the distribution of good health (natural biological differences) or access to appropriate healthcare alone.[33] Health equity is not only about health outcomes but also involves health capabilities—the equal opportunity to achieve one's full health potential.[34] Part of health inequity is caused by unequal distribution of 'social determinants of health', such as income, gender, and geographical location. In other words, especially those people who are part of already marginalized groups are affected by health inequity. Indeed, as health is among the most important conditions of human life, it is also an issue of social justice.

In response to the wider emergence of feminist legal theory in human rights law scholarship, more recent scholarship on health and human rights calls for an *intersectional* approach. Instead of studying the social determinants of health in 'silos' (e.g. the effects of race on health outcomes *or* the effects of gender on health outcomes), it is argued that health inequity emerges at the intersection of various individual characteristics.[35] Crenshaw, inspired by other black feminists before her,[36] first introduced the term 'intersectionality' in legal theory in 1989 in reaction to dominant feminist approaches to law.[37] She describes how various individual characteristics (e.g. race, gender, age, socioeconomic status) overlap and 'intersect' and can create varying discrimination for certain individuals or population groups. To illustrate, treating a black woman only as a 'woman' or only as 'black', ignores the varied discrimination experienced by people with both characteristics. A narrow interpretation of discrimination neglects the existence of multiple systems of oppression in parallel.[38]

In the context of health equity, various legal and policy scholars have demonstrated the importance of taking an intersectional approach. Intersectionality promotes the understanding that human health is determined by multi-factor and multi-level intersecting identities.[39] This understanding is especially important in the context of health law and policy research, because insight into the differential impact of health policy on often highly heterogeneous population groups is necessary to develop appropriate

[31] Yamin and Fukuda-Parr (2023).

[32] See the website of the WHO. Emphasis added by author.

[33] Sen (2002).

[34] Sen (2002), pp. 660–661.

[35] Borras (2021).

[36] See for example: The Combahee River Collective (1977).

[37] Crenshaw (1989).

[38] Crenshaw (1989).

[39] Kapilashrami and Aziz (2023).

health responses without forging unfair health outcomes.[40] This chapter advocates for approaching the right to health from an intersectional lens.

The Covid-19 pandemic powerfully illustrates the need for this approach.[41] While the pandemic affected everyone's health and human rights, research shows that, because of specific risk factors, some—already disadvantaged and marginalized groups—had a greater chance of getting ill and experiencing human rights violations than others.[42] The combination and compounding of these factors exacerbate the harm experienced by the individual. For example, globally, the group of frontline healthcare workers (e.g. nurses, midwives, cleaners)—the group most exposed to the infection—disproportionally consisted of women. Within this group, a disproportionate number of people had a migration background.[43] Further, social distancing measures caused the shutdown of work activities involving interpersonal contact, a sector in which most employees are female, causing a lot of job losses amongst women. Simultaneously, this sector consists primarily of low-income and temporary workers, creating an even larger financial impact for these groups.[44] Mortality rates of migrant workers were two times higher than non-migrant workers, especially for those working in high-risk jobs.[45] In addition, school closures disproportionally affected the mental health of children, with a greater chance of having post-traumatic stress. Female children are generally more affected by mental health issues.[46] At the same time, lockdown measures such as quarantine caused a global surge in domestic violence, especially towards women and children.[47] In other words, only focusing on one 'axis' (e.g. gender or socioeconomic status), does not allow us to fully grasp how health risks are distributed throughout society—and how law and policy can respond to health inequity.

Hankivsky and others have promoted an intersectional approach to inform policies and practices to tackle health inequities. In the context of healthcare, they show how an intersectionality approach is important to combat health inequity by giving the example of cardiovascular diseases. Race and sex are well-recognized as determinants of health outcomes of persons living with cardiovascular diseases. However, intersecting identities such as race, gender, and socioeconomic status affect populations differently.[48] For example, black women with a low income are at a higher risk of developing cardiovascular diseases.[49] In the context of public health, the need for an intersectional approach is illustrated by explaining the ineffectiveness of a uniform response to the HIV pandemic, given the enormous heterogeneity in the global group

---

40 Dhamoon and Hankivsky (2011).

41 See for example: Ryan and El Ayadi (2020) and Siller and Aydin (2022).

42 Olanlesi-Aliu et al. (2024).

43 Singh and Kaur (2022).

44 Maestripieri (2021).

45 Spanikova et al., p. 34.

46 Spanikova et al., p. 34.

47 Kourti et al. (2023).

48 Hankivsky et al. (2017) and Hankivsky (2012).

49 Baiden et al. (2022).

of persons living with HIV caused by the intersections between sexuality, biological sex, gender, and financial wealth.[50]

In the same vein, Davies and others have highlighted the lack of an intersectional approach to gender inequality in the field of global health.[51] They illustrate the importance of intersectionality in global health policy with the example of maternal health: in the USA, maternal and neonatal mortality is significantly greater among black women than among other ethnic groups, which shows the intersection of race and gender.[52] Sekalala and others have advocated the use of an intersectional human rights approach in deciding on the allocation of COVID-19 vaccines. Instead of basing prioritization of scarce resources on a 'single axis', such as age, they argue that taking an intersectional approach (a model based on various individual health criteria such as age and comorbidities *and* sociodemographic vulnerabilities such as living conditions, gender, occupation, etc.) will lead to more health equity.[53] Other scholars underline the importance of the lens of intersectionality in responding to climate change-induced health inequity.[54]

3.3 The Need for an Intersectional Approach to AI in Public Health

When used in the context of public health AI, an intersectional approach enables a deeper understanding of how algorithmic systems can reproduce and exacerbate existing social inequalities. Applying an intersectional approach to public health AI, therefore, means asking who is included in the data, who benefits from technological interventions, who bears the burdens, and whose voices are represented in policy development and oversight.[55] It also allows for a more nuanced assessment of how the right to health is differentially experienced across social groups. For example, racialized and migrant communities may face structural exclusions from health data systems, while women, transgender individuals, or people with disabilities may be rendered invisible or misrepresented in digital health design and implementation.[56] Moreover, intersectionality is not only descriptive but also normative: it calls for legal and policy frameworks that recognize and respond to the complexity of lived experiences.[57] Without this lens, legal frameworks risk reinforcing the status quo of health inequality under the guise of technological neutrality.

---

[50] Hankivsky et al. (2017).

[51] Davies et al. (2019).

[52] Njoku et al. (2023).

[53] Sekalala et al. (2021).

[54] Hefti et al. (2024) and Hefti (2024).

[55] Islam et al. (2023).

[56] Van Kolfschooten (2023).

[57] De Beco (2017).

Importantly, applying an intersectional lens goes beyond identifying algorithmic bias or unequal treatment based on individual characteristics. While anti-discrimination law plays a vital role in flagging differential outcomes, it tends to address protected characteristics, such as race or gender, in isolation.[58] Intersectionality, by contrast, recognizes that health inequities are shaped by interlocking systems of power.[59] It asks how AI technologies reflect and reinforce these systems, not just whether they treat individuals differently. For example, a health AI tool might pass formal fairness tests on race or gender but still disproportionately fail Black women, who face distinctive and intersecting forms of exclusion in healthcare systems.[60] Intersectionality thus enables a shift from formal to substantive equality, and from technical fairness to structural justice. In doing so, it aligns more closely with states' human rights obligations under the right to health, which require not only equal treatment but also equitable outcomes.

The following sections will explore how these challenges manifest in practice and assess how current EU regulatory instruments respond to them.

3.4 *Intersectional Legal Analysis of the Use Cases*

When viewed through the intersectional lens of the right to health, the AI applications outlined above expose specific legal and ethical tensions between public health innovation and human rights protection. Although each use case aims to improve population health, they can simultaneously undermine the principles of availability, accessibility, acceptability, and quality (AAAQ), and states' obligations to respect, protect, and fulfil the right to health, particularly for historically marginalized populations.[61] An intersectional analysis helps reveal not only who is affected but also which questions are being asked, and which are ignored, when designing and deploying these technologies.

3.4.1 Prevention: AI-Assisted Population Cancer Screening

AI-assisted screening programs raise complex questions about who is seen, who is prioritized, and whose health is valued. Public health tools that predict cancer risk or determine eligibility for early screening rely on large datasets, which often reflect the demographics of populations already well-represented in care. This can result in misclassification or exclusion of groups such as racial minorities, migrants, or persons with disabilities. In the UK and Sweden, for example, breast cancer risk models trained predominantly on data from white women may underperform for other

---

[58] Atrey (2019).

[59] Karagianni (2025).

[60] Figueroa et al. (2021).

[61] Borras (2021).

racial and ethnic groups, leading to delayed detection or misallocation of screening resources.[62]

From a right to health perspective, this compromises the principle of non-discrimination and the obligation to ensure equitable access to preventive services. If marginalized groups are systematically excluded from high-quality screening due to biased data or inaccessible digital interfaces, the availability and quality of care are affected in a way that violates international human rights norms. Moreover, opaque decision-making can undermine patients' ability to understand or challenge how they are categorized, raising questions about autonomy and informed consent in population health settings.

An intersectional perspective shifts the focus from statistical inclusion to structural visibility. Instead of merely asking whether women and men have equal access to AI screening, it compels public health authorities to ask who is missing from the data, whose diagnostic experiences are normalized, and whose bodies are treated as outliers.[63] For instance, undocumented migrant women or transgender patients may fall outside the reference categories used to train AI models. If the risk logic embedded in these tools does not reflect their lived experiences, these patients are rendered invisible. Intersectionality thus challenges the assumption that algorithmic accuracy is sufficient to ensure justice in public health decision-making.[64]

3.4.2 Promotion: AI-Driven Healthy Lifestyle Chatbots

AI systems are increasingly used in public health promotion to deliver personalized messages aimed at influencing health behaviours such as vaccination uptake, smoking cessation, or dietary change. These tools, often deployed as chatbots, promise to improve public health communication by tailoring content to individual users based on language, behaviour, or demographic data.[65] First, personalized health messaging can blur the line between persuasion and manipulation, especially when users are unaware that they are interacting with an AI system trained to optimize behavioural change. This raises concerns about autonomy, informed consent, and the acceptability of public health interventions.[66] For example, chatbots that use behavioural nudges without disclosing their logic or objectives may undermine the right to make free and informed health decisions. Where AI tools fail to provide culturally appropriate, linguistically inclusive, or accessible content, for instance, for people with disabilities or low digital literacy, public health messaging may be ineffective.[67] Similarly, WHO's S.A.R.A.H. chatbot initially lacked accessibility features for people with disabilities and offered limited multilingual support, weakening its effectiveness

[62] Dratsch et al. (2023).

[63] Bauer and Lizotte (2021).

[64] Buchbinder et al. (2022).

[65] Passanante et al. (2023), Weingott and Parkinson (2025) and Bendotti et al. (2023).

[66] Ienca (2023).

[67] Nadarzynski et al. (2024).

for vulnerable populations.[68] From a legal standpoint, these deficiencies breach the accessibility and acceptability pillars of the right to health, particularly when tools are rolled out as core channels of public communication.

Intersectionality helps reframe how public health promotion is evaluated.[69] While a health equity perspective might ask whether different communities received comparable chatbot engagement or vaccine uptake, an intersectional lens goes further. It asks: whose communication norms are prioritized, whose distrust is pathologized, and what counts as a successful intervention. Instead of measuring efficacy solely by behavioural change, intersectional analysis urges attention to cultural safety, participatory design, and the power dynamics embedded in digital outreach. A chatbot that is technically functional but fails to account for users' linguistic, cultural, or disability-related needs may not only fall short, but it may even exacerbate inequities.

3.4.3 Protection: Predictive Analytics in Epidemic Control

AI systems designed to predict disease outbreaks can support the availability and quality of public health services, fulfilling part of the state's obligation to provide timely and adequate health infrastructure. However, their effectiveness and fairness hinge on the inclusivity and representativeness of the data they use. When predictive tools rely on datasets that exclude undocumented migrants, unhoused individuals, or digitally disconnected communities, the right to accessibility is compromised.[70] During COVID-19, tools like Google's Mobility Reports and ZIP-code-level hotspot prediction in U.S. cities were deployed to inform public health resource allocation. However, their reliance on smartphone data meant that digitally invisible populations were left out of decision-making, violating the obligation to fulfil the right to health in a non-discriminatory and equitable manner.[71] Moreover, in some cases, high predicted risk in racialized communities led not to increased healthcare access but to increased police surveillance, undermining acceptability and raising concerns about coercion.

Intersectionality pushes public health systems to ask: whose movement is monitored, whose health is prioritized, and whose neighbourhoods are flagged for risk without corresponding support. While a traditional approach might focus on geographic coverage or algorithmic accuracy, intersectionality reveals how predictive systems can reproduce stigmatization and neglect.[72] The same algorithm that flags a migrant neighbourhood as a viral hotspot may be blind to its lack of clinics, clean water, or safe housing. Intersectional governance, therefore, requires more than technical improvements. It demands that AI tools be situated within the broader social and political structures that shape health vulnerability.

68 van Kolfschooten et al. (2025).

69 Heard et al. (2020).

70 Abrar et al. (2023).

71 Erfani and Frias-Martinez (2023).

72 Poteat (2021).

4 Governing the Use of AI in Public Health

4.1 The EU Artificial Intelligence Act: Regulatory Gaps in Public Health AI

The EU AI Act, adopted in 2024, is the world's first comprehensive regulation of AI technologies. It takes a risk-based approach that governs AI systems in accordance with their level of risk. Systems that pose unacceptable risks to fundamental rights or safety are prohibited, while high-risk systems are subject to the most stringent requirements, including human oversight, data quality standards, and accountability obligations. Low-risk systems only need to comply with transparency requirements.[73]

In the context of health, the EU AI Act classifies as high-risk any AI system that is a safety component of a medical device governed by the EU Medical Devices Regulation. It also covers certain public sector uses of AI, including those deployed by public authorities to determine eligibility for essential public services, such as healthcare. This opens the door to regulating some public health applications, such as triage systems used in emergency care or algorithms determining access to health benefits, as high-risk systems. These applications must meet several requirements, including a mandatory fundamental rights impact assessment (FRIA) carried out by the public health authority upon first use (Article 27; Recital 96).[74]

The FRIA obligation applies to both public bodies and private actors delivering services of public interest, including public health services. According to Recital 96, the FRIA must identify risks to individuals and groups and propose mitigation measures, addressing not only individual harms but also structural discrimination.[75] Yet while the AI Act establishes a baseline requirement for a fundamental rights impact assessment, it does not provide detailed guidance on how this assessment should be carried out, nor how it should account for the intersecting inequalities that shape both health outcomes and vulnerability to algorithmic harm.

Several other structural limitations undermine the AI Act's capacity to protect the right to health in public health contexts. First, the regulation primarily targets products, not people. Its technical focus overlooks the social and structural harms that AI systems can perpetuate, especially when used on structurally marginalized populations.[76] Second, the Act does not define key terms such as vulnerability and manipulation, despite explicitly prohibiting AI systems that exploit vulnerabilities under Article 5(1)(a). This omission weakens the Act's ability to prevent discriminatory impacts and foresee unintended consequences for certain population groups,

[73] van Kolfschooten and van Oirschot (2024).

[74] van Kolfschooten and van Oirschot (2024).

[75] Mantelero (2024) and Novelli et al. (2023).

[76] van Kolfschooten (2025).

such as people with intersecting forms of disadvantage.[77] Third, the scope of prohibited practices under Article 5 is narrow and includes broad exemptions. For example, manipulative AI is only banned if it causes 'significant harm', and the prohibition does not apply to systems deployed for national security or law enforcement purposes. These exemptions risk covering public health interventions like border screening or pandemic surveillance.[78] Finally, the AI Act's emphasis on high-risk medical devices reflects a clinical rather than public health focus. It frames risk in terms of individual safety, not collective harm.[79]

Taken together, these limitations reveal that the AI Act offers incomplete and uneven protection for individuals affected by AI-driven public health interventions. As currently designed, it fails to safeguard the right to health in contexts where population-level tools interact with individual rights in complex, intersecting ways. The next section explores how legal frameworks can be updated to close these gaps and ensure algorithmic governance in public health advances, rather than undermines, health equity.

4.2 *Rethinking Legal Protection for AI in Public Health*

The preceding analysis has shown that the EU's current regulatory frameworks for AI, particularly the AI Act, are insufficient to protect the right to health in the digital era, in a manner that meaningfully addresses the intersecting forms of exclusion, discrimination, and marginalisation that shape the impact of AI in public health. This section outlines a practical and normative framework for such an intersectional right to health approach in AI governance.

4.2.1 Beyond Bias Audits: Fundamental Rights Impact Assessment for Health AI (FRIA-H)

As explained in Sect. 4.1, the AI Act does not provide detailed guidance on how the FRIA should be carried out, nor how it should account for structural differences between affected groups. To address this critical gap, we propose the Fundamental Rights Impact Assessment for Health AI (FRIA-H), a sector-specific framework that embeds intersectionality and public health values into every stage of the assessment.

Bias audits, the dominant approach to fairness in AI, are inadequate in healthcare. They tend to treat characteristics like gender or race in isolation, ignoring how intersecting forms of marginalisation (e.g., being a Black woman or a disabled migrant) shape algorithmic harm. They focus on outputs rather than the broader structural context: who is represented in training data, whose values and behaviours

[77] Ćemalović (2024) and Galli and Novelli (2024).

[78] van Kolfschooten (2025).

[79] van Kolfschooten and van Oirschot (2024).

are encoded, and who is involved in the system's design. Moreover, bias audits often reduce fundamental rights to technical metrics, neglecting the normative foundations of public health, such as equality, dignity, consent, access, and redress.

The FRIA-H moves beyond this narrow paradigm. It operationalizes Article 27 in a way that is legally robust and context-sensitive, assessing how AI systems affect structurally marginalised groups and interact with the social determinants of health. Inspired by the Dutch Fundamental Rights and Algorithm Impact Assessment (FRAIA),[80] the FRIA-H is structured around four core components: *Why, What, How,* and *Rights.*

In the proposed FRIA-H, the first component (*Why*) examines the purpose of using AI in a given health-related process, requiring justification for why automation is necessary and whether less intrusive alternatives exist. It considers whether the issue targeted by the AI disproportionately affects excluded groups and risks reinforcing existing distrust or exclusion. *What* focuses on data sources, model design, and anticipated impacts. This includes identifying affected populations and specific risks, using an intersectionality matrix to assess how overlapping disadvantages, such as race, gender, disability, or immigration status, might amplify harm. For example, a digital triage system may perform well overall yet systematically under-assess the needs of women of colour, due to biases embedded in training data.

How addresses implementation, oversight, and redress. The FRIA-H demands not only internal governance mechanisms but also meaningful human oversight, culturally appropriate communication, and accessible complaint procedures. It emphasizes the need for systems that are usable by all affected groups. The final component, *Rights*, brings the assessment together in a legal justification and proportionality analysis. It asks whether infringements on fundamental rights are lawful, necessary, and proportionate, and whether the benefits of the AI system are distributed fairly.

Under Article 27(3), deployers must notify the market surveillance authority once the assessment is complete. The FRIA-H recommends including the intersectional analysis, stakeholder consultation record, and equity-based mitigation measures to ensure transparency and public accountability. The FRIA-H is not merely a best-practice tool; it is a legal mechanism for ensuring that the AI Act's fundamental rights safeguards are meaningful in healthcare settings. It aligns with Recital 96's call for participation of affected groups, civil society, and independent experts. By embedding intersectionality as a core analytical lens, the FRIA-H helps prevent foreseeable harm, promote equitable access, and restore trust in health systems.

4.2.2 Updating Human Rights Frameworks: Digital Health Rights

The growing use of AI in public health exposes not only regulatory gaps but also the inadequacy of existing human rights frameworks to protect individuals in digital health contexts. Core rights such as privacy, non-discrimination, consent, access to care, and participation were shaped in an analogue era and are increasingly strained

[80] Gerards et al. (2022).

by the scale, opacity, and predictive logic of algorithmic systems. Current rights frameworks are ill-equipped to respond to the compounded risks posed by algorithmic profiling, automated decision-making, and data-driven surveillance. The harms involved are often systemic, intersectional, and collective, yet traditional instruments focus on individual violations and linear causality.

What is needed is a new EU framework for the protection of Digital Health Rights: not a replacement of existing rights, but their reinterpretation and expansion to reflect digital realities. This includes protections against algorithmic discrimination; rights to transparency, explainability, and human oversight; the right to contest and seek redress for automated decisions; and the right to equitable access and benefit-sharing in digital health. Such a framework must explicitly embed intersectionality, acknowledging that digital tools are not neutral but shaped by the same structural biases that produce health inequities offline. Such a framework would offer a normative foundation for public health AI that centres human dignity, equity, and human rights.[81]

4.2.3 Collective Redress for Algorithmic Harm in Public Health Interventions

Current legal remedies in Europe remain focused on individual harm and complaints, yet this model fails to capture how AI systems in public health often reproduce structural inequalities. Algorithmic harms are rarely isolated or evenly distributed; they tend to disproportionately affect people at the intersections of race, gender, disability, migration status, and poverty. Misclassification, exclusion from digital services, and invisibility in health data are systemic outcomes of how data and power interact. Individual complaints mechanisms cannot adequately address these collective and intersectional harms. That is why legal frameworks must expand access to collective redress, enabling civil society actors, equality bodies, and grassroots organisations to bring forward claims on behalf of affected groups. Such mechanisms already exist in areas like consumer and environmental law.[82]

The General Data Protection Regulation (GDPR) provides an important legal precedent. Article 80(1) allows individuals to mandate non-profits to pursue data protection claims on their behalf, while Article 80(2) permits Member States to authorise these organisations to act independently in cases of systemic rights violations.[83] Though unevenly implemented across Europe, this provision recognises that digital harms are often diffuse, collective, and difficult to contest individually, especially in contexts involving sensitive health data under Article 9 GDPR.[84] Building on this logic, the AI Act should incorporate equivalent provisions, extending collective standing not only to address data protection violations but also to contest algorithmic

[81] van Kolfschooten (2025).

[82] Hakkarainen (2021).

[83] Federico (2023).

[84] van Kolfschooten (2022, 2024).

discrimination, biased triage, and structural exclusions in digital health systems. These reforms must recognise that intersectional harms often fall through the cracks of existing anti-discrimination frameworks, which are siloed by single grounds such as race or gender. Collective redress, led by actors embedded in affected communities, can surface these layered harms and shift the burden of proof to institutions better placed to produce systemic evidence and implement change.[85]

Effective redress also requires proactive oversight. Regulators must be empowered to investigate algorithmic harms without awaiting individual complaints and to adopt a broader definition of harm, including loss of dignity, algorithmic stigmatisation, and erosion of trust in public health institutions.[86] These harms are harder to quantify but deeply consequential, especially for historically marginalised communities. By embracing collective redress through an intersectional lens, legal systems can begin to evolve from individualised, reactive models of justice toward structural, proactive, and community-driven accountability.[87]

5 Conclusions

Artificial intelligence is transforming public health governance, not only through new tools for surveillance, triage, and prediction, but also by reshaping how health needs are defined, how populations are categorised, and how care is distributed. While often promoted as a means to realise the right to health, AI technologies are also capable of undermining the principles that underpin that right, especially for those situated at the intersection of multiple forms of structural disadvantage. This chapter has argued that public health AI must be governed not only through technical standards, but through legal frameworks that foreground equity. An intersectional interpretation of the right to health reveals how algorithmic systems can reinforce existing inequities in availability, accessibility, acceptability, and quality of care. These are not simply technical failures, but they raise serious legal and ethical concerns tied to states' duties to respect, protect, and fulfil the right to health.

An intersectional approach reveals that digital health cannot be separated from broader systems of inequality, linked to e.g. legal status, race, gender, disability, migration, and socioeconomic precarity. As such, AI governance must move beyond abstract commitments to fairness or transparency and be grounded in a broader social justice agenda. The analysis of the EU AI Act demonstrates that, despite recognising certain risks, the regulation remains largely procedural and technical. It overlooks how AI systems interact with inequalities in public health, and lacks the safeguards to address these dynamics.

To address these challenges, the chapter proposed three complementary interventions. First, a sector-specific Fundamental Rights Impact Assessment for Health AI

[85] Hunter and De Simone (2008).

[86] Busuioc (2021).

[87] Smuha (2021).

(FRIA-H), operationalising Article 27 of the AI Act by embedding intersectional health-specific analysis at every stage of AI deployment, from problem definition to oversight and redress. Second, recognising that algorithmic harms are often collective and relational, it calls for collective redress mechanisms that move beyond the individualised model of justice, drawing on the rationale behind Article 80 GDPR to empower civil society actors to protect affected communities. Third, it argues for the development of a Digital Health Rights framework that reinterprets fundamental rights, such as privacy, equality, and informed consent, for the digital age. Together, these proposals reimagine how law can respond to the risks of health AI. As governments increasingly adopt AI as a tool of public health policy, it is essential to ensure that these systems do not deepen exclusion.

For AI to strengthen rather than weaken the right to health, governance frameworks must adopt an intersectional approach throughout the AI lifecycle. As governments increasingly rely on AI to shape public health interventions, the urgent question is no longer just whether these systems are effective, but whether they are fair, and for whom.

References

Abrar SM, Awasthi N, Smolyak D, Frias-Martinez V (2023) Analysis of performance improvements and bias associated with the use of human mobility data in COVID-19 case prediction models. ACM J Comput Sustain Soc 1:16

Abroms LC, Yousefi A, Wysota CN et al (2025) Assessing the adherence of ChatGPT chatbots to public health guidelines for smoking cessation: content analysis. J Med Internet Res 27:e66896

Adeoye A, Onah CO, Orobator ET et al (2025) AI and machine learning for early detection of infectious diseases in the US: opportunities and challenges. J Med Sci Biol Chem 2:54–63

Aloise I, Migliara G, Franceschetti A et al (2024) Enhancing public health: training an AI chatbot for complex tasks support. Eur J Public Health 34:ckae144.1195

Atrey S (2019) The project: realizing intersectionality in discrimination law. In: Atrey S (ed) Intersectional discrimination. Oxford University Press, Oxford

Baiden D, Parry M, Nerenberg K et al (2022) Connecting the dots: structural racism, intersectionality, and cardiovascular health outcomes for African, Caribbean, and Black mothers. Health Equity 6:402–405

Ball K, Di Domenico M, Nunan D (2016) Big data surveillance and the body-subject. Body Soc 22:58–81

Bauer GR, Lizotte DJ (2021) Artificial intelligence, intersectionality, and the future of public health. Am J Public Health 111:98–100

Bendotti H, Lawler S, Chan GCK et al (2023) Conversational artificial intelligence interventions to support smoking cessation: a systematic review and meta-analysis. Digit Health 9:20552076231211634

Bentley C, Muyoya C, Vannini S et al (2023) Intersectional approaches to data: the importance of an articulation mindset for intersectional data science. Big Data Soc 10:20539517231203667

Bharel M, Auerbach J, Nguyen V, DeSalvo KB (2024) Transforming public health practice with generative artificial intelligence. Health Aff 43:776–782

Borras AM (2021) Toward an intersectional approach to health justice. Int J Health Serv 51:206–225

Broussard M (2023) More than a glitch: confronting race, gender, and ability bias in tech. MIT Press, Cambridge

Browne J, Cave S, Drage E, McInerney K (2023) Feminist AI: critical perspectives on algorithms, data, and intelligent machines. Oxford University Press, Oxford
Buchbinder M, Juengst E, Rennie S et al (2022) Advancing a data justice framework for public health surveillance. AJOB Empir Bioeth 13:205–213
Busuioc M (2021) Accountable artificial intelligence: holding algorithms to account. Public Adm Rev 81:825–836
Ćemalović U (2024) Prohibited artificial intelligence practices according to Article 5 of the European Union's regulation on AI—between the 'too late' and the 'not enough'. Int J Law Inf Technol 32:eaae023
Ciston S (2019) Intersectional AI is essential: polyvocal, multimodal, experimental methods to save artificial intelligence. J Sci Technol Arts 11:3–8
Cochlin FJ, Curran CD, Schmit CD (2024) Unlocking public health data: navigating new legal guardrails and emerging AI challenges. J Law Med Ethics 52:70–74
Collett C, Dillon S (2019) AI and gender: four proposals for future research. Leverhulme Centre for the Future of Intelligence, University of Cambridge, Cambridge
Crenshaw K (1989) Demarginalizing the intersection of race and sex: a Black feminist critique of antidiscrimination doctrine, feminist theory and antiracist politics. U Chi Legal F 1989:139
Crenshaw K, HoSang D (eds) (2023) Under the blacklight: the intersectional vulnerabilities that the twin pandemics lay bare. Haymarket Books, Chicago
Davies SE, Harman S, Manjoo R et al (2019) Why it must be a feminist global health agenda. Lancet 393:601–603
De Beco G (2017) Protecting the invisible: an intersectional approach to international human rights law. Hum Rights Law Rev 17:633–663
del Castillo FA (2024) Generative AI in public health: pathways to well-being and positive health outcome. J Public Health 46:e739–e740
Dhamoon RK, Hankivsky O (2011) Why the theory and practice of intersectionality matter to health research and policy. In: Health inequities in Canada: intersectional frameworks and practices. UBC Press, Vancouver
Dratsch T, Chen X, Rezazade Mehrizi M et al (2023) Automation bias in mammography: the impact of artificial intelligence BI-RADS suggestions on reader performance. Radiology 307:e222176
Eisemann N, Bunk S, Mukama T et al (2025) Nationwide real-world implementation of AI for cancer detection in population-based mammography screening. Nat Med 31:917–924
El Morr C, Ozdemir D, Asdaah Y et al (2024) AI-based epidemic and pandemic early warning systems: a systematic scoping review. Health Inform J 30:14604582241275844
Erfani A, Frias-Martinez V (2023) A fairness assessment of mobility-based COVID-19 case prediction models. PLoS One 18:e0292090
Federico M (2023) European collective redress and data protection: challenges and opportunities. MediaLaws—Rivista di diritto dei media 1:86–103
Figueroa CA, Luo T, Aguilera A, Lyles CR (2021) The need for feminist intersectionality in digital health. Lancet Digit Health 3:e526–e533
Fletcher RR, Nakeshimana A, Olubeko O (2021) Addressing fairness, bias, and appropriate use of artificial intelligence and machine learning in global health. Front Artif Intell 3:561802
Galli N and Novelli C (2024) The many meanings of vulnerability in the AI act and the one missing. BioLaw J 1:53–72
Gentile F, Malara N (2024) Artificial intelligence for cancer screening and surveillance. ESMO Real World Data Digit Oncol 5:100046
Gerards J, Schäfer MT, Muis I, Vankan A (2022, May) Fundamental Rights and Algorithms Impact Assessment (FRAIA). Rijksoverheid. https://www.government.nl/documents/reports/2021/07/31/impact-assessment-fundamental-rights-and-algorithms
Hakkarainen J (2021) Naming something collective does not make it so: algorithmic discrimination and access to justice. Internet Policy Rev 10:1–24
Hankivsky O (2012) Women's health, men's health, and gender and health: implications of intersectionality. Soc Sci Med 74:1712–1720

Hankivsky O, Doyal L, Einstein G et al (2017) The odd couple: using biomedical and intersectional approaches to address health inequities. Glob Health Action 10:1326686
Heard E, Fitzgerald L, Wigginton B, Mutch A (2020) Applying intersectionality theory in health promotion research and practice. Health Promot Int 35:866–876
Hefti A (2024) Intersectional victims as agents of change in international human rights-based climate litigation. Transnat Environ Law, pp 1–26
Hefti A, van Kolfschooten H, Ossom A (2024) A health-centric intersectional approach to climate litigation at the European Court of Human Rights. Harv Hum Rights J 37:351–378
Hernström V, Josefsson V, Sartor H et al (2025) Screening performance and characteristics of breast cancer detected in the Mammography Screening with Artificial Intelligence trial (MASAI): a randomised, controlled, parallel-group, non-inferiority, single-blinded, screening accuracy study. Lancet Digit Health 7:e175–e183
Hunter R, De Simone T (2008) Identifying disadvantage: beyond intersectionality. In: Grabham E, Cooper D, Krishnadas J, Herman D (eds) Intersectionality and beyond: law, power and the politics of location. Routledge-Cavendish, Abingdon, pp 159–182
Hupont I, Tolan S, Gunes H, Gómez E (2022) The landscape of facial processing applications in the context of the European AI Act and the development of trustworthy systems. Sci Rep 12:10688
Ienca M (2023) On artificial intelligence and manipulation. Topoi 42:833–842
Islam R, Keya KN, Pan S et al (2023) Differential fairness: an intersectional framework for fair AI. Entropy 25:660
Kamyabi A, Iyamu I, Saini M et al (2024) Advocating for population health: the role of public health practitioners in the age of artificial intelligence. Can J Public Health 115(3):473–476
Kapilashrami A, Aziz R (2023) Pandemic preparedness with 20/20 vision: applying an intersectional equity lens to health workforce planning. Int J Health Plann Manage 38:1117–1126
Karagianni A (2025) Gender in a stereo-(gender)typical EU AI law: a feminist reading of the AI Act. Cambridge Forum AI Law Govern 1:e25
Kourti A, Stavridou A, Panagouli E et al (2023) Domestic violence during the COVID-19 pandemic: a systematic review. Trauma Violence Abuse 24:719–745
Leslie D, Mazumder A, Peppin A et al (2021) Does 'AI' stand for augmenting inequality in the era of COVID-19 healthcare? BMJ 372:n304
Lupton D (1995) The imperative of health: public health and the regulated body. Sage, London
Lütz F (2024) The AI Act, gender equality and non-discrimination: what role for the AI office? ERA Forum 25:79–95
Maestripieri L (2021) The COVID-19 pandemics: why intersectionality matters. Front Sociol 6:642662
Mantelero A (2024) The Fundamental Rights Impact Assessment (FRIA) in the AI act: roots legal obligations and key elements for a model template. Comput Law Secur Rev 54:106020
Murphy T (2009) New technologies and human rights. Oxford University Press, Oxford
Nadarzynski T, Knights N, Husbands D et al (2024) Achieving health equity through conversational AI: a roadmap for design and implementation of inclusive chatbots in healthcare. PLoS Digit Health 3:e0000492
Njoku A, Evans M, Nimo-Sefah L, Bailey J (2023, February) Listen to the whispers before they become screams: addressing black maternal morbidity and mortality in the United States. Healthcare 11(3):438. https://doi.org/10.3390/healthcare11030438
Novelli C, Casolari F, Rotolo A, et al. (2023) Taking AI risks seriously: a new assessment model for the AI Act. AI Soc
Ó Cathaoir K (2022) Digital healthcare technologies and human rights. In: Health and human rights: global and European perspectives, 2nd edn. Intersentia
Olanlesi-Aliu A, Tulli M, Kemei J et al (2024) A scoping review on the operationalization of intersectional health research methods in studies related to the COVID-19 pandemic. Int J Qual Stud Health Well-being 19:2302305
Olawade DB, Wada OJ, David-Olawade AC et al (2023) Using artificial intelligence to improve public health: a narrative review. Front Public Health 11:1196397

Passanante A, Pertwee E, Lin L et al (2023) Conversational AI and vaccine communication: systematic review of the evidence. J Med Internet Res 25:e42758
Pedersen I, Iliadis A (2020) Embodied computing: wearables, implantables, embeddables, ingestibles. MIT Press, Cambridge
Poteat T (2021) Navigating the storm: how to apply intersectionality to public health in times of crisis. Am J Public Health 111:91–92
Ryan NE, El Ayadi AM (2020) A call for a gender-responsive, intersectional approach to address COVID-19. Glob Public Health 15:1404–1412
Sekalala S, Perehudoff K, Parker M et al (2021) An intersectional human rights approach to prioritising access to COVID-19 vaccines. BMJ Glob Health 6:e004462
Sen A (2002) Why health equity? Health Econ 11:659–666
Siller H, Aydin N (2022) Using an intersectional lens on vulnerability and resilience in minority and/or marginalized groups during the COVID-19 pandemic: a narrative review. Front Psychol 13:894103
Singh N, Kaur A (2022) The COVID-19 pandemic: narratives of informal women workers in Indian Punjab. Gend Work Organ 29:388–407
Smuha NA (2021) Beyond a human rights-based approach to AI governance: promise, pitfalls, plea. Philos Technol 34:91–104
Solaiman B, Cohen IG (eds) (2024) Research handbook on health, AI and the law. Edward Elgar, Cheltenham
The Combahee River Collective (1977) A black feminist statement. In: Eisenstein ZR (ed) Capitalist patriarchy and the case for socialist feminism. Monthly Review Press, New York, pp 362–372
Toebes B (2001) The right to health. In: Eide A, Krause C, Rosas A (eds) Economic, social and cultural rights, 2nd edn. Kluwer Law International, The Hague, pp 169–190
Toebes B (2020) Mediating tensions between public health and individual rights. Eur J Public Health 30:ckaa165.044
Toebes B, Stronks K (2016) Closing the gap: a human rights approach towards social determinants of health. Eur J Health Law 23:510–524
Toupin S (2024) Shaping feminist artificial intelligence. New Media Soc 26:580–595
Tripathi A, Rathore R (2025) AI in disease surveillance—an overview of how AI can be used in disease surveillance and outbreak detection in real-world scenarios. In: AI in disease detection. John Wiley & Sons, Hoboken, pp 337–359
Ulnicane I (2024) Intersectionality in artificial intelligence: framing concerns and recommendations for action. Soc Inclusion 12:7543
van Kolfschooten H (2022) The mHealth power paradox: improving data protection in health apps through self-regulation in the European Union. In: Shachar C, Robertson C, Cohen IG et al (eds) The future of medical device regulation: innovation and protection. Cambridge University Press, Cambridge, pp 63–76
van Kolfschooten H (2023) The AI cycle of health inequity and digital ageism: mitigating biases through the EU regulatory framework on medical devices. J Law Biosci 10:lsad031
van Kolfschooten HB (2024) A health-conformant reading of the GDPR's right not to be subject to automated decision-making. Med Law Rev 32:373–391
van Kolfschooten H (2025) Towards an EU charter of digital patients' rights in the age of artificial intelligence. DISO 4:6
van Kolfschooten H, van Oirschot J (2024) The EU Artificial Intelligence Act (2024): implications for healthcare. Health Policy 149:105152
van Kolfschooten H, van Oirschot J, Lau PL et al (2023) EU Health Policy Platform Thematic Network 2022–23: joint statement—the impact of artificial intelligence on health outcomes for key populations. European Commission, DG SANTE, Brussels
van Kolfschooten H, Goncalves J, Orchard N, Caroline F (2025) AI chatbots for promoting healthy habits: legal, ethical, and societal considerations. Digital Health 11
Yamin AE, Fukuda-Parr F (2023) When misfortune becomes injustice: evolving human rights struggles for health and social equality, 2nd edn. Stanford University Press, Stanford

Weingott S, Parkinson J (2025) The application of artificial intelligence in health communication development: a scoping review. Health Mark Q 42:67–109

Dr. Hannah van Kolfschooten is a postdoctoral researcher at the Centre for Life Sciences Law (ZLSR) University of Basel. Previously, she was a lecturer-researcher at the University of Amsterdam. She has been a visiting fellow at Harvard Law School, University of Verona, and Foundation Brocher. She specialises in the intersection of law, health, and technology.

MIX
Papier aus verantwortungsvollen Quellen
Paper from responsible sources
FSC® C105338

If you have any concerns about our products,
you can contact us on
ProductSafety@springernature.com

In case Publisher is established outside the EU,
the EU authorized representative is:
Springer Nature Customer Service Center GmbH
Europaplatz 3, 69115 Heidelberg, Germany

Printed by Libri Plureos GmbH
in Hamburg, Germany